The **Rough Guide** to

The Netherlands

written and researched by

**Martin Dunford, Phil Lee and
Suzanne Morton-Taylor**

ROUGH
GUIDES

www.roughguides.com

Contents

The Battle with the Sea colour section following p.112

The Dutch Golden Age colour section following p.240

◄◄ Cyclists outside the Rijksmuseum, Amsterdam ◄ De Valk mill, Leiden

GERMANY

Bremen

Hannover

Motorway under construction

Emmen

Groningen

GRONINGEN

Hoogeveen

DRENTHE

Assen

Schiermonnikoog

OVERIJSSEL

Almelo

Enschede

Zwolle

Deventer

Meppel

Apeldoorn

Giethoorn

Kampen

Ameland

FRIESLAND

Leeuwarden

Sneek

Urk

Terschelling

Waddenzee

IJsselmeer

Enkhuizen

FLEVOLAND

Harlingen

Stavoren

Markermeer

Lelystad

Hilversum

Vlieland

Madeblik

Marken

Naarden

Texel

Hoorn

Edam

AMSTERDAM

Den Helder

NOORD-

Volendam

HOLLAND

Alkmaar

Schiphol

Zaandam

IJmuiden

Haarlem

Leiden

Keukenhof

NORTH SEA

N

Newcastle

Hull

Metres	
200	
100	
50	
20	
5	
0	
below sea level	

0   40 km

Contents

The Battle with the Sea colour section following p.112

The Dutch Golden Age colour section following p.240

◄◄ Cyclists outside the Rijksmuseum, Amsterdam ◄ De Valk mill, Leiden

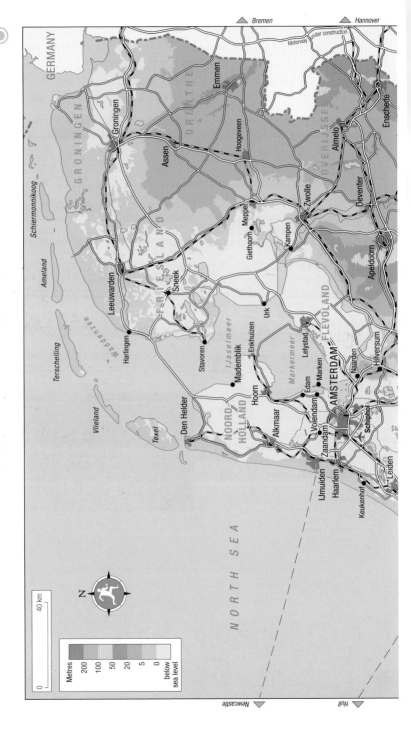

GERMANY

Bremen

Hannover

Motorway under construction

GRONINGEN

Groningen

Schiermonnikoog

DRENTHE

Emmen

Ameland

Assen

Hoogeveen

OVERIJSSEL

Almelo

Enschede

Terschelling

FRIESLAND

Leeuwarden

Sneek

Meppel

Giethoorn

Kampen

Zwolle

Deventer

Apeldoorn

Waddenzee

Harlingen

Stavoren

IJsselmeer

Urk

Enkhuizen

Lelystad

FLEVOLAND

Vlieland

Texel

Den Helder

Mademblik

NOORD-HOLLAND

Hoorn

Alkmaar

Volendam

Zaandam

Markermeer

Edam

Marken

AMSTERDAM

Naarden

Hilversum

Schiphol

IJmuiden

Haarlem

Keukenhof

Leiden

NORTH SEA

N

40 km

0

Metres
200
100
50
20
5
0
below
sea level

Newcastle

Hull

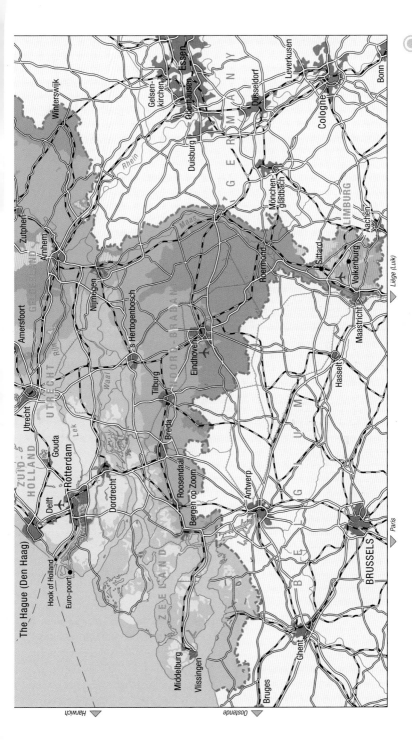

The Hague (Den Haag)

Hook of Holland
Euro-poort

ZUID-&
HOLLAND

Utrecht
Gouda
Delft
Rotterdam
Dordrecht

Amersfoort

UTRECHT

Lek

Waal

Rijn

GELDERLAND

Zutphen
Arnhem
Winterswijk

Nijmegen

's Hertogenbosch

Tilburg

Breda

Roosendaal

Bergen op Zoom

NOORD-BRABANT

Eindhoven

Maas

Roermond

Sittard
Volkenburg

LIMBURG

Aachen

Maastricht

Hasselt

B E L G I U M

Antwerp

Ghent

Bruges

Middelburg
Vlissingen

ZEELAND

BRUSSELS

GERMANY

Essen
Gelsen-
kirchen
Oberhausen
Duisburg
Düsseldorf
Leverkusen
Mönchen-
gladbach
Cologne
Bonn

Rhen

▽ Liège (Luik)

▽ Paris

▽ Oostende

▽ Harwich

www.roughguides.com

5

■

Introduction to

The Netherlands

The Netherlands packs a lot into a relatively small area. No more than the size of the US state of Maryland, and partially reclaimed from the sea (around half lies at or below sea level and around forty percent was once underwater), it's a strikingly unique place. The fertile, pancake-flat landscape, gridded with drainage ditches and canals, beneath huge open skies, is like no other place in the world; the bulbfields provide bold splashes of colour in springtime, and in the west the long coastline is marked by mile upon mile of protective dune, backing onto wide stretches of perfect sandy beach. The country's towns and villages are often pristine and unchanged places of gabled town houses, pretty canals and church spires; each is also profoundly separate, or at least more than you would expect in such a small country – indeed there's perhaps nowhere else in the world where you can hear so many different accents, even dialects, in such a confined area.

A major colonial power, the Dutch mercantile fleet once challenged the English for world naval supremacy, and throughout its seventeenth-century Golden Age, the standard of living was second to none. There have been a few economic ups and downs since then, but today the Netherlands is one of the most developed countries in the world, small and urban, with the highest population density in Europe. It's an international, well-integrated place too: most people speak English, at least in the heavily populated west of the country; and most of the country is easy to reach on a public transport system of trains and buses, whose efficiency may make British and American visitors weep with envy.

Successive Dutch governments have steered towards political consensus – indeed, this has been the drift since the Reformation, when the competing pillars of Dutch society (originally the Calvinists and the Catholics) learnt to live with – or ignore – each other, aided by the fact that trading wealth was lubricating the whole social structure. Almost by accident, therefore, Dutch society became tolerant and, in its enthusiasm to blunt conflict, progressive. These days, many insiders opine that the motive behind liberal Dutch attitudes towards drug use and prostitution isn't freewheeling permissiveness so much as apathy, and the country's avowed multiculturalism has been severely tested of late, with the shootings of Theo Van Gogh and the politician Pim Fortuyn persuading many to reassess the success of the Netherlands' consensus politics.

Where to go

Mention you're going to the Netherlands and most people assume you're going to **Amsterdam**. Indeed for such a small and accessible country, the Netherlands is relatively unknown territory. Some people may confess to a brief visit to Rotterdam or Den Haag (The Hague), but for most visitors Amsterdam *is* the Netherlands, the assumption being that there's nothing remotely worth seeing elsewhere. To accept this is to miss much, but there's no doubt that the capital has more cosmopolitan dash than any other Dutch city, both in its restaurant and bar scene and in the pre-eminence of its three great

Fact file

• The Netherlands has a **population** of just over 16.5 million people. Of these, some 740,000 live in the capital, Amsterdam, 600,000 in Rotterdam and 475,000 in Den Haag (The Hague). "**Holland**" comprises just two of the twelve Dutch provinces: Noord-Holland around Amsterdam, and Zuid-Holland around Rotterdam and Den Haag.

• The country is a constitutional **monarchy**; the present queen, Beatrix, was crowned in 1980. She presides – in a titular sense – over the country's bicameral **parliament**, named the States-General, which comprises an Upper House or First Chamber of 150 directly elected deputies and a Lower House or Senate of 75 senators. Parliament sits in Den Haag.

• Every Dutch city has a municipal **council** with delegated powers over a wide range of social issues, from public order and safety, drugs and housing through to economic development and culture. Currently, the largest national political parties are the left-of-centre PvdA, the right-of-centre CDA and the centrist VVD. The green-left Groenlinks also make a significant showing in the big cities.

• Almost half the population declare no **religious** affiliation. The three largest churches are the Catholics, the Dutch Reformed and its nineteenth-century breakaway, the Reformed; there is also a sizeable Muslim minority.

attractions. These are the Anne Frank Huis, where the young Jewish diarist hid away during the World War II Nazi occupation; the Rijksmuseum, with its wonderful collection of Dutch paintings, including several of Rembrandt's finest works; and the peerless Van Gogh Museum, with the world's largest collection of the artist's work.

In the west of the country, beyond Amsterdam, the provinces of **Noord-** and **Zuid-Holland** are for the most part unrelentingly flat, reflecting centuries of careful reclamation work as the Dutch have slowly pushed back the sea. These provinces are predominantly urban, especially Zuid-Holland, which is home to a grouping of towns known collectively as the Randstad (literally "rim town"), an urban sprawl that holds all the country's largest cities and the majority of its population. Travelling in this part of the country is easy, with trains and buses that are fast, inexpensive and efficient; highlights include amenable **Haarlem**; the old university town of **Leiden**; **Delft**, with its attractive medieval buildings and diminutive, canal-girded centre; and the gritty port city of **Rotterdam**, festooned with prestigious modern architecture. **Den Haag (The Hague)**, is well worth a visit, too, a laidback and relaxing city, seat of the Dutch government and home to several excellent museums. Neither should you miss the **Keukenhof gardens**, with the finest and most extensive bulbfields in the country. To the north of Amsterdam, the old Zuider Zee ports of **Enkhuizen** and **Hoorn** are very enticing, as is the small town of **Alkmaar**, with its unashamedly touristy cheese market, and the small villages and unspoilt dunescapes of the **coast**.

Queen's Day

The Queen in question isn't one of the flamboyant transvestites hanging around Rembrandtplein but Holland's reigning monarch, Queen Beatrix, whose official birthday is celebrated throughout the country on April 30. The ensuing fiesta is Amsterdam's Mardi Gras, Beerfest and street carnival all rolled into one – which, in a city famed for its easy-going, fun-loving population, manages to crank the party volume a few notches higher still. The street party blasts away for a full 24 hours uninterrupted, from the evening of April 29 – Queen's Night – to the evening of April 30, when the citizens of Amsterdam reclaim the streets, parks, squares and canals of the town from tourists, motorists and officialdom for one glorious party.

Beyond lies a quieter, more rural country, especially in the far north where a chain of low-lying islands – the **Frisian Islands** – separates the open North Sea from the coast-hugging Waddenzee. Prime resort territory, the islands possess a blustery, bucolic charm, and thousands of Dutch families come here every summer for their holidays. Apart from **Texel**, the islands lie offshore from the coast of the province of **Friesland**. Friesland's capital, **Leeuwarden**, is a likeable, eminently visitable city, and neighbouring **Groningen** is one of the country's busiest cultural centres.

To the south, the provinces of Overijssel and Gelderland are dotted with charming old towns, notably **Deventer** and **Zutphen**, while their eastern portions herald the Netherlands' first few geophysical bumps as the landscape rolls up towards the German frontier. Here also are two diverting towns: **Arnhem**, much rebuilt after its notorious World War II battle, but a hop and a skip from the open heaths of the **Hoge Veluwe National Park**, and the lively college town of **Nijmegen**.

Further south still are the predominantly Catholic provinces of Limburg, Noord-Brabant and Zeeland. The last of these is well named (literally "Sealand"), made up of a series of low-lying islands and protected from the encroaching waters of the North Sea by one of the country's most ambitious engineering plans, the **Delta Project**. Heading east from here, you reach Noord-Brabant, gently rolling scrub and farmland which centres on the historic cities of **Breda** and **'s Hertogenbosch**, the latter with a famous cathedral, and, not least, the modern manufacturing hub of **Eindhoven**, home to electronics giant Philips. The province of Limburg occupies the slim scythe of land that reaches down between the Belgian and German borders. Its landscape is truly hilly, and it has in its cosmopolitan capital, **Maastricht**, one of the Netherlands' most convivial cities.

9

▼ The Kinderdijk

When to go

The Netherlands enjoys a temperate **climate**, with relatively mild summers and moderately cold winters. Generally speaking, temperatures rise the further south you go. This is offset by the prevailing westerlies that sweep in from the North Sea, making the wetter coastal provinces both warmer in winter and colder in summer than the eastern provinces, where the more severe climate of continental Europe has an influence. As far as rain is concerned, be prepared for it at any time of year.

Average monthly temperatures and rainfall

	Jan	Feb	Mar	Apr	May	Jun	Jul	Aug	Sep	Oct	Nov	Dec
Amsterdam												
Max/min °C	5/1	6/0	9/2	12/4	17/8	19/10	21/13	22/12	18/10	14/7	9/4	7/2
Rainfall (mm)	62	43	59	41	48	68	66	61	82	85	89	75
Sun hrs/day	2	3	4	6	7	7	7	7	4	3	2	1
Leeuwarden												
Max/min °C	5/0	5/0	8/2	11/3	16/7	18/10	20/12	21/12	18/10	13/7	9/3	6/1
Rainfall (mm)	66	42	59	39	51	69	64	60	82	78	84	73
Sun hrs/day	2	3	4	6	7	7	7	6	4	3	2	1
Maastricht												
Max/min °C	5/0	6/0	10/2	13/4	18/8	20/11	23/13	23/13	19/10	14/7	9/3	6/1
Rainfall (mm)	61	51	61	46	64	74	67	58	60	63	66	70
Sun hrs/day	2	3	4	5	6	6	6	6	4	4	2	1
Rotterdam												
Max/min °C	6/1	6/0	10/2	13/4	17/7	19/10	22/13	22/12	19/10	14/7	9/4	7/2
Rainfall (mm)	67	47	65	41	52	72	68	66	82	90	86	80
Sun hrs/day	2	3	4	5	7	6	7	6	4	3	2	1

things not to miss

It's not possible to see everything that the Netherlands has to offer in one trip – and we don't suggest you try. What follows is a selective and subjective taste of the country's highlights, in no particular order: cosmopolitan cities, peaceful villages, memorable landscapes and outstanding museums. They're arranged in five colour-coded categories to help you find the very best things to see, do and experience. All entries have a page reference to take you straight into the Guide, where you can find out more.

01 **Amsterdam** Page **49** • There's plenty to see in the Netherlands apart from Amsterdam, but it would be a strange trip that missed out the picturesque capital altogether.

02 **The Elfstedentocht** Page **224** • Watch, or even better join in with, the speed-skaters of Friesland as they tear round the province's canals in this infrequently staged open-air race.

03 **Delta Project and Expo** Page **116** • The series of huge dykes and flood-barriers in the far-flung western province of Zeeland, which bear witness to the country's long battle to hold the sea at bay, is celebrated in an adjacent exhibition hall.

04 **Maastricht** Page **322** • This atmospheric, laidback city in the far south, squeezed between the porous Belgian and German borders, offers a worldly outlook and a superb old quarter.

05 **Anne Frank Huis, Amsterdam** Page **71** • A poignant and personal evocation of the Nazi persecution of the Jews. The photo below shows the bookcase behind which the Frank family hid for two years.

06 **The Biesbosch** Page **192** • As an escape from Dutch urban life, the reedy marshes and lagoons of the Biesbosch are hard to beat.

07 **Van Gogh Museum, Amsterdam** Page **85** • Quite simply the best and most comprehensive collection of Van Gogh's work anywhere.

08 **'s Hertogenbosch** Page **309** • This lively market town features an intricate old quarter of canals and picturesque bridges, plus a stunning cathedral.

09 **Hoge Veluwe National Park** Page **275** • A richly forested swathe of dunes and woodland in the middle of the country. Cycle your way around thanks to a fleet of free-to-use white bicycles.

10 **Den Haag (The Hague)** Page **155** • Den Haag has a reputation for dourness that is completely undeserved, boasting a first-rate restaurant scene, smart hotels and enough prime museums to exhaust even the most energetic sightseer.

11 **Wadlopen** Page **239** • One novel way of getting to the Frisian Islands is to try guided *wadlopen* or "mud-walking" from the mainland at high tide.

12 Indonesian food Page **32** •
Thanks to the Netherlands' colonial
adventures in Southeast Asia, restaurants
around the country prepare some of the
finest Indonesian cuisine outside Indonesia.

**13 Frans Hals Museum,
Haarlem** Page **112** • Often
neglected, Hals was one of the finest of
the Golden Age painters, his later canvases
acutely dark and broody.

14 Kröller-Müller Museum
Page **277** • This superb art museum
and sculpture garden is set in the heart of the
Hoge Veluwe National Park.

15 Keukenhof gardens Page
154 • Some seven million flowers are
on show in these extensive gardens, which
specialize in daffodils, narcissi, hyacinths and
– of course – tulips.

16 Frisian Islands Pages **232,** **245** & **256** • Of the string of wild and windswept holiday islands off the northern Dutch coast, Terschelling is the most popular, a fine spot for walks and bike-rides amid the dunes.

17 IJsselmeer Page **298** • This beautiful inland lake, formerly the Zuider Zee, lies at the heart of the Netherlands and represents the country at its watery best, with charming old ports like Hoorn and Enkhuizen and former islands like Urk to explore.

18 Cycling Page **26** • No country in Europe is so kindly disposed towards the bicycle than the pancake-flat Netherlands: you'll find bike paths in and around all towns, plus long-distance touring routes taking you deep into the countryside.

19 Delft Page **169** • Eulogized by Vermeer, Delft's centre is particularly handsome, and its market square is one of the country's best.

Basics

Basics

Getting there

UK travellers are spoilt for choice when it comes to deciding how to get to the Netherlands. There are plenty of flights from a bevy of UK airports to Amsterdam, the country's capital, as well as a sprinkling of flights to several second-string airports, primarily Eindhoven and Rotterdam. Alternatively, travelling by train through the Channel Tunnel is just as easy and about the same price as a flight, and neither, if you live in the southeast of the UK, does it take much longer. You can also get there by long-distance bus, which is usually the most affordable option of all, though admittedly more time-consuming. By car, deals for drivers on ferry routes into Dutch and Belgian ports are particularly competitive. From North America and Canada the main decision is whether to fly direct – easy enough as Amsterdam's Schiphol (pronounced skip-oll) is a major international air travel hub – or to route via London, picking up a budget flight onwards from there. From Australia and New Zealand, all flights to Amsterdam require one or two stops on the way; from South Africa, direct flights are available.

Flights from the UK and Ireland

Flights to any of the major airports in the Netherlands – Amsterdam Schiphol, Rotterdam, Eindhoven or Maastricht – take roughly an hour from London, or ninety minutes from Scotland and the north of England. **Amsterdam** is one of the UK's most popular short-haul destinations, and you'll find loads of choice – in carriers, flight times and departure airports. Aside from the major full-service carriers (for example KLM and British Airways), there are plenty of budget airlines operating to Amsterdam, including easyJet, bmibaby and Ryanair. You'll find plenty of choice of daily flights out of London – Heathrow, Gatwick, Stansted, Luton and London City – plus nonstop flights from loads of other airports, including Birmingham, Bournemouth, Cardiff, Coventry, Doncaster–Sheffield, East Midlands, Humberside, Leeds–Bradford, Liverpool, Manchester, Newcastle, Norwich, Southampton, Teesside, Edinburgh, Glasgow and Aberdeen. To **Rotterdam**, you've a choice of Transavia from Luton and the Belgian airline VLM from

London City, Guernsey, Jersey and Manchester. There are also Ryanair flights to **Eindhoven** from Bristol, London Stansted and Dublin, and VLM flights there from London City.

Whichever route you choose, it's hard to say precisely what you'll **pay** at any given time: it depends so much on when you book and when you fly, what offers are available, and how lucky you get. However, flying to any Dutch city with one of the low-cost airlines between April and September, you'll probably pay around £120 return travelling at convenient times at the weekend, including taxes, or £160 with one of the full-service carriers. Weekday travel will cost £50–70 with a budget carrier, and maybe £100 or so with a full-service airline. Of course if you want more flexibility with your ticket you'll pay more, as you will if you book at the last minute – economy return tickets from London to Amsterdam can cost anything up to £400. All carriers offer their lowest prices online.

Flying to the Netherlands from **Northern Ireland**, the most economical option is with easyJet out of Belfast International to

Find everything you need to plan your next trip at ⓦ www.roughguides.com. Read Rough Guides content on destinations worldwide, make use of our unique trip-planner tool, book transport and accommodation, check out other travellers' recommendations and share your own experiences.

Amsterdam (fares are around £100). From the **Republic of Ireland**, Aer Lingus flies five times daily to Amsterdam out of Dublin and twice daily from Cork, for a minimum €80–100 return, depending on the season, with fares rising at peak times.

Flights from the US and Canada

Amsterdam's Schiphol Airport is among the most popular and least expensive gateways to Europe from **North America**, and finding a convenient and good-value flight is rarely a problem. **Direct flights** are operated by KLM/Northwest, Continental and Delta Airlines, but many more airlines fly **via London** and other European centres – and are nearly always cheaper because of it.

Virtually every region of the US is well served by the major airlines. KLM and Northwest, which operate a joint service, offer the widest range of flights, with direct or one-stop flights to Amsterdam from eleven US cities, and connections from dozens more. From elsewhere in the US, the Dutch charter firm Martinair flies year-round from Miami direct to Amsterdam, United also flies direct to Amsterdam from Chicago, while Delta operates from Atlanta and New York, and Continental from Houston.

Booking far enough in advance, you should be able to find a **fare** between April and September for $700–900 return from New York (flight time 7hr 10min) or Chicago (8hr 30min), $900–1000 from Atlanta (10hr), and around $1000 from LA (10hr 30min), though booking less than a couple of weeks in advance can push these prices up considerably.

From **Canada**, KLM flies direct to Amsterdam year-round from Vancouver (9hr 30min) and from Toronto (7hr 10min). There are also plenty of one-stop options via Frankfurt, London and Paris. **Fares** from Toronto go for around Can$1100, from Vancouver around Can$1400.

Flights from Australia, New Zealand and South Africa

There are **no direct flights** to the Netherlands from **Australia and New Zealand**: all involve at least one stop. Singapore Airlines

and Malaysia Airlines offer the most direct routes out of Sydney (stopping in Singapore and Kuala Lumpur respectively). Thai, Austrian and Qantas all have two stops (Bangkok/Munich, Bangkok/Vienna and Singapore/London). Flights from Christchurch go via Sydney and London and from Wellington via Melbourne or Sydney and London. One further option is to pick up a cheap ticket to London, and then continue your journey to Amsterdam with one of the no-frills budget airlines (see below).

From **South Africa**, KLM offers **direct flights** to Amsterdam, with services from Cape Town and Johannesburg. South African Airways offers one-stop flights via London and Frankfurt or Munich; Lufthansa via Frankfurt; and Virgin Atlantic via London.

Fares from Sydney or Melbourne are around A$1800–2000, and from Auckland A$2200. A return flight from Christchurch or Wellington will set you back around NZ$3000. Flights with KLM from Cape Town cost around R8600; from Johannesburg, R7300. Indirect flights via London or Frankfurt cost around R8000.

Airlines and agents

Online booking

ⓦ www.ebookers.com (in UK), ⓦ www
.ebookers.ie (in Ireland)
ⓦ www.expedia.co.uk (in UK), ⓦ www.expedia
.com (in US), ⓦ www.expedia.ca (in Canada)
ⓦ www.lastminute.com (in UK)
ⓦ www.opodo.co.uk (in UK)
ⓦ www.orbitz.com (in US)
ⓦ www.travelocity.co.uk (in UK), ⓦ www
.travelocity.com (in US), ⓦ www.travelocity
.ca (in Canada), ⓦ www.travelocity.co.nz
(in New Zealand)
ⓦ www.travelonline.co.za (in South Africa)
ⓦ www.zuji.com.au (in Australia)

Airlines

Aer Lingus ⓦ www.aerlingus.com
Air Canada ⓦ www.aircanada.com
Air France ⓦ www.airfrance.com
Air New Zealand ⓦ www.airnz.co.nz
American Airlines ⓦ www.aa.com
bmi ⓦ www.flybmi.com
bmibaby ⓦ www.bmibaby.com
British Airways ⓦ www.ba.com
Cathay Pacific ⓦ www.cathaypacific.com

Continental Airlines ⓦ www.continental.com
Delta ⓦ www.delta.com
easyJet ⓦ www.easyjet.com
KLM (Royal Dutch Airlines) ⓦ www.klm.com
Lufthansa ⓦ www.lufthansa.com
Malaysia Airlines ⓦ www.malaysiaairlines.com
Martinair ⓦ www.martinair.com
Northwest ⓦ www.nwa.com
Qantas Airways ⓦ www.qantas.com
Ryanair ⓦ www.ryanair.com
Singapore Airlines ⓦ www.singaporeair.com
South African Airways ⓦ www.flysaa.com
Thai Airways ⓦ www.thaiair.com
Thomsonfly ⓦ www.thomsonfly.co.uk
Transavia ⓦ www.transavia.com
United Airlines ⓦ www.united.com
Virgin Atlantic ⓦ www.virgin-atlantic.com
VLM Airlines ⓦ www.flyvlm.com

Agents and operators

ebookers UK ☎ 0800/082 3000, Republic of
Ireland ☎ 01/431 1311; ⓦ www.ebookers.com. Low
fares on an extensive selection of scheduled flights
and package deals.

North South Travel UK ☎ 01245/608 291,
ⓦ www.northsouthtravel.co.uk. Friendly, competitive
travel agency, offering discounted fares worldwide.
Profits are used to support projects in the developing
world, especially the promotion of sustainable tourism.
STA Travel UK ☎ 0871/2300 040, US
☎ 1-800/781-4040, Australia ☎ 134 STA, New
Zealand ☎ 0800/474 400, SA ☎ 0861/781 781;
ⓦ www.statravel.com. Worldwide specialists in
independent travel; also student IDs, travel insurance,
car rental, rail passes and more. Good discounts for
students and under-26s.
Trailfinders UK ☎ 0845/058 5858, Republic of
Ireland ☎ 01/677 7888, Australia ☎ 1300/780 212;
ⓦ www.trailfinders.com. One of the best-informed
and most efficient agents for independent travellers.

By train from the UK

The simplest and quickest way to travel by
train from the UK to the Netherlands is to
take the **Eurostar** service from London to
Brussels. Trains depart from St Pancras
International station in central London,
Ashford in Kent and Ebbsfleet station, off

Six steps to a better kind of travel

At Rough Guides we are passionately committed to travel. We feel strongly that only
through travelling do we truly come to understand the world we live in and the people
we share it with – plus tourism has brought a great deal of **benefit** to developing
economies around the world over the last few decades. But the extraordinary growth
in tourism has also damaged some places irreparably, and of course **climate change**
is exacerbated by most forms of transport, especially flying. This means that now
more than ever it's important to **travel thoughtfully** and **responsibly**, with respect for
the cultures you're visiting – not only to derive the most benefit from your trip but
also to preserve the best bits of the planet for everyone to enjoy. At Rough Guides
we feel there are six main areas in which you can make a difference:

- Consider what you're contributing to the **local economy**, and how much the
  services you use do the same, whether it's through employing local workers and
  guides or sourcing locally grown produce and local services.
- Consider the **environment** on holiday as well as at home. Water is scarce in
  many developing destinations, and the biodiversity of local flora and fauna can
  be adversely affected by tourism. Try to patronize businesses that take account
  of this.
- Travel with a purpose, not just to tick off experiences. Consider **spending longer**
  in a place, and getting to know it and its people.
- Give thought to how often you **fly**. Try to avoid short hops by air and more harmful
  night flights.
- Consider **alternatives to flying**, travelling instead by bus, train, boat and even by
  bike or on foot where possible.
- Make your trips "**climate neutral**" via a reputable carbon offset scheme. All
  Rough Guide flights are offset, and every year we donate money to a variety of
  charities devoted to combating the effects of climate change.

Junction 2 of the M25; depending on the service, the journey time from all three to Brussels is about two hours. In Brussels, trains arrive at Bruxelles-Midi station (Brussel-Zuid in Dutch), from where plenty of fast trains – including **Thalys** high-speed services (W www.thalys.com) – head on to Amsterdam with a journey time of around two-and-a-half to three hours. En route between Brussels and Amsterdam, Thalys trains call at Rotterdam (1hr 45min) and the Hague (2hr). For other Dutch destinations reachable from Brussels, consult the encyclopedic website of Dutch Railways, **NS** (W www.ns.nl). Eurostar can arrange **through ticketing** from any point in the UK to any point in the Netherlands, as can Rail Europe (see opposite). A standard return **fare** to Amsterdam, with some flexibility, costs around £150, but special deals and bargains are commonplace, especially in the low season, and you can also sometimes reduce costs by accepting certain ticketing restrictions.

A much longer – but cheaper – **rail-and-ferry route**, the **Dutchflyer**, is available through Stena Line in conjunction with National Express East Anglia trains. The journey operates twice daily (early morning and evening) with **trains** departing London's Liverpool Street station bound for Harwich, where they connect with the **ferry** over to the Hook of Holland – the Hoek van Holland. The whole journey takes between nine and eleven hours. From the Hook, there are frequent trains onto Rotterdam (every 30min to 1hr; 30min), from where you can reach a host of other Dutch towns. As for **fares**, a standard return costs £70, £90 on an overnight sailing, cabin included – cabins are compulsory on overnight sailings. Tickets are available from National Express East Anglia trains (for contact details, see opposite) or you can book online with Stena (for contact details, see opposite).

If you're visiting the Netherlands as part of a longer European trip, it may be worth considering a **pan-European rail pass**. There are lots to choose from and **Rail Europe** (W www.raileurope.com), the umbrella company for all national and international passes, operates a comprehensive website detailing all the options, with prices. Note in

particular that some passes have to be bought before leaving home, while others can only be bought in specific countries. For train travel within the Netherlands, see opposite.

Rail contacts

NS (Dutch Railways) International enquiries ☎0900/9296, domestic enquiries ☎0900/9292, both premium lines only operational within the Netherlands; W www.ns.nl.
European Rail UK ☎020/7619 1083, W www.europeanrail.com.
Europrail International Canada ☎1-888/667-9734, W www.europrail.net.
Eurostar UK ☎0870/518 6186, outside UK ☎0044/1233 617575; W www.eurostar.com.
International Rail UK ☎0871/231 0790, W www.international-rail.com.
National Express East Anglia UK ☎0845/600 7245, W www.nationalexpresseastanglia.com.
Rail Europe UK ☎0844/848 4064, W www.raileurope.co.uk.

By ferry from the UK

Three operators run **ferries** from the UK direct to ports in the Netherlands, and all offer year-round services. **Tariffs** vary enormously, depending on when you leave, how long you stay, if you're taking a car, what size it is and how many passengers are in it. There are **discounts** for students and under-26s, though these often involve some travel restrictions. The fastest route is with **Stena Line**, which sails from Harwich in Essex to the Hook of Holland; the journey time is about 6 hours 30 minutes on daytime sailings, seven hours at night, when you have to book a cabin. **P&O Ferries** operates from Hull to the Europoort, 40km west of Rotterdam (11hr); and **DFDS Seaways** sails once daily from Newcastle (North Shields) to IJmuiden near Amsterdam (14hr).

Ferry companies

DFDS Seaways UK ☎0871/522 9955, W www.dfdsseaways.co.uk
P&O Ferries UK ☎0871/664 5645, W www.poferries.com
Stena Line UK ☎0870/570 7070, W www.stenaline.co.uk

Driving from the UK

To reach the Netherlands **by car or motorbike from the UK**, you can either take a ferry (see opposite) or – preferable for its simplicity and hassle-free crossing – use **Eurotunnel's** shuttle train through the Channel Tunnel. Note that Eurotunnel (UK ℡0870/535 3535, ⊛www.eurotunnel.com) only carries cars (including occupants) and motorbikes, not foot passengers, and only takes cyclists by advance booking. Amsterdam is roughly 370km from the Eurotunnel exit in Calais, Rotterdam 200km, Arnhem 260km. There are two shuttle trains per hour (but only 3 in total from midnight to 6am), taking 35min (45min for some night-time departures); you must check in at Folkstone at least 30min before departure. It's possible to turn up and buy your ticket at the toll booths (exit the M20 at junction 11a), though at busy times advance booking through Eurotunnel's website is advisable. **Fares** depend on the time of year, time of day and length of stay: it almost always costs less to travel between 10pm and 6am, while the highest fares are reserved for weekend departures and returns in July and August. Prices are charged per vehicle: short-stay savers between April and October for a car start at around £70. If you wish to stay more than five days, a standard return costs from around £100, while a more flexible "FlexiPlus" fare, which entitles you to change your plans at the last minute, costs more still. Some special offers are usually also available.

By bus from the UK

Travelling by **long-distance bus** is generally the cheapest way of reaching the Netherlands from the UK, but it is very time-consuming: the main route, from London to Amsterdam, takes around twelve hours. There are three or four services daily and all of them use the Eurotunnel. For timetable details, consult the operator, **Eurolines** (⊛www.eurolines .co.uk). A standard single fare works out as £40–50 one-way, £60–70 return, less for seniors (60+) and the under-26s, though promotional return fares can be snapped up for much less.

Getting around

Getting around is hardly ever a problem in the Netherlands: it's a small country, and the longest journey you'll ever make – say from Amsterdam to Maastricht – takes under three hours by train or car. Furthermore, the public transport system is exemplary, a fully integrated network of trains and buses that brings even the smallest of villages within easy reach, and at very reasonable prices too. Train and bus stations are almost always next door to each other, and several of the larger cities also have a tram network.

By train

The best way of travelling around the Netherlands is to take the **train**. The system, largely operated by **Nederlandse Spoor-wegen** (NS – Dutch Railways; international enquiries ℡0900/9296, domestic enquiries ℡0900/9292, both premium lines only opera-tional within the Netherlands; ⊛www.ns.nl), is one of the best in Europe: trains are fast, mostly modern, frequent and very punctual; fares are relatively low; and the network of lines comprehensive. NS domestic services come in two main types: the speedy **Intercity** for city-to-city connections and the normal **Sneltrein**, which stops at most towns and villages. Ordinary **fares** are calculated by the kilometre, diminishing proportionally the further you travel: as sample fares, a standard single from Amsterdam to Maastricht costs €26.60, Rotterdam €13.30 and Leeuwarden €25.80. For a one-way ticket, ask for an *enkele reis*; a return trip is a *retour*. Same-day return tickets (*dagretour*) knock about ten percent off the price of two one-way tickets for the same journey, but otherwise returns are normally double the price of singles. First-class fares cost about fifty percent on top of the regular fare. With any ticket, you're free to stop off anywhere en route and continue your journey later that day, but you're not allowed to backtrack. NS publishes a comprehensive and easy-to-use **timetable** (*spoorboekje*), which is available for €5.50 at all major stations, as well as mounds of information on its various services, passes and fares. Note, however, that you are not allowed to buy a ticket on the train and you cannot pay for a train ticket with a foreign debit card or, in most instances, a credit card.

Treintaxi, discount tickets and deals

In NS's **treintaxi scheme**, rail passengers can be assured of a taxi to or from over 40 major stations. To get to the station at the

MAJOR RAIL ROUTES

N

Roodeschool
Delfzijl
Groningen
Harlingen
Leeuwarden
Sneek
Den Helder
Stavoren
Emmen
Meppel
Enkhuizen
Hoorn
Alkmaar
Kampen
Lelystad
Zwolle
Almelo
Haarlem
Amsterdam
Deventer
Hengelo
Zandvoort
Enschede
Apeldoorn
Schiphol
Hilversum
Zutphen
Leiden
Amersfoort
Den Haag Centraal
Ede-Wageningen
Winterswijk
Den Haag HS
Utrecht
Arnhem
Gouda
Hoek van Holland
Delft
Nijmegen
Rotterdam
Dordrecht
's-Hertogenbosch
Venray
Roosendaal
Breda
Tilburg
Eindhoven
Middelburg
Venlo
Bergen-op-Zoom
Vlissingen
Roermond

GERMANY

Düsseldorf ▶

Bruges
Ghent
Antwerp
Heerlen
BELGIUM
Maastricht
Cologne
Brussels
Aachen

Planning a journey

For pre-departure information on your train journey, the "**Journey Planner**" feature on the NS website (www.ns.nl) is hard to beat. Type in your departure and arrival points (train station, street address or even just the name of a museum or concert hall), and it will not only give you a street map to get to the nearest station, but also tell you what platform your train leaves from, how many changes to make (and where, with platform numbers), and how much your ticket will cost.

start of your journey, call the local *treintaxi* number or 0900/873 4682 (premium line, only within the Netherlands), at least half an hour in advance; the fare is a flat-rate €6 for journeys under 2km, €9 for 2–4km and €12 for 4–6km. On arrival at the local station, you can either book a *treintaxi* at your destination station when you buy your ticket, or wait till you get there and pay the taxi driver. Most major stations have *treintaxi* buttons at the entrance, which you press to summon a *treintaxi* for your onward journey (within the city limits). Note that *treintaxis* are not the same as regular taxis – you may well, for instance, have to share with other people taking a similar route. The cabs are identifiable by a "*treintaxi*" sign on the roof and they have a separate rank outside train stations.

NS discount tickets and deals

NS offers a variety of **discount tickets and deals**, perhaps the most useful of which is the **Dagkaart** (Day Travel Card) for unlimited travel on any train in the system and costing just €44 in second-class; first-class is €75. The **Weekendretour** (Weekend Return) provides substantial discounts on weekend travel (up to forty percent); the family-orientated **Railrunner** charges just €2 per journey for up to three children aged 4–11 travelling with an adult; and the **Vordeeluren-abonnement** (Off-peak Discount Pass) costs €55 and gives a discount of forty percent on all off-peak journeys (Mon–Fri after 9am and on the weekend) to the pass holder and three companions for that day. For further information, consult www.ns.nl.

By bus and tram

Supplementing the train network are **buses** – run by a patchwork of local companies but again amazingly efficient and reaching into

every rural nook and cranny. **Ticketing** is straightforward, using *strippenkaarts* (see box, p.28), though some long-distance buses don't accept them and you must pay the driver instead. Bear in mind also that in more remote rural areas some bus services only operate when passengers have made advance bookings. Local **timetables** indicate where this applies; regional bus timetable books, costing around €3, are sold at some train station bookshops and most VVVs (see p.44).

Within **major towns**, urban public transport systems are extensive, inexpensive and frequent, which makes getting around straightforward and hassle-free; most bus and tram services run from 6am until about midnight and *strippenkaarts* are valid except on special night buses (1–5am). Urban "**Park and Ride**" or **Transferium** schemes are commonplace.

By car

For the most part, **driving** round the Netherlands is pretty much what you would expect: smooth, easy and quick. The country has a uniformly good road network, with most of the major towns linked by some kind of motorway or dual carriageway, though snarl-ups and jams are far from rare. Rules of the road are straightforward: you drive on the right, and **speed limits** are 50kph in built-up areas, 80kph outside, 120kph on motorways – though some motorways have a speed limit of 100kph, indicated by small yellow signs on the side of the road. Drivers and front-seat passengers are required by law to wear seatbelts, and penalties for drunk driving are severe. There are no toll roads, and although **fuel** is expensive, at around €1.60 per litre (diesel €1.30), the short distances mean this isn't too much of a factor.

Travelling on a strippenkaart – and the OV-Chipkaart

On buses, city trams and the metro, from one end of the Netherlands to the other, the most common type of ticket is the **strippenkaart**, a card divided into strips. This universal, nationwide ticketing system is extremely efficient. To make it work the whole country is divided up into **zones**: you need to cancel one strip on your *strippenkaart* for yourself plus one for each of the zones you travel through. On city trams and metro systems you either get the *strippenkaart* cancelled by the conductor or do it yourself by folding the *strippenkaart* over to the right place and inserting it into the on-board franking machine; note that you only have to stamp the last of the strips you need. On buses, you almost always hand the *strippenkaart* to the driver, who will do the stamping for you. In larger towns and cities, two or three strips is enough to take you anywhere in the centre. One *strippenkaart* can be used by any number of people, provided that the requisite number of strips is cancelled for each person's journey. Similarly, strips can be carried over from one *strippenkaart* to another: if you've used up, say, 14 of your 15 strips, you can stamp the 15th strip on one card and the first strip on another, new card in order to travel.

At the time of writing, a two-strip *strippenkaart* **cost** €1.60 and a three-strip €2.40; you can buy these on the bus or tram. However, you're better off buying tickets **in advance**, from tobacconists, magazine stores, the VVV and big-city metro stations: a fifteen-strip costs €7.30 and a 45-strip €21.60. Alternatively, you can opt for a **dagkaart** (day ticket), which gives unlimited travel on buses, city trams and the metro for up to a maximum of three days. Prices are €7 for 24 hours, €11.50 for 48 hours and €15 for 72 hours. Also at time of writing, plans are well advanced for replacing the *strippenkaart* with the **OV-Chipkaart**, a rechargeable payment card which you can buy at any bus or train station for use on all the country's buses, trams and metros. For the latest information, check out ⍉www.ov-chipkaart.nl.

Most foreign **driving licences** are honoured in the Netherlands, including all EU, US, Canadian, Australian and New Zealand ones. If you're **bringing your own car**, you must have adequate insurance, preferably including coverage for legal costs, and it's advisable to have an appropriate breakdown policy from your home motoring organization too.

Renting a car

All the major **international car rental agencies** are represented in the Netherlands and a scattering of contact details are given in the "Listings" section at the end of the Guide accounts of major towns. To rent a car, you'll have to be 21 or over (and have been driving for at least a year), and you'll need a credit card – though some local agencies will accept a hefty cash deposit instead. **Rental charges** are fairly high, beginning around €240 per week for unlimited mileage in the smallest vehicle, but include collision damage waiver and vehicle (but not personal) **insurance**. To cut costs, watch for special deals offered by the bigger companies. If you go to a smaller, local company (of which there are many), you should proceed with care: in particular, check the policy for the excess applied to claims and ensure that it includes a collision damage waiver (applicable if an accident is your fault) as well as adequate levels of financial cover. If you break down in a rented car, you'll get roadside assistance from the particular repair company the rental firm has contracted. The same principle works with your own vehicle's breakdown policy providing you have coverage abroad.

Car rental agencies

Avis ⍉www.avis.com.
Budget ⍉www.budget.com.
Europcar ⍉www.europcar.com.
Hertz ⍉www.hertz.com.
Holiday Autos ⍉www.holidayautos.co.uk.
National ⍉www.nationalcar.com.
SIXT ⍉www.sixt.com.
Skycars ⍉www.skycars.com.
Thrifty ⍉www.thrifty.com.

Cycling

One great way to see the Netherlands, whether you're a keen cyclist or an idle pedaller, is to travel by **bike** (*fiets*). Cycle-touring can be a shortcut into Dutch culture and you can reach parts of the country – its beaches, forests and moorland – that might otherwise be inaccessible. The mostly flat landscape makes travelling by bike an almost effortless pursuit, although you can find yourself battling against a headwind or swallowed up in a shoal of cyclists commuting to work. The short distances involved make it possible to see most of the country with relative ease, using the nationwide system of well-marked **cycle paths**: a circular blue sign with a white bicycle on it indicates an obligatory cycle lane, separate from car traffic. Red lettering on signposts gives distances for fairly direct routes; lettering in green denotes a more scenic (and lengthy) mosey. Long-distance (LF) routes weave through the cities and countryside, often linking up to local historic loops and scenic trails. The Dutch as a nation are celebrated touring cyclists, and bookshops are packed with cycling books; however, for all but the longest trips the maps and route advice provided by most tourist offices are fine.

If you're looking for a **place to stay** after a day in the saddle, the best advice is to visit a member of the **Vrienden op de Fiets** (see p.28), who for a modest fee (❶) will put you up for the night in their home and feed you a princely breakfast the next morning. Many hosts are wonderfully warm and hospitable, as well as experts on cycling in their own country (and often many others).

Cycle rental

You can **rent a bike** from all main train stations for €6.50 a day or €32.50 per week, plus a €50 deposit (€100 in larger centres). Most bikes are single-speed, though there are some 3-speeds to be had, and even mountain bikes in the hillier south. You'll also need some form of **ID**. The snag is that cycles must be returned to the station from which they were rented, making onward hops by rented bike impossible. Most **bike shops** rent bicycles out for around the same amount, and they may be more flexible on deposits – some may accept a passport in lieu of cash. Wherever you're intending to rent your bike from, in summer it's a good idea to reserve in advance. It is possible to take your bike on **trains**, and the bike carriages have a clear cycle symbol on the outside. You'll need to buy a flat-rate ticket (*dagkaart fiets*) for your bike, which is valid for the whole day. Space can be limited, despite the variety of ingeniously folding bikes favoured by locals, and because of this you won't be allowed on at all during the morning and evening rush hours (6.30–9am & 5.30–6pm), except in July and August.

Note that in the larger cities in particular, but really anywhere around the country, you should never, ever, leave your bike **unlocked**, even for a few minutes – bike stealing is a big deal in the Netherlands. Almost all train stations have somewhere you can store your bike safely for less than a euro.

Accommodation

Inevitably accommodation is one of the major expenses of a trip to the Netherlands – indeed, if you're after a degree of comfort and style, it's going to be the costliest item by far. There are, however, budget alternatives, principally private rooms (broadly bed and breakfast arranged via the local tourist office), campsites and a scattering of HI-registered hostels. During the summer and over holiday periods vacant rooms can be scarce, so it's wise to book ahead. In Amsterdam, room shortages are commonplace throughout the year, so advance booking is always required; hotel prices are about thirty percent higher here than in the rest of the country.

Hotels

All **hotels** in the Netherlands are graded on a star system. One-star and no-star hotels are rare, and prices for two-star establishments start at around €60 for a double room without private bath or shower; count on paying at least €80 if you want en-suite facilities. Three-star hotels cost upwards of about €80; for four- and five-star places you'll pay €125-plus. Generally, the stated price includes **breakfast**, except in the most expensive and the very cheapest of hotels.

You can book ahead easily by calling the hotel direct – English is almost always spoken. In the Netherlands itself, you can make advance bookings in person through any tourist office for a nominal fee. Alternatively, two useful **booking websites** are ⓦwww.weekendcompany.nl (in Dutch & German only) and ⓦwww.weekendjeweg.nl (Dutch only).

Private rooms

One way of cutting costs is to use **private accommodation** – rooms in private homes that are let out to visitors on a bed-and-breakfast basis, sometimes known as pensions. Prices are quoted per person and are normally around €20–30 with breakfast usually included. You mostly have to go through the local tourist office to find a private room: they will either give you a list to follow up independently or will book the accommodation themselves and levy a minimal booking fee. Note, however, that not all tourist offices are able to offer private rooms; generally you'll find them only in the larger towns and tourist centres and characteristically a good way from the centre. In some of the more popular tourist destinations the details of these "B&Bs" are listed in tourist brochures.

Vrienden op de Fiets

If you're cycling or walking around the Netherlands, you will find the organization **Vrienden op de Fiets** (Friends of the Bicycle; ☏030/267 9070, ⓦwww.vriendenopdefiets .nl) an absolute bargain. For an annual joining fee of €9, you'll be sent a book of almost two thousand addresses in the Netherlands where you can stay the night in somebody's home for a maximum of €18.50 per person; all you have to do is phone 24 hours in advance. Accommodation can range from stylish town houses to suburban semis to centuries-old farmhouses – you don't know until you turn up – and staying in somebody's home can give a great insight into Dutch life. Hosts are usually very friendly, offer local information about the area and will provide a breakfast of often mammoth proportions to send you on your way.

Hostels

If you're travelling on a tight budget, a **hostel** is likely to be your accommodation of choice. Dutch hostels can often be extremely good value, and offer clean and comfortable dorm beds as well as a choice of rooms (doubles and sometimes singles) at rock-bottom prices. Both city and country locations can

Accommodation price codes

All the **accommodation** listed in this guide has been graded according to the following **price codes**, which indicate the price for the cheapest double room available during high season. In the case of hostels we've given the code if they have double rooms, but otherwise we've stated the price per dorm bed in euros. Single rooms generally cost between sixty and eighty percent of the double-room rate. These codes are above all a guide to price, and aren't intended to indicate the level of facilities available. You'll also find that many bottom-end hotels have a mixture of rooms, some with en-suite facilities, some without; thus, an establishment graded, for example, as a ❸ may also have more comfortable rooms at ❹. Most hotels only charge the full quoted rates at the very busiest times, which means that you'll often pay less than the price quoted in this book; it's always worth asking if there is any discount available either by phone or online, where many of the best deals are posted.

❶ €75 and under   ❹ €126–150   ❼ €201–250
❷ €76–100   ❺ €151–175   ❽ €251–300
❸ €101–125   ❻ €176–200   ❾ €301 and over

---

get very full between June and September, when you should book in advance. If you're planning on spending some nights in hostels, it makes sense to join your home HI organization (see below) before you leave in order to avoid paying surcharges.

Stayokay (@www.stayokay.com), the HI-affiliated Dutch hostel association, runs thirty hostels in the Netherlands. Dorm beds cost €20–30 per person per night including breakfast, depending on the season and the hostel's facilities; there are no age restrictions. Accommodation is usually in small **dormitories**, though most hostels have single- and double-bedded rooms. Meals are often available – about €11 for a filling dinner – and in some hostels there are self-catering facilities. Most Stayokay hostels accept online bookings. In addition to Stayokay HI hostels, the larger cities – particularly Amsterdam – have a number of **private hostels** offering dormitory accommodation (and invariably double- and triple-bedded rooms, too) at broadly similar prices, though standards vary enormously; we've given detailed reviews, where appropriate, in the guide.

Youth hostel associations

Australia Youth Hostels Association @www.yha.com.au
Hostelling International US Hostels @www.hiayh.org
Hostelling International Canada @www.hihostels.ca

Hostelling International Northern Ireland @www.hini.org.uk
Irish Youth Hostel Association @www.anoige.ie
Scottish Youth Hostel Association @www.syha.org.uk
Youth Hostel Association (YHA – England and Wales) @www.yha.org.uk
Youth Hostelling Association New Zealand @www.yha.co.nz

Camping and trekkers' huts

If you're not too averse to rain, then **camping** is a viable proposition in the Netherlands – there are plenty of sites and most of them are very well equipped. Prices vary greatly, depending on the facilities available, but you can generally expect to pay around €3–5 per person, plus the same again for a tent, and another €3–5 or so if you have a car or motorbike. All tourist offices have details of their nearest sites, and we've mentioned a few campsites in the Guide. A list of selected sites is available from the Dutch camping association, Stichting Vrije Recreatie (☎0183/352 741, @www.svr.nl).

If you don't mind having basic facilities, look out for **minicampings**, which are generally signed off the main roads. These are often family-run – you may end up pitched next to a family's house – and are informal, cheap and friendly. Details of registered minicampings can be found in the accommodation section of the provincial guides sold at every tourist office. Some campsites also offer **trekkers' huts** (*trekkershutten*) – frugally furnished wooden affairs that can house a maximum of four people for about €30 a night. You

can get details of the national network, with good information in English and a list of sites in each-province, from the **Stichting Trekkershutten Nederland** (Ⓦwww .trekkershutten.nl).

Food and drink

The Netherlands may not be Europe's gastronomic epicentre, but the food in the average Dutch restaurant has improved by leaps and bounds in recent years, and there are any number of places serving a good, inventive take on home-grown cuisine. All the larger cities also have a decent assortment of ethnic restaurants, especially Indonesian, Chinese and Thai, plus lots of cafés and bars – often known as eetcafés – that serve adventurous, reasonably priced food in a relaxed and unpretentious setting. The Netherlands is also a great country to go drinking, with a wide selection of bars, ranging from the chic and urbane to the rough and ready. Considering the country's singular approach to the sale and consumption of cannabis, you might choose to enjoy a joint after your meal rather than a beer – for which you will have to go to a "coffeeshop" (see p.37).

Food

Dutch **food** tends to be higher in protein content than variety: steak, chicken and fish, along with filling soups and stews, are staples, usually served up in substantial quantities. It can, however, at its best, be excellent, with lots of restaurants – and even bars and eetcafés – offering increasingly adventurous crossovers with French cuisine, all at good-value prices.

Breakfast

In all but the cheapest and most expensive of hotels, **breakfast** (*ontbijt*) will be included in the price of the room. Though usually nothing fancy, it's always substantial: rolls, cheese, ham, hard-boiled eggs, jam and honey or peanut butter are the principal ingredients. Many bars and cafés serve rolls and sandwiches in similar mode, although few open much before 8 or 8.30am.

Dutch **coffee** is normally good and strong, served with a little tub of *koffiemelk* (evaporated milk); ordinary milk is rarely used. If you want coffee with warm milk, ask for a *koffie*

verkeerd. **Tea** generally comes with lemon – if anything; if you want milk you have to ask for it. **Chocolate** (*chocomel*) is also popular, hot or cold; for a real treat, drink it hot with a layer of fresh whipped cream (*slagroom*) on top. Some cafés also sell aniseed-flavoured warm milk (*anijsmelk*).

Snacks and sandwiches

Dutch **fast food** has its own peculiarities. Chips/fries (*friet* or *patat*) are the most common standby; *vlaamse* or "Flemish" style sprinkled with salt and smothered with huge gobs of mayonnaise (*frietesaus*) are the best, or with curry, *sateh*, goulash or tomato sauce. If you just want salt, ask for *patat zonder*; fries with salt and mayonnaise are *patat met*. You'll also come across *kroketten* – spiced minced meat (usually either veal or beef), covered with breadcrumbs and deep fried – and *fricandel*, a frankfurter-like sausage. All these are available over the counter at evil-smelling fast-food places, or, for a euro or so, from coin-op heated glass compartments on the street and in train stations.

Much tastier are the **fish specialities** sold by street vendors, which are good as a snack or a light lunch: salted raw herring, rollmops, smoked eel (*gerookte paling*), mackerel in a roll (*broodje makreel*), mussels and various kinds of deep-fried fish are all delicious. Look out, too, for "green" or *maatje* herring, eaten raw with onions in early summer: hold the fish by the tail, tip your head back and dangle it into your mouth, Dutch-style. Another snack you'll see everywhere is *shoarma* or **shwarma** – another name for a doner kebab, shavings of lamb pressed into a flat pitta bread – sold in numerous Middle Eastern restaurants and takeaways for about €3. Other, less common, street foods include **pancakes** (*pannenkoeken*), sweet or spicy, also widely available at sit-down restaurants; **waffles** (*stroopwafels*), doused with syrup; and, in November and December, *oliebollen*, greasy **doughnuts** sometimes filled with fruit (often apple) or custard (as a *Berliner*) and traditionally eaten on New Year's Eve.

Bars often serve sandwiches and rolls (*boterham* and *broodjes*) – mostly open, and varying from a slice of tired cheese on old bread to something so embellished it's almost a complete meal – as well as more substantial dishes. A **sandwich** made with French bread is known as a *stokbrood*. In the winter, *erwtensoep* (or *snert*) – thick **pea soup** with smoked sausage, served with smoked bacon on pumpernickel – is available in many bars, and – for about €5 a bowl – makes a great buy for lunch. Alternatively, there's an **uitsmijter** (a "kicker-out", derived from the practice of serving it at dawn after an all-night party to prompt guests to depart). Now widely available at all times of day, it comprises one, two or three fried eggs on buttered bread, topped with a choice of ham, cheese, or roast beef; at about €5, it's another good budget lunch.

Cakes and cookies

Dutch **cakes and cookies** are always good, best eaten in a *banketbakkerij* (patisserie) with a small serving area; or bought in a bag and munched on the hoof. Top of the list is the ubiquitous Dutch speciality *appelgebak* – chunky, memorably fragrant apple-and-cinnamon pie, served hot in huge wedges, often with whipped cream (*met slagroom*). Other nibbles include *speculaas*, a crunchy cinnamon cookie with gingerbread texture; *stroopwafels*, butter wafers sandwiched together with runny syrup; and *amandelkoek*, cakes with a crisp cookie outside and melt-in-the-mouth almond paste inside. In and around Maastricht, don't miss *Limburgse Vlaai*, a pie with various fruit fillings.

Full meals

The majority of **bars** serve food, everything from sandwiches to a full menu – in which case they may be known as an **eetcafé**.

Dutch cheese

Abroad, **Dutch cheeses** have an unjustified reputation for being bland – perhaps partly because the Dutch tend to export the lower-quality stuff and keep the best for themselves. On home turf, Dutch cheese can be delicious, although, to be fair, there certainly isn't the variety on show as there is, say, in France or Switzerland. Most Dutch cheeses vary little from the familiar pale yellow, semi-soft **Gouda**, within which differences in taste come with the varying stages of maturity: *jong* cheese has a mild flavour, *belegen* is much tastier, while *oud* can be pungent and strong, with a grainy, flaky texture. The best way to eat it is as the Dutch do, in thin slices (cut with a cheese slice, or *kaasschaaf*) rather than large hunks. Among other names to look out for, best known is **Edam**, also semi-soft in texture but slightly creamier than Gouda; it's usually shaped into balls and coated in red wax ready for export – it's not eaten much in the Netherlands. Leidse is simply a bland Gouda laced with cumin or caraway seeds; most of its flavour comes from the seeds. **Maasdam** is a Dutch version of Emmental or Jarlsberg, strong, creamy and full of holes, sold under brand names such as Leerdammer and Maasdammer. You'll also find Dutch-made Emmental and Gruyère.

This type of place is usually open all day, serving both lunch and an evening meal. Full-blown **restaurants**, on the other hand, tend to open in the evening only, usually from around 5.30pm or 6pm until around 10pm. Especially in the smaller towns, the Dutch eat early, usually around 7.30 or 8pm; after about 10pm you'll find many restaurant kitchens closed.

If you're on a budget, stick to the **dagschotel** (dish of the day) wherever possible, for which you pay around €10. It's usually a meat or fish dish, heavily garnished with potatoes and other vegetables and salad; note, though, that it's often only served at lunchtime or between 6 and 8pm. Otherwise, you can pay up to €20 for a meat or seafood main course in an average restaurant. **Vegetarian** dining isn't a problem. Many eetcafés and restaurants have at least one meat-free menu item, and you'll find a few veggie restaurants in most of the larger towns, offering full-course set meals for €7.50–10 – although bear in mind that they often close early (7/8pm).

As for **foreign cuisines**, the Dutch are particularly partial to **Indonesian** food and Indonesian restaurants are commonplace: *nasi goreng* and *bami goreng* (rice or noodles with meat) are good basic dishes, though there are normally more exciting items on the menu, some very spicy; chicken or beef in peanut sauce (*sateh*) is always available. Or you could try a **rijsttafel** – a sampler meal, comprising rice and/or noodles served with perhaps ten or twelve small, often spicy dishes and hot sambal sauce on the side. Usually ordered for two or more people, you can reckon on paying around €20–25 per person. **Surinamese** restaurants are much rarer, being largely confined to the big cities, but they offer a distinctive, essentially Creole cuisine – try *roti*, flat pancake-like bread served with a spicy curry, hardboiled egg and vegetables.

Italian food is ubiquitous, with pizzas and pasta dishes starting at a fairly uniform €8 or so in most places.

Drinking

Most **drinking** is done in the laid-back surroundings of a brown bar (*bruin kroeg*) – so named because of the colour of the walls, often stained by years of tobacco smoke – or in more modern-looking places, everything from slick designer bars, minimally furnished and usually catering for a younger crowd, to cosy neighbourhood bars. Most bars **stay open** until around 1am during the week and 2am at weekends, though some don't bother to open until lunchtime, a few not until 4 or 5pm.

Though they're no longer common, you may also come across *proeflokaalen* or tasting houses. Originally the sampling premises of small distillers, these are now small, old-fashioned bars that only serve spirits (and maybe a few beers) and sometimes close early (around 8pm).

Beer

The Netherlanders' favourite tipple is **beer**, mostly Pilsener-style lager usually served in a relatively small measure (just under a half-pint, with a foaming head on top) – ask for *een pils*. Prices are fairly standard: about €1.60–1.80 pretty much everywhere. Predictably, beer is much cheaper from a supermarket, most brands retailing at just under €1 for a half-litre bottle. The most common Dutch brands are Heineken, Amstel and Grolsch, all of which you can find more or less nationwide. Expect them to be stronger and more distinctive than the watery approximations brewed abroad under licence. In the south of the country, you'll also find a number of good local brews – Bavaria from Noord-Brabant, De Ridder, Leeuw, Gulpen and Brand (the country's oldest brewer) from Limburg. For something a little less strong, look out for *donkenbier*, which is about half the strength of an ordinary Pilsener beer. There are also a number of seasonal beers: rich, fruity *bokbier* is fairly widespread in autumn, while year-round you'll see *witbier* (a wheaty, white beer) such as Hoegaarden, Dentergems or Raaf – refreshing and potent in equal measure, and often served with a slice of a lemon or lime.

Around the country, you'll also spot plenty of the better-known **Belgian brands** available on tap, like Stella Artois and the darker De Koninck, as well as bottled beers like Duvel, Chimay and various brands of the fruit-flavoured Kriek.

Wine and spirits

Wine is reasonably priced – expect to pay around €6–8 for an average bottle of French white or red in a supermarket, €15 in a restaurant. As for spirits, the indigenous drink is **jenever**, or Dutch gin – not unlike British gin, but a bit weaker and oilier, made from molasses and flavoured with juniper berries. It's served in a small glass (for around €2) and is traditionally drunk straight, often knocked back in one gulp with much hearty back-slapping. There are a number of varieties, principally *Oud* (old), which is smooth and mellow, and *Jong* (young), which packs more of a punch – though neither is extremely alcoholic. The older *jenevers* (including *zeer oude*, very old) are a little more expensive but stronger and less

oily. In a bar, ask for a *borreltje* (straight *jenever*) or a *bittertje* (with angostura); if you've a sweet tooth, try a *bessenjenever* (flavoured with blackcurrant). A glass of beer with a *jenever* chaser is a *kopstoot*. Imported spirits are considerably more expensive, and you can't buy spirits in supermarkets.

Other drinks include numerous **Dutch liqueurs**, notably *advocaat* or eggnog; sweet, blue *curaçao*; and luminous green *pisang ambon*. There is also an assortment of luridly coloured fruit brandies best left for experimentation at the end of an evening – or perhaps not at all – plus a Dutch-produced brandy, *vieux*, which tastes as if it's made from prunes but is in fact grape-based, and various regional **firewaters**, such as *elske* from Maastricht – made from the leaves, berries and bark of alder bushes.

The media

English-speakers will find themselves quite at home in the Netherlands as Dutch TV broadcasts a wide range of British programmes, and English-language newspapers from around the world are readily available.

Newspapers and magazines

British newspapers are on sale in every major city on the day of publication for around €4. Newsagents located at train stations will almost always have copies if no one else does. Current issues of UK and US magazines are widely available too, as is the *International Herald Tribune*.

Of the **Dutch newspapers**, *NRC Handelsblad* is a right-of-centre paper that has perhaps the best news coverage and a liberal stance on the arts; *De Volkskrant* is a progressive, leftish daily; the popular right-wing *De Telegraaf* boasts the highest circulation figures in the country and has a well-regarded financial section; *Algemeen Dagblad* is a right-wing broadsheet; while the middle-of-the-road *Het Parool* ("The Password") and the news magazine *Vrij Nederland* ("Free Netherlands")

are the successors of underground Resistance newspapers printed during wartime occupation. The Protestant *Trouw* ("Trust"), another former underground paper, is centre-left in orientation with a focus on religion. Bundled in with the weekend edition of the *International Herald Tribune* is *The Netherlander*, a small but useful business-oriented review of Dutch affairs in English.

Television and radio

Dutch TV isn't the best, but English-language programmes and films fill up a fair amount of the schedule – and they are always subtitled, never dubbed. Many bars and most hotels have at least two of the big pan-European **cable and satellite** channels – including MTV, CNN and Eurosport – and most cable companies also give access to a veritable raft of foreign television channels, including Britain's BBC1 and BBC2, National Geographic, Eurosport and Discovery, and a host of Belgian, German, French, Spanish, Italian, Turkish and Arabic stations, some of which also show un-dubbed British and US movies.

Dutch **radio** has numerous stations catering for every niche. Of the **public service stations**, Radio 1 is a news and sports channel, Radio 2 plays AOR music, Radio 3 plays chart music and Radio 4 classical, jazz and world music. Of the **commercial stations**, some of the main nationwide players are Radio 538, Veronica, Sky Radio and Noordzee FM; most of them play chart

music. The Dutch Classic FM, at 101.2FM, plays mainstream classical music, with jazz after 10pm. There's next to no **English-language programming**, apart from the overseas-targeted Radio Netherlands (@www.rnw.nl), which broadcasts Dutch news in English, with articles on current affairs, lifestyle issues, science, health and so on, and the BBC World Service (@www.bbc.co.uk /worldservice), which broadcasts pretty much all day in English on 648kHz (AM) around Amsterdam as do the Voice of America (@www.voa.gov) and Radio Canada International (@www.rcinet.ca), whose frequencies are listed on their respective websites.

Festivals and events

Across the Netherlands, most annual festivals are arts- or music-based affairs, confined to a particular town or city, though there is also a liberal sprinkling of folkloric events celebrating one local event or another – the Alkmaar cheese market (see p.134) being a case in point. Most festivals take place during the summer and the local tourist office can be guaranteed to have all the latest details.

January

Elfstedentocht (Eleven Cities' Journey) Friesland @www.elfstedentocht.nl. Annual ice-skating marathon along the frozen rivers of Friesland, starting and finishing in Leeuwarden. Weather permitting.

February

Holland Flowers Festival Zwaagdijk-oost, near Enkhuizen @www.hollandflowersfestival.nl. The world's largest covered flower show held over five days in late February.

Lent carnivals All sorts of shenanigans at the beginning of Lent in Breda, 's Hertogenbosch, Maastricht and other southern towns. Late Feb to early March.

March

Keukenhof Gardens Lisse @www.keukenhof.nl. World-renowned floral displays in the bulbfields and hothouses of this park from mid-March to mid-May. See p.134.

April

Alkmaar Cheese Market Alkmaar @www .vvvalkmaar.nl. Held every Friday (10am–12.30pm), from the first Friday in April to the first Friday in September. See p.134.

Fortis Marathon Rotterdam @www .rotterdammarathon.nl. Popular long-distance run beginning in the city centre. Held on a Sunday in April.

Queen's Day (Koninginnedag) April 30. This is one of the most popular dates in the Dutch diary, a street event *par excellence*. Celebrations in honour of Queen Beatrix take place throughout the Netherlands, but festivities in Amsterdam tend to be the wildest of the lot, with the city's streets and canals lined with people dressed in ridiculous costumes. Anything goes, especially if it's orange – the Dutch national colour. This is also the one day of the year when goods can be bought and sold tax-free to anyone on the streets, and numerous stalls are set up in front of people's houses.

May

Scheveningen Sand Sculpture Festival
Scheveningen ⓦ www.sandsculptures.nl. Hard-working teams descend on the resort from all over Europe to create amazing sand sculptures, which are left for three weeks for visitors to admire. May to mid-June.

Herdenkingsdag (Remembrance Day) There's wreath-laying all over the country and a two-minute silence is widely observed in honour of the Dutch dead of World War II. May 4.

Bevrijdingsdag (Liberation Day) The country celebrates the 1945 liberation from German occupation with music, outdoor festivals and processions. May 5.

Breda Jazz Festival Breda ⓦ www.bredajazz festival.nl. Has open-air concerts and street parades over five days in late May. See p.304.

Pinkpop festival Landgraaf, near Maastricht ⓦ www.pinkpop.nl. A top-notch, three-day open-air rock festival held at the end of May.

June

Holland Festival Amsterdam ⓦ www .hollandfestival.nl. This month-long performing arts festival covers all aspects of both national and international music, theatre, dance and the contemporary arts. Throughout June.

Oerol Festival Terschelling ⓦ www.oerol.nl. A ten-day event featuring theatre and stand-up comedy; mid- to late June.

July

North Sea Jazz Festival Rotterdam ⓦ www .northseajazz.com. Outstanding three-day jazz festival showcasing international names as well as local talent. Multiple stages and a thousand musicians. Mid-July. See p.184.

Woodstock69 Bloemendaal aan Zee ⓦ www .woodstock69.nl. Festival held on Bloemendaal beach and featuring live percussion, dance acts and plenty of revelry. Begins in April and runs through to September, but July and August are best.

Internationale Vierdaagse Afstandmarsen Nijmegen ⓦ www.4daagse.nl. One of the world's largest walking events, with over 30,000 participants walking 30–50km per day over four days. Late July.

August

Sneek Week Sneek ⓦ www.sneekweek.nl. International sailing event in Sneek, with around 1000 boats competing in over thirty classes. Early Aug.

Amsterdam Pride Amsterdam ⓦ www .amsterdamgaypride.nl. The city's gay community celebrates with street parties and performances, as well as a "Canal Pride" flotilla of boats parading along the Prinsengracht. First or second weekend.

Grachtenfestival Amsterdam ⓦ www .grachtenfestival.nl. For nine days, international musicians perform classical music at historic locations in the city centre. Includes the Prinsengrachtconcert, one of the world's most prestigious open-air concerts, featuring a stage over the canal and a promenading audience. Mid-August.

September

Open Monumentendag (Open Monument Day) ⓦ www.openmonumentendag.nl. For two days in September, monuments and historical attractions that are normally closed or have restricted opening times throw open their doors to the public for free. Second weekend.

October

Amsterdam Marathon Amsterdam ⓦ www .amsterdammarathon.nl. Popular city marathon starting and finishing inside the Olympic Stadium and passing through the city centre along the way. Held in early/mid-Oct.

November

Crossing Border The Hague ⓦ www.crossing border.nl. Four-day festival that aims to cross artistic boundaries with performances by over a hundred international acts presenting the spoken word in various forms, from rap to poetry. Second or third week.

Parade of Sint Nicolaas Amsterdam. The traditional parade of Sinterklaas (Santa Claus) through the city on his white horse, starting from behind Centraal Station where he arrives by steam boat, before proceeding down the Damrak towards Rembrandtplein accompanied by his helpers, the Zwarte Pieten ("Black Peters") – so called because of their blackened faces – who hand out sweets and little presents. It all finishes on the Leidseplein. Second or third Sunday.

International Documentary Film Festival Amsterdam ⓦ www.idfa.nl. Arguably the world's largest documentary film festival, held over ten days in Amsterdam and showing around 250 domestic and international documentaries. Mid- to late November.

December

Pakjesavond (Present Evening) Pakjesavond, rather than Christmas Day, is when Dutch kids receive their Christmas presents. If you're in the Netherlands on that day and have Dutch friends, it's worth knowing that it's traditional to give a present together with an amusing poem you have written caricaturing the recipient. For the children, legend asserts that presents are dropped down the chimney by Zwarte Piet (Black Peter) as Sinterklaas rides across the rooftops on his white horse. Traditionally, kids sing songs to make Sinterklaas happy in the weeks before Pakjesavond as there is always the chance of being caught by Zwarte Piet (if you haven't been good) and sent to Spain – where Sinterklaas lives – in a brown bag. December 5.

Travel essentials

Addresses

These are written, for example, as Haarlemmerstraat 15 III, meaning the third-floor (US fourth-floor) apartment at no. 15 Haarlemmerstraat. The ground floor is indicated by **hs** (*huis*, "house") after the number; the basement is **sous** (*sousterrain*). The figures **1e**, **2e**, **3e** and **4e** before a street name are an abbreviation for Eerste, Tweede, Derde and Vierde, respectively – the first, second, third and fourth streets of the same name. Some **sidestreets**, rather than have their own name, take the name of the street that they run off, with the addition of the word *dwars*, meaning crossing – so Palmdwarsstraat is a sidestreet off Palmstraat. **T/O** (*tegenover*, "opposite") in an address shows that the address is a boat: hence "Prinsengracht T/O 26" would indicate a boat to be found opposite building no. 26 on Prinsengracht. Dutch postcodes are made up of four figures and two letters.

Children

In general terms at least, Dutch society is sympathetic to its **children** and the tourist industry follows suit. Extra beds in hotel rooms are usually easy to arrange; many restaurants (but not the smartest) have children's menus; concessions for children are the rule, from public transport through to museums; and baby changing stations are commonplace. Pharmacists (*apotheek*) carry all the kiddy stuff you would expect – nappies, baby food and so forth.

Concessions

Concessionary rates are applied at almost every sight and attraction as well as on public transport. Rates vary, but usually seniors (65+) get in free or for a discounted price, children under 5 go free and kids over 5 and under 15/16 get a substantial discount; family tickets are common too.

Crime and personal safety

By comparison with other parts of Europe, the Netherlands is relatively free of **crime**, so there's little reason why you should ever come into contact with the Dutch police force. However, there is more street crime than there used to be, especially in Amsterdam and the larger cities, and it's advisable to be on your guard against **petty theft**: secure your things in a locker when staying in hostel accommodation, and never leave any valuables in a tent or car. Be cautious when using ATMs, especially late at night, and be wary of suspicious devices fitted around the card slot. If you're on a bike, make sure it is well locked up; bike theft and resale is a major industry here – as is the usual mobile phone theft; keep your network provider's number handy in case you have to bar your phone. If you are **robbed**, you'll need to go to a police station to report it, not least because your insurance company will require a police report; remember to make a note of the report number – or, better still, ask for a copy of the statement itself. Don't expect a great deal of concern if your loss is relatively small – and don't be surprised if the process of completing forms and formalities takes ages.

As for **personal safety**, it's generally possible to walk around without fear of harassment or assault, but certain parts of all the big cities – especially Rotterdam and

Amsterdam – are decidedly dodgy, and wherever you go at night it's always better to err on the side of caution. In particular, Amsterdam's Red Light District can have an unpleasant, threatening undertow (although the crowds of people act as a deterrent), while Rotterdam's docklands are similarly grim. Using public transport, even late at night, isn't usually a problem, but if in doubt take a taxi.

If you're **detained by the police**, you don't automatically have the right to a phone call, although in practice they'll probably phone your consulate for you – not that consular officials have a reputation for excessive helpfulness (particularly in drug cases). If your alleged offence is a minor matter, you can be held for up to six hours without questioning; if it is more serious, you can be detained for up to 24 hours.

Drugs

Thousands of visitors come to the Netherlands in general, and Amsterdam in particular,

just to get **stoned**. Here in the Netherlands the purchase of **cannabis** is decriminalized and this has proved to be a real crowd puller, though it's not without its problems: many Amsterdammers, for instance, get mightily hacked off with "drug tourism", as do folk in border towns, who have to deal with tides of people popping over the international frontier to the first **coffeeshop** they see. However, the Dutch government's attitude to soft drugs is more complex than you might think: the use of cannabis is tolerated but not condoned, resulting in a rather complicated set of rules and regulations that can be safely ignored as long as you buy very small amounts for **personal use only** – which means possession of up to 30g and sales of up to 5g per purchase in coffeeshops, though in practice this is pretty relaxed, and many places will happily sell you much more than this (as they will space-cakes, although these are also technically illegal). Needless to say, never, ever buy dope on the street and don't try to take

Coffeeshops

When you first walk into a **coffeeshop**, how you buy the stuff isn't immediately apparent – it's illegal to advertise cannabis in any way, which includes calling attention to the fact that it's available at all. What you have to do is ask to see the **menu**, which is normally kept behind the counter. This will list all the different hashes and grasses on offer, along with (if it's a reputable place) exactly how many grams you get for your money. The in-house dealer will be able to help you out with queries. Current **prices** per gram of hash and marijuana range from €10 for low-grade stuff up to €25 for top-quality hash and as high as €60 for really strong grass.

The **hash** you come across originates in various countries and is much like you'd find anywhere, apart from **Pollem**, which is compressed resin and stronger than normal. **Marijuana** is a different story, and the old days of imported Colombian, Thai and sensimelia are fading away. Taking their place are limitless varieties of "**Nederwiet**", Dutch-grown under UV lights and more potent than anything you're likely to have come across. Skunk, Haze and Northern Lights are all popular types of Dutch weed, and should be treated with caution – a smoker of low-grade British draw will be laid low (or high) for hours by a single spliff of skunk. You would be equally well advised to take care with **space-cakes** (cakes or biscuits baked with hash), which are widely available: you can never be sure exactly what's in them; they tend to have a delayed reaction (up to two hours before you notice anything strange – don't get impatient and gobble down another one); and once they kick in, they can bring on an extremely intense, bewildering high (10–12hr is common). You may also come across **cannabis seeds** for growing your own: while locals are permitted to grow a small amount of marijuana for personal use, the import of cannabis seeds is illegal in any country, so don't even think about trying to take some home. Finally, one oddity is that since July 2008, smoking tobacco is no longer permitted in coffeeshops (as well as bars and restaurants), though you can mix your joints with tobacco substitutes and these are widely available.

any form of cannabis out of the country. A surprising number of people think (or claim to think) that if it's bought in Amsterdam it can be taken back home legally; this story won't wash with customs officials and drug enforcement officers, who will happily add your stash to the statistics of national drug seizures, and arrest you into the bargain.

As far as **other drugs** go, after a series of serious incidents, the Dutch government has recently enforced a new law on **magic mushrooms**, making them just as illegal as hard drugs. That said, you can still purchase the "grow-your-own" kits or buy truffles, which are claimed to have a similar effect. Despite the existence of a lively and growing trade in cocaine and heroin, possession of either could mean a stay in one of the Netherlands' lively and ever-growing jails. Ecstasy, acid and speed are as illegal in the Netherlands as they are anywhere else.

Electricity

Dutch **electricity** runs at 220V AC. British equipment needs only a plug adaptor; American apparatus requires a transformer and an adaptor.

Entry requirements

Citizens of the EU/EEA, including the UK and Ireland, plus citizens of Australia, New Zealand, Canada and the US do not need a **visa** to enter the Netherlands if staying for three months or less, but they do need a current **passport**. Travellers from South Africa, on the other hand, need a passport and a tourist visa before they leave for the Netherlands for a visit of less than three months; visas are available from the Dutch embassy (see opposite).

EU/EEA residents (with the exception of Bulgaria and Romania) planning on staying longer than three months do not need a residence permit, but they do need to register with **IND**, the Immigration and Naturalization Service (W www.ind.nl). In Amsterdam, go to the **Vreemdelingenpolitie** (Foreign Police), Johan Huizingalaan 757 (T 020/889 3045, W www.immigratiedienst.nl) armed with your birth certificate and proof that you have the funds to finance your stay, a fixed address, and health insurance. Other nationalities wishing to stay in the Netherlands for more

than three months need an **entry visa** and a **residence permit**. The rules are complicated – so consult your Dutch embassy at home before departure. EU and EEA citizens (with the exception of Bulgaria and Romania) do not need a permit to be able to **work** in The Netherlands, but pretty much everyone else does – again enquire at the nearest Dutch embassy before you depart for the latest regulations.

Wherever you're from, a good source of information if you're planning a long-term stay is non-profit organization **Access** (T 020/423 3217, W www.access-nl.org). They operate a very useful English-language information line, as well as running courses on various aspects of Dutch administration and culture.

Dutch embassies abroad

Australia 120 Empire Circuit, Yarralumla, ACT 2600 T 02/6220 9400, W www.netherlands.org.au.
Canada 350 Albert St #2020, Ottawa, ON, K1R 1A4 T 1-877/388 2443, W www.netherlandsembassy.ca.
Ireland 160 Merrion Rd, Dublin 4 T 01/269 3444, W www.netherlandsembassy.ie.
New Zealand PO Box 480, Ballance/ Featherston St, Wellington T 04/471 6390, W www.netherlandsembassy.co.nz.
South Africa 210 Queen Wilhelmina Ave, New Muckleneuk, Pretoria T 012/425 4500, W www .dutchembassy.co.za.
UK 38 Hyde Park Gate, London, SW7 5DP T 020/ 7590 3200, W www.netherlands-embassy.org.uk.
US 4200 Linnean Ave NW, Washington, DC 20008 T 1-877/388 2443, W www.netherlands-embassy .org.

Embassies and consulates in the Netherlands

Australia Carnegielaan 4, 2517 KH The Hague T 070/310 8200, W www.netherlands.embassy .gov.au.
Canada Sophialaan 7, 2514 JP The Hague T 070/311 1600, W www.canada.nl.
Ireland Dr Kuijperstraat 9, 2514 BA The Hague T 070/363 0993, W www.irishembassy.nl.
New Zealand Eisenhowerlaan 77, 2517 KK The Hague T 070/346 9324, W www.nzembassy.com.
South Africa Wassenaarseweg 40, 2596 CJ The Hague T 070/392 4501, W www.zuidafrika.nl.
UK Lange Voorhout 10, 2514 ED The Hague T 070/427 0427, W www.britain.nl; Consulate-General: Koningslaan 44, PO Box 75488, 1070 AL Amsterdam T 020/676 4343.

US Lange Voorhout 102, 2514 EJ The Hague
☏ 070/310 2209, ⊛ www.usemb.nl; Consulate
General: Museumplein 19, 1071 DJ Amsterdam
☏ 020/575 5309.

Gay and lesbian travellers

The Netherlands ranks as one of the top **gay-friendly** countries in Europe. The superstar of the country's gay and lesbian scene is of course Amsterdam, where attitudes are tolerant, bars are excellent and plentiful, and support groups and facilities are unequalled. In the other major cities of the Netherlands, while the scene isn't anywhere near as extensive, it's well organized: Rotterdam, The Hague, Nijmegen and Groningen, for example, each has a visible and enjoyable gay nightlife. The native lesbian scene is smaller and more subdued: many politically active lesbians move in close-knit communities, and it takes time for foreign visitors to find out what's happening.

The **COC** (⊛ www.coc.nl), the national organization for gay men and women, dates from the 1940s and is actively involved in gaining equal rights for gays and lesbians, as well as informing society's perceptions of gayness. The national HQ is at Rozenstraat 8 in Amsterdam (☏ 020/623 4596), but all cities of any size have a branch office, which can offer help, information on events and promotions – and usually a sociable coffee bar. Gay legislation is particularly progressive – for example same-sex marriage and adoption by same-sex partners were legalized in 2001. The age of consent is 16.

Consider timing your visit to coincide with **Amsterdam's Gay Pride** (⊛ www.amster dampride.nl) on the first weekend in August. Celebrations are unabashed, with music, theatre, street parties and floats parading through the streets. Other events of interest might include the Fetish Fantasy Weekend (end of March) and Queen's Day (not that sort of queen, but with lots of gay parties anyway, on April 30, see p.34). Contact the Tourism Board or COC for more details.

Health

As a member of the European Union, the Netherlands has **free reciprocal health agreements** with other member states. **EU**

In emergencies phone ☏ 112.

citizens are entitled to free treatment within the Netherlands' public healthcare system on production of a **European Health Insurance Card (EHIC)**. The EHIC is issued free of charge and is valid for at least three years. **Australians** are able to receive treatment through a reciprocal arrangement with Medicare (check with your local office for details).

In **emergencies**, if you're reliant on **free treatment** within the EU health scheme, try to make this clear to the ambulance staff, and, if you're whisked off to hospital, to the medic you subsequently encounter. If possible, it's a good idea to hand over a photocopy of your EHIC on arrival at the hospital to ensure your status is clearly understood. Without an EHIC you won't be turned away from a hospital, but you will have to pay for any treatment you receive and should therefore get an official receipt, a necessary preamble to the long-winded process of trying to get at least some of the money back. Similarly, if you're visiting a **doctor**, double-check that he/she is both working within, and regarding you as a patient of, the public health care system. Note also that some costs – such as **dental treatment** and repatriation on medical grounds – do not fall within the purview of the EU scheme. Taking out **private health insurance** means the cost of items that do not fall within the EU scheme will be – or should be – covered. Non-EU residents, apart from Australians, will need to insure themselves against all eventualities, including medical costs. In the case of major expense, the more worthwhile policies promise to sort matters out before you pay rather than after, but if you do have to pay upfront, make very sure that you always keep full doctors' reports, signed prescription details and all receipts. Anyone planning to stay for three months or more (even when coming from another EU member state) but still paying taxes back home is required by Dutch law to have private **health insurance**.

Minor ailments can be remedied at a **drugstore** (*drogist*). These sell non-prescription drugs as well as toiletries, tampons, condoms and the like. A **pharmacy** (*apotheek*) – generally open Monday to Friday 9.30am to 6pm, but often closed Monday mornings – is where you go to get a prescription filled. There aren't many 24-hour pharmacies, but the local tourist office, as well as most of the better hotels, will supply addresses of ones that stay open late.

Insurance

Even though EU health care privileges apply in the Netherlands, EU citizens are still best off taking out an **insurance policy** before travelling to cover against theft, loss and illness or injury. For non-EU citizens, an insurance policy is a must. A typical policy usually provides cover for the loss of baggage, tickets and – up to a certain limit – cash or cheques, as well as cancellation or curtailment of your journey. Many policies can be chopped and changed to exclude coverage you don't need: sickness and accident benefits can often be excluded or included at will. Taking out private insurance also means the cost of items not within the scope of the EU scheme, such as dental treatment and repatriation on medical grounds, can be covered. In the case of major expense, the more worthwhile policies promise to sort matters out before you pay rather than after, but if you do have to pay upfront, make very sure that you always keep full doctors' reports, signed prescription details and all receipts. In the event that you have anything stolen, you must obtain an official statement from the police. Note also that visitors planning **longer stays** (of three months or more) are required by Dutch law to take out private health insurance.

Internet

The Netherlands is well geared up for **internet access**. Most hotels provide access for their guests either free or for a small charge and many have also installed wi-fi networks. There are **internet cafés** in all the larger cities, charging around €1 per half hour. You'll also find that most libraries provide internet access for free, sometimes for a fixed period only – usually about an hour.

Mail

As part of a gradual scheme, all existing **Dutch post offices** are scheduled to close by 2012, and postal transactions will be carried out at the new **TNT stores** – or places with the TNT logo. **Stamps** are sold at a wide range of outlets including many supermarkets, shops and hotels. **Postboxes** are everywhere, but be sure to use the correct slot – the one labelled *overige* is for post going outside the immediate locality.

Maps

There are lots of **Netherlands road maps** on the market and for the most part they are widely available both at home and in the Netherlands. The **Hallwag** (Ⓦwww.hallwag .com) offering is particularly good and is also the most detailed (at 1:200,000), a feat it accomplishes by being double-sided; it also includes an index. The problem – and this even applies to the Hallwag – is that the Netherlands is such a crowded country that following any fold-out road map can be very difficult: if you're doing any serious driving, you're best off investing in a **Road Atlas**. The **Michelin Benelux Road Atlas** (1:150,000) does very nicely; it includes an index and has detailed insets of 25 major Dutch towns and cities. Alternatively, the **ANWB** (ⓦwww .anwb.nl), the country's main touring organisation, publishes a whole raft of specialist/ regional maps, including waterproof maps specifically designed for **cyclists**. Of the **city maps**, Falk and Geocart are highly recommended, though the best map of Amsterdam is our own *Rough Guide Map to Amsterdam*, which has the added advantage of being waterproof and rip-proof. This map also marks all the key sights plus the location of many restaurants, bars and hotels.

Money

The **currency** of the Netherlands – like much of the rest of the EU – is the **euro** (€), divided into 100 cents. The **exchange rate** for the euro at time of writing was €0.86 to the British pound; 1.40 to the US dollar; 1.56 to the Canadian dollar; 1.71 to the Australian dollar; 2.09 to the New Zealand dollar; and 11.35 to the South African Rand. There are euro **notes** of €500, €200, €100, €50, €20, €10 and €5, and **coins** of €2, €1, 50c, 20c, 10c, 5c, 2c and 1c, but note that many

retailers will not touch the €500 and €200 notes with a barge pole – you have to break them down into smaller denominations at the bank.

The Netherlands is a **cash** society: as a general rule, people prefer to pay for most things with notes and coins. However, **debit cards** are becoming increasingly popular, and most shops and restaurants accept these as well as **credit cards**. You can use most debit cards (within the Cirrus, Plus or Maestro systems) to withdraw cash from an **ATM**. ATMs also accept major credit cards, but in this case transactions are treated as loans, with interest accruing daily from the date of withdrawal. ATMs usually give instructions in a variety of languages. Otherwise Dutch banks usually offer the best deals on changing money. Banking hours are Monday to Friday 9am to 4pm, with a few big-city banks also open Thursday until 9pm or on Saturday morning. All are closed on public holidays (see p.42).

Museum cards

If you're planning to visit even a handful of Dutch museums, you'll save money with a

Public holidays

Public holidays (*Nationale feestdagen*) provide the perfect excuse to take to the streets. The most celebrated of them all is Queen's Day – Koninginnedag – on April 30, which is celebrated everywhere but with particular vim and gusto in Amsterdam.

January 1 New Year's Day

Good Friday (although many shops are open)

Easter Sunday

Easter Monday

April 30 Queen's Day

May 5 Liberation Day

Ascension Day

Whit Sunday & Monday

December 25 & 26 Christmas

Museumkaart (Museum Card), which gives free entry to over 400 museums and galleries nationwide. It costs €40 for a year (less if you're 24 or under) and you can purchase one at any participating museum – most major museums are in the scheme.

Opening hours

The Dutch weekend fades painlessly into the working week with many smaller shops and businesses, even in Amsterdam, staying closed on Monday mornings until noon. **Normal opening hours** are, however, Monday to Friday 8.30/9am to 5.30/6pm and Saturday 8.30/9am to 4/5pm, and many places open late on Thursday or Friday evenings. **Sunday** opening is becoming increasingly common, with many stores and shops in every city open between noon and 5pm.

Most **restaurants** are open for dinner from about 6 or 7pm, and though many close as early as 9.30pm, a few stay open past 11pm. **Bars**, **cafés and coffeeshops** are either open all day from around 10am or don't open until about 5pm; all close at 1am during the week and 2am at weekends. **Nightclubs** generally function from 11pm to 4am during the week, though a few open every night, and some stay open until 5am at the weekend.

Phones

The **international phone code** for the Netherlands is 31. Numbers prefixed ☏0800 are free; those prefixed ☏0900 are premium-rate – a (Dutch) message before you're connected tells you how much you will be paying for the call, and you can only call these numbers from within the Netherlands. **Phone cards** can be bought at outlets such as tobacconists and tourist offices, and in several denominations, beginning at €5, but **phone boxes** are disappearing fast as a concomitant of the irresistible rise of the mobile phone.

There is good coverage for **mobile phones/cell phones** all over the Netherlands. You need to use a mobile on the 900/1800 MHz band. Prepaid SIM cards are available in telephone shops and in some supermarkets.

To speak to the **Operator** (domestic and international), call ☏0800 0410; for **Directory Enquiries**, dial ☏0900 8008 (domestic), ☏0900 8418 (international).

The Dutch **phone directory** is available (in Dutch) at ✆www.detelefoongids.nl.

Calling home from abroad

Note that the initial zero is omitted from the area code when dialling the UK, Ireland, Australia and New Zealand from abroad.

Australia international access code + 61

New Zealand international access code + 64

UK international access code + 44

US & Canada international access code + 1

Ireland international access code + 353

South Africa international access code + 27

Shopping

The Netherlands has a flourishing retail sector and each of its large towns and cities is jammed with department stores and international chains. More distinctively, the big cities in general, and Amsterdam in particular, play host to scores of specialist shops selling everything from condoms to beads. There are certain obvious Dutch goods – tulips, clogs and porcelain windmills to name the big three – but it's the Dutch flair for design that is the most striking feature, whether it's reflected in furniture or clothes.

Normal **opening hours** are Monday to Friday 8.30/9am to 5.30/6pm and Saturday 8.30/9am to 4/5pm, though many smaller outlets take Monday morning off and larger stores and shops often open late on Thursday or Friday evenings. In the cities, Sunday opening is increasingly common (noon–5pm) and many supermarkets stay open until about 8pm every night. Also in the cities, a handful of night shops – *avondwinkels* – stay open into the small hours or round the clock. Out in the sticks, on the other hand, Saturday afternoon can be a retail desert with just about everywhere closed. Most towns have a **market day**, usually midweek (and sometimes Sat morning), and this is often the liveliest day to visit, particularly when the stalls fill the central square, the *markt*.

Sports and outdoor activities

Most visitors to the Netherlands confine their exercise to **cycling** (see p.26) and **walking**, both of which are ideally suited to the flatness of the terrain and, for that matter, the excellence of the public transport system. The Netherlands also offers all the sporting facilities you would expect of a prosperous, European country, from golf to gymnasia, swimming pools to horse riding. More individual offerings include **Korfbal** (Ⓦ www.korfball.com), a home-grown sport cobbled together from netball, basketball and volleyball, and played with mixed teams and a high basket; **canal ice skating**, though this is of course dependent on the weather being cold enough; and, cream of the idiosyncratic lot, **pole sitting**. The Netherlands also possesses some great sandy **beaches**

on both its western and northern coasts, although it has to be admitted that the weather is notoriously unreliable – some say bracing – and the North Sea is really rather murky. There are a number of fully fledged seaside resorts – such as Zandvoort and Scheveningen – but there are nicer, quieter stretches of coast, most notably amid the wild dunes and beaches that make up the **Nationaal Park Zuid-Kennemerland** near Haarlem (see p.116). There are also long sandy strands right across the islands of the Waddenzee from Texel to Schiermonnikoog and these beaches are popular for **windsurfing** and **kitesurfing** too. The lakes of Friesland and the IJsselmeer are good for **sailing**, particularly the yachting centre of Sneek.

The chief spectator sport is **football** (soccer) and the teams that make up the country's two professional leagues attract a fiercely loyal following. Big-deal clubs include PSV Eindhoven (Ⓦ www.psv.nl); Feyenoord from Rotterdam (Ⓦ www.feyenoord.nl); and Amsterdam's Ajax (Ⓦ www.ajax.nl). The football season runs from September to May, and matches are generally on Sunday at 2.30pm, with occasional games at 8pm on Wednesday. Tickets for key matches are notoriously hard to come by.

Time

The whole of The Netherlands is on **Central European Time** (CET) – one hour ahead of London, six hours ahead of New York, nine hours ahead of Los Angeles and eight hours behind Sydney. **Daylight saving** operates from the end of March to the end of October.

Tipping

Tipping isn't quite as routine a matter as it is in the US or even in the UK. However, you are expected to leave something if you have enjoyed good service – up to around ten percent of the bill should suffice in most restaurants, while hotel porters and taxi drivers may expect a euro or two on top of the fare.

Tourist information

The **Netherlands' Board of Tourism** operates an all-encompassing website (ⓦ www.holland.com), which highlights upcoming events and is particularly strong on practical information. The board also publishes a wide range of brochures and guides. Once in the Netherlands, almost every place you visit will have a **tourist office**, most of which – but certainly not all – are known as a **VVV** (pronounced fay-fay-fay), with a distinctive triangular logo. In towns, the tourist office is usually either in the centre, often on the Grote Markt (the main square), or by the train station. Staff are nearly always enthusiastic and helpful, and speak excellent English. In addition to handing out basic maps (often for free) and English-language information on the main sights, many tourist offices keep lists of local accommodation, which they can book for you for a small fee (around €2.50). Quite often, these lists include lodgings in private houses (see p.28), which are accessible only through the tourist office. Note also that many tourist offices have **premium-rated phone lines**, which cannot be rung from abroad.

Most tourist offices sell **province guides** and these can be very useful as they list every type of accommodation, from plush hotels to mini-campings, albeit almost always in Dutch. However, establishments must pay for inclusion, so by definition the listings are not comprehensive.

Netherlands Board of Tourism offices

UK PO Box 30783, London WC2B 6DH ☏020/7539 7950, ⓔ info-uk@holland.com.

US 355 Lexington Ave, New York, NY 10017 ☏1-212/370-7360, ⓔ information@holland.com. There are no offices in **Australia** or **New Zealand**.

Travellers with disabilities

Despite its general social progressiveness, the Netherlands is only just getting to grips with the requirements of people with **mobility problems**. In Amsterdam and most of the other major cities, the most obvious difficulty you'll face is in negotiating the cobbled streets and narrow, often broken pavements of the older districts, where the key sights are often located. Similarly, provision for people with disabilities on the country's urban **public transport** is only average, although improving – many new buses, for instance, are wheelchair-accessible.

While it can be difficult simply to get around, practically all **public buildings**, including museums, theatres, cinemas, concert halls and hotels, are obliged to provide access, and do. Places that have been certified wheelchair-accessible now bear the **International Accessibility Symbol** (IAS). If you're planning to use the Dutch train network during your stay and would appreciate assistance on the platform, phone the Bureau Assistentieverlening Gehandicapten (Disabled Assistance Office; daily 7am–11pm) on ☏030/235 7822 at least 24 hours before your train departs, and there will be someone to meet and help you at the station. NS, the main train company, publishes information about train travel for people with disabilities online at ⓦ www.ns.nl and in various leaflets, stocked at main stations.

War cemeteries

There was fierce fighting in the Netherlands during World War II, notably at Arnhem (see pp.268–272), where several thousand British and Polish servicemen are remembered at the Oosterbeek cemetery. There are other military cemeteries in the east and south of the country, not least at Margraten, where around eight thousand US soldiers lie buried.

Guide

Guide

www.roughguides.com

Amsterdam

CHAPTER 1 # Highlights

* **Grachtengordel** Amsterdam's "girdle" of canals lattice the city centre – spend a snoozy afternoon viewing the grand facades from the water. See pp.70–77

* **Anne Frank Huis** A poignant memorial to the Holocaust. See p.71

* **Jordaan** This picturesque quarter of tree-shaded canals makes an ideal setting for a stroll. See p.77

* **Rijksmuseum** World-class collection of Dutch paintings, including Rembrandt's *Night Watch*. See p.84

* **Van Gogh Museum** This fabulous collection of the master's paintings are well displayed in a modern, purpose-built gallery. See p.85

* **Bars** Casual bar-hopping is one of the city's greatest pleasures. See p.92

▲ The Grachtengordel

Amsterdam

msterdam has grown up over the last decade. It's a slicker, more cosmopolitan place than it used to be, more business-minded and more integrated into the European mainstream. Yet it still remains one of the continent's most relaxed cities. There's a laid-back feel to its streets and canals that you don't get in many other European capitals, and it has a small city feel: it doesn't take long to get from place to place, and thanks to its canals many parts of the centre are uncongested and peaceful. Having said that, for most people in Holland, it really is the big city, and bears little relation to what you'll find in the rest of the country, which remains extremely provincial by comparison.

The city's layout is determined by a web of **canals**. The historical centre, which dates from the thirteenth century, is girdled by five concentric canals – the **Grachtengordel** – dug in the seventeenth century as part of a planned expansion to create a uniquely elegant urban environment. It is here that the city's merchant class built their grand mansions, typified by tall, gracefully decorated gables, whose fine proportions are reflected in the still, olive-green waters below. The conventional sights are for the most part low-key, the most promoted being the **Anne Frank Huis**. What sways the balance, however, is Amsterdam's world-class museums and galleries. For many, the **Van Gogh Museum** alone is reason enough to visit the city, but add to this the **Rijksmuseum**, with its collections of medieval and seventeenth-century Dutch paintings, and the contemporary and experimental art of the **Stedelijk Museum**, and the international quality of the art on display in the city is self-evident.

But it's Amsterdam's **population** and **politics** that constitute its most enduring characteristics. Notorious during the 1960s and 1970s as the zenith – or nadir – of radical permissiveness, the city mellowed only marginally during the Eighties, and, despite the gentrification of the last ten years or so, retains a uniquely easy-going air, with much to it that is both innovative and comfortably familiar. The city has certainly become a more urban, more homogenized place over the last decade or so, but some things about it haven't changed. The city's unparalleled selection of cosy drinking-places is a delight, whether you choose to visit a traditional, bare-floored **brown café** or one of the many designer bars and grand cafés. Entertainment has a similarly innovative edge, with offerings that are at the forefront of contemporary European film, dance, drama and music. There is any amount of affordable **live music** from all genres and Amsterdam has one of the world's leading classical **orchestras**, with generously subsidized ticket prices and some great new venues. The **club** scene is hopping too, and of course **gay** men will find that Amsterdam has one of Europe's more active and convivial nightlife networks.

Arrival

Arriving in Amsterdam by train and plane could hardly be easier. Schiphol, Amsterdam's international airport, is a quick and convenient train ride away from Centraal Station, the city's international train station, which is itself just a ten-minute metro ride from Amstel Station, the terminus for long-distance and international buses. Centraal Station is also the hub of an excellent public transport network, whose trams, buses and metro combine to delve into every corner of the city and its suburbs.

By air

Amsterdam's international **airport, Schiphol** (℡0900/7244 7465, ⓦwww .schiphol.nl), is located about 15km southwest of the city centre. **Trains** run from there to Amsterdam Centraal Station every ten minutes during the day, every hour at night (midnight–6am); the journey takes 15–20 minutes and costs €3.90, or €6.70 return. There are plenty of **taxis** – the fare from Schiphol to most parts of the city centre is €40–45 – and also hotel shuttles like the Connexxion service (℡038/339 4741, ⓦwww.schipholhotelshuttle.nl), which departs from the designated bus stop outside the arrivals hall every half hour from 6am to 9pm at a cost of €14.50 one-way, €22.50 return. The route varies with the needs of the passengers it picks up at the airport, but buses take about thirty minutes to get from the airport to the city centre. Tickets are available from the Connexxion desk in the arrivals hall.

By train and bus

Amsterdam's **Centraal Station** (CS) has regular connections with key cities in Germany, Belgium and France, as well as all the larger towns and cities of the Netherlands. Amsterdam also has several suburban train stations, but these are principally for the convenience of commuters. As you would expect, Centraal Station has a good spread of facilities, including ATMs, a bureau de change, coin-operated luggage lockers and a staffed left-luggage office (both daily 7am–11pm). In addition, there's a **VVV** tourist office (see opposite) on platform 2 and another directly across from the main station entrance on Stationsplein. Centraal Station is also the hub of the city's excellent public transport system: trams and buses depart from outside on Stationsplein, which is also the location of a metro station and a GVB public transport information office (see p.54). There's a taxi rank on Stationsplein too. For all rail enquiries contact NS (Dutch Railways; international enquiries ℡0900/9296, domestic enquiries ℡0900/9292; ⓦwww.ns.nl). Eurolines (℡020/560 8788, ⓦwww .eurolines.nl) long-distance, international **buses** arrive at **Amstel Station**, about 3.5km to the southeast of Centraal Station. The metro journey to Centraal Station takes about ten minutes.

By car

Arriving **by car** on either the A4 (E19) from Den Haag (The Hague) or the A2 (E35) from Utrecht, you should experience few traffic problems, and the city centre is clearly signposted as soon as you approach Amsterdam's southern reaches. Both roads feed onto the A10 (E22) ring road; on its west side, leave the A10 at either the Osdorp or Geuzenveld exits for the city centre. However, be warned that driving in central Amsterdam – never mind parking – is extremely difficult; see the box on p.54 for further details.

Information and tours

The VVV runs two **tourist offices** in the city centre: on platform 2 of Centraal Station (daily 11am–7pm), and on Stationsplein, across from the entrance to Centraal Station (daily 9am–6pm). These three offices share one premium-rate **information line** on ☎0900/400 4040 and a website at Ⓦwww.iamsterdam .com. They take bookings in person for canal cruises and other organized excursions and operate an extremely efficient accommodation reservation service for just €3 plus a refundable deposit that is subtracted from your final bill, but bear in mind that during peak periods the wait can be exhausting. They also sell tickets for most forthcoming performances, from rock and classical concerts thro ugh to theatre. For cultural events, go to the Amsterdam Uitburo, or **AUB**, operated by the city council, which has a walk-in booking centre tucked away in a corner of the Stadsschouwburg theatre on Leidseplein (Mon–Sat 10am–6pm, Thurs until 9pm, Sun noon–6pm; ☎0900 0191), at which you can get advice on anything remotely cultural, as well as tickets and copies of listings magazines (see p.95).

The VVV's much-touted **IAmsterdam Card** provides free and unlimited use of the city's public transport network, a complimentary canal cruise and free admission to the bulk of the city's museums and attractions. It costs €38 for one day, €48 for two consecutive days and €58 for three. Altogether it's not a bad deal, but you have to work fairly hard to make it worthwhile. It's available from any branch of the VVV. Another option if you're staying for more than a couple of days is the **Museumkaart** (museum card), which gives free entry to most museums in the whole of the Netherlands for a year; it costs €29.95 (€22.45 for the under-24s and over-60s).

Organized tours

No one could say the Amsterdam tourist industry doesn't make the most of its canals, with a veritable armada of glass-topped **cruise boats** shuttling along the city's waterways, offering everything from quick hour-long excursions to fully-fledged dinner cruises. There are several major operators and they occupy the prime pitches – the jetties near Centraal Station on Stationsplein, beside the Damrak and on Prins Hendrikkade. Despite the competition, **prices** are fairly uniform with a one-hour tour costing around €12 per adult, €6 per child (4–12 years old). The big companies, for example Lovers (☎020/530 1090, Ⓦwww .lovers.nl), run a lot of different themed cruises – dinner cruises, literary cruises, etc. All the basic cruises are extremely popular and long queues are common throughout the summer. One way of avoiding much of the crush is to walk down the Damrak from Centraal Station to the jetty at the near end of the Rokin, where the first-rate Reederij P. Kooij (☎020/623 3810, Ⓦwww .rederijkooij.nl), which also has a jetty beside Centraal Station, offers all the basic cruises at cheaper prices.

City transport

The city has a first-rate public transport system, comprising trams, buses, a pint-sized metro and four passenger ferries across the River IJ to the northern suburbs. Centraal Station is the hub of this transit system, which is run by the GVB. Trams, buses and the metro operate daily between 6am and midnight, supplemented by a limited number of nightbuses (*nachtbussen*). All tram and bus

AMSTERDAM

0 | 200 m

JORDAAN

Karthuizerhofje ⑩ ⑨

Noorderkerk ⑦
Pianola
Museum ⑪

Hofje
Van
Brienen

Lutbersekerk

GRACHTENGORDEL
WEST

Anne Frank Huis ⑱

Westerkerk ㉓ Ⓔ ⑳

Nieuwe
Kerk

OLD
CENTRE

Stedelijk
Museum
Bureau

Koninklijk
Paleis

DAM

Woonboot
Museum

De Looier
Market Ⓚ

Rommelmarkt

Bijbels
Museum

Flower
Market

Tassenmuseum
Hendrikje

Kattenkabinet

De
Appel

Melkweg Ⓝ

Stadsschouwburg

American
Hotel

Stadsarchief

GRACHTENGORDEL
SOUTH

Van Loon
Museum

VONDELPARK

Rijksmuseum

Van
Gogh
Museum

MUSEUM
PLEIN

Heineken
Experience

Stedelijk
Museum
(closed) ㊾

MUSEUM
QUARTER

see Central Amsterdam map

CAFÉS, TEAROOMS & LUNCHSPOTS

Arnold Cornelis	34
Bagels & Beans	43
't Blauwe Theehuis	57
Buffet van Odette & Yvette	35
CoBrA	56
Festina Lente	38
De Hortus	42
Keyzer	59
Panini	51
De Roos	58
Spanjer & van Twist	19
Vertigo	55

COFFEESHOPS

Barney's Breakfast Bar	3
The Bulldog	44
Paradox	26

RESTAURANTS

Albatros	10	Duende	4
Bojo	46	éénvistwéévis	28
Bolhoed	11	De Eettuin	14
Burger's Patio	15	Fifteen	17
Cilubang	37	Le Garage	62
Cinema Paradiso	9	Golden Temple	53
Claes Claesz	13	De Gouden Reael	1
Dionysos	49	Greetje	32
Dosa	50	Hemelse Modder	29

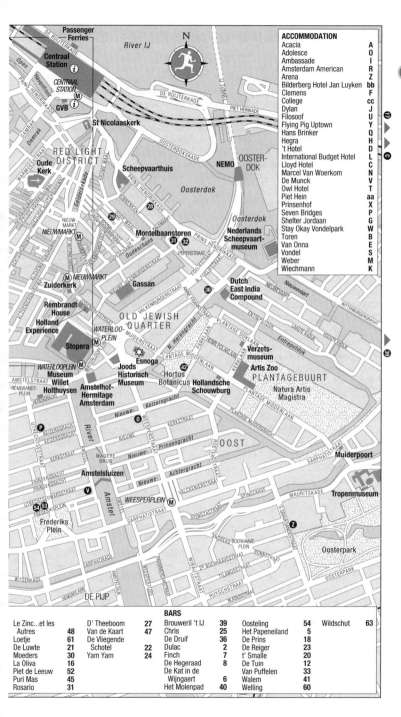

ACCOMMODATION

Acacia	A
Adolesce	O
Ambassade	I
Amsterdam American	R
Arena	Z
Bilderberg Hotel Jan Luyken	bb
Clemens	F
College	cc
Dylan	J
Filosoof	U
Flying Pig Uptown	Y
Hans Brinker	Q
Hegra	H
't Hotel	D
International Budget Hotel	L
Lloyd Hotel	C
Marcel Van Woerkom	N
De Munck	V
Owl Hotel	T
Piet Hein	aa
Prinsenhof	X
Seven Bridges	P
Shelter Jordaan	G
Stay Okay Vondelpark	W
Toren	B
Van Onna	E
Vondel	S
Weber	M
Wiechmann	K

BARS

Le Zinc...et les Autres	48	D' Theeboom	27	Brouweril 't IJ	39	Oosteling	54	Wildschut	63
Loetje	61	Van de Kaart	47	Chris	25	Het Papeneiland	5
De Luwte	21	De Vliegende Schotel	22	De Druif	36	De Prins	18
Moeders	30	Yam Yam	24	Dulac	2	De Reiger	23
La Oliva	16			Finch	7	t' Smalle	20
Piet de Leeuw	52			De Hegeraad	8	De Tuin	12
Puri Mas	45			De Kat in de Wijngaert	6	Van Puffelen	33
Rosario	31			Het Molenpad	40	Walem	41
						Welling	60

Parking

On-street parking is very limited and quite expensive. Every city-centre street where parking is permitted is **metered** between 9am and 7pm every day, with a standard cost of €4 an hour, €30 a day, and maybe €20 or so for the evening. Tickets are available from meters if you are paying by the hour, or from **Stadstoezicht** offices around town – call ☎020/553 0333 for details of the nearest one. If you overrun your ticket, you can expect to be clamped by eager traffic wardens, who can give you a fine of around €55. Car parks in the centre charge comparable rates to the metered street spaces, but those on the outskirts are a good deal less expensive and are invariably but a short journey from the centre by public transport. Note, too, that some of the better hotels either have their own parking spaces or offer special deals with nearby car parks.

stops display a detailed map of the network. For further details on all services, head for the main GVB information office (Mon–Fri 7am–9pm, Sat & Sun 8am–9pm; ☎0900/8011, ⓦwww.gvb.nl) on Stationsplein.

The most common type of ticket, usable on all forms of GVB transport, is the *strippenkaart*, a card divided into strips: fold your *strippenkaart* over to expose the number of strips required for your journey and then insert it into the on-board franking machine. Amsterdam's public transport system is divided into zones, and one person making a journey within one zone costs two strips, two zones three strips, etc. The "Centre" zone covers the city centre and its immediate surroundings (well beyond Singelgracht), and thus two strips will cover most journeys you're likely to make. More than one person can use a *strippenkaart*, as long as the requisite number of strips is stamped. After franking, you can use any GVB tram, bus and the metro for up to one hour. Currently, a two-strip *strippenkaart* costs €1.60, three-strip €2.40, and you can buy these on the bus or tram. However you're better off buying tickets in advance from tobacconists, the GVB, the VVV and metro stations – a fifteen-strip costs €7.30 and a 45-strip €21.60. You can opt instead for a *dagkaart* (day ticket), available from the same places, which gives unlimited access to the GVB system for up to a maximum of three days, and costs €7 for 24 hours, €11.50 for 48 hours, €14.50 for 72 hours and €17.50 for 96 hours.

Finally, note that the GVB tries hard to keep fare dodging down to a minimum and wherever you're travelling, and at whatever time of day, there's a reasonable chance you'll have your ticket checked. If you are caught without a valid ticket, you risk an on-the-spot fine.

Canal transport

One good way to get around Amsterdam's waterways is to take the **Canal Bus** (☎020/623 9886, ⓦwww.canal.nl). This operates on three circular routes, coloured green, red and blue, which meet at various places: at the jetty opposite Centraal Station beside Prins Hendrikkade; on the Singelgracht (opposite the Rijksmuseum), near the Leidseplein; and by the Stadhuis on Waterlooplein. There are fourteen stops in all and together they give easy access to all the major sights. Boats leave from opposite Centraal Station every half an hour or so during high season between 10am and 5.30pm, and a day ticket for all three routes, allowing you to hop on and off as many times as you like, costs €20 per adult, €10 for children (4–12 years old); it's valid until noon the following day and entitles the bearer to minor discounts at several museums.

A similar boat service, the **Museumboot** (☎020/530 1090, ⓦwww.lovers .nl), calls at seven jetties located at or near many of the city's major attractions. It departs from opposite Centraal Station (every 30min; 10am–5pm) and a day ticket costs €20, €10 for children (4–12 years old). Finally **Canal Bikes** (daily 9am–6pm, July & Aug until 9.30pm; ☎020/626 5574, Ⓦwww.canal.nl) are four-seater pedaloes which take a lifetime to get anywhere but are nevertheless good fun unless – of course – it's raining. You can rent them at four central locations: on the Singelgracht opposite the Rijksmuseum; the Prinsengracht outside the Anne Frank Huis; on Keizersgracht at Leidsestraat; and behind Leidseplein. Rental prices per person per hour are €7 (3–4 people) or €8 (1–2 people), plus a refundable deposit of €50; pedaloes can be picked up at one location and left at any of the others.

Bicycles

One of the most agreeable ways to explore Amsterdam is by **bicycle**. The city has an excellent network of designated bicycle lanes (*fietspaden*) and for once cycling isn't a fringe activity – there are cyclists everywhere. Indeed, much to the chagrin of the city's taxi drivers, the needs of the cyclist often take precedence over those of the motorist and by law, if there's a collision it's always the driver's fault. **Bike rental** is straightforward. There are lots of rental companies (*fietsenverhuur*) but MacBike (daily 9am–5.45pm; ☎020/620 0985, Ⓦwww .macbike.nl) is perhaps the most convenient, with three rental outlets in central Amsterdam, one at the east end of Centraal Station, a second beside Waterlooplein at Mr Visserplein 2, and a third near Leidseplein at Weteringschans 2. They charge €6 for three hours, €8.50 per day, €18 for three days and €30 for a week for a standard bicycle; 21-speed cycles cost about half as much again. All companies, including MacBike, ask for some type of security, usually in the form of a cash deposit (some will take credit card imprints) or passport.

Taxis

The centre of Amsterdam is geared up for trams and bicycles rather than cars, with motorists having to negotiate a convoluted one-way system, avoid getting boxed onto tram lines and steer round herds of cyclists. As such, **taxis** are not as much use as they are in many other cities. They are, however, plentiful: taxi ranks are liberally distributed across the city centre and taxis can also be hailed on the street. If all else fails, call ☎020/677 7777. **Fares** are metered and reasonably high, but distances are small: the trip from Centraal Station to the Leidseplein, for example, will cost around €12, €2 more to Museumplein – and about fifteen percent more late at night.

Accommodation

Despite a slew of new **hotels**, from chic designer places through to chain highrises, hotel accommodation in Amsterdam can still be difficult to find, and is often a major expense, especially at peak times of the year – July and August, Easter and Christmas. Such is the popularity of Amsterdam as a short-break

---

Bike rental outlets

Bike City, Bloemgracht 70 ☎020/626 3721, Ⓦwww.bikecity.nl; Damstraat Rent-a-Bike, Damstraat 20 ☎020/625 5029, Ⓦwww.bikes.nl; Holland Rent-a-Bike, Damrak 247 ☎020/622 3207; MacBike, Stationsplein, Mr Visseplein 2, Weteringschans 2 ☎020/620 0985, Ⓦwww.macbike.nl; Macbike Too, Marnixstraat 220 ☎020/626 6964.

destination that you'd be well advised to make an advance **reservation** at any time of the year. In spite of this, most hotels only charge the full quoted rates at the very busiest times, which means that you'll often pay less than the peak-season prices quoted in this book; it's certainly always worth asking if there is any discount available. At least the city's compactness means that you're pretty much bound to end up somewhere within easy reach of the centre.

All accommodation listings are located on a map: the most central ones on pp.32–33, the remainder on p.61.

Hotels

The Old Centre

Hotel des Arts Rokin 154–56 ☎020/620 1558, ⊛www.hoteldesarts.nl. The 22 rooms here are cosy and well furnished, the welcome friendly, and the location excellent. A variety of rooms – and prices. ❹

Le Coin Nieuwe Doelenstraat 5 ☎020/524 6800, ⊛www.lecoin.nl. A good location opposite the swanky *Hotel de l'Europe*, but a quarter of the price, though breakfast is an extra €11.50. All rooms have kitchenettes and are kitted out in contemporary style. ❹

Hotel de l'Europe Nieuwe Doelenstraat 2–8 ☎020/531 1777, ⊛www.leurope.nl. One of the city's top five hotels, and retaining a wonderful fin-de-siècle charm, with large, well-furnished rooms and an attractive riverside terrace. Great central location too – this is about as luxurious as the city gets. ❾

Misc Kloveniersburgwal 20 ☎020/330 6241, ⊛www.hotel.misc.com. Very friendly hotel on the edge of the Red Light District with six good-sized rooms, each decorated with a different theme. Excellent value, and rates include breakfast. ❹

Nes Kloveniersburgwal 137–39 ☎020/624 4773, ⊛www.hotelnes.nl. This pleasant and quiet hotel, with helpful staff, is well positioned away from noise but close to shops and nightlife, and also has a lift. The size and quality of the rooms can vary quite a bit, so don't be afraid to ask to see another if you're disappointed. Prices vary as well and there are also triples and quads. ❹

NH City Centre Spuistraat 288 ☎020/420 4545, ⊛www.nh-hotels.com. This appealing chain hotel occupies a sympathetically renovated 1920s Art Deco former textile factory, and is well situated for the cafés and bars of the Spui, and the Museum Quarter. Rooms vary in size, some have canal views, and all boast extremely comfy beds and good showers. The buffet breakfast is extra, but will set you up for the day. ❺

Sint Nicolaas Spuistraat 1a ☎020/626 1384, ⊛www.hotelnicolaas.nl. More characterful than many of the other budget hotels in the area, the *St Nicolaas* has a cosy downstairs bar-reception which gives way to around 30 smartly refurbished rooms, all with baths and flatscreen TVs. Very conveniently located too, just five minutes' walk from Centraal Station. ❸

Winston Warmoesstraat 129 ☎020/623 1380, ⊛www.winston.nl. This self-consciously young and cool hotel has funky rooms individually decorated with wacko art and a busy ground-floor bar that has occasional live music. It's a formula that works a treat; the *Winston* is popular and often full – though this is probably also due to its low prices. Lift and full disabled access. Ten minutes' walk from Amsterdam Centraal Station. ❷

The Grachtengordel

Agora Singel 462 ☎020/627 2200, ⊛www.hotel agora.nl. Nicely located, small and amiable hotel right near the Flower market. A wide variety of rooms; you'll pay more for a canal view. ❹

Ambassade Herengracht 341 ☎020/555 0222, ⊛www.ambassade-hotel.nl. Elegant canalside hotel made up of ten seventeenth-century houses, with smartly furnished lounges, a well-stocked library and comfortable en-suite rooms. Friendly staff and free 24hr internet access. Breakfast is an extra €16, but well worth it. ❻

Amsterdam American Leidsekade 97 ☎020/556 3000, ⊛www.amsterdamamerican.com. Landmark Art Deco hotel just off Leidseplein, which dates from 1902, though the large double-glazed bedrooms are mostly kitted out in standard modern style. Can be a good source of bargains. ❻–❽

Clemens Raadhuisstraat 39 ☎020/624 6089, ⊛www.clemenshotel.nl. Friendly, well-run budget hotel, with a knowledgeable owner, this is one of the better options along this busy main road. Prices stay the same throughout the year. All rooms have free internet connection, and you can rent laptops for just a few euros. ❷–❸

Dylan Keizersgracht 384 ☎020/530 2010, ⊛www.dylanamsterdam.com. This stylish hotel is housed in a seventeenth-century building that centres on a beautiful courtyard and terrace. Its 41 rooms vary in style but all have flat-screen TVs and stereos. The restaurant combines French and African cuisine and the ambience is hip without being pretentious. Not cheap though, and breakfast is €28 extra. **⑨**

Estherea Singel 303–9 ☏020/624 5146, ⓦwww .estherea.nl. This smart hotel converted from a couple of canal houses is in a great location, and its rooms have been tastefully refurbished; the best overlook the canal. Another place where bargains can be had. **⑤–⑧**

Hegra Herengracht 269 ☏020/623 7877, ⓦwww .hegrahotel.com. Welcoming atmosphere and relatively inexpensive for the location, on a handsome stretch of canal near the Spui. Rooms are small but comfortable, either en suite or with shared facilities. **②**

't Hotel Leliegracht 18 ☏020/422 2741, ⓦwww .thotel.nl. Appealing hotel located in an old high-gabled house along a quiet stretch of canal very close to Dam Square. The eight spacious rooms are decorated in bright, modern style with large beds, TV, fridge and either bath or shower. Minimum three-night stay at weekends. **④**

Marcel van Woerkom Leidsestraat 87 ☏020/622 9834, ⓦwww.marcelamsterdam.com. This popular B&B is run by a graphic designer and artist, who attracts like-minded people to this stylish restored house with four en-suite doubles available for two, three or four people sharing. Relaxing and peaceful amid the buzz of the city, with regulars returning year after year, so you'll need to book well in advance in high season. Breakfast isn't included, but there are tea- and coffee-making facilities. **③**

De Munck Achtergracht 3 ☏020/623 6283, ⓦwww.hoteldemunck.com. This pleasant, family-run hotel off the beaten track, metres from the River Amstel, has neat and trim rooms, and the Sixties-style breakfast room sports a Wurlitzer jukebox with a good collection of 1960s hits. No credit cards. **③**

Prinsenhof Prinsengracht 810 ☏020/623 1772, ⓦwww.hotelprinsenhof.com. This nicely decorated hotel is one of the city's top budget options, with great-value rooms. Booking essential. **①–②**

🏃 **Seven Bridges** Reguliersgracht 31 ☏020/623 1329, ⓦwww.sevenbridges hotel.nl. A long-standing favourite that's excellent value for money. It takes its name from its canalside location, which affords a view of no fewer than seven dinky little bridges. Beautifully decorated in antique style, its spotless rooms are regularly revamped. Small and popular, so reservations are pretty much essential. Breakfast is included in the price and served in your room. **③**

🏃 **Toren** Keizersgracht 164 ☏020/622 6033, ⓦwww.hoteltoren.nl. Cosy, retro-chic boutique hotel, converted from two elegant canal houses, where the emphasis is on intimacy and comfort. All rooms have been recently renovated, and there's an annexe if the main building is full. There's also a nice bar/breakfast room downstairs and they offer a specially adapted menu from nearby *Christophe* if you want to eat in the evening. Very attentive and friendly staff too. **⑤–⑦**

Weber Marnixstraat 397 ☏020/627 2327, ⓦwww.hotelweber.nl. Seven spacious rooms decorated in a brisk, modern style above a popular bar, mainly attracting a youthful clientele. Small in-room breakfast included the rate. **④**

Wiechmann Prinsengracht 328–332 ☏020/626 3321, ⓦwww.hotelwiechmann.nl. Family-run for over fifty years, this medium-sized hotel occupies an attractively restored canal house close to the Anne Frank Huis, with dark wooden beams and restrained style throughout. Large, bright (if old-fashioned) rooms with TVs and showers. Prices stay the same throughout the year. **④**

The Jordaan and the Western Docklands

Acacia Lindengracht 251 ☏020/622 1460, ⓦwww.hotelacacia.nl. Small hotel, situated in the heart of the Jordaan, right on a corner, so some of the rooms have wide views of the canal and its adjoining streets. Rooms, which sleep two to four people, are rather nondescript with small beds and a shower room, but rates are low – and they also have self-catering studios. A 15min walk from Centraal Station. **②–③**

Van Onna Bloemgracht 102 ☏020/626 5801, ⓦwww.hotelvanonna.nl. A quiet, well-maintained place on a tranquil canal. The building dates back over three hundred years and still retains some of its original fixtures, though the rooms themselves are rather modest, with basic furniture and blankets on the beds. Simple setup – no TV, no smoking and cash payment only. Booking advised. Room rates include breakfast. **②**

The Old Jewish Quarter and the Oosterdok

Adolesce Nieuwe Keizersgracht 26 ☏020/626 3959, ⓦwww.adolesce.nl. Popular and welcoming hotel in an old canal house not far from Water-looplein. There are ten neat and trim modern rooms and a large dining room. **③**

Arena 's-Gravensandestraat 51 ☏020/850 2400, ⓦwww.hotelarena.nl. A little way east of the centre, in a renovated old convent on the edge of the Oosterpark, this is a hip three-star hotel complete with split-level rooms and minimalist decor. Despite the odd pretentious flourish, it manages to retain a relaxed vibe, attracting businesspeople and travellers alike. Lively bar, intimate restaurant, and late-night club (Fri & Sat) located within the former chapel. Not cheap, and breakfast is extra, but bargains often abound. ❽ **Lloyd Hotel** Oostelijke Handelskade 34 ☎020/561 3636, ⓦwww.lloydhotel.com. Tram #26 from CS. Situated in the up-and-coming Oosterdok district, this ex-prison and migrant workers' hostel has been renovated to become Amsterdam's coolest hotel. Uniquely, it serves all kinds of travellers, with rooms ranging from one-star affairs to five-star offerings. Some rooms are great, others not, so don't be afraid to ask to change, and the location is better than you might think – just five minutes by tram from Centraal Station. ❸–❽

The Museum Quarter and the Vondelpark

Bilderberg Hotel Jan Luyken Jan Luykenstraat 58 ☎020/573 0730, ⓦwww.janluyken.nl. Good-sized rooms, nicely refurbished, mark out this decent stab at a mini four-star, full-service hotel. A nice lounge and bar downstairs too. ❺

College Roelof Hartstraat 1 ☎020/571 1511, ⓦwww.collegehotelamsterdam.com. Converted from an old schoolhouse, *College* is one of the most elegant and original recent additions to Amsterdam's hotel scene. Original, for it's largely run by students from the city's catering school; elegant because of the sheer class of the refurbishment. ❼

Filosoof Anna van den Vondelstraat 6 ☎020/683 3013, ⓦwww.hotelfilosoof.nl. Tram #1 from CS to Jan Pieter Heijestraat. A lovely, small hotel, with each room decorated according to a different philosophical theme. It's all beautifully kept, nothing is too much trouble, and the garden outside is a rare Amsterdam treat. A bit out of the way but handy for the Vondelpark. A really good choice in this part of town. Breakfast is extra. ❸–❺

Owl Hotel Roemer Visscherstraat 1 ☎020/618 9484, ⓦwww.owl-hotel.nl. The reasonably priced doubles here are relatively bland, but its location is nice and quiet, with a downstairs lounge opening onto a lovely garden, and – run by the same family for nearly forty years – the staff are a welcoming bunch. ❹

Piet Hein Vossiusstraat 53 ☎020/662 7205, ⓦwww.hotelpiethein.nl. Five minutes' walk from Leidseplein, this sleek three-star hotel has large rooms with views over the entrance to the Vondel-park and slightly more expensive rooms in the modern annexe overlooking its peaceful back garden. There's also a comfy bar (with internet access) that's normally open until 1am. ❺

Vondel Vondelstraat 18–30 ☎020/616 4075, ⓦwww.hotelvondel.com. This hotel tries hard to be cool and sleek, and mostly succeeds, with black paint and light natural wood characterizing lovely rooms with flatscreen TVs. There's a pleasant bar and breakfast room and modern art decorates the walls of the common areas. Breakfast is extra. ❺

Hostels

Bob's Youth Hostel Nieuwezijds Voorburgwal 92 ☎020/623 0063, ⓦwww.bobshostel.nl. An old favourite with backpackers, *Bob's* is a lively place with small, basic dorm beds for €18–25 per person, including breakfast in the coffeeshop on the ground floor. They also let four apartments (€70 for two people, €90 for three). However, they kick everyone out at 10.30am to clean. Walk-in policy only. Just 10 minutes' walk from Centraal Station.

Bulldog Low-Budget Hotel Oudezijds Voorburgwal 220 ☎020/620 3822, ⓦwww.bulldoghotel.com. Part of the *Bulldog* coffeeshop chain, with a bar and DVD lounge downstairs complete with leather couches and soft lighting. Beds in dorms with TVs and showers range between €24 and €32, and there are also double rooms for €105–120, plus fully equipped apartments from €150 – all with bathrooms and TVs.

Flying Pig Downtown Nieuwendijk 100 ☎020/420 6822, ⓦwww.flyingpig.nl. Clean, large and well run by ex-travellers familiar with the needs of backpackers. Free use of kitchen facilities, no curfew, there's a late-night coffeeshop next door and the hostel bar is open all night. Justifiably popular, and a very good deal, with mixed dorm beds from just €25 depending on the size of the dorm; queen-size bunks sleeping two also available. During the peak season you'll need to book well in advance. Just a 5min walk from Centraal Station.

Flying Pig Uptown Vossiusstraat 46 ☎020/400 4187, ⓦwww.flyingpig.nl. The better of the two *Flying Pig* hostels, facing the Vondelpark and close to the city's most important museums. Immaculately clean and well maintained by a staff of travellers. Free use of kitchen facilities, no curfew and good tourist information. Fourteen-bed dorm beds start at €21.90, and there are a few two-person queen-size bunks, as well as double rooms. Great value.

Hans Brinker Kerkstraat 136 ☎020/622 0687, ⓦwww.hans-brinker.com. Well-established and raucously popular Amsterdam hostel, with around 500 beds. Dorms are basic and clean and beds go for around €22–25; singles, doubles and triples are also available. All rooms are en suite. The facilities are good: free internet after 10pm, disco every night, and it's near to the buzz of Leidseplein too. A hostel to head for if you're out for a good time (and not too bothered about getting a solid night's sleep). Walk-in policy only in high season.

International Budget Hotel Leidsegracht 76 ☎020/624.2784, ⓦwww.internationalbudget hostel.com. An excellent budget option on a peaceful little canal in the heart of the city. Small, simple rooms sleeping up to four with shared bathroom; breakfast in the café is extra. Young, friendly staff. Singles and twin rooms with private facilities €80, dorm beds €22–32.

Shelter City Barndesteeg 21 ☎020/625 3230, ⓦwww.shelter.nl. A non-evangelical Christian youth hostel smack in the middle of the Red Light District. Beds in large dorms for €22.50, including bed linen, shower and sizeable breakfast, which makes this one of the city's best deals (€24.50 for a bed in a smaller dorm). Dorms are single-sex;

lockers require a €5 deposit and there's a midnight curfew (2am at weekends).

Shelter Jordaan Bloemstraat 179 ☎020/624 4717, ⓦwww.shelter.nl. The second of Amsterdam's two Christian youth hostels, with great-value beds from €22.50 including breakfast. Fri & Sat €3 supplement. Downstairs there is a decent café. Sited in a particularly attractive and quiet part of the Jordaan, close to the Lijnbaansgracht canal.

Stay Okay Stadsdoelen Kloveniersburgwal 97 ☎020/624 6832, ⓦwww.stayokay.com /stadsdoelen. The closest to Centraal Station of the two official hostels, with clean, semi-private dorms at €21.50 for members, who get priority in high season; non-members pay €24. Price includes linen, breakfast and locker, plus use of communal kitchen.

Stay Okay Vondelpark Zandpad 5 ☎020/589 8996, ⓦwww.stayokay.com/vondelpark. Well located and for facilities the better of the city's two HI hostels, with a bar, restaurant, TV lounge, internet access and bike shed, plus various discounts on tours and museums. Rates vary, but in season non-members can expect to pay €33.50 for a dorm bed, members €31. Secure lockers and no curfew. To be sure of a place in high season you'll need to book at least two months ahead.

Campsites

Amsterdamse Bos Kleine Noorddijk 1, Amstelveen ☎020/641 6868, ⓔcamping@dab .amsterdam.nl. Facilities include a bar, shop and restaurant, but this campsite is a long way out, on the southern reaches of the lush and well-kept Amsterdamse Bos (forest). Rates are €5 per person per night (children under 3 are free), hot showers included, plus €5.75 for a tent, €4.50 for a car, €9 for a camper and €6.50 for a caravan. Huts sleeping up to four cost €45 a night, which includes a gas stove. Take yellow NZH bus #172 from Centraal Station to Amstelveen, then bus #171; from Schiphol you can take bus #199 direct. Exit 6 off the A9 towards Aalsmeer. Open April to mid-Oct.

Vliegenbos Meeuwenlaan 138 ☎020/636 8855, ⓦwww.vliegenbos.com. A relaxed and friendly site, just a 10min bus ride into Amsterdam North from CS. Facilities include a general shop, bar and

restaurant. Rates start at €8.30 per night per person with hot showers included. There are also huts with bunk beds and basic cooking facilities for €72.50 per night for four people; phone ahead to check availability. Car parking is €8.30. Bus #32 or #33 from CS or take the ferry to Buiksloterweg and allow a 15min walk; drivers take Exit S116 off the A10. Open April–Sept.

Zeeburg Zuider IJdijk 20 ☎020/694 4430, ⓦwww.campingzeeburg.nl. Well-equipped campsite in the eastern docklands with a bar, restaurant, laundry, kayak and bicycle rental, plus lots of green fields. Tent pitches cost €5 in addition to a €5.50 charge per person per night, and €5 for a car. Two-berth cabins cost €40 and four-berth €80, including bed linen. Tram #26 from CS to Zuiderzeeweg, then a 10min walk; drivers take Exit S114 off the A10. Open all year.

The City

Confined by the circuitous sweep of the Singelgracht canal, Amsterdam's compact centre contains most of the city's leading attractions and it takes only about forty minutes to stroll from one end to the other. **Centraal Station**, where you're most likely to arrive, lies on the centre's northern edge, its back to the River IJ, and from here the city fans south in a web of concentric canals, surrounded by expanding suburbs. The city centre readily divides into a network of distinct neighbourhoods, but it's small enough that just wandering around from one to another to get the flavour of the place is often the most enjoyable way to proceed.

At the heart of the city is Amsterdam's most vivacious district, the **Old Centre**, an oval-shaped area featuring a jumble of antique streets and beautiful, narrow little canals, some of which are the unlikely setting for the sleazy, infamous Red Light District. Forming a ring around it is the first of the major canals, the Singel, followed closely by the Herengracht, Keizersgracht and Prinsengracht – collectively known as the **Grachtengordel**, or "Girdle of Canals". These were part of a major seventeenth-century urban extension and, with the interconnecting radial streets, form the city's distinctive web shape. This is the Amsterdam you see in the brochures: still, dreamy canals, crisp reflections of seventeenth-century town houses, cobbled streets, railings with chained bicycles – an image which, although perhaps a little too familiar, is still utterly authentic. Beyond the Grachtengordel, the **Jordaan** to the west grew up as a slum and immigrant quarter and remains the traditional heart of working-class Amsterdam, though in recent years it has experienced a measure of gentrification. Its mazy streets and narrow canals make it a pleasant area to wander. On the east side of the centre is the **Old Jewish Quarter**; since the Nazi occupation during World War II, this area has changed more than any other – its population gone and landscape altered – but there are several poignant reminders of earlier times, most notably the first-rate Jewish Historical Museum, and a rash of new development in the eastern docklands beyond. A couple of Amsterdam's leading museums can be found just beyond the southern boundary of the Grachtengordel, in what is sometimes known as the **Museum Quarter**, on the edge of Museumplein. This forms a cultural prelude to the sprawling greenery of the nearby **Vondelpark**, Amsterdam's loveliest park, and the residential neighbourhoods of the Old South beyond.

The Old Centre

The **Old Centre** was where Amsterdam began, starting out as a fishing village at the mouth of the River Amstel and then, when the river was dammed in 1270, flourishing as a trading centre and receiving its municipal charter from a new feudal overlord, the Count of Holland, in about 1300. Thereafter, the city developed in stages, each of which was marked by the digging of new canals and, after a particularly severe fire in 1452, by the abandonment of timber for stone and brick as the main building materials. Today, it's the handsome stone and brick buildings of subsequent centuries, especially the seventeenth, which provide the old centre with most of its architectural highlights.

Strolling across the bridge from Centraal Station brings you onto the **Damrak**, the spine of the Old Centre and the thoroughfare that once divided the **Oude Zijde** (Old Side) of the medieval city to the east from the smaller **Nieuwe Zijde** (New Side) to the west. The Damrak culminates in **Dam Square**, flanked by two of the city's most impressive buildings, the Koninklijk

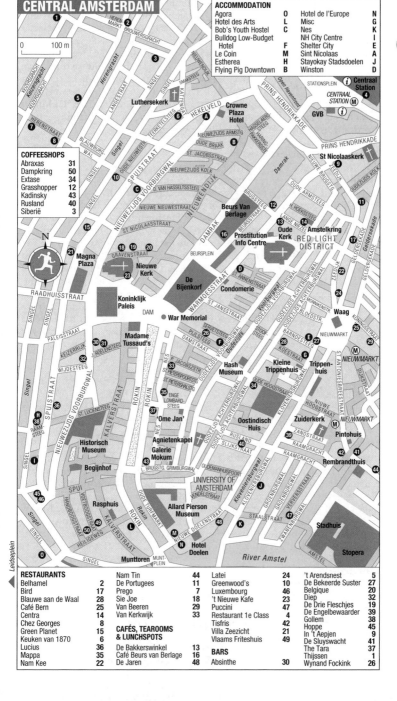

Paleis (Royal Palace) and the Nieuwe Kerk. To the east of Damrak is the **Red Light District**, which stretches up to Nieuwmarkt. It's here that you'll find many of the city's finest buildings, though the seediness of the tentacular red-light zone dulls many charms. That said, be sure to spare time for the district's two delightful churches – the Amstelkring and the Oude Kerk. Just beyond the reach of the Red Light District is careworn **Nieuwmarkt**, an unappetizing start to the **Kloveniersburgwal**, which forms one of the most beguiling parts of the Old Centre, with a medley of handsome old houses lining the prettiest of canals. From here, it's a short walk west to the **Rokin**, a shopping boulevard running south from the Dam to **Muntplein**, a busy junction where you'll find the floating flower market.

Centraal Station and around

With its high gables and cheerful brickwork, the neo-Renaissance **Centraal Station** is an imposing prelude to the city. At the time of its construction in the 1880s, it aroused much controversy because it effectively separated the centre from the River IJ, source of the city's wealth, for the first time in Amsterdam's long history. Nowadays it and **Stationsplein** outside are arousing fresh controversy due to a plan to redevelop the station and the area around it while at the same time, building a new metro line linking Amsterdam's city centre with the south of the city and stations across the IJ in the resurgent north. For the best part of six years now the area around Stationsplein has been a massive construction site, and the chaos looks set to continue for some time, until completion of the project in 2015. There have been huge arguments over the plan: some question whether it's even possible to build a tunnel under a city centre that is mainly built on wooden stilts, and work was halted for a while in 2008 when a number of city-centre buildings began to collapse, but the authorities claim they will deliver not only better connections between the city centre and its outlying districts, but also a more pleasant, pedestrian-friendly Stationsplein and inner harbour.

St Nicolaaskerk

Across the water, to the southeast on Prins Hendrikkade, rise the whopping twin towers and dome of **St Nicolaaskerk** (Mon & Sat noon–3pm, Tues–Fri 11am–4pm; free), the city's foremost Catholic church. Dating back to the 1880s, the cavernous interior holds some pretty dire religious murals, mawkish concoctions only partly relieved by swathes of coloured brickwork. Above the high altar is the crown of the Habsburg emperor Maximilian, very much a symbol of the city and one you'll see again and again. Amsterdam had close ties with Maximilian: in the late fifteenth century he came here as a pilgrim and stayed on to recover from an illness. The burghers funded many of his military expeditions and, in return, he let the city use his crown in its coat of arms – a practice that, rather surprisingly, survived the seventeenth-century revolt against Spain.

Damrak

From Stationsplein, **Damrak**, a wide but unenticing avenue lined with tacky restaurants, bars and bureaux de change, slices south into the heart of the city, first passing an inner harbour crammed with the bobbing canal boats of Amsterdam's considerable tourist industry. Just beyond the harbour is the imposing bulk of the **Beurs**, the old Stock Exchange – known as the "Beurs van Berlage" – a seminal work designed at the turn of the last century by the leading light of the Dutch Modern movement, Hendrik Petrus Berlage (1856–1934). It's used for concerts and occasional exhibitions these days, so you often can't get in to see the graceful exposed ironwork and shallow-arched arcades of the main hall, but you can stop by the café that fronts onto Beursplein around the corner (see p.88) for a coffee and admire the tiled scenes of the past, present and future by Jan Toorop.

De Bijenkorf
Just along from the Beurs, the enormous and long-established **De Bijenkorf** – literally "beehive" – department store extends south along the Damrak. Amsterdam's most upmarket store, De Bijenkorf posed all sorts of problems for the Germans when they first occupied the city in World War II. It was a Jewish concern, so the Nazis didn't really want their troops shopping here, but the store was just too popular to implement a total ban. The bizarre solution was to prohibit German soldiers from shopping on the ground floor, where the store's Jewish employees were concentrated, as they always had been, in the luxury goods section. These days it's a good all-round department store, with the usual floors of designer-wear and well-known brands but none of the snootiness you usually associate with such places.

Dam Square
Situated at the heart of the city just beyond De Bijenkorf, **Dam Square** gave Amsterdam its name: in the thirteenth century the River Amstel was dammed here, and the fishing village that grew around it became known as "Amstelredam". Boats could sail into the square down the Damrak and unload right in the middle of the settlement, which soon prospered by trading herrings for Baltic grain. In the early fifteenth century, the building of Amsterdam's principal church, the Nieuwe Kerk, and thereafter the town hall (now the Royal Palace), formally marked the Dam as Amsterdam's centre, but since World War II it has lost much of its dignity. Today it's open and airy but somehow rather desultory, despite – or perhaps partly because of – the presence of the main municipal **war memorial**, a prominent stone tusk adorned by bleak, suffering figures and decorated with the coats of arms of each of the Netherlands' provinces (plus the ex-colony of Indonesia).

The Koninklijk Paleis
Dominating the Dam is the **Koninklijk Paleis** or Royal Palace (June–Aug daily 11am–7pm; Sept–May Tues–Sun noon–5pm; €7.50, €6.50 concessions; Ⓦwww.koninklijkhuis.nl). The title is deceptive, given that this vast sandstone structure started out as the city's Stadhuis (town hall) in the mid-seventeenth century, and only had its first royal occupant when Louis Bonaparte moved in during the French occupation (1795–1813). At the time of the building's construction, Amsterdam was at the height of its powers. The city was pre-eminent among Dutch towns, and had just resisted William of Orange's attempts to bring it to heel; predictably, the council craved a residence that was a declaration of the city's municipal power and opted for a startlingly progressive design by Jacob van Campen, who proposed a Dutch rendering of the Classical principles revived in Renaissance Italy. Initially there was opposition to the plan from the council's Calvinist minority, who pointed out that the proposed Stadhuis would dwarf the neighbouring Nieuwe Kerk. However, when the Calvinists were promised a new church spire (it was never built) they promptly fell in line, and in 1648 work started on what was then the largest town hall in Europe, supported by no fewer than 13,659 wooden piles driven into the Dam's sandy soil – a number every Dutch schoolchild remembers by adding a "1" and a "9" to the number of days in the year.

The Stadhuis received its royal designation in 1808, when Napoleon's brother Louis, who had recently been installed as king, commandeered it as his residence. Lonely and isolated, Louis abdicated in 1810 and high-tailed it out of the country, leaving behind a large quantity of Empire furniture, most of which is exhibited in the rooms he converted. Possession of the palace subsequently reverted to the city, which sold it to the state in 1935, since when it has been used by royalty on very rare occasions.

The Nieuwe Kerk

Vying for importance with the Royal Palace is the adjacent **Nieuwe Kerk** (daily 10am–6pm; €10; ☎020/638 6909, 🌐www.nieuwekerk.nl), which despite its name – "new church" – is an early-fifteenth-century structure built in a late flourish of the Gothic style, with a forest of pinnacles and high, slender gables. Nowadays it's de-sanctified and used for temporary exhibitions, and opening times vary according to what's on; occasionally it's closed altogether. But it is worth going in if you can: its hangar-like interior holds a scattering of decorative highlights, such as the seventeenth-century tomb of Dutch naval hero Admiral Michiel de Ruyter, complete with trumpeting angels, conch-blowing Neptunes and cherubs all in a tizzy. Ruyter trounced in succession the Spaniards, the Swedes, the English and the French, and his rise from deck hand to Admiral-in-Chief is the stuff of national legend. He was buried here with full military honours and the church is still used for state occasions: the coronations of queens Wilhelmina, Juliana and, in 1980, Beatrix, were all held here.

Magna Plaza

Across the street from the church, you can't miss the old neo-Gothic post office of 1899, now converted into the **Magna Plaza** shopping mall (Mon 11am–7pm, Tues, Wed, Fri & Sat 10am–7pm, Thurs 10am–9pm, Sun noon–7pm; 🌐www.magnaplaza.nl). The building is a grand affair, and makes an attractive setting for the numerous clothes chains that inhabit its redbrick interior.

Rokin and Kalverstraat

Rokin picks up where the Damrak leaves off, cutting south from Dam Square in a wide sweep that follows the former course of the River Amstel. This was the business centre of the nineteenth-century city, and although it has lost much of its prestige it is still flanked by an attractive medley of architectural styles incorporating everything from grandiose nineteenth-century mansions to more utilitarian modern stuff. Running parallel, pedestrianized **Kalverstraat** is a busy shopping street that has been a commercial centre since medieval times, when it was used as a calf market; nowadays it's home to many of the city's chain stores and clothes shops – you could be anywhere in Holland really.

The Allard Pierson Museum

The **Allard Pierson Museum**, off Rokin at Oude Turfmarkt 127 (Tues–Fri 10am–5pm, Sat & Sun 1–5pm; €6.50), is a good, old-fashioned archeological museum in a solid Neoclassical building. The collection is spread over two floors and has a wide-ranging, if fairly small, assortment of finds. The particular highlight is the museum's Greek pottery, with fine examples of both the black-and red-figured wares produced in the sixth and fifth centuries BC. Look out also for the Roman sarcophagi, especially a marble whopper decorated with Dionysian scenes and a very unusual wooden coffin from around 150 AD, which is partly carved in the shape of the man held within.

Hotel Doelen

The **Hotel de l'Europe** on Doelenstraat is one of the city's most luxurious and well-appointed places to stay, but the **Hotel Doelen** next door is perhaps of more historic interest, incorporating as it does the Kloveniers Tower, once the headquarters and meeting place of the company Rembrandt depicted in *The Night Watch*. No one knows for sure whether he painted *The Night Watch* here, but it certainly hung in the building at one time, and if you ask nicely in reception you can stroll up to see where it was, although – despite the tour groups that regularly trundle through – there's not much to look at beyond a crumbling red-brick wall and a bad photo of the painting.

Muntplein and the Bloemenmarkt

Across the street, **Muntplein** is a dishevelled junction where the **Munttoren** of 1480 was originally part of the old city wall. Later, it was adopted as the municipal mint – hence its name – a plain brick structure to which Hendrik de Keyser, in one of his last commissions, added a flashy spire in 1620. A few metres away, the floating **Bloemenmarkt** (Flower Market; daily 9am–5pm, though some stalls close on Sun), extends along the southern bank of the Singel west as far as Koningsplein. Popular with locals and tourists alike, the market is one of the main suppliers of flowers to central Amsterdam; its blooms and bulbs now share stall space with souvenir clogs, garden gnomes and Delftware.

Spui and the Begijnhof

The west end of the **Spui** (rhymes with "cow") opens out into a wide, tram-clanking square flanked by bookshops and popular café-bars. In the middle is a cloying statue of a young boy, known as **'t Lieverdje** ("Little Darling" or "Lovable Scamp"), a gift to the city from a cigarette company in 1960. It was here in the mid-1960s, with the statue seen as a symbol of the addicted consumer, that the playful Sixties pressure group, the **Provos**, organized some of their most successful *ludiek* ("pranks").

A fancy little gateway on the north side of the Spui leads into the **Begijnhof** (daily 10am–5pm; free), where a huddle of immaculately maintained old houses

▲ The Begijnhof

looks onto a central green, their backs to the outside world; if this door is locked, try the main entrance, a couple of hundred metres north of Spui on Gedempte Begijnensloot. The Begijnhof was founded in the fourteenth-century as a home for the *beguines* – members of a Catholic sisterhood living as nuns, but without vows and with the right of return to the secular world. The original medieval complex comprised a series of humble brick cottages, but these were mostly replaced by the larger, grander houses of today shortly after the Reformation, though the secretive, enclosed design survived. A couple of pre-Reformation buildings remain, including the **Houten Huys**, at no. 34, whose wooden facade, the oldest in Amsterdam, dates from 1477 before the city forbade the construction of timber houses as an essential precaution against fire. Of the two churches here, the **Engelse Kerk** (English Reformed Church) is of medieval construction too, but it was taken from the *beguines* and given to Amsterdam's English community during the Reformation. Plain and unadorned, the church is of interest for its carefully worked pulpit panels, several of which were designed by a youthful Piet Mondrian (1872–1944), the leading De Stijl artist. After they had lost their church, the *beguines* were allowed to celebrate Mass inconspicuously in the clandestine Catholic **Begijnhofkapel** (Mon 1–6.30pm, Tues–Fri 9am–6.30pm, Sat & Sun 9am–6pm; free), which they established in the house opposite their old church. It's still used today, a cosy little place with some terribly sentimental religious paintings, one of which – to the left of the high altar – depicts the miracle of the unburnable Host (see "The Oude Kerk", opposite).

The Amsterdams Historisch Museum

Emerging from the east side of the Begijnhof, turn left onto narrow Gedempte Begijnensloot and nearby is the **Schuttersgalerij** – the Civic Guard Gallery. Here, an assortment of huge group portraits of the Amsterdam militia, ranging from serious-minded paintings of the 1540s through to lighter affairs from the seventeenth century, is displayed for free in a glassed-in passageway. The Schuttersgalerij is part of the **Amsterdams Historisch Museum** (entrances at Nieuwezijds Voorburgwal 357 & Kalverstraat 92, Mon–Fri 10am–5pm, Sat & Sun 11am–5pm; €10; Ⓦ www.ahm.nl), which occupies the smartly restored but rambling seventeenth-century buildings of the municipal orphanage. This museum surveys the city's development with a scattering of artefacts and lots of paintings from the thirteenth century onwards. It's a slightly difficult collection to navigate, and you need to pay close attention to the colour-coded signs that attempt to guide you through chronologically – and the labelling, which is in English and Dutch. High points include a number of paintings from the city's Golden Age – Rembrandt's wonderful *Anatomy Lesson of Dr Jan Deijman* stands out – and the section entitled "Social Care & Stern Discipline", where the harsh paternalism of the city's merchant oligarchy is examined with paintings depicting the regents of several orphanages, self-contented bourgeois in the company of the grateful poor.

The Red Light District

The area to the east of Damrak, between Warmoesstraat, Nieuwmarkt and Damstraat, is the **Red Light District**, known locally as "De Walletjes" (Small Walls) on account of the series of low brick walls that contains its canals. The district stretches across the two narrow canals that once marked the eastern part of medieval Amsterdam, **Oudezijds Voorburgwal** and **Oudezijds Achterburgwal**, with the far canal of Kloveniersburgwal forming its eastern boundary. The area is pretty seedy, although the legalized prostitution here has long been one of the city's most distinctive draws. It wasn't always so: the handsome facades of Oudezijds Voorburgwal in particular recall ritzier days when this was one of the wealthiest parts of the city, richly earning its nickname the "Velvet Canal".

Oudezijds Voorburgwal and Oudezijds Achterburgwal, with their narrow connecting passages, are thronged with "window brothels", and at busy times the crass, on-street haggling over the price of sex is drowned out by a surprisingly festive atmosphere – entire families grinning more or less amiably at the women in the windows or discussing the specifications of the sex toys in the shops. There's a nasty undertow to the district, however, oddly enough sharper during the daytime, when the pimps hang out in shifty gangs and drug addicts wait anxiously, assessing the chances of scoring their next hit. Don't even think about taking a picture of one of the windows, unless you're prepared for some major grief from the camera-shy prostitutes and their minders.

Warmoesstraat

Soliciting hasn't always been the principal activity on sleazy **Warmoesstraat**. It was once one of the city's most fashionable streets, home to Holland's foremost poet, **Joost van den Vondel** (1587–1679), who ran his hosiery business from no. 110 in between writing and hobnobbing with the Amsterdam elite. Vondel is a kind of Dutch Shakespeare: his *Gijsbrecht van Amstel*, a celebration of Amsterdam during its Golden Age, is one of the classics of Dutch literature, and he wrote regular, if ponderous, official verses, including well over a thousand lines on the inauguration of the new town hall. He had more than his share of hard luck too. His son frittered away the modest family fortune and Vondel lived out his last few years as doorkeeper of the pawn shop on Oudezijds Voorburgwal, dying of hypothermia at what was then the remarkable age of 92.

The Prostitution Information Centre

Vondel's Warmoesstraat house was knocked down decades ago, and the street holds few attractions apart from the **Condomerie Het Gulden Vlies**, at no. 141, which specializes in every imaginable design and make of condom, in sizes ranging from the small to the remarkable. Also, for the lowdown on the local sex industry, there's the **Prostitution Information Centre**, at Enge Kerksteeg 3, in between Warmoesstraat and the Oude Kerk (Wed & Fri 6–8pm, Sat noon–7pm; ☎020/420 7328, ⓦwww.pic-amsterdam.com), a charitable foundation set up to provide prostitutes, their clients and general visitors with information about prostitution, and which sells books, pamphlets and souvenirs of the Red Light District.

The Oude Kerk

Just to the east of Warmoesstraat, the Gothic **Oude Kerk** is the city's most appealing church (Mon–Sat 11am–5pm, Sun 1–5pm; €5; ⓦwww.oudekerk.nl). There's been a church on this site since the middle of the thirteenth century, but most of the present building dates from a century later, funded by the pilgrims who came here in their hundreds following a widely publicized miracle. The story goes that in 1345 a dying man regurgitated the Host he had received here at Communion and when it was thrown on the fire afterwards, it did not burn. The unburnable Host was placed in a chest and eventually installed here, and although it disappeared during the Reformation, thousands of the faithful still come to take part in the annual commemorative **Stille Omgang** in mid-March, a silent nocturnal procession terminating at the Oude Kerk. Inside you can see the unadorned memorial tablet of Rembrandt's first wife, Saskia van Uylenburg, beneath the smaller of the organs, and three beautifully coloured stained-glass windows beside the ambulatory dating from the 1550s. They depict, from left to right, the Annunciation, the Adoration of the Shepherds and the Dormition of the Virgin. Outside, the Oude Kerk **tower** is open weekends between April and September (1–5pm; €5) and offers predictably great views in a city with relatively few such opportunities.

The Amstelkring

The front of the Oude Kerk overlooks the northern reaches of **Oudezijds Voorburgwal**, where the **Amstelkring** at OZ Voorburgwal 40 (Mon–Sat 10am–5pm, Sun 1–5pm; €7; Ⓦ www.museumamstelkring.nl) was once the city's principal Catholic place of worship and is now one of Amsterdam's most enjoyable museums. The Amstelkring – "Amstel Circle" – is named after the group of nineteenth-century historians who saved the building from demolition, but its proper name is Ons Lieve Heer Op Solder ("Our Dear Lord in the Attic"). The church dates from the early seventeenth century when, with the Protestants firmly in control, the city's Catholics were only allowed to practise their faith in private – such as here in this clandestine church, which occupies the loft of a wealthy merchant's house. The church's narrow nave has been skilfully shoehorned into the available space and, flanked by elegant balconies, there's just enough room for an ornately carved organ at one end and a mock-marble high altar, decorated with Jacob de Wit's mawkish *Baptism of Christ*, at the other. The rest of the house is similarly untouched, its original furnishings reminiscent of interiors by Vermeer or De Hooch.

The Zeedijk

You can cut through from the top end of OZ Voorburgwal to the end of the **Zeedijk**, which was originally just that – a dyke to hold back the sea – and is now a street which girdles the northern end of the Red Light District. A couple of decades ago this narrow thoroughfare was the haunt of drug addicts and very much a no-go area at night, but it's been spruced up and now forms a lively route from Stationsplein through to Nieuwmarkt, on the eastern edge of the Red Light District, as well as being the main hub of Amsterdam's small but vibrant Chinatown. Its seaward end is home to a couple of the oldest bars in the city, and the jazz trumpeter **Chet Baker** famously died here in 1988, when he either fell or threw himself out of the window of the *Prins Hendrik Hotel* - an event remembered by an evocative plaque of the man in full blow. Further down, there are any number of Chinese, Thai and Vietnamese foodie treats, as well as the **Fo Guang Shan He Hua Temple**, on the right at Zeedijk 106, just 100m or so short of Nieuwmarkt (Tues–Sun 10–5pm) – a Buddhist temple heavy with the smell of incense and sounds of chanting. There's not much to see here but for a small donation you can pick your own ready-made dharma out of a box.

The Hash Marihuana Hemp Museum and around

From the Oostindisch Huis (see p.69), it's a couple of minutes' walk west to the **Hash Marihuana Hemp Museum**, Oudezijds Achterburgwal 148 (daily 11am–10pm; €5.70), which features displays on different kinds of dope and the huge number of ways to imbibe and otherwise use it. Amsterdam's reliance on imported dope ended in the late 1980s when it was discovered that a reddish weed bred in America – "skunk" – was able to flourish under artificial lights; nowadays over half the dope sold in the coffeeshops is grown in the Netherlands. There's also an indoor marijuana garden here, samples of textiles and paper made with hemp, and pamphlets explaining the medicinal properties of cannabis. The museum's shop sells pipes, books, videos and plenty of souvenirs.

Nieuwmarkt

Nieuwmarkt was long one of the city's most important market squares and the place where gentiles and Jews from the nearby Jewish Quarter – just southeast along St Antoniebreestraat – traded. All that came to a traumatic end during World War II, when the Nazis cordoned off the Nieuwmarkt with barbed wire and turned it into a holding pen. After the war, the square's old exuberance never returned and these days its focus is the sprawling multi-turreted **Waag**, dating from the 1480s and with a chequered history. Built as one of Amsterdam's fortified gates, the city's expansion soon made it obsolete and the ground floor was turned into a municipal weighing-house (*waag*), with the rooms upstairs taken over by the surgeons' guild. It was here that the surgeons held lectures on anatomy and public dissections, the inspiration for Rembrandt's *Anatomy Lesson of Dr Tulp*, displayed in the Mauritshuis collection in Den Haag. Abandoned by the surgeons and the weigh-masters in the nineteenth century, the building eventually fell into disuse, until being renovated to house the café-bar and restaurant, *In de Waag*.

Kloveniersburgwal

Nieuwmarkt sits at the head of the **Kloveniersburgwal**, a long, dead-straight waterway that was the outermost of the three eastern canals of the medieval city. The canal is framed by a string of old and dignified facades, one of which, the **Trippenhuis**, at no. 29, is a huge overblown mansion complete with Corinthian pilasters and a grand frieze built for the Trip family in 1662. Almost directly opposite, on the west bank of the canal, the **Kleine Trippenhuis**, at no. 26, is, by contrast, one of the narrowest houses in Amsterdam, albeit with a warmly carved facade. Legend asserts that Mr Trip's coachman was so taken aback by the size of the new family mansion that he exclaimed he would be happy with a home no wider than the Trips' front door – which is exactly what he got. His reaction to his new lodgings is not recorded.

Further along the canal, on the corner of Oude Hoogstraat, is the former headquarters of the Dutch East India Company, the **Oostindisch Huis**, a monumental red-brick structure built in 1605 shortly after the founding of the company. It was from here that the company organized and regulated its immensely lucrative trading interests in the Far East, importing shiploads of spices, perfumes and exotic woods. This trade underpinned Amsterdam's Golden Age, but predictably the people of what is now Indonesia, the source of most of the raw materials, received little in return. These days the building is occupied by university classrooms and offices.

The Zuiderkerk

The **Zuiderkerk** (Mon–Fri 9am–4pm, Sat noon–4pm; free), dating from 1611, was the first Amsterdam church built specifically for Protestants. It was designed by the prolific architect and sculptor, Hendrick de Keyser (1565–1621), whose distinctive – and very popular – style extrapolated elements of traditional Flemish design, with fanciful detail and frilly towers added wherever possible. The basic design of the Zuiderkerk is firmly Gothic, but the soaring tower is typical of his work, complete with balconies and balustrades, arches and columns. Now deconsecrated, the church has been turned into a municipal information centre, with displays on housing and the environment, plus temporary exhibitions revealing the city council's future plans. The **tower**, which has a separate entrance, can be climbed during the summer (April–Sept Mon–Sat 1–3.30pm; €3).

St Antoniesbreestraat and the Pintohuis

Stretching south from Nieuwmarkt, **St Antoniesbreestraat** once linked the city centre with the Jewish quarter, but its huddle of shops and houses was mostly demolished in the 1980s to make way for a main road. The plan was subsequently abandoned, but the modern buildings that now line most of the street hardly fire the soul, even if the modern symmetries – and cubist coloured panels – of the apartment blocks that spill along part of the street are at least visually arresting. One of the few survivors of this is the **Pintohuis** (Mon & Wed 2–8pm, Fri 2–5pm, Sat 11am–4pm; free) at no. 69, now a public library. Easily spotted by its off-white Italianate facade, the mansion is named after Isaac De Pinto, a Jew who fled Portugal to escape the Inquisition and subsequently became a founder of the East India Company. Pinto bought this property in 1651 and promptly had it remodelled in grand style, the facade interrupted by six lofty pilasters, which lead the eye up to the blind balustrade. The mansion was the talk of the town, even more so when Pinto had the interior painted in a similar style to the front – pop in to look at the birds and cherubs of the original painted ceiling.

The Grachtengordel

Medieval Amsterdam was enclosed by the Singel, part of the city's protective moat, but this is now just the first of five canals that reach right around the city

The canals

The **canals** of the Grachtengordel were dug in the seventeenth century as part of a comprehensive plan to extend the boundaries of a city no longer able to accommodate its burgeoning population. Increasing the area of the city from two to seven square kilometres was a monumental task, and the conditions imposed by the council were strict. The three main waterways – Herengracht, Keizersgracht and Prinsengracht – were set aside for the residences and businesses of the richer and more influential Amsterdam merchants, while the radial cross-streets were reserved for more modest artisans' homes; meanwhile, immigrants, newly arrived to cash in on Amsterdam's booming economy, were assigned, albeit informally, the Jodenhoek (see p.79) and the Jordaan (see p.77).

Of the three main canals, **Herengracht**, the "Gentlemen's Canal", was the first to be dug, followed by the **Keizersgracht**, the "Emperor's Canal", named after the Holy Roman Emperor and fifteenth-century patron of the city, Maximilian. Further out still, the **Prinsengracht**, the "Princes' Canal", was named in honour of the princes of the House of Orange. In the Grachtengordel, everyone, even the wealthiest merchant, had to comply with a set of strict and detailed planning regulations. In particular, the council prescribed the size of each building plot – the frontage was set at thirty feet, the depth two hundred – and although there was a degree of tinkering, the end result was the loose conformity you can see today: tall, narrow residences, whose individualism is mainly restricted to the stylistic permutations among the gables.

The earliest extant **gables**, dating from the early seventeenth century, are crow-stepped but these were largely superseded from the 1650s onwards by neck gables and bell gables. Some are embellished, others aren't, many have decorative cornices, some don't, and the fanciest, which almost invariably date from the eighteenth century, sport full-scale balustrades. The plainest gables are those of former **warehouses**, where the deep-arched and shuttered windows line up on either side of loft doors, which were once used for loading and unloading goods, winched by pulley from the street down below. Indeed, outside **pulleys** remain a common feature of houses and warehouses alike, and are often still in use as the easiest way of moving furniture into the city's myriad apartments.

centre, extending anticlockwise from Brouwersgracht to the River Amstel in a "girdle of canals" or **Grachtengordel**. This is without doubt the most charming part of the city, its lattice of olive-green waterways and dinky humpback bridges overlooked by street upon street of handsome seventeenth-century canal houses, almost invariably undisturbed by later development. It's a subtle cityscape – full of surprises, with a bizarre carving here, an unusual facade there – but architectural peccadilloes aside, it is the district's overall atmosphere that appeals rather than any specific sight – with the notable exception of the **Anne Frank Huis**. There's no obvious walking route around the Grachtengordel, and indeed you may prefer to wander around as the mood takes you, but the description we've given below goes from north to south, taking in all the highlights on the way. On all three of the main canals – **Herengracht**, **Keizersgracht** and **Prinsengracht** – street numbers begin in the north and increase as you go south.

Brouwersgracht to Leliegracht

Running east to west along the northern edge of the three main canals is leafy **Brouwersgracht**, one of the most picturesque waterways in the city. In the seventeenth century, Brouwersgracht lay at the edge of Amsterdam's great harbour. This was where many of the ships returning from the East unloaded their silks and spices, and as one of the major arteries linking the open sea with the city centre it was lined with storage depots and warehouses. Breweries flourished here too, capitalizing on their ready access to shipments of fresh water. Today, the harbour bustle has moved elsewhere, and the warehouses, with their distinctive spout-neck gables and shuttered windows, formerly used for the delivery and dispatch of goods by pulley from the canal below, have been converted into apartments, some of the most expensive in Amsterdam. There are handsome merchants' houses here as well, plus moored houseboats and a string of quaint little swing bridges.

Strolling south along **Prinsengracht** from Brouwersgracht, past smart canal houses and tumbledown houseboats, it only takes a minute or two to reach the **Hofje Van Brienen**, at Prinsengracht 85–133, which you can walk around for free. This is one of the prettiest of the city's *hofjes*, or courtyard almshouses, built in 1804. Continue walking for a few metres more and you'll come to the first cross-street connecting the main canals, **Prinsenstraat**, which quickly runs into **Herenstraat**, an appealing little street of flower shops and cafés, greengroceries and secondhand clothes shops. At the east end of Herenstraat, turn right onto **Herengracht** and it's a short walk to the **Leliegracht**, one of the tiny radial canals that cut across the Grachtengordel, and home to a number of bookshops and canal-side bars. Though there are precious few extant examples of Art Nouveau and Art Deco architecture in Amsterdam, one of the finest is the tall and striking building at the Leliegracht–Keizersgracht junction. The building was designed by Gerrit van Arkel in 1905.

The Anne Frank Huis

In 1957, the Anne Frank Foundation set up the **Anne Frank Huis** in the house at Prinsengracht 267 (daily: mid-March to mid-Sept 9am–9pm, July & Aug till 10pm; mid-Sept to mid-March 9am–7pm; closed Yom Kippur; €8.50, 10- to 17-year-olds €4, under-9s free; ☎020/556 7100, ⓦ www.annefrank.org), where the young diarist and her family were in hiding for two years (see box, p.72). Since the posthumous publication of her diaries, Anne Frank has become extraordinarily famous, in the first instance for recording the iniquities of the Holocaust, and latterly as a symbol of the fight against oppression and, in

The story of Anne Frank

The story of Anne, her family and friends is well known. Anne's father, **Otto Frank**, was a well-to-do Jewish businessman who ran a successful spice-trading business and lived in the southern part of Amsterdam. After the Nazi occupation of the Netherlands, he felt – along with many other Jews – that he could avoid trouble by keeping his head down. However, by 1942 it was clear that this was not going to be possible: Amsterdam's Jews were isolated and conspicuous, being confined to certain parts of the city and forced to wear a yellow star. Roundups, too, were becoming increasingly commonplace. In desperation, Otto Frank decided – on the advice of two Dutch friends, Mr Koophuis and Mr Kraler – to move the family into the unused back room of his company's warehouse on the Prinsengracht. The Franks went into hiding in July 1942, along with a Jewish business partner and his family, the Van Daans. They were separated from the eyes of the outside world by a bookcase that doubled as a door. As far as everyone else was concerned, they had fled to Switzerland. So began the two-year occupation of the *achterhuis*, or back annexe. The two families were joined in November 1942 by a Mr Dussel, a dentist friend. Koophuis and Kraler, who continued working in the front office, regularly brought supplies and news of the outside world. In her diary Anne Frank describes the day-to-day lives of the inhabitants of the annexe; the quarrels, frequent in such a claustrophobic environment; celebrations of birthdays, or of a piece of good news from the Allied Front; and her own, slightly unreal, growing-up (much of Anne's description of which was edited out by her father, but restored to later editions). Two years later, the atmosphere was optimistic: the Allies were clearly winning the war and liberation seemed within reach. It wasn't to be. One day in the summer of 1944 the Franks were betrayed by a Dutch collaborator and the Gestapo arrived and forced Mr Kraler to open up the bookcase. Thereafter, the occupants of the annexe were all arrested and quickly sent to Westerbork (see p.242) – the transit camp in the north of the country where all Dutch Jews were processed before being moved to Belsen or Auschwitz. Of the eight from the annexe, only Otto Frank survived; Anne and her sister died of typhus within a short time of each other in Belsen, just one week before the German surrender.

particular, racism. The house is now one of the most popular attractions in town, so try to go early (or late) to avoid the crowds.

Anne Frank's **diary** was among the few things left behind in the annexe. It was retrieved by one of the people who had helped the Franks and handed to Anne's father on his return from Auschwitz; he later decided to publish it. Since its appearance in 1947, the diary has been constantly in print, translated into over sixty languages, and has sold millions of copies worldwide. The rooms the Franks lived in for two years are left much the same as they were during the war, even down to the movie star pin-ups in Anne's bedroom and the marks on the wall recording the children's heights. Remarkably, despite the number of visitors, there is a real sense of intimacy here and only the coldest of hearts could fail to be moved. Apposite video clips on the family in particular and the Holocaust in general give the background. Anne Frank was only one of about 100,000 Dutch Jews who died during World War II, but this, her final home, provides one of the most enduring testaments to its horrors. Her diary has been a source of inspiration to many, including Nelson Mandela.

The Westerkerk and around

Immediately to the south of the Anne Frank Huis is the tower of the **Westerkerk** (Mon–Sat: April–Sept 10am–5.30pm, Oct 11am–4pm; free; Ⓦ www.westerkerk.nl) – without question Amsterdam's finest – soaring imperiously above the gables of Westermarkt. On its top perches the crown of the

Habsburg Emperor Maximilian, a constantly recurring symbol of Amsterdam and the finishing touch to what was only the city's second place of worship built expressly for Protestants. The church was designed by Hendrik de Keyser and completed in 1631 as part of the general enlargement of the city, but whereas the exterior is all studied elegance, the interior – as required by the Calvinist congregation – is bare and plain. The church is also the reputed resting place of **Rembrandt**, though the location of his pauper's tomb is not known. Instead, the painter is commemorated by a small memorial in the north aisle, close to which his son Titus is buried. Rembrandt adored his son – as evinced by numerous portraits – and the boy's death dealt a final crushing blow to the ageing and embittered artist, who died just over a year later.

Westermarkt, an open square in the shadow of the Westerkerk, possesses two evocative statues. At the back of the church, beside Keizersgracht, are the three pink granite triangles (one each for the past, present and future) of the **Homo-Monument**. The world's first memorial to persecuted gays and lesbians, commemorating all those who died at the hands of the Nazis, it was designed by Karin Daan and recalls the pink triangles that homosexuals were forced to sew into and display on their clothes during the occupation. The monument's inscription, by the Dutch writer Jacob Israel de Haan, translates as "Such an infinite desire for friendship". Nearby, on the south side of the church by Prinsengracht, is a small but beautifully crafted **statue of Anne Frank** by the gifted Dutch sculptor Mari Andriessen (1897–1979), who is also the creator of the dockworker statue outside Amsterdam's Portuguese Synagogue (see p.81).

Raadhuisstraat to Leidsegracht

Westermarkt flows into **Raadhuisstraat**, the principal thoroughfare into the Old Centre, running east to Dam Square. South of here the main canals are less appealing than the narrow cross-streets, many of which are named after animals whose pelts were used in the local tanning industry – Reestraat ("Deer Street"), Hartenstraat ("Hart Street") and Berenstraat ("Bear Street"), to name but three. The tanners are thankfully long gone, but they've been replaced by some of the most pleasant shopping streets in the city, known collectively as the "Nine Streets", selling everything from carpets and handmade chocolates to designer toothbrushes and beeswax candles. The area's southern boundary is marked by **Leidsegracht**, a mostly residential canal, lined with chic town houses and a medley of handsome gables.

The Bijbels Museum

Just north of Leidsegracht, the **Bijbels Museum** at Herengracht 366 (Mon–Sat 10am–5pm, Sun 11am–5pm; €7.50; ⓦ www.bijbelsmuseum.nl) occupies two of four matching stone mansions, the Cromhouthuizen, frilled with tendrils, carved fruit and scrollwork and graced by dinky little bull's-eye windows and elegant gables. The mansions were built in the 1660s for one of Amsterdam's wealthy merchant families and contain an extravagant painted ceiling portraying Classical gods and goddesses – the work of Jacob de Wit. On display in the museum is a splendid selection of old Bibles, including the first Dutch-language Bible ever printed, dating from 1477, and a series of idiosyncratic models of Solomon's Temple and the Jewish Tabernacle. There's also a scattering of archeological finds from Palestine and Egypt, brought to the Netherlands in the nineteenth century.

Leidseplein and around

Lying on the edge of the Grachtengordel, **Leidseplein** is the bustling hub of Amsterdam's nightlife, a rather cluttered and disorderly open space that has never had much character. The square once marked the end of the road in from Leiden and, as horse-drawn traffic was banned from the centre long ago, it was here that the Dutch left their horses and carts – a sort of equine car park. Today, it's quite the opposite: continual traffic made up of trams, bikes, cars and pedestrians gives the place a frenetic feel, and the surrounding side streets are jammed with bars, restaurants and clubs in a bright jumble of jutting signs and neon lights. On a good night, however, Leidseplein can be Amsterdam at its carefree, exuberant best.

The square has a couple of buildings of architectural note. The grandiose **Stadsschouwburg**, a neo-Renaissance edifice dating from 1894, was so widely criticized for its clumsy vulgarity that the city council of the day temporarily withheld the money for decorating the exterior. Formerly home to the National Ballet and Opera, it is now used for theatre, dance and music performances, as well as hosting visiting English-language theatre companies. However, its most popular function is as the place where the Ajax football team gather on the balcony to wave to the crowds whenever they win anything – as they often do. Almost next door, the **American Hotel** is one of the city's oddest buildings, a monumental and slightly disconcerting rendering of Art Nouveau, with angular turrets, chunky dormer windows and fancy brickwork. Completed in 1902, the present structure takes its name from its demolished predecessor, which was decorated with statues and murals of North American scenes. Inside the present hotel is the *Café Americain*, once the fashionable haunt of Amsterdam's literati, but now a mainstream location for coffee and lunch. The Art Nouveau decor is well worth a peek – an artful combination of stained glass, shallow arches and geometric patterned brickwork.

Leidsestraat

Heading northeast from Leidseplein, **Leidsestraat** is a crowded shopping street, a long, slender gauntlet of fashion and shoe shops of little distinction that leads across the three main canals up towards the Singel and the Flower Market (see p.65). En route, at the corner of Keizersgracht, is **Metz & Co** department store, which was, when it was built, the tallest commercial building in the city – one reason why the owners were able to entice Gerrit Rietveld, the leading architectural light of the De Stijl movement, to add a rooftop glass and metal showroom in 1933. The showroom has survived and is now a café offering one of the best views over the centre in this predominantly low-rise city.

The Spiegelkwartier

One block east of Metz & Co, along Keizersgracht, is Nieuwe Spiegelstraat, an appealing mixture of bookshops and corner cafés that extends south into Spiegelgracht to form the **Spiegelkwartier** – home to the pricey end of Amsterdam's antiques trade. It's a lovely district to browse around; while you're here be sure to pop into **De Appel**, a lively centre for contemporary art at Nieuwe Spiegelstraat 10 (Tues–Sun 11am–6pm; €4; Ⓦ www.deappel.nl).

The Golden Bend

Southeast from Leidsegracht, the elegant sweep of the main **Herengracht** canal reaches the so-called "**Golden Bend**" (De Gouden Bocht), where the canal is overlooked by a long sequence of double-fronted mansions, some of the most opulent dwellings in the city. Most of the houses here date from the eighteenth century, with double stairways leading to the entrance, the small door underneath which was for the servants. Classical references are common, both in form – pediments, columns and pilasters – and decoration, from scrolls and vases through to geometric patterns inspired by ancient Greece. One of the first buildings to look out for on the north side of the canal is **no. 475**, an extravagant edifice surmounted by a slender French-style balustrade and decorated with twin caryatids. It was completed in 1672, whereas the comparable residence at **no. 493**, complete with its good-looking balcony, was finished in the 1730s. In a rather more modest mansion a couple of doors down, at no. 497, is the peculiar **Kattenkabinet** (Tues–Fri 10am–4pm, Sat & Sun 12–5pm; €5; ⓦwww.kattenkabinet.nl), an enormous collection of art and artefacts relating to cats. It was installed by a Dutch financier, whose own cherished moggy, John Pierpont Morgan, died in 1984; feline fanatics will be delighted. Metres away, at the corner of Vijzelstraat, **no. 507** is an imposing building too, all Neoclassical pilasters and slender windows; it was once the home of Jacob Boreel, the one-time major whose attempt to impose a burial tax prompted a riot during which the mob ransacked his house. Opposite, across the canal, is the mammoth lumpiness of the former ABN-AMRO bank, a broadly Expressionist structure dating to 1923.

Rembrandtplein and around

Pushing on along the north side of Herengracht, it takes a couple of minutes to reach pedestrianized **Thorbeckeplein**, a scrawny adjunct to **Rembrandtplein**, itself a dishevelled bit of greenery that was formerly Amsterdam's butter market, renamed after the artist in 1876. Rembrandtplein is one of the city's nightlife centres, though the crowded restaurants are firmly tourist-targeted. The great man's statue stands in the middle, his back wisely turned against the square's worst excesses, which include live (but deadly) outdoor music. Of the prodigious number of cafés and bars here, only the bar of the **Schiller Hotel** at no. 26 stands out, with an original Art Deco interior reminiscent of an ocean liner.

Tacky **Reguliersbreestraat**, leading off the northwest corner of Rembrandtplein, is notable only for the city's most extraordinary cinema, the **Tuschinski**, at nos. 26–28, which boasts a marvellously well-preserved Art Deco interior. Opened in 1921 by a Polish Jew, Abram Tuschinski, the cinema boasts Expressionist paintings, coloured marbles and a wonderful carpet, handwoven in Marrakesh to an original design. Tuschinski died in Auschwitz in 1942, and there's a plaque in the cinema's foyer in his memory.

The Stadsarchief – De Bazel

Opposite **Herengracht 507**, stretching down Vijzelstraat as far as Keizersgracht, is one of Amsterdam's weirdest and most monumentally incongruous buildings, the **Stadsarchief**, or state archives, which started out as the headquarters of a Dutch shipping company, the **Nederlandsche Handelsmaatschappij**, before falling into the hands of the ABN-AMRO bank. Dating from the 1920s, the building is commonly known as **De Bazel** (ⓦwww.debazelamsterdam.nl) after the architect Karel de Bazel (1869–1923), whose devotion to theosophy formed and framed his design. Founded in the late nineteenth-century, theosophy combined metaphysics and religious philosophy, and every facet of de Bazel's building reflects its belief in order and balance, from the pink and yellow brickwork of the exterior to the repeated use of motifs drawn from the Middle East, the source of much of the cult's spiritual inspiration. At the heart of the building is the magnificent **Schatkamer** (Tues–Sat 10am–5pm & Sun 11am–5pm; free), a richly decorated, Art Deco extravagance that feels rather like a royal crypt and holds photographs and documents drawn from the city's archives – anything from 1970s squatters occupying City Hall to hagiographic tracts on the virtues of the Dutch naval hero, Admiral De Ruyter and, perhaps best of the lot, photos of miscreants (or rather the poor and the desperate) drawn from police archives.

The Tassenmuseum Hendrikje

The delightful Tassenmuseum Hendrikje, Herengracht 573 (daily 10am–5pm; €6.50; ⓦwww.tassenmuseum.nl), holds a superb collection of handbags, pouches, wallets, bags and purses from medieval times onwards, exhibited on three floors of a sympathetically refurbished grand old mansion. It has items from the sixteenth to the nineteenth centuries, beautiful Art Nouveau items and a whole cabinet of 1950s specimens as well as temporary displays of contemporary bags – great for inspiration if you're going shopping.

The Museum Willet-Holthuysen

Back on the Herengracht, near the River Amstel, the **Museum Willet-Holthuysen** at no. 605 (Mon–Fri 10am–5pm, Sat & Sun 11am–5pm; €6; ⓦwww.museumwilletholthuysen.nl) is billed as "a peep behind the curtains into an historic Amsterdam canal house", which just sums it up. The coal-trading Holthuysen family occupied this elegant, late-seventeenth-century mansion until the last of the line, Sandra Willet-Holthuysen, gifted her home and its contents to the city in 1895. Modified and renovated on several occasions, the interior has largely been returned to its original eighteenth-century Rococo appearance – a flashy and ornate style that the Dutch merchants held to be the epitome of refinement and good taste. The house also displays a small collection of glass, silver, majolica and ceramics assembled by Sandra's husband, Abraham Willet. At the back of the house are the formal gardens, a neat pattern of miniature hedges graced by the occasional stone statue.

The Museum Van Loon

Southwest of Rembrandtplein, on Keizersgracht, is the **Museum Van Loon** at no. 672 (daily except Tues 11am–5pm; €6; ⓦwww.museumvanloon.nl), which has perhaps the finest accessible canal house interior in Amsterdam. The first tenant of the property built in 1672, was the artist Ferdinand Bol, who seems to have been one of the few occupants to have avoided some sort of scandal. The Van Loons occupied the house from 1884 to 1945, and the last member of the family to live here was Willem van Loon, a banker whose wife, Thora van Loon-Egidius, was *dame du paleis* to Queen Wilhelmina. Of German extraction, Thora was proud of her roots and allegedly entertained high-ranking Nazi officials here during the occupation – a charge of collaboration that led to the Van Loons being shunned by polite society. Recently renovated, the interior of the house has been returned to something akin to its eighteenth-century appearance, with acres of wood panelling and fancy stuccowork. Look out also for the ornate copper balustrade on the staircase, into which is worked the name "Van Hagen-Trip" (after a one-time owner of the house); the Van Loons later filled the spaces between the letters with iron curlicues to prevent their children falling through. The top-floor landing has several pleasant paintings sporting Roman figures, and one of the bedrooms – the "painted room" – is decorated with a Romantic painting of Italy, a favourite motif in Amsterdam from around 1750 to 1820. The oddest items are the fake bedroom doors: the eighteenth-century owners were so keen to avoid any lack of symmetry that they camouflaged the real bedroom doors and created imitation, decorative doors in the "correct" position instead.

The Amstel

The main canals come to an abrupt halt beside the wide and windy **River Amstel**, long the main route into the interior, with goods arriving by barge and boat to be traded for the imported materials held in Amsterdam's many warehouses. Turning left from Herengracht takes you to the **Blauwbrug** ("Blue Bridge") and the Old Jewish Quarter (see pp.79–82), while further down, the **Magere Brug** ("Skinny Bridge") is arguably the cutest of the city's many swing bridges. From here, it's a few metres further to the **Amstelsluizen**, the Amstel Locks. Every night, the municipal water department closes these locks to begin the process of sluicing out the canals. A huge pumping station on an island out to the east of the city then starts to pump fresh water into the canal system from the freshwater IJsselmeer lake; similar locks on the west side of the city are left open for the surplus to flow into the IJ and, from there, out to sea via the North Sea Canal.

The Jordaan and the Western Docklands

Lying to the west of the city centre and the Grachtengordel, its boundaries clearly defined by the Prinsengracht and the Lijnbaansgracht, the **Jordaan** is a likeable and easily explored area of slender canals and narrow streets flanked by an agreeable mix of architectural styles, from modern terraces to handsome seventeenth-century canal houses. In all probability the district takes its name from the French word *jardin* ("garden"), since the area's earliest settlers were Protestant Huguenots, who fled here to escape persecution in the sixteenth and seventeenth centuries. Another possibility is that it's a corruption of the Dutch word for Jews, *joden*. Whatever the truth, the Jordaan developed from open country – hence the number of streets and canals named after flowers and plants – into a refugee enclave, a teeming, cosmopolitan quarter beyond the pale of bourgeois respectability. Indeed, when the city fathers planned the expansion of the city in 1610, they made sure the Jordaan was kept outside the city boundaries. Consequently, the Jordaan was not subject to the rigorous planning restrictions of the Grachtengordel, and its lattice of narrow streets followed the lines of the original polder drainage ditches rather than any municipal outline. This gives the district its distinctive, mazy layout, and much of its present appeal.

Traditionally the home of Amsterdam's working class, the Jordaan has in recent years been transformed by a middle-class influx, with the district now one of the city's most sought-after residential neighbourhoods. Before then, and until the late 1970s, the Jordaan's inhabitants were primarily stevedores and factory workers, earning a crust among the docks, warehouses, factories and boatyards that extended north beyond Brouwersgracht, the Jordaan's northern boundary and nowadays one of Amsterdam's prettiest canals. Specific sights are few and far between but it's still a pleasant area to wander.

Rozengracht to Westerstraat

The streets and canals extending north from **Rozengracht** to **Westerstraat** form the heart of the Jordaan and hold the district's prettiest moments. Beyond Rozengracht, the first canal is the **Bloemgracht** (Flower Canal), a leafy waterway dotted with houseboats and arched by little bridges, its network of cross-streets sprinkled with cafés, bars and idiosyncratic shops. There's a warm, relaxed community atmosphere here which is really rather beguiling, not to mention a clutch of old and handsome canal houses. Pride of architectural place goes to nos. 89–91, a sterling Renaissance building of 1642 complete with mullion windows, crowstep gable, brightly painted shutters and distinctive facade stones, representing a *steeman* (city-dweller), *landman* (farmer) and a *seeman* (sailor).

From Bloemgracht, it's a few metres north to **Egelantiersgracht** (Rose-Hip Canal), where, at no. 12, *Café 't Smalle* is one of Amsterdam's oldest cafés, opened in 1786 as a *proeflokaal* – a tasting house for the (long-gone) gin distillery next door. In the eighteenth century, when quality control was intermittent, each batch of *jenever* (Dutch gin) could turn out very differently, so customers insisted on a taster before they splashed out. As a result, each distillery ran a *proeflokaal* offering free samples, and this is a rare survivor.

A narrow cross-street – Tweede Egelantiersdwarsstraat and its continuation Tweede Tuindwarsstraat and Tweede Anjeliersdwarsstraat – runs north from Bloemgracht, flanked by many of the Jordaan's more fashionable stores and clothing shops as well as some of its liveliest bars and cafés. At the end is workaday **Westerstraat**, a busy thoroughfare, which is home to the small but fascinating **Pianola Museum** at no. 106 (Sun 2–5pm; €5; ⓦ www.pianola.nl), whose collection of pianolas and automatic music-machines dates from the beginning of the twentieth century. Fifteen have been restored to working order.

The Noorderkerk and around

At the east end of Westerstraat, overlooking the Prinsengracht, is Hendrik de Keyser's **Noorderkerk** (Mon, Thurs & Sat 11am–1pm; free), the architect's last creation and probably his least successful, finished two years after his death in 1623. A bulky, overbearing brick building, it represented a radical departure from the conventional church designs of the time, having a symmetrical Greek-cross floor plan, with four equally proportioned arms radiating out from a steepled centre. Uncompromisingly dour, it proclaimed the serious intent of the Calvinists who worshipped here in so far as the pulpit – and therefore the preacher proclaiming the Word of God – was at the centre and not at the front of the church, a symbolic break with the Catholic past. Nevertheless, it's still hard to understand quite how Keyser, who designed such elegant structures as the Westerkerk (see p.72), could have ended up designing this.

The **Noordermarkt**, the somewhat inconclusive square outside the church, holds a statue of three figures bound to each other, a poignant tribute to the bloody Jordaanoproer riot of 1934, part of a successful campaign to stop the government cutting unemployment benefit during the Depression. The inscription reads: "The strongest chains are those of unity". The square also hosts two of Amsterdam's best open-air **markets**: an antiques and general household goods market on Monday mornings (9am–1pm) and a popular Saturday farmers' market, the Boerenmarkt (9am–3pm), a lively affair selling organic fruit and vegetables, freshly baked breads and a plethora of oils and spices.

The Scheepvaartsbuurt and the Western Docklands

Brouwersgracht marks both the northern edge of the Jordaan and the southern boundary of the **Scheepvaartsbuurt** – the Shipping Quarter – an unassuming neighbourhood that focuses on Haarlemmerstraat and Haarlemmerdijk, a long, neighbourly thoroughfare lined with bars, cafés and food shops. In the eighteenth and nineteenth centuries, this district boomed from its location between the Brouwersgracht and the **Westerdok**, a narrow parcel of land dredged out of the River IJ immediately to the north and equipped with docks, warehouses and shipyards. The construction of the artificial islands took the pressure off Amsterdam's congested maritime facilities and was necessary to sustain the city's economic success. The Westerdok hung on to some of the marine trade until the 1960s, but today – bar the odd small boatyard – industry has to all intents and purposes disappeared and the area is busy reinventing itself. There is still an air of faded grittiness here, but the old forgotten warehouses – within walking distance of the centre – are rapidly being turned into bijou studios, and dozens of plant-filled houseboats are moored along the Westerdok itself and the adjoining Realengracht.

The Westerpark and Westergasfabriek

Beyond the Haarlemmerpoort, off to the right, the **Westerpark** is a small park running alongside a narrow sliver of canal with a small lake and some formally planted areas. At its far end, the **Westergasfabriek** is a complex of red-brick nineteenth century buildings that was formerly a gasworks, then a venue for acid house raves in the 1990s, and has since been renovated and is beginning to find its feet as an arts and entertainment complex. There are a number of arts and media-related businesses here, several galleries, a cinema and a number of places to eat and drink, as well as the **Huis van Aristoteles** – a giant play area for kids. You can get in from the park but the Westergasfabriek's main entrance is on Haarlemmerweg.

Het Schip

On the north side of the Westerpark, a pedestrian tunnel leads you to **Het Schip**, the seminal Amsterdam School municipal housing block by Michael de Klerk at Spaarndammerplantsoen 140. Reachable direct by bus #22 from Centraal Station, takes its name from its ship-like shape and is graced by all manner of decorative details such as wavy brick facades and misshapen windows. Housed inside the complex's former post office, the Museum Het Schip (Wed–Sun 1–5pm; €5; ⓦwww.hetschip.nl) explores the history of the architectural movement and provides information on the site's main distinguishing features. Regular half-hour guided tours take you inside one of the restored residences – the block is still used as social housing today – and up to the main turret.

The Old Jewish Quarter and the Eastern Docklands

Originally one of the marshiest parts of Amsterdam, prone to regular flooding, the narrow slice of land sandwiched between the curve of the Amstel, Kloveniersburgwal and the Nieuwe Herengracht was the home of Amsterdam's Jews from the sixteenth century up until World War II. By the 1920s, this **Old Jewish Quarter**, or the **Jodenhoek** ("Jews' Corner"), was crowded with tenement buildings and smoking factories, but in 1945 it lay derelict – and postwar redevelopment has not treated it kindly either. Its focal point, **Waterlooplein**, has been overwhelmed by a whopping town hall and concert hall complex, and the once-bustling Jodenbreestraat is now bleak and very ordinary, with Mr Visserplein, at its east end, one of the city's busiest traffic junctions. Picking your way round these obstacles is not much fun, but you should persevere – among all the cars and concrete are several moving reminders of the Jewish community that perished in the war.

Immediately to the east of the Old Jewish Quarter lies the **Plantagebuurt**, a trim district centred around the **Plantage Middenlaan**, a wide boulevard that was constructed in the mid-nineteenth century as the first part of the creation of this leafy suburb – one of Amsterdam's earliest. The avenue borders the city's largest botanical gardens, the **Hortus Botanicus**, and runs close to the **Artis Zoo**. Just slightly to the north of here are the artificial islands that comprise the **Oosterdok** quarter, dredged out of the River IJ to accommodate warehouses and docks in the seventeenth century. These islands once formed part of a vast maritime complex that spread right along the River IJ. Industrial decline set in during the 1880s, but the area is currently being redefined as a residential district.

Jodenbreestraat and the Rembrandthuis

St Antoniesbreestraat runs into **Jodenbreestraat**, the "Broad Street of the Jews", and once the main centre of Jewish activity. Badly served by postwar development, this ancient thoroughfare is now short on charm, but in these unlikely surroundings, at no. 6, stands the **Rembrandthuis** (daily 10am–5pm; €8; @www.rembrandthuis.nl), whose intricate facade is decorated by pretty wooden shutters and a small pediment. Rembrandt bought this house at the height of his fame and popularity, living here for over twenty years and spending a fortune on furnishings – an expense that ultimately contributed to his bankruptcy. An inventory made at the time details the huge collection of paintings, sculptures and art treasures he'd amassed, almost all of which was confiscated after he was declared insolvent and forced to move to a more modest house on Rozengracht in the Jordaan in 1658. The city council bought the Jodenbreestraat house in 1907 and has subsequently revamped the premises on several occasions, most recently in 1999. A string of period rooms now gives a clear impression of Rembrandt's life and times, while the adjoining modern wing displays an extensive collection of Rembrandt's etchings as well as several of the original copper plates on which he worked. The biblical illustrations attract the most attention, though the studies of tramps and vagabonds are equally appealing. An accompanying exhibit explains Rembrandt's engraving techniques and there are also regular temporary exhibitions on Rembrandt and his contemporaries; to see his major paintings, however, you'll have to go to the Rijksmuseum (see p.84).

The Stadhuis and Muziektheater

Jodenbreestraat runs parallel to the **Stadhuis en Muziektheater**, a sprawling and distinctly underwhelming modern complex dating to the 1980s and incorporating the city hall and a large auditorium. The Muziektheater offers a varied programme of theatre, dance and ballet as well as opera from the first-rate Netherlands Opera (@www.dno.nl). One of the city's abiding ironies is that the title of the protest campaign aiming to prevent the development in the 1980s – "Stopera" – has passed into common usage to describe the finished item. Inside, there are a couple of minor attractions, beginning with the glass columns in the public passageway towards the rear of the complex. These give a salutary lesson on the fragility of the Netherlands: two contain water indicating the sea levels in the Dutch towns of Vlissingen and IJmuiden (below knee level), while another records the levels experienced during the 1953 flood disaster (way above head height). Downstairs a concrete pile shows what is known as "Normal Amsterdam Level" (NAP), originally calculated in 1684 as the average water level in the river IJ and still the basis for measuring altitude above sea level across the Netherlands.

Waterlooplein

The Stadhuis complex dominates **Waterlooplein**, a rectangular parcel of land that was originally swampy marsh. This was the site of the first Jewish Quarter, but by the late nineteenth century it had become an insanitary slum, home to the poorest of the Ashkenazi Jews. The slums were cleared in the 1880s and thereafter the open spaces of the Waterlooplein hosted the largest and liveliest marketplace in the city, the place where Jews and Gentiles met to trade. In World War II, the Nazis used the square to round up their victims, but despite these ugly connotations the Waterlooplein was revived in the 1950s as the site of the city's main **flea market** and remains so to this day (Mon–Sat 9am–5pm). The market is nowhere as large as it once was thanks to the town hall and concert hall development, but nonetheless it's still the final resting place of many a pair of yellow corduroy flares and has some wonderful antique and junk stalls to root through.

Mr Visserplein

Just behind the Muziektheater, **Mr Visserplein** is a busy junction for traffic speeding towards the IJ tunnel. It takes its name from Mr Visser, president of the Supreme Court of the Netherlands in 1939. He was dismissed the following year when the Germans occupied the country, and became an active member of the Jewish resistance, working for the illegal underground newspaper *Het Parool* ("The Password") and refusing to wear the yellow Star of David. He died in 1942, a few days after publicly – and famously – denouncing all forms of collaboration.

The Esnoga

Unmissable on the corner of Mr Visserplein is the brown and bulky brickwork of the **Esnoga** or **Portuguese synagogue** (daily except Sat 10am–4pm; closed Yom Kippur; €6.50; Ⓦwww.esnoga.com), completed in 1675 for the city's Sephardic Jews. One of Amsterdam's most imposing buildings, the central structure, with its grand pilasters and blind balustrade, was built in the broadly Neoclassical style that was then fashionable in Holland. It's surrounded by a courtyard complex of small outhouses, where the city's Sephardim have fraternized for centuries. Barely altered since its construction, the synagogue's lofty interior follows the Sephardic tradition in having the *hechal* (the Ark of the Covenant) and *tebah* (from where services are led) at opposite ends. Also traditional is the seating, with two sets of wooden benches (for the men) facing each other across the central aisle – the women have separate galleries up above. A set of superb brass chandeliers holds the candles, which remain the only source of artificial light. When it was completed, the synagogue was one of the largest in the world, its congregation almost certainly the richest; today, the Sephardic community has dwindled to just 250 families, most of whom live outside the city centre. In one of the outhouses, a video sheds light on the history of the synagogue and Amsterdam's Sephardim; the mystery is why the Nazis left it alone. No one knows for sure, but it seems likely that they intended to turn it into a museum once all the Jews had been polished off.

Jonas Daniel Meijerplein

Next to the synagogue is **Jonas Daniel Meijerplein**, a scrawny triangle of gravel named after the eponymous lawyer, who in 1796, at the age of just 16, was the first Jew to be admitted to the Amsterdam Bar. It was here in February 1941 that around 400 Jewish men were forcibly loaded up on trucks and taken to their deaths at Mauthausen concentration camp, in reprisal for the killing of a Dutch Nazi during a street fight. The arrests sparked off the February Strike (*Februaristaking*), a general strike in protest against the Germans' treatment of the Jews. It was organized by the outlawed Communist Party and spearheaded by Amsterdam's transport workers and dockers – a rare demonstration of solidarity with the Jews whose fate was usually accepted without visible protest in all of occupied Europe. The strike was quickly suppressed, but is still commemorated by an annual wreath-laying ceremony on February 25, as well as by Mari Andriessen's statue of the **Dokwerker** (dockworker) here on the square.

The Joods Historisch Museum

Across J.D. Meijerplein, on the far side of the main road at Nieuwe Amstelstraat 1, the **Joods Historisch Museum** (daily 11am–5pm; closed Yom Kippur; €10;

Ⓦ www.jhm.nl) is cleverly shoehorned into four Ashkenazi synagogues dating from the late seventeenth century. For years after World War II these buildings lay abandoned, but they were finally refurbished – and connected by walkways – in the 1980s to accommodate a Jewish resource centre and exhibition area. Highlights include a display on Jewish life exhibited in the main body of the handsome **Grote Synagoge**, with a fine collection of religious silverware as well as a handful of paintings and all manner of antique artefacts illustrating religious customs and practices. There's a history of the Jews in the Netherlands in the neighbouring Nieuwe Synagoge, which inevitably focuses on the war years, as well as displays on Jewish-Dutch musicians and performers before the war.

The Amstelhof and Hermitage Amsterdam

Right by Amstel, the stern-looking **Amstelhof** is a large *hofje* or almshouse built for the care of elderly women (and ultimately men too) in the 1680s. In time it grew to fill most of the chunk of land between Nieuwe Herengracht and Nieuwe Keizersgracht, becoming a fully fledged hospital in the process, but in the 1980s it became clear that its medical facilities were out of date and it went up for sale. Much municipal huffing and puffing ensued until recently, when it was converted into a museum, **Hermitage Amsterdam**, at Nieuwe Herengracht 14 (daily 10am–5pm; €10; Ⓦ www.hermitage.nl), displaying items loaned from the original Hermitage in St Petersburg. It was – and is – a very ambitious scheme, with a substantial number of galleries now displaying prime pieces. Exhibitions, which usually last about five months, have included "Nicholas & Alexandra" and "Palace Protocol in the Nineteenth Century".

Hortus Botanicus

From Mr Visserplein, it's a short walk east along Muiderstraat to the lush **Hortus Botanicus** at the corner of Plantage Middenlaan and Plantage Parklaan (Mon–Fri 9am–5pm, Sat & Sun 10am–5pm; closes 4pm Dec & Jan, 7pm July & Aug; €7; Ⓦ www.dehortus.nl), the city's botanical gardens, founded in 1682 for medicinal purposes. Thereafter, many of the city's merchants made a point of bringing back exotic species from the East, the result being the 6000-odd plant species exhibited today. The gardens are divided into several distinct sections, each clearly labelled and its location pinpointed by a map available at the entrance kiosk. There's also a three-climates glasshouse, where the plants are arranged according to their geographical origins, a capacious palm house, an orchid nursery and a butterfly house. It's all very low-key – and none the worse for that – and the gardens make a relaxing break on any tour of central Amsterdam, especially as the café, in the old orangery, serves up tasty sandwiches, coffee and cakes (see p.89).

The Hollandsche Schouwburg

Continue down the right-hand side of Plantage Middenlaan to reach another sad relic of the war, **De Hollandsche Schouwburg**, at no. 24 (daily 11am–4pm; closed Yom Kippur; free; Ⓦ www.hollandscheschouwburg.nl). Formerly a Jewish theatre, the building became the main assembly point for Amsterdam Jews prior to their deportation. Inside, there was no daylight and families were interned in conditions that foreshadowed those of the camps they would soon be taken to. The building has been refurbished to house a small exhibition on the plight of the city's Jews, but the old auditorium out at the back has been left as an empty, roofless shell. A memorial column of basalt on a Star of David base stands where the stage once was, an intensely mournful monument to suffering of unfathomable proportions.

Artis Zoo

A brief walk northeast along Plantage Kerklaan is the **Artis Zoo** (daily: April–Oct 9am–6pm; Nov–March 9am–5pm; June–Aug till sundown on Sat with special activities; adults €18.50, 3- to 9-year-olds €15; www.artis.nl). Opened in 1838, the zoo has long been one of the city's top tourist attractions and its layout and lack of bars and cages mean that it never feels overcrowded. Highlights include an African savanna environment, a seventy-metre-long aviary, aquaria and a South American zone with llamas and the world's largest rodent, the capybara. Feeding times – always popular – include: 11am birds of prey; 11.30am and 3.45pm seals and sea lions; 12.30pm crocodiles (Sun only); 3pm lions and tigers (not Fri); and 3.30pm penguins. In addition, the on-site **Planetarium** has five or six shows daily, all in Dutch, though you can pick up a leaflet with an English translation from the desk.

The Verzetsmuseum

Near the zoo, at Plantage Kerklaan 61, is the excellent **Verzetsmuseum** (Mon, Sat & Sun 11am–5pm Tues–Fri 10am–5pm; €6.50; Ⓦ www.verzetsmuseum .org), which outlines the development of the Dutch Resistance from the Nazi invasion of the Netherlands in May 1940 to the country's liberation in 1945. Thoughtfully presented, the main gangway examines the experience of the majority of the population, dealing honestly with the fine balance between cooperation and collaboration. Side rooms are devoted to different aspects of the resistance, from the brave determination of the Communist Party, who went underground as soon as the Germans arrived, to more ad hoc responses like the so-called Milk Strike of 1943, when hundreds of milk producers refused to deliver. Fascinating old photographs illustrate the (English and Dutch) text along with a host of original artefacts, from examples of illegal newsletters to signed German death warrants. Apart from their treatment of the Jews, which is detailed here, perhaps the most chilling feature of the occupation was the use of indiscriminate reprisals to terrify the population. The museum has dozens of little metal sheets providing biographical sketches of the members of the Resistance – and it's this mixture of the general and the personal that is its real strength.

Entrepotdok

At the northern end of Plantage Kerklaan, just beyond the Dutch Resistance Museum, a footbridge leads over to **Entrepotdok**, on the nearest, and most interesting, of the Oosterdok islands. On the far side of the bridge, old brick warehouses stretch right along the quayside, distinguished by their spout gables, multiple doorways and overhead pulleys. Built by the Dutch East India Company in the eighteenth century, they were once part of the largest warehouse complex in continental Europe, a gigantic customs-free zone established for goods in transit. On the ground floor, above the main entrance, each warehouse sports the name of a town or island; goods for onward transportation were stored in the appropriate warehouse until there was enough to fill a boat or barge. The warehouses have been tastefully converted into offices and apartments, a fate that must surely befall the central East India Company compound, whose chunky Neoclassical entrance is at the west end of Entrepotdok on Kadijksplein.

Nederlands Scheepvaartmuseum

The **Nederlands Scheepvaartmuseum**, or Dutch Maritime Museum, is closed until further notice, but occupies the old arsenal of the Dutch navy, a vast sandstone structure built in the Oosterdok on Kattenburgerplein. It's underpinned by no fewer than 18,000 wooden piles driven deep into the riverbed at enormous expense in the 1650s. The building's four symmetrical facades are dour and imposing despite the odd stylistic flourish, principally some small dormer windows and Neoclassical pediments, and they surround a central, cobbled courtyard. It's the perfect location for a maritime museum, and when it reopens promises to be one of the city's key attractions.

NEMO

If you stroll along the waterfront Prins Hendrikkade, the foreground is dominated by a massive elevated hood that rears up above the entrance to the IJ tunnel. A good part of this hood is occupied by the large and lavish **NEMO** centre, Prins Hendrikkade (Tues–Sun 10am–5pm; during school holidays and July & Aug also Mon 10am–5pm; €11.50; ⓦwww.e-nemo.nl) – just follow the signs for the ground-floor entrance. Recently rebranded, this is a young kids' attraction par excellence, with all sorts of interactive science and technological exhibits spread over six floors.

Outside, moored at the NEMO jetty, is a full-scale replica of an East Indiaman, the 78-metre **De Amsterdam** (same times; €2 with NEMO ticket, otherwise €5). The ship has been temporarily relocated here while the Maritime Museum, which owns it, is closed. The original ship first set sail in 1748, but came to an ignominious end, getting stuck on the British coast near Hastings. Visitors can wander its decks and galleys, storerooms and gun bays at their leisure.

The Museum Quarter and the Vondelpark

Just south of Leidseplein, the wide lawns of **Museumplein** extend south from the Rijksmuseum to Van Baerlestraat, and are used for a variety of outdoor activities, from visiting circuses to political demonstrations. The largest of the museums that give it its name is the **Rijksmuseum**, which occupies a huge late-nineteenth-century edifice built in an inventive historic style by Petrus Josephus Hubertus Cuypers, also the creator of Centraal Station, in the early 1880s. The museum possesses one of the most comprehensive collections of seventeenth-century Dutch paintings in the world, with twenty or so of Rembrandt's works, plus a healthy sample of canvases by Steen, Hals, Vermeer and their leading contemporaries. There are also representative displays of every other pre-twentieth-century period of Dutch and Flemish painting. On the right, looking south, the **Van Gogh Museum** boasts the finest assortment of Van Gogh paintings in the world, while the **Stedelijk Museum**, just beyond, focuses on modern and contemporary art, and is due to reopen shortly after a refit. From Museumplein, it's a brief walk northwest along Van Baerlestraat to the sprawling greenery of the **Vondelpark**, Amsterdam's loveliest park.

The Rijksmuseum

The **Rijksmuseum** (daily 9am–6pm, Friday until 8.30pm; €11; audio guide €5; ⓦwww.rijksmuseum.nl)) is without question the country's foremost museum, with an extravagant collection of Dutch art, as well as a vast hoard of applied art and sculpture. The bad news is that there's a major renovation going on at the moment and most of the museum is closed. The exception is the Rijksmuseum's Philips Wing (entrance on Jan Luijkenstraat), whose smallish but eclectic "Masterpieces" exhibition, scheduled to last until the rest of the museum is reopened, is devoted to the paintings of Amsterdam's Golden Age. Bear in mind, though, that queues can be long, especially in summer and at weekends, so try to book online first.

It's worth the wait, as the selection on display is superb. There are paintings by Rembrandt's pupils – Ferdinand Bol, Gerard Dou and Gabriel Metsu; several wonderful canvases by Frans Hals, such as his scatological *Merry Drinker*; the cool interiors of Vermeer, Gerard ter Borch and Pieter de Hooch; soft, tonal river scenes by the Haarlem artist Salomon van Ruysdael and by Albert Cuyp; the cool church interiors of Pieter Saenredam; and the popular carousing peasants of Jan Steen. However, it's the Rembrandts that steal the show, especially *The Night Watch* of 1642 – perhaps the most famous and probably the most valuable of all the artist's pictures – plus other key works, like a late *Self-Portrait*; a touching depiction of his cowled son, Titus the arresting *Staalmeesters*; and *The Jewish Bride*; one of his very last pictures, finished in 1667.

The Van Gogh Museum

The **Van Gogh Museum**, comprising a fabulous collection of the artist's (1853–90) work, is one of Amsterdam's top attractions (daily 10am–6pm, Fri until 10pm; €12.50, children 13–17 years €2.50; audioguide €4; Ⓦwww .vangoghmuseum.nl). It occupies two modern buildings, with the kernel of the collection housed in an angular building designed by a leading light of the De Stijl movement, Gerritt Rietveld, and opened to the public in 1973. Well conceived and beautifully presented, this part of the museum provides an introduction to the man and his art based on paintings that were mostly inherited from Vincent's art-dealer brother Theo.

The **ground floor** of the main museum displays works by some of Van Gogh's well-known friends and contemporaries, many of whom influenced his work – Gauguin, Millet, Anton Mauve, Charles Daubigny and others – while the **first floor** has paintings by the artist himself, displayed chronologically, starting with the dark, sombre works of the early years like *The Potato Eaters* and finishing up with the asylum years at St Rémy and the final, tortured paintings done at Auvers, where Van Gogh lodged for the last three months of his life. It was at Auvers that he painted the frantic *Ears of Wheat* and *Wheatfield with a Reaper*, in which the fields swirl and writhe under weird, light-green, moving skies. A few weeks after completing these paintings, Van Gogh shot and fatally wounded himself.

The two floors above provide backup to the main collection. The **second floor** has a library and study area with access to a detailed computerized account of Van Gogh's life and times, plus a number of sketches and a handful of less familiar paintings. The **third floor** features more drawings and sketches from the permanent collection as well as notebooks and letters. This floor also affords space to temporary exhibitions illustrating Van Gogh's artistic influences, or his own influence on other artists.

To the rear of Rietveld's building, and connected by a ground-floor-level escalator, is the ultramodern curved annexe, an aesthetically controversial structure completed in 1998. Financed by a Japanese insurance company – the same conglomerate who paid $35 million for one of Van Gogh's *Sunflowers* canvases in 1987 – this provides temporary exhibition space. Most of these exhibitions focus on one aspect or another of Van Gogh's art and draw heavily on the permanent collection, which means that the paintings displayed in the older building are regularly rotated.

The Concertgebouw

Across Van Baerlestraat is the **Concertgebouw** (Concert Hall), home of the famed – and much recorded – Royal Concertgebouw Orchestra (Ⓦwww .concertgebouw.nl). When the German composer Brahms visited Amsterdam in the 1870s he was scathing about the locals' lack of culture and in particular their lack of an even halfway suitable venue for his music. In the face of such ridicule, a consortium of Amsterdam businessmen got together to fund the construction of a brand-new concert hall and the result was the Concertgebouw, completed in 1888. Since then it has become renowned among musicians and concert-goers for its marvellous acoustics, and after a facelift and the replacement of its crumbling foundations in the early 1990s it is looking and sounding better than ever. The acoustics of the Grote Zaal (Large Hall) are unparalleled, and the smaller Kleine Zaal regularly hosts chamber concerts, often by the resident Borodin Quartet. Prices are very reasonable; there are free Wednesday lunchtime concerts from September to May, and in July and August they put on a heavily subsidized series of summer concerts. **Guided tours** take place on Sundays (noon–1pm) and Mondays (5–6pm) and cost €10. The tour takes in the Grote Zaal and Kleine Zaal auditoria, as well as various behind-the-scenes activities – control rooms, piano stores, artistes' dressing rooms and the like.

The Vondelpark

Amsterdam's city centre is short of green spaces, which makes the leafy expanses of the **Vondelpark**, just beyond Museumplein, doubly welcome. This is easily the largest and most popular of the city's parks, its network of footpaths used by a healthy slice of the city's population. The park dates back to 1864, when a group of leading Amsterdammers clubbed together to transform the soggy marshland that lay beyond the Leidsepoort into a landscaped park. The group, who were impressed by the contemporary English fashion for natural (as distinct from formal) landscaping, gave the task of developing the new style of park to the Zocher family, big-time gardeners who set about their task with gusto, completing their work in 1865. Named after the seventeenth-century poet Joost van den Vondel, the park proved an immediate success and was expanded to its present size (45 hectares) in 1877. It now possesses over 100 species of tree, a wide variety of local and imported plants, and – among many incidental features – a **bandstand** and excellent **rose garden**. Neither did the Zochers forget their Dutch roots: the park is latticed with ponds and narrow waterways, home to many sorts of wildfowl. There are other animals too: cows,

▲ The Vondelpark

sheep, hundreds of squirrels plus a large colony of bright-green parakeets. The Vondelpark has several different children's **play areas** and during the summer regularly hosts free concerts and theatrical performances, mostly in its own specially designed **open-air theatre**.

De Pijp

Across Boerenwetering, the canal to the east of the Rijksmuseum and Museumplein, lies the busy heart of the **Oud Zuid** (Old South), and specifically the district known as **De Pijp** ("The Pipe"), Amsterdam's first real suburb. New development beyond the Singelgracht began around 1870, but after laying down the street plans, the city council left the actual house-building to private developers. They made the most of the arrangement and constructed long rows of cheaply built and largely featureless five- and six-storey buildings, and it is these that still dominate the area today. The district's name comes from the characteristically narrow terraced streets running between long, sombre canyons of brick tenements: the apartments here were said to resemble pipe-drawers, since each had a tiny street frontage but extended deep into the building. De Pijp remains one of the city's more closely knit communities, and is home to a large proportion of new immigrants – Surinamese, Moroccan, Turkish and Asian.

Albert Cypstraat market

Ferdinand Bolstraat, running north–south, is De Pijp's main street, but the long, slim east–west thoroughfare of **Albert Cuypstraat** is its heart. The general market (daily except Sun 10am–5pm) held here – which stretches for over a kilometre between Ferdinand Bolstraat and Van Woustraat – is the largest in the city, with a huge array of stalls selling everything from cut-price carrots and raw-herring sandwiches to saucepans and Day-Glo thongs. Check out, too, the ethnic shops that flank the market on each side, and the Indian and Surinamese restaurants down the side streets – they're often cheaper than their equivalents in the city centre.

The Heineken Experience

On the northern edge of De Pijp, the former Heineken brewery, a whopping modern building beside the Singelgracht canal at Stadhouderskade 78, now holds the **Heineken Experience** (daily 11am–7pm; €15; Ⓦwww.heinekenexperience .com; tram #16 or #24 from Centraal Station). The brewery was Heineken's headquarters from 1864 to 1988, when the company was restructured and brewing was moved to a more efficient location out of town. Since then, Heineken has developed the site for tourists with lots of gimmicky but fun attractions such as virtual reality tours and displays on the history of Heineken, from advertising campaigns to beer-making. The old brewing facilities with their vast copper vats are included on the tour, but for many the main draw is the free beer you get to quaff at the end in the bar – three drinks, and a souvenir glass, which isn't bad value.

Eating

Amsterdam has never been one of Europe's culinary hotspots, but there has been a resurgence of interest in Dutch cooking in recent years and the city has accumulated a string of excellent homegrown **restaurants**. It's also a city of tremendous diversity, and as well as having some of the best Indonesian food outside Indonesia, at hard-to-beat prices, there are lots of ethnic choices, from

French, Iberian and Italian, to Thai, Middle Eastern and Indian. Amsterdam also excels in the quantity and variety of its **eetcafés and bars**, which serve increasingly adventurous and inexpensive food in a wide range of attractive settings. The city's **cafés and tearooms** – calling themselves this to steer clear of druggy "**coffeeshop**" connotations – correspond to the normal idea of a café: they are generally open all day, might serve alcohol but definitely aren't bars, don't allow dope-smoking, and serve up good coffee, sandwiches, light snacks and cakes.

All the following listings are on the maps on pp.52–53 and p.61.

Cafés, tearooms and lunchspots

The Old Centre

De Bakkerswinkel Warmoesstraat 69. Part of a popular chain that serves great bread and sandwiches, mouthwatering scones, muffins and home-made pies. Expect to queue for a table at lunchtime. Other branches at Roelof Hartstraat in the Old South and at the Westergasfabriek complex. Tues–Sat 8am–6pm, Sun 10am–4pm.

Café Beurs van Berlage Beursplein 1. The best chance to glimpse the interior of the Beurs (see p.62), and an elegantly furnished place to drink coffee or eat lunch. Tables outside too. Mon–Sat 10am–6pm, Sun 11am–6pm.

De Jaren Nieuwe Doelenstraat 20. One of the grandest of the grand cafés, overlooking the Amstel next to the university, with three floors, two terraces and a cool, light feel. A great place to nurse the Sunday papers – unusually you'll find

▲ Puccini café

English ones here. It serves reasonably priced food too, and there's a great salad bar. Daily 10am–1am, Fri & Sat til 2am.

Latei Zeedijk 174. Homely shop and café that sells bric-a-brac as well as serving good coffee and decent lunches. Quite a find if you fancy something different from the Chinese restaurants that dominate this end of Zeedijk. Mon–Wed 8am–6pm, Thurs & Fri 8am–10pm, Sat 9am–10pm, Sun 11am–6pm.

Luxembourg Spui 22. Crowded, trendy grand café with a long and deep bar, a good selection of snacks, and possibly the best hamburgers in town. Daily 9am–1am, Fri & Sat until 2am.

't Nieuwe Kafe Eggerstraat 8. Beside the Nieuwe Kerk, this bistro-style café is popular with shoppers and tourists, serving good, reasonably priced breakfasts, lunches, light meals and great pancakes too. Daily 8am–6pm.

Puccini Staalstraat 21. Lovely café that serves great salads, sandwiches, cakes and pastries, a few doors down from its sister chocolate shop. Mon–Fri 8.30am–6pm, Sat & Sun 10am–6pm.

Restaurant 1e Class Platform 2b, Centraal Station. More of a fully-fledged restaurant than a café, and with a huge menu to prove it. Its location in Centraal Station means that you're most likely to choose to enjoy its sumptuous turn-of-the-century interior and solid menu of omelettes, sandwiches or more substantial meat and fish offerings at lunchtime, and it's certainly the best option in the station's immediate vicinity. Daily 8.30am–11pm.

Villa Zeezicht Torensteeg 4. Excellent sandwiches and light lunches, and some of the best apple cake in the city. Daily 8am–9pm.

Vlaams Friteshuis Voetboogstraat 33. This hole-in-the-wall takeaway has a long-established and pretty much undisputed reputation for serving the best *frites* in town. Mon & Sun noon–6pm, Tues–Sat 11am–6pm.

The Grachtengordel

Bagels & Beans Keizersgracht 504. Bagel specialists, with all sorts of imaginative fillings, attracting a young clientele; their version of straw-berries and cream cheese is a big favourite in the summer. Several other branches, including one in De Pijp. This one is open Mon–Fri 9am–5.30pm, Sat & Sun 10am–6pm.

Buffet van Odette & Yvette Herengracht 309. Just walking past will get your taste buds going: lots of tasty sandwiches, cakes and other good things – a perfect lunch-stop. Mon & Wed–Fri 8.30am–4.30pm, Sat 10am–5.30pm.

Greenwoods Singel 103. Small, English-style teashop in the basement of a canal house. Pies and sandwiches, pots of tea – and a decent breakfast. Mon–Thurs 9.30am–6pm, Fri–Sun till 7pm.

Panini Vijzelgracht 3. Formica may be a thing of the past almost everywhere else, but not here, giving this split-level, Italian café-cum-restaurant a vaguely beatnik air. Great coffee, sandwiches and pasta during the day; reasonably priced meat, fish and pasta dishes at night. Mon–Sat 9.30am–11pm, Sun 11.30am–11pm.

Spanjer & van Twist Leliegracht 60. Hip café-bar with an arty air and tasty snacks and light meals plus an outdoor terrace right on the canal. Lunch served daily 10am–4pm, evening meals from 6pm.

The Jordaan and the Western Docklands

Arnold Cornelis Elandsgracht 78. Long-established confectioner and patisserie with a mouth-watering display of pastries and cakes. Take away or eat in the snug tearoom out the back. Mon–Fri 8.30am–6pm, Sat 8.30am–5pm.

Festina Lente Looiersgracht 40b. Relaxed, mezzanine neighbourhood café-bar with mismatched furniture and armchairs to laze about on. The outside tables overlooking the canal are a sun trap in the summer; inside is equally cosy in the winter, and there's a good selection of board games. Service can be slow. Mon noon–1am, Tues–Fri 10.30am–1/3am, Sat 11am–3am, Sun noon–1am.

The Old Jewish Quarter and the Eastern Docklands

De Hortus Plantage Middenlaan 2a. The amenable café in the orangery of the Hortus Botanicus serves a

good range of tasty sandwiches and rolls plus the best cheesecake in the western world. Unfortunately, you have to pay to get into the gardens to get to the café. Mon–Fri 9am–5pm, Sat & Sun 10am–5pm; Dec & Jan till 4pm; July & Aug till 7pm.

Tisfris St Antoniesbreestraat 142. Colourful, split-level café and bar metres from the Rembrandthuis. Youthful and popular, with hot rolls, sandwiches, salads and so forth. Daily 9am–7pm.

The Museum Quarter and Vondelpark

't Blauwe Theehuis Vondelpark 5. These days this is a slightly shabby tearoom/café/bar in the middle of the Vondelpark, but its building dates from the De Stijl period. Downstairs it's a regular self-service park café; upstairs it's a nice circular bar that hosts DJs on Friday and Saturday nights. April–Sept daily 9am–1am; Oct–March Mon–Wed 9am–7pm, Thurs 9am–11pm, Fri & Sat 9am–1am, Sun 9am–10pm.

CoBrA Hobbemastraat 18. This standalone asymmetric structure behind the Rijksmuseum mainly caters for tourists wanting a convenient place for a drink or quick bite between exhibitions. It's also a popular late-night hangout, open from 10am until 3am at weekends, otherwise until 9pm.

Keyzer Van Baerlestraat 96. In operation since 1905, and right next to the Concertgebouw, this café-restaurant exudes a fin-de-siècle charm, with ferns, gliding bow-tied waiters and a dark carved-wood interior. It's open all day, and you can come here for dinner, but these days it's best as a venue for lunch or coffee. Daily 11am–11pm.

De Roos PC Hooftstraat 183. The downstairs café at this New Age centre on the edge of the Vondelpark is one of the most peaceful spots in the city, selling a range of drinks and organic snacks and meals. There's also an upstairs bookshop, and any number of courses in yoga and meditation. Mon–Fri 8.30am–9pm, Sat & Sun 8.30am–5.30pm.

Vertigo Vondelpark 3. Attached to the Film Museum, this is a pleasant place to while away a summer afternoon at the tables outside overlooking the park, or take refuge in winter in the cosy basement interior. Good food, too, at all times of day. Mon–Fri 11am–1am, Sat & Sun 10am–1am.

Restaurants

The Old Centre

Bird Zeedijk 77 ☏020/420 6289. This Thai canteen is always packed, and rightly so, drawing people from far and wide for its cheap and authentic Thai fare. Its big brother across the road

serves much the same food in slightly more upscale surroundings. Daily 2–10pm.

Blauwe aan de Waal Oudezijds Achterburgwal 99 ☏020/330 2257. Quite a haven, situated down an alley in the heart of the Red Light District, with tremendous French–Dutch food and a wonderfully soothing environment after the mayhem of the streets outside. Not cheap, but worth every cent. Mon–Sat 6–11.30pm.

Café Bern Nieuwmarkt 9 ⓣ020/622 0034 Casual and inexpensive brown café patronized by a predominantly arty clientele. Run by a native of Switzerland, its speciality is, not surprisingly, excellent and alcoholic cheese fondue. Daily 6–11pm.
Centra Lange Niezel 29 ⓣ020/622 3050. This authentic Spanish cantina is a long-standing Red Light District favourite, with a wonderful selection of Spanish food, masterfully cooked and genially served. Cash only. Daily 1.30–11pm.
Green Planet Spuistraat 122 ⓣ020/625 8280. Cute mezzanine café with lots of tofu dishes and a varied international menu. Cash only. Daily 5.30pm–midnight.
Hemelse Modder Oude Waal 9 ⓣ020/624 3203. Sleek restaurant serving a tasty menu of Dutch and vaguely European food in an informal atmosphere. Service is very attentive and – despite the trendy environment – not at all precious, and the food is excellent and reasonably priced. Deservedly popular. Tues–Sun 6–11pm.
Keuken van 1870 Spuistraat 2 ⓣ020/620 4018 This large, light restaurant has been serving hearty Dutch food to cheapskates for years and continues – justifiably – to thrive. Its three-course €7.50 menu is one of the city's best bargains. Mon–Sat 5–10pm.
Lucius Spuistraat 247 ⓣ020/624 1831. This long-established restaurant has been uneven over the years but when it gets it right – as it usually does – it's one of the best fish restaurants in town. Daily 5pm–midnight.
Mappa Nes 59 ⓣ020/528 9170. Classic Italian food with some inventive twists, incorporating good home-made pasta dishes and excellent service in an unpretentious and modern environment. Daily 6–9.45pm (Fri & Sat till 10.45pm).

Nam Kee Zeedijk 111–113 ⓣ020/624 3470. Arguably the best of a number of Chinese diners along this stretch, and attracting a loyal clientele. Quick service, great food. Daily noon–midnight.
De Portugees Zeedijk 39 ⓣ020/427 2005. Truly a little piece of Portugal on the Zeedijk, with chaotic service and authentically hearty and filling (rather than gourmet) food – tasty fish stews, garlicky sausages, salt cod and eggs. Daily 6–10.30pm.
Sie Joe Gravenstraat 24 ⓣ020/624 1830. Small Indonesian café-restaurant whose great value-for-money menu is far from extensive but comprises well-prepared, simple dishes such as *gado gado*, *sateh* and *rendang*. Mon–Sat 11am–7pm, Thurs until 8pm.

Van Beeren Koningstraat 54 ⓣ020/622 2329. This eetcafé serves a satisfying mixture of Dutch staples and modern European fare in relaxed surroundings. Daily 5.30–10.15pm.

Van Kerkwijk Nes 41 ⓣ020/620 3316. This looks like a bar but is more of a restaurant these days, serving steaks, fish and so on from an ever-changing menu that isn't written down but is heroically memorized by the attentive waiting staff. Good food, and cheap too – mains from €12 or so. Daily noon–10pm.

The Grachtengordel

Belhamel Brouwersgracht 60 ⓣ020/622 1095. Smashing restaurant where the Art Nouveau decor makes a delightful setting and the menu is short but extremely well chosen, mixing Dutch with French dishes. Main courses at around €20–25. Daily 6–10pm.
Bojo Lange Leidsedwarsstraat 51 ⓣ020/622 7434. One of the best-value Indonesian places in town, though the food itself is very much a hit-and-miss affair, and you may have to wait a long time both for a table and service. Main courses average €9–13. Mon–Thurs 4pm–2am, Fri 4pm–4am, Sat noon–4am, Sun noon–2am.
Bolhoed Prinsengracht 60 ⓣ020/626 1803. Something of an Amsterdam institution, with a daily changing menu featuring familiar vegan and vegetarian options, with organic beer to wash it down. Mains at around €15. Daily noon–10pm.
Chez Georges Herenstraat 3 ⓣ020/626 3332. Smart-to-formal, split-level, intimate restaurant offering highly rated, upmarket cuisine with an emphasis on meat dishes; mains €23 and up. Open from 6pm, but closed Wed & Sun.
Cilubang Runstraat 10 ⓣ020/626 9755. Tiny but much liked Indonesian restaurant with a friendly atmosphere, serving well-presented, spicy dishes at reasonable prices; mains hover around €14. Tues–Sun 6–11pm.
Golden Temple Utrechtsestraat 126 ⓣ020/626 8560. Laid-back place with a little more soul than the average Amsterdam veggie joint. Well-prepared food and pleasant, attentive service. No alcohol. Daily noon–3pm & 5–9.30pm.
De Luwte Leliegracht 26 ⓣ020/625 8548. This cordial restaurant is kitted out in attractive style, and the small but well-chosen menu offers first-rate Dutch/Mediterranean cuisine – the seafood is especially good. Mains from €20. Daily 6–10pm.
Piet de Leeuw Noorderstraat 11 ⓣ020/623 7181. Arguably Amsterdam's best steakhouse, an old-fashioned, darkly lit, wood-panelled affair dating back to the 1940s. Doubles as a local bar, but the steaks, served in several different ways and

costing around €16, are excellent. Mon–Fri noon–11pm, Sat & Sun 5–11pm.

Prego Herenstraat 25 ☎020/638 0148. Informal Mediterranean restaurant with sharp modern decor offering an inventive menu of rich dishes. Mains €25 and up. Daily 6–10.30pm.

Puri Mas Lange Leidsedwarsstraat 37 ☎020/627 7627. Exceptionally good-value Indonesian restaurant near the Leidseplein. Friendly and informed service preludes spectacular *rijsttafels*, both meat and vegetarian. Main courses from €15. Daily from 6pm.

D'Theeboom Singel 210 ☎020/623 8420. Traditional French restaurant in an old and attractive canal house a short walk from Dam Square. Relaxed atmosphere; attentive service. Mains from around €20. Daily 6–10pm.

Van de Kaart Prinsengracht 512 ☎020/625 9232. Excellent French/Mediterranean basement restaurant decorated in minimalist style and featuring an inventive menu. Main courses for around €28. There's a good cellar too. Mon–Sat 6.30–10.30pm.

Le Zinc…et les Autres Prinsengracht 999 ☎020/622 9044. Wonderfully atmospheric place serving good-quality, simple fare with main courses averaging €25; there's a particularly good wine list too. Mon–Sat 5.30–11pm.

The Jordaan and the Western Docklands

Albatros Westerstraat 264 ☎020/627 9932. This nautically adorned fish restaurant serves excep-tionally good food, making it a great place to splash out and linger over a meal. Mains from €20; three-course menu of the day €30. Mon & Thurs–Sun 6–11pm.

Burger's Patio 2e Tuindwarsstraat 12 ☎020/623 6854. Despite the name (the site used to be occupied by a butcher's), there isn't a burger in sight in this long-established convivial restaurant, which has managed to maintain its informal atmosphere without compromising on taste. Italian-inspired dishes are wonderfully presented with a good choice of daily specials. Mains from €15. Daily 6pm–late.

Cinema Paradiso Westerstraat 186 ☎020/623 7344. Fast-moving restaurant covering all the Italian classics with vim and gusto. It's in a former moviehouse and very popular, so you may have to shout to be heard. Dress to kill/thrill. Pasta and pizzas kick off at around €15. Tues–Sun 6–11pm.

Claes Claesz Egelantiersstraat 24 ☎020/625 5306. This exceptionally friendly Jordaan restaurant attracts a mixed crowd and serves excellent Dutch food. Fridays and Saturdays feature various Dutch theatrical and musical acts between the courses. Three courses €27.Wed–Sun 6–11pm.

Duende Lindengracht 62 ☎020 420 6692. Wonderful and busy tapas bar with a tiled interior, mismatched wood furniture, and a warm and inviting feel. Also includes a small venue out back for live dance and music performances, including regular flamenco every Saturday. Mon–Fri 5–11pm, Sat & Sun 4–11pm.

De Eettuin 2e Tuindwarsstraat 10 ☎020/623 7706. Hefty and eminently affordable portions of Dutch food, with salad from a serve-yourself bar. Non-meat eaters can content themselves with a choice of tasty vegetarian options, and all mains (from €14) come with a choice of rice or potatoes. Daily 5.30–11.30pm.

De Gouden Reael Zandhoek 14 ☎020/623 3883. Fine French food in a unique setting up in the Westerdok. Its relaxed mezzanined interior is a good place for a coffee any time of day. The bar, as described in the novel of the same name by Jan Mens, has a long association with the dockworkers. Main courses hover around €15–20. Daily 6–10.30pm.

🏃 **Moeders** Rozengracht 251 ☎020/626 7957. Really cosy restaurant just across from the Singelgracht whose theme is obvious from the moment you step inside – mothers ("*moeders*"), photos of thousands of whom plaster the walls. Traditional Dutch food, well presented and with the odd modern twist. Mains €13 and up, three-course menus €26–30. Daily 5–10.30pm.

La Oliva Egelantiersstraat 122 ☎020/320 4316. This sleek Jordaan eatery specializes in *pinxtos*, the delectable Basque snacks on sticks that make Spanish bar-hopping such a delight. With a nod to Dutch tastes perhaps, this is more of a restaurant than a bar, and the *pinxtos* anything but bite-sized. Daily except Tues noon–10.30pm.

De Vliegende Schotel Nieuwe Leliestraat 162 ☎020/625 2041. Perhaps the pick of the city's cheap and wholesome vegetarian restaurants, the "Flying Saucer" serves delicious food in large portions. Lots of space and a peaceful ambience. Mains around €10. Daily 4–10.45pm.

Yam Yam Frederik Hendrikstraat 90 ☎020/681 5097. Top pizzeria and trattoria in a simple, tradi-tional dining room, with wipe-clean table covers and an open kitchen. It attracts couples and all the hip young parents from the neighbourhood with its excellent pizza toppings. Booking advised. Pizzas €8–13. Tues–Sun 6–10pm.

The Old Jewish Quarter and the Eastern Docklands

éénvistwéévis Schippersgracht 6 ☎020/623 2894. An uncomplicated fish restaurant serving an

interesting selection of fish and seafood. No menu
– the waiters will tell you what's cooking. Mains at
around €20. Tues–Sun 6–10pm.

Fifteen Jollemanshof 9 ☎0900 343 8336. The
Amsterdam branch of chef Jamie Oliver's
successful formula. Mediterranean, largely Italian-
style menu, with a four-course meal for around
€46. Also has a less formal trattoria and lounge.
Daily noon–3pm & 6–11pm.

Greetje Peperstraat 23 ☎020/779 7450.
A cosy, busy restaurant serving up Dutch
staples with a modern twist. A changing menu
reflects the seasons and the favourite dishes of
the owner's mother – a native of the southern
Netherlands. Superb home cooking in a great
atmosphere. Tues–Sun 5–10pm, Sat till 11pm.

Nam Tin Jodenbreestraat 11 ☎020/428 8508.
Vast cavernous restaurant almost opposite the
Rembrandthuis that serves dim sum every day
between noon and 5pm. Sister restaurant to *Nam
Kee* on Zeedijk (p.90) and one of the best places
for dim sum in the city. It serves a large regular
menu too. Mon–Sat noon–11pm, Sun noon–10pm.

Rosario Peperstraat 10 ☎020/627 0280. Attractive,
canal-side restaurant serving top-quality Italian food.
There's an open kitchen, and the ravioli goes down a
storm. Mains from €21. Tues–Sat 6–11pm.

The Museum Quarter and Vondelpark

Dionysos Overtoom 176 ☎020/689 4441.
Inexpensive Greek restaurant just west of the
Vondelpark, with a good selection of meze and
occasional live music. Tues–Sun 5.30–11pm.

Dosa Overtoom 146 ☎020/616 4838. Halfway
along the Vondelpark, this brightly lit corner restaurant concentrates on Southern Indian dishes at
moderate prices – mains begin at around €15.
Daily 5.30–11.30pm.

Le Garage Ruysdaelstraat 54 ☎020/679 7176.
This elegant restaurant, with an eclectic French
and Italian menu, is popular with a media crowd
since it's run by a well-known Dutch TV cook. Call
to reserve a week ahead and dress to impress.
Prices are moderate to high, with mains around
€30 and three-course menus for around €45. If you
just want a snack, try the cocktail bar next door
instead. Daily noon–2pm and 6–11pm; Sat & Sun
dinner only.

Loetje J. Vermeerstraat 52 ☎020/662 8173.
Excellent steaks, fries and salads are the thing at
this eetcafé. The service can be touch-and-go, but
the food is great, and fairly inexpensive. The
pleasant outdoor terrace in the summer is a bonus.
Mon–Fri 11am–10pm, Sat evening only.

Drinking

Amsterdam's selection of **bars** and **café–bars** is one of the real pleasures of the
city. There are traditional brown cafés, so called because of the dingy colour of
their walls, stained by years of tobacco smoke, and slick, self-consciously modern
designer bars, which tend to be as un-brown as possible and geared towards a
young crowd. We've included details of the more established ones, although these
places come and go – something like seventy percent are said to close down
within a year of opening. Most **café–bars** (often called **eetcafés**) and some bars
sell food – anything from snacks to an extensive menu. Another type of drinking
spot, though increasingly rare, is the **tasting–house** (*proeflokaal*), originally the
sampling rooms of small private *jenever* distillers, now tiny, stand-up places that
often only sell spirits and close around 8pm. For listings of gay bars, see p.100.

All the following listings are on the maps on pp.52–53 and p.61.

The Old Centre

Absinthe Nieuwezijds Voorburgwal 171. Small,
late-night basement lounge bar that specializes in
– you guessed it – absinthe, or at least the turn-of-
the-century decadence that's associated with it.
DJs at the weekend.

In 't Aepjen Zeedijk 1. This building has
been a bar since the days when Zeedijk was
a haunt for sailors gambling away their last few
guilder and having to pay by barter rather than

cash. Its name – literally "In the Monkeys" – refers
to the fact that monkeys were once the stock in
trade here. There are no monkeys now, but not
much else has changed.

De Bekeerde Suster Kloveniersburgwal 6.
Don't waste your time in the unappealing
drinkeries of the Red Light District proper; this
place is a few steps away and offers home-brewed
beer, a good bar menu and a very convivial
atmosphere, just off the top end of Nieuwemarkt.

Belgique Gravenstraat 2. Tiny bar behind the Nieuwe Kerk that serves up Belgian brews with cubes of cheese.

Diep Nieuwezijds Voorburgwal 256. Not much more than an ordinary brown café during the day, but a hip hangout with DJs at night.

De Drie Fleschjes Gravenstraat 18. Tasting house for spirits and liqueurs, which once would have been made on the premises. Clients tend to be well heeled or well soused (often both). Mon–Sat noon–8.30pm, Sun 3–8pm.

De Engelbewaarder Kloveniersburgwal 59. Once the meeting place of Amsterdam's bookish types, this is still known as a literary café. It's relaxed and informal, with live jazz on Sunday afternoons.

Gollem Raamsteeg 4. Small and intimate bar with a superb selection of Belgian beers – and with the correct glasses to drink them from. The genial barman will help you choose.

Hoppe Spui 18. One of Amsterdam's longest-established and best-known bars, frequented by the city's businessfolk on their wayward way home. Summer is especially good, when the throngs spill out onto the street.

 In de Wildeman Kolksteeg 3. This lovely old-fashioned bar has a barely changed wood and tile interior that still boasts its original low bar and shelving. A peaceful escape from the loud, tacky shops of nearby Nieuwendijk, and one of the centre's most appealing watering holes. Daily noon–1am (Fri & Sat til 2am).

The Tara Rokin 85–89. Amsterdam has quite a few Irish pubs these days, but this is one of the best, with decent food (including a great all-day breakfast), regular football and other sports on TV. There's also live music from 10.30pm on Saturdays during the winter.

 Wynand Fockink Pijlsteeg 31. Small and cosy bar hidden just behind the *Krasnapolsky* hotel off Dam Square. One of the older *proeflokalen*, it offers a vast range of its own flavoured *jenevers* that used to be distilled down the street.

The Grachtengordel

 't Arendsnest Herengracht 90. In a handsome old canal house, this bar boasts impressive wooden decor – from the longest of bars to the tall wood-and-glass cabinets – and specializes in Dutch beers, of which it has 130 varieties, twelve on tap. Attracts an older clientele. Daily 4pm–midnight, 2am at the weekend.

De Hegeraad Noordermarkt 34. Lovingly maintained, old-fashioned brown café with a loyal clientele. The back room with red plush furnishings and paintings is the perfect place to relax with a hot chocolate.

 Het Molenpad Prinsengracht 653. This is one of the most appealing brown cafés in the city – a long, dark bar that fills up fast with a young, professional crowd after 6pm.

Oosterling Utrechtsestraat 140. Intimate neighbourhood bar that's been plying its trade for donkey's years. It specializes in *jenever*, with dozens of brands and varieties. No mobile phones.

Het Papeneiland Prinsengracht 2. With its wood panelling, antique Delft tiles and ancient stove, this is one of the cosiest bars in the Grachtengordel, though it does get packed late at night with a garrulous crew.

De Prins Prinsengracht 124. With its well-worn decor and chatty atmosphere, this popular and lively brown bar offers a wide range of drinks and a well-priced bar menu. Food served from 10am to 9pm.

Van Puffelen Prinsengracht 377. This long-established and popular spot is divided into two with a brown café-bar on one side and a (very average) restaurant on the other. The café-bar (daily 3pm to 1 or 2am) is an appealing place to drink, with a good choice of international brews.

Walem Keizersgracht 449. A chic bar-restaurant – cool, light and vehemently un-brown; eat in or chill out at the bar with a mojito. The clientele is stylish, and the food a hybrid of French- and Dutch-inspired dishes. Breakfast in the garden during the summer is a highlight. Usually packed. Kitchen daily 10am–10pm.

The Jordaan and the Western Docklands

Chris Bloemstraat 42. Very proud of itself for being the Jordaan's (and Amsterdam's) oldest bar, dating from 1624. Comfortable, homely atmosphere.

Dulac Haarlemmerstraat 118. A very appealing Art Deco grand café, with lots of nooks to sit in, housed in what was an old city bank – though now the only money changing hands is at the bar, especially on weekends when it stays open till 3am. DJs from Thursday to Saturday play a mixture of jazz, funk and Seventies and Eighties tunes.

Finch Noordermarkt 5. This smart and cosy café-lounge bar situated near the Noorderkerk attracts a stylish, relaxed crowd, drawn by the design-school ambience, good tunes and superb location overlooking the Prisengracht. Lunch from noon, dinner from 6pm.

De Kat in de Wijngaert Lindengracht 160. With the enticing name "Cat in the Vineyard", this small bar is the epitome of the Jordaan local, and quiet enough for conversation.

 De Reiger Nieuwe Leliestraat 34. Situated in the thick of the Jordaan, this is one of the area's many meeting places, an old-style café filled with modish Amsterdammers and with faded portraits on the walls. Dinner from around €19.

't Smalle Egelantiersgracht 12. Candle-lit and comfortable, with a pontoon on the canal out front for relaxed summer afternoons. One of Amsterdam's oldest cafés, it opened in 1786 as a *proeflokaal* – a tasting house for the (long gone) gin distillery next door.

Thijssen Brouwersgracht 107. An old-time favourite with neighbourhood locals. Nothing fancy, but perfect for lingering over coffee or fresh mint tea with a magazine.

De Tuin 2e Tuindwarsstraat 13. The Jordaan has some marvellously unpretentious bars, and this is one of the best: agreeably unkempt and always filled with locals.

The Old Jewish Quarter and the Eastern Docklands

Brouwerij 't IJ De Gooyer windmill, Funenkade 7. Long-established, rudimentary bar and mini-brewery in the old public baths adjoining the windmill. Serves up an excellent range of beers and ales, from the thunderously strong (9%)

Columbus amber ale to the creamier, more soothing Natte (6.5%).

De Druif Rapenburgerplein 83. Claims to be the city's oldest bar and certainly one of its more beguiling, this neighbourhood joint pulls in an easy-going crowd.

De Sluyswacht Jodenbreestraat 1 This pleasant little bar occupies an old and now solitary gabled house that stands sentry by the lock gates opposite the Rembrandthuis. A smashing spot to nurse a beer on a warm summer's night, gazing down the canal towards the Montelbaanstoren.

The Museum Quarter and Vondelpark

Welling J.W. Brouwersstraat 32. Situated right behind the Concertgebouw, this traditional haunt of gloomy Amsterdam intellectuals is usually packed solid with performers and visitors alike before and after evening performances.

Wildschut Roelof Hartplein 1. Not far from the Concertgebouw, this bar is famous for its Art Deco trimmings, and its congenial large interior and outside seating in summer. Much the nicest place to drink in the area, and with a decent menu too.

Coffeeshops

In Amsterdam a "**coffeeshop**" is advertising just one thing: **cannabis**. You might also be able to get coffee and a slice of cake, but the main activity in a coffeeshop is smoking. There are almost as many different kinds of coffeeshops as there are bars: some are neon-lit, with loud music and Day-Glo decor, but there are plenty of others that are quiet, comfortable places to have a relaxed smoke and take it easy. See p.37 for more advice on what to expect, including a rundown on the legal situation and how to go about making your purchase. Be aware that many have closed down since the summer 2008 smoking ban, although others have found creative solutions around this and continue to thrive. The establishments listed here are better than the average, and most of them open around 10am or 11am and close around midnight.

All the following listings are on the maps on pp.52–53 and p.61.

Abraxas Jonge Roelensteeg 12. Quirky, mezzanine coffeeshop with spiral staircases that are challenging after a spliff. The hot chocolate with hash is not for the susceptible. Daily 10am–1am.

Barney's Breakfast Bar Haarlemmerstraat 102. Something of an Amsterdam institution, this extremely popular café-cum-coffeeshop is simply the most civilized place in town to enjoy a big hit with a fine breakfast – at any time of the day. A few doors down, at no. 98, *Barney's Farm* affords a nice sunny spot in the morning and serves alcohol. Daily 7am–10pm.

The Bulldog Leidseplein 15 ⓦ www.bulldog.nl. The biggest and most famous of the coffeeshop chains, and a long way from its poky Red Light District origins, the main branch of *The Bulldog* is here on the Leidseplein, housed in a former police station. It has a large cocktail bar, coffeeshop, juice bar and souvenir shop, all with separate entrances. It's big and brash, not at all the place for a quiet smoke, though the dope they sell (packaged up in neat little brand-labelled bags) is reliably good. Daily 9am–1am, till 3am at weekends.

Dampkring Handboogstraat 29. Colourful coffeeshop with a laid-back atmosphere that is known for its good-quality hash. Daily 10am–1am.

Extase Oude Hoogstraat 2. Part of a chain run by the initiator of the Hash Museum (see p.68). Considerably less chi-chi than a lot of coffeeshops but a handy Red Light District standby. Daily 9am–1am.

Grasshopper Oudebrugsteeg 16. Multi-levelled coffeeshop, with bar, sports screen and restaurant. One of the city's more welcoming places, although its proximity to Centraal Station means that at times it can be overwhelmed by tourists. Another location at Nieuwezijds Voorburgwal 57. Daily 8am–1am.

Kadinsky Langebrugsteeg 9. Small and central branch of this small chain. Strictly accurate deals weighed out to a background of jazz dance. The chocolate chip cookies are to die for. Daily 10am–1am, till 2am at weekends.

Paradox 1e Bloemdwarsstraat 2. If you're fed up with the usual coffeeshop food offerings, Paradox satisfies the munchies with outstanding natural food, including spectacular fresh fruit concoctions and veggie burgers. Daily 10am–8pm.

Rusland Rusland 16. One of the first Amsterdam coffeeshops, a cramped but vibrant place that's a favourite with both dope fans and tea addicts (it has 40 different kinds). A cut above the rest. Daily 10am–1am.

▲ Abraxas coffeeshop

Siberië Brouwersgracht 11. Very relaxed, very friendly, and worth a visit whether you want to smoke or not, with a good selection of magazine and a chessboard. Daily 11am–11pm (Fri & Sat till midnight).

Entertainment and nightlife

Amsterdam offers a broad range of **music, dance and film**, partly due to its relatively young population and partly to government subsidies. Indeed, the city is often at the cutting edge of the arts and its frequent **festivals** and fringe events provide plenty of offbeat entertainment. It's also something of a Mecca for **clubbers**, with numerous venues clustered around Leidseplein and its environs buzzing into the small hours.

For information about what's on, try the Amsterdam Uitburo, or **AUB**, the cultural office of the city council, which is housed in a corner of the Stadsschouwburg theatre on Leidseplein (Mon–Sat 10am–7.30pm, Sun noon–7.30pm). Tickets for most performances can be bought at the Uitburo and VVV offices, or reserved by phone through the AUB Uitlijn (☎020/795 9950, 9am–8pm), although the cheapest way to obtain tickets is to turn up at the venue itself.

For information about what's on, the monthly *Uitkrant* is comprehensive and free, but in Dutch, or there's the VVV's English-language but bland *Day by Day*. Alternatively, the free *NL20* magazine (in Dutch) is the most up-to-date and complete reference source and can be found in many supermarkets, cafés and shops. The Dutch newspaper *Het Parool* has a Wednesday entertainment supplement, and *Amsterdam Weekly* is a free cultural newspaper in English, which comes out every Wednesday and has information on film, music and the arts.

Rock, jazz and folk

Amsterdam is a regular tour stop for many major artists, and something of a testing ground for current rock bands. With the construction of the 50,000-seat ArenA out in the southeastern suburbs, Amsterdam has finally gained the stadium **rock venue** it has craved for years. The Heineken Music Hall, a simple but acoustically impressive black box close to the ArenA, hosts medium-sized acts while in the city centre the **Paradiso** and the **Melkweg** are much smaller, and supply a constantly changing seven-days-a-week programme of music to suit all tastes and budgets. Alongside the main venues, the city's clubs, bars and multimedia centres sporadically host performances by live bands.

Akhnaton Nieuwezijds Kolk 25 ℡ 020/624 3396, ⓦ www.akhnaton.nl. World-music club hosting a wide-ranging programme of events, from salsa nights to Turkish dance parties. On a good night, the place heaves.

Café Alto Korte Leidsedwarsstraat 115 ℡ 020/626 3249, ⓦ www.jazz-cafe-alto.nl. It's worth hunting down this legendary little jazz bar just off Leidseplein for its quality modern jazz, performed every night from around 10pm until 3am (even later at the weekend). It's big on atmosphere, though slightly cramped, but entry is free. Daily from 9pm.

Bimhuis Piet Heinkade 3 ℡ 020/788 2150, ⓦ www.bimhuis.nl. In 2004 the city's premier jazz and improvised-music venue moved to its spanking new building next to the Muziekgebouw (see p.98), featuring events from Dutch and international artists throughout the week, as well as jam sessions and workshops. There's also a modern bar and restaurant for concert-goers with fantastic views over the water.

Maloe Melo Lijnbaansgracht 163 ℡ 020/420 4592, ⓦ www.maloemelo.nl. Dark, low-ceilinged bar with a small back room featuring lively local blues acts every day of the week. Jam sessions Mon–Thurs.

Melkweg Lijnbaansgracht 234a ℡ 020/531 8181, ⓦ www.melkweg.nl. Probably Amsterdam's most famous entertainment venue, plus one of the city's prime multimedia arts centres, with a young, hip clientele. A former dairy (hence the name) just round the corner from Leidseplein, it has two separate halls for live music, and puts on a broad range of bands covering everything from reggae to rock, all of which lean towards the "alternative". Excellent DJ sessions go on late at the weekend, with Que Pasa providing a Latino flavour to Friday nights and anything from dancehall to indie pop on Saturdays. There's also a monthly film programme, a theatre, gallery and café-restaurant (Marnixstraat entrance; Wed–Sun noon–9pm).

Heineken Music Hall ArenA Boulevard ℡ 0900/68742 4255, ⓦ www.heineken-music-hall .nl. Metro or train to Bijlmer station. Hosts dance events featuring well-known Dutch DJs, including the renowned Tiesto.

Paradiso Weteringschans 6–8 ℡ 020/626 4521, ⓦ www.paradiso.nl. A converted church near the Leidseplein, revered by many for its atmosphere and excellent programme, featuring local and inter-national bands ranging from the newly signed to the more established. Popular club nights such as Friday's Paradisoul still draw in the crowds, and look out too for DJ sets featuring live performances on Saturdays. It has been known to host classical concerts as well as debates and multimedia events (often in conjunction with the nearby Balie centre, see p.99).

Winston Warmoesstraat 123 ℡ 020/623 1380, ⓦ www.winston.nl. Adventurous small venue, part of the arty hotel (see p.56), which attracts an eclectic crowd and offers a mix of live bands, electro, drum 'n' bass and cheesy pop nights.

Clubs

Clubbing in Amsterdam used to be a relatively low-key affair, but in recent years the city has established itself as more of a clubbers' city, with a good array of decent venues that are just as style-conscious as those in other European capitals, as well as plenty of bars hosting regular DJs – most playing variations on house, trance, garage and techno. Although all the places listed open at either 10pm or 11pm, there's not much point turning up anywhere before midnight; unless stated otherwise, everywhere stays open until 5am on Friday and Saturday nights, 4am on other nights.

Bitterzoet Spuistraat 2 ☎020/521 3001, ⓦwww
.bitterzoet.com. Spacious but cosy two-floored bar
and theatre hosting a mixed bag of events: DJs
playing acid jazz, R&B, funk and disco, film screenings and occasional urban poetry nights.

't Blauwe Theehuis Vondelpark 5 ☎020/662
0254, ⓦwww.blauwetheehuis.nl. Free open-air
dancing with DJs playing throughout the summer
in the Vondelpark; usually weekends but check
website for programme.

Dansen bij Jansen Handboogstraat 11–13
☎020/620 1779, ⓦwww.dansenbijjansen.nl.
Founded by – and for – students; dance nights
here have an emphasis on disco, club classics
and R&B – and, as you would expect, cheap beer.
Open nightly from 11pm; officially you need
student ID to get in.

Escape Rembrandtplein 11 ☎020/622 1111,
ⓦwww.escape.nl. This vast club has space
enough to house 2000 people, but its glory days –
when it was home to Amsterdam's cutting edge
Chemistry nights – are long gone and it now
focuses on weekly club nights that pull in crowds
of mainstream punters. Thurs–Sun from 11pm.

Jimmy Woo Korte Leidsedwarsstraat 18
☎0202 626 3150. Intimate and stylish club
spread over two floors. Upstairs, the black
lacquered walls, Japanese lamps and cosy
booths with leather couches ooze sexy chic,
while downstairs a packed dance floor throbs
under hundreds of oscillating lightbulbs studded
into the ceiling. Popular with young, well-dressed
locals so look smart if you want to join in.
Thurs–Sun from 11pm.

Melkweg Lijnbaansgracht 234a, near Leidseplein
☎020/624 1777, ⓦwww.melkweg.nl. After the
bands have finished excellent offbeat disco
sessions go on well into the small hours,
sometimes featuring the best DJs in town.

Odeon Singel 460 ☎020/521 8555, ⓦwww
.odeontheater.nl. Originally a brewery, this beautifully restored old canal house has since been a
theatre, cinema and concert hall until it was gutted
in a fire in 1990. Rescued, it's now a stylish
nightclub hosting Eighties parties and regular club
nights (Fri & Sat) with a splendid bar overlooking
the canal. There's also a restaurant (Tues–Sat) and
a café (daily).

▲ Odeon

Panama Oostelijke Handelskade 4 ☎020/311 8686,
ⓦwww.panama.nl. One of Amsterdam's coolest
clubs, *Panama* overlooks the IJ and plays host to
top-name international DJs Thurs–Sun. There's also
a restaurant, which is open daily from noon.

Paradiso Weteringschans 6–8 ☎020/623 7348,
ⓦwww.paradiso.nl. One of the principal venues in
the city, which on Fridays hosts an unmissable club
night, from midnight onwards. Also hosts one-off
events – check listings.

Studio 80 Rembrandtplein 17 ☎020/521 8333,
ⓦwww.studio-80.nl. Right on the Rembrandtplein,
this new club attracts the more fashionable underground scene with techno, soul, funk, minimal and
electro. A creative breeding ground for young and
upcoming DJs, bands and acts.

Zebra Lounge Korte Leidsedwarsstraat 14
☎020/612 6153, ⓦwww.the-zebra.nl. This small,
stylish bar set over two floors attracts a lively,
younger crowd than the neighbouring *Jimmy Woo*
– possibly owing to its less picky door staff. Fri &
Sat only.

Classical music and opera

There's no shortage of **classical music** concerts in Amsterdam, with two major
orchestras based in the city, plus regular visits by other Dutch orchestras.
Amsterdam's Royal Concertgebouw Orchestra (ⓦwww.concertgebouworkest
.nl) is one of the most dynamic in the world, and occupies one of the finest
concert halls to boot. The other resident orchestra is the Dutch Philharmonic

(ⓌWww.orkest.nl), based at the Beurs van Berlage concert hall, which has a wide symphonic repertoire and also performs with the Dutch Opera (ⓌWww .dno.nl) at the Muziektheater. As far as **contemporary classical music** goes, the Muziekgebouw, overlooking the River IJ, is the city's leading showcase for musicians from all over the world. As well as the main concert halls, a number of Amsterdam's churches (and former churches) host regular performances of classical and chamber music; both types of venue are listed below. The most prestigious venue for **opera** is the Muziektheater (otherwise known as the Stopera) on Waterlooplein, which is home to the Dutch Opera company as well as the National Ballet. Visiting companies sometimes perform here, but more often at the Stadsschouwburg and the Carré Theatre.

The best multi-venue event is June's annual **Holland Festival** (ⓌWww .hollandfestival.nl), which attracts the best domestic mainstream and fringe performers in all areas of the arts, as well as an exciting international line-up. Otherwise, one of the more interesting, music-oriented events is the popular **Grachtenfestival** (ⓌWww.grachtenfestival.nl), held at the end of August, a week-long classical music festival which concludes with a piano recital on a floating stage outside the *Pulitzer Hotel* on the Prinsengracht.

Beurs van Berlage Damrak 277 Ⓣ020/521 7575 or 530 4141, ⓌWww.berlage.nl. The splendid interior of the former stock exchange (see p.62) has been put to use as a venue for theatre and music, among other things, and there are regular concerts in its various impressive halls.

Carré Theatre Amstel 115–25 Ⓣ020/524 9452, ⓌWww.theatercarre.nl. A splendid hundred-year-old structure (originally built for a circus) which represents the ultimate venue for Dutch folk artists and hosts all kinds of top international acts, anything from Swedish gospel to Carmen, with reputable touring orchestras and opera companies squeezed in between.

Concertgebouw Concertgebouwplein 2–6 Ⓣ020/671 8345, ⓌWww.concertgebouw.nl. After a recent facelift, the Concertgebouw is looking – and sounding – better than ever. There are two halls here and both boast a star-studded international programme. Prices are very reasonable, €15–50, and around €15 for Sunday-morning events. Free lunchtime concerts are held from Sept to May every Wed at 12.30pm.

Muziekgebouw Piet Heinkade 1 Ⓣ020/788 2000, ⓌWww.muziekgebouw.nl. Amsterdam's newest

concert hall for over a hundred years, with two new medium-sized concert halls, a café, bar and state-of-the-art acoustics, has given new impetus to the redevelopment along the IJ. Its top-quality programme of opera and orchestral music draws a highbrow crowd to this part of town. Worth a visit for the building alone; the café offers great views over the water.

Muziektheater Amstel 3 Ⓣ020/625 5455 or 551 8100, ⓌWww.muziektheater.nl. Part of the €150million complex that includes the city hall. The theatre's resident companies, Netherlands Opera, offer the fullest, and most reasonably priced, programme of opera in Amsterdam. Tickets go very quickly. See p.95.

Stadsschouwburg Leidseplein 26 Ⓣ020/624 2311, ⓌWww.ssba.nl. These days somewhat overshadowed by the Muziektheater, but still staging opera and dance as well as hosting visiting English-language theatre companies.

Waalse Kerk Oudezijds Achterburgwal 159 Ⓣ020/623 2074, ⓌWww.waalsekerk-amsterdam .nl. Weekend afternoon and evening concerts of early and chamber music.

Theatre, cabaret and film

Surprisingly for a city that functions so much in English, there is next to no English-language **theatre** – though English-speaking touring companies do regularly visit. The Stalhouderij is the only company working in English, performing in a broom-cupboard of a theatre in the Jordaan. English-language **comedy** and **cabaret**, on the other hand, has become a big thing in Amsterdam, spearheaded by the resident and extremely successful Boom Chicago comedy company. During the summer in particular, a number of small venues host mini-seasons of English-language stand-up comedy and cabaret featuring touring British performers. As for cinema, most of Amsterdam's commercial cinemas are huge, multiplex picture palaces showing a selection of general releases, but there is also a scattering of film houses (*filmhuizen*) showing revival and art films and occasional retrospectives. All foreign movies playing in Amsterdam (almost no Dutch movies turn up anyway) are shown in their original language and subtitled in Dutch. Amsterdam's only regular film event is the fascinating International Documentary Film Festival in November/December (info ☎ 020/627 3329, ⌨ www.idfa.nl), during which two hundred documentaries from all over the world are shown in ten days.

De Balie Kleine Gartmanplantsoen 10 ☎ 020/553 5151, ⌨ www.debalie.nl. A multimedia centre for culture and the arts, located off the Leidseplein, which often plays host to drama, debates, international symposia and the like, sometimes in conjunction with the *Paradiso* (see p.96) next door. Also has a lovely, roomy, mezzanine bar.

Boom Chicago Leidseplein 12 ☎ 020/423 0101, ⌨ www.boomchicago.nl. Something of a phenomenon in Amsterdam, this rapid-fire improv comedy troupe hailing from the US performs at the Leidseplein Theater nightly to crowds of both tourists and locals, and receives rave reviews. Inexpensive food, cocktails and beer served in pitchers.

Cinecenter Lijnbaansgracht 236 ☎ 020/623 6615, ⌨ www.cinecenter.nl. Opposite the Melkweg, this cinema shows independent and quality commercial films, the majority originating from non-English-speaking countries, shown with an interval.

Filmmuseum Vondelpark 3 ☎ 020/589 1400, ⌨ www.filmmuseum.nl. The Filmmuseum holds literally tens of thousands of prints, and although Dutch films show regularly, there are also regular screenings of all kinds of movies from all corners of the world. Silent movies often have live piano accompaniment, and on summer weekend evenings there are free open-air screenings on the terrace.

Kriterion Roeterstraat 170 ☎ 020/623 1708, ⌨ www.kriterion.nl. Stylish duplex cinema close to Weesperplein metro that shows arthouse and quality commercial films, with late-night cult favourites. Friendly bar attached. Trams #6, #7 or #10.

Melkweg Lijnbaansgracht 234a ☎ 020/531 8181, ⌨ www.melkweg.nl. As well as music, art and dance (see p.96), the *Melkweg* manages to maintain a consistently good monthly film and video programme, ranging from mainstream fodder through to obscure imports.

The Movies Haarlemmerdijk 161 ☎ 020/638 6016, ⌨ www.themovies.nl. A beautiful Art Deco cinema, and a charming setting for independent films. Worth visiting for the bar and restaurant alone. "Filmdiner" nights Mon–Thurs include a three-course meal plus film for €29. Late shows at the weekend.

Nachttheater Sugar Factory Lijnbaansgracht 238 ☎ 020/627 0008, ⌨ www.sugarfactory.nl. Busy Leidseplein's "theatrical nightclub" hosts a stimulating programme of cabaret, live music, poetry and theatre, plus a late-night club that kicks off after the show. Pulls in a young and artistic crowd, and features up to two events per evening. Closed Tues & Wed.

Gay and lesbian Amsterdam

Amsterdam boasts one of the largest gay populations in Europe, and one of the most dynamic gay scenes, with a dense sprinkling of advice centres, bars and clubs. The COC (pronounced "say-oh-say"), the national gay and lesbian pressure group (see p.100), is one of the longest-lived, and largest, groups of its kind in the world. The city has four recognized gay areas: Reguliersdwarsstraat with its trendy bars and clubs tends to attract a young, lively crowd, while quieter Kerkstraat is populated as much by locals as visitors. The streets just north of Rembrandtplein and along Amstel are a camp focus, as well as being home to a number of rent-boy bars, while Warmoesstraat, in the heart of the Red Light District, is cruisey and mainly leather- and denim-oriented. Many bars and clubs have darkrooms, which are legally obliged to provide safe-sex information and condoms. The **bars and clubs** listed below cater either predominantly or exclusively to a gay clientele.

Some venues have both gay-only and mixed gay/straight nights; there are, however, very few **lesbian**-only nights or clubs and bars.

Gay information and bookshops

COC Rozenstraat 14 ☏ 020/626 3087, ⓦ www .cocamsterdam.nl. Amsterdam branch of the national gay and lesbian organization, offering advice and contacts. Mon–Fri 10am–4pm.
Gay and Lesbian Switchboard ☏ 020/623 6565, ⓦ www.switchboard.nl. Mon–Fri noon–10pm, Sat & Sun 4–8pm. An English-speaking service which provides help and advice.
MVS Radio ⓦ www.mvs.nl. Amsterdam's gay and lesbian radio station broadcasts daily 7–8pm on 106.8FM (or 88.1 via cable) – try and catch the English-language talk show *Aliens* (Sun 6–8pm).

Pink Point Near the Homomonument, Westermarkt ☏ 020/428 1070, ⓦ www.pinkpoint.org. Free advice and information point run by a team of volunteers on where to go and what to do in the city, and stocked with flyers and brochures, as well as a range of souvenirs and T-shirts. Also publishes the excellent *Bent Guide*. Daily 11am–6pm.
Vrolijk Paleisstraat 135 ☏ 020/623 5142, ⓦ www .vrolijk.nu. "The largest gay and lesbian bookstore on the continent", with a vast stock of new and secondhand books and magazines, as well as music and videos.

Gay bars and clubs

Argos Warmoesstraat 95. Europe's oldest gay leather bar, with two bars and a raunchy cellar. Not for the faint-hearted. Mon–Thurs & Sun 10pm–3am, Fri & Sat 10pm–4am.
Cockring Warmoesstraat 96 ☏ 020/623 9604, ⓦ www.clubcockring.com. One of Amsterdam's most popular – and cruisey – gay men's clubs with a small dance floor and bars on three levels. Get there early at the weekend to avoid queuing. Daily 11pm–4am (Fri & Sat till 5am); entry €3.50–5.
Cuckoo's Nest Nieuwezijds Kolk 6. A cruisey gay leather bar with a long reputation, this is described as "the best place in town for chance encounters". Vast and infamous darkroom. Daily 1pm–1am (Fri & Sat till 2am).
Downtown Reguliersdwarsstraat 31. Popular café that's a favourite with visitors and locals. Relaxed and friendly, with inexpensive meals. Mon–Wed noon–8pm, Thurs–Sun 10am–8pm.
Entre Nous Halvemaansteeg 14. Camp and often outrageous bar. Can be packed at peak times, when everyone joins in the sing-alongs to cheesy Eighties music. Women welcome. Daily 8pm–3am (Fri & Sat till 4am).

Exit Reguliersdwarsstraat 42 ☏ 020/625 8788, ⓦ www.clubexit.eu. A classic gay club ideally situated for the fallout of the area's surrounding bars and cafés, with four bars each playing different music from R&B to house to an upbeat, cruisey crowd. Predominantly male, though women are admitted. Fri & Sat 11pm–5am.
Prik Spuistraat 109. Voted best gay bar of 2008 with tasty cocktails, smoothies and snacks, plus DJs on weekends. Daily 4pm–1am (Fri & Sat till 3am).
Saarein Elandsstraat 119 ☏ 020/623 4901. Known for years for its stringent women-only policy, *Saarein* finally opened its doors to men in 1999, though its clientele remains mostly female. It's still a warm, relaxing place to take it easy, with a cheerful atmosphere. Also a useful starting point for gay contacts and information. Open 4pm–1am (Fri & Sat til 2am). Closed Mon.
Vive la Vie Amstelstraat 7. Small, campy bar, patronized mostly, but not exclusively, by women. Quiet during the week, it steams on the weekend. Daily 4pm–1am (Fri & Sat till 3am).
The Web St Jacobsstraat 6. Leather and denim bar that attracts an older crowd. Dance floor, darkrooms and a pool table. Daily 1pm–2am (Fri & Sat til 3am).

Shopping

Amsterdam has some excellent, unusual **speciality shops** and a handful of great **street markets**. Where the city scores most though is in its convenience – the centre concentrates most of what's interesting within its tight borders, and the majority of shops are still individual businesses rather than chains, which makes a refreshing change from many big cities.

Broadly, the **Nieuwendijk/Kalverstraat** strip is where you'll find mostly dull, high-street fashion and mainstream department stores. Here, just off Dam Square, is **Magna Plaza**, a massive shopping mall spread over five floors, complete with espresso bars and teenagers joyriding on the escalators. Elsewhere, **Koningsplein** and **Leidsestraat** used to be home to the most exclusive shops, but many of them have fled south, though there is still a surprisingly good selection of affordable designer shoe- and clothes-stores here. The **Jordaan**, by comparison, is where many local artists have set up shop and you can find much original stuff of genuine interest here, from arts and crafts to adventurous clothes shops and affordable antiques. Less affordable antiques – the cream of Amsterdam's renowned trade – can be found in the **Spiegelkwartier**, centred on Nieuwe Spiegelstraat, while to the south, **P.C. Hooftstraat** and **Van Baerlestraat** play host to designer clothiers, upmarket ceramics stores and confectioners.

Books and magazines

American Book Center Spui 12 ⓣ020/625 5537. This store has a vast stock of books in English, as well as lots of imported US magazines and books. Mon 11am–7pm, Tues–Sat 10am–8pm (Thurs till 9pm), Sun 11am–6.30pm.

Athenaeum Spui 14 ⓣ020/514 1460. Excellent all-round bookshop with an adventurous stock, though mostly in Dutch, but also the best source of international newspapers and magazines.

The English Bookshop Lauriergracht 71 ⓣ020/626 4230. Stocks a well-chosen collection of titles on a wide range of subjects, in particular literature, many of which you won't find elsewhere.

Pied-à-Terre Overtoom 135 ⓣ020/627 4455, ⓦwww.piedaterre.nl. The city's best travel bookshop, with knowledgeable staff and a huge selection of books and maps. Also sells inflatable and illuminated globes and hiking maps for Holland and beyond, mostly in English.

Selexyz Scheltema Koningsplein 20 ⓣ020/523 1411, ⓦwww.scheltema.nl. Amsterdam's biggest and arguably best bookshop. Six floors of absolutely everything (mostly in Dutch).

Waterstones Kalverstraat 152 ⓣ020/638 3821. Dutch branch of the UK high-street chain, with four floors of books and magazines. A predictable selection perhaps, but prices are sometimes cheaper here than elsewhere.

Department stores

De Bijenkorf Dam 1 ⓣ020/552 1700. Dominating the northern corner of Dam Square, this is the city's biggest and most diverse department store, a huge bustling place that has an indisputably wide range and little snobbishness. Departments to head for include household goods, cosmetics and kids' wear; there's also a good range of newspapers and magazines.

HEMA Nieuwendijk 174 ⓣ020/623 4176. Nationwide chain that's good for stocking up on toiletries and other essentials, and occasional designer delights – it's owned by De Bijenkorf, and you can sometimes find the same items at knockdown prices. Surprises include wine and salami at the back of the shop, and a good bakery and cheese counter; great sweets too.

Metz & Co Keizersgracht 455 ⓣ020/520 7020. Classic store, with the accent on Liberty prints, stylish ceramics and designer furniture. If your funds won't stretch that far, settle for a coffee in the top-floor restaurant, which gives great views over the city.

Vroom & Dreesmann Kalverstraat 203, entrance also from Rokin ⓣ020/622 0171. The main Amsterdam branch of the middle-of-the-road nationwide chain. It's pretty unadventurous, but check out the listening stands in the CD section on the top floor – the best place for a free Mozart recital with a canal view.

Food and drink

Albert Heijn NZ Voorburgwal 226 ⓣ020/421 8344. Located just behind Dam Square, this is the biggest of the city's forty-odd Albert Heijn supermarkets. None of them take credit cards. There are other central branches at Koningsplein 4 (Grachtengordel south); Vijzelstraat 113 (Grachtengordel south); Westerstraat 79 (Jordaan and Western Docklands); Haarlemmerdijk 1 (Jordaan and

Amsterdam markets

Visiting an Amsterdam market is a must. There's a fine central flea market on Water-looplein, a number of vibrant street markets selling fresh veggies as well as clothes plus smaller, specialist markets devoted to everything from stamps to flowers.

Albert Cuypmarkt Albert Cuypstraat, between Ferdinand Bolstraat and Van Woustraat. The city's principal general goods and food market, with some great bargains to be had. Mon–Sat 9am–5pm. South of the city centre; trams #4, 16, 20, 24 or 25 from Centraal Station.

Amstelveld Prinsengracht. Flowers and plants in a pleasant canalside location near Utrechtsestraat, but much less of a scrum than the Bloemenmarkt. Friendly advice on what to buy too. Mon 10am–3pm.

Bloemenmarkt Singel. Stretching between Koningsplein and Muntplein, this very popular market specializes in flowers and plants, ostensibly for tourists, but is frequented by locals too. Mon–Sat 9am–5pm, but some stalls open on Sunday as well.

Boekenmarkt Spui. Wonderful rambling collection of secondhand books, with many an interesting find lurking in the unsorted boxes. Fri 10am–3pm.

Boerenmarkt Noordermarkt. Next to the Noorderkerk, this organic farmers' market offers all kinds of organically grown produce, fresh bread, exotic fungi and fresh herbs. Sat 9am–4pm.

Kunstmarkt Spui & Thorbeckeplein. Low-key but high-quality art market in two locations, with much lower prices than you'll find in the galleries; prints and occasional books as well. Neither operates during the winter. Both Sun 10am–3pm.

Noordermarkt Noordermarkt. Next to the Noorderkerk, this is a junk-lover's goldmine, with a general market on Mondays full of all kinds of bargains, tucked away beneath piles of useless rubbish. Get here early.

Waterlooplein Behind the Stadhuis. A real Amsterdam institution, sprawling and chaotic, this is the final resting-place of vintage clothes, antique junk and second-hand records. Mon–Sat 9am–5pm.

Western Docklands); Overtoom 454 (Museum Quarter and Vondelpark). Daily 8am–10pm.

De Bierkoning Paleisstraat 125 ☎020/625 2336. The "Beer King" is aptly named: 950 different beers, with the appropriate glasses to drink them from.

Geels & Co Warmoesstraat 67 ☎020/624 0683. Oddly situated among Warmoesstraat's loud bars and porn shops, this is one of the city's oldest and best-equipped coffee and tea specialists, with low prices on beans and utensils, and a fantastic stock of coffees and teas. It also has a small museum of coffee upstairs.

Jacob Hooij Kloveniersburgwal 1. In business at this address since 1778, this is a traditional homeopathic chemist with any amount of herbs and natural cosmetics, as well as a huge stock of drop (Dutch liquorice).

J.G. Beune Haarlemmerdijk 156 ☎020/624 8356. Age-old chocolatier with exquisite confectionery and enticing window displays.

Jordino Haarlemmerdijk 25a ☎020/420 3225. You can sample some of Amsterdam's best ice cream and chocolates at this Haarlemmerdijk institution.

De Kaaskamer Runstraat 7 ☎020/623 3483. Friendly cheese shop, with both Dutch and international cheeses and tapas and olives too.

Kwekkeboom Reguliersbreestraat 36 & Ferdinand Bolstraat 119. One of the city's most famous pastry shops, showered with awards. Serves coffee too.

Oud-Hollandsch Snoepwinkeltje Tweede Egelantierdwarsstraat 2 ☎020/420 7390. All kinds of mouthwatering Dutch sweets, piled up in glass jars – a great place to try Dutch liquorice (drop).

Puccini Staalstraat 17 ☎020/427 8341. Perhaps the best chocolate shop in town – all handmade, with an array of fantastic and imaginative fillings.

Miscellaneous

Broekmans & Van Poppel Van Baerlestraat 92 ☎020/675 6979, ⦿www.broekmans.com. Classical music specialist, with historical recordings, smaller labels, opera and sheet music.
Concerto Utrechtsestraat 54 ☎020/623 5228, ⦿www.concertomania.nl. New and used records and CDs in all categories; equally good on baroque as on grunge. The best all-round selection in the city, with the option to listen before you buy.
Condomerie Het Gulden Vlies Warmoesstraat 141 ☎020/627 4174. Condoms of every shape, size and flavour imaginable, in the heart of the Red Light District. All in the best possible taste.
Frozen Fountain Prinsengracht 465 ☎020/622 9375, ⦿www.frozenfountain.nl. Contemporary furniture and interior design with the emphasis on all things Dutch.
Gerda's Runstraat 16 ☎020/624 2912. Amsterdam is full of flower shops, but this one is the most imaginative and sensual.

P.G.C. Hajenius Rokin 92 ☎020/623 7494. Long-established tobacconist selling its own and other brands of cigars, tobacco, smoking accessories, and every make of cigarette you can think of.
Jacob Hooij Kloveniersburgwal 10–12 ☎020/624 3041. Homeopathic chemist with any amount of herbs and natural cosmetics, as well as a huge stock of *drop* (Dutch liquorice). In business at this address since 1778 – and the shop and its stock seem as if they are the same now as then.
Posthumus Sint Luciensteeg 23 ☎020/625 5812. Upmarket stationery, cards and, best of all, hundreds of rubber stamps.
Witte Tandenwinkel Runstraat 5 ☎020/623 3443. The "White Teeth Shop" sells wacky toothbrushes and just about every dental hygiene accoutrement you could ever need.

Listings

Banks and exchange Bureaux de change are scattered around town – GWK has 24hr branches at Centraal Station and Schiphol Airport and offers competitive rates compared with the others. The VVV tourist office also changes money.
Car rental Avis, Nassaukade 380 ☎020/683 6061; Europcar, Overtoom 197 ☎020/683 2123; Hertz, Overtoom 333 ☎020/612 2441; Sixt, Prins Hendrikkade 20a ☎020/624 2955.
Consulates and embassies UK, Koningslaan 44, Amsterdam ☎020/676 4343; US, Museumplein 19, Amsterdam ☎020/575 5309. For embassies in the Hague see Basics p.38.
Doctors/dentists Your hotel or the VVV should be able to provide the address of an English-speaking doctor or dentist if you need one. Otherwise call Central Doctors Service ☎020/592 3434 or 0900/503 204.
Hospitals Ones with A&E units include: Academisch Medisch Centrum, Meibergdreef 9 ☎020/566 9191; Onze Lieve Vrouwe Gasthuis, 1e Oosterparkstraat at 9 ☎020/599 9111; VU Medisch Centrum, De Boelelaan 117 ☎020/444 4444.
Internet A good central option is Internetcafe at Martelaarsgracht 11 (daily 9am–1am, Fri & Sat until 3am; ☎020/627 1052, ⦿www.internetcafe .nl), just 200m from Centraal Station, serving alcoholic drinks as well as the usual juice and coffee – €1 per half hour, including a drink.
Left luggage Centraal Station has both

coin-operated luggage lockers (daily 7am–11pm) and a staffed left-luggage office (daily 7am–11pm). Small coin-operated lockers cost €4.50, the larger ones €7 per 24hr.
Lost property For items lost on the trams, buses or metro, contact GVB Head Office, Prins Hendrikkade 108–114 (Mon–Fri 9am–4pm; ☎0900 8011). For property lost on a train, first go to the service office at Centraal Station (24hr). Schiphol Airport's lost and found desk is in the Arrivals Hall (daily 8am–6pm; ☎0900 0141).
Pharmacies You'll need an *apotheek* (usually Mon–Fri 9am–6pm, but may be closed Mon mornings) for minor ailments or to get a prescription filled. A complete list – with many opening hours – can be found in the city's yellow pages under "*Apotheken*". Most of the better hotels will be able to assist too.
Police There are city centre police stations at Beurrstraat 33, NZ Voorburgwal 104–108, Lijnbaansgracht 219 and Marnixstraat 148. Or call ☎0900 8844 if it's not an emergency.
Post Post offices are open Mon–Fri 9am–5pm, with larger ones also open Sat 9am–noon. The main post office (Mon–Fri 9am–6pm, Thurs till 8pm, Sat 10am–1.30pm; ☎020/556 3311) is at Singel 250, on the corner with Raadhuisstraat. Stamps are sold at a wide range of outlets including many shops and hotel s. Postboxes are everywhere, but be sure to use the correct slot – the one labelled *overige* is for post going outside the immediate locality.

Travel details

Trains

Amsterdam CS (Centraal Station) to: Alkmaar (every 15min; 35–45min); Amersfoort (every 10min; 35–55min); Apeldoorn (every 30min; 1hr 10min); Arnhem (every 15min; 1hr 10min); Den Helder (every 30min; 1hr 15min); Dordrecht (every 20min; 1hr 20min); Eindhoven (every 20min; 1hr 20min); Enkhuizen (every 20min; 1hr); Groningen (every 30min; 2hr 20min); Haarlem (every 10min; 15min); The Hague/Den Haag (every 15min; 50min); Hoorn (every 20min; 35min); Leeuwarden (every 30min; 2hr 20min); Leiden (every 15min; 35–45min); Maastricht (every 30min; 2hr 30min); Naarden-Bussum (every 30min; 20min); Nijmegen (every 15min; 1hr 30min); Rotterdam (every 15min; 1hr); Schiphol Airport (every 15min; 20min); Utrecht (every 15min; 30min); Weesp (every 15min; 15min); Vlissingen (every 30min; 2hr 45min); Zwolle (every 30min; 1hr 15min).

Buses

Amsterdam CS (Centraal Station) to: Edam (#116, #118; hourly; 40min); Marken (#111; every 30min; 30min); Monnickendam (#111, #116, #118; every 30min; 20min); Volendam (#112; hourly; 30min).
Amsterdam Amstel Station to: Muiden (#136; every 30min; 40min); Naarden (#101; every 30min; 55min).

Noord-Holland

CHAPTER 2 **Highlights**

* **Haarlem** This good-looking old town is home to the outstanding Frans Hals Museum. See p.109

* **Edam** Archetypal Dutch country town of narrow canals and antique cottages that was once famous for its mermaids. See p.120

* **Hoorn** Former Zuider Zee port with an atmospheric old harbour. See p.122

* **Enkhuizen** Handsome old Zuider Zee port of slender waterways, and with the excellent Zuizerzeemuseum thrown in too. See p.126

* **De Brede Duinen route** Among North Holland's myriad cycle routes, this is perhaps the pick, a 42-kilometre-long loop through the pristine coastal scenery that lies to the west of Alkmaar. See p.137

* **Texel** Island hideaway with some magnificent sandy beaches. See p.137

▲ Alkmaar cheese market

2

Noord-Holland

Stretching north from Amsterdam to the island of Texel, the province of **Noord-Holland** (ⓦ www.noord-holland-tourist.nl) remains largely rural, its polder landscapes of green, pancake-flat fields intercepted by hundreds of drainage canals and ditches, its wide horizons only interrupted by the odd farmhouse or windmill. The province's **west coast** is defended from the ocean by a long belt of sand dunes, which is itself shielded by long and broad **sandy beaches**, and it's these that attract holidaying Netherlanders. Very different is the **east coast**, much of which has been reclaimed from what was once the saltwater Zuider Zee and is now, after the construction of two complementary **dykes**, the freshwater Markermeer and IJsselmeer. Here, along this deeply indented coast, lies a string of old seaports which flourished from the fourteenth to the eighteenth century on the back of the sea trade with the Baltic.

Noord-Holland's urban highlight is **Haarlem**, an amenable old town just fifteen minutes by train from Amsterdam. Haarlem has more than its fair share of Golden Age buildings, possesses the province's best art gallery in the **Frans Hals Museum**, and gives ready access to some wild stretches of dune and beach in the **Nationaal Park Zuid-Kennemerland** as well as one of the country's largest coastal resorts, **Zandvoort**.

For investigating the rest of the province, there are two obvious **routes** out of Amsterdam – one along the east coast, the other inland from Zaandam through to Texel, with possible detours to the coast along the way. The east-coast route starts with the villages nearest Amsterdam – **Marken** and **Volendam** – kitsch places full of tourists in search of clogs and windmills during summer, but with considerable charm if you can visit off-season. Neighbouring **Edam** is one of the region's most appealing country towns and one that has somehow managed to elude the tourist hordes. Further north, **Hoorn** and **Enkhuizen** were once major Zuider Zee ports, and their historic wealth is reflected in a liberal scattering of handsome old buildings. Enkhuizen in particular is very attractive and has one of the country's best open-air museums, the **Zuiderzeemuseum**.

The inland route starts a short train ride from Amsterdam in the **Zaanstad** conurbation, whose chief attraction is the antique windmills and canals of **Zaanse Schans**. Further up the line, **Alkmaar** has a much-touted summer cheese market, but is worth a longer visit if you're keen to experience small-town life. Alkmaar also makes a good base for investigating the west coast, especially the network of footpaths and cycle trails that crisscross two protected coastal zones, the **Noordhollands Duinreservaat** (North Holland Dune Reserve) and the **Schoorlse Duinen Nationaalpark**. Beyond, in the far north of the province, lies the island of **Texel**, the most accessible of the Waddenzee islands. It's very crowded during summer, but don't be put off: with

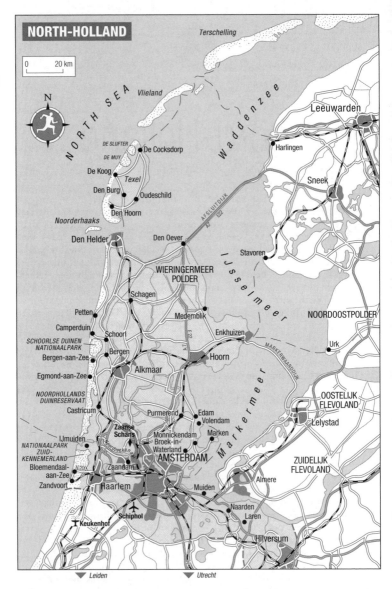

a bit of walking – or cycling – you can soon find some solitude, and the hamlet of **Den Hoorn** is a simply delightful place to stay.

Most of Noord-Holland is located, logically enough, north of Amsterdam, but the borders of the province also dip round the city, taking in an assortment of leafy suburbs. Those to the southeast of Amsterdam are collectively known as **Het Gooi**, where the highlights are the small town of **Muiden** with its castle and the old fortified town of **Naarden**.

Getting around Noord-Holland by **public transport** is easy, with **trains** linking all the major settlements and **buses** filling in the gaps. Distances are small, so the majority of Noord-Holland is easily visited on day-trips from Amsterdam, but to make the most of the province you're much better off **staying over** at least a couple of nights – Haarlem, Edam, Hoorn, Enkhuizen or Den Hoorn on Texel are the most appealing bases. If you want to continue north or east, the two dykes that enclose the Markermeer and the IJsselmeer carry handy road links. The former, the **Markerwaarddijk**, connects Enkhuizen with Lelystad on the reclaimed Flevoland polders (see p.250), and the latter, the **Afsluitdijk**, makes the thirty-kilometre trip from Den Oever to the province of Friesland (see Chapter 4).

Haarlem and around

Though only fifteen minutes from Amsterdam by train, **HAARLEM** has a very different pace and feel from its big-city neighbour, being an easy-going, medium-sized town of around 150,000 souls, and with an old and good-looking centre that is easily absorbed in a few hours or on an overnight stay. Founded on the banks of the River Spaarne in the tenth century, the town first prospered when the counts of Holland decided to levy shipping tolls here; later it developed as a cloth-making centre. In 1572, the townsfolk sided with the Protestant rebels against the Habsburgs, a decision they must have regretted when a large Spanish army besieged them in December of the same year. The siege was a desperate affair that lasted for eight months, but finally the town surrendered after receiving various assurances of good treatment – assurances which the Spanish commander, Frederick of Toledo, promptly broke, massacring over two thousand of the Protestant garrison and all their Calvinist ministers to boot. Recaptured by the Protestants five years later, Haarlem went on to enjoy its greatest prosperity in the seventeenth century, becoming a centre for the arts and home to a flourishing school of **painters**, whose canvases are displayed at the outstanding **Frans Hals Museum**, located in the almshouse where Hals spent his last, and according to some, his most brilliant, years.

Haarlem is also within easy striking distance of the **coast**: every half-hour trains make the ten-minute trip to the clumsy modern resort of **Zandvoort-aan-Zee**, and there are frequent buses to the huddle of fast-food joints that make up **Bloemendaal-aan-Zee** just to the north. Neither is particularly endearing in itself, but both are redeemed by the long sandy beach that stretches for miles along this part of the coast. Equally enticing – perhaps more so – is the **Nationaal Park de Zuid-Kennemerland**, a strip of pristine dune and lagoon, crisscrossed by footpaths and cycling trails, that backs onto Bloemendaal-aan-Zee.

Arrival, information and accommodation

There are fast and very frequent train services between Amsterdam and Haarlem; trains leave every ten minutes or so and take about fifteen minutes. The city's **train station** is just north of the city centre, about ten minutes' walk from the main square, the Grote Markt; **buses** stop just in front. The **VVV** is on the other side of the centre, at Verwulft 11 (April–Sept Mon–Fri 9.30am–5.30pm, Sat 10am–5pm, Sun 11am–3pm; Oct–March Mon–Fri 9.30am–5.30pm, Sat 10am–5pm; ☎0900 616 1600, ⓦwww.vvv.haarlem.nl). The VVV issues free **city maps** and brochures and has details of a small number of **rooms in private houses**, mostly on the outskirts of town and costing in the region of

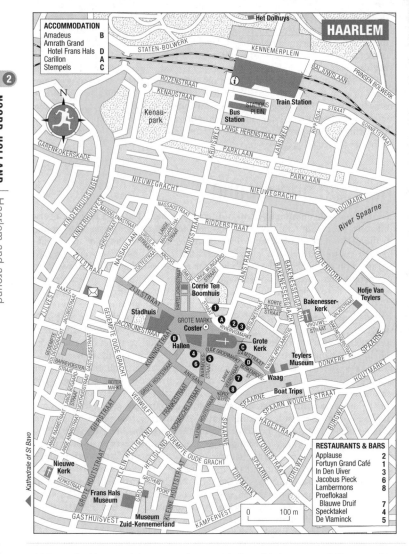

€45 per double per night. It can also provide **hotel** information. **Bike rental** is
available at the train station.

Hotels

Amadeus Grote Markt 10 ☏ 023/532 4530,
Ⓦ www.amadeus-hotel.com. This homely, medium-
sized hotel has plain but perfectly comfortable
en-suite rooms for around €80 a double including
breakfast. The front bedrooms have pleasant views
over the main square. ❷

Amrath Grand Hotel Frans Hals Damstraat 10
☏ 023/518 1818, Ⓦ www.bestwestern.com. Plumb
in the centre of town, this modern chain hotel has
79 smart and well-appointed modern rooms for
around €100, breakfast not included. ❷–❸
Carillon Grote Markt 27 ☏ 023/531 0591, Ⓦ www
.hotelcarillon.com. Bang on the Grote Markt, this

couldn't be more central. Rooms are ok, if a little spartan, but they're well-equipped and good value at €80 a double. Triples and quads available too for €100 or so. ❷

Stempels Klokhuisplein 9 ☎023/512 3910. Housed in a former printworks behind the Grote Kerk is this complex comprising boutique hotel, bar and restaurant. It does its best to be Haarlem's most desirable place to stay, though staff could be friendlier and it could do better. ❸–❹ Still its doubles for €100–140 are reasonable value.

Hostels

Stayokay Haarlem Jan Gijzenpad 3 ☎023/537 3793, ⓦwww.stayokay.com. Spick and span modern HI hostel near the sports stadium about 3km north of the town centre. To get there, take bus #2 from the station – a 10min journey. Dorm beds €27.

The Town

At the heart of Haarlem is the **Grote Markt**, a wide, attractive open space flanked by an appealing ensemble of Gothic and Renaissance architecture, including an intriguing if exceptionally garbled **Stadhuis**, whose turrets and towers, balconies and galleries were put together in piecemeal fashion between the fourteenth and the seventeenth centuries. At the other end of the Grote Markt stands a **statue** of Laurens Coster (1370–1440), who, Haarlemmers insist, is the true inventor of printing. Legend tells of Coster cutting a letter "A" from the bark of a tree, dropping it into the sand by accident, and, hey presto, realizing how to create the printed word. The statue shows him earnestly holding up the wooden letter, but most historians agree that it was the German Johannes Gutenberg who invented printing, in the early 1440s.

The Grote Kerk

The Coster statue stands in the shadow of the **Grote Kerk**, or **Sint Bavokerk** (Mon–Sat 10am–4pm; €2), a soaring Gothic structure supported by mighty buttresses that dwarfs the surrounding clutter of ecclesiastical outhouses. If you've been to the Rijksmuseum in Amsterdam (see p.84), the church may seem familiar, at least from the outside, since it turns up in several paintings of Haarlem by the seventeenth-century artist Gerrit Berckheyde. Finished in 1538, and 150 years in the making, the church is surmounted by a good-looking

▲ Haarlem

lantern tower, which perches above the transept crossing; the tower is made of wood clad in lead, a replacement for a much grander stone tower that had to be dismantled in 1514 when its supports began to buckle.

Entry to the church is round the back, on Oude Groenmarkt, with a humble passageway leading to the southeast end of the **nave**, whose towering beauty is enhanced by the creaminess of the stone and the bright simplicity of the white-washed walls. The Protestants cleared the church of most of its decoration during the Reformation, but the splendid wrought-iron **choir screen** has survived, as have the choir's wooden **stalls** with their folksy misericords. In front of the screen is the conspicuous Neoclassical **tomb** of Haarlem's own Christiaan Brunings (1736–1805), a much-lauded hydraulic engineer and director of Holland's water board.

Close by, next to the south transept, is the **Brewers' Chapel**, where the central pillar bears two black markers – one showing the height of a local giant, the 2.64m-tall Daniel Cajanus, who died in 1749, the other the 0.84m-high dwarf Simon Paap from Zandvoort (1789–1828). In the middle of the nave, the pulpit's banisters are in the form of snakes – fleeing from the word of God – while across the other side is the pocket-sized **Dog Whippers' Chapel**, built for the men employed to keep dogs under control in the church, as evidenced by the rings there to tether them to, and now separated from the nave by an iron grille.

At the west end of the church, the mighty Christian Müller **organ** was manufactured in Amsterdam in the 1730s. It is said to have been played by Handel and Mozart and is one of the biggest in the world, with over five thousand pipes and loads of snazzy Baroque embellishment. You can hear it at work at one of the free organ recitals held in the summer (mid-May to mid-Oct Tues 8.15pm, July & Aug also Thurs 3pm). Beneath the organ, Jan Baptist Xavery's lovely group of draped marble figures represent Poetry and Music offering thanks to the town, which is depicted as a patroness of the arts – in return for its generous support in the purchase of the organ.

The Hallen

Back outside, just beyond the western end of the church, the rambling **Hallen** divides into two; first up is the old meat market, the **Vleeshal**, which boasts a flashy Dutch Renaissance facade and a basement given over to the modest **Archeologisch Museum** (Wed–Sun 1–5pm; free). A couple of doors along is the **Kunstcentrum De Hallen** (Tues–Sat 11am–5pm, Sun noon–5pm; €5), an art gallery where the emphasis is on temporary exhibitions of modern and contemporary art and photography.

The Corrie Ten Boomhuis

Two minutes from the Grote Markt, take time to visit the **Corrie Ten Boomhuis** at Barteljorisstraat 19 (April–Oct Tues–Sat 10am–4pm; Nov–March Tues–Sat 11am–3pm; 1hr guided tours only; free; Ⓦ www.corrietenboom.com), where a Dutch family – the Ten Booms – hid fugitives, resistance fighters and Jews alike above their jewellers shop during World War II. There isn't actually much to look at, but the guided tour is instructive and moving, if a tad drawn-out. The family, whose bravery sprang from their Christian faith, was betrayed to the Gestapo in 1944, and only one member, Corrie Ten Boom, survived – as does the jewellers itself, still doing business at street level.

The Frans Hals Museum

Haarlem's biggest draw, the **Frans Hals Museum** (Tues–Sat 11am–5pm, Sun noon–5pm; €7.50; Ⓦ www.franshalsmuseum.nl), is a five-minute stroll south of

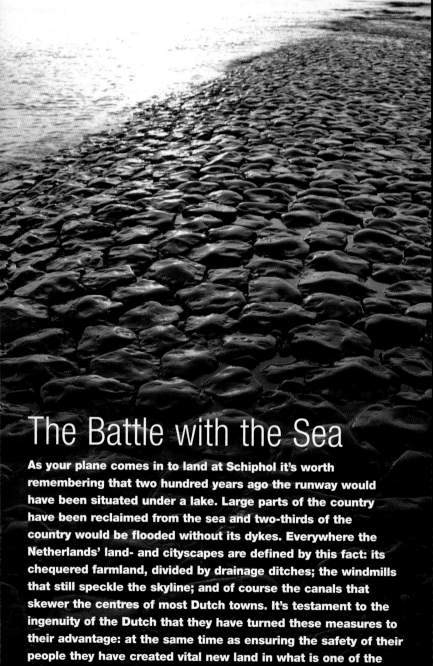

The Battle with the Sea

As your plane comes in to land at Schiphol it's worth remembering that two hundred years ago the runway would have been situated under a lake. Large parts of the country have been reclaimed from the sea and two-thirds of the country would be flooded without its dykes. Everywhere the Netherlands' land- and cityscapes are defined by this fact: its chequered farmland, divided by drainage ditches; the windmills that still speckle the skyline; and of course the canals that skewer the centres of most Dutch towns. It's testament to the ingenuity of the Dutch that they have turned these measures to their advantage: at the same time as ensuring the safety of their people they have created vital new land in what is one of the most congested countries in the world.

The North Sea ▲

Schiphol airport ▼

Water, water, everywhere

The first inhabitants were a wretched but resourceful lot, gathering on higher ground and catching fish in the flooded areas. To protect themselves from flooding, they began to build **dykes**, and in order to cultivate the land efficiently they drained it by whatever means they could. They faced regular threats from breaks in the dykes, with some floods more disastrous than others. After the first St Elizabeth Day Flood of 1404, which mainly affected **Zeeland**, many dykes were reinforced, only to be breached again when North Sea storms flooded South Holland and Zeeland in the second St Elizabeth Day Flood in 1421. In 1916 the areas around the **Zuider Zee** were inundated, but the worst floods in recent memory took place in 1953, when a combination of high tides and heavy storms broke through the North Sea dykes twice, causing nearly 2000 deaths in Zeeland, North Brabant and South Holland, and displacing around 70,000 people.

Draining away

The first land reclamation projects were undertaken in the 1600s, and were the work of **Jan Adriaanszoon**, an engineer who devised the method of draining land using windmills. He patented this in 1605, taking the name Leeghwater, "empty water". Drained land became known as "**polders**", and the first polder, the Beemster, north of Amsterdam, was completed in 1612. Leeghwater was also an advocate of draining the Haarlemmermeer, near Amsterdam, although this didn't happen until the 1850s. It's here that they decided to site **Schiphol** in 1916 – the most tangible example of Dutch success in taming their watery landscape.

▲ Kiteboarding, Frisian Islands

▼ Flooding in Overijssel

▼ The Afsluitdijk

The Zuider Zee

These days the **IJsselmeer** is a shallow lake, but it was formerly the Zuider Zee, or "southern sea" – an inlet of the North Sea that reached deep into Dutch territory and its low-lying areas vulnerable to flooding. In 1932 the creation of the **Afsluitdijk** bridged the gap at the northern end, cutting its connection to the sea, reclaiming land and creating the polderlands that unite western and eastern Netherlands. A massive project, the polders it created included the Wieringermeer, north of Enkhuizen, the North East Polder, drained in 1942, encompassing the two former islands of Schokland and Urk, and two large polders to the south, creating the new province of **Flevoland**. The final part of the plan for a new dyke joining Lelystad to Enkhuizen was begun in 1976. However, there was huge opposition to this from the towns north of Amsterdam who wanted to keep their coastal position, plus the money began to run out, and it was abandoned.

Dyke construction ▲
Storm defences, Rotterdam ▼

The Delta Project

Planned after the inundation of Zeeland in 1953, the **Delta Project** is a complicated series of dams, designed to provide protection from high tides and storm surges. It was over thirty years in the making, partly because of the sheer size of the undertaking and partly because it ran into opposition from environmental groups concerned about local bird habitats and fishermen whose livelihoods were threatened. However, with the completion of the **Stormvloedkering** or "Storm Surge barrier", an ingenious gate designed to only shut when water levels are especially high, it was finally finished, and has kept this part of the country safe ever since.

To drain or not to drain?

The Netherlands' success in overcoming the sea is an inspiring one. But it's also a story of delay and procrastination. The plan to dam and reclaim the **Zuider Zee** was hatched as long ago as 1667, but it wasn't until the early 1900s that the Dutch parliament finally approved the scheme. Similarly with the **Delta Project**: it was known long before the devastating floods of 1953 that the safety of the people living in the low-lying areas of Zeeland and South Holland could not be guaranteed in the event of a major storm, but it took the disaster to force the government to act.

And it's not over yet. It's thought that the sea level around the country will rise by up to ninety centimetres in the next century; plus the ground is sinking, thanks to the Dutch success in draining it. And the threat isn't only from the sea. Higher **rainfall** – the summer of 2004 was the wettest since 1951 – could easily cause widespread **flooding** in an already waterlogged landscape.

Wind turbines, Flevoland ▼

the Grote Markt at Groot Heiligland 62: to get there, take pedestrianized Warmoesstraat and keep going. The museum occupies an old almshouse complex, a much-modified red-brick *hofje* with a central courtyard, where the aged Hals lived out his last destitute years on public funds. The collection comprises a handful of prime works by Hals along with a small but eclectic sample of Dutch paintings from the fifteenth century onwards, all immaculately presented and labelled in English and Dutch. There's also a small separate section consisting of a life-size replica of a seventeenth-century Haarlem street.

Little is known about **Frans Hals** (c.1580–1666), born in Antwerp, the son of Flemish refugees who settled in Haarlem in the late 1580s. His extant oeuvre is relatively small – some two hundred paintings, and nothing like the number of sketches and studies left behind by his contemporary, Rembrandt. His outstanding gift was as a portraitist, showing a sympathy with his subjects and an ability to capture fleeting expression that some say even Rembrandt lacked. Seemingly quick and careless flashes of colour characterize his work, but they are always blended into a coherent and marvellously animated whole.

The museum begins with the work of other artists; first comes a small group of early sixteenth-century paintings, the most prominent of which is a triptych from the School of **Hans Memling**. Next door are two works by **Jan van Scorel** (1495–1562): a polished *Adam and Eve* and *Pilgrims to Jerusalem*, one of the country's earliest group portraits, and, beyond that, **Cornelis Cornelisz van Haarlem**'s (1562–1638) giant *Wedding of Peleus and Thetis*, an appealing rendition of what was then a popular subject, though Cornelisz gives as much attention to the arrangement of his elegant nudes as to the subject. This marriage precipitated civil war among the gods and was used by the Dutch as an emblem of warning against discord, a call for unity during the long war with Spain. Similarly, and in the same room, the same artist's *Massacre of the Innocents* connects the biblical story with the Spanish siege of Haarlem in 1572, while three accomplished pictures by **Hendrik Goltzius** (1558–1617) hang opposite – depictions of Hercules, Mercury and Minerva. Look out also for Adam and Eve by the Haarlem painter **Marten van Heemskerck** (1498–1574), whose work dominates the next room, in particular a brutal and realistic *Christ Crowned with Thorns* and a painting of St Luke with the Virgin and infant Jesus. The next rooms hold several paintings by the **Haarlem Mannerists**, including two tiny and precise works by **Karel van Mander** (1548–1606), leading light of the Haarlem School and mentor of many of the city's most celebrated painters, including Hals; genre works by **Adriaen** (1610–85) and **Isaac van Ostade** (1621–49); and depictions of the Grote Kerk by **Gerrit Berckheyde** (1638–98) and others. Look out also for **Pieter Brueghel the Younger**'s (1564–1638) berserk *Dutch Proverbs*, illustrating a whole raft of contemporary proverbs – a detailed key next to the painting gives the lowdown.

The **Hals paintings** begin in earnest in **Room 14** with a set of five "Civic Guard" portraits – group portraits of the militia companies initially formed to defend the country from the Spanish, but which later became social clubs for the gentry. Getting a commission to paint one of these portraits was a well-paid privilege – Hals got his first in 1616 – but their composition was a tricky affair and often the end result was dull and flat. With great flair and originality, Hals made the group portrait a unified whole instead of a static collection of individual portraits, his figures carefully arranged, but so cleverly as not to appear contrived. For a time, Hals himself was a member of the Company of St George, and in the *Officers of the Militia Company of St George* he appears in the top left-hand corner – one of his few self-portraits. See also Hals's Haarlem contemporary Johannes Verspronck's (1600–62) *Regentesses of the Holy Ghost Orphanage* – one of the most accomplished pictures in the gallery.

Hals's later paintings are darker, more contemplative works, closer to Rembrandt in their lighting and increasingly sombre in their outlook. In **Room 18**, among several portraits of different groups of regents, is Hals's *Regents of St Elizabeth Gasthuis*, a serious but benign work of 1641 with a palpable sense of optimism, whereas his twin *Regents* and *Regentesses of the Oudemannenhuis*, currently displayed in **Room 19**, is deep with despair. The latter were commissioned when Hals was in his 80s, a poor man despite a successful painting career, hounded for money by the town's tradesmen and by the mothers of his illegitimate children. As a result he was dependent on the charity of people like those depicted here: their cold, self-satisfied faces staring out of the gloom, the women reproachful, the men only marginally more affable. Incidentally, although the character just right of centre in the *Regents* painting looks drunk, it is inconceivable that Hals would have depicted him in this condition; it's more likely that he was suffering from some kind of facial paralysis, and his jauntily cocked hat was simply a popular fashion of the time. There are those who claim Hals had lost his touch by the time he painted these pictures, yet their sinister, almost ghostly, power suggests quite the opposite. Van Gogh's remark that "Frans Hals had no fewer than 27 blacks" suddenly makes perfect sense.

Historisch Museum Zuid-Kennemerland
Across the road from the Frans Hals Museum, at Groot Heiligland 47, is the **Historisch Museum Zuid-Kennemerland** (Tues–Sat noon–5pm, Sun 1–5pm; €4), which tracks through a fairly pedestrian history of Haarlem and its region, in premises that were once used as a women's almshouse. A short film illuminates things with the help of some spectacular dramatic effects.

The Teyler's Museum
It's a short stroll from the Grote Markt to the **River Spaarne**, whose wandering curves mark the eastern periphery of the town centre, home to the surly stone facade of the **Waag** (Weigh House) and the country's oldest museum, the **Teylers Museum**, located in a grand Neoclassical building at Spaarne 16 (Tues–Sat 10am–5pm, Sun noon–5pm; €7; ⓦ www.teylersmuseum.nl). Founded in 1774 by a wealthy local philanthropist, one **Pieter Teyler van der Hulst**,

---

Haarlem's hofjes

You could do worse than spend a day exploring Haarlem's **hofjes** – small, unpretentious complexes of public housing built for the old and infirm in the seventeenth century. The best known and perhaps most accessible is the one that was home to Frans Hals in the last years of his life and is now the museum dedicated to him and his contemporaries. But there are others dotted around town, most of them still serving their original purpose but with their gardens at least open to the public. The most grandiose is the riverside **Teylers Hofje**, a little way east of the museum of the same name around the bend of the Spaarne at Koudenhorn 64. Unlike most of the other *hofjes*, which are decidedly cosy, this is a Neoclassical edifice dating from 1787 and featuring solid columns and cupolas. To the west, the elegant fifteenth-century tower of the **Bakenesserkerk** on Vrouwestraat is a flamboyant, onion-domed affair soaring high above the Haarlem skyline, and marks the nearby **Bakenes Hofje**, Haarlem's oldest, with a delightful enclosed garden. On the other side of the city centre, the **Brouweshofje**, just off Botermarkt, is a small, peaceful rectangle of housing, with windows framed by brightly painted red and white shutters, while the nearby **Hofje van Loo**, on nearby Barrevoetstraa, is unlike the rest in being open to view from the road.

the museum is delightfully old-fashioned, its wooden cabinets crammed with fossils and bones, crystals and rocks, medals and coins, all displayed alongside dozens of antique scientific instruments of lugubrious appearance and uncertain purpose. The finest room is the **rotunda** – De Ovale Zaal – a handsome, galleried affair with splendid wooden panelling, and there is also a room of nineteenth-century and early twentieth-century Dutch paintings, featuring the-likes of Breitner, Israëls, Weissenbruch and Wijbrand Hendriks (1774–1831), who was once the keeper of the art collection here.

Het Dolhuys

Perhaps Haarlem's strangest attraction is **Het Dolhuys**, in a pleasant location just the other side of the station in the old moat park at Schotersingerl 2 (Tues–Fri 10am–5pm, Sat & Sun noon–5pm; €7.50; ⓦwww.hetdolhuys.nl). A museum of madness and psychiatric care through the ages, housed in a converted lunatic asylum, it's an imaginative and thought-provoking place, and worth the five-minute stroll from the station. There are isolation cells, exhibits which tell the stories of "mad" people who have done extraordinary things, as well as displays which show different attitudes to mental illness over the years – from medieval imbalances to possession. The central Zorgzaal is the hub of the exhibition, with films, pictures and actual artefacts from asylums around Holland. Most of it is in Dutch, but a helpful booklet on loan from the reception translates the most important stuff.

Eating and drinking

Applause Grote Markt 23a ☎023/531 1425. A chic little bistro serving up Italian food with excellent main courses, hovering around €15. Wed–Sun noon–3pm & 5.30–9.30pm.

Fortuyn Grand Café Grote Markt 21. A popular café-bar with charming 1930s decor, including a tiled entrance and quaint glass cabinets preserved from its days as a shop.

Jacobus Pieck Warmoesstraat 18 ☎023/532 6144. Welcoming café-restaurant that's a good bet for either lunch or dinner, with sandwiches, burgers and salads for €5–8 at lunchtime and a more substantial menu served in the evening. Mon 11am–4pm, Tues–Sat 11am–4.15pm & 5.30–10pm.

In Den Uiver Riviervismarkt 13. Just off the Grote Markt, this lively and extremely appealing brown bar is decked out in traditional Dutch café style; it has occasional live music too.

Lambermons Korte Veerstraat 51 ☎023/542 7804. Large and comfortable restaurant and brasserie that serves both classic Dutch and French food – everything from bouillabaisse to *pot au feu* and oysters and seafood – or just cheese and charcuterie plates if you prefer. Brasserie Tues–Sat noon–10pm, restaurant 6–10pm.

Proeflokaal Blauwe Druif Lange Veerstraat 7. Just off the main square, this is an intimate and amenable bar – typically Dutch.

Specktakel Spekstraat 4 ☎023/532 38 41. Inventive little place that tries its hand at an international menu – everything from kangaroo through to antelope. Mostly, the main courses are very successful and cost around €17. Daily from 5pm, Sat also noon–4pm.

De Vlaminck Warmoesstraat 3. Decent and very central *friterie* if you fancy lunch on the go. Tues–11.30am–6pm, Sat 11.30am–5pm, Sun noon–5pm.

Zandvoort and the Nationaal Park Zuid-Kennemerland

The suburbs of Haarlem ramble out almost as far as **ZANDVOORT-AAN-ZEE**, a major seaside resort just 5km away to the west. As Dutch resorts go, Zandvoort is pretty standard – packed in summer, dead and gusty in winter – and its agglomeration of modern apartment blocks hardly cheers the heart, but its **beach** is wide and sandy, it musters up a casino and a car-racing circuit and it is one of the few places in the Netherlands where the rail network reaches the coast: there's a half-hourly service from Haarlem, and Zandvoort train station is merely a five-minute walk (if that) from the beach.

If, however, you're after more than just a few hours sunbathing, the better option when it comes to exploring the coast is to delve into the pristine woods, dunes and lagoons of the **Nationaal Park Zuid-Kennemerland**, which stretches north from Zandvoort all the way up to the eminently missable industrial town of **IJMUIDEN**, at the mouth of the Nordzeekanaal; maps of the park are available at Haarlem VVV. Hourly **bus** #81 from Haarlem bus station travels west to cut across the national park along the **N200** before reaching the coast at the minuscule beachside settlement of **Bloemendaal-aan-Zee**; it then proceeds the 4km south to Zandvoort bus station, on Louis Davidsstraat, a short, signposted walk from the train station. En route, between Haarlem and Bloemendaal-aan-Zee, several bus stops give access to the clearly marked **hiking trails** that pattern the national park, but the best option is to get off at the **Koevlak** entrance – ask the driver to let you off. Three colour-coded **hiking routes** are posted at Koevlak; the most appealing is the nine-kilometre (3hr) jaunt west through pine wood and dune to the seashore at the *Parnassia* **café** (April–Nov), where you can wet your whistle gazing out across the North Sea. From the café, it's 2km by minor road to Bloemendaal-aan-Zee, where you can catch **bus** #81 back to Haarlem.

The east coast: Marken, Volendam and Edam

The turbulent waters of the **Zuider Zee** were once busy with Dutch trading ships plying to and from the Baltic. This trade was the linchpin of Holland's prosperity in the Golden Age, revolving around the import of huge quantities of grain, the supply of which was municipally controlled to safeguard against famine. The business was immensely profitable and its proceeds built a string of prosperous seaports – most notably Volendam, Hoorn and Enkhuizen – and nourished market towns like Edam, while the Zuider Zee itself supported a batch of fishing villages such as Marken and Urk. In the eighteenth century the Baltic trade declined and the harbours silted up, leaving the ports economically stranded, and, with the rapid increase in the Dutch population during the nineteenth century, plans were made to reclaim the Zuider Zee and turn it into farmland. In the event, the Zuider Zee was only partly reclaimed (see box, p.119), creating a pair of freshwater lakes – the **Markermeer** and **IJsselmeer**.

> ## Hans Brinker
>
> Given that the Dutch have spent most of their history struggling to keep the sea from flooding their land, it's hardly surprising that their folklore abounds with tales of watery salvation, either by luck or the bravery of its inhabitants. One well-known hero is **Hans Brinker**, a young lad who supposedly saved the Haarlem area from disaster by sticking his finger into a hole in the dyke. The village of **Spaarndam**, just north of Haarlem, has a statue in his honour, but in fact, although the tale has the ring of truth, it's all fictitious – invented by the American writer Mary Mapes Dodge in her 1873 children's book, *The Silver Skates*. The monument to the little chap was unveiled in 1950, more, it seems, as a tribute to the opportunistic Dutch tourist industry than anything else.

These placid, steel-grey lakes are popular with day-tripping Amsterdammers, who come here in their droves to sail boats, observe the waterfowl, and visit a string of dinky towns and villages. These begin on the coast just a few kilometres north of Amsterdam with the picturesque old fishing village of **Marken** and the former seaport of **Volendam** just up along the coast. From Volendam, it's a couple of kilometres more to **Edam**, the pick of the local bunch, a small and infinitely pretty little town of narrow canals and handsome old houses.

There are fast and frequent **buses** from Amsterdam's Centraal Station to Marken and an equally efficient service to Volendam and Edam. More poetically, a seasonal **passenger ferry**, the Marken Express (April–Oct daily 11am–5pm, every 30–45min; 30min; €6.50 return, €4 single, bikes €1 one-way; ☎029/936 3331, ⓦwww.markenexpress.nl), skittles along the coast between Marken and Volendam, giving a taste of the pond-like Markermeer. Finally, there are hourly **trains** from Amsterdam's Centraal Station to Hoorn and Enkhuizen.

Marken

Once an island in the Zuider Zee, **Marken** was, until its road connection to the mainland in 1957, pretty much a closed community, supported by a small fishing industry. Despite its proximity to Amsterdam, its biggest problem was the genetic defects caused by close and constant intermarrying, but now it's how to contain the tourists, whose numbers can reach alarming proportions on summer weekends. That said, there's no denying the picturesque charms of the island's one and only village – also called **MARKEN** – where the immaculately maintained houses, mostly painted in deep green with white trimmings, cluster on top of artificial mounds raised to protect them from the sea.

There are two main parts to the village. **Havenbuurt**, around and behind the harbour, is the bit you see in most of the photographs, where many of the waterfront houses are raised on stilts. Although these are now panelled in, they were once open, allowing the sea to roll under the floors in bad weather, enough to terrify most people half to death. One or two of the houses are open to visitors, proclaiming themselves to be typical of Marken, and the waterfront is lined by snack bars and souvenir shops, often staffed by locals in traditional costume. Still you do get a hint of how hard life used to be – both here and in **Kerkbuurt**, five minutes' walk from the harbour around the **church**, an ugly 1904 replacement for its sea-battered predecessor. Kerkbuurt is quieter and less touristy than Havenbuurt, its narrow lanes lined by ancient dwellings and a row of old eel-smoking houses, one of which is now the **Marker Museum** at Kerkbuurt 44 (April–Oct Mon–Sat 10am–5pm, Sun noon–4pm; Oct Mon–Sat 11am–4pm & Sun noon–4pm; €2.50; ⓦwww .markermuseum.nl), furnished as an old fishermen's cottage and devoted to the history of the former island and its fishing industry.

Practicalities

Marken is accessible direct from Amsterdam by **bus** #111, departing from outside Centraal Station (every 30min); the journey takes forty minutes. The bus drops passengers beside the car park on the edge of Marken village, from where it's a five-minute walk to the lakeshore. Marken does not have a VVV. A **passenger ferry**, the Marken Express (☎029/936 3331, ⓦwww.marken express.nl; March–Oct daily 11am–5pm, every 30–45min; 25min journey; €7 return, bikes €2 return) links Marken with Volendam (see p.118), but otherwise travelling between the two means a fiddly bus trip involving a change of buses – and bus stops – at **Monnickendam**, itself a former Zuider

Zee port, but now a busy sailing centre; **bus** #111 stops on the southern edge of Monnickendam at the Swaensborch stop, from where it's a ten-minute walk across Monnickendam to the Bernhardbrug stop for **bus** #110 or #118 north to Volendam and Edam. The *Land en Zeezicht* **restaurant** on the harbour at Havenbuurt 6 (℡0299/601 302) does a decent smoked eel sandwich as well as more substantial meals.

Monnickendam

The former port of **MONNICKENDAM** was named by a group of Benedictine monks, who built a dam here in the fourteenth century. There's not much to it now, but it has the same sleepy charm of the other old Zuider Zee ports, and one or two attractions to divert you on your way to Volendam and Edam. The fifteenth-century clock tower or Speeltoren, right at the heart of the town centre at Noordeinde 4 (April & Oct Sat & Sun 1–4.30pm; May–Sept Tues–Sat 11am–4.30pm, Sun 1–4.30pm; €1.50), houses a fairly typical museum, with displays on the town and surrounding Waterland. The harbour repays a wander too. It has a more rough-and-ready air than that of its neighbours and a more authentically nautical one too, with herring smokehouses and lots of rugged sailing barges alongside the pleasureboats of its marina – all pleasingly not spruced up for tourists.

For **food**, try *De Waegh*, housed in the old weigh house at Middendam 5–7 (℡0299/651 241), a good spot for lunch, with a menu of sandwiches and light meals, or a slap-up fish supper in the evening.

Volendam

The former fishing village of **VOLENDAM** is the largest of the Markermeer towns and has had, by comparison with its neighbours, some rip-roaring cosmopolitan times. In the early years of the twentieth century it became something of an artists' retreat, with both Picasso and Renoir spending time here, along with their assorted acolytes. The artists are, however, long gone and nowadays Volendam is – in season – crammed with day-trippers running the gauntlet of the souvenir stalls arranged along the length of the cobbled main street, whose perky gables line up behind the harbour. The **Volendams Museum**, by the bus stop at Zeestraat 41 (mid-March to mid-Nov daily 10am–5pm; €2.50) has displays of paintings by the artists who have come here over the years, along with mannequins in local costumes and several interiors – a shop, school, and living room. However, the museum's crowning glory is a series of mosaics made from 11 million cigar bands: the bizarre lifetime project of a local artist. You can see more paintings in the antique-filled public rooms of the *Hotel Spaander*, on the waterfront, whose creaking wooden floors, low ceilings, paintings and sketches are pleasant reminders of more artistic times. The hotel was opened in 1881 and its first owner, Leendert Spaander, was lucky enough to have seven daughters, quite enough to keep a whole bevy of artists in lust for a decade or two. Some of the artists paid for their lodgings by giving Spaander paintings – hence today's collection.

Practicalities

In Volendam, **buses** #110 and #118 from Amsterdam and Monnickendam drop passengers on Zeestraat, just across the street from the **VVV**, at Zeestraat 37 (mid-March to Oct Mon–Sat 10am–5pm; Nov to mid-March Mon–Sat 10am–3pm; ℡0299/363 747, ⓦwww.vvvvolendam.nl). From the VVV, it's a five-minute walk to the waterfront, from where there's a regular **passenger**

The closing of the Zuider Zee

The towns and villages that string along the east coast of **Noord-Holland** flourished during Amsterdam's Golden Age, their economies buoyed up by shipbuilding, the Baltic Sea trade and the demand for herring. They had access to the open sea via the waters of the **Zuider Zee** (Southern Sea) and, to the north, the connecting **Waddenzee** (Mud Sea). However, the Zuider Zee was shallow and tidal, and accumulations of silt began to strangle its ports – notably Hoorn and Enkhuizen – from the end of the seventeenth century; shortly afterwards the Baltic trade slipped into decline. By the 1750s the Zuider Zee ports were effectively marooned and the only maritime activity was fishing – just enough to keep a cluster of tiny hamlets ticking over, from Volendam and Marken on the sea's western coast to Stavoren and Urk on the eastern side.

The Zuider Zee may have provided a livelihood for local fishermen, but most of the country was more concerned by the danger of flooding it posed, as time and again storms and high tides combined to breach the east coast's defences. The first plan to seal off and reclaim the Zuider Zee was proposed in 1667, but the rotating-turret windmills that then provided the most efficient way of drying the land were insufficient for the task and matters were delayed until suitable technology arrived – in the form of the steam-driven pump.

In 1891, **Cornelis Lely** (1854–1929) proposed a retaining dyke and his plans were finally put into effect after devastating floods hit the area in 1916. Work began on this dyke, the **Afsluitdijk**, in 1920 and, on May 28, 1932, the last gap in it was closed and the Zuider Zee simply ceased to exist, replaced by the freshwater **IJsselmeer**.

The original plan was to reclaim all the land protected by the Afsluitdijk, turning it into farmland for settlers from the country's overcrowded cities, starting with three large-scale land-reclamation schemes that were completed over the next forty years: the **Noordoostpolder** in 1942 (480 square kilometres), **Oostelijk Flevoland** in 1957 (540 square kilometres) and **Zuidelijk Flevoland** in 1968 (440 square kilometres). In addition, a second, complementary dyke linking Enkhuizen with Lelystad was finished in 1976, thereby creating lake **Markermeer** – a necessary prelude to the draining of another stretch of the IJsselmeer. The engineers licked their contractual lips, but they were out of sync with the majority of the population, who were now opposed to any further draining of the lake. Partly as a result, the grand plan was abandoned and, after much governmental huffing and puffing, the Markermeer was left alone and thus most of the old Zuider Zee remained water.

There were many economic benefits to be had in the closing of the Zuider Zee. The threat of flooding was removed, the country gained great chunks of new and fertile farmland and the roads that were built along the top of the two main retaining dykes brought Noord-Holland within twenty minutes' drive of Friesland. The price was the demise of the old Zuider Zee **fishing fleet**. Without access to the open sea, it was inevitable that most of the fleet would go down the pan, though some skippers wisely transferred to the north coast before the Afsluitdijk was completed. Others learnt to fish the freshwater species that soon colonized the Markermeer and IJsselmeer, but in 1970 falling stocks prompted the government to ban trawling. This was a bitter blow for many fishermen and there were several violent demonstrations before they bowed to the inevitable. Fishing still goes on here, but villages such as Marken and Urk are forced to rely on tourism to survive.

ferry to Marken (see p.117). If you want to **stay** there's no better place than the *Hotel Spaander*, Haven 15–19 (☏0299/363 595, ⓦwww.hotelspaander.com; from €120, not including breakfast).

Edam

You might expect **EDAM**, just 3km from Volendam, to be jammed with tourists, considering the international fame of the rubbery red balls of cheese that carry its name. In fact, Edam usually lacks the crowds and remains a delightful, good-looking and prosperous little town of neat brick houses, high gables, swing bridges and slender canals. Founded by farmers in the twelfth century, it experienced a temporary boom in the seventeenth as a shipbuilding centre with river access to the Zuider Zee. Thereafter, it was back to the farm – the excellent pastureland surrounding the town is still grazed by large herds of cows, though nowadays most Edam cheese is produced elsewhere, even in Germany ("Edam" is the name of a type of cheese and not its place of origin). This does, of course, rather undermine the authenticity of Edam's open-air **cheese market**, held every Wednesday morning in July and August on the Kaasmarkt, but it's still a popular attraction and the only time the town heaves with tourists.

The Town

At the heart of Edam is **Damplein**, a pint-sized main square. Alongside it, an elongated, humpbacked bridge vaults the Voorhaven canal, which now connects the town with the Markermeer and formerly linked it to the Zuider Zee. The bridge stopped the canal flooding the town, which occurred with depressing regularity, but local shipbuilders hated the bridge, as it restricted navigation, and on several occasions they launched nighttime raids to break it down, though eventually they bowed to the will of the local council.

Facing the bridge is the **Edams Museum** (April–Oct Tues–Sat 10am–4.30pm, Sun 1–4.30pm; €3; ⓦwww.edamsmuseum.nl), which occupies an attractive old house whose crow-stepped gables date back to 1530. Inside, a series of cramped and narrow rooms holds a modest display on the history of the town as well as

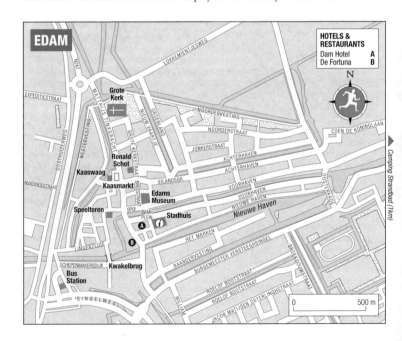

▲ Canal bridge, Edam

an assortment of local bygones, including a couple of splendid box beds. The museum's pride and joy is, however, its **floating cellar**, supposedly built by a retired sea captain who couldn't bear the thought of sleeping on dry land, but actually constructed to stop the house from flooding.

Across the square – over the bridge – stands Edam's eighteenth-century **Stadhuis**, a severe Louis XIV-style structure whose plain symmetries culminate in a squat little tower. The ground floor of the Stadhuis is home to the VVV (see p.122). Upstairs is the second part of the Edams Museum (same times & ticket), comprising a handful of old Dutch paintings; the most curious is the portrait of **Trijntje Kever** (1616–33), a local girl who grew to over 2.5m tall – displayed in front of the portrait is a pair of her specially made shoes.

From Damplein, it's a short walk to the rambling **Grote Kerk** (April–Oct daily 2–4.30pm; free), on the edge of the fields to the north of town. This is the largest three-ridged church in Europe, a handsome, largely Gothic structure whose strong lines are disturbed by the almost comically stubby spire, which was shortened to its present height after lightning started a fire in 1602. The church interior is distinguished by its magnificent stained-glass windows – which date from the early seventeenth century and sport both heraldic designs and historical scenes – and by its whopping **organ**.

Stroll back from the church along Matthijs Tinxgracht, just to the west of Grote Kerkstraat, and you soon reach the **Kaasmarkt**, site of the summer **cheese market** (July to mid-Aug Wed 10.30am–12.30pm). It's a good deal humbler than Alkmaar's (see p.134), but follows the same format, with the cheeses laid out in rows before buyers sample them. Once a cheese has been purchased, the cheese porters, dressed in traditional white costumes and straw boaters, spring into action, carrying them off on their gondola-like trays. Overlooking the market is the **Kaaswaag** (Cheese Weigh House), whose decorative panels feature the town's coat of arms, a bull on a red field with three stars. From the Kaasmarkt, it's a couple of hundred metres south to the fifteenth-century **Speeltoren**, an elegant, pinnacled tower that is all that remains of Edam's second most important medieval church, and roughly the same distance again – south along Lingerzijde – to the impossibly picturesque **Kwakelbrug** bridge.

Practicalities

Every thirty minutes or so, **buses** #110, #116 and #118 leave from outside Amsterdam Centraal Station bound for Edam; the journey takes forty minutes. Edam's **bus station** is on the southwest edge of town, on Singelweg, a five- to ten-minute walk from Damplein, where the **VVV**, in the Stadhuis (mid-March to Nov Mon–Sat 10am–5pm, also Sun 1–4.30pm in July & Aug; Nov to mid-March Mon–Sat 10am–3pm; ☏0299/315 125, ⓦwww.vvv-edam.nl), issues town maps and brochures. The VVV also has details of – and takes bookings for – local **boat trips**, both along the town's canals and out into the Markermeer. **Bike rental** is available at Ronald Schot, in the town centre at Grote Kerkstraat 7 (Tues–Fri 8.30am–6pm & Sat 8.30am–5pm; ☏0299/372 155, ⓦwww.ronaldschot.nl); one-day bike rental costs €6.50.

As regards accommodation, the VVV has a small supply of **rooms in private houses** (averaging €40–50 for a double), which they will book on your behalf for no extra charge. **Hotels** are scarce in Edam, but the charming ⚸ *De Fortuna*, just round the corner from the Damplein at Spuistraat 3 (☏0299/371 671, ⓦwww .fortuna-edam.nl; from €92), is an attractive option. Abutting a narrow canal, this three-star hotel is the epitome of cosiness, its 23 guest rooms distributed among two immaculately restored old houses and three cottage-like buildings round the back. The nearest **campsite**, *Camping Strandbad*, is east of town on the way to the lakeshore at Zeevangszeedijk 7a (☏0299/371 994, ⓦwww.campingstrandbad.nl; April–Sept) – a twenty-minute walk east along the canal from Damplein.

For **food**, ⚸ *De Fortuna* has a first-rate **restaurant**, a lively and eminently agreeable spot decorated in traditional style and with an imaginative, modern menu featuring local ingredients; main courses average around €20. Reservations, especially at the weekend, are essential. The *Dam Hotel* has a nice bar just for a drink, as well as a cosy upscale restaurant and an outside terrace.

Hoorn

The old Zuider Zee port of **HOORN**, some 15km north of Edam, "rises from the sea like an enchanted city of the east, with its spires and its harbour tower beautifully unreal". So wrote the English travel writer E.V. Lucas, who passed through here in 1905, and Hoorn is still a place that is best approached from the water. During the seventeenth century this was one of the richest of the Dutch ports, referred to by the poet Vondel as the "trumpet" of the Zuider Zee, handling the important Baltic trade and that of the Dutch colonies. The Dutch East India Company had one of its centres of operation here; *The Tasman* left Hoorn to "discover" Tasmania and New Zealand; and in 1616 William Schouten sailed out of Hoorn to navigate a passage around South America, calling its tip "Cape Hoorn" after his native town. The good times ended in the early eighteenth century when the harbour silted up, strangling the trade on which the town was reliant and turning Hoorn into one of the so-called "dead cities" of the Zuider Zee – a process completed with the creation of the IJsselmeer in 1932 (see p.119).

Arrival and information

The easiest way to reach Hoorn from Amsterdam is by train (every 30min; 40min); from Edam, take **bus** #114 from the bus station (every 30min, hourly on Sun; 30min). Hoorn's **train station** is on the northern edge of the centre about ten minutes' walk from Rode Steen, and regional buses stop just outside. The

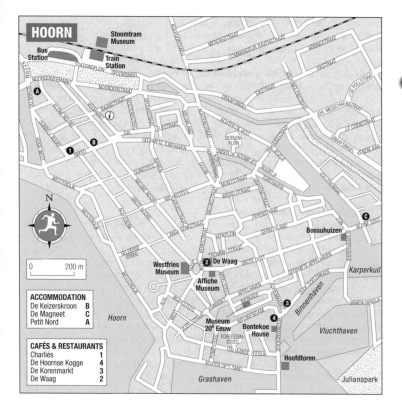

ACCOMMODATION
De Keizerskroon   B
De Magneet   C
Petit Nord   A

CAFÉS & RESTAURANTS
Charliés   1
De Hoornse Kogge   4
De Korenmarkt   3
De Waag   2

VVV is across the road at Veemarkt 4 (May–Aug Mon 1–6pm, Tues, Wed & Fri 9.30am–5.30pm, Thurs 9.30am–6pm & 7–9pm, Sat 9.30am–5pm; Sept–April Mon 1–5pm, Tues–Sat 10am–5pm; ☎072/511 4284, ⓦwww.vvvhoorn.nl), and has the usual info plus a small supply of **rooms** (❶) in private houses.

Accommodation

Keizerskroon Breed 33 ☎0229/212 717, ⓦwww.keizerskroonhoorn.nl. Probably Hoorn's best hotel choice, with mostly large and bright rooms, recent refurbished with wi-fi (€5 for 24hr) and flat-screen TVs. Nicely situated midway between the station and Rode Steen and with a busy bar-restaurant downstairs. No elevator, but there are only two floors of rooms. ❷
De Magneet Kleine Oost 5 ☎0229/215 021, ⓦwww.hoteldemagneet.nl. Friendly long-established

small hotel that's the best option if you want to stay down by the harbour. Well-kept if slightly character-less rooms in both the main building and a series of annexes in the garden behind. Free wi-fi is a plus. ❷
Petit Nord Kleine Noord 53–55 ☎0229/212 750, ⓦwww.hotelpetitnord.nl. Very well-kept and decently furnished rooms that are very slightly more expensive than the town's other hotels. Most rooms have baths, there's wi-fi (€5 for 24hr), and it's only two minutes from the station. ❷

The Town

The centre of Hoorn is **Rode Steen**, literally "red stone", an unassuming square that used to hold the town scaffold and now zeroes in on a swashbuckling **statue** of Jan Pieterszoon Coen (1587–1629), founder of the Dutch East Indies Empire and one of the town's big shots in its seventeenth-century heyday. Coen was a headstrong and determined leader of the Dutch imperial effort and under him the country's Far East colonies were consolidated, and rivals, like the English, kept at bay. His settling of places like the Moluccas and Batavia was something of a personal crusade, and his austere, almost puritanical way of life was in sharp contrast to the wild and unprincipled behaviour of many of his fellow colonialists. On one side of Rode Steen stands the early seventeenth-century **Waag**, whose handsome stone symmetries were designed by Hendrik de Keyser (1565–1621), one of the leading architects of his day. The Waag now accommodates a café-bar, which is enjoyable for its setting amid the ponderous wood and iron appliances that once weighed the cheese here – and is in fact a good place to watch the summer **cheese market** from. The market has made a comeback recently and now takes place on Thursday lunchtimes and evenings (12.30pm & 8.30pm; end-May to end-July), though like Alkmaar's it's basically laid on for tourists.

The Westfries Museum

On the opposite side of the square from the Waag, the **Westfries Museum** at Rode Steen 1 (Mon–Fri 11am–5pm, Sat & Sun 1–5pm; €5; Ⓦ www.wfm.nl) is housed in the former West Friesland government building of 1632, an imposing stone structure whose facade is decorated with the coats of arms of the house of Orange-Nassau and the region's towns. Now a district within the province of Noord-Holland, West Friesland incorporates the chunk of land between Alkmaar, Hoorn and Enkhuizen, but its origins were much grander. The **Frisians**, who speak a distinctive German dialect, once controlled a narrow sliver of seaboard stretching west from Bremerhaven in Germany to Belgium. Charlemagne conquered them in the 780s and incorporated their territory into his empire, chopping it down in size and dividing the remainder into seven regions, two of which – West Friesland and Friesland – are now in the Netherlands.

Inside the museum (where the labelling is only in Dutch) the ground floor holds a string of period rooms that re-create the flavour of the seventeenth- and eighteenth-century seaport, with paintings, silverware, antique furniture and other objects. Most memorable among numerous paintings are the militia portraits of **Jan Rotius** (1624–66) in the old Council Chamber (Room 7) – walk past the figure in the far right of the central painting opposite the fireplace and you'll see his foot change position from left to right, a nifty little trick that was much admired by Rotius's contemporaries. Upstairs, Room 14, the **Chirurgijnskamer** (literally Surgeon's Room, but also, in medieval times, the barber's, the alchemist's and the pharmacist's), holds a mock-up of a medieval "medical" workshop, complete with skeletons, skulls and pickled specimens, while Room 16 has a splendid wooden fireplace carved with tiny scenes of a whaling expedition – Hoorn was once a whaling port of some importance. On the next floor, Room 11 naturally focuses on Coen and the Dutch East India Company, while the loft has exhibits on locals trades and a gruesome holding cell from its time as a prison.

The harbour

East of Rode Steen, **Grote Oost** is shadowed by fine, decorated old mansions, some of which house antique shops and art galleries, and one of which, the **Affiche Museum**, just off Rode Steen at Groot Oost 2–4 (Tues–Fri 11am–5pm, Sat & Sun noon–5pm; €3.50), sports a frieze of the cheese market as well as housing a modest permanent display of political and commercial posters – a treat for students of graphic design. At the far end of Groot Oost, on the corner of Slapershaven, the **Bossuhuizen** has a facade decorated with a long and slender frieze depicting a sea battle of 1573 – which Admiral Bossu actually lost. **Slapershaven** itself has some of the most comfortable houseboats imaginable and leads to Hoorn's inner harbour, the **Binnenhaven**, with its clutter of sailing boats and antique barges alongside **Oude Doelenkade**.

Just over the swing bridge, **Veermanskade** is fringed by elegant merchants' houses mostly dating from the seventeenth century, in particular, the birthplace of **Willem Ysbrantzoon Bontekoe** (1587–1657), set back from the quay at Veermanskade 15, whose facade stone shows a particularly ugly spotted cow, as in *bonte* ("spotted") and *koe* ("cow"). A sea captain with the East India Company, Bontekoe published his journals in 1646, a hair-raising account of his adventures that proved immensely popular. He portrayed himself as astute and brave in equal measure, and his most eventful voyage included the snapping of the mainmast, an epidemic of scurvy and an explosion that forced the crew to abandon ship, all en route from Hoorn to Jakarta. At the end of Veermanskade, the solid brick **Hoofdtoren**, a defensive watchtower from 1532, is now a bar-restaurant and has at its base a lively and realistic bronze sculpture of 1968 of three little boys looking out, that also recalls Bontekoe – it's based on the 1924 classic Dutch novel by Johan Fabricius, *The Cabin Boys of Bontekoe*.

There's a small museum just inland from the Hoofdtoren, the **Speelgoed Museum**, Italiaanse Zeedik 106 (Tues–Sun 11am–5pm; €5), whose antique toys and toyshop may engage the kids for half an hour, while a block back from the inner harbour, the **Museum van de Twintigste Eeuw**, Bierkade 4 (Tues–Fri 10am–5pm, Sat & Sun noon–5pm; €4.50; ⓦ www.museumhoorn .nl), is a museum of nostalgia, documenting life during the twentieth century with products and objects set up in engaging tableaux of everyday life. There are living rooms from the 1940s, 1950s and 1960s, a mock-up of Jacob Blokker's first housewares store at Breed 14 (it's now a nationwide chain), a number of other shops and businesses, and a floor of household appliances, including some fantastic old TVs and radios. The café downstairs serves drinks and snacks and is decorated with photos that tell the story of the last century, and a rather out-of-context scale model of Hoorn as it would have looked during the seventeenth-century Golden Age.

Eating and drinking

Charlie's Dubbele Buurt 4 ☎0229/217 798. One of several cafés on this short yet lively street, just off Grote Noord, this is a classic, cosy Dutch bar.

They serve a good selection of Belgian beers, and a cheap two-course menu on Wed nights, when they also show films. Wed–Sun 4pm–2am.

The Stoomtram

Hoorn is the home of the **Stoomtram Museum**, across the rail tracks from the town's main station, which is the starting point for the **Stoomtram**, an antique steam train that chugs north out of Hoorn across open countryside to Medemblik, 14km away (see p.130). It's a popular family excursion and there are between one and three departures per day in late July and early August, one departure a day the rest of the time, except on Mondays. Pick up a leaflet from the VVV for the rather complicated schedule or contact them direct – ☎0229/214 862, ⓦ www.museumstoomtram.nl; advance booking is in any case recommended. The journey takes an hour and a return ticket costs €19.40 (children 4–12 years, €14.40). Arriving in Medemblik, you can make a day of it by continuing by passenger ferry to Enkhuizen (April–Oct 2–3 daily; 1hr 30min; €9.30 one-way/€15.45 return), from where there is a half-hourly train service back to Hoorn (€3.70). A combination one-way ticket from Hoorn to Enkhuizen using the steam train and boat costs €19.40. Museumcard holders can use both services for free.

De Hoornse Kogge Nieuwendam 2 ☎0229/219 309. In a sympathetically revamped old building right on the harbour, this relatively upscale restaurant offers first-rate French cuisine, with main courses hovering around €20; it is strong on seafood and has a good range of vegetarian dishes too. Daily except Tues 5–10.30pm.

De Korenmarkt Korenmarkt 1 ☎0229/279 826. Mainly Dutch staples at this relaxed and informal brasserie with lots of outside seating right on the harbour quay. There are lots of fish-based starters and usually a catch of the day; otherwise the main courses are the standard steak, chicken and spare ribs options, for €15–20. Daily noon–10pm.

De Waag Rode Steen 8 ☎0229/215 195. Good for both snacks and lunches – and with a small dinner menu too – amid the antiquated paraphernalia of the old municipal weigh house, and with tables outside to watch the action on the square. Mon–Thurs 11am–midnight, Fri–Sun 11am–1am.

Enkhuizen

Like Hoorn, **ENKHUIZEN**, just 19km to the east and 25 minutes away by train, was once one of the country's most important seaports. From the fourteenth to the early eighteenth century, when its harbour silted up, it prospered from both the Baltic sea trade and the North Sea herring fishery – and indeed its maritime credentials were second to none: Enkhuizen was home to Holland's largest fishing fleet and its citizens were renowned for their seamanship, with the Dutch East India Company always keen to recruit here. Enkhuizen was also the first town in Noord-Holland to rise against Spain, in 1572, but unlike many of its Protestant allies it was never besieged – its northerly location kept it safely out of reach of the Habsburg army. Subsequently, Enkhuizen slipped into a long-lasting economic lull, becoming a remote and solitary backwater until tourism has revived its fortunes. It's not a big place – about twenty minutes' walk from end to end – but the town centre, with its ancient streets, slender canals and pretty harbours, is wonderfully well preserved, a rough circle with a ring of bastions and moat on one side, and the old sea dyke on the other. It also has a major attraction in the excellent **Zuiderzeemuseum** and is a good place to visit for its summer passenger **ferry** connections across the IJsselmeer to Stavoren (see p.226) and Urk (see p.251).

Arrival and information

Trains to Enkhuizen, which is at the end of the line, stop right opposite the head of the main harbour – the Buitenhaven, at the southern end of town. **Buses** stop beside the train station, and the **VVV** is about 100m to the east, on the harbourfront at Tussen Twee Havens 1 (daily 9am–5pm; ☎0228/313 164, ⓦwww.vvvenkhuizen.nl). The VVV sells maps and town brochures and has details of local boat trips and has details of **rooms** in private houses (❶).

Campsites

Enkhuizen has two decent **campsites**. The closest is the *Enkhuizer Zand* on the far side of the Zuiderzeemuseum at Kooizandweg 4 (☎0228/317 289, ⓦwww.campingen khuizerzand.nl; April–Sept) – a 10- to 15-minute walk from the station, and very handy for the beach (see p.128). The other is the plainer and slightly cheaper *De Vest*, Noorderweg 31 (☎0228/321 221, ⓦwww.campingdevest.nl; April–Oct), which fits snugly onto one of the old bastions. To get there, follow Vijzelstraat north off Westerstraat, continue along Noorderweg, and turn left by the old town ramparts – a fifteen-minute walk; or **bus** #138 from the station drops you nearby.

ACCOMMODATION

Driebanen	**A**
De Koepoort	**D**
Recuer Dos	**C**
Het Wapen van Enkhuizen	**B**

ENKHUIZEN

De Vest Camping

Enkhuizer Zand Camping

Zuiderzeemuseum

Zuiderzeemuseum Entrance

Westerkerk

Stadhuis

Zuiderkerk

Zuiderzeemuseum

Oosterhaven

Oude Haven

Drommedaris

Buitenhaven

Flessenscheepjesmuseum

Train Station

Ferries to Urk, Stavoren and Zuiderzeemuseum

0   100 m

CAFÉS, RESTAURANTS & BARS

't Ankertje	4
Die Drie Haringhe	3
De Masteman	1
De Smederij	5
Theo Schilder	2

NOORD-HOLLAND | Enkhuizen

Accommodation

Driebanen Driebanen 59 ☎0228/316 381, ⓦwww.hoteldriebanen.com. Right on the canal, in a very peaceful location, this has good-sized if plainly furnished rooms in a slightly faded Sixties building. Quite a large hotel – 37 rooms – but it's a friendly place, and wi-fi only costs €1 a day. ❷

De Koepoort Westerstraat 294 ☎0228/314 966, ⓦwww.dekoepoort.nl. On the edge of the centre, but its wide range of rooms are handy if everywhere else is full. There's a pleasant bar and restaurant downstairs, though the welcome is businesslike rather than friendly. ❷

Recuer Dos Westerstraat 217 ☎0228/562 469, ⓦwww.recuerdos.nl. Probably Enkhuizen's best accommodation option – an immaculate Victorian house on the west side of the centre that has three doubles and one single in a series of chalets outside in the peaceful and elegant garden. The rooms are clean and comfortable, with well-appointed showers, and there are regular Spanish guitar and other concerts in the hotel's purpose-built downstairs music salon – reflecting the owner's occupation as a classical guitar teacher. ❷

Het Wapen van Enkhuizen Breedstraat 59 ☎0228/313 434, ⓦwww.wapenvanenkhuizen.nl. Comfortable if slightly uninspiring rooms in a friendly town centre location, with a downstairs bar and restaurant. Nothing fancy, but very handy for the harbour and Zuiderzeemuseum. ❷

The Town

A good place to start an exploration of Enkhuizen's compact centre is the **Oude Haven**, which stretches east in a gentle curve to the conspicuous **Drommedaris**, a heavy-duty brick watchtower built in 1540 to guard the

127

harbour entrance. On the green by the tower there's a modern statue of the seventeenth-century artist **Paulus Potter**, who was a native of Enkhuizen, painting one of the farm animals he was most famous for. Beyond the Drommedaris is the picturesque Buitenhaven, a jangle of sailing boats and barges, while immediately to the east is the oldest part of town, an extraordinarily pretty lattice of alleys, quays, canals and antique houses. Among these nestles the pocket-sized **Flessenscheepjesmuseum** at Zuiderspui 1 (daily noon–5pm; €3) – actually built above the lock gates at the end of the Zuiderhaven canal – ask and they'll show you the water flowing beneath the house. The museum itself is devoted to that ubiquitous maritime curiosity, the ship-in-a-bottle, and is a well-presented and -labelled collection, with vessels ranging from East Indiamen to steamboats, and containers from light bulbs, even fuses, to a thirty-litre wine flagon. There's also a short film inducting you into the ingenious mysteries of how it's done.

Walk north from the museum along Zuider Havendijk and turn left at the end of the canal to get to the **Zuiderkerk**, a hulking Gothic pile with a massive brick tower that was erected in 1518 – the octagon and then the cupola on top were added later. Close by, just to the east, is the solid, classically styled mid-seventeenth-century **Stadhuis**, an elegant and imposing Neoclassical edifice that still houses the city council. From here stroll up to the end of Enkhuizen's main street, **Westerstraat**, the town's spine, and a busy pedestrianized street that is home to most of its shops and stores. About halfway along stands the **Westerkerk**, an early fifteenth-century, red-brick Gothic church with a free-standing wooden tower. The bare interior of the church, with its three naves of equal height, is distinguished by its **rood-screen**, a mid-sixteenth century extravagance whose six intricately carved panels show biblical scenes in dramatic detail – Moses with the Tablets, St John on Patmos and so forth.

Finally, don't forget that there's a little stretch of sandy **beach** just five to ten minutes' walk from the end of Westerstraat, a shallow spot that's perfect for kids. Right by here, there's also **Sprookjeswonderland**, Kooizandweg 9 (April–Oct

▲ Enkhuizen harbour

daily 10am–5.30pm; €7), a modest theme park with gnome houses, rides, a mini railway, boats and a childrens' farm.

The Zuiderzeemuseum

It's a short walk from the centre of Enkhuizen to the landbound part of the **Zuiderzeemuseum** at Wierdijk 12–22 (daily 10am–5pm; €13; Wwww .zuiderzeemuseum.nl), around a dozen rooms devoted to changing annual exhibitions on different aspects of the Zuider Zee, and with the impressive ship hall at its heart, where you can get up close and personal with a number of traditional sailing barges and other craft. There is an ice-cutting boat from Urk, once charged with the responsibility of keeping the shipping lanes open between the island and the mainland; a dinghy for duck-hunting, complete with shotgun; and some wonderful fully rigged and highly varnished sailing vessels.

The main event though is the so-called **Museumpark**, whose main entrance is about 100m to the north along Wierdijk, and which stretches north along the seaward side of the old dyke that once protected Enkhuizen from the turbulent waters of the Zuider Zee. It's a fantastically well-put-together collection of over 130 dwellings, stores, workshops and even streets that have been transported here from every part of the region, and which together provide the flavour of life hereabouts from 1880 to around 1932. There are many highlights, and just about everything is worth seeing, but the best include a reconstruction of Marken harbour as of 1900, a red-brick chapel and assorted cottages from Den Oever, old fishermen's houses from Urk, a post office, and a pharmacy, which has a marvellous collection of "gapers" – painted wooden heads with their tongues out, which were the traditional pharmacy's sign. The museum works very hard to be authentic: sheep and goats roam the surrounding meadows and its smokehouses smoke (and sell) real herring and eels, the sweetshop sells real old-fashioned sweets, the beautifully kept school rooms offer geography and handwriting classes, and there's even a woman in a 1930s furnished house who will make you a traditional Dutch lunch. There's also a **nature reserve**, where you can take a picnic and walk through the woods for some great views over the water. All in all not be missed, especially if you have children.

Eating and drinking

't Ankertje Dijk 4 T0228/315 767. An atmospheric, old-fashioned kind of place for a drink, with nautical knick-knacks hanging on the walls and lots of tables outside on the quay.

Die Drie Haringhe Dijk 28 T0228/318 610. Housed in an immaculately renovated seventeenth-century building on the harbour, and with a few tables in the courtyard garden outside, this is perhaps the town's best restaurant, with a menu that's strong on seafood and local specialities. Main courses are in the region of €25 – though their three-course set menu is worth trying at €42.50. Daily except Tues noon–2pm & 5–10pm.

De Masteman Compagnieshaven 3 ☎0228/313 691. Down in the marina, this place is great both for a drink or a full meal, lunch or dinner, with a nice short menu of meat and fish dishes for €18–20, along with three- and four-course menus for €29.95–32.95. It's cosy enough inside, but the outside terrace, from which you can watch the yachts chugging by after a long day on the Ijsselmeer, is about as good an end to

a summer's day in Enkhuizen as it gets. Daily 9am–midnight.

De Smederij Breedstraat 158–160 ☎0228/314 604. Inventive, modern Dutch cuisine in a smartly renovated building a block back from the harbour, with main courses around €20–25. Daily except Wed 5–10pm, Oct–March closed Thurs also.

Theo Schilder Dijk 48 ☎0228/317 809. A great fish shop with a pint-sized café and tables outside. Serves a wide variety of fish and seafood snacks. Mon–Sat 9am–7pm, Sun noon–7pm.

Medemblik and around

Nautical **MEDEMBLIK**, just over 20km north along the coast from Enkhuizen, is one of the oldest towns in the Netherlands, a seat of Frisian kings until the seventh century and later a Zuider Zee port of some importance. Unfortunately, there's not a great deal to entice you here nowadays unless you're into yachts: the town's several waterways, harbour and marina are jam-packed with leisure craft.

The Town

The only significant reminder of Medemblik's past is the **Kasteel Radboud**, a dinky little moated fortress beside the entrance to the harbour on Oudevaartsgat (May to mid-Sept Mon–Thurs & Sat 11am–5pm, Sun 2–5pm; €5; ⓦwww .kasteelradboud.nl). The castle is named after the last Frisian king to hold sway here, though the structure that survives is not his at all, but a much-modified thirteenth-century fortress built by a count of Holland, **Floris V** (1254–96), one of the most celebrated of the country's medieval rulers. Nicknamed "God of the Peasants" (Der Keerlen God) for his attempts to improve the lot of his humbler subjects, Floris spent most of his time fighting his enemies, both the nobles within his territories and his archenemy, the duke of Flanders. In the end, it was his own nobles who did for him, capturing Floris when he was out hunting and then murdering him during a skirmish when the peasantry came to the rescue. As for the castle itself, it owes much of its present appearance to Petrus J.H. Cuypers (1827–1921), who repaired and rebuilt what had by then become a dilapidated ruin; Cuypers was a leading architect of his day, who was also responsible – among many other commissions – for Amsterdam's Centraal Station and the Rijksmuseum. Inside the castle, exhibits outline the fort's turbulent history and there's a ragbag of archeological finds from local sites.

The castle apart, Medemblik is short on sights, although the main drag, **Nieuwstraat**, is wide and well appointed. The town is also home to a large lakeside building that was once the main pumping station for the Wieringermeer polder and is now the **Nederlands Stoommachinemuseum**, on the town's southeasterly outskirts at Oosterdijk 4 (mid-Feb to Oct Tues–Sun 10am–5pm; €5.50; ⓦwww.stoommachinemuseum.nl), which is the proud possessor of a batch of antique steam engines.

Practicalities

Buses to Medemblik, as well as the **Stoomtram** from Hoorn (see p.125), pull in on the Dam, at the north end of the town centre – and at the top of Nieuwstraat. The **VVV** is at the foot of Nieuwstraat at Dam 2 (April–June, Sept & Oct

Mon–Sat 10am–4pm; July & Aug Mon–Sat 9.30am–5pm; ☎229/548 000, ⓦwww.medemblik.nl). It sells town maps and has a small supply of **rooms** in private houses (❶). Among the local **hotels**, the *Medemblik*, Oosterhaven 1 (☎0227/543 844, ⓦwww.hetwapenvanmedemblik.nl; ❷), is comfortable and central, and has a decent **restaurant** downstairs.

North of Medemblik

North of Medemblik, the **Wieringermeer Polder** was reclaimed in the 1920s, filling in the gap between the former Zuider Zee island of Wieringen and the mainland. Towards the end of World War II, just three weeks before their surrender, the Germans flooded the polder, boasting they could return the Netherlands to the sea if they so wished. After the war, it was drained again, leaving a barren, treeless terrain that had to be totally replanted. Almost sixty years later, it's indistinguishable from its surroundings, a familiar landscape of flat, geometric fields highlighted by neat and trim farmhouses. The polder leads north to the **Afsluitdijk** highway over to Friesland (see Chapter 4). The sluices on this side of the Afsluitdijk are known as the **Stevinsluizen**, after **Hendrick Stevin**, the seventeenth-century engineer who first had the idea of reclaiming the Zuider Zee. At the time, his grand plan was impracticable – the technology wasn't up to it – but his vision lived on, to be realized by **Cornelis Lely** (see box, p.119), though he too died before the dyke was completed. There's a **statue** of Lely by the modern Dutch sculptor Mari Andriessen at the west end of the dyke. Further out along the dyke, at the point where the barrier was finally closed, there's an observation point on which an inscription reads "A nation that lives is building for its future" – a linking of progress with construction that read well in the 1930s, but seems rather more dubious today.

Zaandam and around

As observed from the train heading north out of Amsterdam, the largely modern town of **ZAANDAM** is not especially alluring, but it does deserve a brief stop. The town was a popular tourist hangout in the nineteenth century, when it was known as "La Chine d'Hollande" for the faintly oriental appearance of its windmills, canals and row upon row of brightly painted houses. Monet spent some time here in the 1870s and, despite being under constant police surveillance as a suspected spy, went on to immortalize the place in a series of paintings.

The Czaar Peterhuisje

Monet's Zaandam is long gone, but the town is home to one real curiosity in the **Czaar Peterhuisje**, at Krimp 23 (Tues–Sun 10–5pm; €3), where the Russian Tsar Peter the Great stayed incognito in 1697. Earlier that year, Peter had attached himself to a Russian trade mission to Holland as an ordinary sailor, Peter Mikhailov. The Russians came to Zaandam, which was then an important shipbuilding centre, and the tsar bumped into a former employee, one Gerrit Kist. Swearing Kist to the utmost secrecy, the tsar moved into Kist's simple home and worked at a local shipyard where he learnt as much as he could about shipbuilding, although it's worth knowing that he was only here for just over a week. Kist's old home is these days a tottering wooden structure, enclosed within a brick museum erected in 1822, and comprises just two small rooms, decorated with a handful of portraits of a benign-looking emperor and the graffiti of tourists going back to the mid-nineteenth century. You can see the cupboard bed in which the tsar is supposed to have slept, together with the calling cards of various visiting Russian delegations, while around the outside of the house displays tell the story of Peter and his western aspirations, and give background on the shipbuilding industry in Zaandam and the modest house itself. As Napoleon is said to have remarked on visiting the building, "Nothing is too small for great men."

The Czaar Peterhuisje is not far from Zaandam train station: cross the main road and walk south to Hogendijk, where you turn left by the garage; follow this for 300m and take the fourth turning on the left.

Zaanse Schans

From Zaandam, it's about 4km north to **Zaanse Schans** (Ⓦ www.zaanseschans .nl), a re-created Dutch village whose antique houses, shops, warehouses and windmills, mostly dating from the eighteenth century, were brought here from all over the region half a century ago and re-erected amid a network of narrow canals. It's a popular day-trip from Amsterdam and can get very crowded in summer. It's pretty well done, and the closest place to Amsterdam to see fully functioning windmills (the other place is Kinderdijk; see p.193).

There's no overall **entry fee**; you just pay per attraction, although you can opt to buy a Zaanse Schans Pass (€9.50) or Pass Plus (€16.50), both of which include entry to the museum and at least one windmill and other discounts. There's an **information centre** (daily 9am–5pm), on the east side of the "village" beside the car park, where you can pick up free maps and other information (such as opening times), from where it's a short stroll to a string of attractions focused on old **crafts** – a Klompenmakerij (clog-making workshop), Bakkerij (bakery) and Kaasmakerij (cheese farm). Next door to the information centre, the **Zaans Museum** and **Verkrade Paviljoen** (daily 10am–5pm; €7.50) have good displays on the Zaanstreek region and a mocked-up chocolate factory. But the real highlight of Zaanse Schans is the **windmills** themselves, eight in all, strung along the River Zaan, giant, insect-like affairs still used – among other things – to cut wood, grind mustard seeds and produce oil (opening times vary; €3 each). Finally, there are also pleasant, 45-minute-long **boat trips** on the River Zaan from the jetty near the De Huisman mustard windmill (April–June & Sept Tues–Sun 11am–4pm, July & Aug daily 11am–4pm; €7.50).

The nearest **train station** is Koog-Zaandijk, two stops up the line from Zaandam. From the station, it's a fifteen-minute walk east to the river, where regular ferries take you across to Zaanse Schans. Or from Amsterdam you can take **bus** #91 right here from Centraal Station.

Alkmaar and around

Forty minutes north from Amsterdam by train, the amenable little town of **ALKMAAR** has preserved much of its medieval street plan, its compact centre surrounded by what was once the town moat and laced with spindly canals. The town is also dotted with fine old buildings, but is best known for its much-touted **cheese market**, an ancient affair that these days ranks as one of the most extravagant tourist spectacles in Noord Holland. Alkmaar was founded in the tenth century in the middle of a marsh – hence its name, which is taken from the auk, a diving bird which once hung around here in numbers, as in *alkeen meer*, or auk lake. Just like Haarlem, the town was besieged by Frederick of

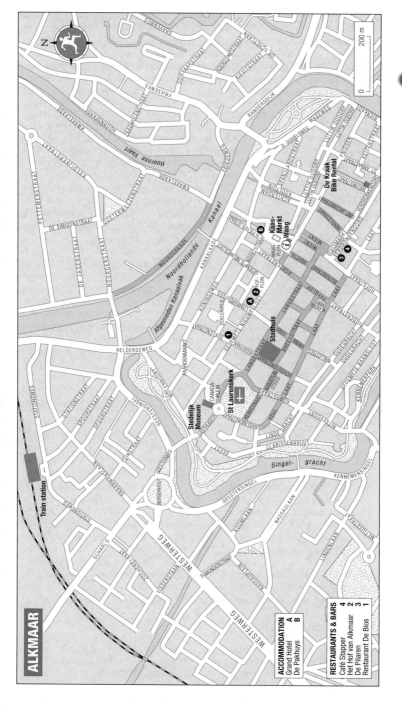

ALKMAAR

N

0 ——— 200 m

De Kraît
Bike Rental

Kaas-
Markt
Waag
B
i

Stadhuis

St Laurenskerk

Stedelijk
Museum

CANADA-
PLEIN

Train station

Singel-
gracht

WESTERWEG

ACCOMMODATION
Grand Hotel   A
De Pakhuys   B

RESTAURANTS & BARS
Café Stapper   4
Het Hof van Alkmaar   2
De Pilaren   3
Restaurant De Bios   1

Alkmaar's cheese market

Cheese has been sold on Alkmaar's main square since the 1300s, and although it's no longer a serious commercial concern, the **kaasmarkt** (cheese market; Fri 10am–12.30pm, from the first Friday in April to the first Friday in Sept) continues to pull the crowds – so get there early if you want a good view. The ceremony starts with the buyers sniffing, crumbling, and finally tasting each cheese, followed by intensive bartering. Once a deal has been concluded, the cheeses – golden discs of Gouda mainly, laid out in rows and piles on the square – are borne away on ornamental carriers by groups of four **porters** (*kaasdragers*) for weighing. The porters wear white trousers and shirt plus a black hat whose **coloured bands** – green, blue, red or yellow – represent the four companies that comprise the cheese porters' guild. Payment for the cheeses, tradition has it, takes place in the cafés around the square.

Toledo, but heavy rain flooded its surroundings and forced the Spaniards to withdraw in 1573, an early Dutch success in their long war of independence. At the time, Alkmaar was small and comparatively unimportant, but the town prospered when the surrounding marshland was drained in the 1700s and it received a boost more recently when the northern part of the old moat was incorporated into the Noordhollandskanaal, itself part of a longer network of waterways running north from Amsterdam to the open sea.

Alkmaar is also within easy striking distance of **Bergen**, a pretty little village halfway between Alkmaar and the North Sea coast, whose immediate hinterland, with its woods and dunes, is protected in the **Noordhollands Duinreservaat** (North Holland Dune Reserve) and, just to the north, the **Schoorlse Duinen Nationaalpark** (Schoorl Dunes National Park). Both the reserve and the park are latticed by hiking and cycling routes, and bike rental is available at Alkmaar and Bergen.

Arrival and information

From Alkmaar's **train** and **bus station**, it's a ten-minute walk to the centre of town: outside the station head straight along Spoorstraat, turn left at the end onto Geestersingel and then turn right over the bridge to get to Kanaalkade; keep going along here until you reach Houttil Pieterstraat. This leads straight to the main square, Waagplein, where you'll find the **VVV** (Mon–Fri 10am–5.30pm, Sat 9.30am–5pm; ☎072/511 4284, ⓦwww.vvvalkmaar.nl). They sell a useful town brochure, have details of the area's walking and cycling routes, and have plenty of **rooms in private houses** for around €40 per double per night, including breakfast, though most places are on the outskirts of town. Among several places, **bike rental** is available at the train station and at De Kraak, Verdronkenoord 54 (May Wed–Fri 11am–6pm, Sat & Sun 10am–8pm; June–Aug daily 10am–9pm; ☎072/512 5840, ⓦwww.dekraak.nl), where they also rent canoes and rowing boats. **Canal trips** leave from the jetty on Mient for a quick zip round the town's central waterways – an enjoyable way to spend 45 minutes (April Mon–Sat hourly 11am–5pm; May–Sept daily, hourly 11am–5pm; 40min; €5.30); tickets are on sale at the VVV or on board.

Accommodation

Grand Hotel Alkmaar Gedempte Nieuwsloot 36 ☎072/576 0970, ⓦwww.grandhotelalkmaar.nl. This new boutiquey option has been stylishly converted from a former post office and has sleek modern rooms. Prices include breakfast and free internet access. ❸

Hotel Pakhuys Peperstraat 1 ℡072/520 2500, ⓦ www.inonshuys.nl. Just off Waagplein, this has lovely canal-side doubles, not including breakfast – a little less in the annexe down the street – some with Jacuzzis and kitchenettes, and with free wi-fi. Slightly cheaper than the *Grand Hotel Alkmaar*. ❸

The Town

Even if you've only come here for the cheese market, it's well worth seeing something of the rest of the town. On the main square, the **Waag** (Weigh House) was originally a chapel – hence the imposing tower – dedicated to the Holy Ghost, and converted and given its delightful east gable shortly after the town's famous victory against the Spanish. The **gable** is an ostentatious Dutch Renaissance affair bedecked with allegorical figures and decorated with the town's militant coat of arms. The Waag holds the VVV and the **Hollands Kaasmuseum** (April–Oct Mon–Sat 10am–4pm; €3; ⓦ www.kaasmuseum.nl), with displays on – predictably enough – the history of cheese, cheese-making equipment and the like. At the far end of the Waagplein, the **Biermuseum de Boom** (Mon–Sat 1–4pm; €3.50), above the *De Boom* bar, has three floors devoted to the art of making and distributing beer – no great shakes, but no worse than the cheese museum. In the other direction, at the south end of Mient, the open-air **Vismarkt** (Fish Market) marks the start of the **Verdronkenoord** canal, whose attractive medley of facades and gables leads east to the spindly **Accijnstoren** (Excise Tower), part harbour master's office, part fortification built in 1622 during the long struggle with Spain. Turn left at the tower along Bierkade and you'll soon reach **Luttik Oudorp**, another attractive corner of the old centre, its slender canal jammed with antique barges.

One block south of the Waag, pedestrianized **Langestraat** is Alkmaar's main and mundane shopping street, whose only notable building is the **Stadhuis**, a florid edifice, half of which (the Langestraat side) dates from the early sixteenth century. At the west end of Langestraat lurks **St Laurenskerk**, a de-sanctified Gothic church of the late fifteenth century whose pride and joy is its **organ**, commissioned at the suggestion of the diplomat and political bigwig Constantijn Huygens in 1645. The case was designed by Jacob van Campen, the architect who was later to design Amsterdam's town hall (see p.63), and decorated with paintings by **Caesar van Everdingen** (1617–78). The artist's seamless brushstrokes – not to mention his willingness to kowtow to the tastes of the burgeoning middle class – were to make van Everdingen a wealthy man. In the apse is the **tomb** containing the intestines of the energetic Count Floris V of Holland (1254–96), who improved the region's sea defences, succoured the poor and did much to establish the independence of the towns hereabouts, until his untimely demise at the hands of his own nobles; the rest of him ended up in Rijnsburg, near Leiden.

Across from the church, Alkmaar's cultural centre holds a theatre, offices and a mildly diverting local museum, the **Stedelijk Museum** (Tues–Sun 10am–5pm; €6; ⓦ www.stedelijkmuseumalkmaar.nl), whose three floors focus on the history of the town. Well displayed, but almost entirely labelled in Dutch only, the collection has a short film on the history of the town (in English), paintings, maps and models of Alkmaar during its seventeenth-century glory years. The many paintings include a typically precise interior of Alkmaar's **St Laurenskerk** by Pieter Saenredam (1597–1665), a striking *Holy Family* by the Mannerist Gerard van Honthorst (1590–1656) and a huge canvas by the medievalist Jacobus Hilverdink (1809–64) depicting the bloody siege of 1573. The top floor explores the history of the town during the twentieth century and hosts a large and well-displayed collection along with pictures by local artist Charley Toorop, daughter of the Dutch impressionist Jan Toorop.

Eating and drinking

Restaurant De Bios Gedempte Nieuwesloot 54
T072/512 4422. Along the street from the *Grand
Hotel Alkmaar, De Bios* is a modern sort of place
whose excellent and well-priced menu has a
French slant. Tues & Wed noon–10pm, Thurs–Sat
10am–1am, Sun noon–10pm.

De Boom Houttil 1. Right in the centre of town, this
small unpretentious bar has a museum of beer
upstairs (see p.135).

Het Hof van Alkmaar Hof van Sonoy 1 T072/512
1222. A delightfully restored medieval nunnery just
off Nieuwesloot, this is pretty good for both lunch
and dinner, with inexpensive omelettes, sandwiches

and pancakes for lunch, and at night tasty Dutch
cuisine with main courses averaging €15–20;
there's an outside terrace too. Daily noon–10pm.

De Notaris Houttil 18 T072/520 7608. A big,
bustling café that does good lunches and evening
meals. Good for food or just a drink. Mon–Thurs &
Sun 10am–2am, Fri & Sat 10am–3am.

Hotel Pakhuys see p.135. A cool wine bar with a
nice selection of bar snacks, as well as a restaurant.

De Pilaren Verdronkenoord 129 T072/511 4997.
A youthful spot catering to a lively crowd, some of
whom take refuge in the *Café Stapper* next door if
the music gets too much.

Bergen and Bergen–aan-Zee

Out towards the coast, just 5km northwest of Alkmaar, lies the village of
BERGEN, a cheerful, leafy sort of place whose main square, the **Plein**, is an
amiable affair crowded by cafés and restaurants. Bergen has been something of a
retreat for artists since the late nineteenth century and the **Museum Kranen-
burgh**, Hoflaan 7 (Tues–Sun 11am–5pm; €7; W www.museumkranenburgh.nl),
in a Neoclassical villa about 700m southwest of the Plein, features the work of
the Expressionist Bergen School, which was founded here in 1915. The group was
greatly influenced by the Post-Impressionists, especially Cézanne, and though
none of the group is original enough to stand out, taken as a whole it's a delightful
collection and one that is supported by an imaginative programme of temporary
exhibitions. These often focus on the two contemporaneous Dutch schools that
were to have much more artistic impact – De Ploeg and De Stijl (see p.359).
Warming to this artistic heritage, the local council organizes all sorts of cultural
events in Bergen, including open-air sculpture displays and concerts, and the
village also boasts a scattering of chi-chi commercial galleries. Bergen has one
other museum of some note, the **Gemeentemuseum Het Sterkenhuis**, in a
seventeenth-century manor house about 100m from the west end of Plein at
Oude Prinsweg 21 (May–Oct Tues–Sat 1–5pm; July & Aug also Sun 1–5pm; €2).
The museum holds regular exhibitions of work by contemporary Dutch artists,
has a string of period rooms and features a local history section, including a display
on a largely forgotten episode in the Napoleonic Wars, when a combined army
of 30,000 English and Russian soldiers were defeated by a Franco-Dutch force
here in 1799.

Bus #160 leaves Alkmaar train station every thirty minutes or so – hourly on
Sunday – for the ten-minute ride to Bergen, dropping passengers in the centre
on Plein, a few metres from **Bergen VVV**, Plein 1 (Mon–Fri 10am–5.30pm,
Sat 9.30am–5.30pm; July & Aug also Sun 11am–3pm; T072/581 3100,
W www.vvvbergen.com). They sell maps of the hiking and cycling routes that
crisscross the coastal woods and dunes just to the west of the village – both in
the Noordhollands Duinreservaat and the Schoorlse Duinen Nationaalpark.
Bike rental is available in Bergen, at, among several places, Fietsverhuur
Bergen, just north of Plein at Breelaan 46 (T072/589 8248).

Bergen-aan-Zee and around

From Bergen, it's just 5km to **BERGEN-AAN-ZEE**, a sprawling, modern
resort that dips and bucks over the dunes. There's nothing special about the

place, apart from the sheer volume of holiday cottages and the first-rate **beach**, a strip of golden sand extending as far as the eye can see to both north and south. The resort also marks the northerly limit of the **Noordhollands Duinreservaat** (North Holland Dune Reserve), whose bumpy sand dunes stretch north from the suburbs of IJmuiden, and the southern boundary of the **Schoorlse Duinen Nationaalpark** (Schoorl Dunes National Park), where a band of sweeping, wooded dunes, up to 5km wide, extends north as far as Camperduin – one of the widest undeveloped portions of the whole Dutch coastline. The dune reserve and the national park are both crisscrossed by footpaths and cycling trails, but the most lauded is the well-signposted, 42-kilometre-long **De Brede Duinen route** that takes cyclists on a loop through Alkmaar, Bergen, Bergen-aan-Zee, Schoorl and Camperduin, passing the highest of the national park's sand dunes (54m) on the way. Both Bergen and Alkmaar VVV sell detailed **maps** of local hiking and cycling routes.

Den Helder

The gritty port, oil supply centre and naval base of **DEN HELDER**, some forty minutes north from Alkmaar by train, was little more than a fishing village until 1811, when Napoleon, capitalizing on its strategic position at the very tip of Noord-Holland, built a fortified dockyard here. It's still the principal home of the Dutch navy, and **national fleet days**, or Vlootdagen, are held in the harbour on one weekend during the summer – usually in July – when, should you so desire, you can check out the bulk of the Dutch navy; for further details, contact the VVV. Otherwise, the town holds little of interest with the possible exception of the **Marinemuseum**, on the seafront – in between the train station and the ferry terminal – at Hoofdgracht 3 (Mon–Fri 10am–5pm, Sat & Sun noon–5pm; €6; Ⓦ www.marinemuseum.nl), which makes a gallant attempt to conjure interest in what is, for most people, hardly a riveting subject. Nevertheless, the sections tracking through the history of the Dutch navy are well presented and entertaining, and in particular you might look out for the stuff on the naval heroes of yesteryear, especially Admiral Michiel de Ruyter (1607–76), who trounced in succession the Spaniards, the Swedes, the English and the French. His most daring exploit was a raid up the River Thames to Medway in 1667 and the seizure of the Royal Navy's flagship, *The Royal Charles*, a raid that drove Charles II almost to distraction. There's lots of technical information too – on shipbuilding techniques and the like – and several decommissioned vessels, including a 1960s submarine, the *Tonijn*, and the veteran World War II minesweeper, the *Abraham Crijnssen*.

It's a five-minute walk north from Den Helder **train station** to the **VVV**, Bernhardplein 4 (Mon 10.30am–5.30pm, Tues–Fri 9.30am–5.30pm, Sat 9.30am–5pm; Ⓣ 0223/625 544, Ⓦ www.vvvkopvannoordholland.nl), and just under 2km to the Texel ferry terminal (for ferry details, see p.138); alternatively, you can miss the town altogether by taking a bus direct from the train station to the ferry dock.

Texel

Stuck out in the Waddenzee, **Texel** (pronounced "tessel") is the westernmost of the string of islands that band the northern coast of the Netherlands. Some 25km long and up to 9km wide, Texel is mostly reclaimed polder, a flattened landscape of green pasture land dotted with chunks of woodland, speckled with small villages and protected in the east by long sea defences. The west coast boasts a magnificent sandy **beach** that stretches from one end of the island to the other, its numbered markers (*paal*) – from 6 in the south to 33 in the north – distinguishing one bit from another. Behind the beach, a belt of sand dunes widens as it approaches both ends of the island. In the north it spreads out into two nature reserves – **De Muy** and **De Slufter** – and the latter incorporates Texel's finest scenery in a tidal inlet where a deep cove of salt marsh, lagoon and dune has been left beyond the sea defences, exposed to the wilfulness of the ocean. The beach, combined with the island's laid-back rural charms, attracts holidaying Netherlanders in their hundreds and the island has scores of holiday bungalows and cottages, plus a scattering of hotels and campsites. As for the island's **villages**, they are disappointingly humdrum with the notable exception of **Den Hoorn**, easily the prettiest place on the island with **De Cocksdorp** a distant runner-up.

Arrival, information and transport

Car ferries, run by Teso (Mon–Sat 6.30am–9.30pm, Sun 7.30am or 8.30am; ☎0222/369 600, ⓦwww.teso.nl), leave Den Helder for Texel hourly on the half hour, and the journey takes about twenty minutes. **Return tickets** cost €3 for foot passengers, plus €2.50 for a bike or moped; cars cost €35 at peak times, which includes most weekend sailings, €24.50 at other times. Ferries dock at the south end of the island, pretty much in the middle of nowhere, but there is a good **island bus** service to – and between – all of Texel's main villages, and connections with each ferry arrival. Pick up an island **bus timetable** at the Den Helder foot passenger ticket window, where you can also buy a one-day, island-wide **bus pass** for €4.50, though passes are sold by the island's bus drivers too. There are also usually plenty of taxis, or at the same ticket window in Den Helder you can arrange for a **Telekomtaxi** (☎0222/322 211) to take you anywhere on the island once you get there. The best way to get around the island is by **bike** – Texel has about 130km of cycle paths. **Bike rental** is available at a number of locations across the island at about €5.50 per day/€20 a week, but there is a very convenient outlet beside the Texel ferry dock – Fietsverhuur Veerhaven Texel (daily 8.30am–6pm; ☎0222/319 588); reservations aren't necessary.

Texel **VVV** is on the southern edge of the island's largest village, **Den Burg**, at Emmalaan 66 (Mon–Fri 9am–5.30pm, Sat 9am–5pm; ☎0222/314 741, ⓦwww .vvv.texel.net), and has a wide range of island information, including booklets detailing **cycling routes** as well as the best places to view the island's many **bird colonies** – the island is one of the most important breeding grounds in Europe. The VVV also operates an **accommodation service**, which is especially useful in the height of the summer when spare rooms can get mighty thin on the ground. The VVV has a substantial supply of **rooms** in private houses (❶–❷), which supplement the island's dozen or so hotels and myriad summer cottages.

De Vriendschap

De Vriendschap (☎0222/316 451, ⓦwww.waddenveer.nl) is a seasonal passenger **ferry** linking De Cocksdorp, at the northern tip of Texel, with the next island along, **Vlieland** (see p.219). It runs between May and September, in July and August operating two services daily every day, and in May, June and September two services daily on Tuesday, Wednesday, Thursday and Sunday. The journey takes thirty minutes and a return ticket costs €22.50 per person. Note that Vlieland is car-free.

TEXEL

Vlieland ▲

Eijerlandse Duinen ▲
De Rottenjäger

De Cocksdorp

Noordzee

DE SLUFTER

DE MUY

De Koog

EcoMare

De Waal   Oosterend

Den Burg

Westerduinen

Den Hoorn

Loodsmansduin

Oudeschild

Waddenzee

't Horntje

De Hors

Marsdiep

▼ Den Helder

N

Dunes

0   3 km

Den Hoorn and around

Ferries from Den Helder dock at the south end of Texel, about 4km from the hamlet of **DEN HOORN**, a leafy little place whose rustic cottages, some of which date back to the eighteenth century, string along the main street, Herenstraat, and out towards the dunes, just 2km away to the west; the beach another 2km further on (at *paal* 10). There are two very appealing **hotels** in the village, beginning with *Loodman's Welvaren*, Herenstraat 12 (☎0222/319 228, ⓦwww.welvaarttexel.nl; ②), which has nine spick-and-span, modern doubles in a sympathetically modernized old building. Similarly enticing is ⚐ *Bij Jef*, in another old building just along the street at Herenstraat 34 (☎0222/319 623, ⓦwww.bijjef.nl; ③) whose rooms are more stylish and whose restaurant is one of the island's best. There's also a large **campsite**, *Loodsmansduin*, Rommelpot 19 (☎0222/317 208, ⓦwww.rsttexel.nl; April–Oct), with plenty of space for tents and caravans on the edge of the dunes just to the southwest of Den Hoorn – about a ten-minute walk. As for **food**, the restaurant of the *Bij Jef Hotel* (Mon–Sat noon–2pm & 6–10pm, Sun noon–9pm)

▲ Horses on the island of Texel

has an island-wide reputation for its excellent Franco-Dutch cuisine, with four-course menus starting at €60. A more economic option is *Klif 23*, on the west side of the village at Klif 23 – Klif being the road running west towards the dunes – where they offer over 150 different sorts of pancake and Texel lamb dishes.

Bike rental is available in Den Hoorn at Vermeulen Bikes, Herenstraat 69 (☎0222/319 213), for €4.50 a day/€20 a week. There are hourly **bus** connections between Den Hoorn and the ferry port Monday through Saturday, five daily on Sundays.

Den Burg, Oudesshild and De Koog

About 5km northeast of Den Hoorn, **DEN BURG** is the island's main village and home to the VVV (see p.138). There's a Monday morning market here and the island's best range of shops, but there's not much to the place to be honest, the only sight being the **Oudheidkamer** local museum (Mon–Fri 11.30am–5.30pm; €3), whose period interiors show how life was on Texel in times gone by.

OUDESCHILD, 3km east on the coast, is home to the **Maritiem & Jutters Museum**, Barentszstraat 21 (Tues–Sat 10am–5pm, Sun noon–5pm; €6), a wonderfully ramshackle collection of maritime junk, with various summertime activities laid on for visitors outside: rope-making, fish-smoking and the like.

In the opposite direction from Den Burg, **DE KOOG** is Texel's busiest resort, equipped with lots of restaurants and hotels, plus a small army of campsites. Pressing on, the coastal road north from De Koog leads, after about 4km, past the first of two turnings that cut down to the sea wall behind **De Slufter** nature reserve, a beautiful tidal inlet whose assorted lagoons, marshes and dunes are exposed to the ocean's tides. Steps enable visitors to clamber up and over the sea wall to the footpaths beyond: it is perhaps the prettiest spot on the island.

De Cocksdorp

Beyond, near the northern tip of Texel, is **DE COCKSDORP**, a middling sort of village whose wedge of mostly modern houses trail along a slender inlet, all protected by a sea wall. The village has a handful of **hotels**, the pick of which is *'t Anker*, a cosy, unassuming little place in a pair of oldish cottages on the main street at Kikkertstraat 24 (℡0222/316 274, ⓦwww.t-anker.texel.com; ❷). There's also a **campsite**, *De Robbenjager*, to the north of the village at Vuurtorenweg 148 (℡0222/316 258; April–Oct). De Cocksdorp heaves with **cafés** and restaurants, and one good choice is the *Pangkoekehuus*, Kikkertstraat 9 (℡0222/316 441), where they serve up a great line in pancakes – and deliver your bill to the table inside a tiny clog.

Ferries to Vlieland (see p.219) leave from the jetty about 1.5km north of De Cocksdorp, and there's an hourly **bus** service between De Cocksdorp, De Koog and the ferry dock.

Het Gooi

Known collectively as **Het Gooi**, the sprawling suburbs that spread southeast from Amsterdam towards Amersfoort and Utrecht (see p.194) are interrupted by open heaths, lakes, canals and woods, reminders of the time when this was a sparsely inhabited district largely devoted to sheep farming. The turning point was the construction of the Amsterdam–Amersfoort railway in 1874, which allowed hundreds of middle-class Amsterdammers to build their country homes here, nowhere more so than in well-heeled **Hilversum**, long the area's main settlement and nowadays pretty much a dormitory town despite the best efforts of the Dutch media, much of which has decamped here. Hilversum is a possible target for a day-trip on account of its modern architecture, most notably the work of Willem Dudok, although Het Gooi's two other prime attractions, the immaculate star-shaped fortifications of **Naarden** and the handsome medieval castle at **Muiden**, are quite frankly more appealing.

The most useful **train line** across Het Gooi passes through **Weesp**, where there are connecting buses onto Muiden, and then proceeds onto Naarden-Bussum (for Naarden) and Hilversum.

Muiden

MUIDEN, just to the north of the A1 motorway about 10km to the southeast of Amsterdam, straddles the River Vecht as it approaches the Markermeer, its several waterways crowded with pleasure boats and yachts. At the far end of the town on the old ramparts is the **Muiderslot** (April–Oct Mon–Fri 10am–4pm, Sat & Sun noon–5pm; Nov–March Sat & Sun noon–4pm; €11; ⓦwww .muiderslot.nl), one of the country's most visited castles, a handsome red-brick structure whose imposing walls are punctuated by mighty circular towers, all set behind a reedy moat. The Muiderslot was built by Count Floris V of Holland (1254–96) – for more on whom, see p.130 – but it has been rebuilt or remodelled on several occasions, most recently after World War II when the interior was returned to its seventeenth-century appearance in honour of the poet Pieter Hooft, one of its most celebrated occupants. Hooft was chatelain here from 1609–47, a sinecure that allowed him to entertain a group of artistic and literary friends who became known as the Muiderkring or Muiden Circle. You have to join one of the half-hourly guided tours to see some of the castle, which take you through a series of period rooms, among them a small dining room and kitchen, and the large Ridderzal, which has a painting showing Hooft and his most famous cronies –Vondel, Huygens, Jacob Cats, Maria Tesselschaede and others – although it's a fake in that not all of the people in the painting were alive at the same time. But really the best bits of the building can be seen on your own, whether it's the chapel which shows a short film about Muiden, Hooft's study and en-suite loo, which enjoys good views over what would have been the Zuider Zee, or the suits of armour and various knightly bits and pieces in one of the towers. Kids may also enjoy the chance to joust or dress in a jester's suit, but really the best thing is the wonderful view over the Markerwaard from the bastions. Bear in mind that entrance tickets also include the gardens, and the regular falconry displays that take place nearby.

Practicalities

To get to Muiden by **public transport**, take the train from Amsterdam Centraal Station to Weesp (every 15min; 15min) and then catch the hourly local **bus** #110 on from there, a five-minute journey. In Muiden, the bus drops you on the edge of town, a short, signposted walk from the centre and the Muiderslot. The centre of Muiden clusters around the big lock gates, where *Ome Ko*, Herengracht 71, is a nice **bar** with an outside terrace overlooking the lock – a good lunch or drink stop, with *uitsmijters*, sandwiches and the like.

Naarden

Look at a postcard of **NAARDEN**, about 8km east along the A1 from Muiden, and it seems as if the old town was created by a giant pastry-cutter, its gridiron of streets encased within a double ring of ramparts and moats that were engineered with geometrical precision between 1675 and 1685 to defend the eastern approaches to Amsterdam.

These formidable defences were used right up until the 1920s, and one of the fortified spurs, on Westwalstraat, is now the wonderfully explorable **Nederlands Vestingmuseum** (March–Oct Tues–Fri 10.30am–5pm, Sat & Sun noon–5pm; Nov–Feb Sun noon–5pm; €5.50; Ⓦ www.vestingmuseum.nl), on whose grassy forks you can clamber around among the cannons, and whose claustrophobic casemates demonstrate how the garrison defended the town for nigh-on 300 years.

Within the ramparts, Naarden's attractive and architecturally harmonious centre mostly dates from the late sixteenth century, its small, low houses erected after the Spanish sacked the town in 1572. Fortunately, the Spaniards spared the late Gothic **Grote Kerk** and its superb vault paintings. Based on drawings by Dürer, these 22 rectangular wooden panels were painted between 1510 and 1518 and show Old Testament scenes on the south side, New Testament scenes on the north; there are also five triangular panels at the east end of the church. To study the paintings without cricking your neck, borrow a mirror at the entrance. The church is also noted for its wonderful acoustics: every year there are several acclaimed performances of Bach's *St Matthew Passion* in the Grote Kerk in the days leading up to Easter – details from the VVV. A haul up the 235 steps of the Grote Kerk's massive square **tower** gives the best view of the fortress. The elaborately step-gabled building opposite the church is the **Stadhuis** (Wed, Sat & Sun 2–3pm; €2.50), built in 1601 and still in use by the town council today.

Naarden is also home to the mildly absorbing **Comenius Museum**, at Kloosterstraat 33 (Tues–Sun noon–5pm; €3.50; Ⓦ www.comeniusmuseum.nl). Jan Amos Komenski, his name latinized as Comenius, was a seventeenth-century philosopher, cartographer and educational reformer who was born in

Moravia, today part of the Czech Republic. A Protestant, he was expelled for his religious beliefs in 1621 and spent the next 36 years wandering round Europe preaching and teaching before finally settling in Amsterdam. The museum outlines Comenius' life and times and takes a stab at explaining his work, notably his plan to improve the Swedish educational system and his 1658 *Orbis Pictus* ("The World in Pictures"), the first-ever picture-book for children. Comenius was buried here in Naarden, and the museum incorporates his **mausoleum**, a rather remarkable affair with an ornamental screen and engraved glass panels decorated with scenes from his life, in what was once the chapel of a Franciscan convent. In the 1930s the Dutch authorities refused the Czechoslovak government's request for the repatriation of the philosopher's remains, and instead sold them the building (and the land it stood on) for the symbolic price of one guilder: the mausoleum remains a tiny slice of Czech territory to this day.

Practicalities

There are three **trains** hourly from Amsterdam Centraal Station to Naarden-Bussum train station, about 4km from the old town – Naarden has spread well beyond its original fortifications. Local buses link the train station with the old town. Naarden's old town is readily explored on foot – it's only 1km long and about 800m wide – and maps are available at the **VVV**, at the south end of the main Marktstraat at Adriaan Dortsmanplein 1B (Tues–Fri 10am–3pm & Sat 10am–2pm; ☎035/694 2836, ⊛www.vvvnaarden.nl). The VVV has a small supply of **rooms** in private houses (❶), though most of these are out of the old town. Naarden has lots of good places to eat. The *Brasserie Sans Doute* at Markstraat 33 is great for sandwiches and coffee, and the *Café De Doelen*, near the Grote Kerk at Markstraat 7, does good *uitsmijters*, sandwiches and more substantial meals. The *Fine* restaurant, Markstraat 66 (☎035/694 4868), a wine bar and fish restaurant with tables outside by the canal, and the wine bar *De Samaritaan*, at Markstraat 41 (☎035/632 1382), are good places for an early evening drink. However the best **restaurant** in town is probably *Het Arsenaal*, housed in the old arsenal shopping complex across the canal from here at Kooltjesbuurt 1 (Mon–Fri noon–4pm & daily from 6pm; ☎035/694 9148), where the well-known Dutch chef Paul Fagel serves excellent French food in both a restaurant and a more informal brasserie (Mon–Fri 10am–5pm).

Hilversum

Sprawling, leafy **HILVERSUM**, some 10km south of Naarden, is the main town of Het Gooi and a prosperous, commuter suburb with a population of around 90,000. Many locals love the place, but for the casual visitor, Hilversum is mainly of interest for its modern architecture – or to be precise the work of **Willem Marinus Dudok** (1884–1974), the director of public works and town architect for over thirty years. Hilversum possesses several dozen buildings by Dudok, who was much influenced by the American Frank Lloyd Wright, but pride of place among them goes to the **Raadhuis**, about 700m northwest of the train station at Dudokpark 1 (tours Sun 2pm; €7.50) – follow Stationstraat and then Melkpad from the station; it's a ten-minute walk. Dating from 1931, the structure has design based on a deceptively simple progression of straw-coloured blocks rising to a clock tower, with long, slender bricks giving it a strong horizontal emphasis. The interior is well worth seeing too: essentially a series of lines and boxes, its marble walls are margined with black, like a monochrome Mondrian painting, all coolly and immaculately proportioned. Dudok also designed the interior decorations, and though some have been altered, his style prevails, right down to the ashtrays and lights. The **Dudok Centrum**, in the basement of the Raadhuis (Wed & Sun noon–4.30pm; €3), presents an overview of Dudok's life and work.

Practicalities

Trains leave Amsterdam's Centraal Station twice an hour for Hilversum, and take about thirty minutes to get there. From Hilversum's **station**, it's a ten-minute walk to the **VVV** at Kerkbrink 6 (Tues–Sat 11am–5pm, Sun noon–5pm; T035/629 2810, W www.vvvhilversum.nl) – take Stationsstraat to the main Groest, turn left and then right onto Kerkstraat and follow it for around 200m. The VVV has a small supply of **rooms** in private houses (❶) and there are a couple of central chain **hotels** too – including the *Grand Hotel Gooiland*, at the far end of Groest in a Dudok-inspired 1930s building at Emmastraat 2 (T035/621 2331, W www.bestwestern.nl; ❷). But with Amsterdam so close, and connections to more interesting towns so easy, there's little reason to stay.

Laren

It's worth making the short trip from Hilversum to the village of **LAREN**, where the **Singer Museum** at Oude Drift 1 (Tues–Sun 11am–5pm; €12; W www.singerlaren.nl) houses an impressive collection of mainly late-nineteenth-century paintings by both local artists and the Hague School, as well as the French Barbizon painters and American Impressionists – in a beautiful, well-lit modern space. It was established in the 1950s by the widow of the American artist William Henry Singer and is well worth the fifteen-minute bus journey from Hilversum station – **bus** #109 runs half-hourly. The same bus also runs from outside Naarden–Bussum station.

Travel details

Trains

Alkmaar to: Haarlem (every 30min; 30min); Hoorn (every 30min; 25min).
Amsterdam CS to: Alkmaar (every 30min; 30min); Den Helder (every 30min; 1hr); Enkhuizen (every 30min; 1hr); Haarlem (every 15min; 15min); Hilversum (every 30min; 30min); Hoorn (every 30min; 40min); Koog-Zaandijk (every 15min; 15min); Naarden-Bussum (every 20min; 20min); Weesp (every 15min; 15min); Zaandam (every 15min; 10min).
Haarlem to: Alkmaar (every 30min; 30min); Hoorn (every 30min; 25min); Zandvoort (every 30min; 10min).
Hilversum to: Amersfoort (every 30min; 15min); Utrecht (every 20min; 20min).

Buses

Alkmaar to: Bergen (every 30min; hourly on Sun; 10min).

Amsterdam to: Edam (every 30min; 40min); Marken (every 30min; 30min); Volendam (every 30min; 30min).
Edam to: Hoorn (every 30min; 25min).
Haarlem to: Bloemendaal-aan-Zee (every 30min– 1hr; 15min).
Hoorn to: Medemblik (every 30min–1hr; 30–40min).
Marken to: Monnickendam (every 30min; 15min).
Monnickendam to: Volendam (every 30min; 15min).

Ferries

Den Helder to: Texel (hourly; 20min).
Enkhuizen to: Medemblik (April–Oct 1–3 daily; 1hr 30min); Stavoren (April–Sept 1–3 daily; 1hr 30min); Urk (mid-July to mid-Aug Mon–Sat 2 daily; 2hr 30min).
Marken to: Volendam (March–Oct daily 11am–5pm, every 30–45min; 25min).

Zuid-Holland and Utrecht

CHAPTER 3   # Highlights

✻ **Den Haag** Enjoyable city that boasts the Mauritshuis, arguably the country's most impressive art gallery. **See p.160**

✻ **Delft** A lovely little town and one-time home of Vermeer, with one of the prettiest market squares in the whole of the Netherlands. **See p.169**

✻ **Rotterdam** This gritty and boisterous port city has resurrected itself in flash modern style after extensive war damage, complete with its own Museumpark. **See p.182**

✻ **Gouda** Archetypal Dutch country town, home of the famous round cheese and a splendid set of stained-glass windows in St Janskerk. **See p.186**

✻ **Utrecht** Lively university town wound around a tight skein of narrow canals. **See p.194**

▲ Kinderdijk windmills

Zuid-Holland and Utrecht

Z uid-Holland (South Holland) is the most densely populated province of the Netherlands, incorporating a string of towns and cities that make up the bulk of what is commonly called the **Randstad** (literally "Rim-Town"). By and large, careful urban planning has succeeded in stopping this from becoming an amorphous conurbation, however, and each town has preserved a pronounced identity. A short hop from Amsterdam is **Leiden**, a university town par excellence, with an antique centre latticed by canals and dotted with fine old buildings. Moving on, **Den Haag** (The Hague) was once a humdrum government town, but has jazzed itself up and is now a very likeable city with a string of good museums and an appealing bar and restaurant scene. Neighbouring **Delft** is a much smaller place, with just 100,000 inhabitants, but it possesses an extremely pretty centre replete with handsome seventeenth-century buildings, in stark contrast to the rough and tumble of big-city **Rotterdam**, the world's biggest port, where an adventurous city council has stacked up a string of first-rate attractions, from fine art through to harbour tours. It's a short journey inland from here to **Gouda**, a good-looking country town historically famed for its cheese market, and to the somnambulant charms of rural **Oudewater**. Back on the coast, **Dordrecht** marks the southern edge of the Randstad and is of some mild interest as an ancient port and for its location, within easy striking distance of the windmills of the **Kinderdijk** and the creeks and marshes of the **Biesbosch**. Finally, the province of **Utrecht** is distinguished by its capital city, Utrecht, a sprawling city with a dramatic history and a bustling, youthful centre.

Historically, Zuid-Holland is part of what was once simply **Holland**, the richest and most influential province in the country. Throughout the Golden Age, Holland dominated the political, social and cultural life of the Republic, overshadowing its neighbours, their economies dwarfed by its success. There are constant reminders of this pre-eminence in the province's buildings: elaborate town halls proclaim civic importance and even the usually sombre Calvinist **churches** allow themselves decorative excesses – the later windows of Gouda's Janskerk being a case in point. Many of the great Dutch **painters** either came from, or worked here, too – Rembrandt, Vermeer, Jan Steen – a tradition that continued into the nineteenth century with the paintings of the Hague School. All the towns offer good **museums** and galleries, most notably The Hague's

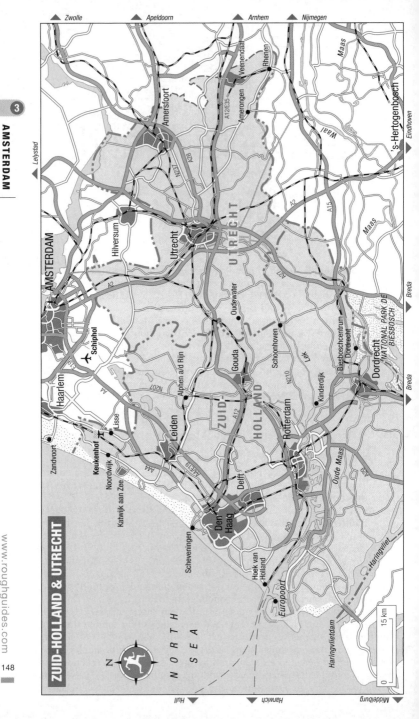

ZUID-HOLLAND & UTRECHT

Zwolle   Apeldoorn   Arnhem   Nijmegen

Lelystad

AMSTERDAM

Schiphol

Haarlem

Zandvoort

Lisse

Noordwijk

Keukenhof

Katwijk aan Zee

Leiden

Scheveningen

Den Haag

Hoek van Holland

Europoort

Hilversum

Utrecht

Alphen a/d Rijn

N207

Gouda

Oudewater

Schoonhoven

N210

Kinderdijk

Delft

Rotterdam

ZUID-HOLLAND

UTRECHT

Amersfoort

Amerongen

Veenendaal

Rhenen

A12/E35

A28

A27

A2

LEK

Lek

A15

Schoonhoven

Biesboschcentrum Dordrecht

Dordrecht

NATIONAL PARK DE BIESBOSCH

Maas

Waal

Waal

's-Hertogenbosch

Eindhoven

Breda

Breda

A20

A29

Oude Maas

Haringvliet

Haringvlietdam

N O R T H
S E A

N

0   15 km

Hull   Harwich   Middelburg

Mauritshuis and Rotterdam's Boijmans Van Beuningen. In addition, the coastal cities – especially Leiden and Den Haag – are only a short bus or tram ride from the wide sandy **beaches** of the North Sea coast, while the pancake-flat Randstad landscape is at least brightened by rainbow flashes of **bulbfields** in spring with the **Keukenhof gardens**, near Leiden, having the finest display.

A fast and efficient rail network makes travelling around Zuid-Holland extremely easy, and where the trains fizzle out, buses take over.

Leiden and around

LEIDEN, just twenty minutes by train from Amsterdam Schiphol airport, is a lively and energetic city of around 120,000 souls that makes for an enjoyable day trip or overnight stay. At its heart, the city's antique, sometimes careworn, centre is a maze of narrow lanes that wriggle and worm their way around a complicated network of canals, one of which marks the line of the medieval walls. It's all very appealing – and appealingly unfussy – with Leiden's multitude of bars and cafés kept afloat by the thirsty students of the city's one great institution, its **university**, one of Europe's most prestigious seats of learning. As for specific sights, top billing goes to the magnificent ancient Egyptian collection at the **Rijksmuseum van Oudheden** (National Museum of Antiquities) and the seventeenth-century Dutch paintings of the **Stedelijk Museum de Lakenhal**, though, perhaps surprisingly, given that this was his home town, the museum is very short of Rembrandts. Leiden is also within easy striking distance of the Dutch bulbfields and the showpiece **Keukenhof gardens** as well as the amenable North Sea resort of **Katwijk-aan-Zee** and its long sandy beach.

Some history

It may well have been the **Romans** who founded Leiden as a forward base on an important trade route running behind the dunes, but, whatever the truth, it was certainly fortified in the ninth century when a local lord built a castle here on an artificial mound. Flemish weavers migrated to Leiden in the fourteenth century and thereafter the town prospered as a minor cloth-making centre, but things didn't really take off until the foundation of its university in 1575. It was **William the Silent** who chose Leiden to be the home of the university as a reward for the city's bravery during the rebellion against Spain: Leiden had declared for William in 1572, but a Habsburg army besieged the city in October 1573. The siege, which lasted a whole year, was a desperate affair during which hundreds of city folk starved to death, but William the Silent finally sailed to the rescue on October 3, 1574, cutting through the dykes around the town and vanquishing the Spaniards in one fell swoop. The event is still commemorated with an annual fair, fireworks and the consumption of two traditional dishes: herring and white bread, which the fleet brought with them, and *hutspot*, a vegetable and potato stew, a cauldron of which was found simmering in the abandoned Spanish camp outside the walls.

Arrival, information and accommodation

Leiden's ultra-modern **train station** is next to the **bus station** on the northwest edge of town, a five-minute walk from the Beestenmarkt at the west end of the centre. Halfway between is the **VVV**, Stationsweg 2 (Mon 11am–6.30pm, Tues–Fri 9.30am–6.30pm, Sat 10am–4pm; April–Aug also Sun

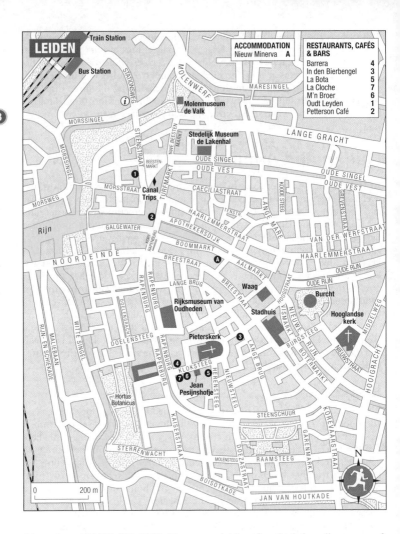

11am–3pm; ☎0900 222 2333, ⓦwww.vvvleiden.nl), which has all manner of local information, including city maps and brochures, as well as an excellent range of walking and touring maps covering most of the country.

Of the town's **hotels**, easily the most appealing is the *Nieuw Minerva*, a cosy, very Dutch hotel that occupies a sequence of old canal-side houses in the centre at Boommarkt 23 (☎071/512 6358, ⓦwww.nieuwminerva.nl; ❸). The tiled breakfast room is particularly pleasant and all the guest rooms are spacious and comfortable, in an undemanding sort of way, though the "honeymoon room" (❻) is up a notch, boasting a four-poster bed and fancy drapes.

The Town

The obvious place to start an exploration of the centre is the **Beestenmarkt**, a large and really rather plain open space that's long been a major meeting point.

The square is also the starting point for **canal trips** around the centre – an enjoyable way to spend forty minutes (March–Sept 3–5 daily; €6). From here, it's a hop and a jump to **Rapenburg**, a gentle, curving canal lined by some of Leiden's grandest mansions.

Rijksmuseum van Oudheden

Down along the Rapenburg, at no. 28, is the town's most important museum, the **Rijksmuseum van Oudheden** (National Museum of Antiquities; Tues–Sun 10am–5pm, plus Mon 10am–5pm in school hols; €8.50; ⓦ www.rmo .nl), whose three floors hold extensive Egyptian and classical collections and also host an ambitious programme of temporary exhibitions. On the ground floor, the museum kicks off in style with the squat and sturdy **Taffeh Temple**, a present from the Egyptian government. It was gifted in gratitude for Dutch help with the 1960s UNESCO excavations that saved scores of ancient monuments from the rising waters of the Nile following the construction of the Aswan dam. Dating back to the first century AD, the Taffeh Temple was originally part of a fortress that guarded the southern border of the Roman province of Egypt. Initially, it was dedicated to Isis, the goddess of love and magic, but in the fourth century it was turned into a Christian church.

On the same floor is the rest of the **Egyptian collection**, which includes wall reliefs, statues, stele and sarcophagi from a variety of tombs and temples, plus a set of mummies as complete as you're likely to see outside Egypt. Particular highlights include magnificent stele from the temple at Abydos and the exceptionally well-preserved double sculpture of Maya and Merit, Maya being the minister of finance under Tutankhamen, Merit his wife. The next floor up exhibits oodles of classical **Greek and Roman sculptures**, including stolid busts, statues and friezes from imperial Rome as well as a scattering of Etruscan artefacts. Moving on, the top floor displays a **Netherlands archeological section**, which has a first-rate selection of Roman stone altars and inscribed tombstones retrieved from the waters of Zeeland in the 1970s.

Hortus Botanicus

Further along Rapenburg, at no. 73, a three-sided courtyard complex includes – on the left – the building that became the university's first home, after previously being part of a medieval monastery. Through the courtyard is the **Hortus Botanicus** (daily: April–Oct 10am–6pm; Nov–March 10am–4pm; €5; ⓦ www .hortusleiden.nl), lushly planted and subtly landscaped botanical gardens that stretch along the Witte Singel canal. Planted in 1587, this is one of the oldest botanical gardens in Europe, a mixture of carefully tended beds of shrubs, ancient gnarled trees and hothouses full of tropical foliage.

Pieterskerk

On the east side of Rapenburg, across from the botanical gardens, lies the network of narrow streets that once constituted the medieval town and now converges on the Gothic **Pieterskerk** (daily 1.30–4pm; free), Leiden's principal church. Deconsecrated now, it has an empty warehouse-like feel, but among the fixtures that remain are a simple and beautiful Renaissance rood screen and a host of memorials to the sundry notables buried here – including one to John Robinson (1575–1625), leader of the Pilgrim Fathers. Robinson lived in a house on the site of what is now the **Jean Pesijnshofje** at Kloksteeg 21, right beside the church – look out for the plaque. A curate in England at the turn of the seventeenth century, he was suspended from preaching in 1604, later fleeing with his congregation to pursue his Puritanism in the more amenable atmosphere of Calvinist Holland. Settling in Leiden, Robinson acted as pastor to growing numbers, but even here he found himself at odds with the religious establishment. In 1620, one hundred of his followers – the **"Pilgrim Fathers"** – sailed via Plymouth for the untrammelled wilderness of America, though Robinson died before he could join them; he's buried in the church.

The Stadhuis and the Waag

From the church, it's a short stroll east to **Breestraat**, which marks the southern edge of Leiden's present commercial centre, but is undistinguished except for the **Stadhuis**, an imposing edifice whose Renaissance facade is a copy of the late-sixteenth-century original destroyed by fire in 1929. Behind the Stadhuis, the canals that cut Leiden's centre into pocket-sized segments converge at the busiest point in town, tiny **Hoogstraat**, the focus of a vigorous general **market** on Wednesdays and Saturdays (9am–5pm). Around Hoogstraat, a tangle of narrow bridges is flanked by a number of fetching buildings, ranging from overblown Art Nouveau department stores to modest terrace houses. Here also, on Vismarkt, is the **Waag**, built to a design by Pieter Post (1608–69) and fronted with a naturalistic frieze showing a merchant watching straining labourers.

The Hooglandsekerk and the Burcht

Stretching southeast from Vismarkt, the **Nieuwe Rijn** is one of the town's prettiest canals, the first of its several bridges topped off by a matching pair of Neoclassical porticoes dating from 1825. Turn left along Burgsteeg and then right at the end for the **Hooglandsekerk** on Nieuwstraat (mid-May to mid-Sept Mon 1–5pm, Tues–Fri 11am–3.30pm, Sat 11am–4pm; free), a light and lofty Gothic structure built in stages over a couple of hundred years. The church holds a monument to Pieter van der Werff, the heroic burgomaster of Leiden at the time of the 1573–74 siege. When the situation became so desperate that the people were all for giving up, the burgomaster, no doubt remembering the massacre at Haarlem (see p.109), offered up his own body to be eaten. The invitation was declined, but it inspired new determination in the town's flagging citizens.

Doubling back to the end of Burgsteeg, go through the gateway and you'll soon pass the steps up to the top of the **Burcht** (daily 10am–10pm; free), the artificial mound where Leiden's first castle stood. The castle is long gone and the circular stone wall which occupies the site today is disappointingly paltry, but the view over the city centre is first-rate. At the far end of the alley is the **Oude Rijn** canal, on the other side of which lies the blandly pedestrian **Haarlemmerstraat**, the town's main shopping street.

The Stedelijk Museum de Lakenhal

From Haarlemmerstraat, it's a short walk north to Leiden's **Stedelijk Museum de Lakenhal** (Tues–Fri 10am–5pm, Sat & Sun noon–5pm; €4; Ⓦwww.lakenhal.nl), housed in the former Cloth Hall at Oude Singel 32. The museum's ground floor holds mixed rooms of furniture, silver, tiles, glass and ceramics as well as a healthy sample of local sixteenth- and seventeenth-century paintings, including examples of the work of Jacob van Swanenburgh (first teacher of the young Rembrandt), Jan Lievens (with whom Rembrandt shared a studio), and Gerrit Dou (1613–75), who is well represented by his exquisite *Astrologer*. Rembrandt's first pupil, Dou began by imitating his master but soon developed his own style, pioneering the Leiden tradition of small, minutely detailed pictures of enamel-like smoothness. There's also Lucas van Leyden's (1494–1533) alarming and spectacularly unsuccessful *Last Judgement* triptych, several paintings devoted to the siege of 1574 and the heroics of burgomaster van der Werff, plus two canvases by the earthy Jan Steen (1626–79) and a splendid *View of Leiden* by Jan van Goyen (1596–1656). **Rembrandt** (1606–69) himself, though a native of Leiden, is poorly represented; he left his home town at the tender age of 14, and although he returned in 1625, he was off again six years later, this time to settle permanently in Amsterdam. Only a handful of his Leiden paintings survive, but there's one here, *Agamemnon before Palamedes*, a stilted and rather unsuccessful rendition of the classical tale, painted in 1626.

The other floors of the museum are of cursory interest only: the next floor up is devoted to Leiden textiles, the next is used for temporary exhibitions, and the top floor has a series of modest displays on the town's history.

The Molenmuseum de Valk

Heading west along Oude Singel from the Stedelijk Museum, turn right at the end and it's a couple of hundred metres to the **Molenmuseum de Valk** (Falcon Windmill Museum; Tues–Sat 10am–5pm, Sun 1–5pm; €3), a restored grain mill that is the last survivor of the twenty-odd windmills built on the town's outer fortifications in the eighteenth century. On the ground floor are the miller's musty living quarters, furnished in simple late-nineteenth-century style, and then it's up the stairs for a short video recounting the history of Dutch windmills. Beyond, up the stairs again, are a series of displays that give the low down on the hard life of the average Dutch miller, who had to be incredibly nimble to survive if the cramped conditions here are anything to go by. The miller was rarely paid in cash, but took a scoop from each sack instead. He was supposed to pay tax on this – some windmills even had a taxman's kiosk next door – but evasion was widespread and many windmills, including this one, had a so-called smuggler's cupboard where the miller could hide the proceeds.

Eating and drinking

Leiden's crowded centre heaves with inexpensive **cafés** and **café-bars**, and there's a cluster of top-flight **restaurants** too. Many of the more interesting places are concentrated in the immediate vicinity of Pieterskerk, among the ancient brick houses that make up this especially pretty part of the city.

Barrera Rapenburg 56. A fashionable café-bar and student favourite, with a good beer menu and a pavement terrace. Opposite the entrance to the Hortus Botanicus. Mon–Sat 10am–1am, Sun 11am–1am.
In den Bierbengel Langebrug 71 ☎071/514 8056. Inhabiting an old building in an attractive corner of the town centre, this popular, informal restaurant has a short but well-chosen menu covering all the Dutch basics. Mains around €20. Daily from 5–10pm.
La Bota Herensteeg 9 ☎071/514 6340. Popular, very informal restaurant serving up some of the best-value Dutch food in town as well as an excellent range of beers. Mains from €12. Daily 5–10pm.
La Cloche Kloksteeg 3 ☎071/512 3053. Small and smart French restaurant with a well-chosen

menu featuring local ingredients – try the Texel lamb. Mains €20–25. Daily 5.30–10.30pm.
M'n Broer Kloksteeg 7 ☎071/512 5024. Agreeable, low-key café-restaurant kitted out in traditional style and offering a tasty range of light snacks and full meals, with Franco-Italian dishes high on the agenda. Main courses €14–18, veggie options €12. Mon–Fri 6–10pm, Sat & Sun 5–10pm.
Oudt Leyden Steenstraat 49 ☎071/513 3144. Pancake specialist on the edge of the Beestenmarkt, whose traditional, wood-panelled interior – and giant Delftware plates – draws in the day-trippers. Delicious pancakes for as little €6. Daily 11.30am–9.30pm.
Petterson Café Turfmarkt. Modern, floating café, where the food is routine, if perfectly OK, but the views of the boats and barges on the busy Galgewater compensate. Daily 9am–8pm.

The Keukenhof gardens

If you're after bulbs, then make a beeline for the bulb growers' showcase, the **Keukenhof gardens** (mid-March to mid-May daily 8am–7.30pm; €14, Ⓦ www.keukenhof.com), located on the edge of the little town of **LISSE**, beside the N208 about 15km north of Leiden. The largest flower gardens in the world, dating back to 1949, the Keukenhof was designed by a group of prominent bulb growers to convert people to the joys of growing flowers from bulbs in their own gardens. Literally the "kitchen garden", its site is the former estate of a fifteenth-century countess, who used to grow herbs and vegetables for her dining table. Several million flowers are on show for their full flowering period, complemented, in case of especially harsh winters, by thousands of square metres of glasshouse holding indoor displays. You could easily spend a whole day here, swooning with the sheer abundance of it all, but to get the best of it you need to come early, before the tour buses descend on the place. There are several restaurants in the grounds, and a network of well-marked footpaths explores every horticultural nook and cranny.

To get to the Keukenhof from Leiden, take **bus** #54 from the bus station direct to the main entrance (every 15min; 30min). To get there from Haarlem, the easiest way is to take the train to Leiden (every 20min; 20min) and then the bus.

Katwijk-aan-Zee

Leiden is just a few kilometres from the North Sea coast, where the prime target is **KATWIJK-AAN-ZEE**, an amenable little resort whose low-slung houses string along behind a wide sandy beach, with a pristine expanse of beach and dune beckoning beyond – and stretching south towards Scheveningen

The bulbfields

The pancake-flat fields stretching north from Leiden towards Haarlem (see p.109) are the heart of the Dutch **bulbfields**, whose bulbs and blooms support a billion-euro industry and some ten thousand growers, as well as attracting tourists in their droves. Bulbs have flourished here since the late sixteenth century, when one **Carolus Clusius**, a Dutch botanist and one-time gardener to the Habsburg emperor, brought the first **tulip bulb** over from Vienna, where it had – in its turn – been brought from Asia Minor by an Austrian aristocrat. The tulip flourished in Holland's sandy soil and was so highly prized that it fuelled a massive **speculative bubble**. At the height of the boom – in the mid-1630s – bulbs were commanding extraordinary prices: the artist Jan van Goyen paid 1900 guilders and two paintings for ten rare bulbs, while a bag of one hundred bulbs was swapped for a coach and horses. When the government finally intervened in 1636, the industry returned to reality with a bang, leaving hundreds of investors ruined – much to the satisfaction of the country's Calvinist ministers, who had long railed against such excesses.

Other types of bulbs apart from the tulip have also been introduced, and nowadays the spring flowering season begins in mid-March with **crocuses**, followed by **daffodils** and yellow **narcissi** in late March, **hyacinths** and **tulips** from mid-April through to May, and **irises** and **gladioli** in August. The views of the bulbfields from any of the trains heading southwest from Schiphol airport can often be sufficient in themselves, the fields divided into stark geometric blocks of pure colour, but, with your own transport – either bicycle or car – you can take in their particular beauty by way of special routes marked by hexagonal signposts; local VVVs sell pamphlets describing the routes in detail. You could also drop by the bulb growers' showpiece, the **Keukenhof** gardens. Bear in mind also that there are any number of local flower festivals and parades in mid- to late April; every local VVV has the details of these too.

(see p.168). Here and there, a row of cottages recalls the time when Katwijk was a busy fishing village, but there are no real sights as such with the possible exception of a chunky, old **lighthouse** by the beach on the southern edge of the resort, and the Katwijk sluices, on the north side of Katwijk. Completed in 1807, this chain of sluice gates regulates the flow of the Oude Rijn as it approaches the sea. Around high tide, the gates are closed, and when they are reopened the pressure of the accumulated water brushes aside the sand deposited at the mouth of the river. This simple system has effectively fixed the course of the Oude Rijn, which for centuries had been continually diverted by its sand deposits, flooding the surrounding area with depressing regularity.

Katwijk is a thirty-minute **bus** ride from Leiden bus station (every 15min, Sun every 30min). The resort's **VVV** is on the main street, a short walk from the beach at Voorstraat 41 (Mon–Fri 10am–5.30pm, Sat 9.30am–5pm; T071/407 5444, Wwww.vvvkatwijk.nl). They have a supply of **rooms** in private houses (❶–❷), as well as a list of hotels and pensions, but even they may struggle to find a vacancy in July and August.

Den Haag

DEN HAAG (The Hague) is markedly different from any other Dutch city. In a country built on municipal independence and munificence, it's been the focus of national institutions since the sixteenth century, but it is not – curiously enough – the capital, which is Amsterdam. Frequently disregarded until the development of central government in the 1800s, Den Haag's older buildings are a comparatively subdued and modest collection, with little of Amsterdam's flamboyance. Indeed, the majority of the canal houses are demurely classical and exude that sense of sedate prosperity which prompted Matthew Arnold's harsh estimation of 1859: "I never saw a city where the well-to-do classes seemed to have given the whole place so much of their own air of wealth, finished cleanliness, and comfort; but I never saw one, either, in which my heart would so have sunk at the thought of living."

Fortunately, much has changed since Arnold's days. His "well-to-do classes" – now mostly diplomats and top-flight executives – are still in evidence, but parts of the centre are now festooned with slick government high-rises and, more promisingly, Den Haag holds a slew of lively and reasonably priced bars and restaurants. A creative city council has done much to jazz the city up, too, organizing a lively programme of concerts and events, and Den Haag boasts a veritable battery of outstanding museums, principally the wonderful Dutch paintings of the **Mauritshuis**, and more modern works of art at the **Gemeentemuseum**. Den Haag is also a brief tram ride from **Scheveningen**, a sprawling kiss-me-quick resort with a long, sandy beach.

Arrival and information

The city has two **train stations**: Den Haag HS (Hollands Spoor) and Den Haag CS (Centraal Station). Of the two, Den Haag CS is the more convenient, sited a five- to ten-minute walk from the town centre; Den Haag HS is 1km to the south. There are frequent rail services between the two or you can catch tram #1 from Den Haag HS direct to the centre.

Den Haag's main **VVV** is bang in the centre of the city, a five- to ten-minute walk west from Den Haag CS at Hofweg 1 (Mon–Fri 10am–6pm, Sat 10am–5pm, Sun noon–5pm; T0900 340 3505, Wwww.denhaag.com). They provide a wide

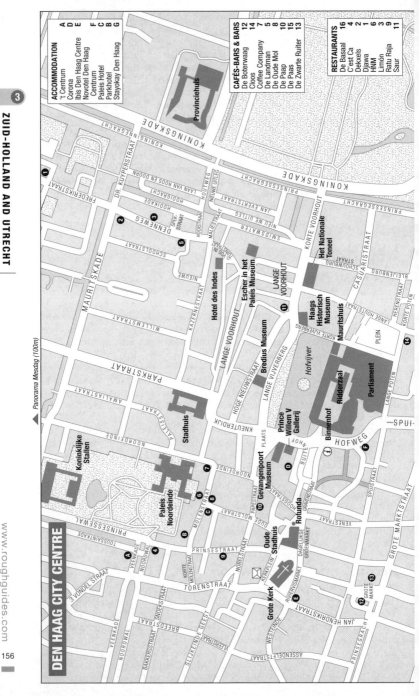

DEN HAAG CITY CENTRE

▲ Panorama Mesdag (100m)

ACCOMMODATION	
't Centrum	A
Corona	D
Ibis Den Haag Centre	E
Novotel Den Haag	F
Centrum	C
Paleis Hotel	B
Parkhotel	B
Stayokay Den Haag	G

CAFÉS-BARS & BARS	
De Boterwaag	12
Cloos	14
Coffee Company	7
De Landman	5
De Oude Mol	10
De Paap	8
De Paas	15
De Zwarte Ruiter	13

RESTAURANTS	
De Basaal	16
C'est Ca	4
Dekxels	2
Djawa	1
HNM	6
Limón	9
Ratu Raja	3
Saur	11

Provinciehuis

Het Nationale Toneel

Escher in het Paleis Museum

Hotel des Indes

Haags Historisch Museum

Bredius Museum

Mauritshuis

Hofvijver

Stadhuis

Koninklijke Stallen

Paleis Noordeinde

Prince Willem V Gallerij

Ridderzaal

Binnenhof

Parliament

Gevangenpoort Museum

Rotunda

Oude Stadhuis

Grote Kerk

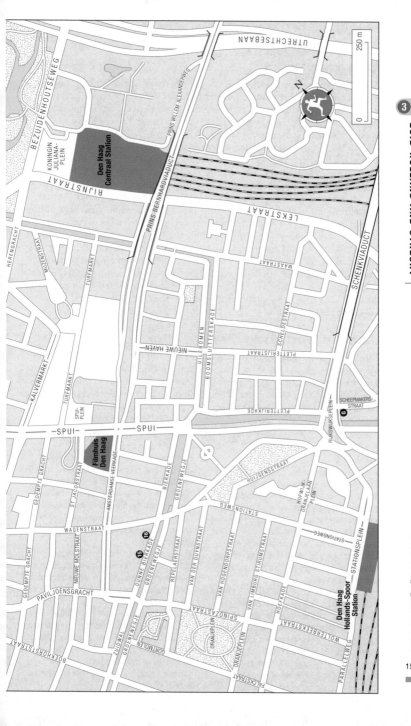

range of information on the city and its surroundings, sell public transport tickets and passes, will reserve accommodation and stock several free listings magazines.

City transport

Most of the city's principal sights are in – or within easy walking distance of – the centre, but this is the country's third-largest city and you may need to catch a **tram or bus** if you're visiting the more outlying attractions. The twin hubs of the tram system, which covers most of where you're likely to want to go, are Centraal Station and the Spui, in the centre of town just south of the VVV; there's also a mini-metro, where some of the trams go underground, to the west of Centraal Station underneath Grote Marktstraat and Prinsegracht.

The city and its immediate environs are divided into twelve or so zones, shown on the public transport map issued free by the VVV. The standard **ticket** is the *strippenkaart*, which you insert into the appropriate franking machine, cancelling one strip per passenger and one for every zone crossed: a journey from Den Haag CS to Scheveningen, for example, takes three strips per passenger per journey. The *strippenkaart* is available at train stations, many news-agents and the VVV. Currently, a two-strip *strippenkaart* costs €1.60, three-strips €2.40, and a fifteen-strip €7.30. To avoid all this stamping, go for the VVV's *dagkaart* (day-card; €6.40, €8.80 with Delft), which grants unlimited use of the system for a day. Finally, tram #1 links Scheveningen and Den Haag with Delft, an alternative to – and slightly cheaper than – the train. **Bike rental** is available at both train stations too.

Accommodation

Den Haag has a good supply of central **hotels**, with many of the more comfort-able (and sometimes luxurious) dotted near the Binnenhof, just to the west of Den Haag CS. Advance reservations are a good idea especially during the week, when business folk arrive in numbers, pushing up hotel prices; weekend rates are usually around thirty percent cheaper. The VVV can help you find a hotel room in either Den Haag or the neighbouring resort of Scheveningen (see p.168) for a small fee; they have a dedicated accommodation booking line ☎070/338 5800.

Hotels

Carlton Ambassador Hotel Sophialaan 2 ☎070/363 0363, ⓦwww.carlton.nl/ambassador. Deluxe, executive four-star hotel with every mod con you can imagine and then some, located in an immaculately maintained nineteenth-century mansion in a smart residential avenue about 1km north of the centre. The rooms are large, well appointed and all decorated in plush, period style. Banquet-like breakfasts included and there's an open-air terrace. ❺

't Centrum Veenkade 5 ☎070/346 3657, ⓦwww .hotelhetcentrum.nl. Small and unassuming two-star hotel in a three-storey terrace house just west of the Paleis Noordeinde. All the rooms are en suite and decorated in neat modern style. ❷

Hotel Corona Buitenhof 39 ☎070/363 7930, ⓦwww.corona.nl. In a great location just across the street from the Binnenhof, this smart chain hotel has large and extremely comfortable double

rooms at a rack rate of €230, but weekend discounts and special deals are often available. ❼

Ibis Den Haag Centre Jan Hendrikstraat 10 ☎070/318 4318, ⓦwww.ibishotels.com. Few would say that Ibis hotels have much character, but they are reliable and inexpensive – and this one, with 200 rooms, has a handy central location too. ❷

Novotel Den Haag Centrum Hofweg 5 ☎070/364 8846, ⓦwww.novotel.com. Efficient, four-star chain hotel with very comfortable rooms right in the centre of things, across the street from the Binnenhof. ❹

Paleis Hotel Molenstraat 26 ☎070/362 4621, ⓦwww.paleishotel.nl. This charming, privately owned hotel is in an old, mostly eighteenth-century town house. Each of the twenty bedrooms is decorated with style and panache – antique furniture, French fabrics and so forth. Great central location as well. ❺

Parkhotel Molenstraat 53 ☎070/362 4371, ⓦ www.parkhoteldenhaag.nl. Smart and immaculately maintained chain hotel in a handy central location. From the outside it doesn't look anything special, but the interior is graced by all sorts of superb Art Deco flourishes. The hotel has over one hundred well-appointed rooms decorated in brisk modern style. Some rooms overlook the Paleis Noordeinde gardens next door. ❹
Residenz Sweelinckplein 35 ☎070/364 6190, ⓦ www.residenz.nl. In a creatively remodelled, late-nineteenth-century villa, this boutique hotel is slick and smart in equal measure with shades of grey, brown and white to the fore. Sweelinckplein

itself is an attractive, garden square to the north of the centre near the Laan van Meerdervoort boulevard. ❻, weekends ❹

Hostel
Stayokay Den Haag Scheepmakersstraat 27 ☎070/315 78 88, ⓦ www.stayokay.com. This large and comfortable HI hostel is located just 400m east of – and across the canal from – Den Haag HS station. A good range of facilities includes luggage and bicycle storage, bike rental, a café, internet terminals and a small library. Doubles ❶; €26.50 for a dorm bed, breakfast included.

The city centre

The prettiest spot in Den Haag – and the logical place to start a visit – is the north side of the **Hofvijver** (Court Pond), a placid lakelet that mirrors the attractive, vaguely Ruritanian symmetries of the extensive **Binnenhof** (Inner Court), the one-time home of the country's bicameral parliament. The Binnenhof is the very heart of the city and it's also metres from its prime attraction, the **Mauritshuis** art gallery. A string of other, lesser museums occupy the handsome mansions that spread north of the Binnenhof, the pick of them being the **Bredius Museum**, with a second superb collection of fine art. To the west of the Binnenhof, by contrast, are the narrow streets of the old centre, where the key building is the **Grote Kerk**.

The Binnenhof

The **Binnenhof** (open access) occupies the site of the medieval castle where Den Haag began. The first fortress was raised by William II, Count of Holland (1227–56) – hence the city's official name, 's Gravenhage, literally "Count's Hedge", but more precisely "Count's Domain". William's descendants became the region's most powerful family, simultaneously acting as Stadholders (effectively provincial governors) of most of the seven United Provinces, which rebelled against the Habsburgs in the sixteenth century. In due course, one of the family, Prince Maurice of Orange-Nassau (1567–1625), established his main residence in Den Haag, which had effectively become the country's political capital. As the embodiment of central rather than municipal power, the Binnenhof was at times feted, at others virtually ignored, until the nineteenth century when Den Haag officially shared political capital status with Brussels during the uneasy times of the United Kingdom of the Netherlands (1815–30). Thereafter it became the seat of government and home to a functioning legislature.

The lack of prestige in the low-slung brick buildings of the Binnenhof long irked Dutch parliamentarians and finally, in 1992, they moved into a flashy new extension next door. Without the politicians, the original Binnenhof became somewhat redundant, but it's still an eye-pleasing architectural ensemble, comprising a broadly rectangular complex built around two connecting courtyards. The main sight as such is the **Ridderzaal** (Knights' Hall), an imposing twin-turreted structure that looks distinctly church-like, but was built as a banqueting hall for Count William's son, Floris V, in the thirteenth century. Now used for state occasions, it's been a courtroom, market and stable, and so often renovated that little of the original remains, but there are regular guided **tours**

▲ The Binnenhof

leaving from the information office round the side at Binnenhof 8 (Mon–Sat 10am–4pm, last tour 3.45pm; 30min; €3; ⓦ www.binnenhofbezoek.nl).

The Mauritshuis

To the immediate east of the Binnenhof, the **Mauritshuis**, Korte Vijverberg 8 (Tues–Sat 10am–5pm, Sun 11am–5pm; April–Aug also Mon 10am–5pm; €10.50 including audioguide, €3 extra for exhibitions; ⓣ070/302 3435, ⓦ www.mauritshuis.nl), is located in an elegant seventeenth-century mansion. The gallery is famous for its eclectic collection of Flemish and Dutch paintings from the fifteenth to the eighteenth century, based on the hoard accumulated by Prince William V of Orange (1748–1806). The collection has examples of the work of all the major Dutch artists, but the Mauritshuis runs an ambitious programme of temporary exhibitions, so quite what paintings are on display – and in which room – varies enormously. Neither are all the rooms numbered, except on the free map issued at reception, which can be confusing, though the museum is not large – just two medium-sized floors. The **museum entrance** is on the east side of the building in the basement; from here, you head up the stairs to reach the **ground floor**, where the medieval paintings are usually displayed; the later paintings either share the same floor or are exhibited on the **upper floor**. The description below focuses on those key paintings from the permanent collection you can expect to see. Finally, the museum shop sells an excellent guidebook detailing the permanent collection for €14 and you can book your own one-hour **guided tour** with the Mauritshuis for €50.

Memling, van der Weyden and Matsys

On the **ground floor**, the room to the east of the old front doors usually holds a small but exquisite sample of late medieval Flemish art. Highlights include *Portrait of a Man* by **Hans Memling** (1440–94), a typically observant work, right down to the scar on the nose, and *The Lamentation of Christ* by **Rogier van der Weyden** (1400–64), a harrowing picture of death and sorrow. Weyden has Christ's head hanging down toward the earth, surrounded by the faces of the mourners, each with a particular expression of anguish and pain. Here also should be *Descent from the Cross* by **Quentin Matsys** (1465–1530), in which Christ's suffering body, bent under the weight of the cross, is contrasted with the grinning, taunting onlookers behind. An influential figure, Matsys was the first major artist to work in Antwerp, where he was made a Master of the Guild in 1519.

Van Hemessen, Cranach, Avercamp and Holbein

Proceeding in an anticlockwise direction, through a series of rooms on either side of the Italianate dining room, you should soon spy a giant allegorical canvas by **Jan Sanders van Hemessen** (1500–66) and **Lucas Cranach the Younger**'s (1515–86) piercing *Man with a Red Beard*. There are also the busy, stick-like figures of *Winter Scene* by **Hendrick Avercamp** (1585–1634), an artist from Kampen, and two fine canvases by **Hans Holbein the Younger** (1497–1543): a striking *Portrait of Robert Cheeseman*, where all the materials – the fur collar, the falcon's feathers and the cape – seem to take on the appropriate texture; and a *Portrait of Jane Seymour*, one of several pictures commissioned by Henry VIII, who sent Holbein abroad to paint matrimonial candidates. Holbein's vibrant technique was later to land him in hot water: an over-flattering portrait of Anne of Cleves swayed Henry into an unhappy marriage with his "Flanders mare" which was to last only six months.

Brouwer and Rubens

The gallery holds three paintings by **Adriaen Brouwer** (1605–38), two of which – *Fighting Peasants* and *Inn with Drunken Peasants* – are typical of his style, with thick, rough brushstrokes recording contemporary Flemish lowlife. Brouwer could approach this subject with some authority, as he spent most of his brief life in either a tavern or a prison. **Peter Paul Rubens** (1577–1640), the acclaimed painter and diplomat, was a contemporary of Brouwer, though the two could hardly be more dissimilar. Rubens moved in much more elevated circles and his *Portrait of Michael Ophovius*, a leading churchman, is a rather formal, somewhat statuesque work, not nearly as intriguing as the dappled, evocative shade and light of his *Old Woman and a Boy with Candles*.

Van Dyck and Jordaens

Rubens' chief assistant was **Anthony van Dyck** (1599–1641), a portrait specialist who found fame at the court of the English king Charles I. His *Peeter Stevens of Antwerp* and *Anna Wake* are good examples of his tendency to flatter and ennoble – which doubtless helped his career prospects no end. Also demonstrating the influence of Rubens are two canvases by **Jacob Jordaens** (1593–1678), the more robust of which is the *Adoration of the Shepherds*.

Rembrandt

The Mauritshuis owns no fewer than twelve paintings by **Rembrandt** (1606–69) and these are almost always exhibited on the **upper floor**. Pride of place among them goes to the *Anatomy Lesson of Dr Tulp*, the artist's first commission in Amsterdam, dating from 1632. The peering pose of the students who lean over the corpse solved the problem of emphasis falling on the body rather than the subjects of the portrait, who were members of the surgeons' guild. Hopefully Tulp's skills as an anatomist were better than his medical advice, which included the recommendation that his patients drink fifty cups of tea a day. Very different is Rembrandt's hauntingly gloomy *Saul and David*, completed when Rembrandt was in his 40s, and his disturbingly flaky *Homer*.

Potter, Hals, Ter Borch and Houckgeest

Look out for *Young Bull* by **Paulus Potter** (1625–54), a massive canvas that includes the smallest of details, from the exact hang of the testicles to the dung at the rear end, while **Frans Hals** (1582–1666) chimes in with the broad brush-strokes of *Laughing Boy* – a far cry from the restrained style he was forced to adopt in his famous paintings of the Haarlem gentry. By contrast, **Gerard Ter Borch** (1617–81) concentrated on domestic scenes with a sentimental undertow, as in the *Lice Hunt* and the *Woman Writing a Letter*, whereas Delft's **Gerard Houckgeest** specialized in church interiors, such as *The Tomb of William of Orange*, a minutely observed study of architectural lines lightened by expanses of white marble.

Fabritius, Vermeer and Steen

Carel Fabritius (1622–54), a pupil of Rembrandt and (possibly) a teacher of Vermeer, was killed in a gunpowder explosion at Delft when he was only 22. Few canvases of his survive but an exquisite exception is *The Goldfinch*, a curious, almost impressionistic work, with the bird reduced to a blur of colour. The Fabritius painting is usually displayed in the same room as two of the museum's most trumpeted paintings, **Johannes Vermeer**'s (1632–75) *Girl with a Pearl Earring* and the same artist's *View of Delft*. The former is not – as is often thought – a portrait, but a "tronie", that is an illustration of a mood or emotion based on a real-life model. In this particular case, the girl looks back over her shoulder expectantly, wide-eyed and with her lips parted, the turban on her head and the sheer size of her earring suggesting her exoticism – as distinct from the rest of her attire, which is ordinary and workaday. The second Vermeer, the superb and somehow thrilling *View of Delft*, is similarly deceptive: the fine lines of the city are pictured beneath a cloudy sky, a patchwork of varying light and shade, but once again all is not quite what it seems. The painting may look like the epitome of realism, but in fact Vermeer doctored what he saw to fit in with the needs of his canvas, straightening here, lengthening there, to emphasize the horizontal. Interestingly, the detached vision implicit in the painting has prompted some experts – like Wilenski – to suggest that Vermeer viewed his subject through a fixed reducing lens or maybe even a mirror.

Finally, dotted throughout the museum are no fewer than fourteen paintings by **Jan Steen** (1625–79), including a wonderfully riotous picture carrying the legend "The way you hear it, is the way you sing it" – a parable on the young learning bad habits from the old – and a typically salacious *Girl Eating Oysters*.

The Haags Historisch Museum

Strolling north from the Mauritshuis, it's a few metres to the **Haags Historisch Museum**, Korte Vijverberg 7 (City Historical Museum; Tues–Fri 10am–5pm, Sat & Sun noon–5pm; €5; ⓦ www.haagshistorischmuseum.nl), which occupies a handsome Neoclassical mansion originally home to the city's leading militia company, the so-called Archers of St Sebastian. The museum's ground floor gives a clear and concise history of the city, illustrating its various twists and turns by means of a fine sequence of paintings. In particular, look out for Jan Steen's charmingly droll *The Merry Homeward Journey* and a lovely, tonal landscape, *River View with Sentry Post* by that pioneer of realistic landscape painting, Jan van Goyen. Here also is a portrait of a lantern-jawed Johan de Witt in all his magisterial pomp and, by way of contrast, a mummified piece of his tongue, rescued from the mob that chopped him and his brother to pieces in 1672 (see p.343). Upstairs are ninety Golden Age paintings, with pride of place going to another canvas by Jan van Goyen, a large and simply wonderful *View of Den Haag*.

Lange Voorhout and the Escher in het Paleis Museum

Across the street from the Historical Museum are the trees and cobblestones of **Lange Voorhout**, a wide L-shaped street-cum-square overlooked by a string of ritzy Neoclassical mansions, many of which are now embassies and consulates. Most conspicuous is the *Hotel des Indes*, an opulent hotel where the ballerina Anna Pavlova died in 1931 and where today you stand a fair chance of being flattened by a chauffeur-driven limousine. Also on the square, at no. 74, is the **Escher in het Paleis Museum** (Tues–Sun 11am–5pm; €7.50; Ⓦ www.escherinhetpaleis.nl), which occupies another of these grand mansions, one that was a favourite royal residence from 1901 to 1934. Nowadays, it's devoted to the work of the Dutch graphic artist, Maurits Cornelis Escher (1898–1972), who churned out dozens of very precise, often disconcerting, lithographs and engravings. The most enjoyable part of the museum is the top floor, which is given over to several hands-on **optical illusions**, all based on Escher's work.

Museum Bredius

From Lange Voorhout, it's a couple of minutes' walk to the delightful **Museum Bredius**, Lange Vijverberg 14 (Tues–Sun noon–5pm; €4.50; Ⓦ www.museum bredius.nl), which displays the collection of paintings bequeathed to the city by art connoisseur and one-time director of the Mauritshuis, Abraham Bredius, in 1946. Squeezed together in this fine old house, with its stuccowork and splendid staircase, are some exquisite paintings, notably **Rembrandt**'s *Head of Christ*, all smooth browns and yellows with the face of Jesus serene and sensitive; interestingly, Rembrandt was the first Dutch artist to use a Jewish model for a portrait of Christ. Among the genre paintings is a charac-teristic *Boar Hunt* by **Roelandt Savery** (1576–1639), all green foliage and fighting beasts, and the careful draughtsmanship of **Aert van de Neer** (1603–77) in his *Winter Landscape*. There are also two noteworthy paintings by **Jan Steen**, the fruity *Couple in a Bedchamber* and the curious *Satyr and the Peasant*, a representation of a well-known Aesop fable in which the satyr, sitting at the table with his hosts, is bemused by human behaviour. The creature's confusion is symbolically represented by the surrounding figures – the man blowing on his soup to cool it down, the woman with the basket of fruit on her head.

Museum Gevangenpoort and the Galerij Prince Willem V

The **Museum Gevangenpoort**, on the west side of the Hofvijver at Buitenhof 33 (Prison Gate Museum; closed for refurbishment; Ⓦ www.gevangenpoort.nl), is sited in the old town prison, which is itself squeezed into one of Den Haag's medieval, fortified gates. The big pull here is – or at least was until it was closed for a revamp – the museum's collection of instruments of torture, interrogation and punishment, which goes down a storm with visiting school parties. Several of the prison's old cells have survived too, including the *ridderkamer* for the more privileged captives. Here Cornelis de Witt, burgomaster of Dordrecht, was imprisoned before he and his brother Johan, another staunch Republican and leader of the States of Holland, were dragged out and murdered by an Orangist mob in 1672. The brothers were shot, beheaded and cut into pieces that were then auctioned to the crowd; Johan's tongue can be seen in the Haags Historisch Museum, along with the toe of poor old Cornelis.

   The adjacent **Galerij Prins Willem V**, Buitenhof 35 (closed for refurbish-ment), was created in 1773 as the private picture gallery of the eponymous prince and Stadholder of the United Provinces. It holds a diverting collection of seventeenth-century paintings exhibited in the style of an eighteenth-century "cabinet" gallery, with the paintings crowded together from floor to ceiling.

The Oude Stadhuis and Grote Kerk

The cobweb of narrow, mostly humdrum streets and squares stretching west of the Buitenhof zeros in on the flamboyant Dutch Renaissance facade of the **Oude Stadhuis** (Old City Hall), a good-looking, sixteenth-century affair complete with mullioned windows, shutters and decorative carvings. To the rear are the plodding symmetries of a later extension, and next door rises the deconsecrated mass of St Jacobskerk, or the **Grote Kerk** (July & Aug Mon–Fri noon–4pm; free; also open for exhibitions & concerts; Ⓦwww.grotekerkdenhaag.nl) easily the pick of Den Haag's old churches. Dating from the middle of the fifteenth century, the building's cavernous interior, with its three naves, has an exhilarating sense of breadth and handsome timber vaulting. Like most Dutch churches, it's short on decoration, but there are one or two highlights, notably the **stained-glass windows** of the choir. Of the two windows right at the back of the church, one depicts the Nativity, while the other shows the Virgin descending from heaven to show the infant Jesus to a kneeling Emperor Charles V, who footed the glaziers' bill. The latter may well have been the work of Dirk Crabeth, one of the craftsmen responsible for the windows in Gouda's St Janskerk (see p.186). To either side are three other key windows, an Annunciation, a Christ in the Temple with the Pharisees and a modern Prophet Zachariah in the Temple. Also at the back of the church stands a memorial to a bewigged Admiral Jacob van Opdam, who was blown up with his ship during the little-remembered naval battle of Lowestoft in 1665.

From the Grote Kerk, it's a short walk north to the sixteenth- and seventeenth-century **Paleis Noordeinde** (no public access), the grandest of several royal buildings that lure tourists onto expensive "Royal Tours" of Den Haag and its surroundings. Outside the palace's main entrance, on Noordeinde, is a jaunty equestrian statue of Holland's principal hero, William the Silent.

North of the city centre

Den Haag's suburbs canter north towards Scheveningen and the North Sea, an apparently haphazard sequence of long boulevards intercepted by patches of woodland. For the most part, this is a prosperous part of town and embedded in it are a string of museums, the most important of which are the **Panorama Mesdag**, a tribute to the endeavours of the nineteenth-century landscape painter Hendrik Mesdag, and the **Gemeentemuseum Den Haag**, with its enormous collection of fine and applied art. The area's attractions are widely dispersed, but it's easy to get around by **tram**.

Panorama Mesdag

The **Panorama Mesdag**, Zeestraat 65 (Mon–Sat 10am–5pm, Sun noon–5pm; €6; Ⓦwww.panorama-mesdag.com), was designed in the late nineteenth century by Hendrik Mesdag (1831–1915), banker-turned-painter and local citizen-become-Hague School luminary. For the most part, Mesdag painted unremarkable seascapes tinged with bourgeois sentimentality, but there's no denying the achievement of his panorama, a delightful depiction of Scheveningen in 1881. Completed in four months with help from his wife and George Hendrik Breitner (1857–1923), the painting is so naturalistic that it takes a few moments for the skills of lighting and perspective to become apparent. Before you get to the Panorama, you pass through three small rooms showing the best of Mesdag's other **paintings**, including a veritable battery of boats on Scheveningen beach beneath cotton-wool skies.

The Panorama is a ten-minute walk north of the Paleis Noordeinde, and accessible by **tram** #10 from Centraal Station and trams #1 and #10 from the Buitenhof.

Museum Mesdag

From the Panorama, it's a ten-minute walk north to the recently revamped **Museum Mesdag** (Tues–Sun noon–5pm; €6; ⓦwww.museummesdag.nl), the house Mesdag bought as a home and gallery at Laan van Meerdervoort 7f. At the time, Mesdag had a view over the dunes, the inspiration for many of his canvases, but the house and its environs were gobbled up by the city long ago and today it is visited for its easily assimilated collection of nineteenth- and early twentieth-century paintings, especially those of the Hague School, whose artists – like Mesdag – took local land and seascapes as their favourite subject. The Dutch canvases are supplemented by a modest collection of French paintings from the likes of Corot, Rousseau, Delacroix and Millet, though none of them represent the artists at their peak.

The museum is readily reached on **tram** #10 from Centraal Station and trams #1 and #10 from the Buitenhof.

The Peace Palace

Flanking the Carnegieplein, round the corner from the Mesdag Museum, the **Vredespaleis** (Peace Palace; guided tours Mon–Fri 10am, 11am, 2pm, & 3pm, plus 4pm May–Sept; €5; reservations required on ☎070/302 4137, ⓦwww.vredespaleis.nl) is home to the **International Court of Justice**, the principal judicial organ of the United Nations and, for all the wrong reasons, a monument to the futility of war. Toward the end of the nineteenth century,

Tsar Nicholas II called an international conference for the peaceful reconciliation of national problems. The result was the First Hague Peace Conference of 1899, whose purpose was to "help find a lasting peace and, above all, a way of limiting the progressive development of existing arms". This in turn led to the formation of a **Permanent Court of Arbitration** housed obscurely in Den Haag until the American industrialist Andrew Carnegie gave $1.5 million for a large new building – the Peace Palace. These honourable aims came to nothing with the onset of World War I: just as the donations of tapestries, urns, marble and stained glass were arriving from all over the world, so Europe's military commanders were preparing their offensives. Backed by a massive law library, fifteen judges still sit at the court today, conducting trade matters in English and diplomatic affairs in French. Widely respected and generally considered neutral, their judgments are nevertheless not binding.

To reach the Peace Palace by **public transport**, take tram #10 from Centraal Station or trams #1 and #10 from the Buitenhof.

The Gemeentemuseum Den Haag

The **Gemeentemuseum Den Haag**, at Stadhouderslaan 41 (Tues–Sun 11am–5pm; €9; ⓦwww.gemeentemuseum.nl), is easily the largest and most diverse of Den Haag's many museums. Designed by Hendrik Petrus Berlage (1856–1934) and completed in 1935, the building itself is often regarded as his masterpiece, an austere but particularly appealing structure with brick facings superimposed on a concrete shell. Inside, the museum displays a regularly rotated selection from its vast permanent collection and also offers an ambitious, headline-making programme of temporary exhibitions.

Among much else, there is a large and diverting collection of Delft pottery, a platoon of period rooms, a fashion section and a wide selection of drawings, prints and posters from the nineteenth and twentieth centuries. The **modern art** section outlines the development of painting since the early nineteenth century and although the bulk of the paintings are Dutch, there's a liberal sprinkling of international artists too. The museum is especially strong on the land and seascape painters of the **Hague School**, which flourished here in the city from 1860 to 1900, and the **De Stijl** movement, that loose but influential group of Dutch painters, sculptors, designers and architects who developed their version – and vision – of modern art and society between the two world wars. The museum has the world's largest collection of paintings from the most famous member of the group, **Piet Mondrian** (1872–1944), and although much of it consists of unfamiliar early works, painted before he evolved the abstraction of form into geometry and pure colour for which he's best known, it does include *Victory Boogie Woogie*, his last and – some say – finest work.

The museum is easy to reach on **tram** #17 from Centraal Station and the Buitenhof.

The Gemeentemuseum campus

There are three other museums on the Gemeentemuseum campus, beside Stadhouderslaan. First up is **GEM**, **Museum voor Actuele Kunst** (Tues–Sun noon–6pm; €5, including Fotomuseum; ⓦwww.gem-online.nl), a gallery of contemporary art featuring an enterprising programme of temporary exhibitions. In the same building is the **Fotomuseum** (Photography Museum; same hours; €5, including GEM; ⓦwww.fotomuseumdenhaag.com), which puts on a minimum of four exhibitions a year and in between times displays photographs from the Gemeentemuseum's permanent collection.

Also close by is the **Museon** (Tues–Sun 11am–5pm; €7.50, children under 12 years €4; ⓦ www.museon.nl), a sequence of non-specialist exhibitions dealing with human activities and the history of the earth – everything from rock formations to the use of tools. Self-consciously internationalist, it's aimed at school parties, as is the neighbouring **Omniversum** at President Kennedylaan 5 (programme on ☏ 0900 666 4837, ⓦ www.omniversum.nl), an IMAX cinema in all but name.

Eating and drinking

Den Haag has an excellent range of **restaurants**, and although some are aimed squarely at the expense account, many more are very affordable, with main courses hovering between €20 and €25. There is a cluster of first-rate places just beyond Lange Voorhout along and around Denneweg and Frederikstraat, and another on Molenstraat, near the Paleis Noordeinde: frankly, you need look no further. These two areas are good for **cafés** and **café-bars** too, though the liveliest **bars** are concentrated on and around the Grote Markt, south of the Grote Kerk, and on the Plein, near the Mauritshuis.

Restaurants

De Basaal Dunne Bierkade 3 ☏ 070/427 6888. With its crisp, modern decor, this smashing restaurant has a short but sharp menu featuring local ingredients – like the catch of the day. Main courses – for example lemon dab and saffron potatoes – average €21.

C'est Ca Prinsestraat 130 ☏ 070/360 1619. New, slickly decorated restaurant that is finding its gastronomic feet, but already scoring full marks for its lively, creative menu. Mains average €24. Tues–Sat 5.30–9.30pm.

Dekxels Denneweg 130 ☏ 070/365 9788. This highly recommended, coolly decorated, chic restaurant serves a superb range of international and Dutch dishes – pheasant with sauerkraut ravioli for example. Main courses average €25. Daily 5.30–10/11pm.

Djawa Mallemolen 12a ☏ 070/363 5763. A favourite with many locals, this smart and long-established Indonesian restaurant offers a tasty range of traditional dishes in smart, modern premises. Full meals for around €30. Mon–Sat 5.30–11pm.

HNM Molenstraat 21 ☏ 070/365 6553. Imaginatively decorated café serving a tasty range of Dutch, Indonesian, French and Italian snacks and meals. The daily specials are especially good value, beginning at just €12. Mon–Wed 4pm–midnight, Thurs & Fri 4pm–1am, Sat noon–1am & Sun noon–6pm.

Limón Denneweg 39a ☏ 070/356 1465. Pastel-painted Spanish tapas restaurant catering to a fashionable, youngish crowd. Good food – though admittedly not all the tapas turn out as well as each other; a very popular spot. Tapas from as little as €5. Daily 5–11pm, midnight at weekends.

Ratu Raja Prinsestraat 30 ☏ 070/3563366. Smooth, richly decorated Franco-Indochinese restaurant that has proved a real Den Haag hit. Mains average €24. Tues–Sat 6–10.30pm.

Saur Lange Voorhout 47 ☏ 070/346 2565. This smart and formal restaurant, with its Art Deco flourishes and French menu, serves some of the best steaks in town. The attached brasserie is a new, ultra modern and informal addition – and the steaks are just as good. Main courses average €25. Mon–Fri noon–2.30pm & 6–10.30pm, Sat 6–10.30pm.

Café-bars and bars

De Boterwaag Grote Markt 8a. Immensely appealing café-bar housed in an old and cavernous brick-vaulted weigh house. It's very popular with a youthful crowd and offers a wide range of beers as well as inexpensive bar food, though this hardly inspires the palate. Large terrace, which fills up quickly when the sun pops out. Daily 10am–1.30am.

Cloos Plein 12a. If you thought Den Haag might be demure, wander down to the Plein, and see the locals getting stuck into the sauce. *Cloos* is one of several large and youthful bars on this square.

Coffee Company Noordeinde 54. Straightforward, modern coffee bar selling the best coffee in town plus good cakes. Mon–Fri 8am–7pm, Sat 9am–7pm, Sun 10am–7pm.

De Landman Denneweg 48. Mellow brown(ish) bar near the southern end of Denneweg with dark panelling and a lively crew. Gay-friendly.

De Oude Mol Oude Molstraat 61. Good old traditional bar and neighbourhood joint down a narrow sidestreet. Oodles of atmosphere and an enjoyable range of beers. Upstairs is a tiny tapas bar, and they serve tapas downstairs too. Daily from 5pm, kitchen Wed–Sat from 5.30pm.

De Paap Papestraat 32 ⓦ www.depaap.nl. Dark and raucous bar with frequent live music showcasing the best of local talent. Tues–Sat from 10pm.

De Paas Dunne Bierkade 16a. Traditional brown bar with lots of zip and over one hundred and fifty beers to sample. Canal-side, central location. Daily from 3pm.

De Zwarte Ruiter Grote Markt 27. This fashionable bar boasts a good selection of beers and ales, and positively heaves on the weekend. Large terrace also.

Listings

Bike rental From either of Den Haag's train stations at standard rates.

Car rental Europcar, Binckhorstlaan 297 ⓣ 070/381 1811; Hertz, Binckhorstlaan 318 ⓣ 070/381 8989. For others – and there are lots of them – look up Autoverhuur in the Yellow Pages or consult ⓦ www.yellowpages .goudengids.nl.

Cinema Filmhuis Den Haag, Spui 191 ⓣ 070/365 6030, ⓦ www.filmhuisdenhaag.nl. The best independent cinema in the city.

Embassies and consulates Australia, Carnegielaan 4 ⓣ 070/310 8200; Canada, Sophialaan 7 ⓣ 070/311 1600; Ireland, Dr Kuyperstraat 9 ⓣ 070/363 0993; New Zealand, Eisenhowerslaan 77 ⓣ 070/346 9324; UK, Lange Voorhout 10 ⓣ 070/427 0427; US, Lange Voorhout 102 ⓣ 070/310 2209. For others, see

Ambassades in the Yellow Pages, or consult ⓦ www.yellowpages.goudengids.nl.

Markets Food market just south of the VVV on Markthof, Gedempte Gracht/Spui (Mon 11am–6pm, Tues–Fri 9am–6pm, Thurs until 9pm & Sat 9am–5pm). Antiques, books and curios markets are on Lange Voorhout (mid-May to late Sept Thurs & Sun 10am–6pm) and on Plein (Oct–May Thurs 10am–6pm).

Pharmacy Hofstad Apotheek, right in the centre at Korte Poten 7a (Mon–Fri 8.30am–6pm, Sat 10am–2pm). For others, see Apotheken in the Yellow Pages, or consult ⓦ www.yellowpages .goudengids.nl.

Post office Main post office on Kerkplein (Mon–Fri 7.30am–6.30pm, Thurs until 9pm, Sat 9am–5pm).

Taxi HTMC ⓣ 070/390 7722.

Scheveningen

Wedged against the seashore about 4km north of the centre of Den Haag, the old fishing port and harbour of **SCHEVENINGEN** is now the Netherlands' biggest coastal resort, a sometimes tacky, often breezy place that attracts more than nine million visitors a year. It also has one curious claim to fame: during World War II, resistance groups tested suspected Nazi infiltrators by getting them to say "Scheveningen" – an impossible feat for Germans, apparently, and not much easier for English-speakers (try a throaty *s-khay-ve-ning-uh*). A thick strip of forested dune once separated Den Haag from Scheveningen, but nowadays it's hard to know where one ends and the other begins. There is, however, no mistaking Scheveningen's principal attraction, its **beach**, a long expanse of golden sand that is hard to resist on a warm day, especially as it only takes about ten minutes to get there from Den Haag on **tram** #1 which leaves from the Spui and from outside the VVV.

A beach without the crowds

If the crowded seaside antics of Scheveningen don't appeal, then help is at hand: take **tram #12** from the city centre to its Duindorp terminus and it's a five-minute walk through the dunes of the **Westduinpark** to the **Zuiderstrand**. This long, sandy beach is often deserted and even at peak times there's oodles of space – and you can watch the ships pulling through the waters of the North Sea.

The seafront

Scheveningen's handiest tram stop (Kurhaus) is a couple of hundred metres from its most impressive building, the **Kurhaus**, a grand hotel of 1885, built when this was one of the most fashionable resorts in Europe. Pop inside for a peek at its central hall, a richly decorated affair with pendulous chandeliers and rich frescoes bearing mermaids and semi-clad maidens cavorting high above the diners and coffee-drinkers. Most of Scheveningen's other attractions are within easy walking distance of the *Kurhaus*: the **casino** is across the street; it's east along the seashore to the **pier** and its amusement arcades; and west to **Sea Life**, Strandweg 13 (daily: Jan & Dec 10am–6pm; Feb–June & Sept–Nov 10am–7pm; July & Aug 10am–8pm; €13.50, children 3–11 years €8.50; ⓦ www.sealifeeurope .com), a glorified aquarium complete with a sea-bed walkway and coral reef. Much more original, and about 200m west of Sea Life, is the **Museum Beelden-aan-Zee**, at Harteveltstraat 1 (Tues–Sun 11am–5pm; €7; ⓦ www .beeldenaanzee.nl), which features an intriguing assortment of modern sculptures arranged around a pavilion built by King William I for his ailing wife, Wilhelmina, in 1826. There are examples of the work of many leading sculptors, including Karel Appel and Wim Quist, Man Ray and Fritz Koenig, and although there is supposed to be a unifying theme – the human experience – it's the variety of forms and materials that impresses.

Practicalities

Scheveningen is best visited on a day-trip from Den Haag, but if you decide to stay, the **VVV**, by the seafront just east of the *Kurhaus* at Gevers Deynootweg 1134 (Mon–Fri 9.30am–5.30pm, Sat 10am–5pm, Sun 11am–4pm; ⓣ 0900 340 3505, ⓦ www.denhaag.com), issues a free brochure listing all the resort's **hotels** and **pensions**. Out of season, there are oodles of vacant rooms, but in the summer it's best to use the VVV's accommodation booking service. Scheveningen also hosts a lively programme of special events, most memorably an international **sand sculpture** competition held in early May.

Delft

DELFT, in between Den Haag and Rotterdam, has a beguiling centre, a medley of ancient red-tiled houses set beside tree-lined canals interrupted by the cutest of bridges. With justification, it's one of the most visited spots in the Netherlands, but most tourists come here for the day, and in the evening, even in the summer, the town can be surprisingly – and mercifully – quiet. Delft boasts a clutch of fascinating old buildings, one of them – the **Prinsenhof** – holding an enjoyable collection of Golden Age paintings. Nevertheless it's the general flavour of the place that appeals rather than any specific sight. That said, the two big pulls as far as the day-trippers are concerned are the **Delftware factories**, stuffed with the blue and white ceramics for which the town is famous, and the **Johannes Vermeer** (1632–75) connection. Precious little is known about Vermeer, but he was certainly born in the town and died here too, leaving a wife, eleven children and a huge debt to the local baker. He had given the baker two pictures as security, and his wife subsequently bankrupted herself trying to retrieve them. Vermeer's most celebrated painting is his 1661 *View of Delft*, now displayed in the Mauritshuis in Den Haag (see p.160), but if you're after a townscape that even vaguely resembles the picture, you'll be disappointed – it doesn't exist and in a sense it never did, no matter how many "Vermeer walks" Delft lays on. Vermeer made no claim to be a realist and his *View* accorded with the landscape traditions

Koninklijke Porceleyne Fles

of his day, presenting an idealized Delft framed by a broad expanse of water and dappled by a cloudy sky. There is a cool detachment here that Vermeer also applied to those scenes of contemporary domestic life which are more typical of his oeuvre – though only 37 Vermeers survive – as exemplified by *The Love Letter*, in Amsterdam's Rijksmuseum (see p.84).

Arrival and information

There are frequent trains from both of Den Haag's stations to Delft **train station** and the journey only takes a few minutes. Delft **bus station** is in front of the train station, and from here it's a five- to ten-minute walk to Delft's main square, Markt. You can also make the trip from Den Haag on **tram #1**, which runs south from Scheveningen to the centre of Den Haag before proceeding onto Den Haag HS station and Delft, where it rattles along Phoenixstraat/Westvest between the train station and the centre; for the centre of Delft, get off at the Prinsenhof tram stop. Allow twenty minutes to get from Den Haag to Delft by tram.

Delft VVV has turned itself into a **Toeristen Informatie Punt (TIP)**, located just north of the Markt at Hippolytusbuurt 4 (April–Sept Mon & Sun 10am–4pm, Tues–Fri 9am–6pm, Sat 10am–5pm; Oct–March Mon 11am–4pm, Tues–Sat 10am–4pm; Sun 10am–3pm ☎015/215 4051, ⊛www.delft.com). They issue free city maps, offer free internet access and sell all manner of local brochures. They can also help with accommodation.

Accommodation

Delft TIP (see p.170) operates an **accommodation booking service**, which can be very useful in the height of summer when spare rooms are thin on the ground. The TIP also has the details of a light scattering of **rooms** in private houses (❶–❷), though most of these are on the outskirts of town, whereas Delft's dozen or so **hotels** are mostly in the old centre.

Hotels

Ark Koornmarkt 65 ☎015/215 7999, ⊛www .deark.nl. Attractive four-star hotel occupying three tastefully restored seventeenth-century canal houses. The bedrooms are perhaps more spartan than you might expect from the public areas, but they are comfortable and well appointed all the same. ❹

Best Western Museumhotels Delft Phoenixstraat 50 ☎015/215 3070, ⊛www.museumhotel.nl. There are two separate sections to this four-star hotel – one in an eighteenth-century building, the other in its grander, seventeenth-century neighbour. Great location, backing onto the Oude Delft canal just along from the Prinsenhof, though the guest bedrooms are themselves uninspiringly modern. ❹

Bridges House Hotel Oude Delft 74 ☎015/212 4036, ⊛www.bridges-house .com. This medium-sized, privately owned hotel occupies an old town house that was once the home of the artist Jan Steen. There's no chain-hotel standardization here and neither is the place excessively spick and span, but the best guest rooms are large, well equipped and have good views of the Oude Delft canal. It has an ideal location, too, the briefest of walks from the Markt. ❸

De Plataan Doelenplein 10 ☎015/212 6046, ⊛www.hoteldeplataan.nl. A little off the beaten track, but still within easy walking distance of the Markt, this three-star hotel has really pushed the decorative boat out, from the cheerful colours of the regular rooms through to the four theme rooms, including a "Garden of Eden" and a "Desert Island" – great fun. ❸

De Vlaming Vlamingstraat 52 ☎015/213 2127, ⊛www.hoteldevlaming.nl. This small, family-run hotel, a short walk from the Markt, occupies a pleasant canal-side location and its handful of guest rooms are cosy in a traditional sort of way – some even have carpet on the wall. ❸

▲ Cycling in Delft

Delftware delights

The origins of the clunky ceramics known as **delftware** can be traced to the Balearic island of Mallorca, where craftsmen had earlier developed **majolica**, a type of porous pottery that was glazed with bright metallic oxides. During the Renaissance, these techniques were exported to Italy from where they spread north, first to Antwerp and then to the United Provinces. Initially, delft pottery designs featured Dutch and Italian landscapes, portraits and biblical scenes, but the East India Company's profitable import of Chinese ceramics transformed the industry. Delft factories freely copied Chinese designs and by the middle of the seventeenth century they were churning out blue-and-white tiles, plates, panels, jars and vases by the boat load – even exporting to China, where they undercut Chinese producers.

From the 1760s, however, the delft factories were themselves undercut by British and German workshops, and by the time Napoleon arrived they had all but closed down. There was a modest revival of the industry in the 1870s and there are several local producers today, but it's mostly mass-produced stuff of little originality. Delft's souvenir shops are jam-packed with delftware, but if that isn't enough, head for the factory of **Koninklijke Porceleyne Fles** (Mon–Sat 9am–5pm; April–Oct also Sun 9am–5pm; frequent guided tours €6.50; ⊛www.royaldelft.com), the leading local manufacturer, where they still produce hand-painted pieces. The factory is located a good twenty minutes' walk south of the centre at Rotterdamseweg 196; alternatively, take bus #121 or #40 from Delft train station and get off at Jaffalaan, from where it's a five-minute walk. More conveniently, **De Porcelijne Lampetkan**, just behind the Nieuwe Kerk at Vrouwenregt 5 (Mon–Sat 10.30am–5.30pm; ☎015/212 1086, ⊛www .antiquesdelft.com), is an appealing little shop selling a good range of antique delftware at (comparatively) reasonable rates, and there's a fine selection on display at Delft's **Museum Lambert van Meerten** (see p.175).

The Town

The obvious place to start an exploration of Delft is the **Markt**, a handsome square and central point of reference with the Stadhuis at one end and the Nieuwe Kerk at the other, and with cafés and restaurants and a **statue** of Delft's own Hugo Grotius lined up in between. A well-known scholar and statesman, Grotius (1583–1645) was sentenced to life imprisonment by Maurice of Orange-Nassau during the political turmoil of the 1610s, but was subsequently rescued by his wife who smuggled him out of jail in a chest. Unfortunately, it didn't save Grotius from a sticky end – he died of exposure after being shipwrecked near Danzig.

The Nieuwe Kerk

The **Nieuwe Kerk** (Mon–Sat: April–Oct 9am–6pm; Nov–March 11am–4pm; €3.30, including Oude Kerk) is new only in comparison with the Oude Kerk, as there's been a church on this site since 1381. Most of the original structure was destroyed in the great fire that swept through Delft in 1536, and the remainder in an explosion a century later – a disaster, incidentally, which claimed the life of the artist Carel Fabritius, Rembrandt's greatest pupil and (debatably) the teacher of Vermeer. The most striking part of the rebuilding is one of the most recent, the church's 100-metre **spire** (same hours; €3 extra), replaced in 1872 and from whose summit there's a great view over the town. Otherwise, apart from the sheer height of the nave, the interior is mainly distinguished by the **mausoleum of William the Silent**, a prodigiously elaborate marble structure built on the orders of the States General between 1614 and 1623. The mausoleum holds two effigies of William, one in his pomp, seated and dressed in his armour, the other showing him recumbent on his deathbed. This second carving is exquisite, down to the finest details of his face, and at his feet is his faithful dog, who – so legend has it – refused to eat or drink after William's death, thereby rejoining his master. The two effigies are surrounded by bronze allegorical figures, representing the likes of Liberty and Justice. The statue of **Fame**, standing on tiptoe behind the recumbent William, caused all sorts of problems: it fell over and the cost of the repairs pushed the whole project way over budget. Look out also for the attractive Art Deco **stained-glass windows** in the north transept and chancel. Inserted between 1927 and 1936, they are a mixed bunch, some illustrating biblical themes, but most singing the praises of the House of Orange, many of whom are interred in the **burial vault** beneath the nave (no public access).

The Stadhuis and the Vermeercentrum

Directly opposite the Nieuwe Kerk, across the Markt, is the **Stadhuis**, whose delightful facade of 1618 is equipped with dormer windows, shutters, fluted pilasters and shell decoration. Most of its medieval predecessor was incinerated in the fire of 1536, but the stern stone tower of the earlier building survived and was incorporated – none too successfully – into the later design.

From the Markt, it's a few metres to Voldersgracht 21, where the new **Vermeercentrum** (daily 10am–5pm; €6; Ⓦ www.vermeerdelft.nl) is an attempt to cash in on Delft's most famous native son, the painter Vermeer. The problem is that the centre doesn't actually own any of the great man's paintings, so it has been forced to bluff its way through, beginning in the basement where a short film introduces the artist and there are copies of all his paintings. A second floor has a mock-up of his studio, making an attempt to explore Vermeer's technique.

The Oude Kerk

From the Markt, it's a short but pretty walk north to the **Oude Kerk** (Mon–Sat: April–Oct 9am–6pm; Nov–March 11am–4pm; €3.30, including Nieuwe Kerk), a rambling Gothic pile whose discordant lines are redeemed by the most magnificent of church towers – a soaring cluster of turrets rising high above the town. Despite its dense buttressing, the tower has long been subject to subsidence and the angle of its lean has been measured by generations of worried town architects. Indeed, there have been periodic panics about its safety, not least in the 1840s when the council almost decided to pull it down; the last repairs were undertaken in the 1990s. Inside, the church boasts a splendid vaulted timber ceiling and a fine set of modern **stained-glass windows** which mostly depict biblical scenes, the key exception being the intense "Liberation Window", installed in the transept in 1956 to celebrate the expulsion of the German army at the end of World War II. Also of interest is the **pulpit**, whose five intricately carved panels depict John the Baptist and the four evangelists in false perspective; dating from 1548, the pulpit did well to survive the attentions of the Protestants when they ransacked the church in the Iconoclastic Fury of 1565.

Among the assorted **tombs** there is a plain floor plaque in honour of Vermeer just to the west of the pulpit and a flashy marble memorial to **Admiral Maarten Tromp** (1598–1653) close by, next to the transept. One of the country's most successful admirals, Tromp was captured twice at sea – once by the English and once by Tunisian Arabs – but survived to lead the Dutch fleet at the start of the First Anglo-Dutch War (1652–54). Tromp famously hoisted a broom at his masthead to "sweep the seas clear of the English", but the Royal Navy had its revenge, shooting him down during a sea battle off Scheveningen in 1653. It's this last battle that is depicted on Tromp's tomb alongside an effigy of the man himself, dressed up in his armour beneath a flock of bawling, trumpeting cherubs. The marble carving depicting the battle, which shows the British fleet burning away, was much admired by no less than Samuel Pepys, who wrote "the smoke [was] the best expressed that ever I saw".

Het Prinsenhof

Down a passageway opposite the Oude Kerk, in what was originally a convent, is **Het Prinsenhof** (Tues–Sat 10am–5pm, Sun 1–5pm; €7.50, including Museum Lambert van Meerten; Ⓦ www.gemeentemusea-delft.nl), which served as the main residence of William the Silent of Orange-Nassau from 1572 to 1584. A sprawling, somewhat confusing building spread over two floors, it was here that William coordinated the Dutch resistance to the Habsburgs and it was here too that he was assassinated. Today, the building has displays celebrating the William connection and also holds the **municipal art collection**, an appealing jumble of works mostly dating from the sixteenth and seventeenth centuries. Free **plans** are issued at reception.

The ground floor

At the beginning, Rooms 3–8 concentrate on the life and turbulent times of **William the Silent** with portraits of some of the protagonists and, in Room 4, the curious *Wretched State of the Netherlands*. This inflammatory canvas by an unknown seventeenth-century Protestant depicts the Habsburg commander, the Duke of Alva, in cahoots with the devil and the pope, enslaving the Low Countries with each province represented by one of the seventeen chained women before him. Meanwhile, in the background, Margaret of Parma, the region's Habsburg governor, can be seen fishing in a pool of blood. Close by, in Room 7, the bottom of the old wooden staircase marks the spot where William the Silent was **assassinated** on July 10, 1584. A former army commander of both Charles V and Philip II, William turned against the Habsburgs during Alva's persecution of the Protestants in 1567. He went on to lead the Protestant revolt against Philip, mustering a series of armies and organizing the Watergeuzen, guerrilla units that played a key role in driving back the imperial army. In return, Philip put a bounty of 25,000 gold crowns on William's head, but in the event the man who shot him was not a professional assassin but a fanatical Catholic, Balthazar Gerard, who did the deed for his religion. Gerard's two bullets passed right through William and the **bullet holes** are now protected by a glass sheet, put there to stop curious fingers enlarging them. Protestant legend asserts that the dying William asked for his assassin to be treated mercifully, but no such luck: Gerard was tortured in the Markt for four whole days.

In Room 8, next door, there's another **painterly curiosity** in the form of a splendidly realistic, almost pointillist canvas entitled *The Disbanding of the Mercenaries in Utrecht, 1618* by Paulwels van Hillegaert. In what now seems a very strange state of affairs, the mercenaries had been hired by Utrecht city council to keep the peace between those Protestants who asserted the primacy of predestination over free will and those who believed it was the other way round. Before matters got even worse, William the Silent's son, Maurits, rode to the rescue. He restored order, disarmed the mercenaries – and gave Hillegaert the chance to produce another of his sycophantic paintings in praise of the House of Orange.

The first floor

Upstairs, Room 16 holds a selection of **militia paintings**, the pick of which is *The Officers of the White Company* by Jacob Willemsz (1619–61). During the long war with Spain, every Dutch city had its own militia, but as the Habsburg threat diminished so the militias devolved into social clubs, each of them keen to immortalize their particular company in a group portrait like these on display here. Nearby, Rooms 17, 18 and 19 also exhibit paintings from Delft's **seventeenth-century heyday**, including a pair of superbly executed anatomy paintings, with *The Anatomy Lesson* by Cornelis de Man (1621–1706) being especially striking.

Museum Lambert van Meerten

Located a few metres north of the Prinsenhof, the canal-side **Museum Lambert van Meerten**, at Oude Delft 199 (Tues–Sat 10am–5pm, Sun 1–5pm; €4, €6.50 with Prinsenhof; ⓦwww.gemeentemusea-delft.nl), exhibits the town's best collection of delftware. There are jars and vases, plates and panels, but the museum's speciality is its **tiles** – a fabulous hoard collected by the eponymous nineteenth-century industrialist who once lived in this grand mansion and gifted the house and its contents to the town when he died. In particular, look out for the vibrant tile picture of the Battle of La Hogue – in which an Anglo-Dutch fleet worsted the French in 1692 – displayed on the staircase.

Eating and drinking

Many of Delft's **cafés** and **restaurants** are geared up for the day-trippers and serve up some pretty routine stuff, but there are also several excellent places dotted within easy strolling distance of the Markt. The same applies to the town's **bars**.

Restaurants and cafés

Kleijweg's Stadskoffyhus Oude Delft 133. Popular café both inside, in a cosily kitted-out old terrace house near the Markt, and outside, on a patio-barge. The best pancakes in town, for €5–10. Very popular with tourists. Mon–Fri 9am–8pm & Sat 9am–6pm.

De Klikspaan Koornmarkt 85 ☎015/214 1562. Smart and polished restaurant in an old canal-side town house just south of the Markt. The food is broadly French, though Dutch dishes do pop up now and then, and you can eat outside on their patio-barge during the summer. Mains €23–27. Wed–Sun 4–11pm.

Le Vieux Jen Heilige Geestkerkhof 3 ☎015/213 0433. Smart but informal French restaurant in old, vaguely rustic premises serving *nouvelle cuisine* (read: small portions) with care and precision. Main courses €23–27; excellent cellar

too. Tues–Fri noon–2.30pm & 6–10.30pm, Sat 6–10.30pm.

Visrestaurant Den Blaeuwen Snoeck Verwersdijk 14 ☎015/213 8850. This sedate restaurant, with its neat, vaguely nautical decor and classical music backdrop, is the best seafood place in town. Prices are very reasonable, with mains averaging around €20. Smashing choice of daily specials. Daily except Tues 5–10.30pm.

Bars

Locus Publicus Brabantse Turfmarkt 67. You don't come to Delft for the nightlife, but this is one of the town's busiest and most youthful bars – and it offers a wide range of beers.

Trappistenlokaal 't Klooster Vlamingstraat 2. Smashing little bar with traditional decor and an excellent range of Belgian beers, both on tap and bottled.

Rotterdam

ROTTERDAM lies at the heart of a maze of rivers and artificial waterways that together form the outlet of the rivers Rijn (Rhine) and Maas (Meuse). After devastating damage during World War II, Rotterdam has grown into a vibrant, forceful city dotted with first-division cultural attractions. Neither has redevelopment obliterated the city's earthy character: its tough grittiness is part of its appeal, as are its boisterous bars and clubs.

An important **port** as early as the fourteenth century, Rotterdam was one of the major cities of the United Provinces and shared its periods of fortune and decline until the nineteenth century when it was caught unawares. The city was ill-prepared for the industrial expansion of the Ruhr, the development of larger ships and the silting up of the Maas, but prosperity did finally return in a big way with the digging of an entirely new ship canal (the "Nieuwe Waterweg") between the city and the North Sea in the 1860s. Rotterdam has been a major seaport ever since, though it has had difficult times, especially during World War II, when the Nazis **bombed** the city centre in 1940 and, in retreat, destroyed much of the harbour four years later, with Allied bombing doing much damage in between.

The postwar period saw the rapid reconstruction of the **docks** and, when huge container ships and oil tankers made the existing port facilities obsolete, Rotterdammers promptly built an entirely new deep-sea port, the **Europoort**, jutting out into the North Sea some 25km to the west of the old town. Completed in 1968, the Europoort can accommodate the largest of ships and now Rotterdam is the largest port in the world, handling some 350 million tonnes of goods a year, with more than half of all goods heading into Europe passing through it. The same spirit of enterprise was reflected in the council's plans to rebuild the devastated **city centre**. There was to be no return to the crowded terrace houses of yesteryear; instead the centre was to be a modern extravaganza of concrete and glass, high-rise and pedestrianized areas. Decades in the making, parts of the plan work very well indeed – such as the *kubuswoningen* ("cube houses") of the Blaak district – but others, such as the Lijnbaan shopping precinct, look tired and sad.

All this modernity may sound unalluring, but Rotterdam's attractions are enticing, most notably the **Kunsthal**, exhibiting contemporary art, and the **Museum Boijmans Van Beuningen**, which has an outstanding art collection holding representative works from almost all the most important Dutch painters. Both are in the city's designated culture zone, the **Museumpark**. Other city highlights include **Oude Haven**, the city's oldest harbour, ravaged during World War II but sympathetically redeveloped, and **Delfshaven**, an antique harbour that managed to survive the bombs pretty much intact. Rotterdam also boasts a string of first-rate **festivals**, including the much lauded **North Sea Jazz Festival** (see p.184), the colourful **Summer Carnival** and the **Dance Parade**, when the entire city centre is swamped by floats booming out ear-splitting house music.

Arrival

Rotterdam has several train stations, but the one you want for the centre is **Centraal Station**. It adjoins Stationsplein, the hub of the RET public transport system, whose metro, trams and buses combine to delve into every urban nook and cranny. Be warned, however, that Centraal Station and its immediate surroundings can be intimidating late at night and was under major reconstruction at the time of writing, making it a grim area indeed. Most visitors arrive by train, but the city also has its own (rapidly expanding) **airport** (Ⓦwww.rotterdam-airport.nl), just 10km or so northwest of Centraal Station; **bus** #33 (every 10–20min; 20min) links the two. A taxi from the airport to the station costs about €20.

Information

There's a **VVV Info Café** on the right as you leave the train station at Stationsplein 45 (Mon–Sat 9am–5.30pm, Sun 10am–5pm), where you can

▲ Erasmus Bridge, Rotterdam

plan your route over coffee and use free internet terminals. The main **VVV** is a five- to ten-minute walk southeast of Centraal Station, at Coolsingel 5 (Mon–Thurs & Sat 9am–5.30pm; Fri 9am–9pm, Sun 10am–5pm; ☎0900 403 4065, ⓦwww.rotterdam.info). They have all the usual tourist information, supply a useful and free mini-guide to the city, issue free city and public transport maps and operate an accommodation booking service. There's a first-rate youth information office too, **Use-it**, in a red-painted building a couple of minutes' walk from the west side of the train station at Schaatsbaan 41 (mid-May to mid-Sept Tues–Sun 9am–6pm; July & Aug also Mon 1–5pm; mid-Sept to mid-May Tues–Sat 9am–5pm; ☎010/240 9158, ⓦwww.use-it.nl); they specialize in budget stuff – from accommodation to cafés and beyond – and offer free internet access as well. If you plan on visiting many cultural sights, you might want to consider the **Rotterdam Welcome Card**, giving you up to fifty-percent discount on many key attractions. The card comes in three versions: without public transport (€5), with two rides included (€8), or with a day card giving you unlimited access to the transport network (€9).

City transport

Operated by **RET** (☎0900 9292, ⓦwww.ret.nl), Rotterdam's public transport system is fast, comprehensive and efficient. Rotterdam is also the first city in the Netherlands to introduce the public-transport **OV-chipcard**, a rechargeable card the size of a credit card, which you can buy at any metro station. Ultimately, when the new system is fully introduced, the chipcard will make the *strippenkaart* redundant, but in the meantime you can still use it (see p.26).

Accommodation

As you might expect of an important industrial city, Rotterdam has a slew of big chain **hotels**. It also possesses a clutch of much less expensive places, occasionally in – or at least near – the centre, including an HI hostel in one of Rotterdam's

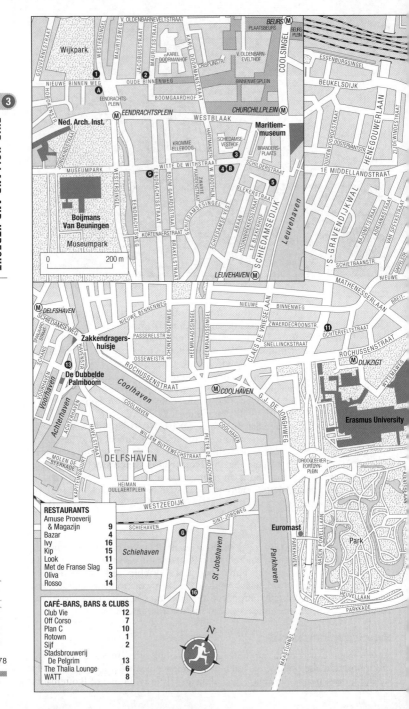

RESTAURANTS

Amuse Proeverij & Magazijn	9
Bazar	4
Ivy	16
Kip	15
Look	11
Met de Franse Slag	5
Oliva	3
Rosso	14

CAFÉ-BARS, BARS & CLUBS

Club Vie	12
Off Corso	7
Plan C	10
Rotown	1
Sijf	2
Stadsbrouwerij De Pelgrim	13
The Thalia Lounge	6
WATT	8

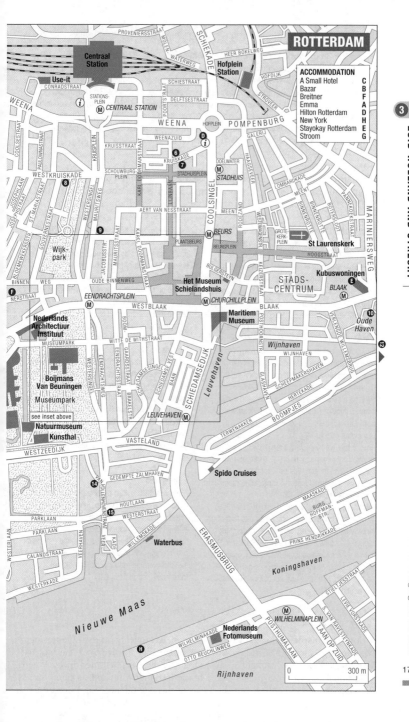

ROTTERDAM

ACCOMMODATION

A Small Hotel	C
Bazar	B
Breitner	F
Emma	A
Hilton Rotterdam	D
New York	H
Stayokay Rotterdam	E
Stroom	G

Centraal Station

Use-it

Hofplein Station

Wijk-park

Nederlands Architectuur Instituut

Boijmans Van Beuningen

Museumpark

see inset above

Natuurmuseum

Kunsthal

St Laurenskerk

Kubuswoningen

STADS-CENTRUM

Het Museum Schielandshuis

Maritiem Museum

Oude Haven

Spido Cruises

Waterbus

Nederlands Fotomuseum

Koningshaven

Nieuwe Maas

Rijnhaven

0   300 m

The Waterbus

Leaving from beside Rotterdam's Erasmusbrug, the Waterbus passenger ferry (℡0900/266 6399 premium line, ⊛www.waterbus.nl) takes an hour to zip down the rivers Nieuwe Maas and Noord bound for Dordrecht (see p.189). It's a great way to see this part of the country and fares are very reasonable – a single to Dordrecht costs just €4.20, €7.20 return; boats leave every half-hour from 7am to 7pm on weekdays, 9.30am to 7pm on Saturdays and 11.30am to 6pm on Sundays. Furthermore, connecting ferries make side journeys to – among several places – the Kinderdijk (see p.193) and the Dordrecht Biesbosch (see p.192).

distinctive *kubuswoningen* (see p.181). Conferences and congresses mean that rooms can sometimes be in short supply, which is one good reason to use the VVV's efficient **accommodation service**, the cost of which is minimal.

Hotels

A Small Hotel Witte de Withstraat 94 ℡010/414 0303, ⊛www.asmallhotel.nl. Incredibly stylish boutique hotel located at the up-and-coming Witte de Withstraat with just six themed rooms, all well equipped and spacious. Free use of mini-bar included. ❺

Bazar Witte de Withstraat 16 ℡010/206 5151, ⊛www.hotelbazar.nl. Lively, very agreeable two-star hotel in a central location near the Museumpark, with great rooms decorated in African, South American and Eastern style. There's also an excellent café-restaurant adjoining it. ❷

Breitner Breitnerstraat 23 ℡010/436 0262, ⊛www.hotelbreitner.nl. Unassuming three-star hotel on a quiet residential street, a short walk from Museumpark. The rooms are pleasant if somewhat spartan. ❸

Emma Nieuwe Binneweg 6 ℡010/436 5533, ⊛www.hotelemma.nl. Recently revamped with a modern glass facade, this trim, modern three-star hotel has a central location, comfortable rooms and a sunny rooftop terrace. ❹

Hilton Rotterdam Weena 10 ℡010/710 8000, ⊛www.rotterdam.hilton.com. Luxurious four-star hotel with large and extremely well-appointed rooms. Occupies a classic early 1970s tower block with a wide sweeping foyer that comes complete with oceans of marble and a broken mirror motif on the walls. First-rate and special weekend deals are abundant. ❺

New York Koninginnenhoofd 1 ℡010/439 0500, ⊛www.hotelnewyork.nl. This prestigious four-star hotel occupies the grand nineteenth-century former head office of a shipping line. It's situated across from the city centre on the south bank of the Nieuwe Maas, and accessible via water taxi from the centre or on the metro – the hotel is a 5min walk from Wilhelminaplein station. All the rooms are extremely well appointed and most have smashing river views. ❹

Stroom Lloydstraat 1 ℡010/221 4060, ⊛www.stroomrotterdam.nl. Twenty-three studios – all varying in size – located in a former power-house to give that urban-industrial feel. All the studios on the second floor are split-level and there's also a modish bar-lounge downstairs. Reachable by tram #8 in the direction of Spangen (Pieter de Hooghweg stop) or metro (Coolhaven stop, 5min walk). ❻

Hostel

Stayokay Rotterdam Overblaak 85 ℡010/436 5763, ⊛www.stayokay.com. Inspired idea to select one of Rotterdam's cube houses – the *kubuswoningen* – as an HI hostel, which was opened in 2009. The facilities are good – there's bike storage and bike rental plus a launderette – and the overnight rate includes breakfast. Doubles ❶, dorm beds €26

The City

From **Stationsplein**, outside Centraal Station, Kruisplein and then Westersingel/Mauritsweg cut south, dividing this part of the city into two: to the west is a largely working-class residential area, while to the east, hemmed in by Weena, Coolsingel and Westblaak, lies a jangle of modern high-rises and shopping streets. The layout is a tad baffling, but the focus of this second area – if indeed there is one – is the **Lijnbaan**, Europe's first pedestrianized shopping precinct, completed in 1953. The Lijnbaan is interesting as a prototype, but the dimensions are disconcerting: the street is too wide and the buildings are too low to create any sense of intimacy. Developers learnt lessons here.

To the east of Coolsingel, just north of Hoogstraat, is the fifteenth-century **St Laurenskerk** or Grote Kerk (Tues–Sat 10am–4pm; free), a mighty brick pile rebuilt after bomb damage in 1940. The church, which now hosts cultural events, has splendid bronze doors, the work of Giacomo Manzu in the 1960s, and you can climb the tower on the third Saturday of the month (April–Sept only, 12.30 & 2pm; €2.50).

From the back of St Laurenskerk it's a short walk south along the wide and windy Binnenrotte to **Blaak**, a compact, one-time working-class district that was comprehensively levelled in World War II, but has since been rebuilt in a full flush of modern design. The architectural high point is a remarkable series of cube-shaped houses, the *kubuswoningen*, completed in 1984 to a design by the architect Piet Blom. One of them, the **Kijk-Kubus** (Show Cube; Jan & Feb Fri–Sun 11am–5pm; March–Dec daily 11am–5pm; €2.50; ⓦwww.kubuswoning.nl), at Overblaak 70, near Blaak train and metro station, is open to visitors, offering a somewhat disorientating tour of what amounts to an upside-down house.

Behind the cube houses is the **Oude Haven**, built in 1325, and now flanked by cafés and crowded with antique barges and boats.

The Maritiem Museum and the Museum Het Schielandshuis

Heading west from the Kijk-Kubus, it's about 600m along Blaak boulevard to Churchillplein and the **Maritiem Museum** (Tues–Sat 10am–5pm, Sun 11am–5pm, July & Aug also Mon 10am–5pm; €7.50; ⓦwww.maritiemmuseum .nl), situated beside the waters of the city's first harbour, the **Leuvehaven**. The museum has an interesting display on the history of Rotterdam as a seaport and shipbuilding centre plus an entertaining section on the life of seamen in the seventeenth and eighteenth centuries. The outside area has been spruced up for the museum's prime exhibit, the *Buffel*, an immaculately restored mid-nineteenth-century ironclad ship, complete with communal sinks shaped to match the angle of the bows and a string of luxurious officers' cabins.

There's more on the history of Rotterdam at the **Museum Het Schielandshuis** (Tues–Sun 11am–5pm; €3; ⓦwww.historischmuseumrotterdam.nl), housed in a seventeenth-century mansion at Korte Hoogstraat 31 – a brief stroll north of the Maritiem Museum on the far side of Blaak boulevard. The main historical display features original footage of the bombing of the city in World War II, and the

---

Spido cruises

The shape and feel of the Leuvehaven, Rotterdam's first artificial harbour, has been transformed by the Boompjes freeway, which scoots along the top of the old enclosing sea dyke. Beside the Boompjes, at the south end of the Leuvehaven, is the departure point for **Spido cruises** (☏010/275 9988, ⓦwww.spido.nl). They have several different tours of the surrounding waterways and port facilities, heading off past the wharves, landings, docks and silos of this, the largest port in the world, but the standard **harbour tour** costs just €9.50 (April–Oct 5–11 daily; Nov–March Thurs–Sun 4 daily; 1hr 15min). In July and August, there are also longer trips to several destinations, most notably the series of colossal dams that make up the Delta Project along the seaboard southwest of Rotterdam (July & Aug 1 weekly on Wed; 6hr 30min; €49.75). For more on the Delta Project and Delta Expo, see p.298.

museum is also home to the Atlas van Stolk collection of drawings and prints, which includes fascinating sketches of pre-colonial Indonesia.

Museumpark

Tram #8 (direction Spangen) links Centraal Station and Coolsingel/ Schiedamsedijk with the southern edge of **Museumpark**, a designated cultural zone where a string of museums fringe a wide, open area. In the south, bordering Westzeedijk, are the **Natuurmuseum** (Tues–Sat 10am–5pm, Sun 11am–5pm; €4; ⓦ www.nmr.nl), where all sorts of stuffed animals are displayed, and the excellent **Kunsthal** (Tues–Sat 10am–5pm, Sun 11am–5pm; €9; ⓦ www .kunsthal.nl), which showcases first-rate exhibitions of contemporary art, photography and design. At the eastern side, right in front of the Erasmus hospital, there's also the **Nederlands Architectuur Instituut** (Dutch Architecture Institute; Tues–Sat 10am–5pm, Sun 11am–5pm; €8; ⓦ www.nai.nl), housed in a modern glass building and showcasing sketches, models and photos by prominent Dutch architects from 1800 onwards in an ambitious programme of temporary exhibitions.

Not located in the museumpark itself, but within easy walking distance is the new **Nederlands Fotomuseum** (Dutch Museum of Photography; Tues–Fri 10am–5pm, Sat & Sun 11am–5pm; €6; ⓦ www.nederlandsfoto museum.nl) with frequently rotated exhibitions of both big-name and up-and-coming photographers. To get there, cross the Erasmusbrug and take the first right.

Museum Boijmans Van Beuningen

A few minutes' walk from the Kunsthal, on the northern edge of Museumpark within shouting distance of the Eendrachtsplein metro stop, is Rotterdam's top attraction, the **Museum Boijmans Van Beuningen** (Tues–Sun 11am–5pm; €9; ⓦ www.boijmans.nl). The museum spreads over two floors with the ground floor used for temporary exhibitions, the first floor for the vast permanent collection. The older paintings are in one wing of the first floor, and those from the late nineteenth century onwards in the other. The information desk provides an updated and simplified diagrammatic outline of the museum, necessary because the exhibits are frequently rotated.

Flemish and Netherlandish paintings

Among the museum's earlier paintings is an excellent **Flemish and Netherlandish** section, where one highlight is the sumptuous *Christ in the House of Martha and Mary* by Pieter Aertsen (1508–75). There are also four exquisite works by Hieronymus Bosch (1450–1516). Usually considered a macabre fantasist, Bosch was actually working at the limits of oral and religious tradition, where biblical themes were depicted as iconographical representations, laden with explicit symbols. In his *St Christopher*, the dragon, the hanged bear and the broken pitcher lurk in the background, representations of danger and uncertainty, whereas the Prodigal Son's attitude to the brothel behind him in *The Peddler* is deliberately ambivalent. Bosch's technique never absorbed the influences of Renaissance Italy, and his figures in the *Marriage Feast at Cana* are static and unbelievable, uncomfortably arranged around a distorted table. Other works in this section include paintings by Jan van Scorel (1495–1562), who was more willing to absorb Italianate styles as in his *Young Scholar in a Red Cap*; the mysterious, hazy *Tower of Babel* by Pieter Brueghel the Elder; and Geertgen tot Sint Jans' (1460–90) beautiful, delicate *Glorification of the Virgin*.

The Golden Age

A fascinating selection of **Dutch genre** paintings reflects the tastes of the emergent seventeenth-century middle class. The idea was to depict real-life situations overlaid with a symbolic moral content as typified by Jan Steen's (1625–79) *The Doctor's Visit* and *Sick Woman*. There's also *The Quack* by Gerrit Dou (1613–75), ostensibly just a passing scene, but littered with small cameos of deception – a boy catching a bird, the trapped hare – that refer back to the quack's sham cures. In this section also are a number of **Rembrandts**, including two contrasting canvases: an analytic *Portrait of Aletta Adriaensdr*, her ageing illuminated but softened by her white ruff, and a gloomy, powerfully indistinct *Blind Tobias and his Wife* painted twenty years later. His intimate *Titus at his Desk* is also in marked contrast to the more formal portrait commissions common to his era. Most of the work of Rembrandt's pupil Carel Fabritius (1622–54) was destroyed when he was killed in a Delft gunpowder explosion in 1654; an exception is his *Self-Portrait*, reversing his master's usual technique by lighting the background and placing the subject in shadow.

Modern paintings

The museum's collection of **modern paintings** is perhaps best known for its **Surrealists**. It's difficult to appreciate Salvador Dalí's *Spain*, de rigueur for students' bedrooms in the 1970s, as anything more than the painting of the poster, but other works by the likes of René Magritte, Max Ernst and Giorgio de Chirico still have the power to surprise. Surrealism was never adopted by Dutch artists, though the **Magic Realism** of Carel Willink (1900–83) has its similarities in the precise, hallucinatory technique he uses to distance the viewer in *Self Portrait with a Pen*. *Three Generations* by Charley Toorop (1891–1955) is also Realism with an aim to disconcert: the huge bust of her father, Jan, looms in the background and dominates the painting. In this section, look out also for paintings from many of Europe's most famous artists, including Monet, van Gogh, Picasso, Gauguin, Cézanne and Munch, as well as a representative sample of the Barbizon and Hague schools, notably *Strandgezicht* by J.H. Weissenbruch (1822–80), a beautiful gradation of radiant tones.

Delfshaven

If little in Rotterdam city centre can exactly be called picturesque, **Delfshaven**, a couple of kilometres southwest of Centraal Station, goes part of the way to make up for it: to get there from the train station, catch tram #8 (direction Spangen) and get off at Spanjaardstraat tram stop, or take the metro to Delfshaven. Once the harbour that served Delft, it was from here that the **Pilgrim Fathers** set sail in 1620, changing to the more reliable *Mayflower* in Plymouth before continuing onward to the New World. Nevertheless, despite this substantial claim to fame, Delfshaven was long a neglected corner of the city until finally, in the 1970s, the council recognized its tourist potential and set about conserving and restoring. Most of the buildings lining the two narrow canals that comprise Delfshaven are eighteenth- and nineteenth-century warehouses, with the more fetching facades on the more westerly Voorhaven.

Eating, drinking and nightlife

Handy for many of the sights, the Oude and Nieuwe Binneweg are two of Rotterdam's grooviest streets, lined with recommendable **cafés**, **café-bars** and **restaurants**. Similarly enticing is Witte de Withstraat, where you'll also find one of the city's more amenable **cannabis coffeeshops**, the *Witte de With*, at no. 92.

The North Sea Jazz Festival

The North Sea Jazz Festival (ⓦ www.northseajazz.nl), held every year in mid-July, is the country's most prestigious jazz event, attracting international media coverage and many of the world's most famous musicians. For many years, the festival was held in Scheveningen near Den Haag, but in 2006 it was transferred to Rotterdam's Ahoy' centre, about 4km south of the city centre at Ahoy'-weg 10. To get to Ahoy' by metro, take the Erasmuslijn and get off at Zuidplein. Details of performances are available online and from the VVV, which will also reserve accommodation – virtually impossible to find after the festival has begun. Various kinds of tickets can be purchased; a *dagkaart*, for example, valid for an entire day, costs a very reasonable €75.

A lively spot in summer is the **Oude Haven**, where outdoor terraces line up overlooking the old harbour, and the **Westelijk Handelsterrein**, an old warehouse area which now holds a dozen very fashionable restaurants, bars and art galleries.

Restaurants

Amuse Proeverij & Magazijn Van Oldenbarn-eveltstrat 139 ⓣ 010/280 7206. Attractive, bistro-style café very much in the French manner, with a simple, tasty and inexpensive menu – set meals start at just €16.50 – and many wines by the glass. Wed & Thurs 11am–11pm, Fri & Sat 11am–midnight, Sun noon–10pm.

Bazar Witte de Withstraat 16. Big and bustling North African restaurant with a good sideline in vegetarian dishes. Laid-back (some would say cool) atmosphere. Daily 9am–11pm (Fri & Sat till midnight).

Ivy Lloydstraat 294 ⓣ 010/425 0520. The newest addition to the in-crowd scene with a speciality in molecular cooking, inspired by the masters of *El Bulli* and *The Fat Duck*. Be sure to book and check the limit on your credit card before splashing out. Tues–Sat noon–2.30pm & 6.30–10.30pm.

Kip Van Vollenhovenstraat 25 ⓣ 010/436 9923. This smooth and chic restaurant in classy premises, kitted out in a modern version of Golden Age style, has won all sorts of gastronomic awards. Finessed food at its finest with mains from €25. Daily 6–10pm.

Look 's Gravendijkwal 140 ⓣ 010/436 7000. As the name might suggest, garlic is the big deal here (*look* is Flemish for "garlic"), in everything from the creamy garlic soup to the garlic-vanilla ice-cream. Tasty surprises at affordable prices, with a three-course set menu costing just €23.50. Wed–Sun from 5.30pm.

Met de Franse Slag Schilderstraat 20a ⓣ 010/413 0143. Delicious French cuisine at this popular café-restaurant, where you sit surrounded by modern paintings and sculptures. Main courses are a very affordable €18 or so. Daily from 5pm.

Oliva Witte de Withstraat 15 ⓣ 010/412 1413. All ingredients in this relaxed restaurant are directly imported from Italy and most are organic. The main courses are written out on a blackboard, guaranteeing you the freshest seasonal produce. A three-course meal sets you back just €34. Daily 5.30–10pm.

Rosso Van Vollenhovenstraat 15 ⓣ 010/225 0705. Located in the happening Westelijk Handelsterrein, this is one of the best of the several fashionable restaurants here, attracting a lively crowd. The menu changes frequently, but if you pick the surprise three-course menu (€39) you can bet on the freshest ingredients with delicacies such as raw marinated tuna or beef from one of countries top butchers. Also many wines by the glass. Daily 6–11pm.

Café-bars and bars

Plan C Slepersvest 1. Bar/club with frequent live music and DJs on weekends. Popular with a youthful clientele and especially appealing in summer on account of the massive, open-air terrace.

Rotown Nieuwe Binnenweg 17. Lively café-bar attracting an alternative crew and serving up a wide variety of snacks and light meals from as little as €3. Regular live music too.

Sijf Oude Binnenweg 115, corner of Jacobstraat. Downbeat café-bar with entertaining decor; serves filling Dutch snacks and light meals. Daily 11am–10pm (Fri & Sat till 11pm).

Stadsbrouwerij De Pelgrim Aelbrechtskolk 12. Rotterdam's one and only brewery is located in the old council hall, which dates back to 1580 and has an attractive terrace overlooking Delfshaven. Their Mayflower Triple beer with a hint of caramel is especially tasty. Closed Mon.

Nightlife

Rotterdam has a vibrant **club scene** as well as a top-notch music venue with regular live performances. Tickets for gigs and concerts are on sale at the VVV (see p.176), which is an authorized outlet for Ticket (@www.ticketmaster.nl). For an up-to-date overview of all nightlife, try to get hold of a copy of the free *NL10* magazine, which can be found in stores, cafés and supermarkets around town.

Club Vie Maasboulevard 300 ☎010/280 0238, @www.clubvie.nl. A stylish venue hosting regular R&B, hip-hop and dance-classics nights as well as many international DJs. Thurs–Sat 10.30pm–4/5am.

Off Corso Kruiskade 22 ☎010/411 3897, @www.off-corso.nl. Large and funky venue near Centraal Station, with top DJs, groovy visuals and even art exhibitions. Fri & Sat 11pm–4/5am.

The Thalia Lounge Kruiskade 31 ☎010/214 2547, @www.thaliarotterdam.nl. Housed in an old cinema in front of *Off Corso*, this style-conscious club is best known for its frequent Latin house nights. Dress to impress. Fri & Sat 11pm–5pm.

WATT West Kruiskade 26 ☎010/217 9199, @www.watt-rotterdam.nl. The best place to catch a live gig is the recently opened *WATT*, hosting many international artists as well as the occasional DJ night.

Gouda and around

GOUDA, a pretty little place some 20km northeast of Rotterdam, is everything you'd expect of a Dutch country town, with its ring of quiet canals encircling ancient buildings set amid a tangle of narrow lanes and alleys. More surprisingly, its **Markt** is the largest in the Netherlands, a wide and airy piazza that remains an attractive reminder of the town's prominence as a centre of the medieval cloth trade, and later of its success in the manufacture of cheeses and that old Dutch favourite, the clay pipe.

Gouda's main claim to fame is its **cheese market**, held on the Markt every Thursday morning (10am–12.30pm) from the middle of June to late August. Traditionally, some one thousand local farmers brought their home-produced cheeses here to be weighed, tested and graded for moisture, smell and taste. These details were marked on the cheeses and formed the basis for negotiation between buyer and seller, the exact price confirmed by an elaborate code of hand-claps. Today, however, the cheese market is a shadow of its former self, comprising a few locals in traditional dress standing outside the Waag with their cheeses, all surrounded by modern, open-air stands. It's mercilessly milked by tour operators who herd their crowds into this scene every week – but don't let this put you off a visit to the town, since Gouda's charms lie elsewhere, especially in the splendid stained-glass windows of **St Janskerk**. Gouda is also a short bus ride from the hamlet of **Oudewater**, home to the curious **Heksenwaag** (meaning "witches' weigh house"), where many medieval women were saved from certain death when it was "proved" they were not witches.

The Town

Slap-bang in the middle of the Markt, the **Stadhuis** is an elegant Gothic structure whose soaring stonework, with its spiky towers and dinky dormer windows, dates from 1450. Statues of Burgundian counts and countesses decorate the building's facades and on its east side is the cheeriest of carillons, where the tiny figures play up and around every half-hour. Opposite, on the north side of the square, is the **Waag**, a tidy seventeenth-century building adorned by a detailed relief of cheese-weighing and now holding a moderately interesting **Kaaswaag** (Cheese Weigh House museum; April–Oct Tues–Sun 1–5pm, Thurs 10am–5pm; €3.50).

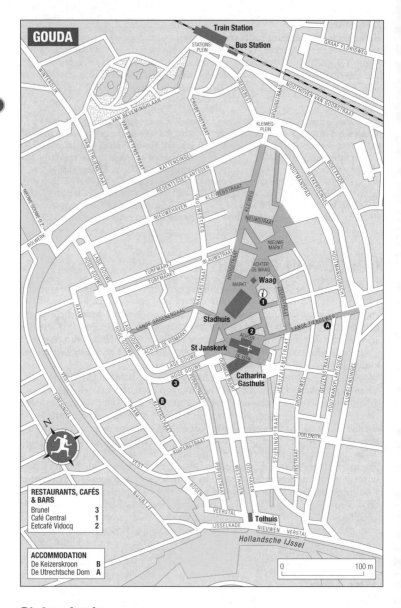

GOUDA

Train Station

Bus Station

STATIONS-PLEIN

GRAAF FLORISWEG

WINTERDIJK

VAN BEVERNINGHLAAN

VAN SWIETENSTRAAT

CARNEHSTRAAT

NIEUWE GOUWE O.Z.

NIEUWE GOUWE W.Z.

VAN STRIENSTRAAT

KATTENSINGEL

REGENTESSEPLANTSOEN

NIEUWEHAVEN

BOLWERK

HOGE GOUWE

LAGE GOUWE

TURFMARKT

TURFMARKT

RAAM

LANGE GROENENDAAL

ACHTER DE VISMARKT

LAGE GOUWE

HOGE GOUWE

PEPERSTRAAT

KEIZERSTRAAT

VEST

RAAM

TURFSINGEL

VEST

BOGEN

BUURTJE

KUIPERSTRAAT

KLEIWEG-PLEIN

PROBEEST

SPOORSTRAAT

NOOTHOVEN VAN GOORSTRAAT

BOELEKADE

BLEKERSSINGEL

HOUTMANSGRACHT

KLEIWEGSTRAAT

HOUTMANSGRACHT

KLEIWEG

NIEUWSTRAAT

NIEUWE MARKT

NAAIERSTRAAT

BLAUWSTRAAT

HOOGSTRAAT

ACHTER DE WAAG

MARKT

♦ Waag

ⓘ
❶

LANGE TIENDEWEG

Ⓐ

LANGE NOODGODSTRAAT

Stadhuis

❷

St Janskerk ✝

ACHTER DE KERK

DUBBELE BUURT

Catharina Gasthuis

❸

JERUZALEMSTRAAT

GROENEWEG

GEUZENSTRAAT

HOUTMANSPLANTSOEN

FLUWELENSINGEL

SPIERINGSTRAAT

WESTHAVEN

OOSTHAVEN

NAAIERSTRAAT

PEPERSTRAAT

DOELENSTR.

TUINSTRAAT

Ⓑ

N

Tolhuis

VEERSTAL

IJSSELKADE

NIEUWEN VERSTAL

VERSTAL

Hollandsche IJssel

0   100 m

RESTAURANTS, CAFÉS & BARS
Brunel   3
Café Central   1
Eetcafé Vidocq   2

ACCOMMODATION
De Keizerskroon   B
De Utrechtsche Dom   A

St Janskerk

To the south, just off the Markt, the lumpy **St Janskerk** (Mon–Sat: March–Oct 9am–5pm; Nov–Feb 10am–4pm; €2.75; Ⓦ www.sintjan.com) was founded in 1280, but the present structure mostly dates from the second half of the sixteenth century, when it was rebuilt following a dreadful fire. The church is famous for its magnificent and stunningly beautiful **stained-glass windows**, which bear witness to the move from Catholicism to Calvinism.

All the windows are numbered and a detailed guide and audioguide are available at the entrance.

The biblical themes executed by **Dirk and Wouter Crabeth** between 1555 and 1571, when Holland was still Catholic, are traditional in content, but they have an amazing clarity of detail and richness of colour. Their last piece, *Judith Slaying Holofernes* (Window no. 6), is perhaps the finest, the story unfolding in intricate perspective – and a gruesome tale it was too. The Assyrian general Holofernes made the mistake of sharing his tent with Judith, a Jewish woman from Bethulia, the town he was besieging; he made things worse by drinking himself into a stupor and Judith, not one to look a gift horse in the mouth, lopped off his head and carried it back to Bethulia in triumph.

By comparison, the **post-Reformation windows**, which date from 1594 to 1603, adopt an allegorical and heraldic style typical of a more secular art. A prime illustration is *The Relief of Leiden* (Window no. 25), which shows William the Silent retaking the town from the Spanish, though Delft and its burgomasters take prominence – no doubt because they footed the bill for the window's manufacture.

The rest of the centre

By the south side of St Jankerk, the fancily carved **Lazarus Gate** of 1609 was once part of the town's leper hospital, until it was moved here to form the back entrance to the **Catharina Gasthuis** (Wed–Fri 10am–5pm, Sat & Sun noon–5pm; €5), a hospice till 1910 and now a fine art museum. The collection, which spreads over two floors, is really rather confusing and short of major paintings, but the Gasthuiskapel does hold a pleasant assortment of sixteenth- and seventeenth-century Dutch paintings, notably a sterling biblical triptych by Dirck Barendsz (1534–92) and, in the corridor between Rooms 10 and 11, a set of four striking Civic Guard group portraits. Upstairs, a modest selection of Hague and Barbizon School canvases is given a bit of artistic sparkle by four small paintings of rural idylls by Anton Mauve (1838–88).

With time to spare, you might stroll south along **Westhaven**, a winsome jumble of old canal-side buildings which rambles off towards the old **Tolhuis** (toll house) beside the Hollandsche IJssel river, on the southern edge of the town centre.

Practicalities

Gouda's **train** and **bus stations** are to the immediate north of the town centre, ten minutes' walk from the **VVV**, at Markt 27 (Mon 1–5.30pm, Tues–Fri 9.30am–5.30pm, Sat 10am–4pm; July & Aug also Sun noon–4pm; ☎0900 468 3288, ⓦwww.vvvgouda.nl). They have a limited supply of **rooms** in private houses (❶–❷), and will make hotel reservations on your behalf for a small charge. There are two reasonably priced **hotels** in the centre, the more enjoyable of which is the excellent-value *De Utrechtsche Dom*, in an airy and pleasantly renovated building five minutes' walk from the Markt at Geuzenstraat 6 (☎0182/528 833, ⓦwww.hotelgouda.nl; ❷). A second choice is *De Keizerskroon*, an unassuming family-run hotel in a terrace house to the west of Westhaven at Keizerstraat 11–13 (☎0182/528 096, ⓦwww.hotelkeizerskroon.nl; ❷).

You don't come to Gouda for the nightlife, but there are several good **cafés**, beginning with ⚔ *Café Central*, Markt 23 (daily 9am–midnight), where they rustle up a tasty and filling range of home-made Dutch stand-bys in resolutely old-fashioned premises – there's been no tacky modernization here, witness the wood panelling. Main courses average around €17, salads and snacks €8, and they serve great pancakes too. There's more good-quality Dutch cuisine at the popular *Eetcafé Vidocq*, Koster Gijzensteeg 8 (daily 5–10.30pm), which is also a pleasant place for a drink. The best **restaurant** in town is *Brunel*, a smart Franco-Dutch split-level joint at Hoge Gouwe 23 (☏0182/518 979; daily 5–10pm); main courses average about €22.

Oudewater

Pocket-sized **OUDEWATER**, deep in the countryside about 11km east of Gouda, is a compact and delightful town that holds a unique place in the history of Dutch witchcraft (see box below). Pride of place here goes to the town's sixteenth-century Waag, which has been turned into the **Heksenwaag** (Witches' Weigh House; April–Oct Tues–Sun 11am–5pm; €4.25; ⓦwww .heksenwaag.nl), a family-run affair where you can be weighed on the original rope and wood balance, as were women accused of witchcraft. The owners dress up in national costume and issue a certificate in olde-worlde English that states nothing much in particular, but does so very prettily. There's not much else to see in Oudewater, but it is a pleasant place, whose old brick houses spread out along the River Hollandsche IJssel as it twists its way through town.

Practicalities

Oudewater is readily reached on **bus** #180 linking Gouda with Utrecht (every 30min, hourly on Sun; 25min from Gouda). Get off at the Molenwal stop, a

---

Witch hunts and Oudewater

It's estimated that over one million European women were burned or otherwise murdered in the widespread **witch-hunts** of the sixteenth century – and not just from quasi-religious fear and superstition: anonymous accusation to the authorities was an easy way of removing a wife, at a time when there was no divorce. Underlying it all was a virulent misogyny and an accompanying desire to terrorize women into submission. There were three main methods for investigating accusations of witchcraft: in the first, **trial by fire**, the suspect had to walk barefoot over hot cinders or have a hot iron pressed into the back or hands. If the burns blistered, the accused was innocent, since witches were supposed to burn less easily than others; naturally, the (variable) temperature of the iron was crucial. **Trial by water** was still more hazardous: dropped into water, if you floated you were a witch, if you sank you were innocent – though very few probably dead by drowning. The third method, **trial by weight**, presupposed that a witch would have to be unduly light to fly on a broomstick, so many Dutch towns – including Oudewater – used the Waag (town weigh house) to weigh the accused. If the weight didn't accord with a notional figure derived from a person's height, the woman was burned. The last Dutch woman to be burned as a witch was a certain Marrigje Ariens, a herbalist from Schoonhoven in Zuid-Holland, whose medical efforts, not atypically, inspired mistrust and subsequent persecution. She was killed in 1597.

The Emperor Charles V (1516–52) made Oudewater famous after seeing a woman accused of witchcraft in a nearby village. The weigh-master there, who'd been bribed, stated that the woman weighed only a few pounds, but Charles was dubious and ordered the woman to be weighed again in Oudewater, where the officials proved unbribable, pronouncing a normal weight and acquitting her. The probity of Oudewater's weigh-master impressed Charles, and he granted the town the privilege of issuing certificates, valid throughout the empire, stating: "The accused's weight is in accordance with the natural proportions of the body." Once in possession of the certificate, a woman could never be brought to trial for witchcraft again. Not surprisingly, thousands of women came from all over Europe for this life-saving piece of paper, and, much to Oudewater's credit, no one was ever condemned here.

five-minute walk from the centre – just follow the signs. The **VVV** is two doors along from the Heksenwaag at Leeuweringerstraat 10 (April–Sept Tues–Sat 10am–4pm, Sun 11am–3pm; Oct–March Tues, Thurs & Fri 10am–1pm, Wed 10am–4pm & Sat 10am–2pm; ☎0900 468 3288, ⓦwww.vvvoudewater.nl). They have lots of local information including bus timetables. For **food**, head for the *Lumière Eetcafé* (daily except Wed 10am–10pm, kitchen from noon), an extremely cosy old place with a tiled fireplace and oodles of wood panelling just opposite the Heksenwaag. They serve traditional, home-made Dutch food here – and very tasty it is too; mains average €16 at night, less at lunchtimes.

Dordrecht and around

Some 20km southeast of Rotterdam, the ancient port of **DORDRECHT**, or "Dordt" as it's often called, sits beside one of the busiest waterway junctions in the world, where tankers and containers from the north pass the waterborne traffic of the Maas and Rijn. Eclipsed by the expansion of Rotterdam – and barely touched by World War II – Dordrecht's old centre has survived in excellent nick, its medley of eighteenth- and nineteenth-century warehouses, town houses and workers' terraces strung along its innermost canals and harbours. It takes about three hours to cover all of the town's main sights, which makes a day-trip the most obvious choice, especially as good hotels are thin on the ground. If, however, you're after exploring the sprawling marshes and tidal flats of the wilderness **Nationaal Park de Biesbosch** just south of town, then Dordrecht is the obvious base, though a long day-trip from, say, Rotterdam, Delft or Den Haag is quite feasible. The other main pull hereabouts is the windmills of the **Kinderdijk**.

Some history

Granted a town charter in 1220, **Dordrecht** was the most important and powerful town in Holland until well into the sixteenth century. One of the first cities to declare against the Habsburgs in 1572, it was the obvious site for the first meeting of the Free Assembly of the United Provinces, and for a series of doctrinal conferences that tried to solve a whole range of theological differences among the various Protestant sects. The Protestants may have hated the Catholics, but they inherited the medieval church's enthusiasm for theological debate; in 1618, at the **Synod of Dordt**, the Remonstrants argued with the Calvinists over the definition of predestination – pretty weighty stuff compared with the Synod of 1574, when one of the main rulings demanded the dismantling of church organs. From the seventeenth century, Dordrecht lost ground to its great rivals to the north, slipping into comparative insignificance, though it did manage to hold on to enough trade and shipbuilding to keep its economy afloat.

Arrival and information

Well connected by train to all of the Randstad's major cities, Dordrecht's adjoining **train** and **bus stations** are a ten-minute walk from the town centre: to get there, head straight down Stationsweg/Johan de Wittstraat and left at the end along Bagijnhof/Visstraat. The **VVV** is located about halfway, at Spuiboulevard 99 (Mon noon–5.30pm, Tues, Wed & Fri 9am–5.30pm, Thurs 9am–9pm, Sat 10am–5pm; ☎0900 463 6888, ⓦwww.vvvdordrecht.nl). It carries a good range of information about the town and its surroundings

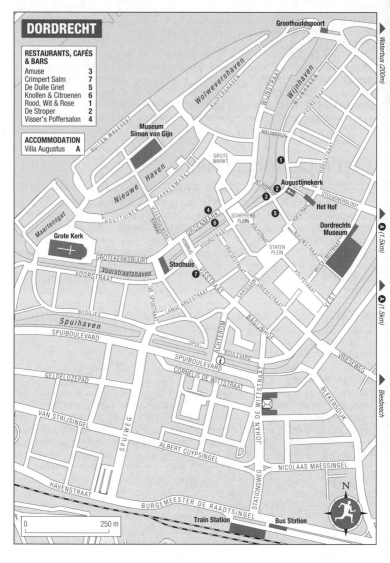

DORDRECHT

RESTAURANTS, CAFÉS
& BARS
Amuse   3
Crimpert Salm   7
De Dulle Griet   5
Knollen & Citroenen   6
Rood, Wit & Rose   1
De Stroper   2
Visser's Poffersalon   4

ACCOMMODATION
Villa Augustus   A

0   250 m

– including the Biesbosch – and operates an accommodation booking service.
There's also a **Waterbus** passenger ferry service from Rotterdam (see p.180)
that drops passengers within easy walking distance of the old centre, a couple
of hundred metres from the **Groothoofdspoort**.

Accommodation

As part of its accommodation service, the VVV has a small supply of **rooms** in
private houses (**1**), which it will reserve on your behalf for a nominal fee. Centrally
located **hotels** are few and far between, and the best bet is to head for the new

🍴 *Villa Augustus*, Oranjelaan 7 (☎078/639 3111, ⓦwww.villa-augustus.nl; ❹), in an old watermill which has been converted into 37 rustic but smart rooms, some with great views; the hotel is about 1.5km east of the centre. They have a huge canteen-like **restaurant** overlooking the kitchen garden too.

Dordrecht also has an HI **hostel**, but it's way out in the boon docks, on the edge of the Biesbosch about 6km east of town on Baanhoekweg (☎078/621 2167, ⓦwww.stayokay.com; ❶, dorm bed €25–31). To get there by public transport, take bus #4 from the station, which will drop you off at the hostel in high season, but otherwise it's a fifteen-minute walk from the Baanhoekweg stop. There's a small **campsite** at the hostel, one of several dotted around the peripheries of the Biesbosch.

The Town

Jutting out into the River Maas, the old part of Dordrecht is interrupted by the three concentric waterways that once protected it from assault. The middle canal runs beside the **Voorstraat**, today's main shopping street, and here, at the junction of Voorstraat and Visstraat, sitting pretty on the **Visbrug**, is a clunky **monument** to the de Witt brothers, Johan and Cornelius, prominent Dutch Republicans who paid for their principles when they were torn to pieces by an Orangist mob in Den Haag in 1672. To the right of the Visbrug, Voorstraat wends its way northeast, a chaotic mixture of the old, the new and the restored, intersected by a series of tiny alleys that once served as the town's docks. About halfway along Voorstraat the Wijnbrug bridge crosses the **Wijnhaven**, the harbour used by the city's merchants to control the import and export of wine when they held the state monopoly from the fourteenth to the seventeenth century. At the end of Voorstraat, the **Groothoofdspoort** was once the main city gate, its grand brick facade of 1618, complete with bronze-green cupola, staring down at the barges and boats that shuttle across the adjacent waterways.

The Wolwevershaven

From the Groothoofdspoort, it's a few metres to the slender **Wolwevershaven**, the first of the two small harbours that together make up the town's innermost canal. The Wolwevershaven is home to an eye-catching mixture of old boats and barges, some of which date back to the 1880s, and is framed by several fine old mansions, one of which has been turned into the **Museum Simon van Gijn**, Nieuwe Haven 29 (Tues–Sun 11am–5pm; €6; ⓦwww.simonvangijn.nl), whose collection of local memorabilia and period rooms is of moderate interest. Best are the eighteenth-century Brussels tapestries and a fine Renaissance chimney-piece of 1550, transferred from the old guild house of the arquebusiers.

The Grote Kerk and the Stadhuis

Lording it over the Nieuwe Haven, the next harbour along, the Gothic **Grote Kerk** (April–Oct Tues–Sat 10.30am–4pm, Sun noon–4pm; Nov–March Sat & Sun 1–4pm; free; ⓦwww.grotekerk-dordrecht.nl) is visible from all over town, its truncated, fourteenth-century **tower** (same hours; €1) topped with incongruous seventeenth-century clocks. One of the largest churches in the country, it was built to emphasize Dordrecht's wealth and importance, but it's heavy and dull, despite its attractive environs, and there's only an elaborately carved choir inside to hold your interest. Climb the tower for a great view over the town and its surrounding waterways.

From beside the church, the harmonious old gables of Grotekerksbuurt lead to the stolid classicism of the **Stadhuis**, on the Voorstraat.

Dordrechts Museum

From the Stadhuis, it's a ten-minute walk east to the town's premier art gallery, the **Dordrechts Museum**, at Museumstraat 40 (closed for renovation at the time of writing; Ⓦ www.dordrechtsmuseum.nl). The museum has a lively programme of temporary exhibitions and a strong permanent collection focused on local artists from the seventeenth century onwards. High points include a couple of finely drawn portraits by Jacob Cuyp (1594–1651), specifically pictures of a very young *Michiel Pompe* and of the eminently bourgeois *Anthonis Repelaer*, and four romanticized land and seascapes by Jacob's son, Aelbert (1620–91). Jan van Goyen (1596–1656), one of the country's finest landscape painters, is well represented by the detailed realism of his exquisite *View of Dordrecht*, the city flat and narrow beneath a wide, cloudy sky. Goyen's vision of Dordrecht bears interesting comparison with Adam Willaertz's (1577–1664) massive *Gezicht op Dordt* ("View of Dordt"), in which the painter abandons proper scale to emphasize the ships in front of the city. More curiously, *De Dordtse Vierling* ("The Dordt Quadruplets") is an odd, unattributed seventeenth-century painting of a dead child and her three swaddled siblings, a simple, moving tribute to a lost daughter.

There's also a selection of work by the later and lesser Ary Scheffer (1795–1858), who was born in Dordrecht, but lived in Paris from 1811. His much-reproduced *Mignon Pining for her Native Land* struck a chord in the sentimental hearts of the nineteenth-century bourgeoisie. Lastly, Jozef Israels' (1824–1911) *Midday Meal at the Inn*, a scream against poverty, and G.H. Breitner's (1857–1923) *Amsterdam's Lauriergracht* are among a small collection of Amsterdam and Hague School paintings.

Eating and drinking

For a small town, Dordrecht has a good spread of **cafés** and **restaurants**. Some of the best are located on **Voorstraat**, the main shopping street, and there's another concentration on narrow **Nieuwstraat**, running off Voorstraat.

Amuse Voorstraat 261 ☎ 078/614 5885. Smart and chic restaurant, where all the dishes – drawn from an inventive menu – are starter-sized. A three-course meal costs €32.50. Wed–Sat noon–11.30pm & Sun 5–11.30pm.

Crimpert Salm Visstraat 5 ☎ 078/614 5557. A French-style café and restaurant, where they serve snacks and light meals during the day and dinner in the evening. The *Crimpert* occupies a handsome old building that once housed the fish merchants' guild, near the Visbrug. Tues–Sat 10am–11.30pm.

De Dulle Griet Nieuwstraat 25 ☎ 078/614 5995. Groovy and inexpensive eetcafé with an international menu including everything from Thai fish curry to Indian vegetable curry and Mexican steak. Side dishes have to be ordered separately. Summer garden terrace. Mon–Sat 6–9.30pm & Sun 5–8.30pm, plus Wed–Sat noon–3pm.

Knollen & Citroenen Groenmarkt 8 ☎ 078/614 0500. Traditional Dutch stews, soups and veggie dishes from – as they say – grandma's kitchen, with decor to match. Wed–Fri 6–10pm, Sat & Sun 5–10pm.

Rood, Wit & Rose Voorstraat 227. An original *vinoteca* serving fifty wines by the glass, many more by the bottle. Specializes in European wines. Thurs noon–9pm, Fri–Sun noon–7pm.

De Stroper Wijnbrug 1 ☎ 078/613 0094. A smart seafood restaurant in modern, well-turned-out premises; main courses cost €20–25. Mon–Fri 11am–2pm & 6–10pm, Sat & Sun 6–10pm.

Visser's Poffersalon Groenmarkt 9 ☎ 078/613 7373. An old-fashioned café which does an especially good lin e in pancakes. Tues, Wed, Fri & Sat 9am–6pm, Thurs 9am–9pm, Sun 2.30–6pm.

The Nationaal Park de Biesbosch

On November 18, 1421, Zuid-Holland's sea defences gave way and the St Elizabeth Day flood formed what is now the Hollands Diep sea channel and the **Biesbosch** (Reed Forest), an expanse of river, creek, marsh and reed covering around fifteen square kilometres to the south and east of Dordrecht. It was a disaster of major proportions, with seventy towns and villages destroyed and a death toll of around 100,000. The effect on the region's economy was catastrophic, too, with the fracturing of links between Zuid-Holland and Flanders accelerating the shift in commercial power to the north. Those villages that did survive took generations to recover, subjected as they were to raids by the wretched refugees of the flood.

Inundated twice daily by the tide, the Biesbosch produced a particular **reed culture**, its inhabitants using the plant for every item of daily life, from houses to baskets and boats, and selling excess cuttings at the local markets. It was a harsh existence that lasted well into the nineteenth century, when machine-manufactured goods largely rendered the reeds redundant. Today, the Biesbosch is protected as a national park, but its delicate ecosystem is threatened by the very scheme that aims to protect the province from further flooding. The dams of the Delta Project (see p.298) have controlled the rivers' flow and restricted the tides' strength, forcing the reeds to give ground to other forms of vegetation incompatible with the area's bird and plant life. Large areas of reed have disappeared, and no one seems to know how to reconcile the nature reserve's needs with those of the seaboard cities, but vigorous attempts are being made.

The national park divides into two main sections, north and south of the Nieuwe Merwede waterway. The undeveloped heart of the park is the **Brabantse Biesbosch**, the chunk of land to the south, whereas almost all tourist facilities have been carefully confined to the north on a strip just east of Dordrecht, along the park's perimeter.

Practicalities

The **Biesboschcentrum Dordrecht**, 7km or so east of town at Baanhoekweg 53 (Visitor Centre: Jan–April & Oct–Dec Tues–Sun 10am–5pm; May–Sept daily 9am–6pm; ⓦ www.hollandsebiesbosch.nl; free), has displays on the flora and fauna of the region and a beaver observatory. Frankly, this is pretty dull stuff, but it's here, from the jetty beside the visitor centre, that you can take a **boat trip** into the untouched reaches of the park, where deep and dense tracts of forest are crisscrossed by narrow waterways inhabited by all manner of wildfowl. Prices vary according to the itinerary, starting at €22.50 for the day ("Dagtochten") or €6.50 for an hour-long excursion ("Rondvaarten"), and you should check what's on offer – and make an advance booking – at Dordrecht VVV (see p.189) before you set out. If you fancy doing it under your own steam, note that there is boat and kayak rental here too.

The other way of visiting the park is by **bike**, for rent at standard rates from Dordrecht train station. The VVV sells detailed maps of the national park and brochures on suggested cycle routes. The ride from town to the Kop van 't Land dock, where ferries shuttle over to the Brabantse Biesbosch, takes about half an hour.

The Kinderdijk

Some 12km north of Dordrecht, the **Kinderdijk** (Child's Dyke; ⓦ www .kinderdijk.nl) sits at the end of a long drainage channel that feeds into the River Lek. Sixteenth-century legend suggests it takes its name from the time when a cradle, complete with cat and kicking baby, was found at the precise spot where the dyke had held during a particularly bad storm. Encompassing a mixture of symbols – rebirth, innocence and survival – the story encapsulates the determination with which the Dutch fought the floods for hundreds of years. Today, the Kinderdijk is famous for its picturesque, quintessentially Dutch

windmills, all nineteen lining the main channel and its tributary beside the Molenkade for some 3km. Built around 1740 to drive water from the Alblasserwaard polders, the windmills are put into operation every Saturday afternoon in July and August and, in addition, one of the windmills is open to visitors from mid-March through to October (daily 9.30am–5.30pm; €3.50).

Easily the best way to get to – and get around – the Kinderdijk is by **bike**; follow signs from Dordrecht or rent one at the shop at Kinderdijk itself for €2.50 for two hours. It is also possible to travel here on the **Waterbus** passenger ferry (see p.180) and by **Arriva bus**, though the bus service from Utrecht (bus #90: hourly; 1hr 30min) and Rotterdam's Zuidplein (bus #90: hourly; 50min) is much better than that from Dordrecht, from where you have to take bus #16 to Alblasserdam and then change onto bus #90 in the direction of Utrecht (2 daily, 45min) or bus #19 to Nieuw Lekkerland and then bus #90 in the direction of Rotterdam (2 hourly; 45min).

Utrecht

First impressions of **UTRECHT** are rarely positive: the mammoth shopping centre that encloses the city's train station is not encouraging and neither is its tangle of busy dual carriageways. But persevere: much of Utrecht's old centre has survived intact, its network of canals, cobbled lanes and old gabled houses at their prettiest around the **Domkerk**, the city's cathedral. Domkerk apart, it's the general appearance and university atmosphere of the place that is its appeal rather than any specific sight – and indeed Utrecht's two key museums, the **Centraal** and the **Catharijne Convent**, both of which have an enjoyable collection of old Dutch paintings, are out of the immediate centre to the south. Utrecht was also the long-time home of the De Stijl luminary **Gerrit Rietveld**, whose assorted furniture decorates the Centraal Museum, which pays further tribute to the man by organizing bus trips to the house that Rietveld built – the **Rietveld Schröderhuis**.

As you might expect of a university town, Utrecht has a vibrant café, bar and restaurant scene and the presence of students ensures that prices are kept down.

Some history

Founded by the **Romans** in the first century AD, Utrecht only came to prominence in the eighth century after the consecration of its first **bishop**. Thereafter, a long line of powerful bishops made Utrecht an independent city-state, albeit under the auspices of the German emperors, extending and consolidating their control over the surrounding region. In 1527, the bishop, seeing which way the historical wind was blowing, sold off his secular rights to the Habsburg Emperor Charles V, and shortly afterwards the town council enthusiastically joined the revolt against Spain. Indeed, the **Union of Utrecht**, the agreement that formalized the opposition to the Habsburgs, was signed here in 1579. The seventeenth century witnessed the foundation of **Utrecht University** and the eighteenth saw Utrecht pop up again as the place where the **Treaty of Utrecht** was signed in 1713, thereby concluding decades of dynastic feuding between Europe's rulers. Fifty years later, it was also the source of one of James Boswell's harsher judgements: "I groaned with the idea of living all winter in so shocking a place," he moaned, which said more about his homesickness – he had just arrived here from England to study law – than it did about the city. Today, with a population of around quarter of a million,

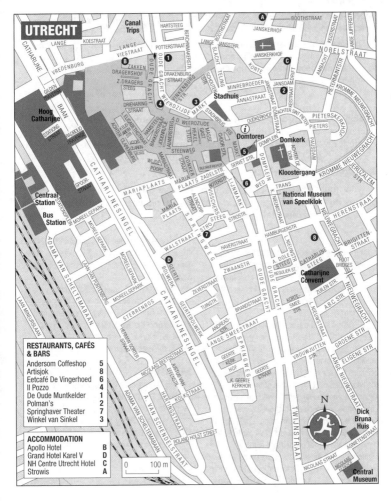

**RESTAURANTS, CAFÉS
& BARS**

Andersom Coffeeshop	5
Artisjok	8
Eetcafé De Vingerhoed	6
Il Pozzo	4
De Oude Muntkelder	1
Polman's	2
Springhaver Theater	7
Winkel van Sinkel	3

ACCOMMODATION

Apollo Hotel	B
Grand Hotel Karel V	D
NH Centre Utrecht Hotel	C
Strowis	A

Utrecht is one of the country's most important cities, its economy buoyed by light industry, academia and IT. One of the best times to visit is during the **Netherlands Film Festival**, ten days of cinematic inspiration held every year at the end of September (Ⓦwww.filmfestival.nl).

Arrival and information

Utrecht's **train and bus stations** are both enmeshed within the sprawling **Hoog Catharijne** shopping centre, on the western edge of the city centre. It's an extremely ugly complex, but there are plans to have it reorganised and revamped. The **VVV** is a ten-minute walk away beside the Domtoren (cathedral tower) at Domplein 9 (April–Sept Mon–Fri 10am–6pm, Sat 10am–5pm & Sun noon–5pm; Oct–March Mon noon–6pm, Tues–Fri 10am–6pm, Sat 10am–5pm & Sun noon–5pm; Ⓣ0900 128 8732, Ⓦwww.utrechtyourway.com). They have

Canal trips

Throughout the summer, Schuttevaer (☎030/272 0111, ⓦwww.schuttevaer.com) operates enjoyable, hour-long **canal trips** (daily 11am–5pm; €8) around the centre of the city. Departures are from Oude Gracht, just south of the Lange Viestraat/Potterstraat junction.

a range of information on the city and its surroundings, sell city maps and operate an accommodation booking service. The best way to explore the city centre is on foot, but **bikes** can be rented from the train station at standard rates.

Accommodation

As you might expect of a big city, Utrecht has a battery of chain **hotels**. Some occupy big modern blocks, but one or two are rather more distinctive, and the city also has a great-value **hostel**.

Hotels

Apollo Hotel Vredenburg 14 ☎030/233 1232, ⓦwww.apollohotelresorts.com. Straightforward, modern, high-rise chain hotel a brief walk from the train station. The rooms aren't anything special, but they are perfectly adequate and the hotel is competitively priced. ❶

Grand Hotel Karel V Geertebolwerk 1 ☎030/233 7555, ⓦwww.karelv.nl. Opened in 2000, this delightful and distinctive five-star hotel is the best in the city by a long chalk and it occupies the site of what was, in medieval times, the headquarters of the Knights of the Teutonic Order. The main building is a cleverly modernised, nineteenth-century edifice that once served as a hospital and there's a modern wing – the Roman wing – too; in between are attractive gardens. All the rooms are well appointed and extremely comfortable, but those in the Roman wing are a tad larger and more luxurious, for the most part being split-level suites. The decor is, as you might expect,

immaculate, all wooden floors and white walls with the odd suit of armour propped up here and there for good measure. A 5min walk south of the train station. ❹

NH Centre Utrecht Hotel Janskerkhof 10 ☎030/231 3169, ⓦwww.nh-hotels.com. Well-equipped chain hotel in a clunkily converted old building from the 1870s. The 45 guest rooms are kitted out in brisk, modern style. A 15min walk east of the train station. ❸

Hostel

Strowis Boothstraat 8 ☎030/238 0280, ⓦwww.strowis.nl. This pleasant hostel, in a seventeenth-century town house, has a good range of facilities including a small library, bike rental, a self-catering kitchen and free internet access. The bedrooms, which range from single rooms to 14-bed dorms, are well kept and painted in cheerful colours. The *Strowis* is situated in the old centre near St Janskerk, 1km east of the station. Dorm beds €15–16, doubles ❶

The Town

The logical place to start a visit to the city is the **Domtoren**, at over 112m the highest church bell tower in the country. It's one of the most beautiful, too, its soaring columns and arches rising to a delicate, octagonal lantern, which was added in 1380 some sixty years after the rest of the tower was completed. Beginning at the adjacent VVV, hour-long guided tours (April–Sept Mon & Sun noon–5pm, Tues–Sat 11am–5pm; Oct–March Mon–Fri & Sun noon–5pm, Sat 11am–5pm; tours hourly; €7.50; ⓦwww.domtoren.nl) take you unnervingly near to the top, from where on a clear day you can see Rotterdam and Amsterdam. Below, the empty space on the east side of the tower was where the nave of the cathedral stood until a storm brought it tumbling down in 1674. However, the monumental transepts and chancel survived and these comprise today's **Domkerk** (May–Sept Mon–Fri 10am–5pm, Sat 10am–3.30pm & Sun 2–4pm; Oct–April Mon–Sat 11am–4pm, Sat 10am–3.30pm & Sun 2–4pm; free;

@www.domkerk.nl), which is distinguished by its strong Gothic lines and funerary monuments. Among the latter, the high point is the exquisitely carved marble sarcophagus of Admiral Willem Joseph van Gendt, who came a cropper at the long-forgotten sea battle of Solebay in 1672.

Next to the Domkerk stands the fifteenth-century **Kloostergang** (cloisters), whose good-looking gables sport low reliefs illustrating the life of the city's fourth-century patron saint, St Martin of Tours.

Around the Domkerk

Kromme Nieuwegracht, just to the east of the Domkerk, is one of the city's most delightful streets, its medley of fine old buildings overlooking a slender canal and its string of mini-footbridges. Follow the canal round and eventually you reach Jansstraat, from where it's a hop, skip and a jump to the **Stadhuis**, whose grandiose, Neoclassical facade dates from 1826. The Stadhuis stands on a bend of the pretty **Oude Gracht**, where, most unusually, a long series of brick cellars, which once served as warehouses and are now bars, cafés and restaurants, are down by the canal and the street level is one storey up.

The Stadhuis is also close to the unusual **Nationaal Museum van Speelklok tot Pierement**, Steenweg 6 (Tues–Sun 10am–5pm; €8; @www.museum speelklok.nl), a collection of fairground organs and ingenious musical boxes worth an hour of (almost) anyone's time. The museum is housed in the **Buurkerk**, once the home of one sister Bertken, who was so ashamed of being the illegitimate daughter of a cathedral priest that she hid away in a small cell here for 57 years, until her death in 1514.

The Museum Catharijne Convent

The **Museum Catharijne Convent** (Tues–Fri 10am–5pm, Sat & Sun 11am–5pm; €9; @www.catharijneconvent.nl), 500m south of the Domtoren at Lange Nieuwstraat 38, has a mass of paintings and church ornaments dating from the ninth century onwards, all superbly exhibited in an imaginatively

▲ Café culture in Utrecht

recycled former convent. Two floors are used for the permanent collection and one for temporary exhibitions, but note that the labelling is almost exclusively in Dutch, whereas the audioguide is available in English. A visit begins in the basement **Schatkamer** (Treasury), which is stuffed with gold and silver chalices, reliquaries, communion cups, ecclesiastical rings, vestments and crucifixes. The next floor up (Floor 0) is divided into two main sections – pre-Reformation and post-Reformation – and both hold statues of the saints and apostles, a battery of retables and several striking paintings, most memorably a Man of Sorrows by Geertgen tot Sint Jans. The top floor – Floor 1 – is devoted to temporary displays.

Centraal Museum and the Dick Bruna Huis

From the Catharijne Convent, it's about 500m south along Lange Nieuwstraat to the **Centraal Museum** at Nicolaaskerkhof 10 (Tues–Sun 11am–5pm; €8 including Rietveld Schröderhuis, see opposite; ⓦwww.centraalmuseum.nl). The museum has an extensive fine-art collection with the paintings of local sixteenth- and seventeenth-century artists playing a star role. One of the most interesting of these painters is **Jan van Scorel** (1495–1562), who lived in Utrecht before and after he visited Rome, from where he brought the influence of the Renaissance back home to his fellow painters. A prime example of this mix of native Dutch observation and Renaissance style is Scorel's vivid *Portraits of Twelve Members of Utrecht's Jerusalem Brotherhood*, in which, incidentally, the fifth figure from the right is the artist himself. Scorel is also thought to have made a trip to Jerusalem sometime in the 1520s and this may well account for his unusually accurate drawing of the city in the *Lokhorst Triptych: Christ's Entry into Jerusalem*.

The Utrecht School

A later generation of city painters known as the **Utrecht School** fell under the influence of Italian art in general and Caravaggio (1572–1610) in particular. One of the group's leading practitioners was **Gerrit van Honthorst** (1590–1656), whose *Procuress* adapted Caravaggio's chiaroscuro technique to a genre subject and also developed an erotic content that would itself influence later genre painters like Jan Steen and Gerrit Dou. Even more skilled and realistic is **Hendrick Terbrugghen**'s (1588–1629) *The Calling of St Matthew*, a beautiful balance of gestures dramatizing Christ summoning the tax collector to become one of the twelve disciples.

Gerrit Rietveld

Gerrit Rietveld (1888–1964), the celebrated De Stijl architect and designer, lived and worked in Utrecht, and the museum has a fine collection of his furniture, especially the brightly coloured geometrical chairs for which he is perhaps best known. The chairs are quite simply beautiful, but although part of the De Stijl philosophy stressed the need for universality, they are undoubtedly better to look at than to actually sit on.

The Dick Bruna Huis

From the Centraal Museum it's a few metres over to the **Dick Bruna Huis**, Agnietenstraat 2 (Tues–Sun 10am–5pm; €8; ⓦwww.dickbrunahuis.com), which celebrates the life and work of Dick Bruna (b.1927), who has established an international reputation for his children's picture books in general and for his star creation, *Miffy* the rabbit, in particular.

The Rietveld Schröderhuis

The **Rietveld Schröderhuis** is located a twenty-minute walk east of the Centraal Museum at Prins Hendriklaan 50 (fixed entry times: Wed at 11am, 1pm, 2pm, 3pm & 4pm; Thurs–Sun at 3pm & 4pm; guided tour €15, including entry to Centraal Museum; otherwise €8, including entry to Centraal Museum; reservations strongly recommended on ☏030/236 2310; ⊛www.rietveldschroderhuis .nl). Rietveld designed and built the house in 1924 for one Truus Schröder and her family. It's hailed as one of the most influential pieces of modern architecture in Europe, demonstrating the organic union of lines and rectangles that was the hallmark of the De Stijl movement. The ground floor is the most conventional part of the building, since its design had to meet the rigours of the building licence; however, Rietveld was able to let his imagination run riot with the top floor living space, creating a flexible environment where only the outer walls are solid – indeed the entire top floor can be subdivided in any way, simply by sliding the modular walls. The admission fee also covers the low-slung modernist **terrace** Rietveld designed nearby at Erasmuslaan 5–11.

Eating and drinking

The old centre of Utrecht literally heaves with inexpensive **cafés**, **bars** and **restaurants**, especially along the Oude Gracht canal. There are several pricier/ smarter restaurants too, but these are very much in the minority and for the most part lack the atmosphere of their more informal competitors. Utrecht also has around thirty **cannabis coffeeshops**, mostly away from the centre, but one central option is *Andersom*, at Vismarkt 23 (Mon–Sat 10am–11pm, Sun noon–11pm).

Artisjok Nieuwegracht 33 ☏030/231 7494. Cosy little place with an imaginative menu featuring variations on a Dutch theme – cod in a mustard sauce for example. Main courses hover around €20. Daily 5–10pm.

Eetcafé De Vingerhoed Donkere Gaard 11. Near the Domtoren, this bustling, brown eetcafé offers a wide range of Dutch dishes, not haute cuisine perhaps but certainly filling. Daily specials cost €13, regular main courses €16. Daily from 11am, but kitchen closed 4–5pm.

De Oude Muntkelder Oude Gracht 112. Long-established, canal-side pancake house. Eighty different sorts of pancake from €7. Daily noon–9pm.

Il Pozzo Oude Gracht 136 ☏030/231 1861. Fantastically popular Italian place with a large canal-side terrace. Covers all the Italian classics, including pizzas (from €13).

Polman's Keistraat 2 ☏030/231 3368. Arguably the pick of Utrecht's smarter restaurants, *Polman's* occupies a large and really rather grand nineteenth-century building – and has its waiters in bow ties to match. The menu mixes Italian and Dutch dishes and mains average €25. Mon–Sat noon–midnight.

Springhaver Theater Springweg 50 ☏030/231 3789, ⊛www.springhaver.nl. Groovy, pint-sized cinema-cum-bar-cum-restaurant that attracts an interesting, arty crew. The food

Amersfoort's Mondriaanhuis

There's one good reason to visit **AMERSFOORT**, a middling sort of town fifteen minutes by train from Utrecht, and that's the **Mondriaanhuis**, Kortegracht 11 (Tues–Fri 11am–5pm, Sat & Sun noon–5pm; €5; ⊛www.mondriaanhuis.nl), which comprises the house where the artist **Piet Mondrian** (1872–1944), the leading light of De Stijl, was born and raised, along with the adjacent school where his father was the head teacher. The museum holds an enjoyable retrospective of the artist's life and work, and although the exhibits are regularly rotated, you can expect to see prime examples of the geometric, non-representational paintings for which Mondrian was internationally famous. There is also an interesting reconstruction of the five-sided studio Mondrian had built for himself in Paris in the 1920s.

The Mondriaanhuis is located on the south side of the city centre, about 1.2km east of the train station.

isn't brilliant, but the atmosphere is – and there's a pavement terrace too.

Winkel van Sinkel Oude Gracht 158. One of the city's best and most distinctive bars with a capacious interior, whose gallery and mirrors date from its previous incarnation as a ballroom. Canalside terrace too. Daily from 11am, Sun from noon.

❸ Travel details

Trains

Amersfoort to: Amsterdam CS (every 20min; 40min); Den Haag CS (every 30min; 1hr); Utrecht (every 15min; 15min); Zwolle (every 30min; 35min).
Amsterdam CS to: Amersfoort (every 20min; 40min); Den Haag CS (every 30min; 50min); Leiden (every 30min; 40min); Utrecht (every 15min; 30min).
Delft to: Den Haag CS (every 15min; 12min); Dordrecht (every 15min; 25min); Rotterdam (every 15min; 10min).
Den Haag CS to: Amersfoort (every 30min; 1hr); Amsterdam CS (every 30min; 50min); Delft (every 15min; 12min); Dordrecht (every 30min; 35min); Gouda (every 20min; 20min); Leiden (every 30min; 20min); Rotterdam (every 15min; 25min); Utrecht (every 20min; 40min).
Dordrecht to: Delft (every 15min; 25min); Den Haag CS (every 30min; 35min); Rotterdam (every 15min; 15min).

Leiden to: Amsterdam CS (every 30min; 40min); Den Haag CS (every 30min; 20min).
Rotterdam to: Delft (every 15min; 10min); Den Haag CS (every 15min; 25min); Dordrecht (every 15min; 15min); Gouda (every 20min; 25min); Utrecht (every 20min; 45min).
Utrecht to: Amersfoort (every 15min; 15min); Amsterdam CS (every 15min; 30min); Arnhem (every 30min; 40min); Den Haag (every 20min; 40min); Leeuwarden (hourly; 2hr); Maarn (for Doorn; every 30min; 15min); Rhenen (every 30min; 30min); Rotterdam (every 20min; 45min); Zwolle (every 30min; 1hr).

Buses

Gouda to: Oudewater (every 30min, hourly on Sun; 25min).
Rotterdam to: Kinderdijk (hourly; 50min).
Utrecht to: Kinderdijk (hourly; 1hr 30min).

The north and the Frisian Islands

CHAPTER 4

Highlights

* **Fries Museum, Leeuwarden** A fine insight into the culture of Friesland, in the heart of this easy-going market town. See p.209

* **Harlingen** Far-flung harbour, with a long history of traditional barge-building. See p.213

* **Terschelling** The most alluring of the Frisian islands, wild and windblown. See p.215

* **Vlieland** Tranquil, low-key island of woods and dunes. See p.219

* **Sneek** This prosperous ship-building town of old is now famous as the location for the Sneek Week sailing regatta every August. See p.220

* **Groningen** Dynamic university town in the far north, with a cosmopolitan outlook and the memorable Groninger Museum of art and culture. See p.232

* **Schiermonnikoog** Atmospheric, little-visited island off the far northern coast. See p.239

* **Wadlopen** The best way to experience the northern landscapes is to copy the Dutch and take a guide for *wadlopen* – mud-flat walking. See p.239

▲ Sneek Week sailing regatta

The north and the Frisian Islands

U
ntil the early twentieth century, the north of the Netherlands was a remote area, a distinct region of small provincial towns far removed from the mainstream life of the Randstad. Yet, in 1932, the opening of the **Afsluitdijk**, a 30-kilometre-long sea wall bridging the mouth of the Zuider Zee, changed the orientation of the country once and for all: the Zuider Zee, once a corridor for great trading ships, became the freshwater IJsselmeer and the cultural gap between the north and west narrowed almost immediately.

One of the three northern provinces, **Friesland**, is a deservedly popular tourist stopover. It offers the cluster of duneswept **Frisian islands** and a chain of eleven immaculate, history-steeped "cities", including **Hindeloopen**, **Stavoren** and **Sloten**, each with a distinct charm. Church towers, cobbled streets, narrow canals, wooden barges and bright window boxes are typical details that add colour to these smartly kept settlements. Like much of the Netherlands, the scenery is predominantly green, bisected by a network of canals and dotted with black-and-white cattle – Friesians, of course – and pitch-black Frisian horses. Breaking the pancake-flat monotony of the landscape, sleek wind turbines make the most of the strong westerlies, a modern counterpart to the last working windmills in the area.

East of Friesland, the province of **Groningen** has comparatively few attractions. But while its villages are less charismatic and more suburban, the university town of Groningen more than makes up for them with its vibrant ambience, contemporary fashions, range of affordable bars and restaurants, a growing international performance-art festival and the best nightlife in the region. It's also home to the **Groninger Museum**, a striking and controversial vision of urban architecture and art, and a definite highlight of the region.

South of Groningen lies **Drenthe**, little more than a barren moor for much of its history. During the nineteenth century, the face of the province was changed by the founding of peat colonies, whose labourers drained the land and dug the peat to expose the subsoil below. As a result of their work, parts of Drenthe are given over to prosperous farmland, with agriculture the dominant industry. Sparsely populated and the least visited of the Dutch provinces, Drenthe is now popular with homegrown tourists, who are drawn by its quiet natural beauty, swathes of wood, wide cycling paths and abundant walking trails. The two main towns have only a couple of attractions: the capital **Assen** has the Drents

THE NORTH & THE FRISIAN ISLANDS

0   10 km

N

Ameland
Nes
Terschelling
Hollum
Oosterend
Wierum
West-Terschelling
Holwerd
Dokkum
Vlieland
Oost-Vlieland
Stiens
Waddenzee
Marssum
A31
Leeuwarden
Harlingen
Franeker
Texel
F R I E S L A N D
A32
Bolsward
Makkum
Sneek
Workum
A7
Hindeloopen
Heerenveen
A6
Den Helder
Stevinsluizen
Stavoren
Sloten
Lemmer
Medemblik
A6
A7
Schagen
Emmeloord
Enkhuizen
Bergen
Urk
Alkmaar
Hoorn
▼ *Lelystad*   ▼ *Kampen*

Museum, with a superb collection of prehistoric finds, while **Emmen** is the best place to see Drenthe's most original feature – its *hunebeds*, or megalithic tombs.

Friesland

A region that prospered during the sixteenth-century heyday of the Zuider Zee trade, **Friesland** is focused around eleven historic cities and seven lakes, the latter symbolized by the seven red hearts on the region's flag, which proudly flutters in many a back garden. Friesland once occupied a much larger chunk of the north

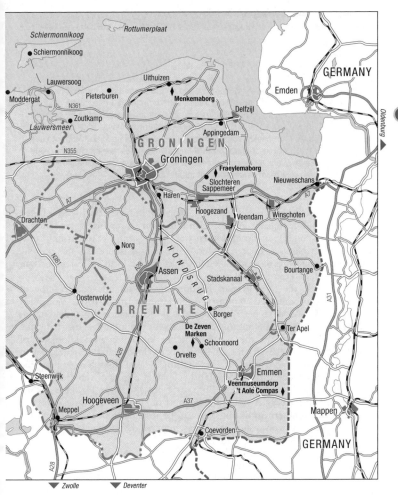

and, in the eighth century, Charlemagne recognized three parts: West Frisia, equivalent to today's West Friesland, across the IJsselmeer; Central Frisia, today's Friesland; and East Frisia, now Groningen province. From earliest times, much of the region was prey to inundation by the sea and the inhabitants built their settlements on artificial mounds (*terpen*) in a frequently forlorn attempt to escape the watery depths. It was a tough existence, but over the centuries the Frisians finessed their skills, extending their settlements by means of a complex network of dykes. You can still see what's left of some of the mounds around the area, though in large settlements they're mostly obscured. Always a maverick among Dutch provinces, the area that is now Friesland proper remained independent of the rest of Holland until it was absorbed into the Habsburg empire by Charles V in 1523.

Since the construction of the Afsluitdijk, Friesland has relied on holidaymakers drawn to its rich history, picturesque lakes and immaculate villages to replace the trading routes and fishing industries of yesteryear. Each city (most

Frisian sports and traditions

The **Frisians** have several unusual sports and traditions that can still raise eyebrows in the rest of the country. Using a large pole to jump over wet obstacles was once a necessity in the Frisian countryside, but the Frisians turned it into a sport: **fierljeppen**. Today Frisian and Dutch pole jumpers compete for the honour during the annual Frisian championships held in Winsum, always on the second Saturday of August.

Skûtjesilen, a fourteen-day sailing race held throughout Friesland in July or August, is another regional rarity. *Skûtjes* are large cargo vessels, but they went out of use after World War II and are now only used for contests and recreational purposes. The VVV in Sneek (see p.221) can give more information on where to see the races. Last but not least is **kaatsen**, a Frisian version of tennis, with over 2000 contests held every year. Instead of a racket a *kaatser* uses a handmade glove to hit the handmade ball; a team of *kaatsers* comprises three players.

of which are town- or village-sized) has a charm of its own: **Harlingen** is noted for its splendid merchant houses; **Hindeloopen** encapsulates the antique neatness of the region; while **Makkum** was once a centre of tile manufacture. Grand old farmhouses, their thatched roofs sloping almost to the ground, remain crowned with *úleboerden,* white gables in the form of a double swan once used as a deterrent to evil spirits.

Further north, the four **Frisian islands** preserve an unexpected sense of wilderness in so populated a country. Each strand of land is barely more than an elongated sandbank, parts of which can be reached by indulging in **wadlopen**, hearty walks along (or ankle-deep in) the mud flats that flank the islands to the south. In the north stretches kilometre after kilometre of hourglass-fine sandy beach and a network of cycleways. A tourist magnet in summertime, busy and developed **Terschelling** is large enough to swallow the holiday crowds, while car-free **Vlieland** resembles a grass-covered dunescape and is popular with young families. Both can be reached from Harlingen, while the access point for busy **Ameland** is the port of Holwerd. The smallest of the four islands is **Schiermonnikoog**; this can be reached from Leeuwarden and Dokkum, but it's actually a shorter journey from neighbouring Groningen, and is covered in that section (see p.239).

Of the larger towns, **Leeuwarden**, the provincial capital, is pleasant if sedate, and boasts two outstanding museums, one of which has the largest collection of tiles in the world. Nearby **Sneek** has access to a tangle of lakes and canals, the busiest watersports area in the country. Boating is one way of getting around and Friesland is also an ideal province to visit by bicycle. The best loop, which takes in all eleven towns, follows the 220-kilometre-long route of the **Elfstedentocht**, a marathon ice-skating race held during winters cold enough for the canals to freeze over. Most VVVs stock maps and guides for cycling, in-line skating, driving or sailing the route all year round.

Leeuwarden

An old market town lying at the heart of an agricultural district, **LEEUWARDEN** was formed from the amalgamation of three *terpen* that originally stood on an expanse of water known as the Middelzee. Later it was the residence of the powerful Frisian Stadholders, who vied with those of Holland for control of the United Provinces. These days it's Friesland's capital, a university town with an amenable provincial air, its centre a haphazard blend of modern glass architecture and traditional design. While it lacks the concentrated historic charm of many other Dutch towns, it does have a number of grand buildings and two outstanding museums. Most appealing is its compact town centre, almost entirely surrounded and dissected by water, along which big barges nudge their way through.

Arrival and information

Leeuwarden's **train** and **bus stations** virtually adjoin each other, five minutes' walk south of the town centre. The **VVV** is on the ground floor of the Achmea Tower, the grey skyscraper 200m north of the train station at Sophialaan 4 (Mon noon–5.30pm, Tues–Fri 9.30am–5.30pm, Sat 10am–3pm; June–Aug Sat until 4pm; ℡0900 202 4060, Ⓦwww.vvvleeuwarden.nl). They publish a map detailing walking tours of the centre (€1.80) and have a short list of **private rooms** that covers the whole of Friesland; they also dispense information on guided boat trips to the Frisian lakes and canal trips through Leeuwarden.

Accommodation

Leeuwarden has its fair share of reasonably priced **hotels** and most are within walking distance of the major sights. Alternatively, a truly authentic experience is sleeping on a large **vessel** (Ⓦwww.slaapschepen.nl) docked in or near the city centre. Prices and availability vary so check in advance with the VVV. There's **camping** at *De Kleine Wielen*, De Groene Ster 14 (℡0511/431 660, Ⓦwww .dekleinewielen.nl; April–Sept), about 6km out towards Dokkum, nicely sited by a lake; take bus #10, #13, #51 or #62 from the station.

Bastion Legedijk 6 ℡058/289 0112, Ⓦwww .bastionhotels.nl. A reliable but very standard fallback, a good walk south of town. ❶
Eden Oranje Stationsweg 4 ℡058/212 6241, Ⓦwww.edenhotelgroup.com. A neat and trim four-star chain hotel right in front of the train station with a large restaurant and comfortable rooms. ❸
Eurohotel Europaplein 30 ℡058/213 1113, Ⓦwww.eurohotel.nl. Located outside the city centre, this hotel is a good option when travelling by car (free parking). The 45 rooms are standard but well equipped and all have free internet access. ❷
Grand Hotel Post Plaza Tweebaksmarkt 25–27 ℡058/215 9317, Ⓦwww.post-plaza.nl. This

brand-new hotel, shoehorned in behind an eighteenth century facade, offers maximum luxury with 43 stylish rooms, a posh bar and every imaginable mod con. ❹
Hotel 't Anker Eewal 69–75 ℡058/212 5216, Ⓦwww.hotelhetanker.nl. This popular and central hotel with adjacent café is one of the cheapest options, though it does need some refurbishing. ❶
Stadhouderlijk Hof Hofplein 29 ℡058/216 2180, Ⓦwww.stadhouderlijkhof.nl. The most elegant option in Leeuwarden is the four-star *Stadhouderlijk Hof*, housed in a former palace with a beautiful inner courtyard. The interior has become a bit weary though. ❸

The Town

If you've just arrived from Friesland's immaculate coast and countryside, first impressions of Leeuwarden are not especially positive, with the southern part of the town centre, near the station, an indeterminate and really rather careless mixture of the old and new. To the north, high-rise blocks and shopping centres line **Wirdumerdijk**, which reaches the centre at **Waagplein**, a long, narrowing open space cut by a canal and flanked by cafés and large department stores. The **Waag** itself, now converted into a restaurant, dates from 1598. Walking west, **Nieuwestad** is Leeuwarden's main shopping street, from where Kleine Kerkstraat leads to the **Oldehoofster Kerkhof**, a large and recently refurbished square near the old city walls, at the end of which stands the

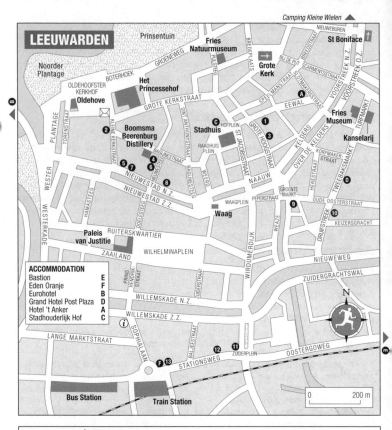

precariously leaning **Oldehove**. Something of a symbol for the city, this is part of a cathedral started in 1529 but never finished because of subsidence, the end result being a lugubrious mass of disproportion that defies all laws of gravity and geometry. To the right stands a statue of the Frisian politician and trade unionist P.J. Troelstra, who looks on impassively, no doubt admonishing the city fathers for their choice of architects. For a better view, climb the 40-metre-high tower (Tues–Sat 2–5pm; €2).

A little further east is the **Prinsentuin**, a small park that was once the pleasure garden of the ruling House of Nassau. It is still a quiet place to wander by the river and admire, on the other side, the rather thoughtful bronze Friesian cow, called *Ús Mem* (Our Mother), donated to the city by the Frisian Cattle Syndicate. *Ús Heit* (Our Father) is also present in Leeuwarden – a statue of Regent Willem Lodewijk, a Frisian hero, which stands on the Gouveneursplein, in front of the majestic *Stadhouderlijk Hof* hotel.

Het Princessehof and around

Grote Kerkstraat leads east from the Oldehoofster Kerkhof, following the line of the track that once connected two of Leeuwarden's original *terpen*, Oldehove and Nijehove. Near the square, at Grote Kerkstraat 11, is **Het Princessehof** (Tues–Sun 11am–5pm; €8; ⓦwww.princessehof.nl), a house from 1650 that was the birthplace of the graphic artist M.C. Escher. It's now a completely renovated ceramics museum, with the largest collection of tiles in the world. Of the many displays, two are outstanding. The first is the collection of **Chinese**, **Japanese** and **Vietnamese ceramics**, which outlines the rise and fall of Far Eastern china production. The second comprises the rooms devoted to the development of **Chinese porcelain** from prehistory onward, with representative examples illustrating major trends. The finest work dates from the Ming Dynasty (1368–1644), with powerful open-mouthed dragons, billowing clouds and sharply drawn plant tendrils. Another section you shouldn't miss is the magnificent range of **Dutch tiles**, with good examples of all the classic designs – soldiers, flowers, ships and so forth – framed by uncomplicated borders. The collection of **European ceramics and porcelain** slots awkwardly around the other exhibits; best are the Art Deco and Art Nouveau pieces. More interesting is the small collection of **Middle Eastern tiles**, including thirteenth-century pieces from Persia and a few flamboyant sixteenth-century Iznik tiles.

A short walk towards the Nieuwestad will lead you to the **Boomsma Beerenburg Distillery**, Bagijnestraat 42a (Tues–Sat 10am–5pm; €1.50; ⓦwww.boomsma.net), where you can get a tour of the small museum and taste the herb-flavoured gin that is a regional speciality.

The Grote Kerk

At the far end of Grote Kerkstraat, the **Grote** or **Jacobijner Kerk** (June Sat 11am–4pm; July & Aug Tues–Thurs & Sat 11am–4pm, Fri 1–4pm), though restored in recent years, remains an unremarkable Gothic construction. Another victim of subsidence, the whole place tilts slightly toward the newer south aisle, where you can see some fragmentary remnants of sixteenth-century frescoes. In front of the church a modernistic monument remembers Leeuwarden's wartime Jewish community, based on the classroom registers of 1942; it's an imaginative and harsh reminder of suffering and persecution.

The Fries Museum

East of here, at Turfmarkt 11, is the **Fries Museum** (Tues–Sun 11am–5pm; €6; ⓦwww.friesmuseum.nl), one of the Netherlands' finest regional museums. Founded by a society that was established in the nineteenth century to develop interest in the language and history of Friesland, the museum traces the development of Frisian culture from prehistoric times up until the present day. It also incorporates the Frisian Resistance Museum, with its story of the local resistance to Nazi occupation, and has an exhibition on Mata Hari, who is – or at least was – something of a local heroine. The main entrance is next to the **Kanselarij**, a superb gabled Renaissance structure of 1571 which is part of the museum, though there are plans to move the whole museum to a new location on the Wilhelminaplein. If construction goes according to schedule, the new museum will open in 2012.

The collections

The museum's extensive collection of **silver** is concentrated in the basement of the Kanselarij. Silversmithing was a flourishing Frisian industry throughout the seventeenth and eighteenth centuries, with most of the work being commissioned by the local gentry, who were influenced by the fashions of the Frisian Stadholder and his court.

The top floor of the Kanselarij has a chronological exhibition tracing the early days of the **Nazi invasion**, through collaboration and resistance and on to the Allied liberation. A range of photographs, Nazi militaria, Allied propaganda and moving personal stories illustrate the text, but the emphasis is very much on the local struggle rather than the general war effort.

Back by the downstairs ticket desk, a passage leads through to the museum's second building, the **Eysingahuis**, where you'll find an exhibition on Leeuwarden's most famous daughter, **Mata Hari** (1876–1917). Born Gertrud Zelle, Hari became a renowned "exotic" dancer after an early but unsuccessful marriage to a Dutch army officer. The Netherlands was neutral during World War I, but it was here in Den Haag that Hari seems to have accepted a German bribe to spy for the kaiser on her return to France. The French intelligence service soon got wind of the bribe – partly because she was also supposed to be working for them – and she was subsequently arrested, tried and shot. What she actually did remains a matter of some debate, but in retrospect it seems likely that she acted as a double agent, gathering information for the Allies while giving snippets to the Germans. Photographs, letters and other mementoes illustrate her forlorn story.

Upstairs, the first floor's most interesting rooms are those devoted to the painted **furniture** of Hindeloopen: rich, gaudy and intense, patterned with tendrils and flowers on a red, green or white background.

St Boniface

A little way north of Turfmarkt is the Catholic church of **St Boniface**, a belated apology to an English missionary killed at nearby Dokkum, along with 52 other Christians, by the pagan Frisians in 754. It's a neo-Gothic building of 1894 designed by P.J.H. Cuypers, its ornamented spire imposing itself on what is otherwise a rather flat skyline. The spire was almost totally destroyed in a storm of 1976 and many people wanted to take the opportunity to pull the place down altogether – even to replace it with a supermarket. Fortunately the steeple was replaced at great expense and with such enormous ingenuity that its future seems secure, making it one of the few Cuypers churches left in the Netherlands.

Eating, drinking and nightlife

Although Leeuwarden does not have a university, it is a real student town, attracting almost 17,000 pupils each year, and where there are students, there are cheap places to eat. Expect to find a good range of **cafés** serving a quick bite at **Nieuwstad**, while **Eewal** is the place for dinner. There are also a few places for a good meal and some nighttime excitement near the station on **Stationweg**.

Café Het Leven Druifstreek 57–59 ☎058/212 1233. This rather smart café is the place for steaks, stews and the occasional curry.

Eetcafé Spinoza Eewal 50–52 ☎058/212 9393. One of the most popular places to eat in Leeuwarden, this is a youthful, reasonably priced restaurant with daily specialities for €7.75 and a range of vegetarian dishes. The hidden inner courtyard is a well-kept treasure.

Humphrey's Nieuwstad 91 ☎058/216 4936. Although part of a chain, *Humphrey's* offers great value for money in a cosy atmosphere, with a three-course meal for the fixed price of €22.50.

Intermezzo Stationsweg 6 ☎058/213 1514. Another stylish establishment near the station, *Intermezzo* is popular with business people during lunch and a slightly younger crowd at night, with its flashy pink and black interior.

Mains like duck breast with orange compote cost €18.75.

Kaldi Kleine Kerkstraat 41. Part of a national chain, but still a great spot for good coffee and a wide range of brownies, scones and salads in a bright orange setting.

De Lachende Koe Grote Hoogstraat 16–20 ☎058/215 8245. A long-time favourite among students with cheap daily specials (€8.50) and a set three-course menu for only €19.95. Great outside yard in summer.

De Vliegende Hollander Berlikumermarkt 15 ☎058/212 1717. Serves daily specialities starting from €7.50 and a wide variety of soups, stews and schnitzels.

Nightlife

For **drinking**, there is a series of lively bars on Doelesteeg, mostly with loud music, plus quieter drinking spots across the bridge on Nieuwesteeg, including *De Bottelier* and *De Twee Gezusters*. Near the station *Café Rembrandt*, with occasional live music and *Café De Rus* are lively options, located on Stationsweg. *Club Noa* hosts Holland's better-known DJs on weekends, while the *Fire Palace* (a former prison), Nieuwestad N.Z. 49, is a big bar that doubles as a disco at weekends.

Listings

Bike rental From the Fietspoint next to the train station (€6.50 per day).
Books Van der Velde, Nieuwstad 57–59, has a good stock of English-language titles.
Car rental AutoRent, Archimedesweg 18 ☎058/299 8882, ⓦwww.autorent.nl.
Internet access At the VVV and the Bibliotheek, Wirdumerdijk 34 ☎058/234 7777.

Market General market on Fridays and Saturdays at Wilhelminaplein.
Pharmacy Details of nearest (emergency) pharmacy on ☎058/288 2338.
Police Holstmeerweg 1 ☎0900/8844.
Post office Oldehoofster Kerkhof 4 (Mon–Fri 7.30am–6pm, Thurs until 8pm, Sat 7.30am–1.30pm).
Taxi Taxi Leeuwarden ☎058/216 1716.

Around Leeuwarden: Popta Slot

The tiny village of **MARSSUM**, on the western outskirts of Leeuwarden, incorporates **Popta Slot** (guided tours only: April–June & Sept–Oct Mon–Sat by appointment; July & Aug Mon–Sat hourly 11am–5pm; €5; ⓦwww.poptaslot .nl), a trim, onion-domed eighteenth-century manor house that sits prettily behind its ancient moat; inside, the period rooms are furnished in the style of the local gentry. Dr Popta was an affluent lawyer who spent some of his excess wealth on the neighbouring **Popta Gasthuis**, neat almshouses cloistered behind an elaborate portal of 1712. Bus #71 heads to Marssum from Leeuwarden bus station, departing each hour.

West of Leeuwarden

West of Leeuwarden, the train line heads straight for **Harlingen** – though the small town of **Franeker**, with its fascinating eighteenth-century planetarium, makes a worthwhile detour. Seventeenth-century Harlingen was very much a naval centre and it remains an important port today, primarily to ferry tourists from the mainland to the Frisian islands of **Terschelling** and **Vlieland**. With a resurgence in the last decades in its tradition of ceramics manufacture, and a strong maritime heritage, Harlingen makes a pleasant stopover for the night en route to the islands.

Franeker

FRANEKER, about 17km west of Leeuwarden, was the cultural hub of the northern Netherlands until Napoleon closed its university in 1810. Nowadays it's a quiet country town with a spruce old centre, the highlight of which is the intriguing planetarium.

All the key sights are beside or near the main street, **Voorstraat**, a continuation of Dijkstraat, which runs east–west to end in a park, **Sternse Slotland** – the site of the medieval castle. Near the park is the **Waag** of 1657 and heading east along Voorstraat you will find the **Museum Martena** (Tues–Fri 10am–5pm, Sat & Sun 1–5pm; €5; ⓦ www.museummartena.nl) in the old **Martenahuis** of 1498, with bits and pieces relating to the former university and its (obscure) alumni. Past the Martenahuis, the Raadhuisplein branches off to the left; opposite, above the Friesland Bank, is the **Kaatsmuseum** (May–Sept Tues–Sat 1–5pm; €2), devoted to the Frisian sport of *kaatsen* (see box, p.206). The nearby **Stadhuis** (Wed–Fri 1.30–5.30pm; free), with its twin gables and octagonal tower, is rather more interesting. It's a magnificent mixture of Gothic and Renaissance styles built in 1591 and is worth a peek upstairs for the leather-clad walls – all the rage until French notions of wallpaper took hold in the eighteenth century.

The Planetarium

Opposite the Stadhuis, at Eise Eisingastraat 3, the fascinating eighteenth-century **planetarium** (Tues–Sat 10am–5pm, Sun 1–5pm; April–Oct also Mon 1–5pm; €4.50; ⓦ www.planetarium-friesland.nl) was built by a local-woolcomber, Eise Eisinga, and is now the oldest working planetarium in the world. Born in 1744, Eisinga was something of a prodigy: he taught himself mathematics and astronomy, and published a weighty arithmetic book when aged only 17. In 1774, the unusual conjunction of Mercury, Venus, Mars and Jupiter under the sign of Aries prompted a local paper to predict the end of the world. There was panic in the countryside, and an appalled Eisinga embarked on the construction of his planetarium, completed in 1781, in order to dispel superstition by demystifying the workings of the cosmos.

The planetarium isn't of the familiar domed variety but was built as a false ceiling in the family's living room, a series of rotating dials and clocks indicating the movement of the planets and associated phenomena, from tides to star signs. The whole apparatus is regulated by a clock, driven by a series of weights hung in a tiny alcove beside a half-size cupboard-bed. Above the face of the main dials, the mechanisms – hundreds of handmade nails driven into moving slats – are open for inspection. A detailed guidebook explains every aspect and every dial, and there's an explanatory film in English, shown on request.

Practicalities

The **train station** is five minutes' walk southeast of the centre: follow Stationsweg round to the left and over the bridge, first left over the second bridge onto Zuiderkade and second right along Dijkstraat to reach the town. **Buses** from Leeuwarden drop off passengers on Kleijenburg, at the northwest corner of the old town centre.

Franeker's unofficial **VVV** is inside the Museum Martena (Tues–Fri 10am–5pm, Sat & Sun 1–5pm; ☏0517/392 192, ⓦ www.beleeffriesland.nl). Of the town's **hotels**, your first choice should be the friendly *De Stadsherberg*, on the continuation of Stationsweg at Oude Kaatsveld 8, situated next to the canal (☏0517/392 686, ⓦ www.stadsherbergfraneker.nl; ❷), with ten neat and trim rooms, and a decent restaurant downstairs. Failing that, try *Pension De Klokgevel*, opposite the modern church at Godsacker 20 (☎0517/392 246; ❶). The town **campsite**, *Bloemketerp* (☎0517/395 099, ⓦwww.bloemketerp.nl), is ten minutes' walk north of the station at Burg. J. Dijkstraweg 3: head up Stationsweg, Oud Kaatsveld and Leeuwarderweg, then turn left.

Eating and drinking

For **snacks**, try the croissanterie *De Lunchkamer*, Zilverstraat 7, or coffee and cakes at the *Planetarium Café*, beside the planetarium at Eise Eisingastraat 2 – the building dates back to 1745 and has fine wooden counters, a mosaic floor and original coffee cabinets from 1910, as well as an attractive back garden. Of the **restaurants**, the upmarket, canal-side *De Grillerije*, Groenmarkt 14 (☎0517/395 7044; closed Mon), offers mains like lamb racks, catch of the day and mixed grill for around €19, or you could try *De Doelen*, a hotel and grand café on the same square, which has main courses for around €15. The trendiest option in town is *Naturel*, Zilverstraat 41 (☎0517/383 838; closed Mon & Tues) with an impeccable white and purple interior and tasty mains for €19.50. *De Bogt Fen Gune*, Vijverstraat 1, is the oldest student **bar** in the country, and worth dropping into for a drink.

Harlingen

HARLINGEN, 30km west of Leeuwarden and just north of the Afsluitdijk, is a more compelling stop than Franeker. An ancient and historic port that serves as the ferry terminus for the islands of Terschelling and Vlieland, the town is something of a centre for traditional Dutch **sailing barges**, a number of which are usually moored in the harbour. Also a naval base from the seventeenth century onwards, the town abuts the Vliestroom channel, once the easiest way for shipping to pass from the North Sea through the shallows that surround the Frisian islands and on into the Zuider Zee. Before trade moved west, this was the country's lifeline, where cereals, fish and other foodstuffs were brought in from the Baltic to feed the expanding Dutch cities.

The Town

From **Harlingen Haven** station the old town, a mass of sixteenth- to eighteenth-century houses which reflect the prosperity and importance of earlier times spreads east, sandwiched between the pretty Noorderhaven and the more functional Zuiderhaven canals. However, Harlingen is too busy to be a twee tourist town: there's a fishing fleet, a small container depot, a shipbuilding yard and a resurgent ceramics industry. The heart of town is **Voorstraat**, a long, tree-lined avenue in between Noorderhaven and Zuiderhaven, home to an elegant eighteenth-century **Stadhuis** and the **Hannemahuis Museum** at no. 56 (Tues–Fri 11am–5pm, Sat & Sun 1.30–5pm; €3.50; ⓦwww.hannemahuis.nl). Sited in an eighteenth-century merchant's house, the museum concentrates on the history of the town and includes some interesting displays on shipping and some lovely locally produced tiles.

Harlingen's tile-making industry flourished until it was undermined by the irresistible rise of wallpaper. The last of the old factories closed in 1933, but the demand for traditional crafts later led to something of a recovery, and the opening of new workshops during the 1970s. If you like the look of Dutch tiles, this is a good place to buy. The **Harlinger Aardewerk en Tegelfabriek**, Voorstraat 84, sells an outstanding range of contemporary and traditional styles – if you've got the money (Dutch handicrafts don't come cheap).

▲ Harlingen harbour

Arrival and information

Trains from Leeuwarden stop on the south side of town at Harlingen's main **train station**, a five- to ten-minute walk from Voorstraat; there's a second station, **Harlingen Haven**, right next to the **docks**, where ferries leave for the islands (see p.216); this is only a couple of minutes from Voorstraat. Harlingen's unofficial **VVV** is currently located at St Odolphisteeg 10, though it will soon move to a kiosk on Grote Bredeplaats, a westerly extension of Voorstraat (May–Oct Mon 1–5pm, Tues–Fri 10am–5pm, Sat 10am–4pm; Nov–April Tues–Fri 1–4pm, Sat 10am–2pm; ☎0517/430 207, ⊛www.harlingen-friesland.nl).

Accommodation

The VVV has a sizeable list of **rooms** and **pensions**, many of which are strung along Noorderhaven. Of the **hotels**, the *Heerenlogement* on the eastern continuation of Voorstraat, at Frankereind 23 (☎0517/415 846, ⊛www .heerenlogement.nl; ❷), has 24 smartly decorated rooms; while the slightly more expensive *Anna Casparii* (☎0517/412 065, ⊛www.annacasparii.nl; ❷), located in three historical buildings at Noorderhaven 67–71, throws in a good restaurant with canal-side terrace as a bonus. The most picturesque option is the *Stadslogement Harlingen*, Kruisstraat 8–14, located in a seventeenth-century warehouse converted into comfortable apartments and hotel rooms (☎0517/417 706, ⊛www.stadslogementharlingen.nl; ❷–❸). Central and close to the ferry is the *Zeezicht*, by the harbour at Zuiderhaven 1 (☎0517/412 536, ⊛www.hotelzeezicht.nl; ❷) with 24 rooms, most of them with sea view.

If you are looking for a really special experience, how about sleeping in a lighthouse or a harbour crane? Both are possible in Harlingen although a room with a view doesn't come cheap and you need to book in advance as they sell out months in advance (☎0515/540 550, ⊛www.vuurtoren-harlingen.nl; ❾).

Harlingen's nearest **campsite**, *De Zeehoeve* (☎0517/413 465, ⊛www .zeehoeve.nl; April–Sept), is a twenty-minute walk along the sea dyke to the south of town at Westerzeedijk 45 – follow the signs from Voorstraat. If you've got your own transport, you're better off heading about 4km south to Kimswerd, to the delightful mini-camping *Popta Zathe* (☎0517/641 205; also a cheap B&B; ➊), just close to the sea wall. There's a small plot of grass, a beautiful garden and bike rental; the sunsets are great and it's a lovely bike ride along the top of the dyke into town.

Eating and drinking

As you might expect, Harlingen's speciality is fresh **fish**, and there are fish stands and restaurants dotted around the centre of town. A good but pricey choice with mains around €30 is *De Gastronoom*, at the Voorstraat 38 (☎0517/412 172; closed Mon), although you do get treated with oysters, bouillabaisse and scallops in a classy environment. Alternatives include *De Tjotter* on the edge of the Noorderhaven at St Jacobstraat 1 (☎0517/414 691), a combined snack bar and restaurant with a wide range of North Sea delicacies, and *Ons* on Voorstraat 73 (☎0517/430 087; closed Mon & Tues) where you can dine on fresh seasonal produce in a retro chic setting. *Café 't Noorderke* at Noorderhaven 17–19 has good-value daily specials (fresh herring in season) and a view of the boats passing by from the terrace.

Nightlife is quiet but there are several decent **bars**, including *'t Skutsje* on the corner of Frankereind and Heiligeweg, and music café *De Wachter*, Voorstraat 64, with a canal pontoon. Sharper places can be found on Grote Bredeplaats, at the west end of the Voorstraat: *Nooitgedagt* and *Eigentijds* are hip venues, attracting a youthful crew.

The islands of Terschelling and Vlieland

A highlight of any visit to Friesland is a trip to **Terschelling** or **Vlieland**, two of the five inhabited islands that string out along the Netherlands' north coast. With kilometres of empty beach and grass-covered dunes, these low-lying sandbank-islands are popular with Dutch tourists in the holiday season and are refuges for scores of plants and animals that thrive in their unique ecological habitat. Known also for their unpredictable weather, the islands are frequently swept by storms throughout the year, though the summer months often boast high temperatures and clear blue skies.

Of the two, Terschelling is by far the more developed, and consequently a lot busier. Visitors' cars are not allowed on smaller and quieter Vlieland, but in any case the best way to explore the islands is by **bike**. There are rental companies near the ferry terminals on both islands, charging roughly €5.50 per day for a basic bike – although given the sometimes steep, stony hills, it's worth shelling out a bit more for a machine with decent gears.

Terschelling

Of all the Frisian Islands, **Terschelling** is both the largest – some 30km long and 3.5km wide – and the easiest to reach. Despite its reputation as a summer teenage hangout, it does offer wilderness, peace and tranquility – you just have to head away from main centres to get it. Quite simply, the further east you go the more attractive the island becomes; eighty percent of the island is a nature reserve, dominated by beach, dunes, forest and polder. Although summer temperatures can soar, out of season Terschelling's wild weather seems to mirror its wild landscape, with storms lending it a brooding air.

Ferries to Terschelling and Vlieland

From Harlingen, **ferries** cross to Terschelling and Vlieland at least three times a day in summer and twice daily in winter (1hr 45min). A return fare is €21.80 for either island (not including nominal taxes), plus €11.98 per bike. Boats dock at West-Terschelling and Oost-Vlieland, the islands' main settlements. There's also a fast **hydrofoil** service from Harlingen (May–Sept 3 daily to Terschelling, 2 daily to Vlieland; Oct–April 2 daily to Terschelling, 1 daily to Vlieland). It costs an extra €11.60 return, but saves you an hour each way in travelling time – perfect for day trips. From May to the end of September there's also a ferry running between Terschelling and Vlieland, once or twice a day (€7.32 one-way, €7.18 for a bike). Check ⓦwww.rederij-doeksen.nl for up to date information.

West-Terschelling

The ferry docks next to the fishing harbour of **WEST-TERSCHELLING**, a tourist resort in its own right that's packed throughout the summer with visitors sampling the restaurants and bars that line the main streets, Torenstraat in particular. West-Terschelling today is a rather unappealing sprawl of chalets, bungalows and holiday complexes that spreads out from what remains of the old village, belying its past importance as a port and safe anchorage on the edge of the Vliestroom channel, the main shipping lane to and from the Zuider Zee. This strategically positioned town boomed throughout the seventeenth century as a centre for the supply and repair of ships and had its own fishing and whaling fleets; it paid the price for its prominence when the British razed it in 1666. The islanders were renowned sailors, much sought after by ships' captains who also needed them to guide vessels through the treacherous shallows and shifting sandbanks that lay to either side of the Vliestroom. All the same, **shipwrecks** were common all along the island's northern and western shores, the most famous victim being the *Lutine*, which sank while carrying gold and silver to British troops stationed here during the Napoleonic wars. The wreck still lies at the bottom of the sea, and only the ship's bell was recovered; it's now in Lloyd's of London and is still rung whenever a big ship goes down.

The museums

The best place to investigate West Terschelling's past is the excellent **Museum 't Behouden Huys**, near the ferry terminus at Commandeurstraat 30 (April–Oct Mon–Fri 10am–5pm & Sat 1–5pm; mid-June to Sept also Sun 1–5pm; €3; ⓦwww.behouden-huys.nl). Prime exhibits here include maps of the old coastline illustrating Terschelling's crucial position, various items from the whaling fleet, lots of sepia photos of bearded islanders and a shipwreck diving room. If you're extra-keen on all things marine, aim for the tiny **Museum "Aike van Stien"**, a fishing museum at the back of a shop on Raadhuisstraat (May–Oct Mon–Sat 10am–12.30pm & 2–5.30pm; Nov–April Thurs & Sat 2–5pm; €2; ⓦwww.visserijmuseumaikevanstien.nl), and the **Centrum voor Natuur en Landschap**, Burgemeester Reedekerstraat 11 (April–Oct Mon–Fri 9am–5pm, Sat & Sun 2–5pm; Nov–March Sat, Sun & Tues 2–5pm; €5; ⓦwww.natuurmuseumterschelling.nl), just east of town, which contains a decent aquarium.

Practicalities

The **VVV** (summer Mon–Sat 9.30am–5.30pm; winter Mon–Fri 9.30am–5pm, Sat 10am–3pm; ☏0562/443 000, ⓦwww.vvvterschelling.nl), near the ferry port, provides a full list of **pensions** and **rooms** and operates a booking service. They also take bookings for the rest of the island, offer a variety of walking tours, sell a good island **map** (€2.75) that includes towns, beaches and cycleways, and dispense information on cycling routes and seal-watching excursions.

You can **rent bikes** from Haantjes, located 50m to the right of the ferry terminal, beyond the VVV – either single-speed (€5.50 per day, €25 per week) or geared bikes (€7 per day, €30 per week); they have various drop-off points around the island, and a handy cycling map. There are other bike-rental shops down by the harbour and at the ferry terminal. The island's **bus** service leaves from right next to the ferry terminus (every 1hr 10min), taking thirty minutes to travel along the south coast to Oosterend.

Accommodation

Accommodation in West-Terschelling is hard to come by in July and August when all the cheaper places tend to be booked up months in advance. At other times you have a wide choice – try the *Hotel Buren*, Burgemeester Mentzstraat 20 (℡0562/442 226, ⓦwww.hotel-buren.nl; ❷) with eleven rooms all in different colour schemes, or the similarly priced *Pension Altijd Wad*, Trompstraat 6 (℡0562/442 050, ⓦwww.altijdwad.nl; ❷), with five hotel rooms, a cosy studio and small private house to choose from. Both are at easy walking distance from the ferry terminus.

There's a HI **hostel** overlooking the harbour at Burgmeester van Heusdenweg 39 (℡0562/442 338, ⓦwww.stayokay.com), with dorm beds (€30) and en-suite doubles (❶): it's a 1.5km walk eastwards along the coast, or you can take any bus to the Dellewal stop. There are also a number of shoreside **campsites** east of town that are popular with the hordes of partying teenagers who descend on the island in summer.

Eating and drinking

For a quick bite to **eat**, the fish-and-chips takeaway at Boomstraat 12 offers the usual fishy suspects fresh from the North Sea, including fried *lekkerbek*, a Dutch fried-fish speciality, for €3.75. At *Strandpaviljoen De Walvis*, at Groene Strand on the western edge of West-Terschelling, you can buy snacks and drinks while taking in the sea view, while the *Brasserie De Brandaris*, Boomstraat 3 (℡0562/442 554) has a suitably nautical atmosphere, with mains around €19 and a typical Terschelling cheese platter for dessert at €7.50. More upmarket and up-to-the-minute is *Storm*, Torenstraat 27 (℡0562/443 232) with lots of dark wood, industrial decor and great cuisine. A good spot for **drinking** is *Het Amsterdamsche Koffijhuis*, tucked away at Willem Barentszstraat 17, serving a wide range of coffees and cheap meals. Similar fare is on offer at nearby *'t Zwaantje*, a typical brown café at Havenstraat 1.

Terschelling Oerol Festival

Every year around June, Terschelling celebrates the beginning of the warmer season with the **Oerol Festival** (ⓦwww.oerol.nl). Oerol, "everywhere" in the Terschelling dialect, is the name of a rural tradition in which the island's cattle were released from their winter stables to frolic and graze in the open fields, an event that marked the changing of the seasons. Today, over 50,000 people head out to the island for the Oerol, transforming Terschelling into a big festival area, with the island serving as both inspiration and stage for theatre producers, musicians and graphic artists. Finding accommodation is almost impossible during the ten-day festival, so book ahead.

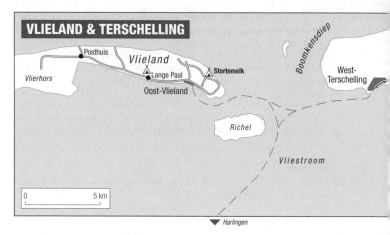

Around the island

From West-Terschelling, plenty of visitors cycle off for the day to the beach 5km away at **WEST-AAN-ZEE**. There's a beach café here, *WestAanZee*, and as much empty beach as you're prepared to look for. There are two cycle routes to get here, the more northerly passing through a cemetery in a wood, with a small Commonwealth forces graveyard; as ever, the inscriptions make sad reading, with few of the downed airmen aged more than 25.

Most of Terschelling's villages are on the south side of the island, sheltered from winter storms by the sand dunes and occasional patches of forest that lie to the immediate north. Cycle routes are almost always traffic-free hereabouts and you can aim to stay in one of the pensions between the villages of Formerum and Oosterend, far enough east to escape most of the crowds; the VVV in West-Terschelling has details.

Definitely worth a visit in **FORMERUM** is the delightful **Wrakken-museum "De Boerderij"**, Formerum Zuid 13 (April–Nov daily 10am–5pm; €2.50; Ⓦ www.wrakkenmuseum.nl). Here, the ground floor is an atmospheric bar decked out with all things nautical, while upstairs there's a collection of items salvaged from the island's beaches and shipwrecks, including cannons and coins, relics from the *Lutine*, and the Netherlands' largest collection of diving helmets. Another Formerum attraction, near the windmill, is the **cranberry factory**, where you can sample and buy all things cranberry (May–Oct; presentation and sampling Mon–Fri at 2pm; €2.50; shop Mon–Fri 10.30am–5pm, Sat 10.30–4pm). Cranberries are a major island crop, harvested from September until the first frost. Located just 2km west of Formerum, tiny **LANDERUM** is the starting point for **horseback rides** which can be arranged through Rijpaarden Verhuur Lok (☎ 0562/448 188). An hour's ride through the woods for beginners costs €19, but if you're an experienced rider, you can set out for the beach (2hr; €31).

The two final settlements, **HOORN** and **OOSTEREND**, are particularly pleasant and within easy reach of empty tracts of beach and the nature reserve **De Boschplaat**, where thousands of birds, including gulls, oystercatchers, green plovers and spoonbills, congregate in the marshy shallows of the southeastern shore. To help protect the birds, De Boschplaat is closed during the breeding season (mid-March to mid-Aug), although the VVV runs guided tours for bird enthusiasts.

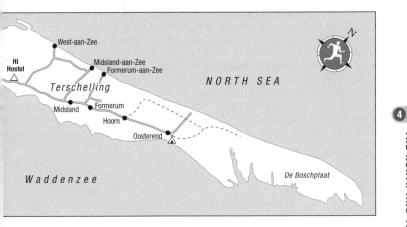

As well as a handful of **campsites**, Oosterend also has a decent **place to eat**, the café *De Boschplaat*, serving hefty Dutch cuisine. Signed 2km north is the *Heartbreak Hotel*, Strandpaviljoen Tordelenweg 2 (March–Nov daily 10am–2am; ⓣ0562/448 634), an American-style **diner** decorated with wall-to-wall 1950s memorabilia, and sited in a superb location overlooking kilometres of white sand and sea.

Vlieland

Compared with its neighbour, **Vlieland** is very low-key. All but car-free, it has just one settlement, **OOST-VLIELAND**, which is little more than a tree-lined street with a string of pavement cafés, bike-rental agencies and a few hotels and B&Bs. Historically isolated by a complex pattern of sandbanks, the island was of minor importance during the Zuider Zee trade; indeed its only other village was swept away by the sea in the eighteenth century and never rebuilt. These days, there's not much to do but enjoy the country walks and relax along the 12km of sandy beach – a sedate lifestyle that is popular with Dutch families, who load up their bikes with panniers, tents, children and animals, and head for one of the island's campsites.

Oost-Vlieland offers all the necessities, including a choice of eateries, bars and supermarkets. There's also a maritime centre geared towards children, the **Centrum "De Noordwester"**, Dorpsstraat 150 (July & Aug Mon–Fri 10am–5pm, Sat 2–5pm & Sun 1–4pm; hours vary out of season; €3; ⓦwww.denoordwester.nl), displaying an assortment of shells, an explanation of dune formation, a couple of aquariums with crabs and rays, and an unexpected elf forest (information is in Dutch only).

To explore the island's woods and dunes, follow one of the many **bike** routes that run the length of the island, passing close to the wide sandy beach that runs along the north shore. The VVV can provide you with details in English of two main cycle routes, and there are also plenty of marked **walking** trails. You can rent bikes, tandems and trailers – for kids as well as canines – all over town.

Arrival and information

Ferries from Harlingen dock at the east end of the island at the village of Oost-Vlieland and there's a limited **bus** service along the southern shore from near the ferry terminus. In addition, private operators organize day-trips to the northern tip of the neighbouring island of **Texel** (see p.137) by means of a tractor-like lorry, which crosses the great expanse of sand (the "Vliehors") on Vlieland's western extremity to connect with a boat (May–Sept; €22.50 for a round trip to Texel; Ⓦwww.waddenveer.nl).

The **VVV**, Havenweg 10 (Mon–Fri 9am–12.30pm & 1.30–5pm, also open for brief periods daily to coincide with ferry arrivals; ℡0562/451 111, Ⓦwww.vlieland.net), does its best with the island's few private rooms, and will help groups rent apartments and "dune houses"; it also has information on birdwatching expeditions.

Accommodation

Accommodation is limited, and virtually impossible to find throughout the summer unless you're camping, although there are several cheap **hotels** and pensions. One of them is the *Duin en Dal*, Dorpsstraat 163 (℡0562/451 684, Ⓦwww.pensionduinendal-vlieland.nl; ❶); along the road is the more comfortable *Badhotel Bruin*, Dorpsstraat 88 (℡0562/451 301, Ⓦwww.badhotelbruin.nl; ❸), and the smart *De Wadden*, Dorpsstraat 61 (℡0562/452 626, Ⓦwww.westcordhotels.nl; ❸). The **campsite** *De Stortemelk*, Kampweg 1 (℡0562/451 225, Ⓦwww.stortemelk.nl; April–Sept), is on the dunes behind the beach, about half an hour's walk or a ten-minute bike ride northeast of the village. More peaceful is the Staatsbosbeheer site a few kilometres west at *Lange Paal* (℡0562/451 639, Ⓦwww.langepaal.com); it's set in the forest clearing of a nature reserve. Facilities are simple but clean and there's a relaxed, friendly atmosphere. Bring some insect repellent though: the mosquitoes here are ruthless.

Southwest Friesland

Trains from Leeuwarden to **Stavoren** pass through a series of small Frisian towns with a speed that belies their earlier isolation. Until well into the nineteenth century, the area's lakes, canals and peat diggings made land communications difficult, and the only significant settlements were built close to the sea or on major waterways. Dependent on water-borne commerce, these communities declined with the collapse of the Zuider Zee trade, but, because of their insularity, some maintained particular artistic and cultural traditions – from the painted furniture and distinctive dialect of **Hindeloopen** to the style and design of many of **Makkum's** tiles. If you're passing through by train, the tiny old towns resemble what in fact they once were: islands in the shallow marshes. Nowadays all are popular holiday destinations; **Sneek**, the centre of a booming pleasure-boat industry, is by far the busiest.

Sneek

Twenty minutes by train from Leeuwarden, **SNEEK** (pronounced *snake*) was an important shipbuilding centre as early as the fifteenth century, a prosperous maritime town protected by an extensive system of walls and moats. Postwar development has robbed the place of some of its charm but there are still some buildings of interest. At the beginning of August, crowds flock in for **Sneek Week**, an annual regatta, when the flat green expanses around town are thick with the white of slowly moving sails.

Arrival and information

Sneek's **train** and **bus stations** are five minutes' walk from the old centre. The town can get exceptionally busy, and accommodation is impossible to find during Sneek Week in early August. At other times, the central **VVV**, near the Stadhuis at Marktstraat 18 (Mon–Fri 9.30am–6pm, Sat 9.30am–5pm; summer Thurs till 9pm; ☎0515/414 096, ⓦwww.vvvsneek.nl), can arrange private **rooms** for a small fee. Here you can also obtain a free map with an overview of the best ways to explore southwest Friesland, either by foot, in-line skate, horse or canoe (ⓦwww.routezuidwestfriesland.nl).

Accommodation

For **hotels**, *Daaldersplaats*, by the station at Stationsstraat 66 (☎0515/413 175, ⓦwww.daaldersplaats.nl; ②), is comfortable, and also has a restaurant which serves a four-course meal for only €14.50, while *De Wijnberg*, Marktstraat 23 (☎0515/412 421, ⓦwww.hoteldewijnberg.nl; ②), is good value and central, with a big restaurant and pub. Alternatively, the recently revamped 🌟 *Hotel Nieuw Hanenburg*, Wijde Noorderhoorne 2 (☎0515/412 570, ⓦwww.hotelhilverda .nl; ②) is the plushest option in town, with smart suites in black and silver shades and a large restaurant downstairs. Sneek also has a brand new HI **hostel**, at Oude Oppenhuizerweg 17 (☎0515/412 132, ⓦwww.stayokay.com; €30), some 1.5km southeast of the centre; head east to the end of Kleinzand, turn right down Oppenhuizerweg, and it's the first major road on the left (bus #99 from the station). The nearest **campsite** is *De Domp*, Domp 4 (☎0515/412 559, ⓦwww .dedomp.nl; April–Oct), 2km northeast of the centre on Sytsingawiersterleane, and a right turn off the main road to Leeuwarden; no buses run near.

The Town

From the station, Stationsstraat leads to the main square, **Martiniplein**, whose ponderous sixteenth-century **Martinikerk** (mid-June to mid-Sept Tues–Sat 2.30–5pm; mid-July to mid-Aug also Tues–Thurs 7–9pm; free) is edged by an old wooden belfry. Around the corner at the end of Grote Kerkstraat, the **Stadhuis**, Marktstraat 15 (mid-July to mid-Aug Mon–Thurs 2–4pm; free), is all extravagance, from the Rococo facade to the fanciful outside staircase; inside there's an indifferent display of ancient weapons in the former guardroom. Heading east along Marktstraat, veer right after the VVV and follow the signs to the nearby **Scheepvaart Museum en Oudheidkamer**, Kleinzand 14 (Mon–Sat 10am–5pm, Sun noon–5pm; €3; ⓦwww.friesscheepvaartmuseum.nl), a well-displayed collection of maritime models, paintings and related miscellany. A little further along, at Kleinzand 32, the **Weduwe Joustra shop** has an original nineteenth-century interior, worth a glance for its old barrels and till, even if you decide not to indulge in a bottle of Beerenburg, a herb-flavoured gin and regional speciality. Turn right at the end of Koemarkt and you reach the grandiose **Waterpoort**, all that remains of the seventeenth-century town walls.

To see more of the lakes outside town, **boat trips** (July & Aug) leave from the Oosterkade, over the bridge by the east end of Kleinzand. Itineraries and prices vary and there's no fixed schedule of sailings: you can request anything from a quick tour of the town's canals to a venture out into the open sea. Contact the VVV or the boat owners at the dock for up-to-date details.

Eating, drinking and nightlife

Sneek has a large number of **restaurants**, few of which have much character. The most appealing is *De Wijsneus*, at Grote Kerkstraat 12 (☎0515/422 387), with a French-style garden and a four-course menu for around €30. *Sneek aan*

Zee, Oosterdijk 10 (☎0515/412 756), is a smart, cheerful fish restaurant with reasonably priced fresh seafood, while *Klein Java*, Wijde Noorderhorne 18, offers Indonesian meals. As for **drinking**, try *Ludiek*, Kruizebroederstraat 77, a bar with dancing after dark, or the *Alcatraz*, a former jail at Kleine Kerkstraat 4/B, which doesn't open until late.

Bolsward

Some 10km west of Sneek, and served by regular bus #99 from Sneek train station, **BOLSWARD** (pronounced *bozwut*) was founded in the seventh century and became a bustling and important textile centre in the Middle Ages, though its subsequent decline was prolonged and deep. It's a tad less touristy than the surrounding towns and possesses two especially handsome old buildings. Your first stop should be the **Stadhuis**, Jongemastraat 2, a magnificent red-brick, stone-trimmed Renaissance edifice of 1613. The facade is topped by a lion holding a coat of arms over the head of a terrified Turk, and below a mass of twisting, curling carved stone frames a series of finely cut cameos, all balanced by an extravagant external staircase. Inside there's a small **museum** (April–Oct Mon 2–4pm, Tues–Fri 9am–noon & 2–4pm; free) holding local historical bits and pieces.

Ten minutes' walk away, the fifteenth-century **Martinikerk**, at Groot Kerkhof (May–Sept Mon–Fri 10am–noon & 2–4pm; July & Aug also Sat 1.30–4pm; Oct–April Mon–Fri 2–4pm; €1.20), was originally built on an earthen mound for protection from flooding. Some of the woodcarving inside is quite superb, particularly the choir with its rare misericords from 1470 and the seventeenth-century pulpit, carved from a single oak tree. Its panels depict the four seasons: the Frisian baptism dress above the young eagle symbolizes spring and the carved ice skates, winter. The stone font dates from around 1000, while the stained glass windows at the back depict the German occupation of World War II and subsequent liberation by the Canadians.

Bolsward is also home to the **Friese Bierbrouwerij**, Snekerstraat 43 (Frisian Brewery; Mon, Tues, Thurs & Fri 3–6pm, guided tour at 4pm; Sat 10am–6pm, guided tours hourly; €5, drink included; ⊛ www.bierbrouwerij-usheit.nl). The smallest brewery in the country, it produces eight different kinds of Us Heit beer and several whiskys. You can learn all about the production process before sampling the product. The brewery also contains a small museum.

Practicalities

The unofficial **VVV**, located in the small Gysbert Japicxhus museum at Wipstraat 6 (mid-June to mid-Sept Mon 1.30–5pm, Tues–Fri 9am–12.30pm & 1.30–5pm, Sat 1.30–4pm, hours vary out of season; ☎0515/577 701), has details of a handful of private **rooms**. There are two convenient **hotels**, the *Stadsherberg Heeremastate*, Heeremastraat 8 (☎0515/573 063, ⊛ www.heeremastate.eu; ❷), which although central is very quiet and has a cosy terrace, and *De Wijnberg*, Marktplein 5 (☎0515/572 220, ⊛ www.wijnbergbolsward.nl; ❷), more centrally located with a terrace right on the market square.

Makkum

Immaculate houses, church towers, cobbled streets, flower pots and wooden boats sum up the agreeable town of **MAKKUM**, just 10km west of Bolsward. It's saved from postcard prettiness by a working harbour, although, as the centre of traditional Dutch **ceramics** manufacture, the town can be overwhelmed by tourists in summer. Ceramics enthusiasts can visit the Tichelaar family workshops, Turfmarkt 65 (Mon–Fri 9am–5.30pm, Sat 10am–5pm; ☎0515/231 341, ⓦwww.tichelaar.nl), take a guided tour (Mon–Fri 11am & 1.30pm; €4.50), or just browse through the shop.

Makkum is served by the irregular **minibus** #102 from Workum train station, and by the much better bus #98 from Bolsward. Makkum **VVV**, Pruikmakershoek 2 (April–May & Sept–Oct Mon, Tues, Thurs & Fri 10am–noon & 1–3pm; June–Aug Mon–Fri 10am–noon & 1–5pm, Sat 10am–3pm; ☎0515/231 190, ⓦwww.hetfriesehart.nl.nl), is sited in the old Waag and can arrange **private rooms** for free. The **campsite** *De Weeren* (☎0515/321 374), 2km out of town on the road to Wons (bus #98 or #99 towards Bolsward), is basic but clean and quiet. The best hotel is the German-run *Villa Mar*, Dominee L. Touwenlaan 5 (☎0515/232 469; ⓦwww.villa-mar.com; ❷–❸), a tastefully renovated old villa with classic rooms, a huge kitchen for communal use and a lush garden. Otherwise, try the central and recently renovated **hotel** *De Waag*, Markt 13 (☎0515/231 447, ⓦwww.hoteldewaagmakkum.nl; ❶), with a low-priced **restaurant**. *It Posthus*, in the old post office building at Plein 15 (☎0515/231 153), has duck breast, salads and daily specialties in a bright and pleasant setting, with a three-course meal for €29.50.

Museumroute Aldfaerserf

If you take the scenic route south from Makkum to Workum you'll pass the **Museumroute Aldfaerserf** (April–Oct Tues–Sun 10am–5pm; €9.50; ⓦwww .aldfaerserf.nl). The villages of Exmorra, Allingawier, Ferwoude and Piaam now serve as open-air museums illustrating Frisian life in the eighteenth and nineteenth centuries. Historical buildings have been restored and refurbished, regaining their historical functions as bakeries, carpenters' shops and smithies. The 25-kilometre route can be done by car or bicycle (which can be rented at Allingawier; €6 a day).

Workum

Heavily protected by its sea defenses, the town of **WORKUM**, ten minutes southwest of Sneek by train, is a long, straggly place with an attractive main street that resembles a prosperous city suburb. Until the early eighteenth century, Workum was a seaport, though nowadays indications of its salad days are confined to the central square, 2km from the train station, with its seventeenth-century **Waag** at Merk 4, now home to both the VVV and a small museum showing a standard nautical-historical collection (same hours as VVV; free). Immediately behind, the **St Gertrudskerk** (Mon–Sat 11am–5pm; hours vary out of season; €1), the largest medieval church in Friesland, contains a small collection of mostly eighteenth-century odds and ends. If you're into religious art, explore the **Museum Kerkelijke Kunst** in the neo-Gothic St Werenfridus Kerk, Noard 175 (mid-May to mid-Sept Mon–Sat 11am–5pm; €2.50) displaying religious silver, tiles and liturgical clothing as well as furniture such as a neo-Gothic confession chair. Just down the road at Noard 6, the likeable **Jopie Huisman Museum** (April–Oct Mon–Sat 10am–5pm, Sun 1–5pm; March & Nov–Dec daily 1–5pm; €5; ⓦwww.jopiehuismanmuseum.nl) is devoted to paintings by Huisman, a contemporary local artist, most of which have an appealingly unpretentious focus on Frisian life.

Practicalities

The **VVV** (April–Oct Mon & Sun 1.30–5pm Tues–Sat 10am–5pm; June–Aug also Mon morning; Nov–March Thurs–Sat 1.30–5pm; ☎0515/541 045,

Ⓦwww.vvvworkum.nl), located in the old Waag at Merk 4, has an overview of private rooms in the area. Alternatively, head for the *Gulden Leeuw*, Merk 2 (Ⓣ0515/542 341, Ⓦwww.deguldenleeuw.nl; ❶), where facilities include a recently revamped restaurant with mainly fish specialities, or the *Herberg van Oom Lammert en Tante Klaasje*, next door at Merk 3 (Ⓣ0515/541 370, Ⓦwww .oomlammertentanteklaasje.nl; ❷), where you can sleep in a *bedstee* (something like an elevated closet, Frisian style). The **campsite** *It Soal* (Ⓣ0515/541 443, Ⓦwww.itsoal.nl; April–Oct) is located on the IJsselmeer, 3km south of the centre.

The most appealing place to **eat** is the recently opened *It Pottebakkershûs* at Merk 18, with tasty veggie dishes, good coffee and high teas. The place doubles as a **ceramics factory** with a permanent exhibition of antique local pottery.

Hindeloopen

The village of **HINDELOOPEN**, the next stop down the rail line from Workum, juts into the IJsselmeer, twenty minutes' walk west of its train station. A highlight of the tour-bus trail during the summer months, it's an appealing little town that blossoms with elderly visitors on sunny weekends. A tidy jigsaw of old streets, canals and wooden bridges makes for an attractive stroll, but unless you visit out of high season it's too touristy to linger for long.

Until the seventeenth century, Hindeloopen prospered as a Zuider Zee **port**, concentrating on trade with the Baltic and Amsterdam. The combination of rural isolation and trade created a specific culture within this tightly knit community, with a distinctive dialect (Hylper–Frisian with Scandinavian influences) and sumptuous local **dress**. Adopting materials imported into Amsterdam by the East India Company, the women of Hindeloopen dressed in a florid combination of colours where dress was a means of personal identification: caps, casques and trinkets indicated marital status and age, and the quality of the print

The Elfstedentocht

The **Elfstedentocht** ("Eleven Towns Race") is Friesland's biggest spectacle, a gruelling **ice-skating** marathon around Friesland that dates back to 1890, when one Pim Muller, a local sports journalist, skated his way around the eleven official towns of the province, simply to see whether it was possible. It was, and twenty years later the first official Elfstedentocht was launched, contested by 22 skaters. Weather – and ice – permitting, it has taken place just fifteen times in the last hundred years, most recently in 1997, attracting skaters from all over the world.

The race is organized by the Eleven Towns Association, of which you must be a member to take part; the high level of interest in the race means that membership is very difficult to obtain. The route, which measures about 200km in total, takes in all the main centres of Friesland, starting in Leeuwarden in the town's Expo Centre, from where the racers sprint – skates in hand – 1500m to the point where they get onto the ice. The first stop after this is Sneek, after which the race takes in Hindeloopen and the other old Zuider Zee towns, plus Dokkum in the north of the province, before finishing in Leeuwarden. The event is broadcast live on national TV, the route lined with spectators. Of the 17,000 or so people who take part, usually no more than three hundred are professional skaters. Casualties are inevitably numerous; the worst year was 1963, when 10,000 skaters took part and only seventy finished, the rest beaten by the fierce winds, extreme cold and snowdrifts along the way. Generally, however, something like three-quarters of the starters make it to the finishing line.

If you're not around for the race itself, the route makes a popular bike ride and is signposted by the ANWB as one of their national cycling routes; four or five days will allow enough time to sightsee as well as cycle.

indicated social standing. Other Dutch villages adopted similar practices, but nowhere were the details of social position more precisely drawn. However, the development of dress turned out to be a corollary of prosperity, for the decline of Hindeloopen quite simply finished it off. Similarly, the local **painted furniture** showed an ornate mixture of Scandinavian and Oriental styles super-imposed on traditional Dutch carpentry. Each item was covered from head to toe with painted tendrils and flowers on a red, green or white background, but the town's decline resulted in the collapse of the craft. Tourism has revived local furniture-making, and countless shops now line the main street selling modern versions, though even the smallest items aren't cheap, and the florid style is something of an acquired taste.

Hindeloopen's attractive **church**, a seventeenth-century structure with a wonky medieval tower, has some graves of British airmen who perished in the Zuider Zee, while the small **Schaats Museum**, Kleine Wiede 1 (Mon–Sat 10am–6pm & Sun 1–5pm; €2.50; ⓦ www.schaatsmuseum.nl), displays some skating mementos relating to the great Frisian ice-skating race "De Friese Elfstedentocht" (see box, p.224), as well as plenty of painted Hindeloopen-ware in its shop. You can see original examples of this in the small village museum, the **Museum Hindeloopen**, beside the church (April–Oct Mon–Fri 11am–5pm, Sat & Sun 1.30–5pm; €3; ⓦ www.museumhindeloopen.nl), although there's a wider display at the Fries Museum in Leeuwarden (see p.209).

Practicalities

From Workum, it's just 6km to Hindeloopen, a pleasant, well-signposted bike-ride across fields, past a windmill and along a dyke. It's a popular route with families as it steers clear of busy roads.

Hindeloopen **VVV**, Nieuwstad 26 (April & May Mon, Wed & Sat 11am–4pm; June also Fri 11am–4pm; July & Aug Mon–Sat 10am–12.30pm & 1–5pm; Sept & Oct Mon, Wed & Sat 10.30am–4pm; ⓣ0514/851 223, ⓦ www.vvvhindeloopen .nl), can organize the odd private **room**. Hindeloopen's popularity makes finding **accommodation** a problem during the summer, with the town's lodgings filling up early. By far the most charming option is to sleep in the old 🅜 *Likhus* at Tuinen 5–7 (ⓣ0514 523 208, ⓦ www.hylperhuis.nl; ❼). This tiny house once served as a residence for the wives and children of ships' captains when they were at sea; the entire place is decorated in old Hindeloopen style. Alternatively, try *De Stadsboerderij*, Nieuwe Weide 9 (ⓣ0514/521 278, ⓦ www.destadsboerderij .nl; ❶) or *Pension De Twee Hondjes*, Paardepad 2 (ⓣ0514/522 873, ⓦ www .detweehondjes.nl; ❶). Both offer the option to sleep in an original *bedstee* (an elevated Frisian-style closet). The **campsite** *Hindeloopen* (ⓣ0514/521 452, ⓦ www.campinghindeloopen.nl; April–Oct) is 1km or so south of the village near the coast at Westerdijk 9.

For **eating**, the intimate *Oost Achterom*, just off the harbour at Kalverstraat 13, is a lovely place to enjoy Italian fare on the terrace in the evening; *De Brabander*, Nieuwe Wiede 7, has main dishes for under €20 and a wide array of excellent pancakes for under €5. Failing that, the stands on the harbour serve fresh fishy snacks during the day for around €5, with grassy verges to picnic on and plenty of passing boat trade for entertainment.

Sloten

With its thicket of boat masts poking out above the rooftops, it's easy to spot **SLOTEN** from afar. It's something of a museum piece, though the village's 1000 inhabitants are proud to call Sloten one of Friesland's eleven "cities", and a medieval one at that. The town comprises little more than a few pavement

▲ Sloten

cafés fronting a central canal, strips of manicured lawn, a windmill, old locks and colourful flower boxes, although it's encircled by water and is a popular spot with Dutch and German tourists alike. The adjoining milk-powder factory may seem a blip in this picture-perfect setting, but if anything it lends the place a welcome sense of realism. There's a small **museum** (April–Oct Tues–Fri 11am–5pm, Sat & Sun 1–5pm; out of season by appointment; €3; Ⓦwww .museumsloten.nl) in the town hall on Heerenwal, but otherwise it's just a case of wandering the cobbled alleyways and admiring the gabled facades.

Practicalities

Reaching Sloten by public transport can be a little awkward; the easiest way is to take **bus** #42 from Sneek train station to the bus change-over point on the motorway at Spannenburg (takes 35min), where connecting bus #41 continues west to Sloten and bus #44 runs on to Sloten and Bolsward. Alternatively, it's a nineteen-kilometre bike ride from Sneek.

The **VVV**, located in the town hall (April–Oct Tues–Fri 11am–5pm, Sat & Sun 1–5pm; Ⓣ0514/531 541, Ⓦwww.gaasterlandpromotion.nl), can suggest a few **places to stay**, including the *Pension 't Brechje*, Voorstreek 110 (Ⓣ0514/531 298, Ⓦwww.pensiontbrechje.nl; ❶). A couple of **restaurants** by the bridge on the canal do good light lunches and more expensive evening meals, and have nice outdoor seating.

The closest **campsite** is *Lemsterpoort*, Jachthaven 3 (Ⓣ0514/531 668), but if you have your own transport, it's worth striking out 2km to neighbouring **Wijckel**: turn left opposite the church, bear right at the first fork, follow the road round, and just past the cow postbox lies the friendly mini-camping *De Tjasker*, Iwert 17 (Ⓣ0514/605 869, Ⓦwww.campingdetjasker.nl), with its own thatched barn and spotless lawn.

Stavoren

Named after the Frisian god Stavo, **STAVOREN** is the oldest town in Friesland and was once a prosperous port; it's now both the end of the train line and the departure point for **ferries** to Enkhuizen (see p.129). Strung out along the coast, Stavoren is an eclectic mix of the old and new: the harbour is flanked by modern "Legoland" housing while the shipyards are linked by cobbled backstreets. Popular with yachty types, it's a great place to admire the carefully restored seventeenth- to nineteenth-century vessels that once plied the Zuider Zee, now moored up and awaiting hire. On a sunny day, watching the old wooden ships go by and listening to the clink of halyards is as an enjoyable pastime as any. At the southern end of town, massive, squat turbines encased in glass can be seen pumping water out of Friesland and into the IJsselmeer.

Practicalities

The glass-shelled **VVV** is on the harbour, two minutes' walk from the train station (April–Oct Tues–Sat 9.15am–noon & 1.30–6pm, opening hours on Sun correspond with ferry departures and arrivals; ☏0514/682 424, ⓦwww .beleeffriesland.nl), and has details of pensions and private rooms. Next door, Zeilvloot Lemmer-Stavoren (☏0514/681 818, ⓦwww.zeilvloot.nl) can provide details on renting **sailboats**, though ideally you'll need to be in a group: keeping up tradition doesn't come cheap.

The best place to **stay** is the hotel *De Vrouwe van Stavoren*, Havenweg 1 (☏0514/681 202, ⓦwww.hotel-vrouwevanstavoren.nl; ❶–❷), attractively sited by the harbour and surprisingly good value. Try sleeping in one of their wine barrels – as long as you're not claustrophobic. Nearby Smidstraat has a pizzeria, café, ice-cream shop and supermarket; Vishandel Doede Bleeker, at no. 21 (summer daily 11am–6.30pm, hours vary out of season), offers a platter of tasty fish and chips for €5.50.

North Friesland

Edged by the Lauwersmeer to the east and protected by interlocking sea dykes to the north, the strip of Friesland **north of Leeuwarden** is dotted with tiny agricultural villages that were once separated from each other by swamp and marsh. The first settlers were forced to confine themselves to whatever higher ground was available, the *terpen* which kept the treacherous waters at bay. The area is home to one of Friesland's oldest towns, **Dokkum**; of interest too are the coastal hamlets of **Moddergat** and **Wierum**. Further west, the unprepossessing port of **Holswerd** provides access to the island of **Ameland**, reached directly from Leeuwarden by a bus service that connects with the ferry. Note too that while the island of Schiermonnikoog can also be reached from Dokkum and Leeuwarden, the quickest and most direct route is from Groningen (for full information on Schiermonnikoog, see p.239).

Cycling around Stavoren

Stavoren is a good base for cycling. Options include following the coastal cycleway 10km north to **Hindeloopen**, or 5km south to **Laaksum**, past dark green and marine-blue lagoons with banks of reeds rustling in the wind. For a longer ride, continue through Laaksum and pick up the signposts to **Oudemirdum**, with its swathes of forest crisscrossed by cycleways and wooden bridges spanning pea-soupy canals. This 40-kilometre loop makes a pleasant day-trip, but bear in mind the winds can be forceful along the coast, and generally blow from the southwest.

Dokkum

From Leeuwarden, the scenic **national bike route** LF3b heads northeast, following the contours of a meandering canal; flat, narrow and predominantly car-less, its only challenges are the minute (but near-vertical) wooden humpback bridges. Before you reach Holwerd, follow signs branching off to **DOKKUM**, which is also just half an hour from Leeuwarden by bus #50. Dokkum is the only significant settlement hereabouts and its early pagan inhabitants made a real name for themselves by murdering the English missionary St Boniface and 52 of his companions here in 754. In part still walled and moated, Dokkum has kept its shape as a fortified town, best appreciated by the side of the Het Grootdiep canal, which cuts the town into two distinct sections. This was the commercial centre of the old town and is marked by a series of ancient gables, including that of the **Admiraliteitshuis** which serves as the town's **museum** (Tues–Sat 1–5pm; €3; ⓦ www.museumdokkum .nl). There's not much else: a couple of windmills, quiet walks along the old ramparts and all sorts of things named after St Boniface as penance for the locals' early misdeeds.

Practicalities

The **VVV**, Op de Fetze 13 (Mon 11am–5.30pm, Tues–Fri 9am–5.30pm, Fri also 7–9pm, Sat 9am–5pm; ⓣ0519/293 800, ⓦ www.vvvlauwersland.nl), issues a map of the town and its surroundings, including outlying Holwerd and Wierum. The best-value **hotel** is 太 *De Abdij van Dokkum*, Markt 30 (ⓣ0519/220 422, ⓦ www.adbij.nl; ②), housed in a former abbey with Frisian-themed rooms and a decent restaurant. If that option fails, try the *Van der Meer*, Woudweg 1 (ⓣ0519/292 380, ⓦ www.hotelvandermeer.nl; ①–②). The closest campsite, *Harddraverspark* (ⓣ0519/294 445, ⓦ www.campingdokkum.nl), is just five minutes' walk east of the centre at Harddraversdijk 1a. At **lunchtime** *De Waegh*, Grote Breedstraat 1, has a decent range of organic dishes, while in the evening your best bet is *'t Raedhus* on Koningstraat 1 (ⓣ0519/294 082; also a hotel), or *Pizzeria Romana* (ⓣ0519/297 756; closed Mon), off the main canal at Koornmarkt 8.

Moddergat and Wierum

Of all the tiny hamlets in north Friesland, two of the most interesting lie on the Waddenzee. **MODDERGAT**, the more easterly of the two, spreads out along the road behind the sea wall 10km northeast of Dokkum, merging with the village of **Paesens**. At its western edge, a memorial commemorates the 1883 tragedy when seventeen ships sank during a storm, with the loss of 83 lives. Opposite, **'t Fiskerhuske Museum**, Fiskerpad 4–8 (March–Oct Mon–Sat 10am–5pm; July & Aug also Sun 1–5pm; €3; ⓦ www.museummoddergat.nl), comprises three restored fishermen's cottages with displays on the history and culture of the village and details of the disaster: as such small museums go, it's pretty good. Huddled behind the sea dyke 5km to the west, **WIERUM** has one main claim to fame, its twelfth-century church with a saddle-roof tower and (as in Moddergat) a golden ship on the weather vane. The dyke offers views across to the islands and holds a monument of twisted anchors to the fishermen who died in the 1883 storm and the dozen or so claimed in the century after. The **Wadloopcentrum Fryslân** here (ⓦ www.wadlopen.net) organizes guided walks across the mud flats; times vary with conditions and tides. There are different routes you can walk depending on tides and seasons, so check the website for details and dates.

Moddergat and Wierum are on the same hourly **bus** #52 route from Dokkum. If you've rented a bicycle from Leeuwarden and ridden to Dokkum, follow the signposted cycleway; it's around 8km to Moddergat and a few kilometres more to Wierum. The best **place to stay** is the farmhouse pension *Recreatiebedrijf Meinsma*, Meinsmaweg 5 in Moddergat (℡0519/589 396, ⓦwww.recreatiebedrijfmeinsma.nl; ❶), which also offers a small campsite and self-contained bungalows.

Ameland

Easy to reach from the tiny port of **HOLWERD**, a few kilometres west of Wierum, the island of **Ameland** is one of the major tourist resorts of the north Dutch coast, with a population that swells from 3000 to a staggering 35,000 during summer weekends. Not that the sun is always shining: at times, clouds jostle for position and the colour of the sky can mirror that of the water. It's during the storms that the island is at its moodiest, the flatness of the land accentuating the action in the sky above.

Ferries dock near Nes, the main village, and there's a summer **bus** service from the ferry to the island's other villages. A variety of **boat trips** depart Nes, including excursions to the islands of Terschelling (see p.215) and Schiermonnikoog (see p.239), and to the sandbanks to watch seals. Details can be given by the VVV or tour operators in Nes.

Nes

NES is a tiny place that nestles among the fields behind the dyke. Once a centre of the Dutch whaling industry, Nes has more than its fair share of cafés, hotels and tourist shops, though quite a bit of the old village has survived. Mercifully, high-rise development has been forbidden, and there's a focus instead on the seventeenth- and eighteenth-century captains' houses, known as *commandeurshuizen*, which line several of the streets. Perhaps surprisingly, the crowds rarely seem to overwhelm the village, but rather to breathe life into it – which is just as well as there's not a lot to do other than wander the streets and linger in cafés. Even if you do hit peak season, it's fairly easy to escape the crowds and you can **rent bikes** at a number of shops in the village. If it's raining, you might consider the **Natuurcentrum**, Strandweg 38 (April–Oct Mon–Fri 10am–5pm, Sat & Sun 1–5pm; Nov & Dec Wed–Sat 1–5pm; €5.75; ⓦwww.amelandermusea.nl), an aquarium and natural history museum – look out for the life-size whale – although there's no information in English.

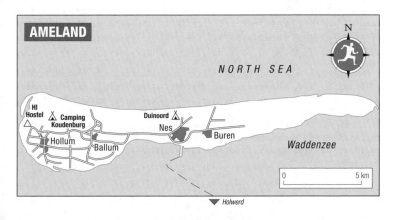

Ferries to Ameland

From Leeuwarden, bus #66 runs to Holwerd (30min), from where the connecting **ferry** departs to Ameland (€12.30 return). In the other direction, the boat leaves Ameland an hour earlier in each case. Timetables are available from Leeuwarden train and bus stations. Check ⓦ www.wpd.nl for up-to-date information.

Practicalities

Nes has a wide range of **accommodation**, but prices do rise dramatically in summer, when vacant rooms can be thin on the ground – indeed, you should reserve ahead if you're visiting in July or August. For a small charge, the **VVV**, Bureweg 2 (Mon–Fri 9am–5pm, Sat 10am–3.30pm; ⓣ0519/546 546, ⓦwww .vvvameland.nl) will fix you up with a pension or private **room** anywhere on the island. Failing that, you could try the central and family-run **hotel** *De Jong*, Reeweg 29 (ⓣ0519/542 016, ⓦwww.hoteldejong.nl; ❷), or the luxurious *Golden Tulip Resort Noordsee*, Strandweg 42 (ⓣ0519/546 600, ⓦwww .westcordhotels.nl; ❹–❺). The best-appointed **campsite** is the sprawling *Duinoord* at Jan van Eijckweg 4 (ⓣ0519/542 070, ⓦwww.campingduinoord .eu; April–Oct); go 1km north out of Nes, then follow Strandweg all the way to the sea, bearing left to enter the camping complex.

Around the island

Ameland is just 2km wide and 25km long, its entire northern shore made up of a fine expanse of **sand** and **dune** laced by foot and cycle paths. The east end of the island is the most deserted, and you can cycle by the side of the marshy shallows that once made up the whole southern shore before the sea dyke was built.

Of the smaller villages that dot the island, the prettiest place to stay is **HOLLUM**, a sedate settlement of old houses and farm buildings west of Nes. Its **VVV**, O.P. Lapstraat 6 (April–Aug Mon–Fri 9am–noon & 1.30–5.30pm, Sat 10am–noon; Sept–March Mon–Fri 9am–noon, Sat 10am–noon, ⓦwww .vvvameland.nl; ⓣ0519/546 546), can offer the same services as the Nes VVV and is generally less crowded. If you're into all things marine, there are a couple of small museums here: the **Sorgdragermuseum**, Herenweg 1 (July & Aug Mon–Fri 10am–5pm, Sat & Sun 1.30–5pm; check hours with the VVV out of season; €3; ⓦwww.amelandermusea.nl), in an old *commandeurshuis*; and the **Reddingsmuseum Abraham Fock**, Oranjeweg 18 (same hours; €4; ⓦwww .amelandermusea.nl), devoted to the local lifeboat teams and the horses that used to drag the boats to the sea. There's also a **lighthouse**, dating from 1880, which offers great views over the island (July & Aug Mon & Sun 1–5pm, Tues–Sat 10am–5pm & 7–10pm, April–June, Sept & Oct closes 9pm, check hours with the VVV out of season; €4; ⓦwww.amelandermusea.nl).

Hollum's best-value place to stay is the homely *Pension Ambla*, Westerlaan 33a (ⓣ0519/554 537, ⓦwww.ambla.nl; ❶). Alternatives include the **campsite** *Koudenburg Oosterhiemweg* (ⓣ0519/554 367, ⓦwww.koudenburg.nl), by the heath to the north at Oosterhemweg 2, and further west, situated dramatically at the tip of the island past the lighthouse and between pine forest and dunes, the *Waddencentrum Ameland* – a good HI **hostel** (ⓣ0519/555 353, ⓦwww .stayokay.com; dorm bed €31.50), with bike rental. To reach it take bus #130 to the last stop.

Groningen

Once known as East Frisia, the province of **Groningen** does not have the high tourist profile of many of the country's other provinces, which is hardly surprising given the relative lack of star attractions. Nonetheless, there are several highlights, most notably **Groningen**, the capital, a lively and very appealing small city that is home to an outstanding art museum, the Groninger, and a population approaching 200,000. The province also includes a large slab of empty coastline, where the **Lauwersmeer National Park** boasts extensive

ACCOMMODATION		RESTAURANTS		CAFÉ-BARS, BARS & NIGHTLIFE	
Asgand Hotel	H	De Biechystoel	7	Café de Keyzer	6
Auberge Corp de Garde	B	Brasserie Groen	17	Café Koster	15
Bud Gett Hostel	F	Brussels Lof	12	Der Witz	13
Eden City Hotel Groningen	D	Diep	3	De Drie Gezusters	8
NH De Ville	C	Four Roses	18	Hooghoudt Café	9
Martini hotel	G	Hemingway's Cuba	16	De Kar	5
Schimmelpenninck Huys	E	De Kleine Heerlijkheid	2	De Oosterpoort	20
Simplon Jongerenhotel	A	Klient Moghul	1	The Palace	14
		Roezemoes	19	De Pintelier	4
		Soestdijk	10	De Spieghel	11

wildlife and **Schiermonnikoog island** offers lovely country walks and cycle rides. Also up north is the **seal sanctuary** of Pieterburen, where sick or underfed seals are nursed until they can be released back into the Waddenzee, and the pick of the old manor houses that dot the province, **Menkemaborg** in **Uithuizen**. To the southeast of Groningen, the old frontier village of **Bourtange** has been painstakingly restored, offering an insight into eighteenth-century life in a fortified town, and nearby **Ter Apel** holds a rare survivor from the Reformation in the substantial remains of its monastery.

Groningen

The most exciting city in the north Netherlands, **GRONINGEN** comes as something of a surprise in the midst of the province's quiet, rural surroundings. Hip, streetwise fashion, a cosmopolitan feel and thriving student life imbue the city with vim and gusto. Competitively priced restaurants dish up exotic curries and fresh falafel alongside the standard Dutch staples, and the arts scene is vibrant, particularly during the academic year. Virtually destroyed during the Allied liberation in 1945, Groningen is now a jumble of arts and architectures: from traditional canal-side townhouses to bright Art Deco tile work along the upper facades of the shopping streets. This eclecticism culminates in the innovative **Groninger Museum**, resplendent in acid-greens and golds on its own little island, its controversial design encasing a superb collection of contemporary art, enhanced by numerous and varied temporary exhibitions.

Groningen may have had humble, swampy beginnings, but by the thirteenth century it had become a powerful trading centre and member of the **Hanseatic League**. Nominally a fiefdom of the bishops of Utrecht from 1040 until 1536, in reality it was an autonomous merchant state ruled by a tightly defined oligarchy, whose power was exercised through the city council. In 1536 Charles V forced the town to submit to his authority, but Groningen was nevertheless still hesitant in its support of the Dutch rebellion against his successors. The dilemma for the city fathers was that, although they stood to gain economically from independence, the majority of the town's citizens were Catholic, deeply suspicious of their Protestant neighbours. In the end, the economic argument won the day, and the town became the capital of its own province in 1594.

Although Groningen does not have a rich culinary tradition, the **Hooghoudt brewery** (Ⓦ www.hooghoudt.nl) is known throughout the country and dates back to 1888. The brewery is most famous for its Graanjevever, but they also produce Beerenburg and other liquors like the Wilhelmus Orange Liquor, which is traditionally served on Queen's Day.

Arrival and information

Groningen's **bus** and **train stations** are side by side on the south side of town. The **VVV** is ten minutes' walk away in the centre at Grote Markt 25 (Mon–Fri 9am–6pm, Sat 10am–5pm; July & Aug also Sun 11am–3pm; ☎ 0900 202 3050, Ⓦ www.tourism.groningen.nl). It offers a range of services, from tourist information on the town and province to online reservations of hotel rooms and tickets for visiting bands, theatre groups and orchestras. Also available is a brochure of city walks for €1.50 and information on exploring Groningen by boat (Ⓦ www.rondvaartbedrijfkool.nl) or canoe. As well as information on the larger hotels, the VVV has a short list of **private rooms** in both Groningen and the surrounding area, though hardly any are near the centre.

Accommodation

Groningen has plenty of good, reasonably priced **accommodation**, though it's a good idea to call ahead to reserve a room. Many hotels offer the use of free bicycles to their guests.

If you're **camping**, *Stadspark*, Campinglaan 6 (☎050/525 1624, ⓦwww.campingstadspark.nl; mid-March to mid-Oct), is the best option, within walking distance of the city centre.

Asgard Hotel Ganzevoortsingel 2 ☎050/368 4810, ⓦwww.asgardhotel.nl. A modern design hotel Scandinavian-style, using only sustainable materials in light shades. The rooms are kitted out with comfy beds, luxurious bathrooms and wireless internet. ❸–❹

Auberge Corps de Garde Oude Boteringestraat 72–74 ☎050/314 5437, ⓦwww.corpsdegarde.nl. A central option located in a seventeenth-century building with high ceilings, close to the Grote Markt. Most of the rooms have recently been revamped, but remain in style with the classic character of the building. ❷–❸

Bud Gett Hostel Rademarkt 3 ☎050/588 6558, ⓦwww.budgetthostels.nl. A brand new hostel, smack in the centre of town and offering well-equipped dorms (€28) and simple but functional twin rooms with private facilities. ❶

Eden City Hotel Groningen Gedempte Kattendiep 25 ☎050/588 6565, ⓦwww.edenhotelgroup.com. Modern and well equipped, with a stunning view over the city from the roof terrace. ❷–❸

NH De Ville Oude Boteringestraat 43 ☎050/318 1222, ⓦwww.deville.nl. Even though now part of a chain, this hotel has maintained its intimate feel with friendly staff and a fine Baroque interior. The cosy courtyard is also a great location for a romantic dinner. ❹

Martini Hotel Gedempte Zuiderdiep 8 ☎050/312 9919, ⓦwww.martinihotel.nl. Large and central, with Martini memorabilia on the walls and a huge grand café with fireplace and piano for an intimate atmosphere. ❷

Schimmelpenninck Huys Oosterstraat 53 ☎050/318 9502, ⓦwww.schimmelpenninckhuys.nl. The origins of this hotel, listed as a state monument, date back to 1100, and there is a fourteenth-century wine cellar and an Art Deco lounge. By far the prettiest inner courtyard in town. ❹

Simplon Jongerenhotel Boterdiep 73 ☎050/313 5221, ⓦwww.simplon-jongerenhotel.nl. The lowest prices in town are found at the edge of the city, with clean doubles and well-kept dorms (€14.50); from the Grote Markt follow Oude Ebbingestraat north over the canal, take the first right and then first left. ❶

The City

Still encircled by what was once the moat, Groningen's compact city centre is the enjoyable part of town and all the main sights are within easy walking distance of each other. One exception, just to the south of the centre, is the **train station**, which was built in 1896 at enormous cost; it was one of the finest of its day, decorated with the strong colours and symbolic designs of Art Nouveau tiles from the Rozenburg factory in The Hague. The grandeur of much of the building has disappeared under a welter of concrete, glass and plastic suspended ceilings, but the old first- and second-class waiting rooms have survived pretty much intact, and have been refurbished as restaurants.

The Groninger Museum

The town's main draw is the excellent **Groninger Museum** (Tues–Sun 10am–5pm; €8; ⓦwww.groningermuseum.nl), set on its own island on the southern edge of the centre, directly across from the train station. It consists of **six pavilions**, each designed in a highly individual style. The museum entrance is under the shimmering golden tower of the central pavilion: think Gaudí on holiday in Miami, and you'll have some inkling of the interior decor. In between the stylish café and museum shop, a striking mosaic stairwell flummoxes most visitors by sweeping downwards, depositing you among two bulbous lemon-yellow pillars on a baby-blue floor. From here moat-level

▲ Groninger Museum

corridors head off to pavilions either side: east to Mendini, Mendini 1 and Coop Himmelb(l)au, west to Starck and De Ploeg.

Highlights include Rubens' energetic *Adoration of the Magi*; Isaac Israels' inviting *Hoedenwinkel* from a modest sample of Hague School paintings; a number of later works by the Expressionists of the Groningen De Ploeg school, principally Jan Wiegers, whose *Portrait of Ludwig Kirchner* is typically earnest; and the bizarre *Can the Bumpsteers While I park the Chariot* by Henk Tas. The paintings are regularly rotated, so don't pin your hopes on catching any particular item.

The pavilions

To the west, the **Philippe Starck pavilion** is a giant disc clad in aluminium plating. A simple vase motif on the exterior hints at the collection of **Chinese and Japanese porcelain** within, beautifully displayed in circular glass cases, softened by gauzy drapes. Starck's disc pavilion sits atop the **De Ploeg pavilion**, created by Michele De Lucchi in the form of a trapezium constructed from red bricks, a traditional building material around here. The De Ploeg art movement

---

Pedal power in Groningen

One of the best things about Groningen is the lack of motor traffic: much of the centre is **car-free**, the result of municipal decisions dating back to the mid-1970s, when the city suffered some of the worst road congestion in Europe. In a bold move, the city council dismantled a huge motorway intersection in the city centre, closed most of its roads to cars and invested heavily in a network of cycle paths and bus lanes. Today the park-and-ride scheme goes from strength to strength and two-thirds of residents travel regularly by **bike**, the highest percentage in the country.

began in Groningen in 1918, and is characterized by intense colour contrasts, exaggerated shapes and depiction of landscapes. As founding member Jan Altink put it: "There wasn't much going on in the way of art in Groningen, so I thought of cultivation and thus also of ploughing. Hence the name De Ploeg." The group often depicted the landscape north of Groningen in their works.

To the east of the mosaic stairway, **three pavilions** house the museum's collection of **contemporary art**. On the lower and ground levels, the **Mendini pavilion** is dedicated to temporary exhibitions. The **Mendini 1 pavilion**, on the first floor, displays a selection of the museum's collection of contemporary visual art, with particular emphasis on art, architecture, design, graffiti and photography. The galleries are individually colour-schemed: cool blues and purples, or the toastier cherry and peach.

A large concrete stairway links Mendini 1 to the final, and most controversial, pavilion. Designed by Wolfgang Prix and Helmut Swiczinsky, who together call themselves **Coop Himmelb(l)au**, this is a Deconstructivist experiment: double-plated steel and reinforced glass jut out at awkward angles, and skinny aerial walkways crisscross the exhibition space. It all feels – probably deliberately – half-built. Look out for the glasswalk holes, where the concrete floor stops and suddenly between your feet the canal gapes, two storeys below. This pavilion is given over to temporary exhibitions that exist in a harsh industrial sound-scape, created by the movement of visitors through metal doors and on the unworked concrete and resonating steel gantries.

Grote Markt and around

The effective centre of town is **Grote Markt**, a wide open space that was badly damaged by wartime bombing and has been rather unimaginatively recon-structed. At its northeast corner is the tiered tower of the **Martinikerk** (May, June & Sept Tues–Sat noon–5pm; July & Aug Mon–Sat 11am–5pm; €1; ⓦwww .martinikerk.nl). Though the oldest parts of the church date back to 1180, most of it dates from the mid-fifteenth century, the nave being a Gothicized rebuilding undertaken to match the added choir.

Adjoining the church is the essentially seventeenth-century **Martinitoren** (April–Oct Mon–Sat 11am–5pm; July & Aug also Sun 11am–5pm; rest of year Mon–Sat noon–4pm; €3), which offers a view that is breathtaking in every sense of the word. Behind the church is the lawn of the **Kerkhof**, an ancient piece of common land that's partly enclosed by the **Provinciehuis**, a rather grand neo-Renaissance building of 1915, seat of the provincial government. On the opposite side of the Grote Markt, the classical **Stadhuis** dates from 1810, tucked in front of the mid-seventeenth-century **Goudkantoor** (Gold Office); look out for the shell motif above the windows, a characteristic Groningen decoration.

Around the A-kerk

From the southwest corner of the Grote Markt, the far side of Vismarkt is framed by the **Korenbeurs** (Corn Exchange) of 1865. The statues on the facade represent, from left to right, Neptune, Mercurius (god of commerce) and Ceres (goddess of agriculture). Just behind, the **A-kerk** is a fifteenth-century church with a Baroque steeple, attractively restored in tones of yellow, orange and red. The church's full name is Onze Lieve Vrouwekerk der A ("Our Dear Lady's Church of the A"), the A being a small river which forms the moat encircling the town centre.

Just west of the church along A-Kerkhof N.Z., the **Noordelijk Scheepvaart Museum**, Brugstraat 24–26 (Tues–Sat 10am–5pm, Sun 1–5pm; €4; ⓦwww .noordelijkscheepvaartmuseum.nl), is one of the best-equipped and most comprehensive maritime museums in the country, tracing the history of north Holland's shipping from the sixth to the twentieth centuries. Housed in a warren of steep stairs and timber-beamed rooms, each of the museum's twenty displays deals with a different aspect of shipping, including trade with the Indies, the development of peat canals and a series of reconstructed nautical workshops. The museum's particular appeal is its imaginative combination of models and original artefacts, which are themselves a mixture of the personal (seamen's chests, quadrants) and the public (figureheads, tile designs of ships).

Smaller museums

As for the city's smaller museums, there's contemporary art at the **Centrum Beeldende Kunst** (Visual Arts Centre) in the Oosterpoort, Trompsingel 27 (Wed–Sun 1–5pm; free; Ⓦwww.cbkgroningen.nl), while the **Grafisch Museum**, Rabenhauptstraat 65 (Graphic Museum; Tues–Sun 1–5pm; €4; Ⓦwww.grafisch museum.nl), southeast of the train station, has everything from a nineteenth-century steam-driven printing press to modern word processors. For exhibitions by up-and-coming photographers, head for the **Galerie Noorderlicht**, A-Kerkhof 12 (Wed–Sun noon–6pm; free; Ⓦwww.noorderlicht.com).

Northwest of Grote Markt, down a passage off Zwanestraat, the **Universiteits-museum** (Tues–Sun 1–5pm; €2.50; Ⓦwww.rug.nl/museum) gives a taste of the university's history, with exhibits ranging from scientific equipment to photos of derby-hatted students clowning around at the turn of twentieth century.

Eating, drinking and nightlife

As Groningen is a student town, there are many budget options for a decent meal, and nightlife is vibrant around the clock. The nicest places to **eat and drink** can be found around **Poelestraat**, just east of Grote Markt, where an array of open-air cafés pulls in a mainly young crowd. The south side of the **Grote Markt** serves all tastes with large terraces and loud music at night, while in the **Kleine** or **Grote Kromme Elleboog** areas, you are in the heart of the university district.

The free *Uitloper* has listings of all events. There are several **music venues** in the city, and the main **theatre**, the Stadsschouwburg, overlooks the water at Turfsingel 86 (Ⓣ050/312 5645). Most plays are in Dutch, but they also have contemporary dance and music performances.

Restaurants

De Biechtstoel Schuitendiep 88 Ⓣ050/313 8246. Cosy restaurant hidden in a small alley and crammed with holy relics (hence the name 'confession chair'). The menu offers everything from stew to scallops for around €18.

Brasserie Groen Carolieweg 16 Ⓣ050/311 3962. Agreeable multi-level lunchroom-cum-restaurant with fresh green accents and very decent coffee. A seasonal three-course menu sets you back €22.50.

Brussels Lof A-Kerkstraat 24 Ⓣ050/312 7603. Serves a wide range of vegetarian dishes and good fondues, but also known for fresh fish; pure and simple cuisine with mains like tuna, artichoke pie or scallops for around €20.

Diep Schuitendiep 44 Ⓣ050/589 0009. Once a residence for monks, now a stylish

restaurant with lime-green hues and a hidden inner courtyard. The friendly staff serve mains like salmon fillet, steak Japanese-style and goat's cheese salad for around €18.

Four Roses Oosterstraat 71 Ⓣ050/314 3887. Tex-Mex food such as nachos, burritos and rib-eyes, at the junction of Oosterstraat and Gedempte Zuiderdiep. Also great cocktails.

Hemingway's Cuba Gedempte Kattendiep 23/1 Ⓣ050/589 3409. This restaurant is part of the Via Vecchia, consisting of four restaurants located around a tiny Mediterranean-style alley. It serves tapas Cuban-style and steaks with Caribbean vegetables for around €18.

De Kleine Heerlijkheid Schuitendiep 42 Ⓣ050/313 1370. Located in one of the oldest buildings just outside the city walls, the smallest

Festival Noorderzon

Every year in mid-August, Groningen hosts the increasingly popular **Festival Noorderzon** (Ⓦwww.noorderzon.nl), a ten-day blend of theatre, music, film and performance art. About a third of the events are free, many of them staged in the Noorderplantsoen park, a fifteen-minute walk north along Nieuwe Kijk in 't Jatstraat. Come nighttime, food stalls and drinking-holes surround the lake in the park, while folk stroll along the lantern-lit paths or chill on the lake's stone steps to the sound of Afrobeat, Latin, funk, rock, jazz or ambient music. Other entertainment includes circuses, mime, puppetry, videos and installations. Hotels get busy, so if you're planning to visit around this time you'd do well to book in advance.

restaurant in Groningen serves mains such as barramundi or lamb shoulder for around €19, in an agreeable atmosphere.

Kleine Moghul Nieuwe Boteringestraat 62 ℡050/318 8905. A 10min walk north from the Grote Markt is this excellent-value and busy Indian takeaway and restaurant, well worth the trek for its kitsch decor.

Roezemoes Gedempte Zuiderdiep 15 ℡050/314 8854. For an original *stamppot* (mashed potatoes with veggies and meat) you're in the right place – they even serve this typical Dutch winter dish in summer. There are also non-mashed mains on the menu for around €13.

Soestdijk Grote Kromme Elleboog 6 ℡050/314 5050. A bit pricier and posher than average with *sateh* chicken skewers, steaks and lamb racks on the menu. Also a popular spot for an afternoon drink.

Café-bars, bars and nightlife

Café de Keyzer Turftorenstraat 4. Amenable brown café – very popular with local students – with many beers on draught and free peanuts in the shell.
Café Koster Hoogstraat 7. Hidden down an alley, this music café focuses on live blues, funk and rock music.

Der Witz Grote Markt 47. This German-style brown café has eight different beers on draft and some strong chilled *korns* (the German version of *jenever*).

De Drie Gezusters Grote Markt 39. A civilized bar with a great old interior that interlinks with neighbouring bars – handy on cold winter nights.

Hooghoudt Café Grote Markt 42. Located in the old Lloyds Insurance building, with a huge terrace and attractively priced daily specials.

De Kar Peperstraat 15. A popular bar among students, it's also open late during weekdays and has dancing. Closed Sun.

De Oosterpoort Trompsingel 27 ℡050/313 1044. This well-known and modern music centre, just east of the train station, hosts many of the bigger visiting bands.

The Palace Gelkingestraat 1. A good club that occasionally hosts live bands and attracts a younger crowd.

De Pintelier Kleine Kromme Elleboog 9. Busy Belgian beer café with 23 beers on draught and another ninety by the bottle. Also has a very large selection of whiskys.

De Spieghel Peperstraat 11. This jazz café has live performances most nights, including some reasonably big names, and a nice terrace in summer.

Listings

Bike rental At the train station (€6.50 per day, €32.50 per week; ℡050/312 4174).
Boat trips Along the old town moat (€9 for 1hr). Bookings and schedules at the VVV.
Books There's a good range of English-language titles at Selexyz Scholtens on Guldenstraat.
Cinema Images, Poelestraat 30 (℡050/312 0433, Ⓦwww.images.nu) is an arthouse cinema with a pleasant open-air café. Mainstream films are shown at the Pathé Megabioscoop, Gedempte Zuiderdiep 78 (℡050/584 4050).
Internet access Bibliotheek, Oude Boteringestraat 14 ℡050/368 3683.

Laundry Self- or service wash at Handy Wash, Schuitendiep 56 ℡050/318 7587.
Markets Vegetables, fruit, flowers, fish and fabrics at A-Kerkhof (Tues, Fri & Sat 9am–5pm). Organic food market at Vismarkt (Wed 9am–5pm). Non-food general market at the Grote Markt (Thurs 1–9pm).
Pharmacy Apotheek Hanzeplein, Hanzeplein 122 (open 24hr; ℡050/311 5020).
Police Rademarkt 12 ℡0900 8844.
Post office By the A-kerk on Munnekeholm (Mon 10am–6pm, Tues–Fri 9am–6pm, Sat 10am–1.30pm).
Taxi TaxiCentrale ℡050/366 6663.

Around Groningen

For day-tripping from Groningen city, the most agreeable journey is to the village of **UITHUIZEN**, 25km northeast, where the moated manor house of **Menkemaborg** (March–May Tues–Sun 10am–5pm; June–Sept daily 10am–5pm; Oct–Dec Tues–Sun 10am–4pm; €6; ⓦwww.menkemaborg.nl) is a signed ten-minute walk from the station. Dating from the fifteenth century and surrounded by formal gardens in the English style, the house has a sturdy, compact elegance and is one of the very few mansions, or *borgs*, of the old landowning families to have survived. The interior consists of a sequence of period rooms furnished in the style of the seventeenth century, displaying some of the Groninger Museum's applied art and history collection.

The trip to Uithuizen can be combined with *wadlopen* (see box opposite) – a guided walk across the coastal mud flats to the uninhabited sand-spit island of **Rottumeroog**. Excursion buses head out to the coast from Menkemaborg two or three times monthly (June–Sept); the trip costs from €27.50 per person, and booking is essential – contact Stichting Uithuizer Wad (ⓦwww.wadlopen.nl). Without a guide, it's too dangerous to venture onto the mud flats, but it is easy enough to **walk** along the enclosing dyke that runs behind the shoreline for the whole length of the province. There's precious little to see, but when the weather's clear, the browns, blues and greens of the surrounding land and sea are unusually beautiful. From Uithuizen, it's a good hour's stroll north to the nearest point on the dyke, and you'll need a large-scale map (available from Groningen VVV) for directions.

Pieterburen

For the Dutch, the first thing that springs to mind when you mention **PIETERBUREN**, 27km north from Groningen, is the **seal sanctuary** (Zeehondencreche Pieterburen; daily 9am–6pm; €3; ⓦwww.zeehondencreche .nl). Founded almost 40 years ago by Lenie 't Hart, a local animal welfare heroine, the sanctuary rescues abandoned or weak seals with the purpose of releasing them back into the wild. The best time to see seal pups is during the summer, when many will be nursed and fed until they are strong enough to make it on their own. Pieterburen is also the start and end point for the longest unbroken walking tour in the Netherlands, the 464-kilometre long **Pieterpad** to Maastricht. More information and a map of the walking route can be obtained at the VVV, Hoofdstraat 83 (☎0595/528 522).

Just 5km from Pieterburen you'll find the smallest hotel in the world, mentioned in the *Guinness Book of Records*. De Kromme Raake (☎0595/491 600, ⓦwww.hoteldekrommeraake.nl; ❺) in **EENRUM** is an old grocery shop transformed into a hotel with nothing more than a reception and one room.

The Lauwersmeer National Park

Lauwersmeer National Park, some 35km northwest of Groningen, comprises a broken and irregular lake that spreads across the provincial boundary into neighbouring Friesland. Once an arm of the sea, it was turned into a freshwater lake by the construction of the Lauwersoog dam, a controversial 1960s project that was vigorously opposed by local fishermen, who ended up having to move all their tackle to the coast. Spared intensive industrial and agricultural development because of the efforts of conservationists, it's a quiet and peaceful region with a wonderful variety of sea birds, and is increasingly popular with anglers, windsurfers, sailors and cyclists.

Wadlopen

Wadlopen, or mud-flat walking, is a popular and strenuous Dutch pastime, and the stretch of coast on the northern edge of the provinces of Friesland and Groningen is one of the best places to do it: twice daily, the receding tide uncovers vast expanses of mud flat beneath the Waddenzee. It is, however, a sport to be taken seriously, and far too dangerous to do without an experienced guide: the depth of the mud is variable and the tides inconsistent. In any case, channels of deep water are left even when the tide has receded, and the currents can be perilous. The timing of treks depends on weather and tidal conditions, but most start between 6am and 10am. It's important to be properly equipped; recommended gear includes shorts or a bathing suit, a sweater, wind jacket, knee-high socks, high-top trainers and a complete change of clothes stashed in a watertight pack. In recent years, *wadlopen* has become extremely popular, and as excursions are infrequent, between May and August it's advisable to book a place at least a month in advance.

Prices are around €25 a head, and include the cost of a return ferry crossing; the VVVs in Leeuwarden, Dokkum and Groningen can provide details, or you could contact one of the *wadlopen* organizations direct. Dijkstras Wadlopencentrum, Hoofdstraat 118, Pieterburen (℡0595/528 345, Ⓦ www.wadloop-dijkstra.nl), has the most multi-lingual guides; there's also Stichting Wadloopcentrum Pieterburen, Hoofdstraat 105, Pieterburen (℡0595/528 300, Ⓦ www.wadlopen.com) or the Wadloopcentrum Fryslân (phone numbers vary so check the website, Ⓦ www.wadlopen.net).

The local villages are uniformly dull, however; the most convenient base is **ZOUTKAMP**, near the southeast corner of the lake on the River Reitdiep and accessible by bus #65 from Groningen. The **VVV**, Reitdiepskade 11 (April–Sept Mon–Fri 9am–5pm, Sat 10am–4pm; Oct Mon–Fri 10am–5pm, Sat 10am–4pm; Nov–March Mon–Fri 10am–noon & 1–3pm; ℡0595/401 957; Ⓦ www.vvvlauwersland.nl), has a limited supply of private rooms, which can be reserved here or at Groningen VVV.

At the mouth of the lake, some 10km north of Zoutkamp, the desultory port of **LAUWERSOOG** is where **ferries** leave for the fifty-minute trip to the island of Schiermonnikoog.

Schiermonnikoog

Until the Reformation, the island of **Schiermonnikoog** belonged to the monastery of Klaarkamp on the mainland; its name means literally "island of the grey monks". Nothing remains of the monks, however, and these days Schiermonnikoog's only settlement is a prim and busy village bordering long stretches of muddy beach and sand dune to the north and farmland and mud flats to the south. At low tide, these motionless pools of water reflect the colours in the sky, particularly atmospheric at dawn and dusk. Schiermonnikoog is the smallest of the Frisian islands at 16km long and 4km wide, and, once you're

Ferries to Schiermonnikoog

For **Schiermonnikoog**, head to the port of **Lauwersoog** on either bus #163 from Groningen (7 daily; 1hr) or bus #50 from Dokkum (6 daily; 30min) and Leeuwarden (6 daily; 1hr 30min). From Lauwersoog, there are frequent ferries to the island (45min; €12.65 return; Ⓦ www.wpd.nl). The returning boat leaves from the island one hour *later* in each case. Taking your bike over will cost extra (€7.90 return); only residents' cars are allowed on Schiermonnikoog.

clear of the weekend homes that fringe the village, it's a wild, uncultivated place, crisscrossed by cycle paths – a popular spot for day-trippers.

Ferries from Lauwersoog dock at the island jetty, some 3km from the village; a connecting bus drops you off outside the VVV in the centre. It's even possible to walk to the island across the mud flats from Kloosterburen, a distance of about 8km, but you must do this accompanied by a guide; see the box on p.239 for details.

Practicalities

Finding **accommodation** is difficult in season, when prices rise sharply, and it's essential to ring ahead. The **VVV**, Reeweg 5 (May–Sept Mon–Fri 9am–1pm & 2–6pm, Sat 9.30am–1pm & 2–4.30pm; Oct–April Mon–Sat closes 30min earlier; ☎0519/531 233, ⓦwww.vvvschiermonnikoog.nl) will help by booking **private rooms** and pensions. The large *Van der Werff*, Reeweg 2 (☎0519/531 203, ⓦwww.hotelvanderwerff.nl; ❸) is the most pleasant **hotel** in town; the two-star *De Tjattel* (☎0519/531 133, ⓦwww .detjattel.nl; ❸), at Langestreek 94, in the heart of the village, is a second possibility, with a large restaurant and bar. On the east side of the village at Knuppeldam 2, fifteen minutes' walk from the VVV, is the *Herberg Rijsbergen* (☎0519/531 257, ⓦwww.rijsbergen.biz; ❷), located in a historical building with a huge grass lawn around it. Schiermonnikoog's **campsite**, *Seedune* (April–Sept; ☎0519/531 398, ⓦwww.seedune.nl), is to the north, in the woods just east of Badweg at Seeduneweg 1.

The *Strandhotel* has windsurfing equipment for rent; bikes are available from several small shops in the village, and the VVV sells good maps. Places to eat and drink are scattered along Langestreek and Badweg to the north of the VVV.

Bourtange and Ter Apel

BOURTANGE (ⓦwww.bourtange.nl), some 60km southeast of Groningen close to the German frontier, is a superbly restored fortified village. Founded by William of Orange in 1580 to help protect the eastern approaches to Groningen, Bourtange fell into disrepair during the nineteenth century, only to be entirely refurbished as a tourist attraction in 1964. The design of the village is similar to that of Naarden (see p.142) and is best appreciated as you walk around the old bastions of the star-shaped fortress. You enter the village through the **VVV** building and information centre (April–Oct Mon–Fri 9am–5.30pm, Sat & Sun 10am–5pm; Nov–March Mon–Fri 9am–noon; ☎0599/354 600). Entry to the village is free, but there is a charge of €4 if you want to see the slide-show, which gives a history of Bourtange, and to visit the various exhibitions depicting traditional life. There's a **campsite**, *'t Plathuis*, Vlagtwedderstraat 88 (☎0599/354 383, ⓦwww.plathuis.nl; April–Oct), and one **hotel**, *De Staakenborgh*, up the road at no. 33 (☎0599/354 216, ⓦwww.staakenborgh.nl; ❷).

Ter Apel

Some 30km to the south of Bourtange, in the small town of **TER APEL**, the **Museum Klooster** (Tues–Sat 10am–5pm, Sun 1–5pm; €5; ⓦwww.museum klooster-terapel.com) is a highlight of this part of the country. This was the monastery of the Order of the Holy Cross – or Croziers – dating back to the Middle Ages and probably unique among rural Dutch monasteries in surviving the ravages of the Reformation. The chapel, superbly restored, preserves a number of unusual features, including the tripartite sedilia, where the priest and his assistants sat during Mass, and a splendid rood screen that divides the chancel from the nave. Elsewhere, the east wing is a curious hybrid of Gothic and

The Dutch Golden Age

Ever wondered about those grim-faced portraits of black-hatted Dutch burghers who stare at us out of the gloom? The Dutch Golden Age of the seventeenth century was an amazing phenomenon: the Netherlands was the dominant economic force of Europe and its people, for a brief period at least, grew richer than they could ever have imagined. This prosperity was matched by an unparalleled progressive and tolerant attitude to religion, the poor and the elderly, and an explosion of creativity in art that has left us with a magnificent record of the time - its values, its achievements and its people.

The history

After the death of Philip II, Spain was forced to accept the independence of the United Provinces in 1609. The country was then formally recognized with the Peace of Westphalia in 1648, which also enforced the closure of the Scheldt river to sea traffic – a key factor in the decline of Antwerp as a sea port and the rise of Amsterdam, to which the upturn in trade brought extraordinary wealth. This was a bourgeois revolution, the people who benefited most weren't aristocrats, and it was taking place in a country that had spent the past fifty years getting rid of the Catholic Church. Amsterdam's burghers didn't build churches and fill them with art glorifying God, and their architecture was domestic rather than monumental in scale. Though certain families became very rich, and displayed their success at every opportunity, there was also a subtlety and relative humility to their efforts. This attitude also underlied the aims of the authorities – such as with the extension of Amsterdam's canals – that in some ways make seventeenth-century Holland the world's first example of a modern welfare state.

Despite being a product of the religious conflicts of the Reformation, Calvinist Holland was an unusually tolerant place. With the Inquisition dispatched, Catholic worship was tolerated, as long it was conducted behind closed doors, and Jews and other religious refugees were welcomed. Partly as a result of this, the population of Amsterdam quadrupled in the first half of the seventeenth century, with a knock-on effect in other towns and the ports of the Zuider Zee – Hoorn and Enkhuizen – which benefited from the flourishing Baltic trade. Other Dutch

King Philip of Spain ▲

Map of Amsterdam, 1662 ▼

Tulipomania

Nothing exemplifies the economic bubble of seventeenth-century Holland better than the **tulip**. As a relatively exotic flower (from Turkey) it had already captured the imagination of other parts of Europe, and its arrival in **Holland**, coinciding with an abrupt rise in personal wealth, led to it becoming the bloom of choice. New varieties were developed voraciously and the trade in bulbs boomed in the 1630s, with **prices** spiralling out of control. By this time it was less about flowers, and more about speculation, with tulips seen as a way of getting **rich** quick. This couldn't be sustained, and the bottom fell out of the market in 1637. Today tulips still define the Dutch landscape. Get up close at the **Keukenhof gardens** (see p.154) or indulge yourself at Amsterdam's wonderful **Bloemenmarkt** (see p.65).

▲ Tulips, c.1630

▼ Majolica Dutch clipper, Cornelis Boumeester

institutions date back to this time, not least the university at Leiden, which was founded in 1575 as a reward to the people of the city for withstanding a famous siege by the Spanish (see p.149). Its motto, Presidium Libertatis, or "Bastion of Liberty", deliberately reflected its founding principles of freedom and tolerance, particularly when it came to religion.

The organization that kept the country's coffers full during the Golden Age was the East India Company. Formed in 1602, it enjoyed a trading monopoly with the territories of the East, and effectively became the governing power in the countries the Dutch controlled – Malaysia, Sri Lanka and Indonesia. In 1632 the West India Company was formed, and had the same function, extending Dutch dominion over parts of South America and the Caribbean (and even New York at one point), to bring back the goods that oiled the wheels of the Dutch economy.

▼ Leiden university

Sailing Boats on a River, Salomon van Ruisdael ▲

Rembrandt's Night Watch ▼

The art

The first half of the seventeenth century in Holland was a time of extraordinary creative output, with the arts benefiting from the society that was its sponsor. But here works of art weren't commissioned by the church; the patrons were businesspeople who had grown rich on the success of the Dutch republic. Paintings were designed to hang in smaller spaces, and portraiture flourished, as did landscapes and "genre" painting (scenes of everyday domestic life).

Portraits were intended to dignify the sitters' roles and glorify their achievements, either in stiff formal pose, as in **Jan Lievens**' depiction of the politician Constantijn Huygens, in Amsterdam's Rijksmuseum, or with their wives, as in **Frans Hals**' twin portraits of Jacon Olycan and his wife-to-be, in the Mauritshuis in Den Haag; or, more informally, as in the same painter's marriage portrait of Isaac Massa, also in the Rijksmuseum. Groups were painted together, for example in the so-called Civic Guard portraits of ex-military luncheon clubs, of which **Rembrandt**'s *Night Watch* is the best-known example. It was also common for the groups that ran the country's almshouses and orphanages to have their portraits captured for posterity.

Among genre painters, **Gerrit Dou**, **Gerard ter Borch** and **Jan Steen** stand out, as does **Johannes Vermeer** of Delft, whose small output belies the popularity of his work. Most people know the bucolic landscapes of **Jacob van Ruisdael**. He, his namesake **Salomon van Ruisdael**, and **Jan van Goyen** capture perfectly the huge skies and expanses of water that characterize the Dutch landscape. All these painters are represented in Amsterdam's Rijksmuseum, but you should find examples of their work in most big Dutch galleries.

Jan Steen's The Physician's Visit ▼

Baroque styles, the cloister has a small herb garden and the other rooms are normally given over to temporary exhibitions of religious art. The monastery is surrounded by extensive beech woods and magnificent old horse chestnut trees; follow one of the marked walks or simply ramble at your leisure. Opposite, the **hotel** and **restaurant** *Boschhuis* (☎0599/581 208, ⓦwww.hotelboschhuis.nl; ❶) is ideal for a good meal, or for spending a quiet night in the country.

Drenthe

Until the early nineteenth century, the sparsely populated province of **Drenthe**, by the German border, was little more than a flat expanse of empty peat bog, marsh and moor. In recent decades, it's accumulated a scattering of small towns, but it remains the country's least populated province, whose main pull is its woods and countryside. Its only conspicuous geographical feature is a ridge of low hills that runs northwest for some 50km from Emmen, its largest town, toward Groningen. This ridge, the **Hondsrug**, was high enough to attract prehistoric settlers whose *hunebeds* (megalithic tombs) have become Drenthe's main tourist attraction. Otherwise, **Assen**, the provincial capital, is a dull place with a good museum, and **Emmen**, its only real rival, can only be recommended as a convenient base for visiting some of the *hunebeds* and three neighbouring open-air folk culture museums.

Governed by the bishops of Utrecht from the eleventh century, Drenthe was incorporated into the **Habsburg Empire** in 1538. The region sided with the Protestants in the rebellion against Spain, but it had little economic or military muscle and its claim to provincial status was ignored until the French occupation – and the days of the Batavian Republic. In the nineteenth century, work began in earnest to convert the province's peat bogs and moors into farmland. *Veenkolonies* (peat colonies) were established over much of the south and east of Drenthe, where the initial purpose of the labourers was to dig drainage canals and cut the peat for sale as fuel to the cities. Once cleared of the peat, the land could be used to grow crops, and today the region's **farms** are some of the most profitable in the country.

Assen

ASSEN, about 16km south of Groningen, is a possible first stop, though not somewhere you're likely to want to stay. Its train and bus station are about five minutes' walk from the centre of town – keep straight ahead across the main road down Stationsstraat. On the eastern side of Brink, the main square, is the **Drents Museum** (Tues–Sun 11am–5pm; €6; ⓦwww.drentsmuseum.nl), which, spread over a pleasant group of old houses, is the only thing that makes a stop in town worthwhile. The museum's most important exhibit is its collection of prehistoric skeletons brought here from the neighbouring *hunebeds*. There is also the much-vaunted Pesse Canoe, the oldest water vessel ever found and dating from about 6800 BC; it looks its age.

Assen's **VVV**, Marktstraat 8–10 (Mon 1–6pm, Tues–Thurs & Sat 9am–6pm, Fri 9am–9pm; ☎0592/243 778, ⓦwww.ditisassen.nl), is located in the main shopping street. The only **hotel** in the centre of town is *Hotel de Jonge*, Brinkstraat 85 (☎0592/312 023, ⓦwww.hoteldejonge.nl; ❷), which has a reasonable **restaurant** and terrace.

Around Assen

If you have your own transport, you might want to detour to the **Herinneringscentrum Kamp Westerbork** (Mon–Fri 10am–5pm, Sat & Sun 1–5pm; July & Aug Sat & Sun also 11am–1pm; €5; ⓦwww.kampwesterbork.nl), a little south of town on the road between the villages of Amen and Hooghalen. It was here during World War II that the Nazis assembled Dutch Jews before transporting them to the death camps in the east. Although little remains of the camp itself, the documents and artefacts on display are deeply affecting.

Emmen

To all intents and purposes **EMMEN** is a new town, a twentieth-century amalgamation of strip villages that were originally peat colonies. The centre is a modern affair, mixing the remnants of the old with lumpy boulders, trees and shrubs and a job lot of concrete and glass. Emmen is known for two things: its *hunebeds* and its zoo. The **zoo** (daily 10am–6pm; March–May & Oct closes 5pm, Sept closes 5.30pm, Nov–Feb closes 4.30pm; €18.50; ⓦwww.noorderdierenpark.nl), right in the middle of town at Hoofdstraat 18, boasts an imitation African savanna, where the animals roam "free", a massive sea-lion pool and a giant hippo house. In the newer part of the park you can find Humboldt penguins.

The best of Emmen's *hunebeds* is **Emmerdennen Hunebed**, in the woods 1km or so east of the station along Boslaan. This is a so-called passage-grave, with a relatively sophisticated entrance surrounded by a ring of standing stones.

Practicalities

Emmen's **train** and **bus stations** adjoin each other, five minutes' walk north of the town centre: head straight down Stationsstraat into Boslaan and turn left down Hoofdstraat, the main drag. The unofficial **VVV**, Hoofdstraat 22 (Mon 1–5pm, Tues–Sat 10am–5pm; ☎0591/649 712, ⓦwww.drenthe.nl), can arrange **accommodation** at pensions, private rooms and hotels. A cheap hotel-pension is *De Wanne*, Stortweg 1 (☎0591/611 250, ⓦwww.hoteldewanne.nl; ❶), 1.5km southwest of the zoo. Up a notch in price is hotel *Boerland*, Hoofdstraat 57 (☎0591/613 746, ⓦwww.stads-hotelboerland.nl; ❷), which is across the street from the zoo.

Borger and the open-air museums

BORGER, some 20km northwest of Emmen, has the largest *hunebed* in the country, located on the northeast edge of the village. At 22.5m long, the

---

Motor racing in Assen

The only time Assen is the centre of attention is during the **TT Assen** (ⓦwww.tt-assen.com), the only Grand Prix motor race in the Netherlands. More than 100,000 people visit the circuit on the last Saturday in June, making the TT the largest one-day sports event in the Netherlands. On the three nights leading up to the TT, Assen's centre is packed with people enjoying live music and lots of beer. If you are visiting while it's on, make sure to book accommodation well ahead of time.

hunebed is an extraordinary feat (in prehistoric terms at least) and its origins are explained at the adjoining information centre (Mon–Fri 10am–5pm, Sat & Sun 11am–5pm; €5.75, Ⓦwww.hunebedcentrum.nl). However, you will need to use your imagination: these bulges in the ground, sprouting tufts of grass and small trees, aren't up to much. Back in town, the *hunebed* theme is everywhere, from street names and pancakes to special menus. Should you decide to stay, the unofficial **VVV**, Grote Brink 3 (Mon 1–6pm, Tues–Thurs 9am–6pm, Fri 9am–9pm, Sat 9am–5pm; Ⓣ0599/234 430, Ⓦwww.drenthe .nl), has a list of private rooms, or you could try the hotel-pension *Nathalia*, Hoofdstraat 87 (Ⓣ0599/234 791; Ⓦwww.hotelpensionnathalia.nl; ➊). **Bus** #59 runs to Borger on its way between Emmen and Groningen; from Assen, take bus #24.

The Veenpark
About 11km east of Emmen, towards the German border, the **Veenpark** (daily Easter–Oct 10am–5pm, July & Aug until 6pm; €12; Ⓦwww.veenpark .nl), served by bus #45 from Emmen station (hourly; 25min) followed by a forty-minute walk, is a massive open-air museum-village that traces the history and development of the peat colonies of the moors of southern Groningen and eastern Drenthe. The colonies were established in the nineteenth century, when labour was imported to cut the thick layers of peat that lay all over the moors. Isolated in small communities, and under the thumb of the traders who sold their products and provided their foodstuffs, the colonists were harshly exploited and lived in abject poverty until well into the 1930s. Built around some old interlocking canals, the museum consists of a series of reconstructed villages that track through the history of the colonies. It's inevitably a bit folksy, but very popular, with its own narrow-gauge railway, a canal barge, and working period bakeries, bars and shops. A thorough exploration takes a full day.

Travel details

Trains

Emmen to: Zwolle (every 30min; 1hr).
Groningen to: Amsterdam (every 30min; 2hr 20min); Assen (every 20min; 20min); Leeuwarden (every 30min; 50min); Uithuizen (every 30min; 35min); Zwolle (every 20min; 1hr 10min).
Leeuwarden to: Amsterdam (every 30min; 2hr 20min); Franeker (every 30min; 15min); Groningen (every 30min; 50min); Harlingen (every 30min; 25min); Hindeloopen (hourly; 40min); Sneek (every 30min; 20min); Stavoren (hourly; 50min); Zwolle (every 30min; 50min–1hr 5min).

Buses

Bolsward to: Makkum (Mon–Sat every 30min; Sun hourly; 20min).
Bourtange to: Ter Apel (Mon–Fri hourly; Sat every 2hr; Sun 3 daily; 30min).

Dokkum to: Wierum & Moddergat (Mon–Sat hourly, Sun 5 daily; 25min & 35min).
Groningen to: Emmen (every 20min; 1hr 10min); Zoutkamp (Mon–Fri every 30min, Sat hourly; 1hr).
Leeuwarden to: Dokkum (Mon–Fri 3 hourly, Sat & Sun hourly; 30–50min); Marssum (Mon–Sat 5 hourly, Sun 2 hourly; 15min).
Sneek to: Bolsward (Mon–Fri 4 hourly, Sat 2 hourly, Sun hourly; 20min).
Workum to: Makkum (Mon–Fri every 2–3hr; 30min).

Buses to connecting ferries

Groningen to: Lauwersoog (bus #163: 7 daily; 1hr) for boats to Schiermonnikoog.
Leeuwarden to: Holwerd (bus #66: hourly; 50min) for boats to Ameland; and to Lauwersoog (bus #50: 6 daily; 1hr 30min) for boats to Schiermonnikoog.

Ferries and hydrofoils

Harlingen to: Terschelling (2–3 ferries daily; 1hr 45min; 2–3 hydrofoils daily; 50min direct, 1hr 20min via Vlieland); Vlieland (2–3 ferries daily; 1hr 45min; 1–2 hydrofoils daily; 45min direct, 1hr 30min via Terschelling).
Holwerd to: Ameland (4–14 ferries daily; 45min).

Lauwersoog to: Schiermonnikoog (3–6 ferries daily; 45min).
Stavoren to: Enkhuizen (May–Sept 3 ferries daily; 1hr 20min).
Terschelling to: Vlieland (1–2 hydrofoils daily; 30min).
Vlieland to: Terschelling (1–2 hydrofoils daily; 30min).

The eastern
Netherlands

CHAPTER 5

Highlights

* **Giethoorn** A postcard-pretty hamlet set amid lakes and wetlands, Giethoorn is an ideal place for pottering around on the water. See p.259

* **Blokzijl** Lovely little town and former Zuider Zee port perched on the edge of moors and wetlands. See p.261

* **Zutphen** Quintessential Dutch country town tucked up against the River IJssel. See p.263

* **Arnhem** This garden city with a searing wartime history makes a good base for exploring this attractive region. See p.268

* **Hoge Veluwe National Park** Spacious area of heath and forest, crossed by footpaths and cycle routes galore. See pp.275–278

* **Kröller-Müller Museum** Outstanding museum of modern European art, with a large sculpture garden and an impressive collection of works by van Gogh. See p.277

▲ Sculpture garden at the Kröller-Müller Museum

The eastern Netherlands

I n the **eastern Netherlands** the flat polder landscapes of the west gradually give way as the countryside ripples up towards the border with Germany. Arriving from Amsterdam, the first province you reach is **Flevoland**, whose three pancake-flat, reclaimed polders – the twin Flevoland polders and the Noordoostpolder – are decidedly tedious. Neither is the main town, modern **Lelystad**, of much appeal, though at least the fishing village of **Urk**, an island until the damming of the Zuider Zee (see p.119), is of some considerable interest. The boundary separating Flevoland from the province of **Overijssel** runs along the old Zuider Zee shoreline and it's here that the region comes up trumps with a string of former seaports, most strikingly the pretty little towns of **Elburg** (in Gelderland), **Kampen** and **Blokzijl**. These three, along with nearby **Zwolle**, the provincial capital, enjoyed a period of immense prosperity during the heyday of the Zuider Zee trade, from the fourteenth to the sixteenth century, but the bubble burst in the seventeenth when the great merchant cities of Zuid- and Noord-Holland simply out-played and undercut them. Later, these four towns – along with neighbouring **Deventer** and **Zutphen** – were bypassed by the Industrial Revolution, one happy consequence being that each of them boasts a medley of handsome late medieval and early modern houses and churches.

Blokzijl also shares its part of the province – **northwest Overijssel** – with the lakes and waterways that pattern the hamlet of picture-perfect **Giethoorn**, the region's most popular tourist target. By contrast, the district of **Twente**, which makes up southeast Overijssel, is an industrial region of one-time textile towns that remains one of the least visited parts of the country and with good reason: only **Enschede**, the main town, provides a reason to visit, with an excellent museum and an enjoyable set of distinctive 1930s public buildings.

The third province covered in this chapter, **Gelderland**, spreads east from Utrecht to the German frontier, taking its name from the German town of Geldern, its capital until the late fourteenth century. As a province it's a bit of a mixture, varying from the uninspiring agricultural land of the **Betuwe** (Good Land), south of Utrecht, to the more distinctive – and appealing – **Veluwe** (Bad Land), an expanse of heath, woodland and dune that sprawls down from the old Zuider Zee coastline to **Arnhem**. Infertile and sparsely

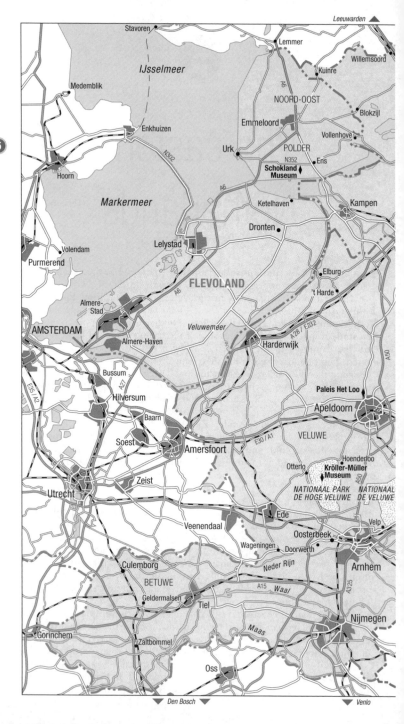

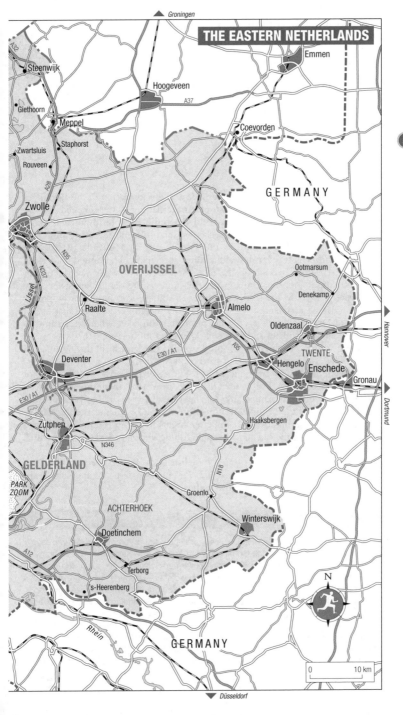

populated in medieval times, today the Veluwe constitutes one of the most popular holiday destinations in the country, strewn with campsites, second homes and bungalow parks. Some people use sedate **Apeldoorn** as a base to visit the fine **Hoge Veluwe National Park**, which holds the outstanding **Kröller-Müller Museum** of modern art, but you'd be better off choosing **Arnhem**, which is considerably livelier. The ancient town of **Nijmegen**, 21km south, is a fashionable university city, with a lively contemporary music and arts scene, and it makes a good, if brief, stop on the way south into Limburg (see pp.316–332).

Flevoland

Following the damming of the Zuider Zee and the formation of the IJsselmeer (see box, p.119), the coastline east of Amsterdam was transformed by the creation of the **Zuidelijk Flevoland** and **Oostelijk Flevoland** polders, which together form one large chunk of reclaimed land in front of the old shoreline. This polder-island also comprises the greater part of Holland's twelfth and newest province – **Flevoland** – with a third (and separate) reclaimed polder, the **Noordoostpolder**, making up the rest. The Noordoostpolder was drained in the 1930s and it soon became apparent that there were design faults: very few trees were planted, so the land was subject to soil erosion, and both the polder and the adjacent mainland dried out and started to sink – problems that persist today. The Dutch did, however, learn from their mistakes when they came to drain Zuidelijk Flevoland and Oostelijk Flevoland in the 1950s: they created an encircling waterway, which successfully stopped the land from drying out and sinking. The government also tried hard to make the new polders more attractive – they're fringed by trees and parks – but nevertheless the Dutch have not exactly queued up to live here. There are now two medium-sized towns, **Almere** and **Lelystad**, named after Cornelis Lely (1854–1929), the pioneering engineer who had the original idea for the Zuider Zee scheme, though frankly neither has much going for it. Much better targets are the intriguing **Schokland Museum** as well as the old and amenable fishing village of **Urk**, both of which are on the Noordoostpolder.

The Noordoostpolder is easy to reach by **bus** from Zwolle (see p.253) and the towns of northwest Overijssel (see p.258). There's a fast and frequent **train** service to Zwolle from Amsterdam Centraal.

Wind turbines

Strung along the shores of the IJsselmeer, and popping up on many rural horizons, **wind turbines** dot the Dutch landscape from Friesland to Zeeland. In the countryside, solitary turbines provide electricity for farmers, while on the coast and out to sea, banks of turbines harness the incoming weather systems, providing electricity for thousands of households. Erected in the 1930s, the first wind turbines provided electricity for remote communities in the USA and the Australian outback. However, their full potential wasn't realized until research into cleaner forms of energy, carried out in Denmark and Germany during the 1970s, produced mechanisms that were both more efficient and more powerful. Ideally suited to the flat, windswept polders of the Netherlands, the first Dutch turbines generated 40 kilowatts of electricity; output is now a beefier 600 kilowatts – enough for a single wind farm of 50 turbines to provide power to 6500 households.

The Noordoostpolder

Drained in the early 1930s, the **Noordoostpolder** was the first major chunk of land to be reclaimed after the damming of the Zuider Zee (see p.119). The original aims of the scheme were predominantly agricultural, with the Noordoostpolder providing 500 square kilometres acres of new farmland, which the government handed out to prospective smallholders. Little consideration was given to the needs of the new settlers, however, and even now much of the Noordoostpolder remains dull in the extreme. If you're looking for a crumb of scenic comfort, then the wide skies – and wide-skied sunsets and sunrises – can be breathtaking, and there is also compensation in the agreeable old fishing port of **Urk** and the fascinating **Schokland Museum**, a UNESCO World Heritage Site since 1995.

Schokland Museum

The southern reaches of the Noordoostpolder incorporate the former Zuider Zee islets of Urk and **Schokland**, a slender sliver of land that was abandoned in 1859 by royal decree – the authorities decided it was just too dangerous for the islanders to soldier on. Given the turbulent waters of the Zuider Zee, it's a wonder that the islanders hung on for as long as they did: approaching from the east along the N352, you can only just spot the gentle ridge that once kept the islanders out of the water. Neither did their heroic efforts win the respect of their fellow Netherlanders, a *schokker* (the colloquial name for the islanders) being a piece of cow dung. And neither did the islanders necessarily like each other: the north end was Catholic, the south Protestant and intermarriage was rare indeed.

The main reminder of those precarious times is the **Schokland Museum** (April–Oct Tues–Sun 11am–5pm; July & Aug also Mon 11am–5pm; Nov–March Fri–Sun 11am–5pm; €3.80; Ⓦ www.schokland.nl), a huddle of buildings lying just to the south of the N352 on the site of what was once the island's largest village. The museum kicks off with an excellent film tracking the history of Schokland. Just beyond is a display of all sorts of bits and pieces found during the draining of the polder – incidental tools, a rusty cannon, pottery and even mammoth bones. Footsteps away is the plain and dour **church** of 1834, with part of the stockade that once protected the village immediately behind.

From the museum, a combined footpath and cycleway follows the old Schokland shoreline, a loop trail about 10km long. There's not much to see as such – the remains of the other three island villages are extremely scant – but it's a pleasant way to while away a few hours.

Getting to the museum by public transport is awkward: the museum is located some 3km west of Ens – and about 300m south of the minor road between Ens and Nagele/Urk. **Buses** from Zwolle (see p.284) go to Ens bus station, but you have to walk the rest of the way.

Urk

Easily the most interesting town on the Noordoostpolder is **URK**, a burgeoning harbour and fishing port, where a series of narrow lanes – and tiny terraced houses – indicate the extent of the old village. Before it was pressed into the mainland, centuries of hardship and isolation had bred a tight-knit island community, one that had a distinctive dialect and its own version of the national costume. Most of Urk's individuality may have gone, but its earlier independence does still resonate, rooted in a fishing industry that marks it out from the surrounding agricultural communities. As if to prove the point, some of the islanders still wear traditional costume, further examples of which are on display

Urk irked

The damming of the Zuider Zee (see box, p.119) posed special problems for the **deep-sea fishermen of Urk** and it's hardly surprising that they opposed the IJsselmeer scheme from the beginning. Some villagers feared that when the Noordoostpolder was drained they would simply be overwhelmed by new settlers, but the fishermen were really irritated by the loss of direct access to the North Sea. After futile negotiations at national level, the fishermen of Urk decided to take matters into their own hands: the larger ships of the fleet were sent north to fish from ports above the line of the Afsluitdijk, particularly Delfzijl, and transport was organized to transfer the catch straight back for sale at the Urk fish auctions. In the meantime, other fishermen decided to continue to fish locally and adapt to the freshwater species of the IJsselmeer. These were not comfortable changes for the islanders and the whole situation deteriorated after the Dutch government passed new legislation banning trawling in the IJsselmeer in 1970. When the inspectors arrived in Urk to enforce the ban, years of resentment exploded in ugly scenes of dockside violence and the government moved fast to sweeten the pill by offering substantial subsidies to compensate those fishermen affected. This arrangement continues today and the focus of conflict has moved to the attempt to impose EU quotas on the catch of the deep-sea fleet.

in the **Museum Het Oude Raadhuis,** in the heart of Urk at Raadhuisstraat 2 (April–Sept Mon–Fri 10am–5pm & Sat 10am–4pm; Oct–March Mon–Sat 10am–1pm; €4). There's not much else to the old centre, but there are handsome views out across the IJsselmeer from the lakeshore **Vissersmonument** (Fisherman's Monument), where a plaque commemorates local seamen lost at sea and there's a statue of a woman gazing westward, presumably awaiting the return of her man. Down below is a small sandy **beach** and just along the shore is the **lighthouse**. Incidentally, the insignificant rock sticking out of the water about seventy metres from the lighthouse is the **Ommelebommelestien**, a rock from where, according to legend, all newly born Urkers spring: all Dad has to do is row out to the rock and pick up a baby – very handy.

Practicalities

There are regular **buses** to Urk from Zwolle, but note that some buses cut a circuitous route through the village's sprawling, modern outskirts; the stop you want is just north of the traffic roundabout on the Singel. From here, it's a five-minute walk to the harbour and the old village, which rolls along the low hill immediately to the north of the harbour. During the summer, there is also a limited **sailing boat** service across the IJsselmeer between Urk and Enkhuizen on the *Willem Barentsz* (mid-July to mid-Aug Mon–Sat 2 daily; 2hr; €12 one-way, €18 day-return; ⓦwww.willem-barentsz.nl). Tickets and sailing times are available from Urk VVV; advance reservations are required.

Urk **VVV** is in the same building as the museum, in the centre of the old village at Raadhuisstraat 2 (April–Oct Mon–Sat 10am–3pm; Nov–March Mon–Fri 10am–1pm; ☏0527/684 040, ⓦwww.touristinfourk.nl). They issue maps and sell tickets for local boat trips, including the excursion over to Enkhuizen on the *Willem Barentsz*. They also have a list of Urk **pensions** and **B&Bs**. Among several inexpensive options in the old village, one pleasant choice is the *Pension 't Anker*, in a cosy terrace house metres from the VVV at Prins Hendrikstraat 13 (☏0527/685 307; ❷). Incidentally, one peculiarity of the village is its addresses: all the streets now have names, but traditionally Urk was just divided into areas called 'Wijks': thus, the *Pension 't Anker* is at Prins Hendrikstraat 13 and/or Wijk 4–13.

The Urk fishing fleet specialises in sole, plaice and eel, and the best place to sample them is *Visrestaurant De Kaap*, a long-established **restaurant** down on the old harbour just below the lighthouse (℡0527/681 509, ⓦwww.dekaap-urk.nl; daily from 10am). A 500-gram plaice will cost you around €30 and there's the added bonus of a fine view over the IJsselmeer from the window tables.

Zwolle

A major railway junction, **ZWOLLE** is the compact capital of **Overijssel**. An ancient town, it achieved passing international fame when Thomas à Kempis settled here in 1399, and it went on to prosper throughout the fifteenth century as one of the principal towns of the Hanseatic League, its burghers commissioning an extensive programme of public works designed to protect its citizens and impress their rivals. Within the city walls, German textiles were traded for Baltic fish and grain, or more exotic products from Amsterdam like coffee, tea and tobacco. The boom lasted some two hundred years, but by the middle of the seventeenth century the success of Amsterdam and the general movement of trade to the west had undermined its economy – a decline

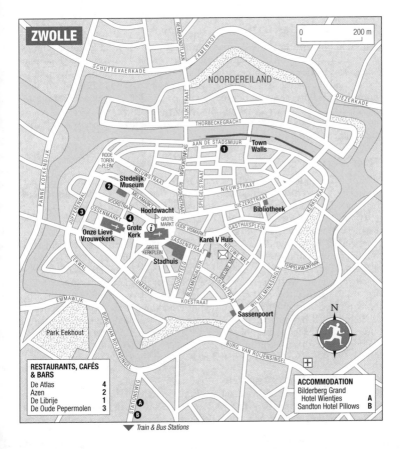

reflected in Zwolle's present-day status as a small market town of middling significance.

Strategically important, medieval Zwolle was protected by a strong **city wall**, a small section of which has survived on the north side of town, but the star shape of today's town centre, comprising nine roughly triangular earthen bastions that encircle the old town and its harbour, mostly dates from the seventeenth century. The approach from the train station is particularly pleasant, as fountains play in the moat and the city's fortifications are clearly visible among the trees.

Arrival and information

Zwolle is well connected by train to many of the Netherlands' major cities and by bus to most of Overijssel's larger towns and villages. From Zwolle **train** and **bus station**, it's about ten minutes' walk to the centre: head north along Stationsweg and then proceed east round the moat. If you're intending to travel to and around northwest Overijssel (see p.258) by bus, it's worth buying a regional bus timetable from Zwolle **VVV**, which is in the **Hoofdwacht**, beside the **Grote Kerk** in the centre of town at Grote Kerkplein 15 (Mon 1–5pm, Tues–Fri 10am–5pm, Sat 10am–4pm; ☏0900 112 2375, ⓦwww.vvvzwolle.nl). They also have oodles of information on the city and its surroundings.

Accommodation

Central **accommodation** is limited, but there are two good **hotels** a couple of minutes' walk from the station on Stationsweg. The four-star *Bilderberg Grand Hotel Wientjes* occupies a large and good-looking early-twentieth-century villa at Stationsweg 7 (☏038/425 4254, ⓦwww.bilderberg.nl; ❸). The rooms here are bright and modern, though hardly inspiring, whereas those of the adjacent *Sandton Hotel Pillows*, Stationsweg 9 (☏038/425 6789, ⓦwww.hotelpillows.nl; ❸), have been kitted out in sharp modernist style with browns and creams to the fore.

The Town

Right in the middle of Zwolle is the **Grote Markt**, a large and somewhat discordant square that surrounds the sandstone mass of the **Grote Kerk** (July–Sept Tues–Fri 11am–4pm, Sat 1.30–4pm; free), one of the unluckiest churches in Overijssel: the townsfolk were once inordinately proud of the church's soaring bell tower, but after it had been hit by lightning no fewer than three times (in 1548, 1606 and 1669), they gave up and sold the bells. Inside, you'll find the familiar austerity of Dutch Protestantism, with the cavernous nave bare of decoration and the seats arranged on a central pulpit plan. The pulpit itself is an intricate piece of Renaissance carving, but it's the Baroque organ of 1721 that really catches the eye, a real musical whopper with no less than four thousand pipes. Attached to the outside of the church is the **Hoofdwacht**, an ornately gabled building of 1614, which once served as the municipal guard-house. Public executions took place in front of the Hoofdwacht and the building bears the inscription *Vigilate et Orate* ("Watch and Pray"), a stern warning to the crowds who gathered to witness the assorted mutilations.

Onze Lieve Vrouwekerk

A little way to the west, down an alley off the Grote Markt, the prim and proper **Onze Lieve Vrouwekerk** (Sat 1.30–3.30pm; free, tower €2) has had some hard times too: in the sixteenth century, the congregation stuck to their Catholic faith, so the Protestants closed the place down and the last priest had to hotfoot it out of town after he delivered a final sermon in 1580. Thereafter, the church was used for all sorts of purposes – including a cart shed and a musket range – until it was returned to the Catholics in 1809 during the far more tolerant days of the Batavian Republic (see p.343). Today, the interior is firmly neo-Gothic, all ornate paintings and painted walls, but the church does boast an unusual tower, nicknamed *De Peperbus* (The Pepper Mill) after its distinctive shape.

The Stedelijk Museum and the old town walls

Heading northwest from the Grote Markt, it's a brief stroll through to the **Stedelijk Museum**, at Melkmarkt 41 (Tues–Sat 10am–5pm, Sun 1–5pm; €4). The museum is divided into two halves – the modern wing, which is used for temporary exhibitions, and the old wing in the eighteenth-century Drosten-huis. The latter mainly consists of a string of period rooms and these are enlivened by a modest selection of Golden Age paintings, the highlights being the finely detailed genre scenes of Gerard ter Borch (1617–81) and Hendrick ten Oever (1639–1716).

From Melkmarkt, it's another brief stroll northeast to the old city **harbour** and Aan de Stadsmuur, a pedestrianized lane flanked by heavily restored portions of the medieval **town wall**, complete with defensive parapets and a couple of fortified towers. The wall is, however, small architectural beer in comparison with the massive **Sassenpoort**, a mighty brick construction whose spiky turrets stand guard over the southern entrance to the old town; dating from 1409, it's the town's only surviving medieval gate.

Eating and drinking

The classiest **restaurant** in Zwolle is the award-winning *De Librije*, Broerenkerk-plein 13 (☎038/421 2083; Tues–Sat 7–10pm, Wed–Fri noon–1.30pm, 7–10pm), where an eclectic, international menu features the freshest of seasonal ingredients. The restaurant occupies an old monastery library and main courses will set you back €25–30, though most people opt for the set menus from €50; reservations are well-nigh essential. A second upmarket choice is the *Azen*, Melkmarkt 47 (☎038/429 0634; daily 5.30–10pm), a smooth and polished place in a handsome old mansion that also offers an international menu with mains from about €17. If your wallet is a little lighter, you might try *De Oude Pepermolen*, a steakhouse at Jufferenwal 21 (daily 5–10pm). Zwolle has something of a **bar scene** with *De Atlas*, a large and youthful café-bar beside the Onze Lieve Vrouwekerk at Ossenmarkt 9, leading the alcoholic rush.

Kampen

KAMPEN, just ten minutes by train from Zwolle, strings along the River IJssel, its bold succession of towers and spires recalling headier days when the town was a bustling seaport with its own fleet. The good times came to an abrupt end in the sixteenth century, when rival armies ravaged its hinterland and the IJssel silted up – Amsterdam then mopped up what was left by undercutting its trade prices. Things have never been the same since and, although Kampen did experience a minor boom on the back of its **cigar factories** in the nineteenth century, it remains, in essence, a sleepy provincial town, the main advantage being that literally scores of late medieval and early modern buildings have survived intact.

The Town

Not much more than six roughly parallel streets flanking the river, **central Kampen** only takes a couple of hours to explore and the logical place to start is the **IJssel bridge**, which hits the town centre about halfway along. From the bridge, it's a few metres to the **Raadhuis**, which is divided into two: the red-brick Oude Raadhuis, dating from 1543 and topped by a distinctive onion-shaped dome, and the Neoclassical Nieuwe Raadhuis, which was built in the eighteenth century. Together, the two buildings comprise the **Stedelijk Museum** (Tues–Sat 10am–5pm, Sun 1–5pm; €5), which is devoted to the history of Kampen with a particular focus on its most prosperous days. The highlight is, however, the **Schepenzaal** ("Magistrates' Hall") in the Oude Raadhuis, a claustrophobic medieval affair with dark-stained walls capped by a superbly preserved barrel-vault roof. The hall's magnificent stone **chimney-piece** – a grandiloquent, self-assured work – was carved by Colijn de Nole in tribute to the Habsburg Charles V in 1545, though the chimney's typically Renaissance representations of Justice, Prudence and Strength speak more of municipal pride than imperial glory. To the right, the magistrate's bench is the work of an obscure local carpenter, a Master Frederik, who didn't get on with de Nole at all: angry at not getting the more important job of the chimneypiece, his legacy can be seen on the left-hand pillar, where a minute, malevolent satyr laughs maniacally at the chimney.

The Nieuwe Toren

Just across the street from the Oude Raadhuis is a second tower, the seventeenth-century **Nieuwe Toren**, which becomes Kampen's main attraction for one morning each year, usually in mid-July (contact the VVV for the exact date and time), when the "Kampen cow" is pulled up to its top. The story goes that when grass began growing at the top of the tower, a local farmer asked if he could graze his cattle up there. To commemorate this daft request, an animal has been hoisted up the tower every year ever since, though thankfully it's now a plastic model rather than a real one.

The Bovenkerk and the old town gates

The Raadhuis and the Nieuwe Toren straddle Kampen's innocuous main street, pedestrianized **Oudestraat**, which runs south to the **Bovenkerk** (May to early Sept Mon–Tues 1–4pm, Wed–Fri 10am–4pm; free). A finely proportioned Gothic church with a light and spacious interior it is generally regarded as one of the most important of the country's medieval churches. Its choir – with thirteen radiating chapels – was the work of Rotger of Cologne, a member of the Parler family of masons who worked on Cologne Cathedral among other commissions. In the south transept an urn contains the heart of Admiral de Winter, a native of Kampen who loathed the House of Orange. A staunch Republican, he took part in the successful French invasion of 1795 that created the Batavian Republic; the rest of him lies in the Pantheon in Paris.

Beside the Bovenkerk is the earliest of Kampen's three surviving gates, the fourteenth-century **Koornmarktspoort**. The others – the **Cellebroeder-spoort** and the **Broederpoort** – are of a later, more ornamental design and lie on the west side of town along Ebbingestraat, reached from the Bovenkerk via Schoolstraat.

Practicalities

Trains leave Zwolle for end-of-the-line Kampen every half an hour (hourly on Sundays) and the journey takes ten minutes. From Kampen **train station**, it's a five-minute walk over the bridge to the town centre, where the **VVV**, on the main street just along from the Stadhuis at Oudestraat 151 (mid-April to Sept Mon–Fri 9.30am–5.30pm & Sat 10am–4pm; Oct to mid-April Mon & Wed–Fri 10am–5pm, Tues 10am–1pm & Sat 10am–4pm; ☏0900 112 2375, ⓦwww.vvvkampen.nl), sells town maps and issues local info. There's only one **hotel** in the centre, the riverside *Van Dijk*, an amenable, modern, three-star place near the bridge at IJsselkade 30 (☏038/331 4925, ⓦwww.hotelvandijk .nl; ❷); advance reservations are advised.

For **food**, there are tasty sandwiches and snacks at *'t Trappetje*, a pleasant little café at Oudestraat 25, and seafood dishes for around €22 at *D'Olde Vismark*, near the bridge at IJsselkade 45 (☏038/331 3490; Wed–Fri noon–10pm, Sat & Sun 3–10pm).

Elburg

Once a Zuider Zee port of some importance, tiny **ELBURG**, 10km south of Kampen, abuts the **Veluwemeer**, the narrow waterway separating the mainland from the Oostelijk Flevoland polder. In recent years, the town has become a popular day-trip destination, awash with visitors who come here to wander Elburg's old streets, drink at one of its many cafés, and taste the local delicacy, **smoked eel**.

Elburg was a successful port with its own fishing fleet from as early as the thirteenth century, but the boom times really began in the 1390s when the governor, a certain Arent thoe Boecop, redesigned the whole place in line with the latest developments in town planning, imposing a central grid of streets encircled by a protective wall and moat. Not all of Elburg's citizens were overly impressed – indeed the street by the museum is still called Ledige Stede, literally "Empty Way" – but the basic design, with the notable addition of sixteenth-century ramparts and gun emplacements, survived the decline that set in when the harbour silted up, and can still be observed today. Elburg's two main streets are **Beekstraat**, which forms the northeast–southwest axis, and **Jufferenstraat/Vischpoortstraat**, which runs southeast–northwest; they intersect at right angles to form the main square, the Vischmarkt.

The Town

Entering Elburg from the southeast, it's a few metres from the moat to the mildly enjoyable **Museum Elburg**, Jufferenstraat 6–8 (Tues–Fri 10am–5pm, Sat 11am–5pm; €4.50, including Kazematten, see below), which is housed in an old convent and offers period rooms and objects of local interest. From the museum, it's a couple of minutes walk north to **St Nicolaaskerk** (June–Aug Mon–Fri 2–4.30pm, Tues also 10am–noon), a lumpy fourteenth-century structure that dominates the landscape, even without its spire, which was destroyed by lightning in 1693. Northwest of the church, down Van Kinsbergenstraat, is the old balconied **Stadhuis**, which once served as Boecop's home, and just beyond, a left turn onto Beekstraat brings you to the town's main square, **Vischmarkt**. From here, Vischpoortstraat leads straight to the best preserved of the medieval town gates, the **Vischpoort**, a much restored brick rampart tower dating from 1594.

Beyond the Vischpoort, the pattern of the sixteenth-century defensive works is clear to see – from interior town wall to dry ditch, to earthen mound and moat. One of the subterranean artillery casements, the **Kazematten**, is open in summer (mid-June to Aug Mon 2–5pm, Tues–Fri 10am–5pm); it's easy to see why the Dutch called such emplacements, cramped and poorly ventilated, Moortkuijl, literally "Pits of Murder". From the Kazematten, it's a lovely, leafy, one-hour stroll right round the old **ramparts**.

Practicalities

Elburg is not on the train network, but bus #100 (1–3 hourly) links it with Zwolle train station to the northeast (35min) and Nunspeet train station (on the Amersfoort/Zwolle line) to the southwest (20min). **Buses** drop passengers just outside the southern entrance to the old town, a couple of minutes' walk from Elburg **VVV**, at Jufferenstraat 8 (Tues–Fri 10am–12.30pm & 1–4pm, Sat 11am–12.30pm & 1–4pm; ☎0525/681 520, ⊛www.vvvelburg.nl). They have the details of **boat trips** along the Veluwemeer, or you can go it alone by renting a sailing boat from any one of several companies – again the VVV has the latest information. The VVV also has a long list of private rooms (❶–❷) and will phone around to make a booking; try to get a room in the old centre and come early in the day in high season, when accommodation gets tight. There's one **hotel** here, the three-star *Elburg*, Smedestraat 5 (☎0525/683 877, ⊛www .hotelelburg.nl; ❷), in a pleasantly maintained, eighteenth-century building in the old town just off Beekstraat with straightforward, unassuming rooms.

Of Elburg's many **restaurants** it's difficult to find any of real note, though the *Grand Café Derde Hoofdstuk,* in the old town at Beekstraat 39 (☎0525/690 445), will do very nicely, being a cosy little place which casts a wide gastronomic net, from Italian and Dutch classics to tapas; mains average €18. In summertime, the town's favourite nibble, smoked eel in jelly, is available at any number of pavement stalls and is sold by weight – a *pond* is 500g.

Northwest Overijssel

The closing of the Zuider Zee and the draining of the Noordoostpolder (see p.251) transformed **northwest Overijssel**, the parcel of land lying just beyond Kampen and Zwolle: not only were the area's old seaports cut off from the ocean, but – as if to add injury to insult – they were placed firmly inland with only a narrow channel, the **Vollenhover Kanaal**, separating them from the new polder. In the event, however, it all turned out rather well: **Vollenhove** and more especially **Blokzijl**, the two main seaports concerned, speedily reinvented themselves as holiday destinations and today hundreds of Dutch city folk come here to sail and cycle.

Traditionally, both Vollenhove and Blokzijl looked firmly out across the ocean, doing their best to ignore the moor and marshland villages that lay **inland**. They were not alone: for many centuries this was one of the most neglected corners of the country and things only began to pick up in the 1800s, when the "Society of Charity" established a series of agricultural colonies here. The Dutch bourgeoisie were, however, as apprehensive of the pauper as their Victorian counterparts in Britain and the 1900 *Baedeker*, when surveying the colonies, noted approvingly that "the houses are visited almost daily by the superintending officials and the strictest discipline is everywhere observed". The villagers were reliant on **peat** for fuel and their haphazard diggings, spread over several centuries, created the canals, lakes and ponds that now lattice the area, attracting tourists by the boatload. The big pull is picture-postcard **Giethoorn**, whose mazy canals are flanked by splendid thatched cottages, but try to avoid visiting

From Steenwijk train station bus #70 (Mon–Fri hourly) goes to Giethoorn (10min), Zwartsluis (30min) and Zwolle (1hr 10min). Bus #75 (Mon–Fri hourly) goes to Blokzijl (20min) and Marknesse (30min).

From Zwolle train station bus #70 (Mon–Fri hourly) goes to Zwartsluis (40min), Giethoorn (1hr) and Steenwijk (1hr 10min). Bus #71 (Mon–Sat every 30min, Sun hourly) goes to Zwartsluis (30min), Vollenhove (50min), Marknesse (55min) and Emmeloord on the Noordoostpolder (1hr 15min).

For timetables, ask at the nearest VVV or consult ⓦ www.connexxion.nl.

5

in the height of the season, when the crowds can get oppressive. And, finally, the area makes a handy base for venturing out onto the Noordoostpolder – specifically to Urk (see p.251) and Schokland (see p.251).

Buses crisscross northwest Overijssel (see box above), but you really won't get the full flavour of the area unless you take at least one **boat** ride – or, even better, paddle away under your own steam: boat rental hereabouts is almost ubiquitous.

Giethoorn

GIETHOORN's origins are really rather odd. No one gave much thought to this marshy, infertile chunk of land until the thirteenth century, when the local landowner gifted it to an obscure religious sect. Perhaps to his surprise, the settlers made a go of things, eking out a living from local peat deposits and discovering, during their digs, the horns of hundreds of goats, which are presumed to have been the victims of the great St Elizabeth's Day flood of 1170; duly impressed, the residents named the place Geytenhoren ("goats' horns"). Later, the settlers dug canals to transport the peat and the diggings flooded, thus creating the watery network that now attracts herds of day-trippers, the scenic supplement being the village's thatched cottages and dinky, humpbacked footbridges.

www.roughguides.com

259

▲ Giethoorn

Messing about on the water

Most of Giethoorn's campsites and hotels **rent boats** in a variety of shapes and sizes, from canoes to motorboats and dinghies. Prices vary, but reckon on €12 per hour for a whisper boat (a quiet, environmentally friendly, electric-powered motorboat) down to €12 per day for a kayak. **Water taxis** are similarly commonplace and a trip round the village costs about €5 per hour.

Giethoorn runs parallel to – and just east of – the N334, which links Zwartsluis (see p.261) and Steenwijk. The village is about 4km from top to bottom and never more than 900m wide. Most visitors make a beeline for the centre of Giethoorn, which spreads out along **Ds. Hylkemaweg**, between the N334 and lake Bovenwijde, but this is in fact the least appealing section. Much more agreeable, with little of the tourist congestion, is **northern Giethoorn**, where you'll find pristine thatched cottages, immaculate gardens, the cutest of wooden bridges and the first-rate *Hotel De Harmonie*. If this appeals, there's more of the same along **Dwarsgracht**, about 4km west of Giethoorn on the other side of the N334, and yet more in the **Nationaal Park De Weerribben**, a slice of protected canal and marshland starting about 8km to the west of the village. The VVV can suggest cycle routes through the park and has details of the summer boat trips that explore its waterways.

Practicalities

Bus #70 travels the length of Giethoorn, pulling in at several stops, including Ds. Hylkemaweg and the *Hotel De Harmonie* (see below). The **VVV** is metres from the Ds. Hylkemaweg bus stop, just off the N334 at Eendrachtsplein 1 (April to mid-May, Sept & Oct Mon–Fri 9am–5pm, Sat 10am–4pm; mid-May to June Mon–Sat 9am–5pm, Sun 10am–4pm; July & Aug Mon–Sat 9am–6pm, Sun 10am–4pm; Nov–March Mon–Fri 9am–5pm; ☎0900 567 4637, ⓦwww .kopvanoverijssel.nl).

The VVV has a long list of **private rooms** (❶–❷), though only a few of them are in the north part of Giethoorn, which is where you want to be. Accommodation can get very tight between June and August. Giethoorn's best **hotel** by a long chalk is the four-star ⚓ *De Harmonie*, a warm and extremely friendly modern place at the north end of the village at Beulakerweg 55 (☎0521/361 372, ⓦwww.harmonie-giethoorn.nl; ❸). The hotel consists of two two-storey buildings, one of which is thatched, and although the rooms are not especially stylish, they are attractive enough in a simple sort of way and they are spacious. The hotel also rents out bikes and boats and organises its own boat trips, beginning on the adjacent jetty. A second good place to stay is *Hotel De Jonge* (☎0521/361 360, ⓦwww.dejonge-giethoorn .nl; ❷), which occupies several intelligently converted old buildings across the street from the *Hotel De Harmonie* at Beulakerweg 30. Alternatively, Lake Bovenwijde has no fewer than six **campsites** on its western shore, including the well-kept *Botel Giethoorn*, at Binnenpad 49 (☎0521/361 332, ⓦwww .botel-giethoorn.nl; April to mid-Oct).

The *Hotel De Harmonie* has a first-rate, attractively decorated **restaurant**, serving a tasty range of Dutch dishes with main courses costing about €20. This is *the* place to try a local delicacy, perch and pike (*snoekbaarsfilet*) from the IJsselmeer. The best-known **café-bar** hereabouts is the *Eetcafé Fanfare*, in the centre of the village at Binnenpad 68.

Zwartsluis and Vollenhove

Heading south from Giethoorn, the N334 cuts a watery course over a couple of lakes before clipping on into **ZWARTSLUIS**, a modest sort of place which was once the site of an important fortress at the junction of waterways from Zwolle and Meppel. From Zwartsluis, it's 11km west to **VOLLENHOVE**, whose former role as a Zuider Zee port is recalled by the remains of its bastions and ramparts, which now nudge up against the Vollenhover Kanaal, separating the mainland from the Noordoostpolder. The old **harbour** has survived too, a cramped, circular affair encased in steep grass banks. Neighbouring Kerkplein holds a clutch of handsome old buildings, most notably the elegant, arcaded **Raadhuis**, the large and rambling Gothic **St Nicolaaskerk** and the seventeenth-century **Latin School**, now an antique shop, which boasts charming crow-stepped gables.

Buses stop on Clarenberglaan, a five-minute walk from Kerkplein – straight up Doelenstraat and then Kerkstraat. The **VVV** is beside the harbour, just north of Kerkplein at aan Zee 4 (May–June Mon–Fri 10am–12.30pm & 2–4pm, Sat 10.30am–12.30pm; July & Aug Mon–Sat 10am–12.30pm & 1.30–4.30pm; ☎0900 567 4637, ⓦwww.kopvanoverijssel.nl). As for **food**, *De Cartouwe*, Kerkplein 12 (daily from 10am), serves inexpensive daily specials at €11. More appealing – and more expensive – is the *Restaurant Seidel* in the old Raadhuis at Kerkplein 3 (☎0527/241 262; Tues–Sat noon–2pm & 5–10pm, Sun 2–10pm), which is worth popping into, even for just a snack – the decor is delightfully antique.

Blokzijl

Tiny **BLOKZIJL**, some 5km north of Vollenhove, is easily the prettiest of the area's former seaports, its cobweb of narrow alleys and slim canals surrounding a trim little harbour that is now connected to the Vollenhover Kanaal. The town boasts dozens of seventeenth-century houses, the most conspicuous being the **Grote Kerk** (May–Aug daily 10am–6pm; free), which, with its splendid wooden pulpit and ceiling, was one of the country's first Protestant churches.

Buses to Blokzijl drop passengers beside the N333 on the west edge of town, a five-minute walk from the harbour, where the shop at Bierkade 9 operates as an informal **tourist office**. The pick of Blokzijl's several **hotels and pensions** is *Kaatjes Résidence*, a deluxe, four-star place in a substantial nineteenth-century villa not far from the harbour – and beside a canal – at Zuiderstraat 1 (☎0527/208 580, ⓦwww.kaatjesresidence.nl; ⑥). The town is stuffed with **restaurants**, including the *Auberge aan Het Hof*, a smart little French place at Kerkstraat 9 (☎0527/291 844; daily noon–10pm); mains here average about €22.

Deventer, Zutphen and around

South of Zwolle, the **River IJssel** marks the provincial boundary between Overijssel and Gelderland as it twists its way through flat, fertile farmland. For two hundred years the towns of the lower IJssel, **Deventer** and **Zutphen**, shared with Zwolle and Kampen a period of tremendous prosperity at the junction of trade routes from Germany, the Baltic and Amsterdam. Both towns suffered grievously during the wars with Spain, but the real reasons for their subsequent decline were economic: they could do little to stop the movement of trade to the west and could not compete with the emerging cities of Noord- and

Zuid-Holland. By the eighteenth century, they had slipped into provincial insignificance – and this remains the case today, though both, especially Zutphen,
have a clutch of handsome old buildings and an amenable small-town air.

Deventer

Glued to the east bank of the IJssel, **DEVENTER**, some 30km from Zwolle,
is an intriguing and – in tourist terms – rather neglected town, whose origins
can be traced back to the missionary work of the eighth-century Saxon monk,
Lebuinus. An influential centre of medieval learning, it was here in the late
fourteenth century that Gerrit Groot founded the **Brotherhood of the
Common Life**, a semi-monastic collective that espoused tolerance and
humanism within a philosophy known as *Moderne Devotie* ("modern devotion").
This progressive creed attracted some of the great minds of the time, and
Thomas à Kempis and Erasmus both studied here. Nowadays, Deventer makes
a pleasant stop on any itinerary with a handful of fine old buildings and a good
bar and restaurant scene.

The Town

Enclosed by the river and the remains of its moat, Deventer's busy, broadly
circular centre has kept its medieval street plan, which zeroes in on the **Brink**,
a surprisingly large, cobbled marketplace that runs roughly north to south. At
the square's southern end is the **Waag**, a late-Gothic red-brick structure of
1528, whose good-looking medley of towers and turrets is fronted by a stone
portico that was added a century later. Oddly enough, there's a large **pan** nailed
to the outside of the Waag's western wall, which must once have served as a
warning: when the city council learnt that the mint master was debasing the
town's coins, he was promptly put in the pan and boiled alive. The bullet holes
weren't an attempt to prolong the agony, however, but the work of idle French
soldiers garrisoned here, who were taking, quite literally, "pot shots".

The Lebuinuskerk and around

From the Waag, it's a short walk south then west along L-shaped Polstraat to
the **Lebuinuskerk** (Mon–Sat 1–5pm; free), a vast Gothic edifice built during
Deventer's fifteenth-century pomp. Inside, the church's soaring, three-aisled
nave, with its high-arched windows and slender pillars, rises to a vaulted ceiling
adorned by intricate tracery. Look out also for the medieval murals on the
walls of the nave – they may be faded, but enough remains to see the skill of
their original execution. Back outside, the large square flanking the church, the
Grote Kerkhof, is a good deal prettier than the Brink and here, attached to
the south end of the Lebuinuskerk, are the bruised remains of the fourteenth-
century **Oude Mariakerk**. Services haven't been held here since 1591 and the
town council considered demolishing the church as early as 1600, but in the

event it survived as the town's arsenal and now houses a smart restaurant – the *Arsenal* (see below).

The Bergkwartier

Back at the Brink, take Rijkmanstraat from the square's east side – from just behind the Waag – and you're in the **Bergkwartier**, an area of old housing that was tastefully refurbished during the 1960s in one of the region's first urban renewal projects. Proceeding up Rijkmanstraat, turn left onto **Kerksteeg**, at the end of which is the medieval **Bergkerk**. Fronted by two tall towers, the church is a serious-looking affair where the differences in the colouring of the brick indicate the two main stages of its construction.

From the west side of the church, Roggestraat leads down to the east side of Brink and on the way, at no. 3, you'll pass the **Etty Hillesum Centrum** (Wed, Sat & Sun 1–4pm; Ⓦwww.ettyhillesumcentrum.nl), which celebrates the life of the eponymous Jewish woman who perished in Auschwitz in 1943; Hillesum lived in Deventer from 1924 to 1932. Moving on, Roggestraat arrives at the Brink opposite the **Penninckshuis**, whose florid Renaissance frontage is decorated with statuettes of six virtues. The inscription *Alst Godt behaget beter benyt als beclaget* is smug indeed: "If it pleases God it is better to be envied than to be pitied".

Practicalities

Deventer's **bus** and **train stations** are on the north side of the town centre, a five- to ten-minute walk from the Brink: veer left out of the train station and go over the footbridge straight down Keizerstraat. The **VVV** is bang in the centre of town, in the Waag on the Brink (Mon & Sun 1–5pm, Tues–Sat 10am–5pm; ☎0570/693 781, Ⓦwww.vvvdeventer.nl).

Hotels are thin on the ground, but there is the excellent *Sandton Gilde Hotel*, Nieuwstraat 41 (☎0570/641 846, Ⓦwww.gildehotel.nl; ❷), which occupies an intelligently revamped, nineteenth-century convent hospital with an attractive arcaded courtyard. The cheapest rooms here are a tad spartan, but others have their own little balconies. The hotel is located a five- to ten-minute walk west of the Brink – take Kleine Overstraat and keep straight ahead.

Deventer does well for **cafés and restaurants**. Among a score of places lining up along the Brink, one good choice is the region's oldest cake shop, *Jacob Bussink's Koekwinkel*, at no. 84, where they serve a tasty cup of coffee along with the local speciality, *Deventer koek*, a spiced and very chewy gingerbread biscuit. Moving on up the food chain, *Restaurant 't Arsenal*, at the back of Lebuinuskerk on Grote Kerkhof (Tues–Sat 5.30–10pm; ☎0570/616 495), is a smart little place offering a wide, modern menu with mains averaging €25; and *Chez Antoinette*, just east off the Brink at Roggestraat 10 (Tues–Sun from 5pm; ☎0570/616 630), is a smart Franco-Portuguese place with a first-rate wine cellar; main courses here average €20. Finally, don't leave Deventer without popping into 🅰️ De Leeuw, an old-fashioned, but incredibly cutesy sweet shop and café at Nieuwstraat 25.

Zutphen

ZUTPHEN, 12km south of Deventer, is everything you might hope for in a Dutch country town: there's no crass development here and the centre musters dozens of old buildings set amid a medieval street plan that revolves around three long and very appealing piazzas – Groenmarkt, Houtmarkt and Zaadmarkt. Much of the centre is pedestrianized and, without a supermarket in sight, the town's old-fashioned shops still flourish, as do its cafés and, in a quiet sort of way, its bars, but not, it appears, its pigeons: strangely, there aren't any.

Zutphen was founded in the eleventh century as a fortified settlement at the confluence of the Berkel and IJssel rivers. It took a hundred years for the town to become an important trading post, but thereafter its very success brought torrid times. Habsburg armies sacked Zutphen on several occasions, but the worst came in 1572, when Spanish troops massacred its citizens, an outrage that became part of Protestant folklore, strengthening their resolve against Catholic absolutism right across Europe. It was also here in Zutphen that **Sir Philip Sidney**, the English poet, soldier and courtier, met his end while fighting against the Spanish in 1586. Every inch the Renaissance man, Sidney even managed to die with some measure of style: mortally wounded in the thigh – after having loaned his leg-armour to a friend – he offered his last cup of water to a wounded chum, protesting "thy need is greater than mine".

The Town

From the train station, it's a couple of minutes' walk south along Stationsstraat to the narrow passageway that leads through the old city wall to the town centre. Here, at the junction of Groenmarkt and Houtmarkt, is the **Wijnhuis**,

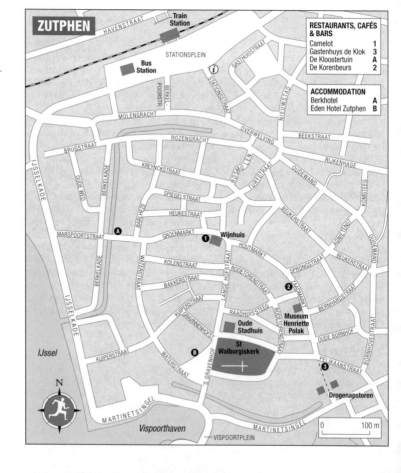

ZUTPHEN

RESTAURANTS, CAFÉS & BARS
Camelot	1
Gastenhuys de Klok	3
De Kloostertuin	A
De Korenbeurs	2

ACCOMMODATION
| Berkhotel | A |
| Eden Hotel Zutphen | B |

0   100 m

a conspicuous if somewhat disjointed clock tower, whose assorted pillars and platforms date from the seventeenth century. Keep straight ahead from here, along Lange Hofstraat, and you soon reach **St Walburgiskerk** (June Tues–Sat 1.30–4.30pm; July to early Sept Mon 1.30–4.30pm, Tues–Sat 10.30am–4.30pm; €1.20, €3.50 with library; @www.walburgiskerk.nl), an immense, Gothic church whose massive, square tower rises high above the town. Inside, the most impressive features are the extravagant brass baptismal font and a remarkable medieval **library**, sited in the sixteenth-century chapterhouse. The library boasts a beautiful low-vaulted ceiling that twists around in a confusion of sharp-edged arches above the original wooden reading desks. It has all the feel of a medieval monastery, but it was in fact one of the first Dutch libraries to be built for the general public, a conscious effort by the Protestant authorities to dispel ignorance and superstition. The library owns over 700 items, ranging from early illuminated manuscripts to sixteenth-century books, a selection of which are still chained to the lecterns on which they were once read. Curiously, the tiles on one side of the floor are dotted with paw marks, which some contemporaries attributed to the work of the Devil.

Across from St Walburgiskerk is the **Oude Stadhuis**, an elegant Neoclassical building whose main portal is decorated with military carvings in the style of ancient Rome.

The Drogenapstoren and Zaadmarkt

Proceeding south from St Walburgiskerk, you cross the old town **moat** to reach Martinetsingel, which curves east offering exquisite views of the town centre on its way to the **Drogenapstoren**, one of the old city gates – and a fine example of a brick rampart tower – that takes its name from the time when the town trumpeter, one Thomas Drogenap, lived here.

The Drogenapstoren is a few metres from **Zaadmarkt**, a wide and especially handsome street that leads back towards the Wijnhuis. Zaadmarkt is also home to the **Museum Henriette Polak**, at no. 88 (Tues–Sun 11am–5pm; €3.50), which features temporary displays of modern, usually Dutch, art. The house itself looks nineteenth century, but in fact it is much older, as evidenced by the tiny chapel on the top floor. When the Protestants took control of the Netherlands in the sixteenth century, Catholics were allowed to hold services in any private building providing that the exterior revealed no sign of their activities – hence the development of clandestine churches (*schuilkerken*) all over the country, of which this is one of the few to have survived.

Practicalities

Zutphen's **train** and **bus stations** are on the north side of the town centre; the **VVV** is across from the station at Stationsplein 39 (Mon 10am–5.30pm, Tues–Fri 9am–5.30pm, Sat 10am–4pm; ☏0900 269 2888, @www.vvvzutphen .nl). There are two good **hotels**, both handily located in the centre. These are the *Eden Hotel Zutphen*, a four-star hotel in a fine old mansion across from St Walburgiskerk at 's Gravenhof 6 (☏0575/596 868, @www.edenhotelzutphen .com; ❷), though the least expensive rooms here are a tad poky; and the much more low-key, distinctly cosy, three-star ⌘ *Berkhotel*, in a pleasant, two-storey, late nineteenth-century building at Marschpoortstraat 19 (☏0575/511 135, @www.berkhotel.nl; ❷); this hotel is a short walk west of the Wijnhuis via Groenmarkt.

For **food**, the *Berkhotel* has a competent vegetarian café called *De Kloostertuin* (Tues–Sun 5–9pm) and there's also the very pleasant *Gastenhuys de Klok* (☏0575/517 035; Tues–Sat noon–9pm), in antique, wood-panelled premises at

Pelikaanstraat 6 – at the foot of Zaadmarkt. During the day, they serve up tapas and salads and at night the menu offers a mix of French and Dutch dishes with mains from €22; they also have a charming garden terrace. *Camelot*, a dark bar with a wide range of beers at Groenmarkt 34, is a good place for a **drink**; or, even better, try *De Korenbeurs*, a little, old-fashioned place complete with a splendid wooden stairway at Houtmarkt 84.

The Achterhoek

Extending some 30km southeast from Zutphen to the German border, the **Achterhoek** ("Back Corner") is aptly named, comprising a sleepy rural backwater of pocket-sized towns and villages. The easy hills here have made it a popular spot for **cyclists**, with Zutphen as the obvious base. There are no noteworthy attractions per se, with the possible exception of the old frontier settlement of **'S-HEERENBERG**, where a resolutely modern centre edges the medieval town hall, church and castle that once belonged to the counts van de Bergh. Of the three, it's the castle – the **Huis Bergh** – that dominates, its impressive red-brick walls rising abruptly above the moat. Its present appearance dates from 1912 when an Enschede industrialist, a certain J.H. van Heek, bought the place and had it restored. Guided tours (mid-April to Oct Tues–Sun 12.30–4.30pm; Nov & Dec Sun 12.30–4.30pm; outside season call ☎0314/661 281; €8; ⓦwww.huisbergh.nl) whisk you round an interior littered with sundry late medieval paintings, statues, prayer books and other paraphernalia, all installed by van Heek. The quickest way to reach 's-Heerenberg is to take the train from Zutphen to Arnhem, where you change for **Doetinchem**; from Doetinchem train station, take bus #24.

Through the Veluwe

Stretching west of the River IJssel, Gelderland's **Veluwe** (literally "Bad Land") is an expanse of heath, woodland and dune that lies sandwiched between **Apeldoorn** in the east, Amersfoort to the west, **Arnhem** in the south and the Veluwemeer waterway to the north. For centuries these infertile lands lay almost deserted, but today they make up the country's busiest holiday centre, dotted with a profusion of campsites, bungalow parks and second homes, with the exception of the area's southeast corner, which has been conserved and protected as the **Hoge Veluwe National Park** (see pp.275–278). The park is much the prettiest part of the Veluwe and the best place to experience the area – though, unless you're camping, it's best to visit the park from Arnhem (see p.268).

Apeldoorn

The administrative capital of the Veluwe, **APELDOORN** was no more than a village a century ago, but it's grown rapidly to become an extensive garden city; a rather characterless modern place that spreads languidly into the surrounding countryside. However, as one-time home of the Dutch royal family, Apeldoorn is now a major tourist centre, particularly popular with those Dutch senior citizens who flock here to visit the **Paleis Het Loo**. If you're staying here in August, it's worth catching the **Veluwe Highlands Music and Film Festival** (ⓦwww .veluwehighlands.nl) at the Natuurpark Berg & Bos, featuring live performances by Dutch artists and international films (but with only Dutch subtitles); details are available from the VVV. Finally, in July and August an old **steam train** is put back into service between Apeldoorn and Dieren (€12.50 return ticket), facilitating a pleasant half-day excursion of one hour and a quarter each way.

The Paleis Het Loo

Apeldoorn is most famous for the **Paleis Het Loo** (Tues–Sun 10am–5pm; €10; Ⓦ www.paleishetloo.nl), situated on the northern edge of town and reachable by half-hourly bus #5, #96 or #102 from the train station or a fifteen-minute ride by bicycle. Looking something like an imposing military academy, it was designed in 1685 by Daniel Marot for William III and his queen, Mary, shortly before he acceded to the throne of England and Scotland. Later the palace was the favourite residence of Queen Wilhelmina, who lived here until her death in 1962. No longer used by the Dutch royal family – they moved out in 1975 – it was opened as a national museum in the early 1980s to illustrate three hundred years of the history of the House of Orange-Nassau. Years of repair work have restored an apparently endless series of bedrooms, ballrooms, living rooms and reception halls to their former glory. A self-guided tour, with information in English, leads you along a warren of passageways with each room packed with displays of all things royal, from lavish costumes and silk hangings to documents and medals, via roomfuls of sombre dynastic portraits. If you are partial to royalty, it's a fascinating and infinitely detailed snapshot of Orange-Nassau life, and you can view the rooms of William and Mary, including their colourful individual bedchambers, as well as the much later study of Queen Wilhelmina.

Outside, the formal **gardens** (both William and Mary were apparently keen gardeners) are a relaxing place to wander. A maze of miniature hedgerows and a series of precise and neatly bordered flowerbeds are accessible by long walkways ornamented in the Dutch Baroque style, with tiered fountains, urns, statuettes and portals. The other part of the palace, the **Royal Stables** of 1906, has displays of some of vintage royal cars and carriages, including a baby carriage that's rigged up against gas attack.

Apenheul monkey reserve

Apeldoorn's second draw is the **Apenheul monkey reserve** (April–Oct daily 9.30am–5pm; July & Aug until 6pm; €17.50; Ⓦ www.apenheul.nl), just west of

▲ Paleis Het Loo

town on bus #3. The highlight is the **gorillas** − among the world's largest colonies of the creatures − living on wooded islands that isolate them from the visitors and from the dozen or so species of monkey that roam around the rest of the park, with some of the least aggressive species allowed to roam among the visitors. It's best to go early to catch the young gorillas fooling around and antagonizing the elders; as the day warms up they all get a bit more slothful. The park is well designed, with a reasonable amount of freedom for most of the animals (at times it's not obvious who is watching who), and you'll see other wildlife including otters, deer and capybara.

Practicalities

From Apeldoorn **train and bus stations**, it's a ten- to fifteen-minute walk to the centre straight down Stationstraat. As you approach the centre, Stationstraat crosses Deventerstraat, which is where, at no.18, you will find the **VVV** (Mon–Fri 9am–5.30pm, Sat 9am–5pm; ☎055/526 0200, ⓦ www.vvvapeldoorn.nl), which stocks maps of the town and the surrounding area. They also have information on walking trails in the forests around the Paleis Het Loo and on local cycle routes. Bikes can be rented from the train station (€7.50 per day). As regards accommodation, the VVV has a list of **rooms** − in season it's advisable to ask them to ring ahead to confirm vacancies. The most reasonably priced **hotel** near the centre, with only ten rooms, is the *Abbekerk*, Canadalaan 26, a ten-minute walk north (☎055/522 2433, ⓦ www.hotelabbekerk.nl; ❷): head up Stationstraat and Canadalaan is the fourth left turn after the Marktplein. More conveniently located is the *Hotel Le Paris* (☎055/522 1822, ⓦ www.paris .nl; ❷), smack in the centre of town on Raadhuisplein 5, with a decent café downstairs and recently revamped rooms. There's also a **HI hostel**, 4km west at Asselsestraat 330 (☎055/355 3118, ⓦ www.stayokay.com; €28.50 for a dorm bed), which is open year-round and reachable on bus #6 (Mandala stop) or #7 (Ordenplein stop). The nearest **campsite** is *De Parelhoeve*, Zwolseweg 540 (☎055/312 1332, ⓦ www.deparelhoeve.nl), in the village of **Wenum Wiesel** some 5km north of Apeldoorn centre (bus #90 or #96 from the train station). The VVV also has a list of nearby mini-campsites.

Eating and drinking

Don't expect a lot of nighttime excitement. The main hive of evening activity is the **Caterplein**, where Hoofdstraat meets Nieuwstraat. For **food** head to the nearby Van Kinsbergenstraat where you'll find *Gijs en Katrien* at number 4, an amenable restaurant with a modern but warm interior serving mains including monkfish and sateh for around €18 − very decent cappuccino too. *Central Park*, an excellent **lunchroom** with a rickety rack interior, serves smoothies, bagels and coffee close by at Kapelstraat 1, while *Eetcafé 't Pakhuys*, Beekpark 9, has reasonable Dutch food. Further south on Hoofdstraat, Raadhuisplein has several good **café-bars**, and the *Blues Café* on Nieuwstraat has occasional live music.

Arnhem

ARNHEM, about 20km south of Apeldoorn, on the far side of the Hoge Veluwe National Park, was once a wealthy resort, a watering hole to which the merchants of Amsterdam and Rotterdam would flock to idle away their fortunes. In World War II, however, it became better known as the place where thousands of British and Polish troops died in the failed Allied airborne operation of September 1944, codenamed **Operation Market Garden** (see

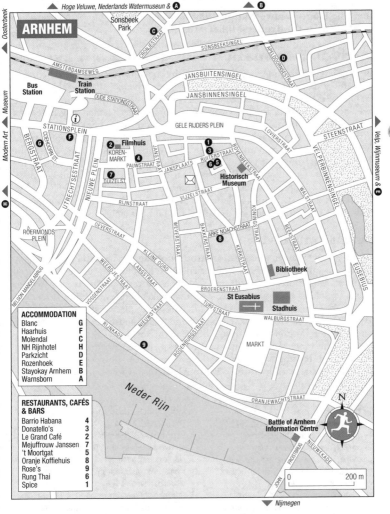

Hoge Veluwe, Nederlands Watermuseum & **A**

ARNHEM

Sonsbeek
Park

C

SONSBEEKSINGEL

D

AMSTERDAMSEWEG

Bus
Station

Train
Station

JANSBUITENSINGEL

OUDE STATIONSSTRAAT

JANSBINNENSINGEL

STATIONSPLEIN

GELE RIJDERS PLEIN

LOVIERSTRAAT

STEENSTRAAT

G   **F**

Filmhuis

2   **1**

KOREN-
MARKT

4

PAUWSTRAAT

3

6 5

ROGGENBEELSTRAAT

JANSPLAATS

RUITERSTRAAT

7

Historisch
Museum

DUIZELST

VIJZELSTRAAT

RIJNSTRAAT

WEVERSTRAAT

KONINGSTRAAT

ROERMONDS
PLEIN

OEVERSTRAAT

ARKE NOACHSTRAAT

BAKKERSTRAAT

BEEKSTRAAT

8

KLEINE OORD

Bibliotheek

KERKSTRAAT

LANGSTRAAT

VOSSENSTRAAT

WEERDJESSTRAAT

NIEUWSTRAAT

BROERENSTRAAT

TURFSTRAAT

St Eusabius

Stadhuis

St Eusabius

WALBURGSTRAAT

RIJNKADE

RODENBURGSTRAAT

MARKT

9

ORANJEWACHTSTRAAT

Neder Rijn

ACCOMMODATION

Blanc	G
Haarhuis	F
Molendal	C
NH Rijnhotel	H
Parkzicht	D
Rozenhoek	E
Stayokay Arnhem	B
Warnsborn	A

RESTAURANTS, CAFÉS & BARS

Barrio Habana	4
Donatello's	3
Le Grand Café	2
Mejuffrouw Janssen	7
't Moortgat	5
Oranje Koffiehuis	8
Rose's	9
Rung Thai	6
Spice	1

Battle of Arnhem
Information Centre

N

0   200 m

Nijmegen

box, p.275). The city is most famous for its bridge, a key objective in Field Marshal Montgomery's audacious attempt to shorten the war by dropping parachute battalions behind enemy lines to secure a string of advance positions across the rivers of southeast Gelderland. Much of Arnhem was destroyed as a result of the operation, and most of what you see today is a postwar reconstruction. Perhaps inevitably, Arnhem is something of a place of pilgrimage for English visitors, who congregate here every summer to visit the crucial sites of the battle, but it's also a lively town where the fashion academy has nurtured a number of young designers, whose boutique stores are now a feature of the city centre. Arnhem also makes a first-rate base for seeing the numerous attractions scattered around its forested outskirts – the war museums and memorials near **Oosterbeek** (see p.272), the **Nederlands Openluchtmuseum**, the **Burgers' Zoo** and one of the highlights of the area, the **Hoge Veluwe National Park**, incorporating a superb collection of modern art at the **Kröller-Müller Museum**.

Arrival, information and getting around

A major transport junction, Arnhem's **train** and **bus stations** are only a few minutes' walk from the centre. The **VVV**, Stationsplein 13 (Mon–Fri 9.30am–5.30pm, Sat 9.30am–5pm; ☏0900 112 2344, ⓦwww.vvvarnhem.nl), has a good selection of Dutch maps, books on Operation Market Garden, brochures and up-to-date cultural information. One of their most useful booklets is Discover Arnhem (€5), comprising five themed walking routes and a cycling route. **Walking** is the best way to get around the centre, although to see any of the outlying attractions and for some of the accommodation you'll need at some point to use a **trolley bus**. Arnhem has a rather odd system of trolley buses which follow a figure-of-eight route around town. This means there'll often be two buses at the station with the same number and different destinations, so it's important to get the direction as well as the number right.

Accommodation

The VVV operates an **accommodation booking** service, which is especially useful in July and August when Arnhem's handful of reasonably priced pensions and hotels can fill up fast. The nearest **campsite** is *Camping Warnsborn*, 6km northwest of the centre at Bakenbergseweg 257 (☏026/442 3469; ⓦwww.campingwarnsborn.nl; bus #2, direction Schaarsbergen; April–Oct), attractively situated on a large estate and hemmed in by beech and oak trees. You can **rent bikes** here for the lovely cycle ride through the trees to the Hoge Veluwe National Park, 5km further north. There are many other campsites around the edge of the park, including one by the Hoenderloo entrance in the park itself (☏055/378 2232; April–Oct) – an ideal spot for a quiet night's camping.

Hotels

Blanc Coehoornstraat 4 ☏026/442 8072, ⓦwww.hotel-blanc.nl. This small hotel has only 22 stylishly decorated rooms, a few with balconies, located in one old and one more modern building. Breakfast is served in the attractive next-door café. ❸

Haarhuis Stationsplein 1 ☏026/442 7441, ⓦwww.hotelhaarhuis.nl. The reassuringly comfortable *Haarhuis* is conveniently located opposite the train station. Breakfast can be somewhat of a letdown though. ❺

🏃 **Hotel Molendal** Cronjéstraat 15 ☏026/442 4858, ⓦwww.hotel-molendal.nl. Located right behind the train station and in a beautifully renovated Art Nouveau building, this grand hotel boosts sixteen elegant rooms – all varying in size – with great views onto the Sonsbeek park. ❹

NH Rijnhotel Onderlangs 10 ☏026/443 4642, ⓦwww.nh-hotels.com. Located just ten minutes' walk from the train station in the direction of Oosterbeek, this four-star hotel offers luxury with great views over the River Rhine. Don't be put off by its concrete facade; the interior is stylish with a Spanish twist. ❸–❹

Parkzicht Apeldoornsestraat 16 ☏026/442 0698, ⓦwww.parkzichthotel.nl. Friendly if a bit old-fashioned, a family-run hotel with fourteen rooms, all in traditional style. Some rooms have shared facilities. ❶–❷

Rozenhoek Rozendaalselaan 60 ☏026/364 7290, ⓦwww.derozenhoek.nl. If you have problems finding a room in town, this is a good alternative outside the city in the leafy suburb of Velp. *Rozenhoek* is located in an old villa, just five minutes from the Rosendael castle. Untouched by the war, parts of Velp are still much as they were a century ago – comfortable country mansions and landscaped streets and gardens. ❷

🏃 **Warnsborn** Schelmseweg 1 ☏026/442 5994, ⓦwww.pensionwarnsborn.nl. By far the cheapest option is located near all Arnhem's main attractions and the Hoge Veluwe National Park, just north of the centre of town. This family-run B&B in an eighteenth-century house has spacious rooms, some with private balconies. ❶

Hostels

Stayokay Arnhem Diepenbrocklaan 27 ☏026/442 0114, ⓦ www.stayokay.com. Some 5km north of town in the woods and within walking distance of Burgers' Zoo and the Nederlands Openluchtmuseum. Facilities include a pool table, internet access, a restaurant and bicycle hire. Take bus #3, direction Altaveer, to the Rijnstaete hospital stop. €26.50 for a dorm bed, double rooms ❶.

The Town

Predictably, postwar rebuilding has left Arnhem a patchy place with the usual agglomerations of concrete and glass; however, five minutes' walk southeast of the train station is the **Korenmarkt**, a small square that escaped much of the destruction. The streets leading off it are choc-a-block with restaurants and bars, while the **Filmhuis**, at Korenmarkt 42, has an excellent programme of international films and late-night showings, and a small gallery on the ground floor.

Arnhem deteriorates as you walk southeast from the Korenmarkt and into the area most badly damaged by the fighting. Here stands the "Bridge Too Far", the **John Frostbrug**, named after the commander of the battalion that defended it for four days. It's a plain modern bridge, but it remains a symbol of people's remembrance of the battle, Dutch and British alike. Located right under the north side of the bridge is the **Battle of Arnhem Information Centre** (April–Oct Mon–Sat 10am–5pm & Sun noon–5pm; Nov–March Mon–Sat 11am–5pm & Sun noon–5pm), where you can find detailed information and stories from witnesses to the battle, from a Dutch, British and German point of view.

Around the north end of the bridge you can see the results of the rebuilding: wide boulevards intersect broad open spaces edged by haphazardly placed tower blocks and car parks. Overlooking this rather desolate spot, at the end of the characterless **Markt**, is the church of **St Eusebius** (April–Oct Tues–Sat 10am–5pm, Sun noon–5pm; Nov–March Tues–Sat 11am–4pm, Sun noon–4pm; free), with the dainty fifteenth-century **Stadhuis** tucked in behind. The church is a fifteenth- to sixteenth-century structure surmounted by a valiantly attempted but rather obvious replacement tower which was extensively renovated for the fiftieth anniversary of Operation Market Garden in 1994; you can take a lift to the top (€2.50) for fine views over the surrounding area.

The museums

From outside the train station, it's a fifteen-minute walk west along Utrechtsestraat (or take bus #1 direction Oosterbeek) to the **Museum voor Moderne Kunst**, Utrechtseweg 87 (Modern Art Museum; Tues–Fri 10am–5pm, Sat & Sun 11am–5pm; €6; ⓦ www.mmkarnhem.nl), whose speciality is exhibitions of modern Dutch art. The nucleus of the permanent collection is the work of the Magic Realists, particularly Carel Willink and Pyke Koch, whose *Vrouwen in de Straat* is a typically disconcerting canvas, the women's eyes looking out of the picture in a medley of contrasting emotions.

The more centrally located **Historisch Museum** (Historical Museum; Tues–Fri 10am–5pm, Sat & Sun 11am–5pm; €3.75; ⓦ www.hmarnhem.nl) is in an old orphanage at Bovenbeekstraat 21. The collection includes a display of Chinese, Japanese and Delft ceramics from the seventeenth and eighteenth centuries; Dutch silver, notably several guild beakers, whose size and degree of decoration indicated the status of the owner; and a modest selection of paintings from the sixteenth to the nineteenth centuries, with the emphasis on views of the landscape, villages and towns of Gelderland.

Wine lovers will enjoy the **Nederlands Wijnmuseum**, Velperweg 23 (Dutch Wine Museum; Tues–Fri 2–5pm, Sat 11am–5pm; €4; wine tasting and guided tour on Saturday at 1.30 & 3pm; €11; ⓦ www.wijnmuseum.nl), towards Velp, where the entire process from grape to bottle is explained. On Saturday you can visit the immense wine cellars below the museum, where thousands of litres of wine are kept in barrels, waiting to be drunk. Ask for their English guidebook.

Eating, drinking and nightlife

Arnhem has plenty of decent places for reasonably priced **food** and a good range of **bars**. For a drink, most people head for the pavement cafés of **Korenmarkt**, and there's bargain-basement food on and around the **Jansplein**, and several stylish restaurants along **Pauwstraat**. The bars and restaurants dotted along the **Rijnkade** are especially appealing on warm summer evenings. There's often **live music** at one bar or another – get hold of a copy of the listings magazine *Uit Loper* for details of what's on.

Barrio Habana Pauwstraat 3 ☏026/442 8669. Gigantic restaurant and bar with a deliberately rundown Cuban feel. Don't mind Che looking over your shoulder while you enjoy large tapas or one of their cocktails.

Donatello's Jansplein 50 ☏026/443 7444. Cheap Italian chain restaurant, frequented by students on a tight budget. All pizzas and pastas are under €8 and a three-course meal comes at the amazingly low price of €10 (Mon–Wed).

Le Grand Café Korenmarkt 16. Probably the most popular spot for drinking on Korenmarkt, complete with fake palm trees and tacky lampshades. If it's too crowded there are a dozen or so other places around here to choose from.

Mejuffrouw Janssen Duizelsteeg 7 ☏026/351 4069. Just south of Korenmarkt, this restaurant offers excellent value for money with a three-course meal for €14.95; the menu changes regularly but you can expect tasty dishes like *sateh*, shrimp skewer and steak in an amenable atmosphere.

't Moortgat Ruiterstraat 35. This brown-style café, with beer memorabilia on the walls and over 120 beers to choose from, caters to an older crowd. There's also a billiards table to pass the time on a rainy day.

Oranje Koffiehuis Arke Noachstraat 7. Tiny café with Art Deco interior that, despite its name (coffeehouse), also serves stronger drinks. A nice detail is the miniature glass of liquor that they serve with their coffee. Live music twice a week.

Rose's Rijnkade 49 ☏026/442 5798. Lounge bar and restaurant overlooking the River Rhine with kitsch velvet sofas, Chesterfields and an intimate fireplace where you can choose from a large selection of mixed platters and a creative à la carte menu. Occasional salsa and 70s and 80s dance nights.

Rung Thai Ruiterstraat 43 ☏026/445 0032. Trendy Thai place with bright pink walls and a wicked *Tom Yam Kai*. Main dishes around €16. Also does takeaway.

Spice Jansplein 49 ☏026/443 2963. Cheap and tastefully decorated restaurant with a varied menu, serving everything from curry to spareribs. Starters never exceed €6 and mains are around €11.

Around Arnhem

Most people who visit Arnhem do so for the attractions outside the city and you could certainly spend several days here, visiting the wartime sites of Operation Market Garden around **Oosterbeek**, taking in the countryside of the **Hoge Veluwe National Park** and its superb modern art collection, the **Kröller-Müller Museum**, heading off to the **Nederlands Openluchmuseum**, the country's largest open-air museum of Dutch vernacular architecture, and dropping by **Burgers' Zoo**, which has a sizeable menagerie of animals housed in sensitively re-created and attractive habitats.

Oosterbeek's World War II memorials

The area around Arnhem is scattered with the graveyards of thousands of soldiers who died during Operation Market Garden (see box, p.275). Arnhem

▲ Airborne Cemetery, Oosterbeek

VVV sells specialist books on the campaign for devotees of militaria and provides details of organized tours (minimum twenty people). Otherwise, the easiest way to get some idea of the conflict and its effect on this part of the Netherlands is to visit **OOSTERBEEK**, once a small village and now a prosperous suburb of Arnhem – take the train or bus #1 to get there.

Following the signs from beside Oosterbeek train station, it's a five-minute walk east to the **Airborne Cemetery**, a neat, symmetrical tribute to nearly two thousand paratroopers, mostly British and Polish, whose bodies were brought here from the surrounding fields. It's a quiet, secluded spot and the personal inscriptions on the gravestones are especially poignant.

Ten minutes' walk (or take bus #1) south of the station down Stationsweg, the village proper has spruced lawns and walls dotted with details of the battle – who held out where and for how long – as the Allied forces were pinned back within a tighter and tighter perimeter.

The Airborne Museum

The **Airborne Museum**, Utrechtseweg 232 (closed for renovation at the time of writing; Ⓦwww.airbornemuseum.nl), just to the west of the village centre along Utrechtseweg – and reachable direct from Arnhem on bus #1 or #86 – is housed in the former Hotel Hartenstein, where the British forces were besieged by the Germans for a week before retreating across the river. With the use of an English commentary, photographs, dioramas and original military artefacts – from rifles and light artillery to uniforms and personal memorabilia – the museum gives an excellent outline of the battle and, to a lesser extent, aspects of World War II as it affected the country as a whole. The Army Film and Photographic Unit landed with the British forces, and it's their photographs that stick in the memory: grimly cheerful soldiers hauling in their parachutes; tense, tired faces during the fighting; and shattered Dutch villages.

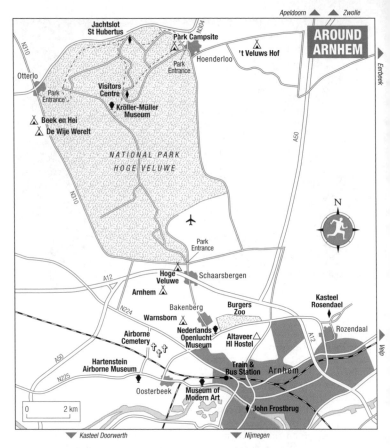

Map: AROUND ARNHEM

The Nederlands Openluchtmuseum and Burgers' Zoo

Located immediately to the north of Arnhem, the **Nederlands Openlucht-museum**, Schelmseweg 89 (Dutch Open-Air Museum; daily: April–Oct 10am–5pm; Dec to mid-Jan 11am–7pm; €14; ⓦ www.openluchtmuseum.nl), comprises an impressive collection of old Dutch buildings. One of the first of its type, the museum was founded in 1912 in order to "present a picture of the daily life of ordinary people in this country as it was in the past and has developed in the course of time". Over the years, original buildings have been taken from all over the country and assembled here in a large area of the Veluwe forest. Where possible, buildings have been placed in groups that represent the different regions of the Netherlands – from the farmsteads of Friesland to the peat colonies of Drenthe. There are about eighty buildings in all, including examples of every type of Dutch windmill, most sorts of farmhouse, a variety of bridges and several working craftshops, demonstrating the traditional skills of papermaking, milling, baking, brewing and bleaching. Other parts of the museum include one of the most extensive regional costume exhibitions in the country and a modest herb garden. Altogether, it's an imaginative attempt to re-create the rural Dutch way of life over the past two centuries. The museum is reachable from Arnhem by bus #3 (direction Alteveer; every 20min), or direct by special bus #13 (July & Aug only; every 20min),

The Burgers' Zoo

Near the Nederlands Openluchtmuseum is another of Arnhem's major attractions, **Burgers' Zoo**, Antoon van Hooffplein 1 (April–Oct 9am–7pm; Nov–March 9am–5pm; €18; ⓦ www.burgerszoo.nl). The zoo started in 1913 with a small private collection and has since grown to become one of the largest zoos in the Netherlands. Artificial ecosystems like Burgers' Ocean, Safari and Desert copy the animals' habitats as accurately as possible. The most recent addition to the zoo is the Rimba, with a wide selection of animals from the Malaysian jungle.

The Hoge Veluwe National Park

Spreading north from the Open-Air Museum is the **Hoge Veluwe National Park** (ⓦ www.hogeveluwe.nl), an area of sandy heath, lake, dune and woodland crisscrossed by cycle trails and inhabited by wild game. At its heart is one of the country's most prestigious art galleries, the **Kröller-Müller Museum**, and

---

Operation Market Garden

By September 1944, most of France and much of Belgium had been liberated from German occupation. Fearing that an orthodox campaign would take many months and cost many lives, **Field Marshal Montgomery** decided that a pencil-thrust north through the Netherlands and subsequently east into the Ruhr, around the back of the Siegfried Line, offered a good chance of ending the war early. To speed the advance of his land armies, Montgomery needed to cross several major rivers and canals in a corridor of territory stretching from Eindhoven, a few kilometres north of the front, to Arnhem. The plan, codenamed **Operation Market Garden**, was to parachute three Airborne Divisions behind enemy lines, each responsible for taking and holding particular bridgeheads until the army could force their way north to join them. On Sunday, September 17, the 1st British Airborne Division parachuted into the fields around Oosterbeek, their objective to seize the bridges over the Rhine at Arnhem. Meanwhile, the 101st American Airborne Division was dropped in the area of Veghel to secure the Wilhelmina and Zuid-Willemsvaart canals, and the 82nd was dropped around Grave and Nijmegen, for the crossings over the Maas and the Waal.

The American paratroopers were successful, and by the night of September 20, sections of the main British army, 30 Corps, had reached the American bridgehead across the River Waal at Nijmegen. However, the landings around Arnhem ran into serious problems: Allied Command had estimated that opposition was unlikely to exceed three thousand troops, but, as it turned out, the entire 2nd SS Panzer Corps was refitting near Arnhem just when the 1st Division landed. Taking the enemy by surprise, 2nd Parachute Battalion, under **Lieutenant-Colonel John Frost**, did manage to capture the north end of the road bridge across the Rhine, but it proved impossible to capture the southern end. Surrounded, out-gunned and out-manned, the 2nd Battalion held their position from September 17th to the morning of the 21st, a feat of extraordinary courage and determination. Meanwhile, other British and Polish battalions had concentrated around the bridgehead at Oosterbeek, which they held at tremendous cost under the command of **General Urquhart**. By the morning of the 25th it was apparent that reinforcements in sufficient numbers would not be able to get through in support, so under cover of darkness, a dramatic and supremely well-executed withdrawal saved 2163 soldiers out of an original force of 10,005.

sprinkled across it are a number of other attractions, from a handsome hunting lodge through to a sculpture garden.

The park was formerly the private estate of **Anton and Helene Kröller-Müller**. Born near Essen in 1869, Helene came from a wealthy family who made their money in the manufacture of blast furnaces, while her husband, the ever-so-discreet Anton came from a Rotterdam shipping family. Super-rich, the couple had a passionate desire to leave a grand bequest to the nation: a mixture of nature and culture, which would, Helene felt, "be an important lesson when showing the inherent refinement of a merchant's family living at the beginning of the century". She collected the art, Anton the land and its animals – the moufflons (wild sheep) were, for example imported from Corsica – and in the 1930s ownership of the whole estate was transferred to the nation on the condition that a museum was built in the park. The museum opened in 1938 and Helene acted as manager until her death in 1939. The parkland is carefully managed and there are hides sprinkled across the park from which you can observe its varied fauna.

Park practicalities

The park has **three entrances**: one near the village of **Otterlo** on the northwest perimeter, another near **Hoenderloo** on the northeast edge, and a third to the south at Rijzenburg, near the village of **Schaarsbergen**, just 7km from Arnhem. It has long **opening hours** (daily: April 8am–8pm; May & Aug 8am–9pm; June & July 8am–10pm; Sept 9am–8pm; Oct 9am–7pm; Nov–March 9am–6pm), but during the deer rutting season, in September and early October, certain areas of the park are off-limits. **Admission** is €7 (park only) or €14 (park and Kröller-Müller museum); cars cost an extra €6.

There are very few roads in the park, so easily the best way to explore it is on one of the many **white bicycles**, which lie in wait at each of the park's three entrances and are free to use. These famous white bikes come in all shapes and sizes and several have children's seats at the front and rear. There are also trikes, tandems and wheelchair bikes available from next to the **Bezoekerscentrum** (Visitors' Centre; April–Oct daily 9.30am–6pm; Nov–March 9.30am–5pm), located in the middle of the park near the museum. The Bezoekerscentrum also sells maps of the park marked with several themed cycle routes, such as the 14km "Images in the Landscape" taking in the best of the open-air art.

There are a number of ways to get to the park by **bus**. From Arnhem, bus #107 runs hourly to Otterlo; here, you can change to bus #106 which runs 4km east to the Kröller-Müller Museum, or you can walk to the park entrance (5min) and pick up a free white bike. Alternatively, bus #110 runs hourly on a handy route between Ede-Wageningen and Apeldoorn, stopping midway at the Otterlo entrance, the Bezoekerscentrum and the Hoenderloo entrance. To get to the park from Arnhem, you can **rent a bike** at Arnhem train station and cycle in from there; the round trip from Arnhem station to the Kröller-Müller museum and back is a total of about 28km.

Around the park

In **OTTERLO** village, a ten-minute walk west of the park entrance and across from the VVV at Eikenzoom 12, is the small **Tegel Museum** (Tile Museum; Tues–Fri 10am–5pm, Sat & Sun 1–5pm; €4; ⓦ www.nederlandstegelmuseum .nl), which is worth an hour of your time. Displays here trace the development of the Dutch tile from the sixteenth to the twentieth century, and include themes such as biblical scenes, shipping and sea monsters. Slideshows and guided tours in English are available on request.

In the park itself, beneath the Bezoekerscentrum, the engrossing, subterranean **Museonder** (April–Oct daily 9.30am–6pm; Nov–March 9.30am–5pm; free), investigates the unusual ecosystems that sustain the park through an array of interactive presentations – great for children, and adults will find themselves morbidly fascinated too. Look out for the giant beetle-mites, a rabbit morgue and a 23-metre-long beech-tree banister.

The Jachtslot St Hubertus

The **Jachtslot St Hubertus** (open only for guided tours, book at the Bezoekerscentrum; €3), some 3km north of the Visitors' Centre, is a hunting lodge and country home built in 1920 for the Kröller-Müllers by the modernist Dutch architect H.P. Berlage. Dedicated to the patron saint of hunters, it's an impressive Art Deco monument, with lots of plays on the hunting theme. The floor plan – in the shape of branching antlers – is representative of the stag bearing a crucifix that allegedly appeared to St Hubert, the patron of hunters, and each room of the sumptuous interior symbolizes an episode in the saint's life: all in all, a somewhat unusual commission for a committed socialist who wrote so caustically about the haute bourgeoisie.

The Kröller-Müller Museum

Most people who visit the Hoge Veluwe Park come for the **Kröller-Müller Museum** (Tues–Sun 10am–5pm; €14 with park admission included; ⓦ www .kmm.nl), made up of the private art collection of the Kröller-Müllers. It's one of the country's finest museums, comprising a wide cross section of modern European art from Impressionism to Cubism and beyond. It's housed in a low-slung building that was built for the collection in 1938 by the much-lauded Belgian architect Van de Velde. In the 1970s a new wing was added to a design by the Dutch architect Wim Quist.

Charley Toorop and Mondrian

The bulk of the collection is in one long wing, starting with the most recent painters and working backwards. There's a good set of paintings, in particular some revealing self-portraits by **Charley Toorop**, one of the most skilled and sensitive of twentieth-century Dutch artists. Her father, Jan, also gets a good showing throughout the museum, from his pointillist studies to later, turn-of-the-century works more reminiscent of Aubrey Beardsley and the Art Nouveau movement. **Piet Mondrian** is well represented, too, his 1909 *Beach near Domburg* a good example of his more stylized approach to landscape painting, a development from his earlier sombre-coloured scenes in the Dutch tradition. In 1909 Mondrian moved to Paris, and his contact with Cubism transformed his work, as illustrated by his *Composition* of 1917: simple flat rectangles of colour with the elimination of the object complete, the epitome of the De Stijl approach. One surprise is an early Picasso, *Portrait of a Woman*, from 1901, a classic post-Impressionist canvas very dissimilar from his more famous works.

Vincent van Gogh

The building as a whole gravitates toward the works of **Vincent van Gogh**, with one of the most complete collections of his work in the world, housed in a large room around a central courtyard and placed in context by accompanying contemporary pictures. The museum owns no fewer than 272 Van Gogh pieces (both paintings and drawings), and exhibits are rotated, with the exception of his most important paintings. Of earlier canvases, *The Potato Eaters* and *Head of a Peasant with a Pipe* are outstanding: rough, unsentimental paintings of labourers from around his parents' home in Brabant. His penetrating *Self-portrait* from 1887 is a superb example of his work during his years in Paris, the eyes fixed on the observer, the head and background a swirl of grainy colour and streaky brush-strokes. One of his famous sunflower paintings also dates from this period, an extraordinary work of alternately thick and thin paintwork in dazzlingly sharp detail and colour. The joyful *Café Terrace at Night* and *Bridge* at *Arles*, with its rickety bridge and disturbed circles of water spreading from the washerwomen on the riverbank, are from his months in Arles in 1888, one of the high points of his troubled life.

The Sculpture Garden

Outside the museum, behind the main building, the **Sculpture Garden** (Tues–Sun 10am–4.30pm; free entrance with museum ticket) is one of the largest in Europe. Some frankly bizarre creations reside within its 25 hectares, as well as works by Auguste Rodin, Jacob Epstein and Barbara Hepworth. In contrast to the carefully conserved paintings of the museum, the sculptures are exposed to the weather and you can even clamber all over Jean Dubuffet's *Jardin d'email*, one of his larger and more elaborate jokes.

Nijmegen

The oldest town in the Netherlands, **NIJMEGEN**, some 20km south of Arnhem, was built on the site of the Roman frontier fortress of Novio Magus, from which it derives its name. Situated on the southern bank of the River Waal, just to the west of its junction with the Rhine, the town has long been strategically important. The Romans used Nijmegen as a buffer against the unruly tribes to the east; and Charlemagne, Holy Roman Emperor from 800 to 814, made the town one of the principal seats of his administration, building the **Valkhof Palace**, an enormous complex of chapels and secular buildings completed in the eighth century. Rebuilt in 1155 by another emperor, Frederick Barbarossa, the complex dominated Nijmegen right up until 1769, when the palace was demolished and the stonework sold; what was left suffered further demolition when the French occupied the town in 1796. In September 1944, the town's bridges were captured by the Americans in Operation Market Garden (see box, p.275), but the failure at Arnhem put Nijmegen on the front line for the rest of the war. The results are clear to see: the old town was largely destroyed and its modern replacement is pleasant if largely undistinguished.

Arrival, information and accommodation

From Nijmegen's **train** and **bus stations**, it's a good ten-minute trudge northeast to the town centre; if you can't face the walk, take any local bus from the station. The **VVV** is housed in the **Stadsschouwburg** at Keizer Karelplein 32/H, halfway between the stations and the town centre (Mon–Fri 9.30am–5.30pm, Sat 10am–5pm; ℡0900 112 2344, Ⓦwww.vvvnijmegen.nl).

Accommodation is fairly thin on the ground, so it's a good idea to book in advance. The basic but clean *Apollo* is on the street running east off Keizer Karelplein, at Bisschop Hamerstraat 14 (℡024/322 3594, Ⓦwww.apollo-hotel -nijmegen.nl; ❷), and there's a small B&B, with two rooms and a self-service breakfast, at the *Stadsbrouwerij De Hemel* brewery, Franse Plaats 1 (℡024/360 6167, Ⓦwww.brouwerijdehemel.nl ❷). If you're stuck, try the recently renovated *Atlanta*, right in the centre at Grote Markt 38 (℡024/360 3000,

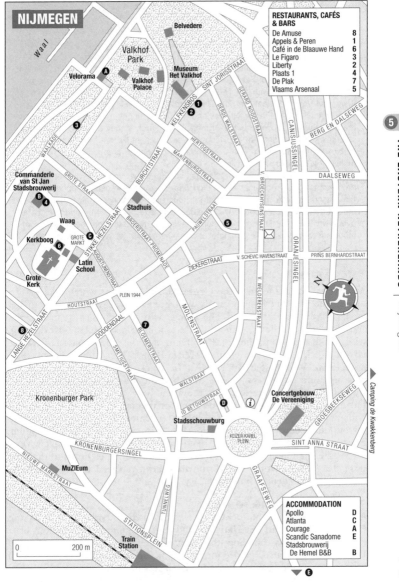

NIJMEGEN

Waal

Belvedere

Valkhof Park

Museum Het Valkhof

Velorama Ⓐ

Valkhof Palace

SINT JORISSTRAAT

DERDE WALSTRAAT

GERARD NOODSTRAAT

CANISIUSSINGEL

BERG EN DALSEWEG

KELFKENSBOS ❶
❷

❸

WAALKADE

GROTE STRAAT

BURCHTSTRAAT

HERTOGSTRAAT

MARIENBURGSTRAAT

DAALSEWEG

V. BROECKHYSENSTRAAT

Commanderie van St Jan Stadsbrouwerij Ⓑ ❹

STIKKE HEZELSTRAAT

Stadhuis

BROERSTRAAT PROMENADE

PAUWELSTRAAT

❺

Waag
Ⓒ GROTE MARKT

Kerkboog ❻

AUGUSTIJNENSTRAAT

Latin School

ZIEKERSTRAAT

V. SCHEVIC HAVENSTRAAT

ORANJESINGEL

PRINS BERNHARDSTRAAT

Grote Kerk

HOUTSTRAAT

PLEIN 1944

V. WELDERENSTRAAT

LANGE HEZELSTRAAT

❽

DODDENDAAL

BLOEMERSTRAAT

❼

MOLENSTRAAT

N

Kronenburger Park

SMETIUSSTRAAT

WALSTRAAT

10 BETOUWSTRAAT

Ⓓ

Stadsschouwburg

ⓘ

Concertgebouw De Vereeniging

GROESBEEKSEWEG

► Camping de Kwakkenberg

KEIZER KAREL PLEIN

SINT ANNA STRAAT

KRONENBURGERSINGEL

NIEUWE MARKTSTRAAT

MuZIEum

TUNNELWEG

STATIONSPLEIN

GRAAFSEWEG

Train Station

0   200 m

▼ Ⓔ

RESTAURANTS, CAFÉS & BARS

De Amuse	8
Appels & Peren	1
Café in de Blaauwe Hand	6
Le Figaro	3
Liberty	2
Plaats 1	4
De Plak	7
Vlaams Arsenaal	5

ACCOMMODATION

Apollo	D
Atlanta	C
Courage	A
Scandic Sanadome	E
Stadsbrouwerij De Hemel B&B	B

Ⓦwww.atlanta-hotel.nl; ❷), which is reasonably priced for its central location, although it can be rather noisy. Overlooking the river Waal, the *Courage*, Waalkade 108 (☎024/360 4970, Ⓦwww.hotelcourage.nl; ❸), is a classy alternative, right next to the Velorama museum. More luxury can be found a bit further out of town at the *Scandic Sanadome*, Weg door Jonkerbos 90 (☎024/359 7280, Ⓦwww.sanadome.nl; ❼), and although rooms here are expensive, the use of their indoor and outdoor thermal baths is included in the price.

5

The Four-Day Marches

Every year on the third Tuesday of July, Nijmegen is flooded with walking fanatics taking part in the **Nijmeegse Vierdaagse**, the world's largest walking event, (🅦www.4daagse.nl) attracting more than 45,000 participants, who go for the 30-, 40- or 50-kilometre route depending on age and gender, all receiving the much-coveted **Four Day Marches Cross** at the end. The event dates back to 1909 when "four days" was a popular theme, with events like four days' cycling, rowing and horseback riding. It was not until 1928 that the Four Day Marches became international, with delegations from Germany, France, Norway and the United Kingdom taking part. Even after the war, which destroyed much of Nijmegen, the marches carried on, thanks to many volunteers and fundraisers. Nowadays over 60 countries are represented in the exhausting walking event, with everyone from children to grandparents taking part, making this a real family occasion.

The image of the marches was damaged in 2006 when two people died on the first day because of extreme heat. The march was cancelled amid debates about whether the authorities could have prevented it, though the traditional **parties** that happen around the event continued (🅦www.vierdaagsefeesten.nl), with live performances all over town. If you're planning to visit during the event, make sure you book your accommodation well ahead either at a hotel or with a host family (🅦www.vierdaagsebed.nl).

The Town

At the heart of the town is the **Grote Markt**, much of which managed to survive the war and is surprisingly well preserved, in stark contrast to the modern shops across the road. The **Waag**, with its traditional stepped gables and shuttered windows, stands beside a vaulted passage, the **Kerkboog**, which leads through to the peaceful precincts of the much-renovated Gothic **Grote Kerk** (May–Oct Mon 10.30am–1pm, Tues, Thurs, Fri & Sun noon–5pm, Wed & Sat 10.30am–5pm; check 🅦www.stevenskerk.nl for opening hours out of season). The church, dedicated to St Stephen, is entered around the back to the left, past the attractively carved facade of the old **Latin School**; inside there's some fine Renaissance woodwork. The **tower**, with its vaguely oriental spire, offers a commanding vista over the surrounding countryside (June–Aug Mon 11am, Wed & Sat 2pm & 3.30pm; €4), but the view over the streets beside and behind the church isn't what it used to be: the huddle of medieval houses that once sloped down to the Waal were flattened in World War II and have been replaced by a hopeful but rather sterile residential imitation.

Around the Grote Markt

A few metres north of the Grote Markt, down toward the river, is the **Commanderie van St Jan**, an authentic-looking reconstruction of a seventeenth-century building that now houses the **Stadsbrouwerij De Hemel**, Franse Plaats 1 (guided tours €7 with a drink included, call ☎024/360 6167 for reservations; 🅦www.brouwerijdehemel.nl), which features a brewery museum and a tasting room. To the east of the Grote Markt, Burchtstraat runs roughly parallel to the river to pass the dull reddish-brown brick of the **Stadhuis**, a square, rather severe edifice with an onion-domed tower – another reconstruction after extensive war damage.

The Velorama Nationaal Fietsmuseum

Bike enthusiasts shouldn't miss the **Velorama Nationaal Fietsmuseum**, just a few minutes' walk east of the Grote Markt at Waalkade 107 (National

Bicycle Museum; Mon–Sat 10am–5pm, Sun 11am–5pm, €5; ⓦwww
.velorama.nl). This museum has the largest collection of bicycles and other
human-powered vehicles in Western Europe, over 200 contraptions dating
from the early nineteenth century and displayed over three floors. There
are delicately carved wooden bicycles, a bicycle for five people, penny-
farthings, recumbents and quadricycles – anything and everything that has
helped shape bicycle design in the last few centuries, all lovingly restored and
beautifully displayed – making this the perfect museum to visit in a country
where the bicycle rules.

The Valkhof

In a park beside the east end of Burchtstraat lie the scant remains of the
Valkhof Palace, specifically a ruined fragment of the Romanesque choir of
the twelfth-century palace chapel and, just to the west, a sixteen-sided chapel
built around 1045, in a similar style to the palatinate church at Charlemagne's
capital, Aachen. These bits and pieces are connected by a footbridge to a
belvedere, which was originally a seventeenth-century tower built into the
city walls; today it's a restaurant and a lookout platform with excellent views
over the river.

The neighbouring **Museum Het Valkhof**, Kelfkensbos 59 (Tues–Fri
10am–5pm, Sat & Sun noon–5pm; €7; ⓦwww.museumhetvalkhof.nl), houses a
variety of exhibits with a local flavour, including innumerable paintings of
Nijmegen and its environs, most notably Jan van Goyen's *Valkhof Nijmegen*,
which used to hang in the town hall. Painted in 1641, it's a large, sombre-toned
picture – pastel variations on green and brown – where the Valkhof shimmers
above the Waal, almost engulfed by sky and river. The museum also holds a
substantial collection of more modern paintings, including work by Carel
Willink, Pyke Koch and Raoul Hynckes, as well as a large archeological collection, which gives a good idea of the first Roman settlements both here in
Nijmegen and elsewhere in the Netherlands.

MuZIEum

The most recent addition to the museum scene is the **MuZIEum**, a
ten-minute walk north of the train station at Nieuwe Marktstraat 54
(Museum of Sight; Tues–Fri 1.45–5pm, Sat & Sun 11am–6pm, longer opening
hours during school hols; €8.50; ⓦwww.muzieum.nl). This lively, modern
museum is dedicated entirely to sight – or the lack of it. Visitors can experience what it's like to be blind during a guided tour in pitch black, where you
have to rely on your senses to find your way round; reservations are essential
on ⓣ024/382 8181.

Eating, drinking and nightlife

As you'd expect in a student town, Nijmegen has a wide range of places to
eat and drink at sensible prices. Kelfkensbos and Lange Hezelstraat are
good areas for restaurants (sse p.282) while the Waalkade turns into one big
riverside terrace on summer evenings. Every inch a fashionable town,
Nijmegen attracts some top-name rock **bands**, especially during the
academic year. Most perform at the Concertgebouw De Vereeniging, Keizer
Karelplein 2/D, or the Stadsschouwburg, Keizer Karelplein 32/H; for the
latest information about what's on, check with the VVV. For **films**, the Lux,
Marienburg 38–39, has a good international programme of independent
flicks and some late-night shows.

De Amuse Lange Hezelstraat 64 ☎024/324 5570. With a menu comprising over fifty small bites (nothing exceeding €8.95), this is the ideal fingerfood restaurant. The neighbouring cocktail bar is as trendy as anything you'll find in Amsterdam. Closed Mon.

Appels & Peren Kelfkensbos 29 ☎024/324 1627. Trendy place with lime green accents and appealing dishes like tuna *carpaccio* or grilled halibut. Not expensive either, with mains for €13.50.

Café in de Blaauwe Hand Achter de Hoofdwacht 3. The oldest bar in town, behind the Grote Kerk – a typical brown café with a wide array of beers and *jenevers*.

Le Figaro Waalkade 19. As good as any other café along the Waalkade with a seasonal menu and a three-course meal for €19.50.

Liberty Kelfkensbos 21 ☎024/360 6656. Stylish restaurant with an eclectic mix of European, Asian and South American food. Mains around €22. Closed Mon & Tues.

Plaats 1 Franseplaats 1 ☎024/365 6708. A must in summer – located in the Commanderie van St Jan – with a tree-covered terrace. Creative dishes including poached wolffish and a *confit* of duck go for the amazingly low price of €9. Closed Mon.

De Plak Bloemerstraat 90 ☎024/322 2757. Cheap and mainly organic food, with a large selection of vegetarian dishes.

Vlaams Arsenaal Arsenaalpoort 1 ☎024/324 1750. Traditional Flemish cuisine in an up-to-the-minute setting. One side of the building houses the café, the other the brasserie. A three-course menu will set you back €27.50.

Twente

East of the River IJssel, the flat landscapes of the west give way to the lightly undulating, wooded countryside of **Twente**, an industrial region within the province of Overijssel whose principal towns – Almelo, Hengelo and Enschede – were once dependent on the textile industry. Hit hard by cheap Asian imports, all three have been forced to diversify their industrial base, with mixed success. The largest town, **Enschede**, still has a serious unemployment problem, but it's the only one you're likely to visit on account of its excellent train connections and first-rate museum, the **Rijksmuseum Twente**.

Enschede

The university town of **ENSCHEDE**, some 50km east of Zutphen, may have a desultory modern centre, but it's a lively place and it hosts regular festivals, events and exhibitions. As ever, the obvious place to start a visit is the main square, the **Markt**, which is home to both the nineteenth-century **Grote Kerk** and the rather more interesting **St Jacobuskerk**, which was completed in 1933 in a sort of neo-Byzantine-meets-Art Deco style with angular copper-green roofs, huge circular windows and an inconclusively lumpy main tower. The **Stadhuis**, a couple of minutes away down Langestraat, was finished in the same year and is also something of an architectural landmark, its brown brick tower topped by four eye-catching blue and gold clocks.

Rijksmuseum Twente

Housed in an Art Deco mansion of 1930, the **Rijksmuseum Twente**, at Lasondersingel 129 (Tues–Sun 11am–5pm; €6; ⓦwww.rijksmuseumtwenthe .nl), possesses an outstanding collection of fine art gifted to the city by a wealthy mill-owning family, the van Heeks. The museum contains two key sections – fifteenth- to nineteenth-century art and modern and contemporary art, primarily Dutch with the emphasis on Expressionism. It is located a fifteen-minute walk north of the centre: go over the train tracks at the crossing beside the station, take the first right, then second left and follow the road to the end.

The collection

Among a fine sample of early religious art, three particular highlights are a set of brilliant blue and gold fragments from a French hand-illuminated missal; a primitive twelfth-century wood carving of Christ on Palm Sunday; and a delightful cartoon strip of contemporary life entitled *De Zeven Werken van Barmhartigheid* ("The Seven Acts of Charity"). Of later canvases, Hans Holbein's *Portrait of Richard Mabott* is typical of his work, the stark black of the subject's gown offset by the white cross on his chest and the face so finely observed it's possible to make out the line of his stubble. Pieter Brueghel the Younger's *Winter Landscape* is also fastidiously drawn, down to the last twig, and contrasts with the more loosely contoured figures and threatening clouds of his brother Jan's *Landscape*. Moving on, Jan Steen's *The Alchemist* is all scurrilous satire, from the skull on the chimneypiece to the lizard suspended from the ceiling and the ogre's whispered advice. Steen also mocks sex, most memorably here in his *Lute Player*, which features a woman with bulging breasts and flushed countenance in the foreground, while on the wall behind is the vague outline of tussling lovers.

High points of the modern and contemporary section include Monet's volatile *Falaises près de Pourville*; a characteristically unsettling canvas by Carel Willink, *The Actress Ank van der Moer*; and examples of the work of less well-known Dutch modernists like Theo Kuypers, Jan Roeland and Emo Verkerk.

Practicalities

Enschede **train** and **bus stations** are on the northwest edge of the town centre, about 600m from the Markt – just follow the signs. The **VVV** is right at the train station, at Stationsplein 1 (Tues–Fri 10am–5.30pm, Sat 10am–2pm; ☎053/432 3200, ⓦwww.vvvenschede.nl). They have a small supply of **private rooms** (❶) and the town also has a couple of central **hotels**, the more promising of which is the three-star *Amadeus*, in an older, two-storey block at Oldenzaalsestraat 103 (☎053/435 7486, ⓦwww.amadeushotel.nl; ❷–❸), on the east side of the town centre.

For something to **eat**, there are plenty of choices around the Markt, with *De Beiaard*, Oude Markt 24, being one of the better places, offering a good selection of draft beers and inexpensive daily specials.

Travel details

Trains

Apeldoorn to: Amersfoort (every 30min; 25min); Deventer (every 30min; 10min); Zutphen (every 30min; 20min).
Arnhem to: Amsterdam CS (every 20min; 1hr 10min); Nijmegen (every 10min; 15min); Roosendaal (every 30min; 1hr 45min); Velp (every 30min; 10min).
Enschede to: Amsterdam CS (every 30min; 2hr); Deventer (every 30min; 45min).
Lelystad to: Amsterdam CS (every 15min; 40min).

Zutphen to: Arnhem (every 30min; 25min); Deventer (every 30min; 15min).
Zwolle to: Amersfoort (every 20min; 35–55min); Amsterdam CS (every 30min; 1hr 15min); Arnhem (every 30min; 1hr); Deventer (every 30min; 25min); Emmen (every 30min; 55min); Groningen (3 hourly; 1hr–1hr 10min); Kampen (every 30min; 10min); Leeuwarden (every 30min; 55min–1hr 5min); Nijmegen (every 30min; 1hr 30min); Schiphol airport (every 30min; 1hr 25min); Steenwijk (every 30min; 25min); Zutphen (every 30min; 35min).

Buses

Doetinchem to: 's-Heerenberg (Mon–Fri every 30min, Sat & Sun hourly; 20min).
Kampen to: Lelystad (Mon–Sat every 30min, Sun hourly; 1hr).
Lelystad to: Kampen (Mon–Sat every 30min, Sun hourly; 55min).
Steenwijk to: Blokzijl (Mon–Fri hourly; 20min); Giethoorn (hourly; 15min); Zwartsluis (hourly; 30min); Zwolle (Mon–Fri hourly; 1hr 10min).

Zwartsluis to: Vollenhove (Mon–Sat every 30min, Sun hourly; 20min).
Zwolle to: Elburg (Mon–Sat every 30min, Sun hourly; 35min); Ens (Mon–Fri every 30min, Sat & Sun hourly; 50min); Giethoorn (Mon–Fri hourly; 1hr); Steenwijk (Mon–Fri hourly; 1hr 10min); Urk (Mon–Fri every 30min; 1hr 30min); Vollenhove (Mon–Fri every 30min, Sat & Sun hourly; 50min); Zwartsluis (Mon–Sat every 30min, Sun hourly; 30min).

The south and Zeeland

CHAPTER 6 # Highlights

✳ **Middelburg** Attractive maritime town, capital of the watery province of Zeeland. See p.289

✳ **The Walcheren coast** Zeeland's windswept coast has some dramatic footpaths and cycle routes. See p.294

✳ **Delta Expo** The Delta Project – a monumental engineering project to protect the Netherlands from flooding – is commemorated in this outstanding exhibition. See p.298

✳ **Carnival at Bergen-op-Zoom** If you're around in February, don't miss the country's most exuberant carnival. See p.303

✳ **Breda** Pretty little town with a stunning Gothic cathedral. See p.304

✳ **'s Hertogenbosch** This lively market town has a picturesque old quarter of alleys and little bridges. See p.309

✳ **Roermond** A popular holiday spot, Roermond makes a good base for exploring the nearby lakes on the Maasplassen and the woods of the National Park De Meinweg. See p.318

✳ **Maastricht** Alluringly cosmopolitan city in the far south, squeezed between the Belgian and German borders. See pp.322–329

▲ Limburg landscape

6

The south and Zeeland

L
ook at a map and you'll see that the southern part of the Netherlands doesn't make much geographical sense at all: in the west it's all islands and rivers, while in the east a dangling sliver of land hooks deep into Belgium, its shape defined by centuries of dynastic wrangling. The west, which comprises the province of **Zeeland**, is classically Dutch, the inhabitants of its small towns and villages spending much of their history either at sea or keeping the sea away from hearth and home. Zeeland suffered its last major flood in 1953 and it was this disaster that kick-started the **Delta Project**, whose complex network of dykes, dams and sea walls, completed in 1986, has prevented any watery repetition. Zeeland has mile upon mile of sandy beach and wide-open landscapes, but many of its old towns and villages have been badly mauled by the developers. Two have, however, survived – **Middelburg**, with its splendid old centre, and **Veere**, every inch a nautical, seafaring port.

Inland lies **Noord–Brabant**, whose arc of industrial towns long bore the brunt of the string of invading armies who marched up from the south. Each of these towns has lots of history but not much else, though both **Breda** and **'s–Hertogenbosch** have fine churches. Noord-Brabant's largest town is **Eindhoven**, home to the multinational electrical company Philips, and from here it's just a few kilometres to the region's third province, **Limburg**, which was badly damaged in World War II. Limburg's principal attraction is **Maastricht**, a city of vitality and virtuosity, which comes complete with a lively restaurant and bar scene as well as a set of first-rate medieval buildings.

Zeeland

Luctor et Emergo, reads **Zeeland**'s slogan: "I struggle and I emerge", a reference to the interminable battle the province has waged with the sea. As its name suggests, the southwestern corner of the Netherlands is bound as much by water as land. Comprising three main peninsulas within the delta of the Rijn (Rhine), the Schelde and the Maas, this cluster of islands and semi-islands is linked by a

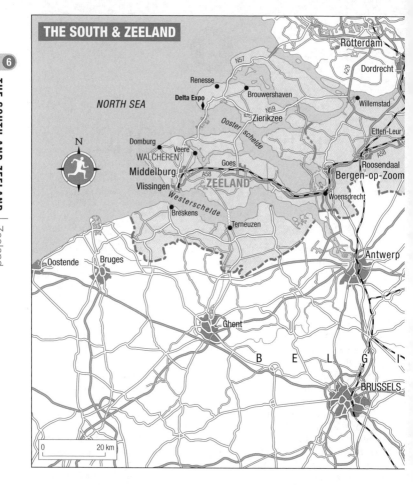

THE SOUTH & ZEELAND

complex network of dykes. This concrete web not only gives protection from flooding but also forms the main lines of communication between each sliver of land. The northernmost landmass, **Goeree-Overflakkee**, a little south of Rotterdam, is connected by two dams to **Schouwen-Duiveland**, while further south are **Noord and Zuid Beveland**, the western tip of which adjoins **Walcheren**. Furthest south of all is **Zeeuws Vlaanderen**, lying across the blustery waters of the Westerschelde on the Belgian mainland.

Before the Delta Project (see p.298) secured the area, fear of the sea's encroachment had prevented any large towns developing and consequently Zeeland remains a condensed area of low dunes and nature reserves, popular with holidaymakers escaping the cramped conurbations nearby. The province also has more sun than anywhere else in the Netherlands: the winds blow the clouds away, with spectacular sunsets guaranteed. Getting around is easy, with bus services making up for the lack of north–south train connections, though undoubtedly the best way to see these islands is to **cycle**, using **Middelburg** as a base and venturing out into its environs.

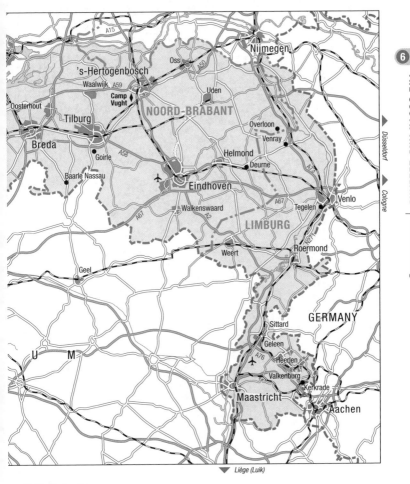

Liège (Luik)

Middelburg

Compact **MIDDELBURG**, the largest town in Zeeland, is also its most likeable. The town's streets preserve some snapshots of medieval Holland, its cobbled alleyways echo the sea-trading days of the sixteenth century, and a scattering of museums and churches provide targets for your wanderings. Middelburg's centre holds a large Thursday **market** and if you can only make it for a day, this is the best time to visit. Set against the imposing backdrop of the Stadhuis and packed with local produce, it's an atmospheric event that's guaranteed to draw a crowd – including, if you're lucky, elderly couples in traditional costume. With a reasonable range of accommodation, Middelburg also makes an ideal base for exploring the surrounding area, including Veere, Domburg and the Delta Project, with good bus connections and excellent cycling along Walcheren's windswept coast.

One of the town's most colourful **festivals** is **Ringrijderij**, a horseback competition where riders try to pick off rings with lances. It takes place in

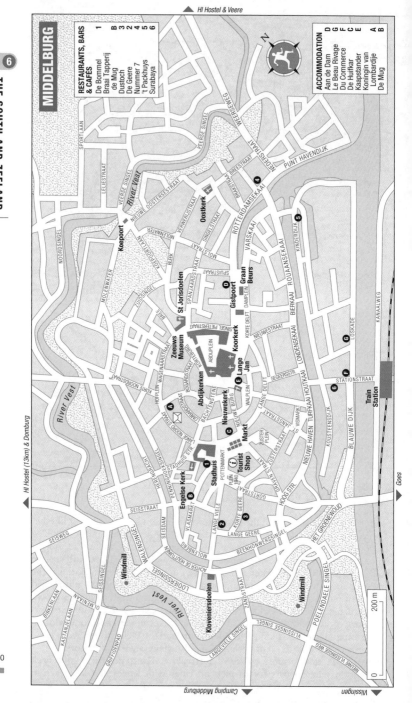

MIDDELBURG

RESTAURANTS, BARS & CAFÉS
De Bommel	1
Braai Tapperij de Mug	B
Dustoch	3
De Geere	2
Nummer 7	4
't Packhuys	5
Surabaya	6

ACCOMMODATION
Aan de Dam	D
Le Beau Rivage	G
Du Commerce	F
De Huifkar	C
Kaapstander	E
Koningin van Lombardije	A
De Mug	B

August at the Koepoort city gate near Molenwater, and in the central Abdijplein on one day in July; check with the tourist office for dates. Another major draw is the annual **Mosselfeesten** (Ⓦwww.mosselfeesten.nl) on the last weekend in July, celebrating the arrival of the fresh black mussels, of which Zeeland is particularly proud. The festival takes place around the Vlasmarkt, with live music and restaurants offering their own version of this regional speciality.

Arrival and information

From the **train station** and **bus station**, it's just a short walk to the town centre, across the bridge on Loskade, opposite the hotel *Du Commerce*. Head up Segeersstraat and Lange Delft and you find yourself on the Markt. Middelburg does not have an official VVV office, but you should be able to find whatever you need at the privately run **Tourist Shop** at Markt 65/C (Mon–Fri 9.30am–5.30pm, Sat 9.30am–5pm; ℡0118/674 300, Ⓦwww.touristshop.nl), which has details of summer events in the city, a list of **private rooms** and is well stocked with cycling maps for touring Zeeland's coast.

Boat trips and guided tours

Open-top **boats** offer trips on the canals, leaving from the Lange Viele bridge on Achter de Houttuinen (April–Oct daily 11am–5pm; €6; Ⓦwww.rondvaart middelburg.nl). The return boat trip to Veere (May–Sept daily 10.15am & 2pm; €13; Ⓦwww.rederij-dijkhuizen.nl) leaves from near the train station. The Tourist Shop has a **guided walking tour** (April–Oct daily except Fri 1.30pm; €4.75), which leaves from their office and lasts an hour and a half, taking in the city's main landmarks. **Horse-drawn carriage rides** operate from Nieuwe Burg 38–40 (July & Aug Mon–Sat 11.30am–4.30pm, Sun 1–4.30pm; €3; 20min).

Accommodation

Most of Middelburg's **hotels** and **pensions** are just minutes from the Markt. There is not an awful lot to choose from, so it's wise to book in advance, especially in summer.

The nearest **campsite**, *Camping Middelburg*, Koninginnelaan 55 (℡0118/625 395, Ⓦwww.campingmiddelburg.nl; April–Oct), is about 2km out of town: head down Zandstraat and Langeviele Weg, or take bus #53 or #55 (every 30min) from the station.

Aan de Dam Dam 31 ℡0118/643 773, Ⓦwww .aandedamhotel.nl. A well-kept treasure with only seven suites, all in different styles and varying sizes, plus a garden that's a real oasis in summer. ❷–❺

Du Commerce Loskade 1 ℡0118/636 051, Ⓦwww.hotelducommerce.nl. You really can't miss this hotel right in front of the train station, with great views over the canal. The weary interior could do with a makeover. ❹

De Huifkar Markt 19 ℡0118/612 998, Ⓦwww .hoteldehuifkar.nl. Located above the cafés of the Markt, this hotel can be noisy. Book ahead as they only have five rooms. ❷

Kaepstander Koorkerkhof 10 ℡0118/640 767, Ⓦwww.kaepstander.nl. Small rooms, but with great views of the Abbey Churches and a relaxing café downstairs. Breakfast is very simple. ❶

Koningin van Lombardije Blindehoek 12 ℡0118/637 099. The cheapest option in town is this friendly hotel, which also boasts a gargantuan breakfast. ❶

Le Beau Rivage Loskade 19 ℡0118/638 060, Ⓦwww.lebeaurivage.nl. This small hotel has only nine rooms, all elegantly furnished with old Chesterfields and the like. Free wi-fi is included. ❸–❹

De Mug Vlasmarkt 54–56 ℡0118/614 851, Ⓦwww.demug.nl. Four spacious rooms are located in a completely renovated building, also housing a restaurant, popular bar and shop with local specialities, and with friendly owners who'll make you feel at home immediately. By far the most appealing and authentic option in town. ❸

The Town

Sitting pretty on Walcheren island, **Middelburg** is an appealing town to explore, small enough to cover on foot and dotted with architectural clues that bear witness to its rich maritime past. The town owes its early growth to its position on a bend in the River Arne, making it easy to defend. The slight elevation on which it was built gave the settlement protection from the sea and its streets slope down to the harbour. Look out for the surviving stone blocks at the end of **Brakstraat**, into which wooden planks were slotted, then bolstered with sandbanks, acting as a temporary dyke when floods threatened.

Though its **abbey** was founded in 1120, Middelburg's isolation restricted its development until the late Middle Ages when, being at the western end of the Scheldt estuary, it became rich off the back of the wool and cloth trade with Antwerp, Bruges and Ghent. Thereafter, it became both the market and administrative centre of the region. The town's **street names** – Houtkaai ("Timber Dock"), Korendijk ("Grain Dyke"), Bierkaai ("Beer Dock") – reveal how diverse its trade became, while house names like "London" and "Samarkand" tell of the routes Middelburg's traders plied. Kuiperspoort ("Barrelmaker's Port") is an alleyway off **Rouaansekaai** along which a string of warehouses have been restored, many of them now occupied by artists and musicians.

The Stadhuis

The town's **Stadhuis** is generally agreed to be Zeeland's finest building, a wonderfully eclectic mix of architectural styles. The towering Gothic facade is especially magnificent, dating from the mid-fifteenth century and built to a design by the Keldermans family from Mechelen in modern-day Belgium. Inside is the **Vleeshal**, a former meat hall that now houses changing exhibitions of contemporary art, which can be visited on conducted tours. A forty-minute **tour** of the Stadhuis (April–Oct daily except Fri 11.30am & 3.15pm; €4.25) takes in the mayor's office, council chambers and various reception rooms.

The Stadhuis's impressive pinnacled **tower** was added in 1520, but it's as well to remember that this, along with the Stadhuis itself and much of Middelburg's city centre, is only a reconstruction of the original. On May 17, 1940, the city was all but flattened by German bombing in the same series of raids that destroyed Rotterdam. Restoration was a long and difficult process, but so successful that you can only occasionally tell that the city's buildings have been patched up.

The Abdijkerken

Badly damaged on several occasions, most recently by the Germans in 1940, Middelburg's **Abdijkerken** ("Abbey Churches") complex, on Onderdentoren, comprises three churches (April–Oct Mon–Fri 10.30am–5pm; May–Aug also Sat & Sun 1.30–5pm; free), parts of which date back to the thirteenth century. Not that much remains from the abbey's salad days as a centre of Catholic worship and there's a reason for this: Middelburg was an early convert to Protestantism following the uprising against the Spanish, and in 1574 William the Silent's troops ejected the monks and converted the abbey to secular use. Thereafter, the complex was used by all and sundry, becoming at one time a gun factory and at another a mint, before the three churches were turned over to the Protestants.

Among the ecclesiastical trio, the **Nieuwe Kerk** has an organ case of 1692; the **Wandel Kerk** holds the triumphalist tomb of admirals Jan and Cornelis Evertsen, brothers killed fighting in a naval battle against the English in 1666; and the **Koor Kerk** retains the oldest decoration, including a fine Nicolai organ of 1478. Best of all, however, is the complex's landmark 91-metre **tower**, known locally as **Lange Jan** (Long John; April–June, Sept & Oct Mon–Sat 10am–4pm;

July & Aug daily 10am–5pm; €4), whose **carillon** plays every quarter-hour, with additional concerts year-round. Climb the 207 steps of the **tower** and you'll be treated to some fine views: in clear weather, the view from the top of the tower stretches across Walcheren and as far as the Zeelandbrug and the eastern Scheldt, all of which gives a good idea of how vulnerable the province is to the ebbs and flows of the sea.

The Zeeuws Museum and the Damplein

At the rear of the abbey, housed in what were once the monks' dormitories, the recently revamped **Zeeuws Museum** (Tues–Sun 10am–5pm; €8; ⓦwww .zeeuwsmuseum.nl) holds a mixed bag of a collection with the emphasis on the Zeeland area. The museum has a small but fine collection of paintings by Adriaan Coorte, Joris Hoefnagel and the twentieth-century realist painter Charley Toorop. There are also lively tapestries, commissioned by the local authorities between 1591 and 1604 to celebrate the naval battles against the Spanish, and a comprehensive display of local costumes. Take note that regular changing exhibitions often take over large parts of the museum, so the permanent collection is not always on display.

East of the abbey, **Damplein** was restored to its original width by the demolition of a couple of rows of houses. It forms a quieter focus for bars than the Markt and is the site of the **Graanbeurs**, a grain exchange rebuilt in the nineteenth century and today containing some intriguing and humorous stone plaques by international artists – a project known as "Podio del Mondo per l'Arte".

Kloveniersdoelen

While the streets around the Abdijkerken and Stadhuis are the most atmospheric, it's worth walking to the western edge of town to reach the landmark of the **Kloveniersdoelen** at the end of Langeviele. Built in 1607 in exuberant Flemish Renaissance style, this was the home of the city's civic guard, the Arquebusiers, until the end of the eighteenth century, later becoming the local headquarters of the East India Company, and later still a military hospital. Restored in 1969 (as you might guess if you spot the weather vane), it's now a recital hall and is renowned for presenting new and experimental music.

Eating and drinking

Most of Middelburg's **bars**, **cafés** and **restaurants** are on or near the Markt with a particular concentration along Vlasmarkt. Many are tourist-oriented and pricey for what you get, but there is a sprinkling of top-notch places too.

On Thursdays, **market** stalls supply limitless cheap and tasty snacks, especially fresh fish and seafood. Look out for *bolus*, a circular sweetbread first brought to Middleburg by Portuguese Jews and best served hot with butter and a cup of coffee.

De Bommel Markt 85. This is the pick of the bars along here, although there's not much to choose between them at weekends; it's open seven days a week and is convenient for a quick bite.

Braai Tapperij De Mug Vlasmarkt 56 ☏0118/614 851. Good Dutch–French cooking (mussels in season) at moderate prices, an excellent array of beers, and occasional live jazz, all in an old-fashioned setting decorated with aged cognac barrels.

Dustoch Korte Geere 16. This colourful and cheap café is part of a project placing people with mental disabilities in jobs, and includes a children's menu.

De Geere Lange Viele 55 ☏0118/613 083. Daily specials for €8.50 and cheap beer are on offer at this centrally located café with red-brick walls and smart chandeliers. Closed Mon.

Nummer 7 Rotterdamsekaai ☏0118/627 077. This cosy restaurant with only a few tables serves a seven-course appetizers menu for €45, including tasty dishes like sea bass with lime dressing and scallops combined with fresh seasonal products. Closed Mon.

't Packhuys Kinderdijk 82 ☏0118/647 064. Located in an old warehouse with a great water-front terrace, this maritime-themed restaurant serves fabulous food like lobster soup, salads and lambs racks. Mains around €20.

Surabaya Stationstraat 20 ☏0118/635 914. A slightly run-down Indonesian restaurant specializing in Javan food, with reasonably priced rijsttafels and a €19.50 evening buffet. Closed Mon.

Listings

Bookshop De Drukkerij, Markt 51, has a wide selection of books, internet access and a popular café centred around a communal table.

Markets General market on the Markt is on Thurs (8.30am–4pm); there's also a book and curio market on Mon (April–Oct, 11am–5pm). Vismarkt has a flea market on the first Sat of the month (except Jan; 8am–4pm), and an art and antique market in summer (June–Aug Thurs 9am–4pm).

Police Achter de Houttuinen 10 ☏0900 8844.

Post office Lange Noordstraat 48 (Mon 10am–5.30pm, Tues–Fri 9am–5.30pm, Sat 9am–5pm).

Taxi Taxicentrale ☏0118/612 600 or 601 100.

Around Middelburg: the Walcheren coast

The **coast** north and west of Middelburg offers some of the Netherlands' finest beaches and excellent walking and cycling, although on midsummer weekends parts of it virtually disappear beneath the crowds of Dutch and German holidaymakers. Bus #53 from Middelburg station (hourly) cuts a pleasant rural route northwest to **OOSTKAPELLE**, just 12km away and notable for its striking church tower. It then proceeds on past the thirteenth-century **Kasteel Westhove**, now home to the fine ⚑ **Domburg HI hostel** (☏0118/581 254, ⓦwww.stayokay.com; dorms €30), which comes complete with a moat and is set amid a nature reserve. You can rent bikes here (€8.25 per day) and it's only a short stroll to the beach. Next door at Duinvlietweg 6, the **Terra Maris Museum** (May–Oct daily 10am–5pm; Nov–April Wed–Fri noon–4pm, Sat & Sun noon–5pm; €5.25; ⓦwww.terramaris.nl) has an aquarium, displays on local flora and fauna and a comprehensive explanation of the history of Zeeland. Oostkapelle's **VVV** is at Lantsheerstraat 1 (hours vary but usually Mon–Sat 9.30am–5pm; closed lunch; ☏0118/582 910, ⓦwww.vvvzeeland.nl).

Domburg and around

A couple of kilometres further on from Oostkapelle, also on the route of bus #53, **DOMBURG** is the area's principal resort, a favourite haunt for artists since early last century when Jan Toorop gathered together a group of like-minded painters (including, for a while, Piet Mondrian), inspired by the coastal scenery and the fine quality of the light. Toorop built a pavilion to exhibit the paintings and the building has been recycled as the **Marie Tak van Poortvliet Museum Domburg**, Ooststraat 10a (April–Oct Tues–Sun 1–5pm; €3; ⓦwww.marietakvanpoortvlietmuseumdomburg.nl), where exhibitions display works by members of the group. Museum apart, the main reason to come to Domburg is to walk over the dunes and through the woods or to cycle the coastal path. An easy ride 7km southwest of Domburg is **WESTKAPELLE**, a quieter beach resort with a picturesque lighthouse and a critical spot where the dyke was breached during the 1953 flood (see box, p.298).

Cycling around Walcheren

Countless **cycling** options are available to make the most of **Walcheren's** handsome coastline, with plenty of refreshments en route. With limited public transport available to transport bikes, most routes are best completed as loops. As a rule of thumb, red cycleway signs indicate utility paths, often parallel to a main road, while the green signs denote more scenic alternatives.

Possible day-trips include cycling west to **Domburg**, picking up signs to the Domburg HI hostel and continuing through the woods to **Breezand**. A cycleway follows the polder to **Veere**, from where you can ride alongside the Walcheren canal, cutting back to Middelburg. Alternatively, pick up the same canal out of town to **Vlissingen**, joining the cycleway that runs between dune and woodland to **Zoutelande** and **Westkapelle**: there's a fabulous stretch of dyke to cycle along in the direction of Domburg with spectacular sunsets out to sea and a photogenic lighthouse. A red-signposted cycle path leads directly back to Middelburg.

If Zeeland's well-founded reputation for blustery winds is putting you off, pay a visit to one of Middelburg's more unusual factories. **M5**, at Nieuwe Kleverskerkseweg 23 (℡0118/628 759, ⑳www.m5-ligfietsen.com), is a company at the cutting edge of bicycle technology: it specializes in **recumbents**, or *ligfietsen* in Dutch. With their low-slung riding position, recumbents are not only fun and comfortable to ride but will also slice through Zeeland's fiercest headwinds – though it might take a few minutes to learn to ride one. You can rent from M5 for around €20 a day, with significant discounts if renting for a week or more. Otherwise, you can **rent bikes** from Middelburg train station. Alternatively, head for Delta Cycles at Zusterplein 8 (down the alleyway next to the ING bank on Marktplein; ℡0118/639 245). Single-speed bikes here cost €5 per day.

Practicalities

Domburg's **VVV** is at Schuitvlotstraat 32 (April–June, Sept & Oct Mon–Sat 9.30am–12.30pm & 1–5pm; July & Aug Mon–Sat 9.30am–6pm, Sun noon–4pm; Nov–March Mon–Fri 10am–5pm, Sat 10am–2pm, Sun 10am–4pm; ℡0118/581 342, ⑳www.vvvzeeland.nl) – ask the bus driver to drop you nearby. They'll help with accommodation and provide you with a map of the village. Staff can recommend dozens of **pensions** – *Duinlust* is a safe bet at Badhuisweg 28 (℡0118/582 943, ⑳www.hotelduinlust.nl; ❶–❷), within easy walking distance of the beach. For something more upmarket try the *Strandhotel Duinheuvel* (℡0118/581 100; ⑳www.wilduin.nl; ❸) with 35 tastefully decorated rooms in minimalist style and an art gallery downstairs, or the next-door *Hotel Wilhelmina* (same contact information; ❸–❹). There are several **campsites**, the nearest being *Hof Domburg* at Schelpweg 7 (℡0118/588 200, ⑳www.hofdomburg.nl), a few minutes' walk west of town.

If you plan on staying a bit longer, a truly unique experience is staying right on the beach in a modern and well-equipped **beach house** (⑳www.slaapzand.nl; €440 for a weekend, €680 for a week) sleeping up to five people. Advance reservations are advised.

Domburg has plenty of simple **cafés**: try the great pizzas at *Pizzeria Milano* at 't Groentje 11 (℡0118/581 251) or the excellent seafood at *MarktZes* located at Markt 6 (℡0118/582 373). *Tramzicht*, on Stationstraat 8, is the best **bar**, with themed parties attracting a youthful crowd.

Vlissingen

VLISSINGEN (Flushing), just 5km south of Middelburg, was previously an important ferry terminus, but its role as a hub for transport to Belgium has been reduced by the completion of the tunnel between Ellewoutsdijk and Terneuzen, a little way to the east. There's not an awful lot to see in the town, although the maritime museum warrants a couple of hours, and the assorted shipping that plies the choppy Westerschelde estuary has an appeal of its own.

Arrival, information and accommodation

Vlissingen **train station** is located in the harbour, next to the ferry terminal to Breskens (see box below) and an inconvenient ten-minute bus ride from the town centre. Coming from Middelburg, it is wiser to catch **bus** #55, #56 or #58 from Middelburg train station as these services drop you off right in the centre of Vlissingen; the journey takes about 25 minutes. Vlissingen **VVV** is at Oude Markt 3 (July & Aug Mon 11am–5.30pm, Tues–Fri 9.30am–5.30pm, Sat 9.30am–5pm; Sept–June Mon 1–5.30pm, Tues–Fri 9.30am–5.30pm, Sat 9.30am–5pm; ☎0118/422 190, ⓦwww.vvvzeeland.nl). It has a list of **pensions**, including the nearby *Pension Marijke*, Coosje Buskenstraat 88 (☎0118/415 062, ⓦwww.pensionmarijke.nl; ❶), with simple rooms, and *Belgische Loodsen Societeit*, on the seafront near the end of Nieuwendijk at Boulevard de Ruyter 4 (☎0118/413 608, ⓦwww.bsoos.nl; ❶–❷), with plain and basic rooms, but a fabulous view of passing ships; the VVV also has information on local cycling routes.

The Town

Vlissingen's workaday centre should not detain you long, though you might drop by the improbably named **Cornelia Quackhofje**, an eighteenth-century almshouse for sailors, just north of the Lange Zelke shopping precinct. For more atmosphere, head for the **harbour**, whose bundle of pavement cafés and fresh fish-and-chip stalls is popular with Dutch and German tourists. The **Zeeuws Maritiem "Muzeeum"** at Nieuwendijk 11 (Mon–Fri 10am–5pm, Sat & Sun 1–5pm; €8; ⓦwww.muzeeum.nl) is the place to gen up on Zeeland's strong maritime traditions. The museum is divided into four themes – the sea, trade, glory and adventure. Multimedia presentations (in Dutch) explain the sea's crucial role in shaping Zeeland's livelihood, while excellent audiovisuals reconstruct scenes of naval battles to dramatic effect. Displays include wares shipped along the trading routes of the Dutch East Indies – nutmeg, ginger, salt, tea, silver, porcelain and even bricks.

Vlissingen to Belgium by tunnel and ferry

The 6.6-kilometre **tunnel** beneath the Westerschelde, linking Ellewoutsdijk and Terneuzen, is open 24 hours a day; the toll for cars is €4.70. The **ferry** across the Westerschelde between Vlissingen and Breskens takes 20min and carries foot passengers and bicycles only. Buses #56 and #57 from Vlissingen town centre, via the train station, run to the port. Ferry departures from Vlissingen are daily (every 30min 5.45am–9.55pm), and there are buses on the other side from Breskens to the Belgian town of Bruges. In the opposite direction, the ferry departs Breskens daily (every 30min 6.15am–10.25pm). Tickets are €2.65 per person each way, with a 90c surcharge for bicycles. Check ⓦwww.bba.nl for up-to-date information.

Families will enjoy **Het Arsenaal**, on Arsenaalplein (July & Aug daily 10am–8pm; hours vary outside season but generally daily 10am–7pm; last admission 2hr before closing; €13; ⓦ www.arsenaal.com), a theme park where you can go on a simulated sea voyage, climb an observation tower and walk on a mock-up sea bed among tanks of sharks.

The Westerschelde

The blustery **walk** along the Nieuwendijk offers views of the enormous vessels that sail the Westerschelde. Keeping to a narrow, often tortuous route, these container ships must negotiate the shallow waters and shifting sandbanks that sometimes reveal centuries-old wrecks. Further round the harbour, the promenade has a pleasant seaside feel, with a **beach** at the end. Alternatively, you can **rent a bike** from the train station next to the ferry terminal – it has a wide selection, including recumbents – and continue past the promenade on the green-signposted cycle path to Dishoek and Zouteland; along the way there are plenty of opportunities to lock your bike and hike up and over the dunes, emerging onto a beach that runs for miles.

Eating and drinking

Vlissingen has a fair share of decent places to **eat** and – as you might expect – fresh seafood is the lead item on many a menu. *De Gecroonde Liefde* (☎0118/441 194), next to the maritime museum, is your best bet for lunch, with tasty sandwiches and home-baked apple pie. *Soif* (☎0118/410 516), close to the harbour at Bellamypark 14, specialises in fresh oysters and salmon and has occasional live music, while *De Beurs* (☎0118/410 295), located in a beautifully restored building on Beursplein 11, has a good terrace overlooking the harbour.

Veere

VEERE, some 8km northeast of Middelburg, is an attractive little town by the banks of the Veerse Meer that makes for an amenable half-day visit. Nowadays, it's a centre for all things maritime, its small harbour jammed with yachts and its cafés packed with weekend admirals, but a handful of buildings and a large church point to a time when Veere was wealthy and quite independent of other, comparable towns in Zeeland.

Veere went down the economic tubes with the decline of the wool trade. The opening of the Walcheren canal linking the town to Middelburg and Vlissingen, in the nineteenth century gave it a stay of execution, but the construction of the Veersegatdam and Zandkreekdam in the 1950s finally sealed off the port to seagoing vessels, and simultaneously created a freshwater lake ideal for watersports.

The Town

Veere made its fortune through a fortuitous Scottish connection: in 1444 a certain Wolfert VI van Borssele, the lord of Veere, married Mary, daughter of James I of Scotland. As part of the dowry, van Borssele was granted a monopoly on trade with Scottish wool merchants and, in return, Scottish merchants living in Veere were granted special privileges. A number of their houses still stand, best of which are those on the dock facing the harbour: **Het Lammetje** (The Lamb) and **De Struys** (The Ostrich), dating from the mid-sixteenth century, were combined offices, homes and warehouses for the merchants. They now house the **Museum Schotse Huizen** (April–Oct daily 1–5pm; €3;

The Delta Project and the Delta Expo

On February 1, 1953, a combination of an exceptionally high spring tide and powerful northwesterly winds drove the North Sea over the dykes to **flood** much of Zeeland. The results were catastrophic: 1855 people drowned, 47,000 homes and 500km of dykes were destroyed and some of the country's most fertile agricultural land was ruined by salt water. Towns as far inland as Bergen-op-Zoom and Dordrecht were flooded and Zeeland's road and rail network was wrecked. The government's response was immediate and massive. After patching up the breached dykes, work was begun on the **Delta Project**, one of the largest engineering schemes the world has ever seen and one of phenomenal complexity and expense.

The aim was to ensure the safety of Zeeland by radically shortening and strengthening its coastline. The major estuaries and inlets would be dammed, thus preventing unusually high tides surging inland to breach the thousands of kilometres of small **dykes**. Where it was impractical to build a dam – such as across the Westerschelde or Nieuwe Waterweg, which would have closed the seaports of Antwerp and Rotterdam respectively – secondary dykes were to be reinforced. New roads across the top of the dams would improve communications to Zeeland and Zuid-Holland and the freshwater lakes that formed behind the dams would enable precise control of the water table of the Zeeland islands.

It took thirty years for the Delta Project to be completed. The smaller, secondary dams – the **Veersegat**, **Haringvliet** and **Brouwershaven** – were built first to provide protection from high tides as quickly as possible, a process that also enabled engineers to learn as they went along. In 1968, work began on the largest dam, intended to close the Oosterschelde estuary that forms the outlet of the Maas, Waal and Rijn rivers. It soon ran into intense opposition from **environmental groups,** who pointed out that the mud flats were an important breeding ground for birds, while the estuary itself was a nursery for plaice, sole and other North Sea fish. The inshore fishermen saw their livelihoods in danger too: if the Oosterschelde were closed the oyster, mussel and lobster beds would be destroyed, representing a huge loss to the region's economy.

The environmental and fishing lobbies argued that strengthening the estuary dykes would provide adequate protection; the water board and agricultural groups raised the emotive spectre of the 1953 flood. In the end a compromise was reached, and in 1976 work began on the **Stormvloedkering** ("Storm Surge Barrier"), a gate that would stay open under normal tidal conditions, allowing water to flow in and out of the estuary, but close ahead of potentially destructive high tides.

Delta Expo

It's on the Stormvloedkering, completed in 1986, that the fascinating **Delta Expo** (April–Oct daily 10am–5.30pm, check website for opening hours out of season; €18.50; ⓦwww.neeltjejans.nl), signposted as Waterland Neeltje Jans, is housed. Only once you're inside the Expo, though, do you get an idea of the scale of the project. It's best to start with the half-hour video presentation before taking in the exhibition, which is divided into three areas: the historical background of the Netherlands' water management problems; the technological developments that enabled the country to protect itself; the environmental consequences of applying the technologies and the solutions that followed. The Surge Barrier (and the Delta Project as a whole) has been a triumphant success: computer simulations predict most high tides, but if an unpredicted rise does occur, the sluice gates close automatically in a matter of minutes.

Transport to the Delta Expo is easy: from Middelburg take bus #133 (2 hourly in summer) from Langevieleweg on the west side of town, or cycle there (1hr 30min) following national cycleway LF16 (noord) alongside open beaches and dunes, past wind turbines and onto the storm barrier itself; there are ample opportunities to peer into the sluice gates and appreciate the full scale of the project. Allow for blustery winds on the way back.

▲ The Delta Project

Ⓦ www.schotsehuizen.nl), a rather lifeless collection of local costumes, old books, atlases and furniture, along with an exhibit devoted to fishing.

Elsewhere, the town centre holds many other fine old buildings, whose ornate workmanship leaves you in no doubt that the Scottish wool trade earned a bundle for the sixteenth- and seventeenth-century burghers of Veere: many of the buildings (which are usually step-gabled with distinctive green and white shutters) are embellished with whimsical details that play on the owners' names or their particular line of business. The **Stadhuis** at Markt 5 (May–Oct daily 1–5pm; €1.50; Ⓦ www.schotsehuizen.nl) is similarly opulent, dating from the 1470s, with an out-of-scale Renaissance tower added a century later. Its facade is decorated with statues of the lords of Veere and their wives (Wolfert VI is third from the left) and, inside, a small museum occupies what was formerly the courtroom.

The Grote Kerk

Of all Veere's buildings the **Grote Kerk** (May–Sept Tues–Sun 11am–5pm; €3) seems to have suffered most: finished in 1560, it was badly damaged by fire a century later and subsequent restorations removed much of its decoration. In 1808 invading British troops used the church as a hospital and three years later Napoleon's army converted it into barracks and stables, destroying the stained glass, bricking up the windows and inserting five floors in the nave. Despite all this damage, the church's blunt 42-metre **tower** (same hours and ticket; last admission 4.30pm) adds a glowering presence to the landscape, especially when seen from the town's watery surroundings. According to the original design, the tower was to have been three times higher, but even as it stands there's a great view from the top, back towards the pinnacled skyline of Middelburg and out across the Veerse Meer.

Practicalities

To reach Veere from Middelburg, catch **bus** #54, which runs hourly, or rent a bike from Middelburg train station (€7.50) and take either the cycle path beside the main road or the circuitous but more picturesque route from the north side of town. Veere **VVV**, Oudestraat 28 (mid-April to June & Sept to mid-Oct daily noon–4pm; July & Aug daily 10am–4.30pm; mid-Oct to mid-April Fri–Sun noon–4pm; ☎0118/506 110, ⓦwww.vvvzeeland.nl), can advise on the rental of all types of watercraft and has details of **private rooms**. The cheaper of Veere's two **hotels** is the recently renovated *'t Waepen van Veere*, Markt 23–27 (☎0118/501 231, ⓦwww.waepenvanveere.nl; ❷–❸), while the *De Campveerse Toren*, Kade 2, is divided over four buildings, all beautifully situated overlooking the water (☎0118/501 291, ⓦwww.campveersetoren.nl; ❹). There are a couple of recommendable **cafés** around the Markt including the *Suster Anna Pannekoekhuis* at Markt 8, which serves pancakes, sandwiches and cakes.

Schouwen-Duiveland

Heading north, the Storm Surge Barrier spans the mouth of the Oosterschelde estuary over to **Schouwen-Duiveland**. Most of the Dutch and German tourists who come here head directly to the western corner of this island for the acres of beach, pine forest and dune that stretches out between **Burgh-Haamstede** and **Renesse**, two villages situated 6km apart. In the summer, this western flank of the island is packed with families and predominantly young holidaymakers, making the most of its waterborne activities. **Zierikzee** further east is a more traditional affair, a miniature Middelburg that makes an appealing base for exploring the area, with some fine trips through the countryside out over one of Europe's longest (and perhaps windiest) bridges nearby.

If you're coming for peace and quiet, you should steer clear of the school holidays. Travel over the season's bookends in June and September and you'll find you have much of the long, pristine beaches to yourself, though the weather can be unpredictable, facilities dwindle with the approach of autumn, and storms can blot the sky.

Renesse

RENESSE, about 8km north of the Barrier, is a modern sprawl of bungalows set just a kilometre from the beach, making an appealing base. Popular with the surfing and windsurfing crowd, its sixteen-kilometre beach is divided in summer into sectors, catering for families, surfers, kite-flyers and naturists. A free, open-top electric **bus** (9am–7pm) plies the length of the beach, linking hotels, campsites and the "Transferium" – the modern bus station on the edge of town that offers changing rooms, showers and bike rental, in an attempt to encourage holidaymakers to abandon their cars at the free car park alongside. Parking at the beach is limited to two hours. **Surfboards** cost €30 a day from Windsurfing Renesse, De Zoom 15 (ⓦwww.windsurfingrenesse.nl), who also provide lessons. Windsurfing equipment can be rented too, but the best spot for windsurfing is at the Brouwersdam, 8km away.

Surfcentrum

The **Surfcentrum**, at Ossenhoek 1, Kabbellaarsbank (☎0111/671 480, ⓦwww.brouwersdam.nl), is an invigorating detour from Renesse, with views across the Grevelingenmeer inlet. Reached by bus #104 (ask the driver for the Port Zélande stop), it's situated halfway along the Brouwersdam, linking Schouwen-Duiveland to Goeree-Overflakkee. The centre offers excellent windsurfing on one side, and one of Europe's cleanest beaches on the other;

renting a board and wetsuit costs €65 a day, or €97.50 for a weekend. Tuition, small sailboats and four-bed dorms (€57.50 per room) are also available.

Practicalities

The area is teeming with hotels, campsites and holiday homes, many of which operate as B&Bs. If you're planning on visiting over the summer, you should book accommodation well in advance. One **hotel** option, situated within walking distance of both town and beach, is *Hotel de Logerij*, Laône 15 (☎0111/462 570, ⊛www.delogerij.nl; ❷), with simple but clean rooms. The **VVV**, Roelandsweg 1 (July & Aug Mon–Sat 9am–7pm; Sept–June Mon–Sat 9am–5pm; mid-May to mid-Sept also Sun 10am–4pm; ☎0900/2020 233, ⊛www.vvvzeeland.nl), has a list of available accommodation, or try the English-language website ⊛www.renesse.nl, which includes lists of accommodation and services. Travel with a tent and you're likely to find a plot of grass to squeeze onto. The VVV sells an excellent map detailing beach allotment, as well as walking and cycling trails on the island (€3) and has a free booklet, *Toegankelijk Schouwen-Duiveland*, on areas suitable for travellers with disabilities.

Zierikzee and around

Schouwen-Duiveland's most interesting town, **ZIERIKZEE**, is situated about 14km east of the Barrier. The town's position at the intersection of shipping routes between England, Flanders and Holland made it an important port in the late Middle Ages and it was famed for its salt and madder – a root that, when dried and ground, produces a brilliant red dye. Nowadays, it's a picturesque town of narrow cobbled streets and traditional gabled facades, and one that makes an ideal base for exploring the area.

Encircled by a defensive canal – and best entered by one of two sixteenth-century watergates – Zierikzee's centre is small and easily explored, easier still if you arm yourself with a map from the **VVV** at Nieuwe Haven 7 (Mon–Sat 10am–4pm; ☎0900 202 0233, ⊛www.vvvzeeland.nl). A few minutes' walk from their office, the Gothic **'s Gravensteen** building, Mol 25 (April–Oct Mon–Sat 10am–5pm, Sun noon–5pm; €2), was once the jail and is today home to a maritime museum, although the building is more interesting than the exhibits: the removal of plaster walls from the old prison cells in 1969 uncovered graffiti and drawings by the prisoners, and the basements contain the most primitive of iron-cage cells. Zierikzee's **Stadhuis** is easy enough to find – just head for the tall spire on Meelstraat 6. Inside, the **Stadhuismuseum** (closed for renovation at the time of writing) has collections of silver, costumes and a regional history exhibition. Also worth seeing is the **Monstertoren** (March–Oct daily 11am–4pm; €2), a tower designed by the Keldermans family, on which work was stopped when it reached 97 of its planned 167 metres.

Practicalities

The VVV has details of **private rooms**, including a lovely self-contained apartment at Minderbroederstraat 36–38 (☎0111/416 759; ❶). Other options include the *Pension Klaas Vaak*, Nieuwe Bogerdstraat (☎0111/414 204, ⊛www .pensionklaasvaak.nl; ❶), with simple rooms but a lovely garden, and the *Hotel Van Oppen China Garden*, Verrenieuwstraat 11 (☎0111/412 288, ⊛www .hotel-van-oppen.nl; ❶–❷), which offers a bit more luxury. Book early during the summer – like the rest of the island, Zierikzee is a magnet for Dutch, German and Belgian tourists. **Bus** #132 shuttles between Goes and Zierikzee in half an hour; it's an hour to Rotterdam on the hourly bus #395.

Dreischor and the Watersnoodmuseum

If you have your own transport – or rent a bike from Bike Totaal, Weststraat 5 – you have plenty of scope for discovering the surrounding countryside and coastline. **DREISCHOR**, 8km northeast, makes a pleasant half-day ride. There, the fourteenth-century St Adriaanskirche lies surrounded by a moat and lush green lawns, encircled by a ring of attractive houses. Complete with waddling geese and a restored *travalje* (livery stable), it's an idyllic setting – although busy on weekends.

Six kilometres out of Zierikzee in the opposite direction in the recently enlarged **Watersnoodmuseum**, Weg van de Buitenlandse Pers 5 **OUWERK-ERIC** (Tues–Sun: April–Oct 11am–5pm; Nov–March 1–5pm; €6; Ⓦ www .watersnoodmuseum.nl), commemorates the great floods of 1953 (see box, p.298), the catalyst for the massive Delta Project. Atmospherically set in four desolate caissons – the original concrete bunkers manoeuvred into plugging a break in the dyke – the museum tells the story chronologically from the disaster to the current and future plans to keep the waters at bay. The first caisson holds construction machinery used in the 1950s, scale models showing the extent of the damage, old photographs and original newsreel footage beamed onto the wall. The second caisson focuses more on the human aspect, with interactive stories about the many victims of the flood. The third and fourth caissons give an insight into the reconstruction phase and future plans to keep Zeeland safe.

Finally, to put colour in your cheeks, you could follow the bike lane over the wind-tunnel-like **Zeelandbrug**, a graceful bridge that spans the Oosterschelde south of Zierikzee. Refreshments are available in **Colijnsplaat** on the other side, where you can rest up having cycled one of the longest bridges in Europe, at 5022m. Prevailing winds will be against you on the way out; expect the journey back to take half the time.

Noord-Brabant

Noord–Brabant, the Netherlands' largest province, stretches from the North Sea to the German border. Woodland and heath make up most of the scenery, the gently undulating arable land in striking contrast to the watery polders of the west. While it's unlikely to form the focus of an itinerary, the instantly likeable provincial capital of **Den Bosch** is well worth an overnight visit, as is **Breda**, whose cobbled and car-free centre enjoys a lively market that pulls in the crowds from far and wide. In contrast, **Eindhoven** lacks the historic interest of these towns, as hardly anything here was spared during World War II. It is, however, renowned for its modern architecture and design and has a fairly vibrant nightlife. North of **Tilburg** is the province's other highlight, for kids at least – the **Efteling** theme park, set deep in the woods.

Originally part of the independent Duchy of Brabant, Noord-Brabant was occupied by the Spanish, and eventually split in two when its northern towns joined the revolt against Spain. This northern part was ceded to the United Provinces in 1648; the southern half formed what today are the Belgian provinces of Brabant and Antwerp. The Catholic influence is still strong here: the region takes its religious festivals seriously and if you're here in February and March, the boozy **carnivals** (especially in **Bergen–op–Zoom** and Den

Bosch) are must-sees. Towns even change their names for the occasion: Den Bosch becomes Oeteldonk, Tilburg is Kruikenstad and people in Bergen-op-Zoom live in Krabbegat during the festivities – tradition deriving from the Burgundy version of carnival. The names refer to what the main industry of the cities used to be. Eindhoven for example becomes Lampegat, referring to Philips producing light bulbs.

Bergen-op-Zoom

BERGEN-OP-ZOOM, just 30km north of Antwerp and about 60km east of Middelburg, is an untidy town, a jumble of old and new buildings that are the consequence of being shunted between various European powers from the sixteenth century onwards. In 1576 Bergen-op-Zoom sided with the United Provinces against the Spanish and as a result was under near-continuous siege until 1622. This war-ravaged theme continued thereafter: the French bombarded the city in 1747 and took it again in 1795, though it managed to withstand a British attack in 1814. Bergen-op-Zoom's saving grace is its famous **February carnival** when almost every inhabitant – as well as revellers from all over Europe – joins in the Tuesday procession. It's a great time to be in the town, although you shouldn't expect to find any accommodation – the whole place gets packed out - so just do as the locals do and party all night. Contact the VVV for the exact dates.

The Town

Walk straight out of the train station and you'll soon find yourself on the **Grote Markt**, most cheerful during summer when it's decked out with open-air cafés and the like. The **Stadhuis**, on the north side of the square (May–Oct Tues–Sun 1–4.30pm; €1.20), is Bergen's most attractive building, spruced up in recent years and comprising three separate houses: to the left of the gateway an alderman's house of 1397, to the right a merchant's house of 1480 and on the far right a building known as "De Olifant", whose facade dates from 1611. All of this is a lot more appealing than the blunt ugliness of the **Grote Kerk**, an unlucky building that's been destroyed by siege and fire innumerable times over the past four hundred years.

Left of the Stadhuis, Fortuinstraat leads to the recently renovated **Markiezenhof Museum**, Steenbergsestraat 8 (Tues–Sun 11am–5pm; €5; Ⓦ www.markiezenhof.nl), a first-rate presentation of a collection that has a little of everything: domestic utensils and samplers from the sixteenth century onwards, sumptuous period rooms and architectural drawings as well as a permanent exhibition on fairground attractions on the top floor. All this is housed in a palace built by Anthonis Keldermans between 1485 and 1522 to a late-Gothic style that gives it the feel of an Oxford college. As for the rest of old Bergen-op-Zoom, little survives: at the end of Lievevrouwestraat, near the entrance to the Markiezenhof, the **Gevangenpoort** is practically all that remains of the old city defences, a solid-looking fourteenth-century gatehouse that was later converted into a prison.

Practicalities

The **VVV**, just off the Grote Markt at Kortemeestraat 19 (Mon 1–5pm, Tues–Sat 10am–5pm; May–Oct also Sun noon–4pm; Ⓣ 0164/277 482, Ⓦ www .vvvbrabantsewal.nl), has details of **private rooms** and issues free maps of the centre. The most central **hotel** is *De Bourgondiër*, Grote Markt 2 (☎0164/254 000, ⓦwww.grandcafehoteldebourgondier.nl; ❷), with thirteen classy, recently revamped rooms and a pleasant café downstairs overlooking the market square. Alternatively, *Beursplein 5* (☎0164/266 377, ⓦwww.hotelrestaurantbeursplein5 .nl; ❷) is a slightly less upmarket option located on the handsomely restored Beursplein square near the Markiezenhof museum. The city also possesses an **HI hostel** (☎0164/233 261, ⓦwww.stayokay.com; dorms €28), which is 4km out of town at Boslustweg 1; take bus #22 from the station and it's a fifteen-minute walk from the Ziekenhuis (hospital) stop.

A variety of **restaurants** are grouped around the Grote Markt and, while the town's drinking scene is not exactly buzzing, *De Hemel* is a lively spot at Moere-grebstraat 35, just off Steenbergsestraat.

Breda

BREDA, about 30km east of Bergen-op-Zoom, is one of the prettier towns of Noord-Brabant, a pleasant, easy-going place to while away a night, maybe two. A magnificent Gothic **cathedral** looms above the three-storey buildings that front its stone-paved main square, which is crammed with stallholders and shoppers on market days. There's a range of well-priced accommodation here too, plus inexpensive restaurants and lively bars, though ultimately it's less appealing than Den Bosch (see p.309) as a base for exploring central Noord-Brabant.

While there's little evidence of it today, Breda developed as a strategic fortress town and was badly damaged following its capture by the Spanish in 1581. The local counts were scions of the House of Nassau, which married into the House of Orange in the early sixteenth century. The first prince of the Orange-Nassau line was **William the Silent**, who spent much of his life in the town and would probably have been buried here, had Breda not been in the hands of the Spanish at the time of his assassination in Delft (see p.174). In 1566 William was among the group of Netherlandish nobles who issued the **Compromise of Breda** – an early declaration against Spanish domination of the Low Countries. The town later fell to the Spanish, was retaken by Maurice, William's son, then captured once more by the Spanish, but finally ceded to the United Provinces in 1648. Curiously, King Charles II of England lived in Breda during part of his long exile and it was here, in 1660, that he issued his **Declaration of Breda**, an offer of amnesty to his former foes which greased the wheels of his return to the English throne.

Breda has an excellent **carnival**, which is celebrated with vim and gusto, and a top-notch, four-day annual **jazz festival** (ⓦwww.bredajazzfestival.nl), when some twenty stages are scattered around the centre; it usually starts on Ascension Day.

Arrival, information and accommodation

Breda has two **VVV** offices, one at Willemstraat 17–19 (Mon 1–5.30pm, Tues–Fri 9.30am–5.30pm, Sat 10am–4pm; ☎0900 522 2444, ⓦwww.vvvbreda .nl), just outside the **train station**, about five minutes' walk from the Grote Markt, where the second office is located at no. 38 (Wed–Fri 10.30am–5.30pm, Sat 10.30am–5pm; July & Aug also Tues 10.30am–5.30pm).

Hotels and **B&Bs** include the classic ☀ *B&B Aan de Singelgracht*, Delpratsingel 14 (☎076/521 6271; ⓦwww.desingelgracht.nl; ❷–❸), within walking distance of the train station and with elegantly redecorated rooms and an amazing eye for detail. Two of the rooms have original *bedstedes*, a bed built in a closet which was used until well into the nineteenth century. A bargain-basement alternative is the surprisingly inexpensive and conveniently located *De Klok* at Grote Markt 26–28 (℡076/521 4082, ⓦwww.hotel-de-klok.nl; ❷), though this fills up quickly in summer. With more money, the *Bliss* hotel, Torenstraat 9 (℡076/533 5980, ⓦwww.blisshotel.nl; ❼), is a must, with nine exclusive suites, located in the chic shopping area in the centre of town.

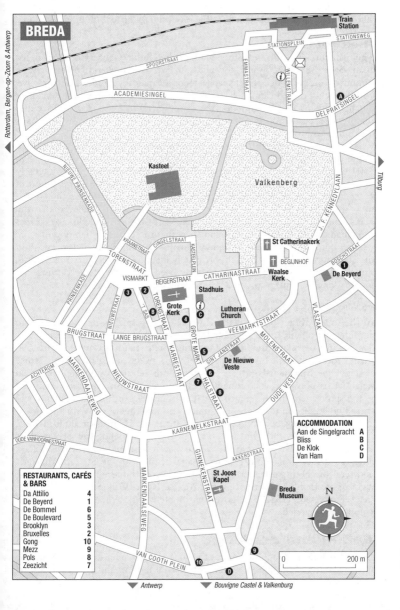

BREDA

Rotterdam, Bergen-op-Zoom & Antwerp

Train Station

STATIONSPLEIN   STATIONSWEG

SPOORSTRAAT

ACADEMIESINGEL

EMMASTRAAT

WILLEMSTRAAT

DELPRATSINGEL

Ⓐ

Tilburg

Kasteel

Valkenberg

NIEUWE PRINSENKADE

J. F. KENNEDYLAAN

KRAANSTRAAT   CINGELSTRAAT

TORENSTRAAT

KASTELPLEIN

† St Catharinakerk

BEGIJNHOF

Waalse Kerk

BOSCHSTRAAT

Ⓑ De Beyerd

VISMARKT   REIGERSTRAAT   CATHARINASTRAAT

PRINSENKADE

NIEUWSTRAAT

'T SAS

Ⓒ③ ②

TORENSTRAAT

Stadhuis

Grote Kerk   ⓘ
Ⓒ ④

Lutheran Church

VEEMARKTSTRAAT

VLASZAK

BRUGSTRAAT   LANGE BRUGSTRAAT

KARRESTRAAT

GROTE MARKT

SINT JANSTRAAT

⑤

De Nieuwe Veste

MOLENSTRAAT

ACHTEROM   MARKENDAALSEWEG

NIEUWSTRAAT

⑦   ⑥

HALSTRAAT   ⑧

OUDE VEST

KARNEMELKSTRAAT

OUDE VANHOORNESTRAAT

MARKENDAALSEWEG

GINNEKENSTRAAT

AKKERSTRAAT

St Joost Kapel

Breda Museum

ACCOMMODATION
Aan de Singelgracht   A
Bliss   B
De Klok   C
Van Ham   D

N

RESTAURANTS, CAFÉS & BARS
Da Attilio   4
De Beyerd   1
De Bommel   6
De Boulevard   5
Brooklyn   3
Bruxelles   2
Gong   10
Mezz   9
Pols   8
Zeezicht   7

VAN COOTH PLEIN

⑩   Ⓓ

⑨

0   200 m

▼ Antwerp   ▼ Bouvigne Castel & Valkenburg

The Town

From the train station, head down Willemstraat and cross the park for the town centre. The **Grote Markt** is the focus of life, site of a general **market** every Tuesday and Friday morning and a secondhand market every Wednesday morning, when stalls loaded with books, bric-a-brac, clothes and small furniture pieces push up against the **Grote Kerk**. From here, head southbound for Breda's main **shopping street** – the Karrestraat, which turns into the Ginnekenstraat – where you'll primarily find large chain stores and the chic covered mall De Barones. There's more upmarket shopping nearby on Hallstraat, lined with boutique stores.

The Grote Kerk

The main attraction on the Grote Markt is the Gothic **Grote Kerk** (Mon–Sat 10am–5pm, Sun 1–5pm; free, tower €4.50; Ⓦwww.grotekerkbreda.nl), whose stunningly beautiful bell tower reaches high into the sky. Inside, the main nave, with its richly carved capitals, leads to a high and mighty central crossing. Like the majority of Dutch churches, the Grote Kerk had its decorations either removed or obscured after the Reformation, but a few murals have been uncovered and they reveal just how colourful the church once was. The Grote Kerk's most remarkable feature is the **Mausoleum of Count Engelbrecht II**, a one-time stadholder and captain-general of the Netherlands who died in 1504 of tuberculosis – vividly apparent in the drawn features of his intensely realistic face. Four kneeling figures (Caesar, Regulus, Hannibal and Philip of Macedonia) support a canopy that carries his armour, so skilfully sculpted that their shoulders seem to sag slightly under the weight. It's believed that the mausoleum was the work of Tomaso Vincidor of Bologna, but whoever created it imbued the mausoleum with grandeur without resorting to flamboyance; the result is both eerily realistic and oddly moving. During the French occupation the choir was used as a stable, but fortunately the sixteenth-century misericords, showing rustic scenes of everyday life, survived. A couple of the carvings are modern replacements – as you'll see from their subject matter.

The Kasteel and around

At the top of Kasteelplein sits the **Kasteel** – too formal to be forbidding and considerably rebuilt since the Compromise of Breda was signed here in 1566. Twenty-five years later the Spanish captured Breda, but it was regained in 1590 thanks to a neat trick by Maurice of Nassau's troops using the Trojan Horse strategy. The **Spanjaardsgat**, an early sixteenth-century watergate with twin defensive bastions just west of the Kasteel, is usually (but inaccurately) identified as the spot where this happened. Today the Kasteel is a military academy and there's no admission to its grounds, unless you join one of the VVV tours.

To the east of Kasteelplein on Catherinastraat, the **Begijnhof**, built in 1531, was until quite recently the only *hofje* in the Netherlands still occupied by Beguines. Today it has been given over to elderly women, some of whom look after the dainty nineteenth-century chapel at the rear, the St Catherinakerk, and tend the herb garden that was laid out several hundred years ago. To the right of the Begijnhof entrance is the **Waalse Kerk** (Walloon Church), where Peter Stuyvesant (1612–72), governor of New York when it was a Dutch colony, was married.

Eating and drinking

Breda has a decent range of places to **eat**, many of them located around the Grote Markt and the streets running off it. Kebab joints and Turkish pizzas are plentiful at Havermarkt, a square packed with hole-in-the-wall eateries for late-night snacks. This is also the best place for **drinking** with plenty of bars that stay open late into the night.

De Beyerd Boschstraat 26. The place to be for connoisseurs of Low Countries' beer, just outside the centre. Closed Wed.
De Bommel Halstraat 3. A large and lively café-bar frequented by a mix of customers – with occasional live music and DJs on weekends.
De Boulevard St Janstraat 3 ⑦076/514 6399. Located in an old theatre, this eetcafé mainly attracts large families and people on a tight budget with its extremely cheap three-course meals and a wide variety of dishes – anything from French to Mexican.
Brooklyn Havermarkt 21 ⑦076/522 8670. Cosmo-politan bar-cum-restaurant with an appetizing menu comprising of a selection of starter-size bites which never exceed €12. Also has a large cocktail list.
Bruxelles Havermarkt 5. This is a great place for Low Countries' beer and cheap daily specialities; also popular for after-work drinks.

Da Attilio Grote Markt 35 ⑦076/514 3900. A decent pizzeria right on the market square, with the classic wine bottles hanging from the ceiling and paintings depicting typical Italian scenes on the walls; there's also a pleasant terrace in summer.
Gong Van Coothplein 24 ⑦076/521 6696. If you're looking for something trendy, stylishly decorated *Gong* is your best bet; Asian food for around €17. Closed Mon.
Mezz Keizerstraat 1 ⑩www.mezz.nl. This concert hall is the best place in town for live music and the occasional DJ on weekends.
Pols Halstraat 15 ⑦076/514 8674. A small and excellent eetcafé with an intimate garden and four courses for €32.50.
Zeezicht Halstraat 2a. This upmarket café is good for its large choice of beers, which makes up for their overprized snacks. Live music on Fridays.

Tilburg and De Efteling

Tilburg, 20km east of Breda, is a humdrum industrial town, its streets a maze of nineteenth-century houses and anonymous modern shopping precincts. The main reason you might find yourself passing through is to change transport on your way to the action-packed **De Efteling** theme park. However, three decent museums within easy walking distance of the train station provide a worthwhile detour. There's no need to explore further – if that's as far as you get, you haven't missed much. That said, thrill seekers shouldn't miss the largest **funfair** in Benelux (⑩www.tilburgsekermis.nl), a ten-day event held annually at the end of July. Surprisingly, Monday is the busiest day of the fair as it was declared Pink Monday about a decade ago, attracting thousands of gays and lesbians from all over the country.

The Town

TILBURG developed as a textile town, though today most of its mills have closed in the face of cheap competition from India and Southeast Asia. The **Nederlands Textielmuseum** is housed in an old mill with an adjacent modern glass building at Goirkestraat 96 (out of the station, walk west along Spoorlaan, turn right along Gasthuisring, and Goirkestraat is the fourth turn on the right; Tues–Fri 10am–5pm, Sat & Sun noon–5pm; €6.50; ⑩www.textielmuseum.nl), and displays aspects of the industry relating to design and textile arts. It houses a collection of textile designs by Dutch artists, a range of looms and weaving machines from around the world, and puts on demonstrations of weaving and spinning.

The **Scryption**, Spoorlaan 434a (Tues–Fri 10am–5pm, Sat & Sun noon–5pm; €5; ⑩www.scryption.nl), is a fancy name for a collection of writing implements – everything from lumps of chalk to word processors. Particularly interesting are the old, intricate typewriters, some of which you can operate yourself.

The **De Pont** modern art museum in a converted woolspinning mill (Tues–Sun 11am–5pm; €6; ⓦwww.depont.nl), a fifteen-minute walk behind the station at Wilheminapark 1, has both a permanent international collection with renowned artists such as James Turrell, Marlene Dumas and Thierry de Cordier, and annual exhibitions; its main gallery space is complemented by more intimate side rooms, previously used for wool storage.

Koningshoeven

Worth a detour is **Koningshoeven monastery** (April–Oct Tues–Sun 11am–7pm; guided tours Tues–Fri 2pm, Sat & Sun 1.30pm & 3.30pm; €10, beer included; ⓦwww.koningshoeven.nl), home to the brewery of **La Trappe**, the only Dutch Trappisten beer. Trappist does not refer to the type of beer, but to the fact that it has been brewed by monks; worldwide there are only seven monasteries that brew this beer. Take bus #141 in the direction of Eindhoven and ask to be dropped at the Trappistenklooster.

Practicalities

The **VVV** is at Spoorlaan 364 (Mon 1–6pm, Tues–Fri 9.30am–6pm, Sat 10am–4pm; ⓣ0900 202 0815, ⓦwww.vvvtilburg.nl), a few minutes' walk from the station – cross the main road and head left. There's little reason to **stay** in Tilburg, but the least expensive room in town is at the *Het Wapen van Tilburg* hotel, next to the VVV at Spoorlaan 362 (ⓣ013/542 2692, ⓦwww.hetwapenvantilburg.nl; ❶), with a decent restaurant and one room fit for backpackers (dorm beds €22.50). There are several good **cafés** around Korte Heuvel; *Studio* at number 7 would be your best bet for some nighttime entertainment with DJs and live jam sessions, while *Stoffel* at number 13 has cheap and decent **food**. Tilburg's largest music venue, *013* at Veemarktstraat 44, hosts many gigs by national and international artists as well as regular dance parties.

De Efteling

Hidden in the woods fifteen minutes' drive north of Tilburg, the prize-winning **De Efteling theme park** (April–Oct daily 10am–6pm, €28; mid-July to late-Aug until 9pm; check website for opening hours in winter; €30; ⓦwww.efteling.nl) is one of the country's principal attractions. It's an excellent day out, and not just for children. The setting is superbly landscaped, especially in spring when the tulips are out. And while it's not Disney, it's certainly vast enough to swallow up the crowds.

Of the rides, Python is the most hair-raising, a rollercoaster twister with great views of the park before plunging down the track; De Bob, a bobsleigh run, is almost as exhilarating although over far too quickly, especially if you've queued for ages. Piranha takes you through some gentle whitewater rapids (expect to get wet). Of the quieter moments, Villa Volta is a slightly unsettling room that revolves around you, after a rather lengthy introduction in Dutch. For kids, the Fairy-Tale Wood, where the park began – a hop from Gingerbread House to Troll King to Cinderella Castle – is popular. Vogel Rok and Droomvlucht are the best of the rides, and there are afternoon shows in the Efteling Theatre. In addition, there are a number of fairground attractions, canoes and paddleboats, and a great view over the whole shebang and the surrounding woods from the Pagoda. A sedate way to check whether you've missed anything is to take the steam train around the park. Prepare yourself for long queues on summer weekends; if you're not up to doing it all, skip the disappointing Haunted Castle and the Carnaval Festival.

Bus #137 runs to De Efteling every half-hour from Tilburg (15min) and from Den Bosch (40min); in summer, the direct services #169 from Tilburg and #168 from Den Bosch are slightly faster. The park is well signposted just off the A261 between Tilburg and Waalwijk; parking costs €8. Though there's little need to **stay**, if you're eager for another day's fun, the *Efteling Hotel* is right by the park (☎0416/287 111, ⓦwww.efteling.nl; ❸). There are plenty of **maps** posted around the complex, and snack bars and refreshment stops at every turn.

's-Hertogenbosch (Den Bosch) and around

Capital of Noord-Brabant, **'s-HERTOGENBOSCH** is a lively town, particularly on Wednesdays and Saturdays, when its Markt fills with traders from all over the province. Better known as **Den Bosch** (pronounced "bos"), it merits exploration over a day or two. The town's full name – "the Count's Woods" – dates from the time when Henry I, Duke of Brabant, established a hunting lodge here in the twelfth century. Beneath the graceful town houses of the old city flows the Binnendieze, its gloomy depths spanned by small wooden bridges. Staggered crossroads, winding streets and the twelfth-century town walls are

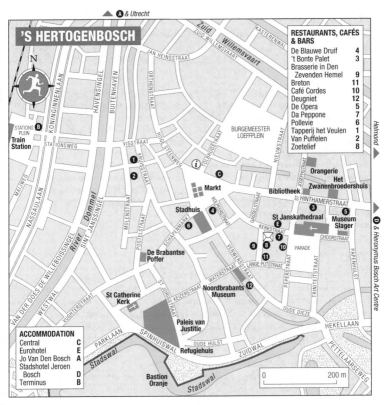

'S HERTOGENBOSCH

▲ Ⓐ & Utrecht

RESTAURANTS, CAFÉS & BARS	
De Blauwe Druif	4
't Bonte Palet	3
Brasserie in Den Zevenden Hemel	9
Breton	11
Café Cordes	10
Deugniet	12
De Opera	5
Da Peppone	7
Pollevie	6
Tapperij het Veulen	1
Van Puffelen	2
Zoetelief	8

ACCOMMODATION	
Central	C
Eurohotel	E
Jo Van Den Bosch	A
Stadshotel Jeroen Bosch	D
Terminus	B

vestiges of interminable warfare between the Protestants to the north and the Catholics to the south. The town's history is written into its street and house names: "Corn Bridge", "The Gun Barrel", "Painters' Street" and more, while its most famous son is the fifteenth-century artist **Hieronymous Bosch**, whose statue now stands, palette in hand, in the middle of the Markt.

Arrival, information and tours

Den Bosch's centre is fifteen minutes' walk east of the **train station**. Stop by the **VVV** office, housed in De Moriaan, the oldest brick building in town, at Markt 77 (Mon 1–6pm, Tues–Fri 9.30am–6pm, Sat 9am–5pm; ☏073/613 9629, ⓦ www.vvvdenbosch.nl), to pick up the useful *Tourist Information Guide* (€1.50) and *Walking tour 's-Hertogenbosch* (€1.90), which unearths all kinds of historical and architectural nuggets.

One good way to see a lot of the town is on a **boat trip**. Traditional open boats depart from Molenstraat 15a, next to *Café van Puffelen* (mid-April to Oct Mon 2–5.20pm, Tues–Sun 10am–5.20pm; every 20min; €6; reserve on ☏0900 202 0178, ⓦ www.kringvriendenvanshertogenbosch.nl). Closed boats depart from St Janssingel near the Wilhelmina bridge, and tours take in the River Aa, Dommel and the Oude Dieze (May–Sept Tues–Sun noon, 1.30pm & 3pm; €7.50). Rederij Wolthuis, Leunweg 17 (☏073/631 2048, ⓦ www.rederijwolthuis .nl), has information and takes reservations for closed-boat tours.

Accommodation

Den Bosch does not have an awful lot of **hotels** to choose from in the city centre, so you would be wise to book in advance. If the central hotels are filled up, there are a couple of large chain hotels just out of the city centre. The VVV has a list of the town's **B&Bs**.

Central Burgemeester Loeffplein 98 ☏073/692 6926, ⓦ www.hotel-central.nl. Located on the Markt with spacious rooms and occasional live jazz in one of the bars. Breakfast is served in a fourteenth-century vault. ❺
Eurohotel Kerkstraat 56 ☏073/613 7777, ⓦ www.eurohotel-denbosch.com. Family-run with well-equipped rooms and a lively terrace. ❸
Jo van den Bosch Boschdijkstraat 39a ☏073/613 8205, ⓦ www.jovandenbosch.nl. Small but intimate family-run hotel, with a restaurant downstairs serving a three-course meal for only €22.50. ❷–❸

Stadshotel Jeroen Bosch Jeroen Boschplein 6 ☏073/610 3556, ⓦ www.stadshoteljeroenbosch .nl. The most appealing option in town, located right next to the Hieronymus Bosch Art Centre and with only four rooms and two suites, kitted out in basic but elegant style. ❸
Terminus Boschveldweg 15 ☏073/613 0666, ⓦ www.hotel-terminus.nl. The cheapest option just west of town and near the train station, with a traditional folk pub downstairs. Shared facilities. ❶

The Town

If you were to draw a picture of the archetypal Dutch marketplace, it would almost certainly look like the **Markt** in Den Bosch. It's broad and cobbled, home to the province's largest market (Wed & Sat) and lined with typical seventeenth-century houses. The sixteenth-century **Stadhuis** (guided tours Wed 3pm & Sat 1pm; €4) has a carillon that's played every Wednesday between 10 and 11am and that chimes the half-hour to the accompaniment of a group of mechanical horsemen.

St Janskathedraal

From just about anywhere in the centre of town it's impossible to miss **St Janskathedraal** (Mon–Sat 10–11.30am & 1.30–4pm; restricted entrance

▲ St Janskathedraal

during services; ⓦ www.sint-jan.nl). Generally regarded as the finest Gothic church in the country, it was built between 1330 and 1530 and has recently undergone a massive restoration. But if Breda's Grote Kerk is Gothic at its most intimate and exhilarating, then St Jan's is Gothic at its most gloomy, the garish stained glass – nineteenth-century or modern – only adding to the sense of dreariness that hangs over the nave. You enter beneath the oldest part of the cathedral, the western **tower** (guided tours at 1.30pm & 3pm: April, May & Oct Wed, Sat & Sun; June–Sept Tues–Sun; €3.50): blunt and brick-clad, it's oddly prominent amid the wild decoration of the rest of the exterior, which includes some nasty-looking creatures scaling the roof – symbols of the forces of evil that attack the church.

Inside, there's much of interest. The **Lady Chapel** near the entrance contains a thirteenth-century figure of the Madonna known as *Zoete Lieve Vrouw* ("Sweet Dear Lady"), famed for its miraculous powers in the Middle Ages and still much venerated today. The brass **font** in the southwest corner was the work of Alard Duhamel, who worked on the cathedral in the late fifteenth century. It's thought that the stone pinnacle, a weird twisted piece of Gothicism at the eastern end of the nave, was the sample piece that earned him the title of master mason.

Almost filling the west wall of the cathedral is an extravagant **organ case**, assembled in 1602. It was described by a Victorian visitor as "certainly the finest in Holland and probably the finest in Europe…it would be difficult to conceive a more stately or magnificent design". Equally elaborate, though on a much smaller scale, the south transept holds the **Altar of the Passion**, a retable made in Antwerp in around 1500. In the centre is a carved Crucifixion scene, flanked by Christ bearing the Cross on one side and a Lamentation on the other. Though rather difficult to make out, a series of carved scenes of the life of Christ run across the retable, made all the more charming by their attention to period (medieval) costume detail.

Hieronymus Bosch Art Centre

Den Bosch's most prominent native son was the late Gothic painter **Hieronymus Bosch** (1450–1516), who lived in the town all his life: his fantastically vivid and tormented religious paintings won him the epithet "The master of the monstrous…the discoverer of the unconscious" from no less than Carl Jung. The **Hieronymus Bosch Art Centre** located in the St Jacobskerk on Jeroen Boschplein 2 (April–Oct Tues–Fri 10am–6pm, Sat & Sun noon–6pm; Nov–March Tues–Fri 10am–5pm, Sat & Sun noon–5pm; €5; Ⓦ www .jheronimusbosch-artcenter.nl) pays tribute to his life and work, although all the paintings on display are replicas of the original work. At the time of writing, the mayor was trying to raise funds to get more original paintings to the city for the big exhibition in 2016, exactly 500 years after Hieronymus Bosch's death. Until then a collection of his prints can been seen in the town's Noordbrabants Museum.

The museums

Opposite the cathedral at Hinthamerstraat 94, the **Zwanenbroedershuis** (Tues & Thurs 1.30–4.30pm; €5; Ⓦ www.zwanenbroedershuis.nl) has an intriguing collection of artefacts, liturgical songbooks and music scores that belonged to the Brotherhood of which Bosch was a member. Founded in 1318, there's nothing sinister about the Brotherhood: membership is open to all and its aim is to promote and popularize religious art and music.

South and east of the cathedral, the **Museum Slager**, Choorstraat 16 (closed for renovation at the time of writing; Ⓦ www.museum-slager.nl), contains the works of three generations of the Slager family who lived in Den Bosch. The paintings of the family's doyen, P.M. Slager (1841–1912), such as *Veterans of Waterloo*, have the most authority, but some of the other works are competent, encompassing the major trends in European art as they came and went.

A few minutes' walk southwest of the cathedral, the **Noordbrabants Museum**, Verwersstraat 41 (Tues–Fri 10am–5pm, Sat & Sun noon–5pm; €7; Ⓦ www.noordbrabantsmuseum.nl), is housed in an eighteenth-century building that was once the seat of the provincial commissioner and has been enlarged with two wings and complemented by a sculpture garden. The good-looking collection of local art and artefacts from prehistory to the present is uniformly excellent and interesting, and the downstairs galleries often hold superb temporary exhibitions of modern art. The permanent collection includes drawings and prints by Hieronymus Bosch, works by other medieval painters and assorted early torture equipment.

Finally, the **Stedelijk Museum 's-Hertogenbosch**, at Magistratenlaan 100 (Tues & Thurs 1–9pm, Wed & Fri–Sun 1–5pm; €4; Ⓦ www.sm-s.nl), is the museum for contemporary art and design, with varied exhibitions.

The rest of the town

Just down the road from the museum, St Jorisstraat leads down to the site of the old city walls, which still marks the southern limit of Den Bosch. The **Bastion Oranje** once defended the southern section of the city walls but, like the walls themselves, it has long gone. Still remaining is a large cannon, **De Boze Griet** ("The Devil's Woman"), cast in 1511 in Cologne and bearing in German the inscription "Brute force I am called, Den Bosch I watch over". The only action she sees now is from the cows, chewing away in the water-meadows below.

The rest of the backstreets of Den Bosch are a mass of intriguing buildings and facades. Particularly pleasant is the **Uilenburg** quarter, with pint-sized houses squashed up against each other; look out for the restored farmhouse opposite Molenstraat 29, and the picturesque Uilenburgstraatje bridge.

Eating and drinking

You can find anything from inexpensive eetcafés to pricey **restaurants** in Den Bosch. Make sure to try the "Bossche Bol", a local speciality with chocolate and whipped cream – an absolute calorie bomb. **Nightlife** isn't particularly exciting but it's easy enough to wander up and down Hinthamerstraat or the streets that radiate from the Markt and find somewhere convivial to drink.

De Blauwe Druif Markt 13. At the corner of Markt and Kolperstraat, this big and boozy pub takes off on market days.

't Bonte Palet Hinthamerstraat 97. A tiny, popular bar with a cornucopia of kitsch hanging from the ceiling and occasional live music.

Brasserie in den Zevenden Hemel Korte Putstraat 13–17. Located on the cosiest street for a romantic dinner, this restaurant uses seasonal produce with an international twist and has a three-course meal for €33.50.

Breton Korte Putstraat 26. Soberly decorated restaurant with an intimate terrace. The menu consists of numerous starter-sized dishes inspired by French, Italian and Japanese cuisine.

Café Cordes Parade 4. This aluminium-clad café-bar brings in Den Bosch's bright young things.

Da Peppone Kerkstraat 77. A little more chic than your standard kitschy pizzeria, *Da Peppone* serves tasty pizzas from €8.50 but also classic dishes such as *ossobuco* or *merluzzo* for around €19.

Deugniet Verwersstraat 55. A deftly decorated bar near the Noordbrabants Museum, specializing in beer, with tastings available on request.

De Opera Hinthamerstraat 115–117. This small restaurant offers a range of wonderful Dutch–French cooking in a relaxed setting: well worth a splurge.

Pollevie Minderbroederstraat 22–24. Cheerful eetcafé with traditional dishes as well as the rare oddity such as crunchy grasshopper spring rolls or falafel. Mains around €14.

Tapperij het Veulen Korenbrugstraat 9. Typical brown café with oodles of atmosphere and at least forty beers by the bottle, mainly attracting an older clientele.

Van Puffelen Molenstraat 4. A short distance from the centre, this is an attractive eetcafé above the canal, with affordable *dagschotels* (daily specialities).

Zoetelief Korte Putstraat 10. Large and stylish restaurant with a very decent menu comprising of delicacies such as sashimi of scallops and saltimbocca of monkfish. A three-course meal sets you back €32.50.

Camp Vught

Opened in January 1943, **Camp Vught** (Tues–Fri 10am–5pm, Sat & Sun noon–5pm; free; ⓦwww.nmkampvught.nl) was the only official SS concentration camp in the Netherlands, modelled on camps in Germany. It was divided into two sections, one for political prisoners brought here from Belgium and the Netherlands, the other for Jews, who were, for the most part, subsequently moved to Westerbork (see p.242) before being transported onto the death camps in the east. Predictably, many people died here in the cruelest of circumstances or were executed in the woods nearby. Although it's a reconstruction, and only a fraction of the size it used to be, Camp Vught still provides a vivid impression. Next to the old camp are the walls of a high security prison, giving the location a rather eerie feel. All information is in Dutch, but an English-speaking guide is available for €3.50. From Den Bosch take **bus** #203 (hourly) and get off at the Lunettenlaan stop.

Eindhoven

EINDHOVEN, 25km south of Den Bosch, is not your typical Dutch city and has few historical sights of interest. This is mainly because the town – which was granted city rights in 1232 – only grew to any size in the twentieth century: in 1900 Eindhoven's population was approximately 4700, but a century later it had passed 200,000, making it the country's fifth largest city. What happened in between was **Philips**, the multinational electrical firm: the town is home to Philips' research centre (the manufacturing plant had such trouble recruiting here, it relocated to Amsterdam), and the name of Eindhoven's benevolent dictator is everywhere – on bus stops, parks, even the stadium of the famous local football team, PSV Eindhoven. The town even moved the main train station (in the shape of a Philips transistor radio) to make sure all the company's employees could get to work faster.

What little there was of old Eindhoven was bombed to smithereens during World War II, but being a very modern city does have its advantages, with a leading modern **design academy** and many hi-tech multinationals based here.

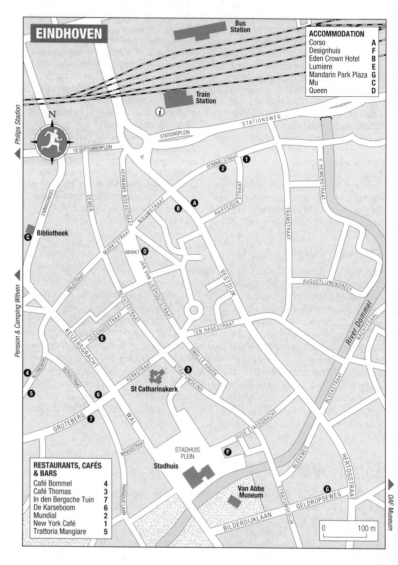

EINDHOVEN

ACCOMMODATION
Corso	A
Designhuis	F
Eden Crown Hotel	B
Lumiere	E
Mandarin Park Plaza	G
Mu	C
Queen	D

RESTAURANTS, CAFÉS & BARS
Café Bommel	4
Café Thomas	3
In den Bergsche Tuin	7
De Karseboom	6
Mundial	2
New York Café	1
Trattoria Mangiare	5

The annual internationally renowned **Dutch Design Week** draws almost 80,000 visitors, and all sorts of design projects can be found around town as well as at the recently opened **Designhuis**. The technical university draws in many international students making nightlife vibrant, with many bars and clubs to choose from.

Arrival and information

Most people will arrive by train, but Eindhoven also possesses an **airport** (ⓦwww.eindhovenairport.nl) with direct flights to London, Bristol and Dublin. As airport taxes are low, flying directly to Eindhoven is often cheaper than going to Schiphol airport. From the airport, bus #401 will get you to the centre of town. Eindhoven's **VVV** (Mon 10am–5.30pm, Tues–Fri 9am–5.30pm, Sat 10am–5pm; ⓣ0900 112 2363, ⓦwww.vvveindhoven.nl) is a great source of information, maps and walking routes. If design is your thing, consider purchasing the **Art & Design card**, which gives you free entrance to the city's main museums as well as discount in many design shops; it's available at the VVV for €12.50.

Accommodation

For a city which is not a key tourist attraction, Eindhoven has a wide range of **hotels**, many of them located in the heart of town. The VVV can help you with your booking for a small fee. They can also provide a handy brochure on the city and a list of **pensions**.

Corso Vestdijk 17 ⓣ040/244 9131. The cheapest option in town, with basic but adequate rooms. An upcoming restyling should add some extra comfort. Shared facilities. ❶

Eden Crown Hotel Vestdijk 14–16 ⓣ040/844 4000, ⓦwww.edencrownhotel.com. Mainly catering to a corporate clientele, so you can expect luxury with all mod cons in a trendy setting. Special deals are abundant. ❺

🏃 **Lumiere** Hooghuisstraat 31a ⓣ040/239 4950, ⓦwww.hotellumiere.nl. The newest addition right in the heart of town, this boutique hotel with 25 rooms has all the luxury you can

wish for with free wireless internet, comfortable beds and a separate toilet. Breakfast is served in the next-door bakery. ❹

Mandarin Park Plaza Geldropseweg 17 ⓣ040/214 6500, ⓦwww.parkplaza.com. This modern hotel offers a high level of comfort and great Chinese and Japanese cuisine. The entire lobby and most of the rooms have recently had an upgrade. ❺

Queen Markt 7 ⓣ040/245 2480, ⓦwww.queeneindhoven.nl. Recently revamped and enlarged, this hotel is conveniently located above the Markt right in the principal shopping area. ❸

The Town

Eindhoven's prime attraction is the first-rate **Van Abbe Museum**, Bilderdijk-laan 10 (Tues–Sun 11am–5pm; €8.50; ⓦwww.vanabbemuseum.nl), with its superb collection of modern paintings that includes works by Picasso, Klein, Chagall, Kandinsky and Bacon. The museum, built in 1936 by architect Kropholler and expanded with a new wing designed by Cahen, is an attraction itself with a very pleasant café overlooking the Dommel river. Just across the river, the new **Designhuis**, located in a former courthouse at Stadhuisplein 3 (Tues–Sun 11am–6pm; €5; ⓦwww.designhuis.com), is the Netherlands' first design museum, with frequently rotated themed exhibitions by renowned and up-and-coming designers. Another exhibition space devoted solely to contemporary art and design – although a lot smaller – is the **MU** at Emmasingel 20, inside a building called Witte Dame (Mon–Fri 10am–6pm, Sat 11am–5pm, Sun 1–5pm; €2; ⓦwww.mu.nl), where you'll need a broad imagination to catch the artists' message. Less brain-stretching is the **DAF Museum**, Tongelresetraat 27 (Tues–Sun 10am–5pm; €7; ⓦwww.dafmuseum.nl), which is devoted to the history of the only Dutch truck manufacturer.

Eating and drinking

Eindhoven comes alive at night with the Kleine and Grote Berg being the best places for **eating**, with restaurants offering a diverse range of international food. The main strip for **drinking** is the Stratumseind, which starts just south of Cuypers' gloomy neo-Gothic St Catherinakerk. This street, with its loud music and cheap beer, has the honour of being the longest bar street in the Netherlands. A little less crowded is the Dommelstraat, with a good range of restaurants and trendy bars.

Café Bommel Kleine Berg 32. An old-fashioned, traditional bar, good for a quiet drink.
Café Thomas Stratumseind 23. As good as any pick on the busy Stratumseind, with ear-splitting music attracting a young student crowd.
In den Bergsche Tuin Grote Berg 17 ☎040/243 7727. Cosy eetcafé-cum-restaurant, very popular with both students and large groups, and specialising in meat dishes for around €18. Closed Mon.
De Karseboom Grote Berg ☎040/243 9597. An old-time favourite, this restaurant has been here for over thirty years and still pulls in the crowds. Great yard for warm evenings.

Mundial Dommelstraat 13. A relaxing spot with comfy lounge seats, wicked cocktails and a menu comprising dishes from all over the globe. Mains around €17.
New York Café Dommelstraat 9. One of the newest additions to the drinking scene, with a decent menu, a good range of cocktails and DJs on weekends.
Trattoria Mangiare Kleine Berg 67 ☎040/236 7088. The best place for spaghetti and risotto in an industrial setting. Also a beautiful inner courtyard for summer.

Limburg

Pressed between Belgium and Germany, **Limburg**, the Netherlands' southernmost province, is shaped like an hourglass and is only 13km across at its narrowest. By Dutch standards, this is a geographically varied province: the north is a familiarly flat landscape of farmland and woods until the town of **Roermond**, where the River Maas loops and curls its way across the map; in the south, and seemingly out of nowhere, rise rolling hills studded with vineyards and châteaux. The people of Limburg are as distinct from the rest of the Netherlands in their landscape – their dialects incomprehensible to "Hollanders", their outlook more closely forged by Belgium and Germany than the distant Randstad. Nowhere is this international flavour more apparent than in the main city, **Maastricht**, an energetic and cosmopolitan blend of the very old (Imperial Rome) and very new (European Union). **South Limburg's** distinctive, and notably un-Dutch, atmosphere makes it popular with tourists from the rest of the Netherlands, who head to its many caves and scenic cycle routes, and in summertime resorts like **Valkenburg** are jam-packed with young people and families. North and central Limburg are less colourful, but still have some places that are well worth visiting. **Venlo**, with its stunning Stadhuis, is a good starting point for heading on to the **National War and Resistance Museum**, and **Roermond** makes a good base to explore the **National Park De Meinweg**.

Pinkpop Festival

What started as a small gathering forty years ago is now mentioned in the *Guinness Book of Records* as the oldest unbroken festival in Europe. Limburg's **Pinkpop** (ⓦwww.pinkpop.nl), a three-day event starting on Whitsun, has its roots in Geleen but soon moved to **Landgraaf**, close to the German border in eastern Limburg, where it grew into a festival attracting more than 90,000 alternative pop and rock fans. It's hosted many big names, from Elvis Costello to Lenny Kravitz and from the Counting Crows to Crowded House, and has always been a trendsetter for other festivals in the country. Traditionally Monday is the busiest day. Die-hards who don't want to miss a thing can stay on the purpose-built campsite on the premises; if that's not your thing, be sure to book accommodation ahead. During the festival, frequent trains connect Maastricht and Heerlen to Landgraaf station, from where a shuttle service will get you to the festival site.

Venlo and around

Just a few kilometres from the German border, **VENLO** has been repeatedly destroyed and recaptured throughout its history, particularly during World War II, when most of its ancient buildings were knocked down during the Allied invasion of Europe. As a result the town is short of sights, but makes a good base for the **National War and Resistance Museum** at neighbouring Overloon (see p.318).

The cramped streets of Venlo's centre wind around the town's architectural highlight, the fancily turreted and onion-domed **Stadhuis**, a much-modified building dating from the sixteenth century. Nearby, along Grote Kerkstraat, is the imposing pile of **St Martinus Kerk** (Mon & Sun 2–4pm, Tues–Fri 10.30am–12.30pm & 2–4pm, Sat 10am–4pm; free), rebuilt after bombing in 1944, but still holding a brilliant golden seventeenth-century reredos. Near the station is the **Limburgs Museum**, Keulsepoort 5 (Tues–Sun 11am–5pm; €6; ⓦwww.limburgsmuseum.nl), which houses the city's historical collection. Best exhibit is the nineteenth-century kitchenware, the largest such assortment in western Europe. Venlo's other museum, the **Van Bommel Van Dam**, Deken van Oppensingel 8 (Tues–Sun 11am–5pm; €4; ⓦwww.vanbommelvandam.nl), shows temporary exhibitions of the work of contemporary, mostly local, artists; from the train station, take the third right off the roundabout.

Practicalities

Venlo's **VVV**, Nieuwstraat 40–42 (Mon–Fri 10am–5.30pm, Sat 10am–5pm; ☎077/354 3800, ⓦwww.vvvvenlo.nl), is located about 600m west from the train station, towards the pedestrianized part of town. They have details of **boat trips** and can help find **accommodation**. The trendiest hotel in town is ⚹ *Puur*, Parade 7 (☎077/351 5790, ⓦwww.hotelpuur.nl; ❷), a hospitable place with basic but stylish rooms and a breakfast area with an industrial feel.

Flanking the train station are *Hotel Wilhelmina*, Kaldenkerkweg 1 (☎077/351 6251, ⓦwww.hotel-wilhelmina.nl; ❷–❸), with spacious rooms and a decent restaurant, and the cheaper *American*, Keulsepoort 14 (☎077/351 5454, ⓦwww.hotelamerican.nl; ❷), which boasts a big terrace.

Try the *D'n Dorstigen Haen*, Markt 26, for **snacks** and a few samples of their huge range of **beers**. Several cafés around the Stadhuis and the Parade are other options for cheap light lunches.

National War and Resistance Museum

The cosy residential town of Venray, a few minutes north of Venlo by train, is a stepping-stone to **OVERLOON** in Noord-Brabant, site of the **Nationaal Oorlogs- en Verzetsmuseum** (National War and Resistance Museum). To reach the museum from Venray, take the *treintaxi* (see p.24; €4.60 each way). Alternatively, you could rent a bike from Venlo and follow route LF33, turning off at Venray to cycle the last 6km through the wheat fields to Overloon. This affluent little town was rebuilt following its destruction in World War II during a fierce battle in October 1944 in which 2400 men died. The final stages took place in the woods to the east, where hand-to-hand fighting was needed to secure the area, and it's on this site that the **museum** (daily: July & Aug 10am–6pm; Sept–June 10am–5pm; €12; ⓦwww.oorlogsmuseum-overloon.nl) now stands, founded with the military hardware that was left after the battle. Its purpose is openly didactic: "Not merely a monument for remembrance, it is intended as an admonition and warning, a denouncement of war and violence". In showing the machinery of war, including tanks, rocket launchers, armoured cars, a Bailey bridge and a V1 flying bomb, the museum powerfully achieves this, making it a moving experience and a poignant prelude to its excellent collection of documents and posters. **Touring** the museum takes a couple of hours.

Roermond and around

ROERMOND, the focal point of central Limburg, is something of an oddity. While not especially exciting, it does have a rich Catholic heritage, as numerous shrines to the Virgin attest – a legacy of several hundred years of Hapsburg hegemony. It was also the hometown of that most prolific of architects, P.J.H. Cuypers, who dotted the whole country with his fancy neo-Gothic structures. Today, the town's greatest asset is its position: Roermond lies on the banks of the **River Maas**, at the point where it meanders into the small, artificial lakes of the **Maasplassen**. Come summertime, these lakes fill with small boats, windsurfs and water-skis as holidaymakers take to the water or fish under the town's skyline. For those less aquatically inclined, it's only 9km to **De Meinweg**, the Netherlands' largest national park, with forests and fens that extend to the German border. Roermond is also useful as a base for visiting nearby **Thorn**, and a handy stopover on the way to **Maastricht** and the south, or Aachen, Düsseldorf and Cologne in Germany.

The Town

Walk into town from the train station and you'll come to the **Munsterkerk** (April–Oct daily 2–5pm, Sat closes 4pm; Nov–March Sat 2–4pm; free), on Munsterplein, built in Romanesque style in the thirteenth century, but much altered and gothicized by P.J.H. Cuypers, who lived and worked here in Roermond for much of his life. Inside, the main thing to see is the polychrome thirteenth-century tomb of Gerhard III and his wife Margaret of Brabant. From here it's a short walk to the large sloping square of the **Markt**, on the eastern side of which is the early eighteenth-century **Stadhuis**, a dull building that's easily overlooked.

Making your way down the larger streets leading south from the Markt – Marktstraat, Neerstraat and Minderbroeders Singel – you'll come across some later and much more attractive architecture. Wherever you are in town, it's worth keeping an eye open for Roermond's alluring twentieth-century **facades**: the

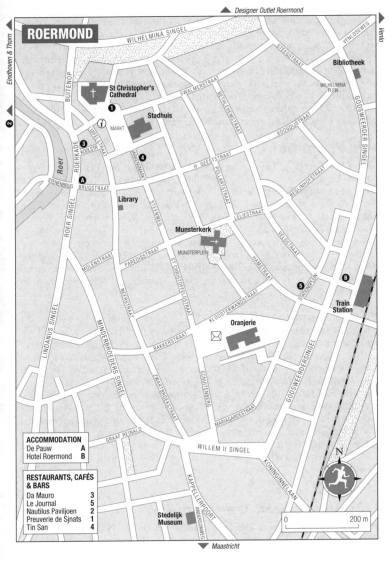

ROERMOND

Designer Outlet Roermond

Eindhoven & Thorn

Venlo

WILHELMINA SINGEL

St Christopher's Cathedral

Stadhuis

MARKT

Bibliotheek

WILHELMINA PLEIN

Library

Munsterkerk

MUNSTERPLEIN

Oranjerie

Train Station

Stedelijk Museum

Maastricht

N

0   200 m

ACCOMMODATION
De Pauw   A
Hotel Roermond   B

RESTAURANTS, CAFÉS & BARS
Da Mauro   3
Le Journal   5
Nautilus Paviljoen   2
Preuverie de Sjnats   1
Tin San   4

majority are Art Nouveau, often strongly coloured with heavily moulded vegetal patterns and designs, sometimes with stylized animal heads and grotesque characters. Some examples can be found at Neerstraat 38 and 10.

The Stedelijk Museum – and P.J.H. Cuypers

Roermond's principal claim to architectural fame is celebrated at the **Stedelijk Museum**, Andersonweg 2–8 (Tues–Fri 11am–5pm, Sat & Sun 2–5pm; €2; Ⓦwww.museum.roermond.nl). **P.J.H. Cuypers** (1827–1921) was the Netherlands' foremost ecclesiastical architect in the nineteenth century, his work paralleling that of the British Gothic revivalist, Augustus Pugin. Almost every large city in the country has a Catholic church by him – those in Eindhoven, Leeuwarden and Hilversum are notable – though his two most famous buildings are secular: the Rijksmuseum and Centraal Station in Amsterdam. Roermond's museum is the building in which Cuypers lived and worked for many years, and preserves a small private chapel as well as a large extension in which masses of decorative panels, mouldings and fixtures were produced. Other exhibits show his plans and paintings, along with a collection of works by other local artists, chiefly Hendrik Luyten.

Practicalities

The **VVV**, Markt 17 (April–Oct Mon–Fri 10am–5pm, Sat 10am–4pm; Nov–March Mon–Fri 9.30am–5pm, Sat 9.30am–4pm; ☎0475/335 847, ⓦwww .vvv-middenlimburg.nl), is a ten- to fifteen-minute walk from the train station. They can provide details of **fishing** and **boat trips** along the River Maas (April–Sept). If you want to rent a boat, visit Watersportschool Frissen, Hatenboer 75 (☎0475/327 873), where a five-person boat costs €60 a day.

Roermond has a good range of **hotels**, including *De Pauw*, on Roerkade 1 overlooking the water (☎0475/316 597, ⓦwww.hoteldepauw.nl; ❷), and the *Hotel Roermond*, Stationsplein 9 & 13 (☎0475/332 325, ⓦwww.hotelroermond .nl; ❷), which has modern rooms, an inviting terrace and three restaurants to choose from.

Eating and drinking

The three main areas to **eat** and **drink** are around the Markt, the Munsterkerk and the train station. On Stationsplein, *Le Journal*, at no. 17, is an inexpensive café-bar that stays open till late at weekends. *Tin San* is the best of several Chinese places, just south of the Markt at Varkensmarkt 1, while *Da Mauro* (closed Wed), Koolstraat 8, is an Italian restaurant that serves a three-course meal for €27.50. In summertime, the *Nautilus Paviljoen* at Maasboulevard 2 is a popular café overlooking the yachts moored up in the marina. Roermond lacks first-rate watering holes, though the cafés at Stationsplein are often the liveliest nightspots; otherwise try *Preuverie de Sjnats*, Markt 24, for a good range of beers. For a cultural night out, check out the *Orangerie* (ⓦwww .oranjerieroermond.nl), at Kloosterwandplein 12–16, which is a hotel and a theatre, showcasing musicals, ballet and cabaret. Check their website for up-to-date information.

Nationaal Park De Meinweg

Roermond makes a good base for exploring the nearby **Nationaal Park De Meinweg**, an excellent region for walking and cycling by the German border. It comprises 16 square kilometres of oak, birch and pine trees, dotted with small lakes and heathland, and home to adders and (shy) wild boars. Entrance to De Meinweg is free (open daily, unlimited access), and the **Bezoekerscentrum** (visitors' centre; April–Oct daily 10am–5pm; ⓦwww.nationaal-parkdemeinweg .nl), just before the park entrance, sells maps with routes and starting points for walkers and cyclists, and has a small nature museum.

To get to the park, you're best off using your own **transport** as bus connections aren't great – rent a bike from the Rijwielshop at Roermond station (€7 per day for a three-geared bike) and cycle the 9km, following signs to the village of **Herkenbosch**, or drive. From Herkenbosch, follow Keulsebaan, then turn left down Meinweg to reach the Bezoekerscentrum and the entrance to the park. In Herkenbosch, Manege de Venhof at Venhof 2 (☏0475/531 495), can arrange group **horseriding** in the park.

Thorn

The village of **THORN** makes for an enjoyable half-day outing from Roermond. Regular buses link the two, but it's more fun to rent a bike from the train station and cycle along the River Maas, following LF Route 5b (Roermond to Thorn). Take a map (available at the Roermond VVV), as the signposting is patchy. To return, follow the 5a signs; the round trip is roughly 30km.

Once you get here, it's easy to see why Thorn is a favourite for travel agents' posters, and something of a tourist honeypot. Its houses and farms are all painted **white**, a tradition for which no one seems to have a credible explanation, but one which has a striking photogenic effect. The farms intrude right into the village itself, giving Thorn a barnyard friendliness that's enhanced by its cobblestone streets, the closed-shuttered propriety of its houses and, at the centre, the Abdijkerk.

The Abdijkerk

The **Abdijkerk** (March–Sept daily 10am–5pm; Oct–Feb Sat & Sun 11am–4pm; €3) was founded at the end of the tenth century by a powerful count, Ansfried, and his wife Hilsondis, as a sort of religious retirement home after Ansfried had finished his tenure as bishop of Utrecht. Under his control the abbey and the land around it was granted the status of an independent principality under the auspices of the Holy Roman Empire, and it was in the environs of the abbey that the village developed.

The abbey was unusual in having a **double cloister** that housed both men and women (usually from local noble families), a situation that carried on right up until the French invasion of 1797, after which the monks and nuns were dispersed and all the abbey buildings, save the church, destroyed. Most of what can be seen of the church today dates from the fifteenth century, with some tidying up by P.J.H. Cuypers in the nineteenth. The interior decoration, though, is congenially Baroque, with some good memorials and side chapels. If you're into the macabre, aim for the **crypt** under the chancel, which has a couple of glass coffins containing conclusively dead members of the abbey from the eighteenth century: this and other highlights are described in the notes that you can pick up on entry (in English) for a self-guided walking tour.

Thorn has one small museum, the **Museum Land of Thorn**, in the historic heart of the village at Wijngaard 14 (April–Oct Mon noon–5pm, Tues–Sun 10am–5pm; Nov–March Tues–Sun 11am–4pm; €3; ⓦwww.museumhetland vanthorn.nl), which details the history of Thorn, hosts temporary exhibitions of art and houses a three-dimensional painting of the village.

Practicalities

The **VVV**, near the entrance to the museum at Wijngaard 8 (April–Oct Mon 1–5pm, Tues–Fri 10am–5pm, Sat 10am–4pm, Sun 11am–3pm; Nov–March Tues–Fri 11am–4pm, Sat & Sun 11am–3pm; ☏0900/202 5588), can help with regional information. The cheaper of the town's two **hotels** is the *Crasborn*, Hoogstraat 6 (☏0475/561 281, ⓦwww.hotelcrasborn.nl; ❷–❸), though the atmospheric *Hostellerie La Ville Blanche*, Hoogstraat 2 (☏0475/562 341, ⓦwww .villeblanche.nl; ❸), offers surprisingly affordable luxury. There's also a private **campsite**, *Vijverbroek*, Kessenicherweg 20 (☏0475/561 914; April–Oct), reached by turning right halfway down Hofstraat.

Maastricht

MAASTRICHT is one of the most vibrant cities in the Netherlands. With its cobbled streets and fashionable boutiques in the old town, contemporary architecture in the Céramique district, a fantastic art fair and excellent cuisine, the city literally buzzes with excitement and its multilingual, multinational population epitomizes the most positive aspects of the European Union.

Though its claim to be the oldest town in the Netherlands is disputed by Nijmegen, Maastricht was certainly settled by the **Romans**, who took one look at the River Maas and dubbed the town Mosae Trajectum or "Crossing of the Maas". An important stop-off on the trading route between Cologne and the North Sea, the town boasted a Temple of Jupiter, whose remains are now on view in a hotel basement. A millennium later, **Charlemagne** beefed up the city too, though his legacy is ecclesiastical, his two churches representing some of the finest extant Romanesque architecture in the whole of the country.

Maastricht has also had its hard times, hitting the economic skids in the 1970s after the last of the region's coal mines closed, but its fortunes have been revived by a massive **regeneration** scheme, which has pulled in foreign investors by the busload. The town is now popular as a day-trip destination with the Dutch, the Germans and the Belgians, and it is also home to students from around the world studying at over forty international institutes, including the European Journalism Centre and the University of the United Nations. Redevelopment continues apace today with the addition of **'t Bassin**, a spruced-up inland harbour north of the Markt, with a hatful of restaurants, cafés and galleries. The most recent construction in the centre of town is the **Mosae Forum**, a shopping centre with an attractive blend of classical and modern architecture. Finally, Maastricht is especially appealing during **Carnival**, with colourful parades and locals and visitors alike dressed up in the most creative outfits, mostly handmade.

Arrival

The centre of Maastricht is on the west bank of the River Maas and most of the town spreads out from here toward the Belgian border. You're likely to arrive, however, on the east bank, in the district known as **Wyck**, a sort of extension to the centre that's home to the **train** and **bus stations** and many of the city's hotels. The train station itself is about ten minutes' walk from the St Servaas bridge, which takes you across the river into the centre. All local buses from either station connect with the Markt, but it's easy enough to walk. Maastricht **airport** (ⓦwww.maa.nl) is 12km north of the city at Beek; from here it's a twenty-minute ride on bus #59 to the Markt and the train station; a taxi costs about €25. Arriving by **car**, follow signs for Q-Parking; there's no free parking in the town centre. The VVV has a detailed "Parking in Maastricht" leaflet.

TEFAF art and antiques fair

Once a year, art and antique lovers gather at the **TEFAF** fair (ⓦwww.tefaf.com), held in the congress centre (MECC) in Maastricht. From its modest beginnings in 1975 as a fair specializing in old master paintings, the TEFAF now claims to be the world's leading fine art and antiques fair, attracting visitors from all over the world. It usually takes place in March, but check the exact dates in advance on the website. Even if you're not an art lover it's worth checking the dates, as finding accommodation is almost impossible when it's on.

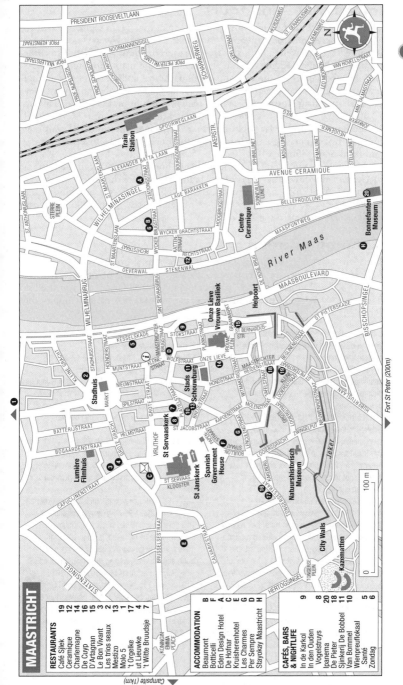

MAASTRICHT

RESTAURANTS

Café Sjiek	19
Ceramique	12
Charlemagne	14
De Cuyp	16
D'Artagnan	15
Le Bon Vivant	3
Les trios seaux	2
Mestizo	13
Molo 5	1
't Orgelke	17
ut Lieuwke	4
't Witte Bruudsje	7

ACCOMMODATION

Beaumont	B
Botticelli	F
Eden Design Hotel	A
De Hofnar	C
Kruisherenhotel	E
Les Charmes	G
Per Sempre	D
Stayokay Maastricht	H

CAFÉS, BARS & NIGHTLIFE

In de Karkol	9
In den Ouden Vogelstruys	8
Ipanema	20
De Pieter	18
Sjinkerij De Bobbel	11
Van Bommel	10
Wienpreuflokaal Santé	5
Zondag	6

Information and tours

The main **VVV** (May–Oct Mon–Sat 9am–6pm, Sun 11am–3pm; Nov–April Mon–Fri 9am–6pm, Sat 9am–5pm; ☎043/325 2121, ⊛www.vvvmaastricht.nl) is housed on the west side of the river in the Dinghuis, a tall, late-fifteenth-century building at Kleine Staat 1, at one end of the main shopping street. As well as information on the city and on film, theatre and music events around town, they have decent maps and good walking guides. In July and August they organize **walking tours** in English, which leave from the office daily at 12.30pm (€4.50) and last about an hour and a half. From March until November, City Tour Maastricht offers a ride through the historical centre of town by **horse carriage**, departing from the Onze Lieve Vrouweplein (Tues–Sun from noon; 45min; €10).

Between May and September, Stiphout runs hourly **cruises** from the bottom of Graanmarkt down the Maas (daily 10am–5pm; check hours out of season; 50min; €7; ☎043/351 5300, ⊛www.stiphout.nl), and offers trips taking in the St Pietersberg caves (3hr; €11.90). Since not all cruises are available every day, phone to confirm or ask at the VVV.

Accommodation

For a small city, Maastricht has a wide range of central **hotels**, though they do tend to be a tad pricey. Alternatively, the VVV has a list of **private rooms**, which they will either book on your behalf for a small fee or sell you the list. There are several good **pensions** and a brand new **HI hostel**, overlooking the River Maas.

Beaumont Wyckerbrugstraat 2 ☎043/325 4433, ⊛www.beaumont.nl. Grab a style magazine at random and you might just find this hotel in it. Wooden floors, natural colours and chandeliers combined with modern elements make this hotel a picture-perfect example of a contemporary designer hotel. ❺

Botticelli Papenstraat 11 ☎043/352 6300, ⊛www.hotelbotticelli.nl. Located in two monumental buildings right in the heart of town, this luxurious hotel in Italian style has oodles of atmosphere. The intimate inner courtyard is a perfect spot to rest your feet after a day of shopping. ❺

Eden Design Hotel Stationsstraat 40 ☎043/328 2525, ⊛www.edenhotelgroup.com. The Netherlands' first design hotel has recently been taken over by the Eden chain, but hasn't lost its spunk. Funky colours, daring art and a great champagne breakfast make this one of the trendiest spots in the up-and-coming Wyck area. Special deals are abundant so check in advance. ❹

De Hofnar Capucijnenstraat 35 & Keizer Karelplein 13 ☎043/351 0396. Cosy B&B divided over two buildings with perfectly adequate rooms, all varying in size and shape. A very homely atmosphere right in the heart of the city. ❶

Kruisherenhotel Kruisherengang 19–23 ☎043/329 2020, ⊛www.chateauhotels.nl. Definitely not cheap, but worth every penny just for its location this is a fifteenth-century monastery and Gothic church which have been transformed into a luxurious design hotel with sixty well-equipped rooms. ❼

Les Charmes Lenculenstraat 18 ☎043/321 7400, ⊛www.hotellescharmes.nl. Located in an old mansion dating from 1725, this small hotel has only fifteen rooms, which are stylish but still cosy. ❹

Per Sempre Maastrichter Smedenstraat 28 ☎043/321 9969, ⊛www.persempre.nl. This smart guesthouse, located right above the store with the same name, is great value for money, with large rooms (ask for the ones in front) and a friendly owner. No private facilities. ❶

Stayokay Maastricht Maasboulevard 101 ☎043/750 1790, ⊛www.stayokay.com. Modern hostel sleeping as many as 199 guests, right on the banks of the River Maas and within walking distance of the Onze Lieve Vrouweplein. Dorm beds for €33.50. ❶

The Town

The busiest of Maastricht's squares is the **Markt**, which hosts a general market on Wednesday and Friday mornings. At the centre of the square is the seventeenth-century **Stadhuis** (Mon–Fri 8.30am–12.30pm & 2–5pm; free), a square, grey limestone building that is a typical slice of Dutch civic grandeur. Its double staircase was constructed so that the rival rulers of Brabant and nearby Liège didn't have to argue about who should go first on the way in. Inside, the building has an imposing main hall which leads to an octagonal dome supported by heavy arches.

On your way to **Vrijthof**, the second of the town's main central squares, pop your head into the thirteenth-century **Dominicanerkerk**, just off Helmstraat, for a bit of a surprise. Inside the church you'll find Maastricht's largest **bookstore**, with a great view of the old frescoes which have been restored. **Vrijthof** itself is just west of the Markt, a larger, rather more grand open space flanked by a couple of churches on one side and a line of cafés on the other, with tables taking over the wide pavement in summer. During the Middle Ages, Vrijthof was the scene of the so-called "Fair of the Holy Relics", a seven-yearly showing of the bones of St Servaas, the first bishop of Maastricht, which brought plenty of pilgrims into the town but resulted in such civil disorder that it was eventually banned.

The Basiliek van St Servaas

The church that holds the relics of St Servaas today, the **Basiliek van St Servaas** (Mon–Sat 10am–5pm, Sun 12.30–5pm; €3.70), dominates the west side of Vrijthof. Dating from 950, it was built on the site of an earlier shrine, which marked the spot where the saint was supposedly buried in c.384. Only the crypt remains of the tenth-century church, containing the tomb of the saint himself, and the rest is mostly of medieval or later construction. You enter on the north side, where a fifteenth-century Gothic cloister leads into the **treasury**, which holds a large collection of reliquaries, goblets and liturgical accessories. Among them a bust reliquary of St Servaas is decorated with reliefs telling the saint's story, which is carried through the town in Easter processions. There's also a coffin-reliquary of the saint, the so-called "Noodkist", dating from 1160 and bristling with saints, stones and ornate copperwork, as well as a jewelled crucifix from 890 and a twelfth-century Crucifixion in ivory. Beyond the treasury is the entrance to the rich and imposing interior, the round-arched nave supporting freshly painted Gothic vaulting. Don't miss the mid-thirteenth-century **Bergportaal** on the south side of the church, the usual entrance during services.

St Janskerk and the Museum aan het Vrijthof

The second most prominent building on the square is Maastricht's main Protestant church, the fourteenth-century **St Janskerk** (April–Oct Mon–Sat 11am–4pm), which was the baptistery of the church of St Servaas when it was a cathedral and now comes complete with its own late-medieval Gothic tower. The church has some medieval murals, but a climb up the tower (€1.50) is the church's main appeal. On the south side of the square, the sixteenth-century Spanish Government House holds the **Museum aan het Vrijthof** (Wed–Sun 1–5pm; €4; Ⓦwww.museumaanhetvrijthof.nl), which has a number of period rooms furnished in Dutch, French and the more local Liège–Maastricht style. Among various exhibits are statues and figurines, porcelain and applied arts and a handful of seventeenth-century paintings.

The Onze Lieve Vrouwe Basiliek

Another prominent Maastricht church, the **Onze Lieve Vrouwe Basiliek**, is a short walk south of Vrijthof down Bredestraat, in a small, shady square crammed with café tables in summer. It's unusual for its fortified west front, with barely more than one or two slits for windows. First built around the year 1000, it's a solid, dark and deeply devotional place after the relative sterility of St Servaaskerk. The Gothic vaulting of the nave springs from a Romanesque base, while the galleried choir is a masterpiece of proportion, raised under a high half-dome, with a series of capitals exquisitely decorated with Old Testament scenes. Off the north aisle, the **treasury** (Easter to mid-Oct Mon–Sat 11am–5pm, Sun 1–5pm; €3) holds the usual reliquaries and ecclesiastical garments, most notably the dalmatic of St Lambert – the evangelical bishop of Maastricht who was murdered at Liège in 705, allegedly by a local noble whom he had rebuked for adultery. Entrance to the church is through a side chapel on the Onze Lieve Vrouweplein, which houses the statue of **Stella Mare**, an object of pilgrimage for centuries and one which attracts as many devotees as the church itself.

Stokstraat Kwartier and the city walls

Around the corner from the Onze Lieve Vrouweplein is a district of narrow streets known as the **Stokstraat Kwartier** after its main gallery- and boutique-lined spine, Stokstraat. This quarter has an intimate feel, with its vermilion town houses, scattered sculptures and Maasland-Renaissance-style houses in warm Namur stone. On Plankstraat, the **Museumkelder Derlon** (Sun noon–4pm; free), in the basement of the hotel of the same name, contains one of the few remnants of Roman Maastricht – the remains of a temple to Jupiter, a well and several layers of pavement, discovered before the building of the present hotel in the mid-1980s.

On the other side of Onze Lieve Vrouweplein lies another of Maastricht's most appealing quarters, narrow streets winding out to the remains of the town battlements alongside the River Jeker. The best surviving part of the walls is the **Helpoort** of 1229, close to a stretch overlooking the river at the end of St Bernadusstraat; and from here you can walk along the top of the walls almost as far as the **Natuurhistorisch Museum** at De Bosquetplein 6–7 (Mon–Fri 10am–5pm, Sat & Sun 2–5pm; €4.50; Ⓦwww.nhmmaastricht.nl), where there's a small collection on the geology, flora and fauna of the surrounding area, along with a compact lush garden.

The Kazematten

Located a little way southwest of the Natuurhistorisch Museum, in the Waldeck Park, the **Kazematten** (Casemates; tours July & Aug daily at 2pm; outside these months, check with the VVV; €4.90) are further evidence of Maastricht's once-impressive fortifications. Built between 1575 and 1825, these subterranean galleries are all that remains of a whole network which once protected the garrison from enemy attack and housed a string of complimentary gun batteries. The tour takes you through a string of damp passages, a mildly interesting way to spend an hour. Trivia buffs might be interested to know that the famous fourth "musketeer", d'Artagnan, was killed here, struck down while engaged in an attack on the town as part of forces allied to Louis XIV in 1673.

The east bank

Ten minutes' walk south of the St Servaas bridge is the **Bonnefanten Museum**, Avenue Céramique 250 (Tues–Sun 11am–5pm; €8; Ⓦwww.bonnefanten.nl), one of Maastricht's highlights. Named after the Bonnefanten monastery where it used to be housed, the museum now inhabits an impressive modern building on the banks of the Maas. Its space-rocket-style cupola is instantly recognizable, zooming skywards. Inside is a permanent collection of old masters and contemporary fine art, including works from the Minimal Art and Arte Povera movements. The rest of the museum is given over to various temporary exhibitions, superbly displayed: you could find anything from giant spider installations to Titians. Don't miss the cupola space, which is usually given over to a single piece of art.

Not far from the Bonnefanten Museum on Plein 1992, with its low horizons and euro symbols impressed into the paving stones, is the **Centre Céramique**, Avenue Céramique 50 (Mon–Fri 10.30am–5pm, Tues & Thurs until 8.30pm, Sat 10am–3pm, Sun 1–5pm; ⓦ www.centreceramique.nl). This huge modern building is home to the European Journalism Centre, the city archives and the library (which has free internet access).

Outside the centre: St Pietersberg

There are more dank passageways to explore fifteen minutes' walk from the Casemates on the southern outskirts of Maastricht, where the flat-topped hill of **St Pietersberg** rises to a height of about 110m. The galleries here were hollowed out of the soft sandstone, or marl, that makes up the hill – an activity that has been going on here since Roman times. There are more than 20,000 passages, but nowadays only 8000 of them are accessible. The galleries used to claim the lives of people (usually children) who never found their way out, but these days it's almost impossible to enter the caves without guidance. Of the two cave systems, the **Zonneberg** is probably the better, situated on the far side of the St Pietersberg hill at Casino Slavante (guided tours in English July & Aug daily 1.50pm; €4.90). These caves were intended to be used as air-raid shelters during World War II and were equipped accordingly, though they were in fact only used during the final days of the German occupation. There is some evidence of wartime usage, plus what everyone claims is Napoleon's signature on a graffiti-ridden wall. Also on the walls are recent charcoal drawings, usually illustrating a local story and acting as visual aids for the guides, not to mention the ten varieties of bat that inhabit the dark (and cold) corridors.

The other, more northerly system of caves, the **Grotten Noord**, is easier to reach (a 15min walk from the centre of town). The entrance is at Chalet Bergrust on the near side of St Pietersberg close by **Fort St Pieter**, and has panoramic views over the town and surrounding countryside. The fort is a low brick structure, pentagonal in shape and built in 1702 (tours July & Aug daily at 12.30pm and 2pm; outside these months, check with the VVV; €3.95).

Preuvenemint

Maastricht is often known as the culinary capital of the Netherlands, and never more so than during **Preuvenemint**, an annual four-day culinary event held on the last full weekend in August (ⓦ www.preuvenemint.nl), when Vrijthof square is filled with over thirty stands functioning as restaurants. "Preuvenemint" is a contraction of the Maastricht words "*preuve*" (to taste) and "*evenemint*" (event), and it's a great way to explore the richness of Dutch cuisine. The main attraction, though, has to be the crowd the event attracts. Posh Maastricht comes out to show off its latest purchases, but also to contribute to a good cause, since all the proceeds go to charity.

Eating, drinking and nightlife

Maastricht has some of the best cooking in the Netherlands, so options for good **eating** and **drinking** abound. Regional delicacies include asparagus, cave mushrooms, Limburgse Vlaai (fruit tart) and Romm edou cheese. Limburg is also the only wine-producing province in the Netherlands, although not everyone will be charmed by the slightly sour taste of its produce.

For drinking, the **bars** on the east side of the Vrijthof have most pulling-power, particularly in summer when the pavement cafés are jam-packed. A more intimate environment can be found around the Onze Lieve Vrouweplein, while heavy nighttime entertainment is concentrated around the Platielstraat.

Lumière Filmhuis, Bogaardenstraat 40b (℡043/321 4080), regularly shows interesting, often English-language, **movies**.

Restaurants

Café Sjiek Sint Pieterstraat 13 ℡043/321 0158. Anyone from a carpenter to a top lawyer feels at home in this pleasant eetcafé, which serves a wide selection of regional dishes at affordable prices. Their cheese platter is a must for connoisseurs.

Céramique Rechtstraat 78 ℡043/325 2097. Located in the Wyck, an area burgeoning with many restaurants, this eetcafé serves no-nonsense food, with mains like salmon, steak and sea bass for around €20.

Charlemagne Onze Lieve Vrouweplein 24 ℡043/321 9373. Cosy café with reasonably priced steaks, salads and a wide variety of beers. Great terrace in summer and attentive staff.

De Cuyp Tongersestraat 30 ℡043/321 8382. Located in the university district, a few minutes from the centre, this restaurant serves Dutch–French dishes (around €20) and seasonal specialities. There's also a tiny terrace which is shared with the neighbours across the street.

D'Artagnan Graanmarkt 3 ℡043/325 5164. Despite the slightly posh-looking terrace, this is a traditional brown-café-style place that serves a great range of daily specialities, with a better-than-average wine list. Main dishes around €20.

Le Bon Vivant Capucijnenstraat 91 ℡043/321 0816. Pure French cuisine such as foice gras, scallops, pigeon and fish soup. A three-course meal in this seventeenth-century vault starts at €35.

Les Trois Seaux Markt 41 ℡043/321 2038. Just off the crowded Markt, this fish restaurant offers fresh lobster, oysters and seasonal products in a maritime setting. Mains around €20.

Mestizo Bredestraat 18 ℡043/327 0874. A funky little place offering tasty Latin cuisine. Great starters such as raw tuna with lemon mayonnaise or chorizo quesadillas, all under €8.50. Mains around €17.

Molo 5 Bassinkade 5 ℡043/327 0033. There are a few good restaurants and art galleries situated in this inland harbour; *Molo 5* serves Italian food with price starting from €13 for a pasta dish and €24 for a main course. Great terrace.

't Orgelke Tongersestraat 40 ℡043/321 6982. This restaurant is famous for its *sateh* and stews, but they also serve a wide variety of fish and meat dishes for around €18. If you beat the record holder in *sateh* eating, your name will be added to the wall of fame.

Ut Lieuwke Grote Gracht 62 ℡043/321 0459. Great classic Dutch/French cuisine in an informal setting with very amenable owners. Make sure to book as the tiny restaurant fills up quickly with regular customers.

't Witte Bruudsje Platielstraat 12. Late-night snack attacks can be assuaged here from their choice of baguettes, salads and hot staples such as chilli con carne and fish and chips. Open until 2am (Fri & Sat 3am).

Cafés, bars and nightlife

In de Karkol Stokstraat 5. If you're up for a true authentic Maastricht experience, this tiny café is the place to be, with music in dialect by regional artists which is loudly sung along to by the local crowd.

In den Ouden Vogelstruys Vrijthof 15. One of the nicest bars on the otherwise touristy Vrijthof, just on the corner of Platielstraat.

Ipanema Avenue Céramique 250. Located in a wing of the Bonnefanten Museum, this trendy bar occasionally turns into a club at weekends.

De Pieter Sint Pieterstraat 22. Typical brown café with sand on the floor and a good array of beers. Occasional live *chanson* music.

Sjinkerij De Bobbel Wolfstraat 32. Just off Onze Lieve Vrouweplein, this is a bare-boards place, lively in the early evening.

▲ Vrijthof Square, Maastricht

Van Bommel Platielstraat 13–15. While the neighbouring bars mainly attract students, *Van Bommel* aims at an older crowd. Open till late.
Wienpreuflokaal Santé Kesselskade 56. Tiny wine bar, great for tasting rare Dutch wines.
Zondag Wyckerbrugstraat 42. The place to go for a coffee and grandma's apple pie. Also has live DJs at weekends and stiff cocktails.

Listings

Bike rental Aon de Stasie, Stationsplein (☏043/321 1100; Mon–Fri 6am–midnight, Sat & Sun 7.30am–1am; from €7.50 per day with a €50 deposit).
Books The best bookstore is Selexyz in the Dominicanerkerk, which has a good selection of new English-language titles. There's also a branch of De Slegte at Grote Straat 53, good for second hand English-language paperbacks and much else besides.

Bureau de change There's a GWK office at the train station, open daily.
Car rental Europcar, Sibemaweg 1 ☏043/361 2310. The major companies also have desks at the airport.
Markets General market on Markt (Wed & Fri 8am–1pm). Antique and curiosities market on Stationsstraat (Sat 8am–4pm).
Post office Statenstraat, just off the northwest corner of Vrijthof.
Taxis Crals, Posthoornstraat 75 ☏043/362 2222.

South Limburg

South Limburg boasts the Netherlands' only true **hills** and as such is a popular holiday destination for those Netherlanders who are keen to escape the pancake-flat landscapes of the north. Several long-distance **walking routes** converge on Maastricht, including the popular and scenic Grand Randonné 5 "Traject der Ardennen", the Pieterpad (from St Pietersberg to Groningen's Pieterburen), and the Krijtlandpad, which winds its way to the German border. The countryside is green and rolling, studded with castles (many of which have been converted into hotels), seamed with river valleys and dotted with the crooked timber-framed houses that are unique to this area. Everywhere is within easy reach of Maastricht, but since public transport connections are patchy it makes more sense to take a **car**. This puts you within easy reach of

Liège in Belgium (Luik in Dutch) and Aachen in Germany, and just an hour away from the cities of Brussels, Düsseldorf and Cologne – or the wild river valleys and peaks of Belgium's Ardennes.

Valkenburg is South Limburg's main resort, perhaps the easiest place to visit as it's on the main train line from Maastricht to Aachen, though it does get packed throughout the summer. Further east down the line, **Heerlen** is also easily reached, though it's of limited appeal. To the south of the train line, toward the Belgian border, the countryside is wilder and more impressive, though there are no specific targets of note.

East of Maastricht

Take bus #54 east from Maastricht to get to **MARGRATEN** where, just before the town proper, there's an **American War Cemetery** (daily sunrise–sunset), a moving memorial to over eight thousand American servicemen who died in the Dutch and Belgian campaigns of late 1944 and 1945. Buses stop right outside. The centrepiece is a stone quadrangle recording the names of the soldiers, together with a small visitors' room and a pictorial representation and narrative describing the ebb and flow of the local campaign; beyond the quadrangle, the white marble crosses that mark the burial places of the soldiers cover a depressingly huge area.

The small town of **VAALS**, at the end of bus route #54, is perched on a hillside whose peak is the highest point in the Netherlands, at a lofty 321m. Just a few metres further on are three flags in a graffiti-covered concrete block symbolizing the **Drielandenpunt**, where the borders of Belgium, Germany and the Netherlands meet. A nearby labyrinth (April–Oct 10am–6pm; €3.25; Ⓦ www.drielandenpunt.nl), an observation tower (€3.25), car parks and fast-food outlets contrive to make this a truly underwhelming experience.

Valkenburg

Set in the gently wooded valley of the River Geul, **VALKENBURG**, ten minutes northeast of Maastricht by train, is southern Limburg's major tourist resort. A medieval castle, its ruins starkly silhouetted on crags above the town, surveys the ersatz castle train station and the garish centre, where busloads of tourists arrive every day throughout the summer. While you probably wouldn't want to stay here, it's certainly a change from the rest of the Netherlands, with a feel more akin to a Swiss or Austrian alpine resort. Valkenburg is famed for its Christmas markets, held in Fluweelengrot and Gemeentegrot, with all manner of special foodstuffs, decorations and street entertainment. It is also where the **Amstel Gold Race** (Ⓦ www.amstelgoldrace.nl), one of the country's leading cycle events, finishes sometime each April.

The Town

Theodoor Dorrenplein, five minutes' walk from the train station, is the centre of town, fringed with cafés and home to the VVV. From here, the main Grotestraat leads up through the pedestrianized old centre to the old **Grendelpoort** arch beyond which is **Grendelplein**, a second focus, with streets leading off to Valkenburg's main attractions. A great many of these are aimed at children – things like bobsleigh runs, a fairy-tale wood and a hopeful reconstruction of Rome's catacombs.

It's worth a walk up to the **castle** (entrance off Grendelplein; daily: April–June 10am–5.30pm; July–Sept 10am–6pm; Oct–Dec 10am–4.30pm; hours vary outside season; €3.50, joint ticket with Fluwelengrot €6.80; Ⓦ www.kasteelvalkenburg.nl).

The edifice was blown up in 1672 on the orders of William III, after he had recaptured it from the French. Repair and restoration began in 1921 and continue still; in the process a series of long-forgotten underground passages has been discovered.

The caves

These passages form part of the **Fluweelengrot** (guided tours only: Jan–March Mon–Fri 11am & 1pm, Sat & Sun 11am–3pm on the hour; April–June daily 11am–4pm on the hour; July & Aug daily 10.30am–5pm every half-hour and at 8pm; Sept & Oct daily 11am–4pm on the hour; closed Nov & Dec for Christmas market; extra tours during school and public hols; €5.20, joint ticket with castle €6.80), further up the road on the left are a series of caves that were formed – like those of St Pietersberg in Maastricht – by the quarrying of marl, which has long been used for much of the building hereabouts. On the whole they're a damp, cold way to spend an hour, the most interesting features being the signatures and silhouettes of American soldiers who wintered here from 1944 to 1945 and a clandestine chapel that was used during the late eighteenth-century French occupation.

There are several other caves you can visit in the area, including ones you can cycle through – the **Grotbiken** (cave biking; ☎043/6040 675; ⓦwww.asp adventure.nl; €17 per hr) – and the **Gemeentegrot** (check website for hours; €5; ⓦwww.gemeentegrot.nl), which does the trip to an underground lake by train.

A day's cycling in South Limburg

On a leisurely cycle route east from Maastricht to Vaals, right on the German border, scenic villages nestle among vineyards and orchards, linked by quiet lanes dotted with shrines. The pace of life is slow – the pony and trap is still a common sight – and cycling is a perfect way to appreciate this rolling landscape and its un-Dutch hills. Allow a day for this seventy-kilometre round-trip ride, and pick up a Limburg province map from Maastricht VVV.

From Maastricht train station, follow the river south to **Gronsveld**, picking up signs to the eleventh-century village of St Geertruid. The black and white half-timbered farmsteads in these villages are known as *vakwerkhuisjes*, built from clay, wood and dried dung. The road snakes over hills draped with vineyards before swooping into the villages **Mheer**, **Noorbeek** and **Slenaken** – all very pretty and popular with walkers throughout the year. At Slenaken, the road develops some hairpin tendencies as it climbs the valley side above. Continue through **Eperheide** and **Epen**, with sweeping views across to the rolling valleys of Belgium on the right. Between Epen and **Vaals**, there's a gradual eight-kilometre climb on narrow roads, winding between woods of red oaks, with glimpses of bright green farmland below. For a six-kilometre round-trip to the highest point in the Netherlands, follow the signs to the **Drielandenpunt** (see opposite) from Vaals – the monument celebrating 321m of altitude is just in front of the concrete observation tower. Otherwise, follow the main road out of Vaals (there's a dedicated cycle lane), turning left to **Vijlen** where ploughed fields and potatoes take up as much space on the main street as the houses. Surrounding you is a panoramic view over Belgium, Germany and the Netherlands, beautiful on a clear day with the wind turbines swishing away in the distance. From **Mechelen** and **Gulpen**, you're in striking distance of **Valkenburg** to the north, approached through the old town. Climb the steep but brief Cauberg hill to return to Maastricht, enjoying a speedy descent between orchards and farmland with the city locked in your sights. Once on the outskirts, follow the cycle route signs to bring you back to the station.

An alternative (and shorter) return route is to continue from Gulpen to Maastricht on a straight route via **Margraten** and **Cadier-en-Keer**.

Practicalities

The **VVV**, Theodoor Dorrenplein 5 (April–June Mon–Sat 9am–5pm, Sun 10am–2pm; July & Aug Mon–Fri 9am–5.30pm, Sat 9am–5pm, Sun 10am–2pm; Sept–March Mon–Fri 9am–5pm; ☎043/609 8600, ⓦwww.vvvzuidlimburg.nl), has maps and information on all Valkenburg's attractions, as well as lists of the dozens of **hotels** and **pensions**.

Among the cheapest hotels is *La Casa* at Grotestraat 25–27 (☎043/601 2180, ⓦwww.la-casa.nl; ❶), with eight recently redone rooms and a kitsch Spanish/Italian restaurant. Slightly more upmarket are the family-run *Hostellerie Valckenborgh*, Hovetstraat 3 (☎043/601 2484, ⓦwww.valckenborgh.nl; ❷), and *Gaudi*, Grendelplein 14 (☎043/601 5333, ⓦwww.hotelgaudi.nl; ❶–❷), inspired by the Spanish architect and centrally located with fifteen rooms. The nearest **campsite** is *Den Driesch*, a short walk up Dahlemerweg from Grendelplein on the left (☎043/601 2025, ⓦwww.campingdendriesch.nl; April to mid-Dec), which attracts a young crowd. Virtually every second building in Valkenburg is a **restaurant**, though they're all very touristy and fairly cheap, and nowhere stands out.

Heerlen

HEERLEN, ten minutes northeast of Valkenburg by train, is an ugly modern town, but it does have one enjoyable attraction, the excellent **Thermen Museum**, Coriovallumstraat 9 (Tues–Fri 10am–5pm, Sat & Sun noon–5pm; €5.50; ⓦwww.thermenmuseum.nl), which incorporates the remains of a bath complex from the Roman city of Coriovallum – a key settlement on the Cologne–Boulogne trade route. These have been enclosed in a gleaming, purpose-built hi-tech structure, with walkways leading across the ruins and tapes (in English) explaining what's what. An adjacent room displays finds and artefacts from the site, including glasswork from Cologne, shards of pottery, tombstones and coins, all neatly labelled. To get to the museum, follow Saroleastraat from the station as far as Raadhuisplein and turn right.

Travel details

Trains

Breda to: Dordrecht (every 20min; 20min); 's Hertogenbosch (every 30min; 30min); Maastricht (every 30min; 1hr 50min); Middelburg (every 30min; 1hr 15min); Roosendaal (every 30min; 17min).
Eindhoven to: Roermond (every 30min; 30min); Venlo (every 30min; 35min).
's Hertogenbosch to: Eindhoven (every 10min; 25min).
Maastricht to: Amsterdam (every 30min; 2hr 35min); Den Haag/The Hague (every 30min; 2hr 45min); Roermond (every 30min; 40min).
Middelburg to: Bergen-op-Zoom (every 30min; 40min); Goes (every 30min; 13min); Roosendaal (every 30min; 50min).

Roermond to: Venlo (every 30min; 24min).
Roosendaal to: Breda (every 30min; 17min); Dordrecht (every 20min; 25min).
Tilburg to: Eindhoven (every 20min; 35min); 's Hertogenbosch (every 30min; 15min).
Vlissingen to: Middelburg (every 30min; 8min).

Buses

Middelburg to: Delta Expo (Mon–Fri 2 hourly, Sat hourly, Sun every 2hr; 30min); Renesse (hourly; 45min); Veere (Mon–Sat hourly; 12min).
Renesse to: Brouwershaven (hourly; 30min).
Zierikzee to: Goes (every 30min; 30min).

Ferries

Vlissingen to: Breskens (every 30min; 30min).

Contexts

Contexts

History

T he country now known as the **Netherlands** didn't reach its present delimitations until 1830. Until then the borders of the entire region, formerly known as the **Low Countries** and including present-day Belgium and Luxembourg, were continually being redrawn following battles, treaties and alliances. Inevitably, then, what follows is, in its early parts at least, an outline of the history of the whole region, rather than a straightforward history of the Netherlands as such. Please note, incidentally, that the term "Holland" refers to the province – not the country – throughout.

Beginnings

Little is known of the **prehistoric** settlers of the Low Countries, their visible remains largely confined to the far north of the Netherlands, where mounds known as *terpen* were built to keep the sea at bay in Friesland and Groningen. There are also megalithic tombs (*hunebeds*) among the hills near Emmen in the northeast corner of the Netherlands, but quite how these tie in with the Iron Age culture that had established itself across the region by the fifth century BC is impossible to say.

Clearer details of the region begin to emerge at the time of Julius Caesar's conquest of Gaul (broadly France) in 57 to 50 BC. He found three tribal groupings living in the region: the mainly Celtic **Belgae** (hence the nineteenth-century term "Belgium") settled by the Rhine, Maas and Waal to the south; the Germanic **Frisians** living on the marshy coastal strip north of the Scheldt; and the **Batavi**, another Germanic people, inhabiting the swampy river banks of what is now the southern Netherlands. The Belgae were conquered and their lands incorporated into the imperial province of **Gallia Belgica**, but the territory of the Batavi and Frisians was not considered worthy of colonization. These tribes were granted the status of allies, a source of recruitment for the Roman legions and curiosity for imperial travellers. In 50 AD **Pliny** observed: "Here a wretched race is found, inhabiting either the more elevated spots or artificial mounds… When the waves cover the surrounding area they are like so many mariners on board a ship, and when again the tide recedes their condition is that of so many shipwrecked men."

Romans and Merovingians

The Roman occupation of Gallia Belgica continued for 500 years until the legions were pulled back to protect the heartlands of the crumbling empire. As the empire collapsed in chaos and confusion, the Germanic **Franks**, who had been settling within Gallia Belgica from the third century, filled the power vacuum, establishing a **Merovingian** kingdom around their capital Tournai (in modern Belgium) with their allies the Belgae. A great swathe of forest extending from the Scheldt to the Ardennes separated this Frankish kingdom from the more confused situation to the north and east, where other tribes of Franks settled along the Scheldt and Leie, Saxons occupied parts of Overijssel and Gelderland, and the Frisians clung to the seashore.

Towards the end of the fifth century, the Merovingian king Clovis was converted to **Christianity** and the faith slowly filtered north, spread by energetic missionaries like St Willibrord, first bishop of Utrecht, from about 710, and St Boniface, who was killed by the Frisians in 754 in a final act of pagan resistance before they too were converted. Meanwhile, after the death of the last distinguished Merovingian king, Dagobert, in 638, power passed increasingly to the so-called "mayors of the palace", a hereditary position whose most outstanding occupant was **Charles Martel** (c.690–741). Martel inherited a large but all-too-obviously shambolic kingdom, whose military weakness he determined to remedy. Traditionally, the Merovingian (Frankish) army was comprised of a body of infantry led by a small group of cavalry. Martel replaced this with a mounted force of highly trained knights who bore their own military expenses in return for land – the beginnings of the **feudal system**. These reforms came just in time to save Christendom: in 711 the extraordinary Arab advance, which had begun early in the seventh century in modern-day Saudi Arabia, reached the Pyrenees and a massive Muslim army occupied southern France in preparation for further conquests. In the event, Martel defeated the invaders outside Tours in 732, one of Europe's most crucial engagements and one that saved France from Arab conquest for good.

The Carolingians

Ten years after Martel's death, his son, Pepin the Short, formally usurped the Merovingian throne with the blessing of the pope, becoming the first of the **Carolingian** dynasty, whose most famous member was **Charlemagne**, son of Pepin and king of the west Franks from 768. In a dazzling series of campaigns, Charlemagne extended his empire south into Italy, west to the Pyrenees, north to Denmark and east to the Oder. His secular authority was bolstered by his coronation as the first **Holy Roman Emperor** in 800, a title bestowed on him by the pope in order to legitimize his claim as the successor to the emperors of imperial Rome.

The strength and stability of Charlemagne's court at Aachen spread to the Low Countries, bringing a building boom that created a string of superb Romanesque churches like Maastricht's St Servaas, and a trading bonanza along the region's principal rivers. However, unlike his Roman predecessors, Charlemagne was subject to the divisive inheritance laws of the Salian tribe of Franks, and after his death in 814, his kingdom was divided between his grandsons into three roughly parallel strips of territory, the precursors of France, the Low Countries and Germany.

The growth of the towns

The tripartite division of Charlemagne's empire placed the **Low Countries** between the emergent French- and German-speaking nations, a dangerous location, which was subsequently to decide much of its history. Amid the cobweb of local alliances that made up **early feudal western Europe** in the ninth and tenth centuries, however, this was not apparent. During this period, French kings and German emperors exercised a general authority over the region, but power was effectively in the hands of local lords who, remote from central control, brought a degree of local stability. From the twelfth century, feudalism slipped into a gradual decline, the intricate pattern of localized allegiances undermined by the increasing strength of certain lords, whose power and wealth often exceeded that of their nominal sovereign. Preoccupied by territorial squabbles, this streamlined nobility was usually willing to assist the growth of towns by granting charters that permitted a certain amount of **autonomy** in exchange for tax revenues and military and labour services. The first major cities were the cloth towns of Flanders – Bruges, Ieper (Ypres) and Ghent. Meanwhile, their smaller northern neighbours concentrated on trade, exploiting their strategic position at the junction of the region's main waterways – Amsterdam being a case in point.

Burgundian rule and the Habsburgs

By the late fourteenth century the political situation in the Low Countries was fairly clear: five lords controlled most of the region, paying only nominal homage to their French or German overlords. In 1419 **Philip the Good** of Burgundy succeeded to the countship of Flanders and by a series of adroit political moves gained control over Holland, Zeeland, Brabant and Limburg to the north, and Antwerp, Namur and Luxembourg to the south. He consolidated his power by establishing a strong central administration in Bruges and restricting the privileges granted in the towns' charters. During his reign Bruges became a showcase for the Hanseatic League, a mainly German association of towns which acted as a trading group and protected their interests by an exclusive system of trading tariffs. Philip died in 1467 to be succeeded by his son, **Charles the Bold**, who was killed in battle ten years later, plunging his father's carefully crafted domain into turmoil. The French seized the opportunity to take back Arras and Burgundy and before the people of Flanders would agree to fight the French, they kidnapped Charles's daughter, Mary, and forced her to sign a charter that restored the civic privileges removed by her grandfather Philip.

After her release, Mary married the **Habsburg** Maximilian of Austria, who assumed sole authority when Mary was killed in a riding accident in 1482. **Maximilian** continued to implement the centralizing policies of Philip the Good, but in 1494, when he became Holy Roman Emperor, he transferred control of the Low Countries to his son, Philip the Handsome. The latter died in 1506 and his territories were passed on to Maximilian's grandson **Charles V**, who also became King of Spain and Holy Roman Emperor in 1516 and 1519, respectively. Charles was suspicious of the turbulent burghers of Flanders and, following in Maximilian's footsteps, favoured Antwerp at their expense; it soon became the greatest port in the empire, part of a general movement of trade and prosperity away from Flanders to the cities to the north.

Through sheer force of will and military might, Charles bent the merchant cities of the Low Countries to his will, but regardless of this display of force, a spiritual trend was emerging that would soon question not only the rights of the emperor but also rock the power of the Catholic Church itself.

Stirrings of the Reformation

An alliance of Church and State had dominated the medieval world: pope and bishops, kings and counts were supposedly the representatives of God on earth, and they combined to crush religious dissent wherever it appeared. Much of their authority depended on the ignorance of the population, who were entirely dependent on their priests for the interpretation of the scriptures, their view of the world carefully controlled.

There were many complex reasons for the **Reformation**, the stirring of religious revolt that stood sixteenth-century Europe on its head, but certainly the **development of typography** was key. For the first time, printers were able to produce relatively cheap bibles in quantity, and the religious texts were no longer the exclusive property of the Church. Consequently, as the populace snaffled up the bibles, so a welter of debate spread across much of western Europe under the auspices of theologians like **Erasmus of Rotterdam** (1465–1536), who wished to cleanse the Catholic Church of its corruptions, superstitions and extravagant ceremony; only later did many of these same thinkers – principally **Martin Luther** (1483–1546) – decide to support a breakaway church. In 1517, Luther produced his 95 theses against indulgences, rejecting – among other things – Christ's presence in the Eucharist and denying the Church's monopoly on the interpretation of the Bible. There was no way back, and when Luther's works were disseminated his ideas gained a European following among reforming groups that were soon branded **Lutheran** by the Catholic Church. Luther asserted that the Church's political power was subservient to that of the state, whereas the supporters of another great reforming thinker, **John Calvin** (1509–64), emphasized the importance of individual conscience and the need for redemption through the grace of Christ rather than the confessional.

These seeds of **Protestantism** fell on fertile ground among the Low Countries' merchants, whose wealth and independence could not easily be accommodated within a rigid caste society. Similarly, their employees, the guildsmen and their apprentices, had a long history of opposing arbitrary authority, and were soon convinced of the need to reform an autocratic, venal church. In 1555, **Charles V abdicated**, transferring his German lands to his brother Ferdinand, and his Italian, Spanish and Low Countries territories to his son, the fanatically Catholic **Philip II**. In the short term, the scene was set for a bitter confrontation, while the dynastic ramifications of the division of the Habsburg Empire were to complicate European affairs for centuries.

The revolt of the Netherlands

After his father's abdication, Philip decided to teach his heretical subjects a lesson they wouldn't forget. He garrisoned the towns of the Low Countries with Spanish mercenaries, imported the Inquisition and passed a series of anti-Protestant edicts. However, other pressures on the Habsburg Empire forced him into a tactical withdrawal and he transferred control to his sister, **Margaret of Parma**, in 1559. Based in Brussels, the equally resolute Margaret implemented the policies of her brother with gusto. In 1561 she reorganized the Church and created fourteen new bishoprics, a move that was construed as a wresting of power from civil authority, and an attempt to destroy the local aristocracy's powers of religious patronage. Protestantism – and Protestant sympathies – now spread to the nobility, who formed the "League of the Nobility" to counter Habsburg policy. The League petitioned Philip for moderation, but was dismissed out of hand by one of Margaret's Walloon advisers, who called them *ces geux* ("those beggars"), an epithet that was to be enthusiastically adopted by the rebels. In 1565 a harvest failure caused a winter famine among the workers, and, after years of repression, they struck back: a Protestant sermon in the tiny Flemish textile town of Steenvoorde incited the congregation to purge the local church of its "papist idolatry". The crowd attacked the church's reliquaries and shrines, smashed the stained-glass windows and terrorized the priests, thereby launching the **Iconoclastic Fury**, which spread like wildfire: within ten days churches had been ransacked from one end of the Low Countries to the other, nowhere more so than in Antwerp.

The ferocity of this outbreak shocked the upper classes into renewed support for Spain, and Margaret regained the allegiance of most nobles – with the principal exception of the country's greatest landowner, Prince William of Orange-Nassau, known as **William the Silent** (though William the Taciturn is a better translation of the Dutch moniker). Of Germanic descent, William was raised a Catholic but the excesses and rigidity of Philip had caused him to side with the Protestant movement. A firm believer in individual freedom and religious tolerance, William became a symbol of liberty, but after the Fury had revitalized the pro-Spanish party, he prudently slipped away to his estates in Germany.

Philip II was encouraged by the increase in support for Margaret and so, in 1567, he sent the **Duke of Alva**, with an army of 10,000 men, to the Low Countries to suppress his religious opponents absolutely. Margaret was, however, not at all pleased by Philip's decision and, when Alva arrived in Brussels, she resigned in a huff, thereby abandoning the Low Countries to military rule. One of Alva's first acts was to set up the Commission of Civil Unrest, which was soon nicknamed the "**Council of Blood**", after its habit of executing those it examined: no fewer than 12,000 citizens were polished off by the commission, mostly for participating in the Fury. Initially the repression worked: in 1568, when William attempted an invasion from Germany, the towns, garrisoned by the Spanish, offered no support. William waited and considered other means of defeating Alva. In April 1572, a band of privateers entered Brielle on the Maas and captured it from the Spanish. This was one of several commando-style attacks by the so-called **Waterguezen**, or sea-beggars, who were at first obliged to operate from England, although it was soon possible for them to secure bases in the Netherlands, whose citizens had grown to loathe Alva and his Spaniards.

After the success at Brielle, the revolt spread rapidly: by June the rebels controlled most of the province of Holland and William was able to take command of his troops in Delft. Alva and his son Frederick fought back, taking Gelderland, Overijssel and the towns of Zutphen and Naarden, and then Haarlem, where they massacred the Calvinist ministers and most of the defenders. But the Protestants retaliated: utilizing their superior naval power, the dykes were cut and the Spanish forces, unpaid and threatened with watery destruction, were forced to withdraw. Frustrated, Philip replaced Alva with **Luis de Resquesens**, who initially had some success in the south, where the Catholic majority was more willing to compromise with Spanish rule than their northern neighbours.

William's triumphant relief of Leiden in 1574 increased the confidence of the rebel forces, and when de Resquesens died in 1576, his unpaid garrison in Antwerp mutinied and attacked the town, slaughtering some eight thousand of its people in what was known as the **Spanish Fury**. Though Spain still held several towns, the massacre alienated the south and pushed its inhabitants into the arms of William, whose troops now swept into Brussels, the heart of imperial power. Momentarily, it seemed possible for the whole region to unite behind William, and all signed the **Union of Brussels**, which demanded the departure of foreign troops as a condition for accepting a diluted Habsburg sovereignty. This was followed, in 1576, by the **Pacification of Ghent**, a regional agreement that guaranteed freedom of religious belief, a necessary precondition for any union between the largely Protestant north (the Netherlands) and Catholic south (Belgium and Luxembourg).

The end of the revolt

Philip was, however, not inclined to compromise, especially when he realized that William's Calvinist sympathies were giving his newly found Walloon and Flemish allies the jitters. The king bided his time until 1578, when, with his enemies still arguing among themselves, he sent another army from Spain to the Low Countries under the command of Alessandro Farnese, the **Duke of Parma**. Events played into Parma's hands. In 1579, tired of all the wrangling, seven northern provinces (Holland, Zeeland, Utrecht, Groningen, Friesland,

Overijssel and Gelderland) broke with their southerly neighbours to sign the **Union of Utrecht**, an alliance against Spain that was to be the first unification of the Netherlands as an identifiable country – the so-called **United Provinces**. The agreement stipulated freedom of belief within the provinces, an important step since the struggle against Spain wasn't simply a religious one: many Catholics disliked the Spanish occupation and William did not wish to alienate this possible source of support. This liberalism did not, however, extend to freedom of worship, although to all intents and purposes a blind eye was turned to the celebration of Mass if it was done privately and inconspicuously – giving rise to the "hidden churches" found throughout the Netherlands today. Meanwhile, in the south – and also in 1579 – representatives of the southern provinces signed the **Union of Arras**, a Catholic-led agreement that declared loyalty to Philip II in counterbalance to the Union of Utrecht in the north. Parma used this area as a base to recapture all of Flanders and Antwerp, which fell after a long and cruel siege in 1585. But Parma was unable to advance any further north and the Low Countries were, de facto, divided into two – the Spanish Netherlands and the United Provinces – beginning a separation that would lead, after many changes, to the creation of three modern countries – Belgium, Luxembourg and the Netherlands.

The United Provinces 1579–1648

To follow the developments of the sixteenth and seventeenth centuries in the **United Provinces**, it's necessary to have an idea of its organization. Throughout the period, Holland, today comprising Noord- and Zuid-Holland, was by far the dominant province economically and politically, and although the provinces maintained a degree of decentralized independence, as far as the United Provinces as a whole were concerned, what Holland said pretty much went. The assembly of these United Provinces was known as the **States General** and it met at Den Haag (The Hague); it had no domestic legislative authority, and could only carry out foreign policy by unanimous decision, a formula designed to make potential waverers feel more secure. The role of **Stadholder** was the most important in each province, roughly equivalent to that of governor, though the same person could occupy this position in any number of provinces – and mostly did, with the Orange-Nassaus characteristically picking up five or six provinces at any one time. The **Council Pensionary** was another major post. The man who held either title in Holland was a centre of political power. Pieter Geyl, in his seminal *Revolt of the Netherlands*, defined the end result as the establishment of a republic which was "oligarchic, erastian [and] decentralized".

In 1584, a Catholic fanatic assassinated William the Silent at his residence in Delft. It was a grievous blow to the provinces and, as William's son **Maurice** was only 17, power passed to **Johan van Oldenbarneveldt**, the country's leading statesman and Council Pensionary of Rotterdam and ultimately Holland. Things were going badly in the war against the Spanish: Nijmegen had fallen and Henry III of France refused to help even though the States General had made him tentative offers of sovereignty. In desperation, Oldenbarneveldt turned to **Elizabeth I** of England, who suggested the Earl of Leicester as governor general. Leicester was accepted, but he completely mishandled the military situation, alienating the Dutch into the bargain. Short of options, Oldenbarneveldt and Maurice then stepped into the breach and, somewhat to their surprise, drove the Spanish back. International events then played into their hands: in 1588, the English defeated the Spanish Armada and the following year the powerful king Henry III of France died. Most important of all, Philip II of Spain, the scourge of the Low Countries, died in 1598, a necessary preamble to the **Twelve Year Truce** (1609–21) signed between the Habsburgs and the United Provinces, which grudgingly accepted the independence of the new republic.

The early seventeenth century

In the breathing space created by the Twelve Year Truce, the **rivalry** between Maurice and Oldenbarneveldt intensified and an obscure argument within the Calvinist church on predestination proved the catalyst for Oldenbarneveldt's downfall. The quarrel, between two Leiden theologians, began in 1612: one of them, Armenius, argued that God gave man the choice of accepting or rejecting faith; Gomarus, his opponent, that predestination was absolute – to the degree that God chooses who will be saved and who damned, with man powerless in the decision. This row between the two groups (known respectively as Remonstrants and Counter-Remonstrants) soon became attached to the political divisions within the republic. When a synod was arranged at Dordrecht to resolve the doctrinal matter, the province of Holland, led by Oldenbarneveldt, refused to attend, insisting on Holland's right to decide its own religious orthodoxies. At heart, he and his fellow deputies supported the provincial independence favoured by Remonstrant sympathizers, whereas Maurice sided with the Counter-Remonstrants, who favoured a strong central authority. The Counter-Remonstrants won at Dordrecht and Maurice, with his troops behind him, quickly overcame his opponents and had Oldenbarneveldt arrested. In May 1619 Oldenbarneveldt was **executed** in Den Haag "for having conspired to dismember the states of the Netherlands and greatly troubled God's church".

The Thirty Years' War

With the end of the Twelve Year Truce in 1621, fighting with Spain broke out once again, this time part of the more general **Thirty Years' War** (1618–48), a largely religious-based conflict between Catholic and Protestant countries that involved most of western Europe. In the Low Countries, the Spanish were initially successful, but they were weakened by war with France and by the fresh attacks of Maurice's successor, his brother **Frederick Henry**. From 1625, the Spaniards suffered a series of defeats on land and sea that forced them out of what is today the southern part of the Netherlands, and in 1648 they were compelled to accept the humiliating **Peace of Westphalia**, the general treaty that ended the Thirty Years' War. Under its terms, the independence of the United Provinces was formally recognized and the Dutch were even able to insist that the Scheldt estuary be closed to shipping, an action designed to destroy the trade and prosperity of Antwerp, which – along with the rest of modern-day Belgium – remained part of the Habsburg empire. By this act, the commercial expansion and pre-eminence of Amsterdam was assured, and the Golden Age began.

The Golden Age

The brilliance of **Amsterdam**'s explosion onto the European scene is as difficult to underestimate as it is to detail. The size of the city's merchant fleet carrying Baltic grain into Europe had long been considerable and even during the long war with Spain it had continued to expand. Indeed, not only were the Spaniards unable to undermine it, but they were, on occasion, even obliged to use Dutch ships to supply their own troops – part of a burgeoning cargo trade that was another key ingredient of Amsterdam's economic success.

It was, however, the emasculation of Antwerp by the Treaty of Westphalia that launched a period of extraordinarily dynamic growth – the so-called **Golden Age** – and Amsterdam quickly became the emporium for the products of north and south Europe and the new colonies in the East and West Indies. Dutch banking and investment brought further prosperity, and by the mid-seventeenth century Amsterdam's wealth was spectacular. The Calvinist bourgeoisie indulged themselves in fine canal houses and commissioned images of themselves in group portraits. Civic pride knew no bounds: great monuments to self-aggrandizement, such as Amsterdam's new town hall, were hastily erected, and, if some went hungry, few starved, as the poor were cared for in municipal almshouses. The arts flourished and religious tolerance extended even to the traditional scapegoats, the Jews, and in particular the Sephardic Jews, who had been hounded from Spain by the Inquisition but were guaranteed freedom from religious persecution under the terms of the Union of Utrecht of 1579. By the end of the eighteenth century, Jews accounted for ten percent of the city's inhabitants. Guilds and craft associations thrived, and in the first half of the seventeenth century the city's population quadrupled. Furthermore, although Amsterdam was the centre of this boom, economic ripples spread across much of the United Provinces. Dutch farmers were, for instance, able to sell all they could produce in the expanding city and a string of Zuider Zee ports cashed in on the flourishing Baltic trade.

The East and West India companies

Throughout the Golden Age, one organization that kept the country's coffers brimming was the **Dutch East India Company**. Formed in 1602, this Amsterdam-controlled enterprise sent ships to Asia, Indonesia, and China to bring back spices, woods and other assorted valuables. The States General granted the company a trading monopoly in all lands east of the Cape of Good Hope and, for good measure, threw in unlimited military powers over the lands it controlled. As a consequence, the company became a colonial power in its own right, governing, at one time or another, parts of Malaya, Sri Lanka and parts of modern-day Indonesia. In 1621, the **West India Company** was inaugurated to protect Dutch interests in the Americas and Africa. However, this second company never achieved the success of its sister, expending most of its energies in waging war on Spanish and Portuguese colonies from its base in Surinam. The company was dismantled in 1674, ten years after its nascent colony of New Amsterdam had been captured by the British and renamed **New York**. Elsewhere, the Netherlands held on to its colonies for as long as possible: Java and Sumatra remained under Dutch control until 1949.

Johan de Witt versus William III of Orange

Although the economics of the Golden Age were dazzling, the **politics** were dismal. The United Provinces were dogged by interminable wrangling between those who hankered for a central, unified government under the pre-eminent **House of Orange-Nassau** and those who championed provincial autonomy. Frederick Henry died in 1647 and his successor, William II, lasted just three years before his death from smallpox. A week after William's death, his wife bore the son who would become William III of England, but in the meantime the leaders of the province of Holland seized their opportunity. They forced measures through the States General that abolished the position of Stadholder, thereby reducing the powers of the Orangists and increasing those of the provinces, chiefly Holland itself. Holland's foremost figure in these years was **Johan de Witt**, Council Pensionary to the States General. He guided the country through wars with England and Sweden, concluding a triple alliance between the two countries and the United Provinces in 1678. This didn't last, however, and when France and England marched on the Provinces two years later, the republic was in deep trouble – previous victories had been at sea – and the army, weak and disorganized, could not withstand an attack. In panic, the country turned to **William III of Orange** for leadership and Johan de Witt was brutally murdered by a mob of Orangist sympathizers in Den Haag. By 1678, William had defeated the French and made peace with the English – and was rewarded (along with his wife Mary) with the English crown ten years later.

The United Provinces in the eighteenth century

Though William III had defeated the French, Louis XIV retained designs on the United Provinces and the pot was kept boiling in a long series of dynastic wars that ranged across northern Europe. In 1700, Charles II of Spain, the last of the Spanish Habsburgs, died childless, bequeathing the Spanish throne and control of the Spanish Netherlands to Philip of Anjou, Louis' grandson. Louis promptly forced Philip to cede the latter to France, which was, with every justification, construed as a threat to the balance of power by France's neighbours. The **War of the Spanish Succession** ensued, with the United Provinces, England and Austria forming the Triple Alliance to thwart the French king. The war itself was a haphazard, long-winded affair distinguished by the spectacular victories of the Duke of Marlborough at Blenheim, Ramillies and Malplaquet. It dragged on until the **Treaty of Utrecht** of 1713 in which France finally abandoned its claim to the Spanish Netherlands.

All this fighting had, however, drained the United Provinces' reserves and its slow economic and political decline began, accelerated by the ossification of its ruling class. This reflected the emergence of an increasingly socially static society, with power and wealth concentrated within a small, immovable elite. Furthermore, with the threat of foreign conquest effectively removed, the Dutch ruling class divided into two main camps – the **Orangists** and the pro-French "**Patriots**" – whose interminable squabbling soon brought political life to a virtual standstill. The situation deteriorated even further in the latter half of the century and the last few years of the United Provinces present a sorry state of affairs.

French occupation and the United Kingdom of the Netherlands

In 1795 the French, aided by the Patriots, invaded, setting up the **Batavian Republic** and dissolving the United Provinces – and much of the hegemony of the rich Dutch merchants. Effectively part of the Napoleonic empire, the Netherlands also obliged to wage unenthusiastic war with England, and in 1806 Napoleon appointed his brother **Louis** as king in an attempt to create a dynastic gulf between the country and England. Louis, however, wasn't willing to allow the Netherlands to become a simple satellite of France; he ignored Napoleon's directives and after just four years of rule his brother forced him to abdicate. The country was then formally incorporated into the French Empire, and for three gloomy years suffered occupation and heavy taxation to finance French military adventures.

Following Napoleon's disastrous retreat from Moscow, the Orangist faction surfaced to exploit weakening French control. In 1813, Frederick William, son of the exiled William V, returned to the country and eight months later, under the terms of the **Congress of Vienna** which concluded the Napoleonic Wars, was crowned King William I of the **United Kingdom of the Netherlands**, incorporating both the old United Provinces and the Spanish (Austrian) Netherlands. A strong-willed man, he spent much of the latter part of his life trying to control his disparate kingdom, but failed primarily because the Catholic south did not trust him. The southern provinces revolted against his rule and in 1830 the independent Kingdom of Belgium was proclaimed.

From 1830 to the early twentieth century

In 1839, a final fling of the military dice gave William most of Limburg, and all but ended centuries of territorial change within the Low Countries. The Netherlands benefited from this new stability both economically and politically, emerging as a unitary state with a burgeoning industrial and entrepot economy. The outstanding political figure of the times, **Jan Rudolph Thorbecke**, formed three ruling cabinets (1849–53, 1862–66 and 1872, in the year of his death) and steered the Netherlands through these changes. The political parties of the late eighteenth century had wished to resurrect the power and prestige of the seventeenth-century Netherlands; Thorbecke and his allies resigned themselves to the country's reduced status and eulogized the advantages of being a small power. For the first time, from about 1850, liberty was seen as a luxury made possible by the country's very lack of power, and the malaise that had long disturbed public life gave way to a positive appreciation of the very narrowness of its national existence. One of the results of Thorbecke's liberalism was a gradual extension of the franchise, culminating in the **Act of Universal Suffrage** of 1917.

The war years

The Netherlands remained neutral in **World War I** and although it suffered privations from the Allied blockade of German war materials, this was offset by the profits accrued by continuing to trade with both sides. Similar attempts to remain neutral in **World War II** failed: the Germans invaded on May 10, 1940, destroying Rotterdam four days later, a salutary lesson that made prolonged resistance inconceivable. The Dutch army was quickly overwhelmed, Queen Wilhelmina fled to London to set up a government-in-exile, and members of the **NSB**, the Dutch fascist party, which had welcomed the invaders, were rewarded with positions of authority. Nevertheless, in the early stages of the occupation, life for the average Netherlander went on pretty much as usual, which is just what the Germans wanted – they were determined to transform the country by degrees. Even when the first roundups of the **Jews** began in late 1940, many managed to turn a blind eye, though the newly outlawed Dutch Communist Party did organize a widely supported strike to protest, a gesture perhaps, but an important one all the same.

As the war progressed, so the German grip got tighter and the Dutch **Resistance** stronger, its activities focused on destroying German supplies and munitions as well as the forgery of identity papers, a real Dutch speciality. The Resistance also trumpeted its efforts in a battery of underground newspapers, most notably *Het Parool* (The Password), which survives in good form today. Inevitably, the Resistance paid a heavy price with some 23,000 of its fighters and sympathizers losing their lives, but Amsterdam's Jews took the worst punishment: in 1940, Amsterdam's Jewish population, swollen by refugees from Hitler's Germany, was around 140,000, but by the end of the war there were only a few thousand left, rendering the Jodenhoek deserted and derelict.

Liberation began from the south in the autumn of 1944. To speed the process, the British determined on **Operation Market Garden**, an ambitious plan to finish the war quickly by creating an Allied corridor stretching from Eindhoven to Arnhem. If it had been successful, the Allies would have secured control of the country's three main rivers and been able to drive on into Germany, thereby isolating the occupying forces in the western Netherlands. On September 17, 1944, the 1st Airborne Division parachuted into the countryside around Oosterbeek, a small village near the most northerly target of the operation, the **bridge at Arnhem**. However, German opposition was much stronger than expected and after heavy fighting the paratroopers could only take the northern end of the bridge. The advancing British army was unable to break through fast enough, and after four days the decimated battalion defending the bridge was forced to withdraw.

With the failure of Operation Market Garden, the Allies were obliged to resort to more orthodox military tactics. In their push towards Germany, they slowly cleared the east and south of the country in the winter and spring of 1944–45, leaving the coastal provinces pretty much untouched, though here lack of food and fuel created desperate conditions, with hundreds starving to death. Finally, on **May 5, 1945**, the remains of the German army in the Netherlands surrendered to the Canadians at Wageningen.

Reconstruction: 1945 to 1960

The **postwar years** were spent patching up the damage of occupation and liberation: Rotterdam was rebuilt in double-quick time, the dykes blown during the war were speedily repaired, and the canals and waterways were soon cleared of their accumulated debris. At the same time, the country began a vast construction programme, with modern suburbs mushrooming around every major city, especially Amsterdam, where almost all the land projected for use by the year 2000 was in fact used by 1970. But an ill-advised foreign adventure was to mar the late 1940s and early 1950s: the former **Dutch colonies** of Java and Sumatra had been occupied by the Japanese at the outbreak of the war and they were now ruled by a nationalist Republican government that refused to recognize Dutch sovereignty. Following the failure of talks between Den Haag and the islanders in 1947, the Dutch sent in the army in a colonial enterprise that soon became a bloody debacle. International opposition was intense and, after much condemnation, the Dutch reluctantly surrendered their most important Asian colonies, which were incorporated as **Indonesia**, in 1950.

Back home, **tragedy** struck on February 1, 1953, when an unusually high tide was pushed over Zeeland's sea defences by a westerly wind, flooding around 150 square kilometres of land and drowning over 1800 people. The response was to secure the area's future with the **Delta Project**, closing off the western part of the Scheldt and Maas estuaries with massive sea dykes. A brilliant and graceful piece of engineering, the main storm surge barrier on the Oosterschelde was finally completed in 1986. Amsterdam itself had already been secured by the completion of the **Afsluitdijk** between Noord-Holland and Friesland in 1932. This dyke separated the North Sea from the former Zuider Zee, which now became the freshwater **IJsselmeer**, and in 1976 a second dyke was added, calving the Markermeer from the IJsselmeer. For more on the Netherlands' sea defences see the *The Battle with the Sea* colour section.

The 1960s to the 1980s

The radical and youthful mass movements that swept across the West in the 1960s transformed Amsterdam from a middling, rather conservative city into a turbocharged hotbed of hippy action – and where Amsterdam led, all the big cities of the Randstad followed. Initially, it was the Provos (see box below) who led the counter-cultural charge, but in 1967 they dissolved themselves and many of their supporters moved on to the **squatter movement**, which opposed the wholesale destruction of low-cost (often old) urban housing as envisaged by many municipal councils. For many squatters, it seemed as if local councils were neglecting the needs of their poorer citizens in favour of business interests, and in Amsterdam, the epicentre of the movement, there were regular confrontations between the police and the protestors at a handful of symbolic squats. The first major incident came in Amsterdam in March 1980 when several hundred police evicted squatters from premises on **Vondelstraat**. Afterwards there was widespread rioting, but this was small beer in comparison with the protests of

The Provos and the Kabouters

In 1963, one-time window cleaner and magician extraordinaire **Jasper Grootveld** won celebrity status by painting "K" – for *kanker* ("cancer") – on cigarette billboards throughout Amsterdam. Two years later, he proclaimed the statue of the *Lieverdje* ("Lovable Rascal") on the Spui (see p.65) the symbol of "tomorrow's addicted consumer" – since it had been donated to the city by a cigarette manufacturer – and organized large-scale gatherings there once a week. His actions enthused others, most notably **Roel van Duyn**, a philosophy student at Amsterdam University, who assembled a left-wing-cum-anarchist movement known as the **Provos** – short for *provocatie* ("provocation"). The Provos participated in Grootveld's meetings and then proceeded to organize their own street "**happenings**", which proved fantastically popular among young Amsterdammers. The number of Provos never exceeded about thirty and the group had no coherent structure, but they did have one clear aim – to bring points of political or social conflict to public attention by spectacular means. More than anything they were masters of publicity, and pursued their "games" with a spirit of fun rather than grim political fanaticism. The reaction of the Amsterdam police, however, was aggressive: the first two issues of the Provos' magazine were confiscated and, in July 1965, they intervened at a Saturday night "happening", setting a pattern for future confrontations. The magazine itself contained the Provos' manifesto, a set of policies which later appeared under the title "**The White Plans**". These included the famously popular **white bicycle plan**, which proposed that the council ban all cars in the city centre and supply 20,000 bicycles (painted white) for general public use.

There were regular police–Provo confrontations throughout 1965, but it was the **wedding of Princess Beatrix** to Claus von Amsberg on March 10, 1966, that provoked the most serious unrest. Amsberg had served in the German army during World War II and many Netherlanders were deeply offended by the marriage. Consequently, when hundreds took to the streets to protest, pelting the wedding procession with smoke bombs, a huge swathe of Dutch opinion supported them – to some degree or another. Amsberg himself got no more than he deserved when he was jeered with the refrain "Give us back the bicycles", a reference to the commandeering of hundreds of bikes by the retreating German army in 1945. The wedding over, the next crisis came in June when, much to the horror of the authorities, it appeared that students, workers and Provos were about to combine. In panic, the Hague government ordered the dismissal of Amsterdam's police chief, but in the event the Provos had peaked and the workers proved far from revolutionary, settling for arbitration on their various complaints instead.

The final twist in the Provos' tale was the formation of a splinter group called the **Kabouters**, named after a helpful gnome in Dutch folklore. Their manifesto described their form of socialism as "not of the clenched fist, but of the intertwined fingers, the erect penis, the escaping butterfly…" – appealing perhaps, but never massively popular.

April 30, 1980 – the **coronation day of Queen Beatrix** – when a mixed bag of squatters and leftists vigorously protested both the lavishness of the proceedings and the expense of refurbishing Beatrix's palace in Den Haag. Once again there was widespread rioting and this time it spread to other Dutch cities, though the unrest was short-lived.

Now at its peak, Amsterdam's squatter movement boasted around ten thousand activists, many of whom were involved in two more major confrontations with the police – the first at the Lucky Luyk squat, on Jan Luykenstraat, the second at the Wyers building in February 1984, when the squatters were forcibly cleared to make way for a hotel. Thereafter, the movement faded away, at least partly because of its repeated failure to stop the developers, who could now claim, with some justification, to be more sensitive to community needs.

The 1990s and the rise of Pim Fortuyn

In the 1990s, the country's street protests and massive squats became an increasingly distant memory, but some of the old ideas – and ideals – were carried forward by the **Greens**, who attracted – and continue to attract – a small but significant following in every national election. One of the recurring political problems was that the country's finely balanced system of **proportional representation** brought little rapid change, often getting mired in interminable compromise and thus becoming a bland if necessary business conducted between the three main parties, the **Protestant–Catholic CDA** coalition, the **Liberal VVD** and the **Socialist PvdA**. However, the entire political class received a jolt in the national elections of May 2002 when a brand-new Rightist grouping – **Leefbaar Neederlands** (Liveable Netherlands) – led by Rotterdam's **Pim Fortuyn**, swept to second place behind the CDA, securing seventeen percent of the national vote. Stylish and witty, openly gay and a former Marxist, Fortuyn managed to cover several popular bases at the same time, from the need for law and order through to tighter immigration controls. Most crucially, he also attacked the liberal establishment's espousal of multiculturalism even when some representatives of minority groups were deeply reactionary, anti-gay and sexist. Politically, it worked a treat, but a year later Fortuyn was assassinated and his party rapidly unravelled, losing most of its seats in the general election of January 2003. One of the reasons for Fortuyn's electoral success reflected the other shock to the Dutch system, which came with the publication of a damning report on the failure of the Dutch army to protect the Bosnian Muslims ensconced in the UN safe haven of **Srebrenica** in 1995. Published in April 2002, the report told a tale of extraordinary incompetence: the UN's Dutch soldiers were inadequately armed but still refused American assistance, and watched as Serb troops separated Muslim men and women in preparation for the mass executions, which the Dutch soldiers then did nothing to stop (though they were never involved). In a country that prides itself on its internationalism, the report was an especially hard blow and the whole of the PvdA-led government, under **Wim Kok**, resigned in April 2002 – coincidentally in the same year as the Netherlands dropped the guilder in favour of the euro.

To the present

The general election of 2003 was a close-run thing, and there was certainly a revival in PvdA fortunes, but a **rightist alliance** – consisting of the VVD, the CDA and the Lijst Pim Fortuyn (formerly Leefbaar Neederlands) – still managed to cobble together an administration under the leadership of **Jan Peter Balkenende**. In the event, this coalition proved most unstable, but Balkenende soldiered on (with different partners) until the national election of November 2006. This saw modest gains for the far right and left, but not enough to unseat Balkenende, who is currently the head of a majority CDA, PvdA and Christian Union (CU) administration. Superficially, therefore, and with Leefbaar Neederlands dead and gone (the party dissolved itself), it seemed that normal political service had been resumed, but although the CDA and the PvdA were once again the largest parties, there was an uneasy undertow. In truth, Fortuyn's popularity had pushed certain sorts of social debate, particularly on **immigration**, to the right.

The situation got much worse – and race relations much more tense – when, in late 2004, filmmaker **Theo van Gogh** was shot dead on an Amsterdam street by a Moroccan who objected to a film he had made – *Submission* – about Islamic violence against women. Shown on Dutch TV, the film was scripted by **Ayaan Hirsi Ali**, a Dutch politician and one-time Somali refugee, whose pronouncements on this same subject have been hard-hitting and headline-grabbing in equal measure. In an interview with the UK's *Daily Telegraph* in December 2004, she is reported to have said: "But tell me why any Muslim man would want Islamic women to be educated and emancipated? Would a Roman voluntarily have given up his slaves?". Unfortunately for Ali, she was engulfed by controversy of a different kind in 2006, when it turned out that her application for asylum had not been entirely truthful – and the ensuing furore created parliamentary panic. In the meantime, race relations had eased not least because Amsterdam city council in general – and the mayor, Job Cohen, in particular – handled the tension with great aplomb.

The crisis initiated by the murder of Theo van Gogh may have passed its peak, but the Netherlands is still a troubled country – the angst coming from the gap between how the Dutch conceive of themselves and how things seem to be turning out. The vast majority want their country to be liberal and tolerant, and yet there are undoubtedly racial tensions; nearly everyone wants the Netherlands to be prosperous, and yet they have been stung by the worldwide recession; and while most of the Dutch are still proud of the progressive social policies they introduced in the 1960s and 1970s, these very policies are not wearing too well. The best illustration is in Amsterdam, where the country's liberal attitude to soft drugs and prostitution may once have seemed sane and pragmatic, but has now turned the city into a target for thousands of tourists hellbent on pursuing the city's twin indulgences. To a solid bloc of Amsterdammers, the Red Light District now seems unpleasant, if not downright offensive, and there have been political rumblings about closing the "window brothels" down. Other Netherlanders are voting with their feet: in 2006, 132,000 mostly middle-class Dutch citizens emigrated, the largest number ever.

Art

D
esigned to serve only as a quick reference, the following **outline** is the very briefest of introductions to a subject that has rightly filled volumes. Inevitably, it covers artists that lived and worked in both the Netherlands and Belgium, as these two countries have – along with Luxembourg – been bound together as the "**Low Countries**" for most of their history. For in-depth and academic studies, see the recommendations in "Books" on p.361.

Beginnings: the Flemish Primitives

Throughout the medieval period, **Flanders**, in modern-day Belgium, was one of the most artistically productive parts of Europe, and it was here that the solid realist base of later Dutch painting developed. Today, the works of these early Flemish painters, the **Flemish Primitives**, are highly prized, and although examples are fairly sparse in the Netherlands, all the leading museums – especially Amsterdam's Rijksmuseum and Den Haag's Mauritshuis – have a healthy sample.

Jan van Eyck (1385–1441) is generally regarded as the first of the Flemish Primitives, and has even been credited with the invention of oil painting – though it seems more likely that he simply perfected a new technique by thinning his paint with turpentine (at the time a new discovery), thus making it more flexible. The most famous of his works still in the Low Countries is the altarpiece in Belgium's Ghent Cathedral, which was revolutionary in its realism, for the first time using elements of native landscape in depicting biblical themes. Van Eyck's style and technique were to influence several generations of the region's artists.

Weyden, Bouts and Goes

Firmly in the Eyckian tradition were the **Master of Flemalle** (1387–1444) and **Rogier van der Weyden** (1400–64), one-time official painter to the city of Brussels. The Flemalle master is a shadowy figure: some believe he was the teacher of van der Weyden, others that the two artists were in fact the same person. There are differences between the two, however; the Flemalle master's paintings are close to van Eyck's, whereas van der Weyden shows a greater degree of emotional intensity in his religious works. Van der Weyden also produced serene portraits of the bigwigs of his day and these were much admired across a large swathe of western Europe. His style, never mind his success, influenced many painters, one of the most talented of these being **Dieric Bouts** (1415–75). Born in Haarlem but active in (Belgium's) Leuven, Bouts is recognizable by his stiff, rather elongated figures and penchant for horrific subject matter – the tortures of damnation for example – all set against carefully drawn landscapes. **Hugo van der Goes** (d.1482) was the next Ghent master after van Eyck, most famous for the Portinari altarpiece in Florence's Uffizi gallery. Van der Goes died insane and his later works have strong hints of his impending madness in their subversive use of space and implicit acceptance of the viewer's presence.

Memling, David and Bosch

Few doubt that **Hans Memling** (1440–94) was a pupil of van der Weyden. Active in Bruges throughout his life, he is best remembered for the pastoral charm of his landscapes and the quality of his portraiture, much of which survives on the rescued side panels of triptychs. **Gerard David** (1460–1523) was a native of Oudewater, near Gouda, but he moved to Bruges in 1484, becoming the last of the great painters to work in that city, producing formal religious works of traditional bent. Strikingly different, but broadly contemporaneous, was **Hieronymus Bosch** (1450–1516), who lived for most of his life in the Netherlands, though his style is linked to that of his Flemish contemporaries. His frequently reprinted religious allegories are filled with macabre visions of tortured people and grotesque beasts, and appear faintly unhinged at first, though it's now thought that these are visual representations of contemporary sayings, idioms and parables. While their interpretation is far from resolved, Bosch's paintings draw strongly on subconscious fears and archetypes, giving them a lasting, haunting fascination.

The sixteenth century

At the end of the fifteenth century, Flanders was in economic and political decline and the leading artists of the day were drawn instead to the booming port of **Antwerp**, also in present-day Belgium. The artists who worked here soon began to integrate the finely observed detail that characterized the Flemish tradition with the style of the Italian painters of the Renaissance. **Quentin Matsys** (1464–1530) introduced florid classical architectural details and intricate landscapes to his works, influenced perhaps by the work of Leonardo da Vinci. As well as religious works, he painted portraits and genre scenes, all of which have recognizably Italian facets – and in the process he paved the way for the Dutch genre painters of later years. **Jan Gossaert** (1478–1532) made the pilgrimage to Italy too, and his dynamic works are packed with detail, especially finely drawn classical architectural backdrops. He was the first Low Countries artist to introduce the subjects of classical mythology into his paintings, part of a steady trend towards secular subject matter.

The middle of the sixteenth century was dominated by the work of **Pieter Bruegel the Elder** (c.1525–69), whose gruesome allegories and innovative interpretations of religious subjects are firmly placed in Low Countries settings. Pieter also painted finely observed peasant scenes, though he himself was well connected in court circles in Antwerp and, later, Brussels. **Pieter Aertsen** (1508–75) also worked in the peasant genre, adding aspects of still life; his paintings often show a detailed kitchen scene in the foreground, with a religious episode going on behind. Bruegel's two sons, **Pieter Bruegel the Younger** (1564–1638) and **Jan Bruegel** (1568–1625), were lesser painters; the former produced fairly insipid copies of his father's work, while Jan developed a style of his own – delicately rendered flower paintings and genre pieces that earned him the nickname "Velvet". Towards the latter half of the sixteenth century highly stylized Italianate portraits became the dominant fashion, with **Frans Pourbus the Younger** (1569–1622) the leading practitioner. Frans hobnobbed across Europe, working for the likes of the Habsburgs and the Médicis.

Meanwhile, there were artistic rumblings in the province of Holland. Leading the painterly charge was **Geertgen tot Sint Jans** (Little Gerard of the Brotherhood of St John; d.1490), who worked in Haarlem, initiating – in a strangely naive style – an artistic vision that would come to dominate the Dutch in the seventeenth century. There was a tender melancholy in his work which was very different from the stylized paintings produced in Flanders, and, most importantly, a new sensitivity to light. **Jan Mostaert** (1475–1555) took over after Geertgen's death, developing similar themes, but the first painter to effect real changes in northern painting was **Lucas van Leyden** (1489–1533), born in Leiden. His bright colours and narrative technique were refreshingly novel, and he introduced a new dynamism into what had become a rigidly formal treatment of devotional subjects. There was rivalry, of course. Eager to publicize Haarlem as the artistic capital of the northern Netherlands, **Karel van Mander** claimed **Jan van Scorel** (1495–1562) as the better painter, complaining, too, of van Leyden's dandyish ways. Certainly van Scorel's influence should not be underestimated. Like many of his contemporaries, van Scorel hotfooted it to Italy to view the works of the Renaissance, but in Rome his career went into overdrive when he found favour with Pope Hadrian VI, one-time bishop of Utrecht, who installed him as court painter in 1520. Van Scorel stayed in Rome for four years and when he returned to Utrecht, armed with all that papal prestige, he combined the ideas he had picked up in Italy with those under-pinning Haarlem realism, thereby modifying what had previously been an independent artistic tradition once and for all. Among his several students, probably the most talented was **Maerten van Heemskerck** (1498–1574), who duly went off to Italy himself in 1532, staying there for five years before doubling back to Haarlem.

The Golden Age

The seventeenth century begins with **Karel van Mander** (1548–1606), Haarlem painter, art impresario and one of the few contemporary chroniclers of the art of the Low Countries. His *Schilderboek* of 1604 put Flemish and Dutch traditions into context for the first time, and in addition specified the rules of fine painting. Examples of his own work are rare – though Haarlem's Frans Hals Museum (see p.112) weighs in with a couple – but his followers were many. Among them was **Cornelius Cornelisz van Haarlem** (1562–1638), who produced elegant renditions of biblical and mythical themes; and **Hendrik Goltzius** (1558–1616), who was a skilled engraver and an integral member of van Mander's Haarlem academy. The enthusiasm these painters had for Italian art, combined with the influence of a late revival of Gothicism, resulted in works that combined **Mannerist** and **Classical** elements. An interest in realism was also felt, but, for them, the subject became less important than the way in which it was depicted; biblical stories became merely a vehicle whereby artists could apply their skills in painting the human body, landscapes, or copious displays of food. All of this served to break the religious stranglehold on art, and make legitimate a whole range of everyday subjects for the painter.

In what is now the Netherlands (and this was where the north and the south finally diverged) this break with tradition was compounded by the **Reformation**: the austere Calvinism that had replaced the Catholic faith in the United Provinces had no use for images or symbols of devotion in its churches. Instead, painters catered to the burgeoning middle class, and no longer visited (Catholic) Italy to learn their craft. Indeed, the real giants of the seventeenth century – Hals, Rembrandt, Vermeer – stayed in the Netherlands all their lives. Another innovation was that painting split into more distinct categories – genre, portrait, landscape – and artists tended (with notable exceptions) to confine themselves to one field throughout their careers.

Historical and religious painting

The artistic influence of Renaissance Italy may have been in decline, but Italian painters still had clout with the Dutch, most notably **Caravaggio** (1571–1610), who was much admired for his new realism. Taking Caravaggio's cue, many artists – Rembrandt for one – continued to portray classical subjects, but in a way that was totally at odds with the Mannerists' stylish flights of imagination. The Utrecht artist **Abraham Bloemaert** (1564–1651), though a solid Mannerist throughout his career, encouraged these new ideas, and his students – **Gerard van Honthorst** (1590–1656), **Hendrik Terbrugghen** (1588–1629) and **Dirck van Baburen** (1590–1624) – formed the nucleus of the influential **Utrecht School**, which followed Caravaggio almost to the point of slavishness. Honthorst was perhaps the leading figure, learning his craft from Bloemaert and travelling to Rome, where he was nicknamed "Gerardo delle Notti" for his ingenious handling of light and shade. In his later paintings, however, this was to become more routine technique than inspired invention, and though a supremely competent artist, Honthorst is somewhat discredited among critics today. Terbrugghen's reputation seems to have aged rather better; he soon forgot Caravaggio and developed a more individual style, his later, lighter work having a great influence on the young Vermeer. After a jaunt to Rome, Baburen shared a studio with Terbrugghen and produced some fairly original work – work which also had some influence on Vermeer – but today he is the least studied member of the group and few of his paintings survive.

Rembrandt

The gilded reputation of **Rembrandt van Rijn** (1606–69) is still relatively recent – nineteenth-century connoisseurs preferred Gerard Dou – but he is now justly regarded as one of the greatest and most versatile painters of all time. Born in Leiden, the son of a miller, he was a boy apprentice to Jacob van Swanenburgh, a then quite important, though singularly uninventive, local artist. Rembrandt shared a studio with Jan Lievens, a promising painter and something of a rival, though now all but forgotten, before venturing forth to Amsterdam to study under the fashionable Pieter Lastman. Soon he was painting commissions for the city elite and became an accepted member of their circle. The poet and statesman Constantijn Huygens acted as his agent, pulling strings to obtain all of Rembrandt's more lucrative jobs, and in 1634 the artist married Saskia van Ulenborch, daughter of the burgomaster of Leeuwarden and quite a catch for a relatively humble artist.

Without doubt, Rembrandt was the most original historical artist of the seventeenth century, also chipping in with religious paintings throughout his career. In the 1630s, Huygens procured for him his greatest commission – a series of five paintings of the Passion, beautifully composed and uncompromisingly realistic. Later, however, Rembrandt drifted away from the mainstream, ignoring the smooth brushwork of his contemporaries and choosing instead a rougher, darker and more disjointed style for his biblical and historical subjects. This may well have contributed to a decline in his artistic fortunes and it is significant that while the more conventional Jordaens, Honthorst and van Everdingen were busy decorating the Huis ten Bosch near Den Haag for the Stadholder Frederick Henry, Rembrandt was having his monumental *Conspiracy of Julius Civilis* – painted for the new Amsterdam town hall – thrown out. The reasons for this rejection have been hotly debated, but it seems likely that Rembrandt's rendition was thought too suggestive of cabalistic conspiracy – the commissioners wanted to see a romantic hero and certainly not a plot in the making. Julius had organized a revolt against the Romans, an important event in early Dutch history, which had obvious resonance in a country just freed from the Habsburgs. Even worse, perhaps, Rembrandt had shown Julius to be blind in one eye, which was historically accurate but not at all what the city's burghers had in mind for a Dutch hero.

Genre painting

Often misunderstood, the term **genre painting** was initially applied to everything from animal paintings and still lifes through to historical works and landscapes, but later – from around the middle of the seventeenth century – came to be applied only to **scenes of everyday life**. Its target market was the region's burgeoning middle class, who had a penchant for non-idealized portrayals of common scenes, both with and without symbols – or subtly disguised details – making one moral point or another. One of its early practitioners was Antwerp's **Frans Snijders** (1579–1657), who took up still-life painting where Aertsen (see p.350) left off, amplifying his subject – food and drink – to even larger, more sumptuous canvases. Snijders also doubled up as a member of the Rubens art machine (see p.357), painting animals and still-life sections for the master's works. In Utrecht, Hendrik Terbrugghen and Gerard van Honthorst adapted the realism and strong chiaroscuro learned from Caravaggio to a number of tableaux of everyday life, though they were more concerned with religious works (see p.351), while Haarlem's Frans Hals dabbled in genre too, but is better known as a portraitist. The opposite is true of one of Hal's pupils, **Adriaen Brouwer** (1605–38), whose riotous tavern scenes were well received in their day and collected by, among others, Rubens and Rembrandt. Brouwer spent only a couple of years in Haarlem under Hals before returning to his native Flanders, where he influenced the inventive **David Teniers the Younger** (1610–90), who worked in Antwerp and later in Brussels. Teniers' early paintings are Brouwer-like peasant scenes, although his later work is more delicate and diverse, including *kortegaardje* – guardroom scenes that show soldiers carousing. **Adriaen van Ostade** (1610–85), on the other hand, stayed in Haarlem most of his life, skilfully painting groups of peasants and tavern brawls – though his later acceptance by the establishment led him to water down the realism he had learnt from Brouwer. He was teacher to his brother **Isaak** (1621–49), who produced a large number of open-air peasant scenes, subtle combinations of genre and landscape work.

Jan Steen

The English critic E.V. Lucas dubbed Teniers, Brouwer and Ostade "coarse and boorish" compared with **Jan Steen** (1625–79) who, along with Vermeer, is probably the most admired Dutch genre painter. Steen's paintings offer the same Rabelaisian peasantry in full fling, but they go their debauched ways in broad daylight, and nowhere do you see the filthy rogues in shadowy hovels favoured by Brouwer and Ostade. Steen offers more humour, too, as well as more moralizing, identifying with the hedonistic mob and reproaching them at the same time. Indeed, many of his pictures are illustrations of well-known proverbs of the time – popular epithets on the evils of drink or the transience of human existence that were supposed to teach as well as entertain.

Rembrandt's pupils and their contemporaries

Leiden's **Gerrit Dou** (1613–75) was one of Rembrandt's first pupils. It's difficult to detect any trace of the master's influence in his work, however, as Dou initiated a (genre) style of his own: tiny, minutely realized and beautifully finished views of a kind of ordinary life that was decidedly more genteel than Brouwer's – or even Steen's for that matter. He was admired, above all, for his painstaking attention to detail and he would, it's said, sit in his studio for hours waiting for the dust to settle before starting work. Among his students, **Frans van Mieris** (1635–81) continued the highly finished portrayals of the Dutch bourgeoisie, as did **Gabriel Metsu** (1629–67) – perhaps Dou's most talented pupil – whose pictures often convey an overtly moral message. Another pupil of Rembrandt's, though a much later one, was **Nicholas Maes** (1629–93), whose early works were almost entirely genre paintings, sensitively executed and with an obvious didacticism. His later paintings show the influence of a more refined style of portraiture, which he had picked up in France.

Gerard ter Borch and Pieter de Hooch

As a native of Zwolle, **Gerard ter Borch** (1619–81) found himself far from all these Leiden/Rembrandt connections; despite trips abroad to most of the artistic capitals of Europe, he remained very much a provincial painter. He depicted the country's merchant class at play and became renowned for his curious doll-like figures and his ability to capture the textures of different cloths. His domestic scenes were not unlike those of **Pieter de Hooch** (1629–84), whose simple depictions of everyday life are deliberately unsentimental and have little or no moral commentary. De Hooch's favourite trick was to paint darkened rooms with an open door leading through to a sunlit courtyard, a practice that, along with his trademark rusty red colour, makes his work easy to identify and, at its best, exquisite. That said, his later pictures lose their spartan quality, reflecting the increasing opulence of the Dutch Republic; the rooms are more richly decorated, the arrangements more contrived and the subjects far less homely.

Johannes Vermeer

It was **Johannes Vermeer** (1632–75) who brought the most sophisticated methods to painting interiors, depicting the play of natural light on indoor surfaces with superlative skill – and the tranquil intimacy for which he is now famous the world over. Another observer of the better-heeled Dutch household and, like de Hooch, without a moral tone, he is regarded (with Hals and Rembrandt) as one of the big three Dutch painters – though he was, it seems, a slow worker. As a result, only about forty paintings can be attributed to him with any certainty. Living all his life in Delft, Vermeer is perhaps the epitome of the seventeenth-century Dutch painter – rejecting the pomp and ostentation of the High Renaissance to record quietly his contemporaries at home, painting for a public that demanded no more than that: bourgeois art at its most complete.

Portraiture

Predictably enough, the ruling bourgeoisie of the United Provinces was keen to record and celebrate its success, and consequently portraiture was a reliable way for a young painter to make a living. **Michiel Jansz Miereveld** (1567–1641), court painter to Frederick Henry of Orange-Nassau in Den Haag, was the first real portraitist of the Dutch Republic, but it wasn't long before his stiff and rather conservative figures were superseded by the more spontaneous renderings of **Frans Hals** (1585–1666). Hals is perhaps best known for his "corporation pictures" – group portraits of the Dutch civil guard regiments that had been formed in most of the larger towns during the war with Spain, but subsequently became social clubs. These large group pieces demanded superlative technique, since the painter had to create a collection of individual portraits while retaining a sense of the group, and accord prominence based on the relative importance of the sitters and the size of the payment each had made. Hals was particularly good at this, using innovative lighting effects, arranging his sitters subtly, and putting all the elements together in a fluid and dynamic composition. He also painted many individual portraits, making the ability to capture fleeting and telling expressions his trademark; his pictures of children are particularly sensitive. Later in life, however, his work became darker and more akin to Rembrandt's, spurred – it's conjectured – by his penury.

Jan Cornelisz Verspronck (1597–1662) and **Bartholomeus van der Helst** (1613–70) were the other great Haarlem portraitists after Frans Hals – Verspronck recognizable by the smooth, shiny glow he always gave to his sitters' faces, van der Helst by a competent but unadventurous style. Of the two, van der Helst was the more popular, influencing a number of later painters and leaving Haarlem as a young man to begin a solidly successful career as portrait painter to Amsterdam's elite.

Rembrandt again

Rembrandt's early portraits and self-portraits show the confident face of security – on top of things and quite sure where he's going. Rembrandt would not always be the darling of the Amsterdam burghers, but his fall from grace was still some way off when he painted *The Night Watch* (see p.85), a group portrait often – but inaccurately – associated with the artist's decline in popularity. Indeed, although Rembrandt's fluent arrangement of his subjects was totally original, there's no evidence that the military company who commissioned the painting was anything but pleased with the result. More likely culprits are the artist's later pieces, whose obscure lighting and psychological insights took the conservative Amsterdam merchants by surprise, and his personal irascibility. Whatever the reason, his patrons were certainly not sufficiently enthusiastic about his later work to support both his taste for art collecting and his expensive house on Jodenbreestraat (see p.80), the result being that Rembrandt was declared bankrupt in 1656. Rembrandt died thirteen years later, a broken and embittered old man – as his last self-portraits show. Throughout his career he maintained a large studio, and his influence pervaded the next generation of Dutch painters. Some – Dou and Maes – more famous for their genre work, have already been mentioned. Others turned to portraiture.

Rembrandt's pupils

Govert Flinck (1615–60) was perhaps Rembrandt's most faithful follower, and he was, ironically enough, given the job of decorating Amsterdam's new town hall after his teacher had been passed over. Unluckily for him, Flinck died before he could execute his designs and Rembrandt took over, but although the latter's *Conspiracy of Julius Civilis* was installed in 1662, it was discarded a year later. The early work of **Ferdinand Bol** (1616–80) was also heavily influenced by Rembrandt, so much so that for centuries art historians couldn't tell the two apart, though Bol's later paintings are readily distinguishable, blandly elegant portraits which proved very popular with the wealthy. At the age of 53, Bol married a wealthy widow and promptly hung up his easel – perhaps he knew just how emotionally tacky his work had become. Most of the pitifully scarce extant work of **Carel Fabritius** (1622–54) is portraiture, but he too died young, before he could properly realize his promise as perhaps the most gifted of all Rembrandt's students. Generally regarded as the teacher of Vermeer, he forms a link between the two masters, combining Rembrandt's technique with his own practice of painting figures against a dark background, prefiguring the lighting and colouring of Vermeer.

Landscapes

Aside from Pieter Bruegel the Elder (see p.350), whose depictions of his native surroundings make him the first true Low Countries landscape painter, **Gillis van Coninxloo** (1544–1607) stands out as the earliest Dutch landscapist. He imbued his native scenery with elements of fantasy, painting the richly wooded views he had seen on his travels around Europe as backdrops to biblical scenes. In the early seventeenth century, **Hercules Seghers** (1590–1638), apprenticed to van Coninxloo, carried on his mentor's style of depicting forested and mountainous landscapes, some real, others not; his work is scarce but is believed to have had considerable influence on the landscape work of Rembrandt himself. **Esaias van der Velde**'s (1591–1632) quaint and unpretentious scenes show the first real affinity with the Dutch countryside, but while his influence was likewise considerable, he was soon overshadowed by his pupil **Jan van Goyen** (1596–1656), a remarkable painter who belongs to the so-called "tonal phase" of Dutch landscape painting. Van Goyen's early pictures were highly coloured and close to those of his teacher, but it didn't take him long to develop a marked touch of his own, using tones of green, brown and grey to lend everything a characteristic translucent haze. His paintings are, above all, of nature, and if he included figures it was just for the sake of scale. A long-neglected artist, van Goyen only received recognition with the arrival of the Impressionists, when his fluid and rapid brushwork was at last fully appreciated.

Another "tonal" painter, Haarlem's **Salomon van Ruysdael** (1600–70) was also directly affected by Esaias van der Velde, and his simple and atmospheric, though not terribly adventurous, landscapes were for a long time consistently confused with those of van Goyen. More esteemed is his nephew, **Jacob van Ruysdael** (1628–82), generally considered the greatest of all Dutch landscapists, whose fastidiously observed views of quiet flatlands dominated by stormy skies were to influence European landscapists right up to the nineteenth century. John Constable, certainly, acknowledged a debt to him. Ruysdael's foremost pupil was **Meindert Hobbema** (1638–1709), who followed the master faithfully, sometimes even painting the same views as in his *Avenue at Middelharnis*.

The Italianizers

Nicholas Berchem (1620–83) and **Jan Both** (1618–52) were the "Italianizers" of Dutch landscapes. They studied in Rome, taking back to the Netherlands rich, golden views of the world, full of steep gorges and hills, picturesque ruins and wandering shepherds. **Allart van Everdingen** (1621–75) had a similar approach, but his subject matter stemmed from his travels in Norway, which, after his return to the Netherlands, he reproduced in all its mountainous glory. **Aelbert Cuyp** (1620–91), on the other hand, stayed in Dordrecht all his life, painting what was probably the favourite city skyline of Dutch landscapists. He inherited the warm tones of the Italianizers, and his pictures are always suffused with a deep, golden glow.

The specialists

Of a number of specialist seventeenth-century painters who can be included here, **Paulus Potter** (1625–54) is rated as the best painter of domestic animals. He produced a surprisingly large number of paintings in his short life, the most reputed being his lovingly executed pictures of cows and horses. The accurate rendering of architectural features also became a specialized field in which **Pieter Saenredam** (1597–1665), with his finely realized paintings of Dutch church interiors, is the most widely known exponent. **Emanuel de Witte** (1616–92) continued in the same vein, though his churches lack the austere crispness of Saenredam. **Gerrit Berckheyde** (1638–98) worked in Haarlem soon after, but he limited his views to the outside of buildings, producing variations on the same townscapes. Nautical scenes in praise of the Dutch navy were, on the other hand, the speciality of **Willem van der Velde II** (1633–1707), whose melodramatic canvases, complete with churning seas and chasing skies, are displayed to greatest advantage in the Nederlands Scheepvaartmuseum in Amsterdam (see p.83).

A further thriving category of seventeenth-century painting was the still life, in which objects were gathered together to remind the viewer of the transience of human life and the meaninglessness of worldly pursuits. Thus, a skull would often be shown alongside a book, pipe or goblet, and some half-eaten food. Two Haarlem painters dominated this field – **Pieter Claesz** (1598–1660) and **Willem Heda** (1594–1680).

Rubens and his followers

Down in the south, in Antwerp, **Pieter Paul Rubens** (1577–1640) was easily the most important exponent of the Baroque in northern Europe. Born in Siegen, Westphalia, he was raised in Antwerp, where he entered the painters' guild in 1598. Two years later, he became court painter to the Duke of Mantua and thereafter he travelled extensively in Italy, absorbing the art of the High Renaissance and classical architecture. By the time of his return to Antwerp in 1608 he had acquired an enormous artistic vocabulary and, as with his Dutch contemporaries, the paintings of Caravaggio were to greatly influence his work. His first major success was *The Raising of the Cross*, painted in 1610 and displayed today in Antwerp cathedral. A large, dynamic work, it caused a sensation at the time, establishing Rubens' reputation and leading to a string of commissions that enabled him to set up his own studio.

The division of labour in Rubens' studio, and the talent of the artists working there (who included Anthony van Dyck and Jacob Jordaens) ensured an extraordinary output of excellent work. The degree to which Rubens personally worked on a canvas would vary – and would determine its price. From the early 1620s onwards he turned his hand to a plethora of themes and subjects – religious works, portraits, tapestry designs, landscapes, mythological scenes, ceiling paintings – each of which was handled with supreme vitality and virtuosity. From his Flemish antecedents he inherited an acute sense of light, and used it not to dramatize his subjects (a technique favoured by Caravaggio and other Italian artists), but in association with colour and form. The drama in his works comes from the vigorous animation of his characters. His large-scale allegorical works, especially, are packed with heaving, writhing figures that appear to tumble out from the canvas.

The energy of Rubens' paintings was reflected in his private life. In addition to his career as an artist, he also undertook diplomatic missions to Spain and England, and used these opportunities to study the works of other artists and – as in the case of Velázquez – to meet them personally. In the 1630s, **gout** began to hamper his activities, and his painting became more domestic and meditative. Hélène Fourment, his second wife, was the subject of many portraits and served as a model for characters in his allegorical paintings, her figure epitomizing the buxom, well-rounded women found throughout his work.

Rubens' influence on the artists of the period was enormous. The huge output of his studio meant that his works were universally seen and also widely disseminated by the engravers he employed to copy his work. Chief among his followers was the portraitist **Anthony van Dyck** (1599–1641), who worked in Rubens' studio from 1618, often taking on the depiction of religious figures in his master's works, or at least those that required particular sensitivity and pathos. Like Rubens, van Dyck was born in Antwerp and travelled widely in Italy, though his initial work was influenced less by the Italian artists than by

Rubens himself. Eventually, van Dyck developed his own distinct style and technique, establishing himself as court painter to Charles I of England, and creating portraits of a nervous elegance that would influence the genre there for the next 150 years. **Jacob Jordaens** (1593–1678) was also an Antwerp native who studied under Rubens. Although he was commissioned to complete several works left unfinished by Rubens at the time of his death, his robustly naturalistic works have an earthy – and sensuous – realism that is quite different and distinct in style and technique.

The eighteenth century

Accompanying the Netherlands's economic decline was a gradual deterioration in the quality and originality of Dutch painting. The subtle delicacies of the great seventeenth-century painters was replaced by finicky still lifes and minute studies of flowers, or overly finessed portraiture and religious scenes: the work of **Adrian van der Werff** (1659–1722) is typical. Of the era's other big names, **Gerard de Lairesse** (1640–1711) spent most of his time decorating a rash of brand-new civic halls and mansions, but, like the buildings he worked on, his style and influences were French. **Jacob de Wit** (1695–1754) continued where Lairesse left off, painting burgher ceiling after ceiling in flashy style. He also benefited from a relaxation in the laws against Catholics, decorating several of their (newly legal) churches. The eighteenth century's only painter of any real talent was **Cornelis Troost** (1697–1750) who, although he didn't produce anything stunningly original, painted competent portraits and some neat, faintly satirical pieces that have since earned him the title of "The Dutch Hogarth". Cosy interiors also continued to prove popular, and the Haarlem painter **Wybrand Hendriks** (1744–1831) satisfied demand with numerous proficient examples.

The nineteenth century

Born in Overijssel, **Johann Barthold Jongkind** (1819–91) was the first important Dutch artist to emerge in the nineteenth century, painting landscapes and seascapes that were to influence Monet and the early Impressionists. He spent most of his life in France and his work was exhibited in Paris with the Barbizon painters, though he owed less to them than to van Goyen and the seventeenth-century "tonal" artists of the United Provinces. Jongkind's work was a logical precursor to the art of the **Hague School**. Based in and around Den Haag between 1870 and 1900, this prolific group of painters tried to re-establish a characteristically Dutch school of painting. They produced atmospheric studies of the dunes and polders around Den Haag, nature pictures that are characterized by grey, rain-filled skies, windswept seas, and silvery, flat beaches – pictures that, for some, verge on the sentimental. **J.H. Weissenbruch** (1824–1903) was a founding member, a specialist in low, flat beach scenes dotted with stranded boats. The banker-turned-artist **H.W. Mesdag** (1831–1915) did the same but with more skill than imagination, while **Jacob Maris** (1837–99), one of three artist brothers, was perhaps the most typical, with his rural and sea scenes heavily covered by grey, chasing skies. His brother **Matthijs** (1839–1917) was less predictable, ultimately tiring of his colleagues' interest in straight observation and going to London to design windows, while the youngest brother **Willem** (1844–1910) is best known for his small, unpretentious studies of nature.

Anton Mauve (1838–88) is better known, an exponent of soft, pastel landscapes and an early teacher of van Gogh. Profoundly influenced by the French Barbizon painters – Corot, Millet et al. – he went to Hilversum near Amsterdam in 1885 to set up his own group, which became known as the "Dutch Barbizon". **Jozef Israëls** (1826–1911) has often been likened to Millet, though it's generally agreed that he had more in common with the Impressionists, and his best pictures are his melancholy portraits and interiors. Lastly, **Johan Bosboom**'s (1817–91) church interiors may be said to sum up the romanticized nostalgia of the Hague School; shadowy and populated by figures in seventeenth-century dress, they seem to yearn for the country's Golden Age.

Very different, and slightly later, **Jan Toorop** (1858–1928) went through multiple artistic changes, radically adapting his technique from a fairly conventional pointillism through a tired Expressionism to Symbolism with an Art Nouveau feel. Roughly contemporary, **George Hendrik Breitner** (1857–1923) was a better painter, and one who refined his style rather than changed it. His snapshot-like impressions of his beloved Amsterdam figure among his best work.

Vincent van Gogh

Vincent van Gogh (1853–90) was one of the least "Dutch" of Dutch artists, and he spent most of his relatively short painting career in France. After countless studies of Dutch peasant life – studies which culminated in his sombre *Potato Eaters* – he went to live in Paris with his art-dealer brother Theo. There, under the influence of the Impressionists, he lightened his palette, following the pointillist work of Seurat and "trying to render intense colour and not a grey harmony". Two years later he went south to Arles, the "land of blue tones and gay colours", and, struck by the brilliance of the Mediterranean light, began to develop his characteristic style. A disastrous attempt to live with Gauguin, and the much-publicized episode in which he cut off part of his ear and presented it to a local prostitute, led to his committal in an asylum at St-Rémy. Here he produced some of his most famous, and most Expressionistic, canvases – strongly coloured and with the paint thickly, almost frantically, applied. Van Gogh is now one of the world's most popular – and popularized – painters, and Amsterdam's Van Gogh Museum has the world's finest collection of his work (see p.85).

The twentieth century: De Stijl

Each of the major modern art movements has had – or has – its followers in the Netherlands and each has been diluted or altered according to local taste. Of many lesser names, **Jan Sluyters** (1881–1957) stands out as the Dutch pioneer of Cubism, but this is small beer when compared with the one specifically Dutch movement – **De Stijl** (The Style). **Piet Mondrian** (1872–1944) was De Stijl's leading figure, developing the realism he had learned from the Hague School painters – via Cubism, which he criticized for being too cowardly to depart totally from representation – into a complete abstraction of form which he called Neo-Plasticism. Mondrian was something of a mystic, and this was to some extent responsible for the direction that De Stijl – and his paintings – took: canvases painted with grids of lines and blocks made up of the three primary colours plus white, black and grey. Mondrian believed this freed his art from the vagaries of personal perception, making it possible to obtain what he called "a true vision of reality".

De Stijl took other forms too: there was a magazine of the same name, and the movement introduced new concepts into every aspect of design, from painting to interior design and architecture. But in all these media, lines were kept simple, colours bold and clear. **Theo van Doesburg** (1883–1931) was a De Stijl co-founder and major theorist. His work is similar to Mondrian's except for the noticeable absence of thick, black borders and for the diagonals that he introduced into his work, calling his paintings "contra-compositions" – which, he said, were both more dynamic and more in touch with the twentieth century. **Bart van der Leck** (1876–1958) was the third member of the circle, identifiable by white canvases covered by seemingly randomly placed interlocking coloured triangles. Mondrian split with De Stijl in 1925, going on to attain new artistic extremes of clarity and soberness before moving to New York in the 1940s and producing atypically exuberant works such as *Victory Boogie Woogie* – named for the artist's love of jazz and now owned by Den Haag's Gemeentemuseum (see p.166).

From De Stijl to the present day

During and after De Stijl, a number of other movements flourished in the Netherlands, though their impact was not so great and their influence was largely local. The Expressionist **Bergen School** was probably the most localized, its best-known exponent, **Charley Toorop** (1891–1955), daughter of Jan, developing a distinctively glaring but strangely sensitive realism. **De Ploeg** (The Plough), centred in Groningen, was headed by **Jan Wiegers** (1893–1959) and influenced by Ernst Ludwig Kirchner and the German Expressionists; the group's artists set out to capture the uninviting landscapes around their native town, and produced violently coloured canvases that hark back to van Gogh. Another group, known as the **Magic Realists**, surfaced in the 1930s, painting quasi-surrealistic scenes that, according to their leading light, **Carel Willink** (1900–83), revealed "a world stranger and more dreadful in its haughty impenetrability than the most terrifying nightmare."

Postwar Dutch art began with **CoBrA** – a loose grouping of like-minded painters from Denmark, Belgium and the Netherlands, whose name derives from the initial letters of their respective capital cities. Their first exhibition at Amsterdam's Stedelijk Museum in 1949 provoked a furore, at the centre of which was **Karel Appel** (1921–2006), whose brutal abstract Expressionist pieces, plastered with paint inches thick, were, he maintained, necessary for the era – indeed, inevitable reflections of it. "I paint like a barbarian in a barbarous age," he claimed. In the graphic arts, the most famous twentieth-century Dutch figure was **Maurits Cornelis Escher** (1898–1972), whose Surrealistic illusions and allusions were underpinned by his fascination with mathematics. Many remain unconvinced by Escher, but the Dutch took a liking to his work and he now has his own museum in Den Haag (see p.162).

As for today, the Netherlands boasts a vibrant contemporary art scene with all the major cities possessing at least a couple of art galleries that showcase regular exhibitions of contemporary art. Among modern Dutch artists, look out for the abstract work of **Edgar Fernhout** (1912–74) and **Ad Dekkers** (1938–74); the reliefs of **Jan Schoonhoven** (1914–94); the multimedia productions of **Jan Dibbets** (b.1941); the imprecisely coloured geometric designs of **Rob van Koningsbruggen** (b.1948); the smeary Expressionism of **Toon Verhoef** (b.1946); the exuberant figures of **Rene Daniels** (b.1950); the exquisite realism of Karel Buskes (b.1962) and Joke Frima (b.1952); and the witty, hip furniture designs of **Piet Hein Eek** (b.1967) – to name just ten of the more important figures.

Books

Most of the books listed below are **in print** and **in paperback**, and those that are **out of print** (o/p) should be easy to track down either in secondhand bookshops or through Amazon's used and second-hand book service (Ⓦ www.amazon.co.uk or Ⓦ www.amazon.com). Note also that while we recommend all the books we've listed below, we do have favourites – and these have been marked with 🎂.

History, politics and general

Ayaan Hirsi Ali *Infidel: My Life.* This powerful and moving autobiography, written by one of the Netherlands's most controversial figures, begins with Ali's harsh and sometimes brutal childhood in Somalia and then Saudi Arabia, where – among other tribulations – her grandmother insisted she have her clitoris cut off when she was 5. Later, in 1992, Ali wound up in the Netherlands at least partly to evade an arranged marriage. Thereafter, she made a remarkable transition from factory cleaner to MP, becoming a leading light of the rightist VVD political party and remaining outspoken in her denunciations of militant Islam (see p.348). Due to death threats, Ali was forced to go into hiding in 2004, only returning to parliament in 2005. She now lives in the US.

J.C.H. Blom (ed.) *History of the Low Countries.* Books on the totality of Dutch history are thin on the ground, so this heavyweight volume fills a few gaps, though it's hardly sun-lounger reading. A series of historians weigh in with their specialities, from Roman times onwards. Taken as a whole, its forte is in picking out those cultural, political and economic themes that give the region its distinctive character. Blom has also edited a second, top-notch anthology, *The History of the Jews in the Netherlands.*

Mike Dash *Tulipomania.* An examination of the introduction of the tulip into the Low Countries at the height of the Golden Age – and the extraordinarily inflated and speculative market that ensued. There's a lot of padding and scene-setting, but it's an engaging enough read, and has nice detail on seventeenth-century Amsterdam, Leiden and Haarlem.

Pieter Geyl *The Revolt of The Netherlands 1555–1609* and *The Netherlands in the Seventeenth Century 1609–1648.* Geyl presents a detailed account of the Netherlands during its formative years, chronicling the uprising against the Spanish and the formation of the United Provinces. First published in 1932, these two complementary titles have long been regarded as the classic texts on the subject, though they make for a hard and ponderous read.

A.C. Grayling *Descartes: The Life and Times of a Genius.* One of the greatest philosophers of all time, René Descartes (1596–1650) was a key figure in the transition from medieval to early modern Europe. He also made key contributions to optics and geometry and, among his miscellaneous travels, spent time living in Amsterdam. This crisply written, erudite biography deals skilfully with the philosophy – Grayling is himself a philosophy professor – and argues that Descartes was almost certainly a Jesuit spy acting on behalf of the Habsburg interest during his time here in the Netherlands.

Han van der Horst *The Low Sky: Understanding the Dutch* (o/p). Thoughtful, thorough attempt to explain the Dutch mentality to the outside world, from the peripheral – herring eating and gardening – to weightier sections on attitudes to egalitarianism and conspicuous consumption.

Lisa Jardine *The Awful End of Prince William the Silent*. Great title for an intriguing book on the premature demise of one of the country's most acclaimed heroes, who was assassinated in Delft in 1584. At just 160 pages, the tale is told succinctly, but – unless you have a particular interest in early firearms – there is a bit too much information on guns.

Carol Ann Lee *Roses from the Earth: the Biography of Anne Frank*. Among a spate of publications trawling through and over the life of the young Jewish diarist, this is probably the best, written in a straightforward and insightful manner without sentimentality. Working the same mine is the same author's *The Hidden Life of Otto Frank* – clear, lucid and equally as interesting.

Geert Mak *Amsterdam: A Brief Life of the City*. First published in 1995, this infinitely readable trawl through the city's past is a simply wonderful book – amusing and perceptive, alternately tart and indulgent. It's more a social history than anything else, so – for example – it's here you'll find out quite why Rembrandt lived in the Jewish Quarter and why the city's merchant elite ossified in the eighteenth century. It's light and accessible enough to read from cover to cover, but its index of places makes it easy to dip into.

Geoffrey Parker *The Dutch Revolt* and *The Army of Flanders and the Spanish Road 1567–1659*. The compelling account of the struggle between the Netherlands and Spain, quite the best thing you can read on the period. The latter has a title which may sound academic, but this book gives a fascinating insight into the Habsburg army that occupied the Low Countries for well over a hundred years – how it functioned, was fed and moved from Spain to the Low Countries along the so-called Spanish Road.

Simon Schama *The Embarrassment of Riches: An Interpretation of Dutch Culture in the Golden Age*. Long before his reinvention on British TV, Schama had a reputation as a specialist in Dutch history, and this chunky volume draws on a huge variety of archive sources. Also by Schama, *Patriots and Liberators: Revolution in the Netherlands 1780–1813* focuses on one of the less familiar periods of Dutch history and is particularly good on the Batavian Republic set up in the Netherlands under French auspices. Both are heavyweight tomes, and leftists might well find Schama too reactionary. See also Schama's *Rembrandt's Eyes* (p.363).

Andrew Wheatcroft *The Habsburgs*. Excellent and well-researched trawl through the family's history, from eleventh-century beginnings to its eclipse at the end of World War I. Enjoyable background reading.

Manfred Wolf (ed.) *Amsterdam: A Traveler's Literary Companion*. One of a series published by Whereabouts Press, an independent American company, this anthology – like its companion titles – tries to get to the heart of the city it covers. Contains a well-chosen mixture of travel pieces, short fiction and reportage, uncovering a low-life aspect to the city of Amsterdam that exists beyond the tourist brochures. A high-quality and evocative selection, and often the only chance you'll get to read some of this material in translation. Published in 2001.

Art and architecture

Svetlana Alpers *Rembrandt's Enterprise*. Intriguing 1988 study of Rembrandt, positing the theory – in line with the findings of the Leiden-based Rembrandt Research Project – that many paintings previously accepted as Rembrandt are not his at all, but merely the products of his studio. Bad news if you own one.

Anthony Bailey *A View of Delft*. Concise, startlingly well-researched book on Vermeer, complete with an accurate and well-considered exploration of his milieu.

R.H. Fuchs *Dutch Painting* (o/p). As complete an introduction to the subject – from Flemish origins to the postwar period – as you could wish for, in just a couple of hundred pages. Published in the 1970s and sadly out of print, there's still nothing better.

Melissa McQuillan *Van Gogh*. Extensive, in-depth look at Vincent's paintings, as well as his life and times. Superbly researched and illustrated.

Simon Schama *Rembrandt's Eyes*. Published in 1999, this erudite work received good reviews, but it's very, very long – and often very long-winded.

Mariet Westerman *The Art of the Dutch Republic 1585–1718*. This excellently written, immaculately illustrated and enthralling book tackles its subject thematically, from the marketing of works of art to an exploration of Dutch ideologies. Highly recommended. Also by Westerman is an all-you-could-ever-want-to-know book about *Rembrandt*.

Christopher White *Rembrandt*. White is something of a Rembrandt specialist, writing a series of books on the man and his times. Most of these books are expensive and aimed at the specialist art market, but this particular title is perfect for the general reader. Well illustrated with a wonderfully incisive and extremely detailed commentary. Published in 1984, but still very much on song.

Frank Wynne *I was Vermeer: The Forger who Swindled the Nazis*. The art forger Han van Meegeren fooled everyone, including Hermann Goering, with his "lost" Vermeers, when in fact he painted them himself. This story of bluff, bluster and fine art is an intriguing tale no doubt, but Wynne's book of 2007, though extremely well informed, is overly written.

Literature

A.C. Baantjer *De Kok and the Dead Harlequin*. An ex-Amsterdam policeman, who racked up nearly forty years service, Baantjer is currently the most widely read author in the Netherlands. This rattling good yarn, the latest in the Inspector De Kok series, has all the typical ingredients – crisp plotting, some gruesomeness and a batch of nice characterizations on the way. More? Try *De Kok and the Somber Nude*.

Tracy Chevalier *Girl with a Pearl Earring*. Chevalier's novel is a fanciful piece of fiction, building a story around the subject of one of Vermeer's most enigmatic paintings. It's an absorbing read – if a tad too detailed and slow-moving for some tastes – that paints a convincing picture of seventeenth-century Delft, exploring its social structures and mores.

Anne Frank *The Diary of a Young Girl*. Lucid and moving, the most revealing book you can read on the plight of Amsterdam's Jews during the German occupation. An international bestseller since its original publication in 1947.

Nicolas Freeling *Love in Amsterdam*; *Dwarf Kingdom*; *A Long Silence*; *A City Solitary* (all o/p). Freeling wrote detective novels, and his most famous creation was the rebel cop van der Valk. These are light, carefully crafted tales, with just the right amount of twists to make them classic cops 'n' robbers reading – and with good Amsterdam (and Dutch) locations. London-born, Freeling (1927–2003) evoked Amsterdam (and Amster-dammers) as well as any writer ever has, subtly and unsentimentally using the city and its people as a vivid backdrop to the fast-moving action.

Willem Frederik Hermans *The Dark Room of Damocles* Along with Wolkers (see p.365), Mulisch (see p.365) and Gerard Reve, Hermans is considered one of the four major literary figures of the Dutch postwar generation. This particular title, published in 1958, but only recently translated, is all about the German occupation and its concomitants – betrayal, paranoia and treason. Indeed, the reader is rarely certain what is truth and what is falsehood. If this whets your appetite for Hermans, try the same author's *Beyond Sleep*, which has also been translated recently. Hermans died in 1995.

Etty Hillesum *An Interrupted Life: the Diaries and Letters of Etty Hillesum, 1941–43*. The Germans transported Hillesum, a young Jewish woman, from her home in Amsterdam to Auschwitz, where she died. As with Anne Frank's more famous journal, penetratingly written – though on the whole a tad less readable.

Arthur Japin *The Two Hearts of Kwasi Boachi*. Inventive re-creation of a true story in which the eponymous

Ashanti prince was dispatched to the court of King William of the Netherlands in 1837. Kwasi and his companion Kwame were ostensibly sent to Den Haag to further their education, but there was a strong colonial subtext. Superb descriptions of Ashanti-land in its pre-colonial pomp. Also try Japin's *Lucia's Eyes*, an imaginative extrapolation of a casual anecdote found in Casanova's memoirs and set for the most part in eighteenth-century Amsterdam.

Sylvie Matton *Rembrandt's Whore*. Taking its cue from Chevalier's *Girl with a Pearl Earring*, this slim novel tries hard to conjure Rembrandt's life and times, with some success. Matton certainly knows her Rembrandt – she worked for two years on a film of his life.

Sarah Emily Miano *Van Rijn*. Carefully composed re-creation of Rembrandt's milieu, based on the (documented) visit of Cosimo de Medici to the artist's house. As an attempt to venture into Rembrandt's soul it does well – but not brilliantly.

Deborah Moggach *Tulip Fever*. At first Deborah Moggach's novel seems no more than an attempt to build a story out of her favourite domestic Dutch interiors, genre scenes and still-life paintings. But ultimately the story is a basic one – of lust, greed, mistaken identity and tragedy. The Golden Age Amsterdam backdrop is well realized, but almost incidental.

Marcel Moring *In Babylon*. Popular Dutch author with an intense style spliced with thought-provoking, philosophical content. *In Babylon* has an older Jewish man and his niece trapped in a cabin in the eastern Netherlands and here they ruminate on their family's history. Moring's *Dream Room* is also gracefully nostalgic in its concentration on the family of Boris and his son, David, while Moring's latest novel, *In a Dark Wood*, is set in the town of Assen, again in the east of the country, during the annual Dutch TT motorbike races.

Harry Mulisch *The Assault*. Set partly in Haarlem, partly in Amsterdam, this novel traces the story of a young boy who loses his family in a reprisal raid by the Nazis. A powerful tale, made into an excellent and effective film. Mulisch also wrote *The Discovery of Heaven*, a gripping yarn of adventure and happenstance; *The Procedure*, featuring a modern-day Dutch scientist investigating strange goings-on in sixteenth-century Prague; and *Siegfried: a Black Idyll*, whose central question is whether a work of imagination can help us to understand the nature of evil in general and Hitler in particular.

Multatuli *Max Havelaar: Or, The Coffee Auctions of the Dutch Trading Company*. Classic, nineteenth-century Dutch satire of colonial life in the East Indies. Eloquent and intermittently amusing. If you have Dutch friends, they will be impressed (dumbstruck) if you have actually read it, not least since it's 352 pages long.

Cees Nooteboom *Rituals* (o/p). Nooteboom published his first novel in 1955, but only hit the literary headlines with this, his third novel, in 1980. The central theme of all his work is the phenomenon of time; *Rituals* in particular is about the passing of time and the different ways of controlling the process. Inni Wintrop, the main character, is an outsider, a well-heeled, antique-dabbling dilettante as he describes himself. The book is almost entirely set in Amsterdam, and although it describes the inner life of Inni himself, it also paints a strong picture of the city.

Janwillem van de Wetering *Tumbleweed*; *Hard Rain*; *Corpse on the Dyke*; *Outsider in Amsterdam*. Offbeat detective tales set in Amsterdam and the Dutch provinces. Humane, quirky and humorous, Wetering's novels have inventive plots and feature unusual characters in interesting locations, though the prose itself can be a tad indigestible.

Jan Wolkers *Turkish Delight* (o/p). Wolkers is one of the Netherlands' best-known artists and writers, and this is one of his early novels, a close examination of the relationship between a bitter, working-class sculptor and his young, middle-class wife. A compelling work, at times misogynistic and even offensive, by a writer who seeks reaction above all. If you like it, try Wolkers' *Horrible Tango* (o/p).

Language

Language

Dutch

I n the Netherlands, the native language is **Dutch**. Most Dutch-speakers, however, particularly in the bigger towns and the tourist industry, speak English to varying degrees of excellence. The Dutch have a seemingly innate talent for languages, and your attempts at speaking theirs may be met with some bewilderment – though this can have as much to do with your pronunciation (Dutch is very difficult to get right) as their surprise that you're making an effort.

Dutch is a Germanic language – the word itself is a corruption of "Deutsche", a label inaccurately given by English sailors in the seventeenth century and indeed, although the Dutch are at pains to stress the differences between the two languages, if you know any German you'll spot many similarities.

For such a small country, the Netherlands has many dialects and even an official language other that Dutch; Fries is the pride of inhabitants from Friesland and incomprehensible to people from other provinces. Similarly, the dialect spoken in Limburg is closer to German and Flemish than to Dutch, and its inhabitants are keen on using it. Variation in pronunciation can even be found between cities. Inhabitants from Amsterdam have a very different accent and slang than someone from The Hague, although this variation is hardly noticeable for visitors.

As noted above, English is very widely spoken, and even in smaller towns and in the countryside, where things aren't quite as cosmopolitan, the following words and phrases should be the most you'll need to get by. We've also included a basic food and drink glossary, though **menus** are nearly always multilingual and where they aren't, ask and one will almost invariably appear.

As for **phrasebooks**, the *Rough Guide to Dutch* is pocket-sized, and has a good dictionary section (English–Dutch and Dutch–English) as well as a menu reader; it also provides a useful introduction to grammar and pronunciation.

Pronunciation

Dutch is **pronounced** much the same as English. However, there are a few Dutch sounds that don't exist in English, which can be difficult to get right without practice.

Consonants

Double-consonant combinations generally keep their separate sounds in Dutch: **kn**, for example, is never like the English "knight". Note also the following consonants and consonant combinations:

j is an English **y**

ch and g indicate a throaty sound, as at the end of the Scottish word lo**ch**.

ng as in bri**ng**

nj as in o**nio**n

y is not a consonant, but another way of writing **ij**

Vowels and diphthongs

A good rule of thumb is that doubling the letter lengthens the vowel sound.

a is like the English **a**pple

aa like c**a**rt

e like l**e**t

ee like l**a**te

o as in p**o**p

oo in p**o**pe

u is like the French t**u** if preceded by a consonant; it's like w**oo**d if followed by a consonant

uu is the French t**u**

au and ou like h**ow**

ei and ij as in f**i**ne, though this varies strongly from region to region; sometimes it can sound more like l**a**ne

oe as in s**oo**n

eu is like the diphthong in the French l**eu**r

ui is the hardest Dutch diphthong of all, pronounced like h**ow** but much further forward in the mouth, with lips pursed (as if to say "oo").

Words and phrases

yes	ja	I don't understand	Ik begrijp het niet
no	nee	women/men	vrouwen/mannen
please	alstublieft	children	kinderen
thank you	dank u or bedankt	men's/women's toilets	heren/dames
hello	hallo or dag	I want…	Ik wil…
good morning	goedemorgen	(+verb) I don't want to…	Ik wil niet…
good afternoon	goedemiddag		
good evening	goedenavond	(+noun) I don't want any…	Ik wil geen…
goodbye	tot ziens		
see you later	tot straks	How much is…?	Wat kost…?
Do you speak English?	Spreekt u Engels?		

Travel and shopping

post office	postkantoor	railway platform	spoor or perron
stamp(s)	postzegel(s)	ticket office	loket
money exchange	geldwisselkantoor	here/there	hier/daar
cash desk	kassa	good/bad	goed/slecht
How do I get to…?	Hoe kom ik in…?	big/small	groot/klein
Where is…?	Waar is…?	open/closed	open/gesloten
How far is it to…?	Hoe ver is het naar…?	push/pull	duwen/trekken
When?	Wanneer?	new/old	nieuw/oud
far/near	ver/dichtbij	cheap/expensive	goedkoop/duur
left/right	links/rechts	hot/cold	heet or warm/koud
straight ahead	rechtdoor	with/without	met/zonder

Numbers

0	nul	3	drie
1	een	4	vier
2	twee	5	vijf

6	zes	22	twee en twintig
7	zeven	30	dertig
8	acht	40	veertig
9	negen	50	vijftig
10	tien	60	zestig
11	elf	70	zeventig
12	twaalf	80	tachtig
13	dertien	90	negentig
14	veertien	100	honderd
15	vijftien	101	honderd een
16	zestien	200	twee honderd
17	zeventien	201	twee honderd een
18	achttien	500	vijf honderd
19	negentien	525	vijf honderd vijf en twintig
20	twintig	1000	duizend
21	een en twintig		

Days and times

Monday	maandag	It's…	Het is…
Tuesday	dinsdag	3.00	drie uur
Wednesday	woensdag	3.05	vijf over drie
Thursday	donderdag	3.10	tien over drie
Friday	vrijdag	3.15	kwart over drie
Saturday	zaterdag	3.20	tien voor half vier
Sunday	zondag	3.25	vijf voor half vier
yesterday	gisteren	3.30	half vier
today	vandaag	3.35	vijf over half vier
tomorrow	morgen	3.40	tien over half vier
tomorrow morning	morgenochtend	3.45	kwart voor vier
year	jaar	3.50	tien voor vier
month	maand	3.55	vijf voor vier
week	week	8am	acht uur 's ochtends
day	dag	1pm	een uur 's middags
hour	uur	8pm	acht uur 's avonds
minute	minuut	1am	een uur 's nachts
What time is it?	Hoe laat is het?		

Menu reader

Basic terms

boter	butter	eieren	eggs
boterham/broodje	sandwich/roll	groenten	vegetables
brood	bread	honing	honey
dranken	drinks	hoofdgerechten	main courses

huzarensalade	potato salad with pickles	suiker	sugar
kaas	cheese	uitsmijter	ham or cheese with eggs on bread
koud	cold	vegetarisch	vegetarian
nagerechten	desserts	vis	fish
patat/friet	chips/french fries	vlees	meat
peper	pepper	voorgerechten	starters/hors d'oeuvres
pindakaas	peanut butter	vruchten	fruit
sla/salade	salad	warm	hot
soep	soup	zout	salt
stokbrood	french bread		

Meat and poultry

biefstuk (duitse)	hamburger	kip	chicken
biefstuk (hollandse)	steak	kroket	spiced veal or beef hash, coated in breadcrumbs
eend	duck		
fricandeau	roast pork	lamsvlees	lamb
fricandel	frankfurter-like sausage	lever	liver
		ossenhaas	tenderloin beef
gehakt	minced meat	rookvlees	smoked beef
kalfsvlees	veal	spek	bacon
kalkoen	turkey	worst	sausages
karbonade	a chop		

Fish

forel	trout	oesters	oysters
garnalen	prawns	paling	eel
haring	herring	schelvis	haddock
kabeljauw	cod	schol	plaice
makreel	mackerel	tong	sole
mosselen	mussels	zalm	salmon

Cooking terms

belegd	filled or topped	geraspt	grated
doorbakken	well-done	gerookt	smoked
gebakken	fried or baked	gestoofd	stewed
gebraden	roast	half doorbakken	medium-done
gegrild	grilled	rood	rare
gekookt	boiled		

Vegetables

aardappelen	potatoes	erwten	peas
bloemkool	cauliflower	hutspot	mashed potatoes and carrots
bonen	beans		
champignons	mushrooms	knoflook	garlic

komkommer	cucumber	stampot boerenkool	mashed potato and cabbage
prei	leek	uien	onions
rijst	rice	wortelen	carrots
sla	salad, lettuce	zuurkool	sauerkraut
stampot andijvie	mashed potato and endive		

Sweets and desserts

appelgebak	apple tart or cake	pannenkoeken	pancakes
drop	Dutch liquorice, available in *zoet* (sweet) or *zout* (salted) varieties	pepernoten	Dutch ginger nuts
		poffertjes	small pancakes, fritters
gebak	pastry	(slag)room	(whipped) cream
ijs	ice cream	speculaas	spice and cinnamon-flavoured biscuit
koekjes	biscuits		
oliebollen	traditional sweet sold at New Year – something like a doughnut	stroopwafels	waffles
		taai-taai	spicy Dutch cake
		vla	custard

Fruits and nuts

aardbei	strawberry	hazelnoot	hazelnut
amandel	almond	kers	cherry
appel	apple	kokosnoot	coconut
appelmoes	apple purée	peer	pear
citroen	lemon	perzik	peach
druiven	grape	pinda	peanut
framboos	raspberry	pruim	plum/prune

Drinks

anijsmelk	aniseed-flavoured warm milk	melk	milk
		met ijs	with ice
appelsap	apple juice	met slagroom	with whipped cream
bessenjenever	blackcurrant gin	pils	Dutch beer
chocomel	chocolate milk	proost!	cheers!
citroenjenever	lemon gin	sinaasappelsap	orange juice
droog	dry	thee	tea
frisdranken	soft drinks	tomatensap	tomato juice
jenever	Dutch gin	vruchtensap	fruit juice
karnemelk	buttermilk	wijn	wine
koffie	coffee	(wit/rood/rosé)	(white/red/rosé)
koffie verkeerd	coffee with warm milk	vieux	Dutch brandy
kopstoot	beer with a jenever chaser	zoet	sweet

Glossary

Dutch terms

Abdij Abbey

Amsterdammertje Phallic-shaped bollard placed in rows alongside many Amsterdam streets to keep drivers off pavements and out of the canals

A.U.B. *Alstublieft* – "please" (also shown as S.V.P., from French)

BG *Begane grond* – "ground floor" ("basement" is **K** for *kelder*)

Begijnhof Similar to a hofje but occupied by Catholic women (*begijns*) who led semi-religious lives without taking full vows

Beurs Stock exchange

Botermarkt Butter market

Brug Bridge

B.T.W. *Belasting Toegevoegde Waarde* – VAT (sales tax)

Fietspad Bicycle path

Gasthuis Hospice for the sick or infirm

Geen toegang No entry

Gemeente Municipal, as in *Gemeentehuis* (town hall)

Gerechtshof Law Courts

Gesloten Closed

Gezellig A hard term to translate – something like "cosy", "comfortable" and "inviting" in one – which is often said to lie at the heart of the Dutch psyche.

Gilde Guild

Gracht Canal

Groentenmarkt Vegetable market

Grote Kerk Literally "big church" – the main church of a town or village

Hal Hall

Hijsbalk Pulley beam, often decorated, fixed to the top of a gable to lift goods and furniture. Essential in canal houses whose staircases were narrow and steep, *hijsbalken* are still very much in use today

Hof Courtyard

Hofje Almshouse, usually for elderly women who could look after themselves but needed small charities such as food and fuel; usually a number of buildings centred around a small, enclosed courtyard

Huis House

Ingang Entrance

Jeugdherberg Youth hostel

Kasteel Castle

Kerk Church

Koning King

Koningin Queen

Koninklijk Royal

Kunst Art

Let Op! Attention!

Luchthaven Airport

Markt Central town square and the heart of most Dutch communities, normally still the site of weekly markets

Mokum A Yiddish word meaning "city", originally used by the Jewish community to indicate Amsterdam; now in general usage as a nickname for the city

Molen Windmill

Nederland The Netherlands

Nederlands Dutch

Noord North

Oost East

Paleis Palace

Plein A square or open space

Polder An area of land reclaimed from the sea

Poort Gate

Postbus Post office box

Raadhuis Town hall

Randstad Literally "rim-town", this refers to the urban conurbation that makes up much of Noord- and Zuid-Holland, stretching from Amsterdam in the north to Rotterdam and Dordrecht in the south

Rijk State

Schouwburg Theatre

Sierkunst Decorative arts

Spionnetje Small mirror on a canal house enabling the occupant to see who is at the door without descending the stairs

Spoor Train station platform

Stadhuis The most common word for a town hall

Stedelijk Civic, municipal

Steeg Alley

Steen Stone

Stichting Institute or foundation

Straat Street

T/M *Tot en met* – "up to and including"

Toegang Entrance

Toren Tower

Tuin Garden

Uitgang Exit

V.A. *Vanaf* – "from"

V.S. *Verenigde Staten* – "United States"

Vleeshuis Meat market

Volkskunde Folklore

VVV Tourist office

Waag Old public weigh house, a common feature of most towns

Weg Way

West West

Wijk District (of a city)

Z.O.Z. Please turn over (page, leaflet, etc)

Zuid South

Architectural terms

Ambulatory Covered passage around the outer edge of the choir of a church.

Apse Semi-circular protrusion (usually) at the east end of a church.

Art Deco Geometrical style of art and architecture popular in the 1930s.

Art Nouveau Style of art, architecture and design based on highly stylized vegetal forms. Especially popular in the early part of the twentieth century.

Baroque The art and architecture of the Counter-Reformation, dating from around 1600 onwards. Distinguished by extreme ornateness, exuberance and by the complex but harmonious spatial arrangement of interiors.

Carillon A set of tuned church bells, either operated by an automatic mechanism or played by a keyboard.

Carolingian Dynasty founded by Charlemagne; mid-eighth to early tenth century. Also refers to art of the period.

Caryatid A sculptured female figure used as a column.

Chancel The eastern part of a church, often separated from the nave by a screen (see "rood screen"). Contains the choir and ambulatory.

Classical Architectural style incorporating Greek and Roman elements – pillars, domes, colonnades etc – at its height in the seventeenth century and revived, as Neoclassical, in the nineteenth century.

Clerestory Upper story of a church with windows.

Diptych Carved or painted work on two panels. Often used as an altarpiece – both static and, more occasionally, portable.

Expressionism Artistic style popular at the beginning of the twentieth century, characterized by the exaggeration of shape or colour; often accompanied by the extensive use of symbolism.

Flamboyant Florid form of Gothic.

Fresco Wall painting – durable through application to wet plaster.

Gable The triangular upper portion of a wall – decorative or supporting a roof – which is a feature of many Amsterdam canal houses. Initially fairly simple, they became more ostentatious in the late seventeenth century, before turning to a more restrained Classicism in the eighteenth and nineteenth centuries.

Genre painting In the seventeenth century the term "genre painting" applied to everything from animal paintings and still lifes through to historical works and landscapes. In the eighteenth century, the term came only to be applied to scenes of everyday life.

Gothic Architectural style of the thirteenth to sixteenth centuries, characterized by pointed arches, rib vaulting, flying buttresses and a general emphasis on verticality.

Merovingian Dynasty ruling France and parts of the Low Countries from the sixth to the middle of the eighth century. Refers also to art, etc, of the period.

Misericord Ledge on choir stall on which the occupant can be supported while standing; often carved with secular subjects (bottoms were not thought worthy of religious subjects).

Nave Main body of a church.

Neoclassical A style of Classical architecture revived in the nineteenth century, popular in the Low Countries during and after French rule in the early nineteenth century.

Neo-Gothic Revived Gothic style of architecture popular between the late eighteenth and nineteenth centuries.

Renaissance The period of European history marking the end of the medieval period and the rise of the modern world. Defined, among many criteria, by an increase in classical scholarship, geographical discovery, the rise of secular values and the growth of individualism. Began in Italy in the fourteenth century. Also refers to the art and architecture of the period.

Retable Altarpiece

Rococo Highly florid, light and intricate eighteenth-century style of architecture, painting and interior design, forming the last phase of Baroque.

Romanesque Early medieval architecture distinguished by squat, heavy forms, rounded arches and naive sculpture.

Rood screen Decorative screen separating the nave from the chancel. A rood loft is the gallery (or space) on top of it.

Stucco Marble-based plaster used to embellish ceilings, etc.

Transept Arms of a cross-shaped church, placed at ninety degrees to nave and chancel.

Triptych Carved or painted work on three panels. Often used as an altarpiece.

Tympanum Sculpted, usually recessed, panel above a door.

Vauban Seventeenth-century military architect, whose fortresses still stand all over Europe – including the Low Countries; hence the adjective Vaubanesque.

Vault An arched ceiling or roof.

Travel store

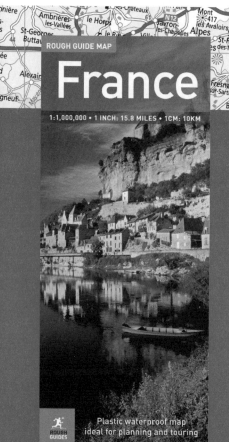

information on over 25,000 destinations around the world

- **Read** Rough Guides' trusted travel info
- **Access** exclusive articles from Rough Guides authors
- **Update** yourself on new books, maps, CDs and other products
- **Enter** our competitions and win travel prizes
- **Share** ideas, journals, photos & travel advice with other users
- **Earn** points every time you contribute to the Rough Guide community and get rewards

Book Aid International
www.bookaid.org

Books change lives

Poverty and illiteracy go hand in hand. But in sub-Saharan Africa, books are a luxury few can afford. Many children leave school functionally illiterate, and adults often fall back into illiteracy in adulthood due to a lack of available reading material.

Book Aid International knows that books change lives.

Every year we send over half a million books to partners in 12 countries in sub-Saharan Africa, to stock libraries in schools, refugee camps, prisons, universities and communities. Literally millions of readers have access to books and information that could teach them new skills – from keeping chickens to getting a degree in Business Studies or learning how to protect against HIV/AIDS.

What can you do?

Join our Reverse Book Club and with your donation of only £6 a month, we can send 36 books every year to some of the poorest countries in the world. For every two pounds extra you can give, we can send another book!

Support Book Aid International today!

 Online. Go to our website at **www.bookaid.org**, and click on 'donate'

 By telephone. Start a Direct Debit or give a donation on your card by calling us on 020 7733 3577

Book Aid International is a charity and a limited company registered in England and Wales.
Charity No. 313869 Company No. 880754 39-41 Coldharbour Lane, Camberwell, London SE5 9NR
T +44 (0)20 7733 3577 F +44 (0)20 7978 8006 E info@bookaid.org www.bookaid.org

Small print and
Index

A Rough Guide to Rough Guides

Published in 1982, the first Rough Guide – to Greece – was a student scheme that became a publishing phenomenon. Mark Ellingham, a recent graduate in English from Bristol University, had been travelling in Greece the previous summer and couldn't find the right guidebook. With a small group of friends he wrote his own guide, combining a highly contemporary, journalistic style with a thoroughly practical approach to travellers' needs.

The immediate success of the book spawned a series that rapidly covered dozens of destinations. And, in addition to impecunious backpackers, Rough Guides soon acquired a much broader and older readership that relished the guides' wit and inquisitiveness as much as their enthusiastic, critical approach and value-for-money ethos.

These days, Rough Guides include recommendations from shoestring to luxury and cover more than 200 destinations around the globe, including almost every country in the Americas and Europe, more than half of Africa and most of Asia and Australasia. Our ever-growing team of authors and photographers is spread all over the world, particularly in Europe, the US and Australia.

In the early 1990s, Rough Guides branched out of travel, with the publication of Rough Guides to World Music, Classical Music and the Internet. All three have become benchmark titles in their fields, spearheading the publication of a wide range of books under the Rough Guide name.

Including the travel series, Rough Guides now number more than 350 titles, covering: phrasebooks, waterproof maps, music guides from Opera to Heavy Metal, reference works as diverse as Conspiracy Theories and Shakespeare, and popular culture books from iPods to Poker. Rough Guides also produce a series of more than 120 World Music CDs in partnership with World Music Network.

Visit www.roughguides.com to see our latest publications.

Rough Guide travel images are available for commercial licensing at www.roughguidespictures.com

Rough Guide credits

Text editor: Helen Ochyra
Layout: Jessica Subramanian
Cartography: Deshpal Dabas
Picture editor: Mark Thomas
Production: Rebecca Short
Proofreader: Richard Lim
Photographers: Tim Draper, Natascha Sturny and Mark Thomas
Editorial: Ruth Blackmore, Andy Turner, Keith Drew, Edward Aves, Alice Park, Lucy White, Jo Kirby, James Smart, Natasha Foges, Róisín Cameron, James Rice, Emma Traynor, Emma Gibbs, Kathryn Lane, Monica Woods, Mani Ramaswamy, Harry Wilson, Lucy Cowie, Alison Roberts, Joe Staines, Peter Buckley, Matthew Milton, Tracy Hopkins, Ruth Tidball; **Delhi** Madhavi Singh, Karen D'Souza, Lubna Shaheen
Design & Pictures: **London** Scott Stickland, Dan May, Diana Jarvis, Nicole Newman, Sarah Cummins, Emily Taylor; **Delhi** Umesh Aggarwal, Ajay Verma, Ankur Guha, Pradeep Thapliyal, Sachin Tanwar, Anita Singh, Nikhil Agarwal, Sachin Gupta

Production: Liz Cherry
Cartography: **London** Ed Wright, Katie Lloyd-Jones; **Delhi** Rajesh Chhibber, Ashutosh Bharti, Rajesh Mishra, Animesh Pathak, Jasbir Sandhu, Karobi Gogoi, Alakananda Bhattacharya, Swati Handoo, Deshpal Dabas
Online: **London** Faye Hellon, Jeanette Angell, Fergus Day, Justine Bright, Clare Bryson, Aine Fearon, Adrian Low, Ezgi Celebi; **Delhi** Amit Verma, Rahul Kumar, Narender Kumar, Ravi Yadav, Debojit Borah, Rakesh Kumar, Ganesh Sharma, Shisir Basumatari
Marketing & Publicity: **London** Liz Statham, Louise Maher, Jess Carter, Vanessa Godden, Vivienne Watton, Anna Paynton, Rachel Sprackett, Laura Vipond; **New York** Katy Ball, Judi Powers; **Delhi** Ragini Govind
Reference Director: Andrew Lockett
Operations Assistant: Becky Doyle
Operations Manager: Helen Atkinson
Publishing Director (Travel): Clare Currie
Commercial Manager: Gino Magnotta
Managing Director: John Duhigg

SMALL PRINT

Publishing information

This fifth edition published March 2010 by
Rough Guides Ltd,
80 Strand, London WC2R 0RL
14 Local Shopping Centre, Panchsheel Park, New Delhi 110017, India
Distributed by the Penguin Group
Penguin Books Ltd,
80 Strand, London WC2R 0RL
Penguin Group (USA)
375 Hudson Street, NY 10014, USA
Penguin Group (Australia)
250 Camberwell Road, Camberwell, Victoria 3124, Australia
Penguin Group (Canada)
195 Harry Walker Parkway N, Newmarket, ON, L3Y 7B3 Canada
Penguin Group (NZ)
67 Apollo Drive, Mairangi Bay, Auckland 1310, New Zealand
Cover concept by Peter Dyer.

Typeset in Bembo and Helvetica to an original design by Henry Iles.
Printed in Singapore
© Martin Dunford, Phil Lee and Suzanne Morton-Taylor
Maps © Rough Guides

No part of this book may be reproduced in any form without permission from the publisher except for the quotation of brief passages in reviews.

392pp includes index
A catalogue record for this book is available from the British Library
ISBN: 978-1-84836-506-3

The publishers and authors have done their best to ensure the accuracy and currency of all the information in **The Rough Guide to The Netherlands**, however, they can accept no responsibility for any loss, injury, or inconvenience sustained by any traveller as a result of information or advice contained in the guide.

1   3   5   7   9   8   6   4   2

Help us update

We've gone to a lot of effort to ensure that the fifth edition of **The Rough Guide to The Netherlands** is accurate and up-to-date. However, things change – places get "discovered", opening hours are notoriously fickle, restaurants and rooms raise prices or lower standards. If you feel we've got it wrong or left something out, we'd like to know, and if you can remember the address, the price, the hours, the phone number, so much the better.

Please send your comments with the subject line "**Rough Guide The Netherlands Update**" to ©mail@roughguides.com. We'll credit all contributions and send a copy of the next edition (or any other Rough Guide if you prefer) for the very best emails.

Have your questions answered and tell others about your trip at ⑩www.roughguides.com

Acknowledgements

Phil Lee would like to thank his editor, Helen Ochyra, for her patient efficiency during the preparation of this new edition of the Netherlands. Special thanks also to Malijn Maat for her help with all sorts of queries; Jeroen Beelen of Delft Marketing; and my co-authors, Martin Dunford and Suzanne Morton-Taylor.

Suzanne Morton-Taylor would like to thank Catharina Jansen, Carien Kirkels, Morien Janse, Mathijs Wilmink, Rens Kalsbeek and Stephanie Hameleers for their hospitality and help with all sorts of queries. Special thanks also to Helen Ochyra for her thoroughness and to co-authors Phil Lee and Martin Dunford.

SMALL PRINT

Readers' letters

Thanks to all the readers who took the trouble to write and email in with their comments and suggestions. In particular, thanks to:

Douglas Adler; Julie Beckford; Johanneke Braam; J. G. Brekelmans; Anne Brittain; David Buckley; Mark Burns; Richard Butler; A M Castro; Martin Christlieb; Lyndsey Daley; Rik Feije; Kay Fraser; Annette Gahlings; Claes De Groot; Maarten van der Gulik; David Jenkins; Jenny Jensen; Michael Kirby; Leo Lacey; Richard Lamey; Keith Lawson; Stav Louizou; Tom Marrinan; Roelof Mooiweer; Leann Nelson; Margery Nzerem; Judith Orford; Alice Park; Jill Pearson; Bill Paton; Nick Reeves; Fiona Rempt; Mandy Revel; Lesa Rollo; Bobby Russell; Nigel Sandford; Toby Screech; Dennis Simmonds; Carolien Selderijk; Johanna Sleeswijk; Damian Smith; Hilary Smith; Jean Smith; Taco Spanbroek; Anja Spaninks; K Tan; Dunya Verwey; Anna Vidou; Ronald Walgreen; Clare Webster; Susan Webster; Christel van Weezep; Paul Weston; Lucy White; B. White; J Wood; Karen Woods; C A Yates; Alison Young; Liz Young.

www.roughguides.com

Photo credits

All photography by Tim Draper, Natascha Sturny and Mark Thomas © Rough Guides except the following:

Title page
Cyclists outside the Rijksmuseum © Beth Perkins/Getty

Full page
Leiden at dusk © Simeon Huber/Getty

Introduction
Queen's Day © Mark Thomas
Erasmus bridge, Rotterdam © Michele Falzone/Getty

Things not to miss
02 Elfstedentocht ice race © Brian Harris/Alamy
05 Secret door in Anne Frank's House, courtesy of Anne Frank Huis
08 St Jan Cathedral, 's Hertogenbosch © Werner Otto/Alamy
11 *Wadlopen* © Picture Contact/Alamy
15 Keukenhof Gardens © Nagelstock/Alamy

The Battle with the Sea colour section
Sunset over sea wall © Dann Toner/Alamy
Kiteboarding, Frisian Islands © Wolfgang Kaehler/Alamy
Flooding, Overijssel © Peter Horree/Alamy
Zuider Zee dam © Art Kowalsky/Alamy
Dyke construction © Avatra Images/Alamy
Rotterdam lock © Picture Contact/Alamy
Schiphol Airport © Isifa Image Service/Alamy

The Dutch Golden Age colour section
The Milkmaid, c.1658–60 (oil on canvas) by Vermeer Johannes (1632–75). Rijksmuseum, Amsterdam, The Netherlands/The Bridgeman Art Library
King Philip II of Spain © London Art Archive/Alamy
Old map of Amsterdam © The London Art Archive
Tulips from "Verzameling van Bloemen naar deNatuur getekend" (Collection of flowers drawn from nature) c.1630 © The Bridgeman Art Library
Dutch clipper © Peter Horree/Alamy
The Nightwatch (oil on canvas) by Rembrandt Harmenszoon van Rijn (1606–69) © The Bridgeman Art Library
The Physician's Visit (oil on panel); by Jan Steen (1625/26–79) © The Bridgeman Art Library

Black and whites
p.106 Alkmaar cheese market © Ball Miwako/Alamy
p.202 Boats at Sneek Week © Peter Horree/Alamy
p.226 Sloten © Bildarchiv Monheim GmbH/Alamy
p.234 Groninger Museum © Frans Lemmens/Alamy

Index

Map entries are in colour.

INDEX

www.roughguides.com

Map symbols

maps are listed in the full index using coloured text

▪▪▪▪▪	International boundary	Ⓜ	Metro station
▪▪▪	Chapter division boundary	Ⓣ	Tram stop
▪▪▪▪	Provincial boundary	⊙	Statue
▬▬▬	Motorway	♠	Museum
═══	Main road	⊠	Post office
═══	Minor road	✈	Airport
▪▪▪▪▪	Tunnel	⊞	Hospital
▬▬▬	Pedestrianized street	♁	Garden
▪▪▪▪▪	Footpath	✡	Synagogue
▬▬▬	Railway	△	Hostel
▬▬▬	River/canal	⚠	Campsite
▬ ▬	Ferry route	♱	Cemetery
▬▬▬	Wall	✛	Church
⌣	Bridge	▪	Building
♦	Point of interest	▦	Park
⊠	Gate	▦	Beach/dune
ⓘ	Tourist information (VVV)		

So now we've told you about the things not to miss, the best places to stay, the top restaurants, the liveliest bars and the most spectacular sights, it only seems fair to tell you about the best travel insurance around

WorldNomads.com
keep travelling safely

Recommended by Rough Guides